KUKULCAN'S REALM

Gulf of
Mexico

Isla
Mujeres
Isla Cancun

CHIKINCHEL
Emal

TASES

CHIKIN CHEL

CUPUL

Chichen
Itza

ECAB
Xcaret

AH CANUL

Mayapán

Isla
de Cozumel

Uxmal

Coba
Xelha
Tulum

CHANRAHOL

Caribbean
Sea

COCHUAH

CANPECH

CHANPUTUN

ACALAN -TIXCHEL

UAYMIL

CEHACHE

Sta. Rita

CHETUMAL

Lamanai

DZULUINICOB

ITZA

The Yucatán Peninsula
• = Town
○ = Village, Hacienda
    or Rural
▲ = Ruins

0   50   100
        km

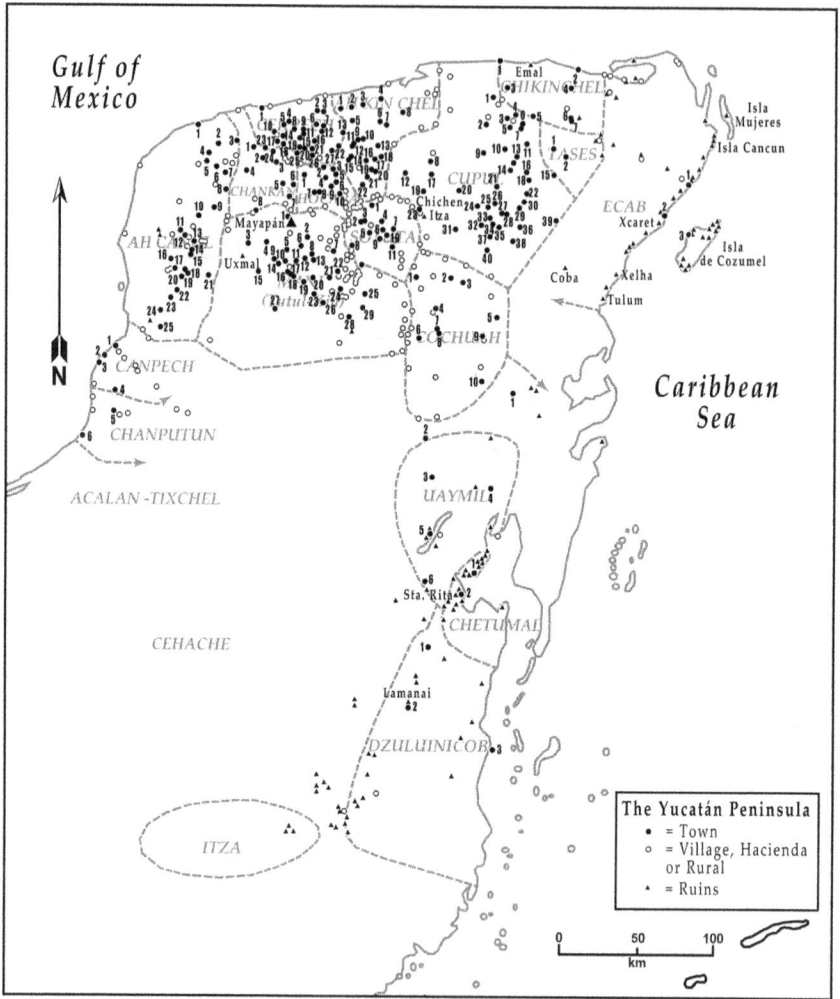

FIG. 0.1. *Towns in Contact Period Yucatán. Compiled by Bradley Russell, from Roys (1957).*

KUKULCAN'S REALM

URBAN LIFE AT ANCIENT MAYAPÁN

Marilyn A. Masson and Carlos Peraza Lope

with contributions by Timothy S. Hare

UNIVERSITY PRESS OF COLORADO

Boulder

Published by University Press of Colorado
5589 Arapahoe Avenue, Suite 206C
Boulder, Colorado 80303

The University Press of Colorado is a proud member of
The Association of American University Presses.

The University Press of Colorado is a cooperative publishing enterprise supported, in part, by Adams State University, Colorado State University, Fort Lewis College, Metropolitan State University of Denver, Regis University, University of Colorado, University of Northern Colorado, Utah State University, and Western State Colorado University.

Library of Congress Cataloging-in-Publication Data
Masson, Marilyn A.
  Kukulcan's realm : urban life at ancient Mayapán / Marilyn A. Masson and Carlos A. Peraza Lope with contributions by Timothy S. Hare.
    pages ; cm.
  Includes bibliographical references.
  ISBN 978-1-60732-319-8 (cloth) — ISBN 978-1-60732-320-4 (ebook) — ISBN 978-1-60732-427-0 (pbk)
  1. Mayapan Site (Mexico) 2. Mayas—Urban residence—Mexico—Mayapan. 3. Maya architecture—Mexico—Mayapan. 4. Mayas—Mexico—Mayapan—Antiquties. 5. Excavations (Archaeology)—Mexico—Mayapan. 6. Mayapan (Mexico)—Antiquities. I. Title.
  F1435.1.M3M28 2014
  972'.6—dc23

                     2013041205

Front cover illustrations: stucco portrait of Xipe Totec from a column at Hall Q-163 (left); stucco portrait of a merchant deity from a column at Hall Q-163 (right), photographs by Bradley Russell.

To Alec, Annika, Rylen, Christopher, Nayvi, and Gibran

This book was conceived of thirteen years ago when Marilyn Masson approached the University Press of Colorado about writing a sequel to her monograph on the small hinterland site of Laguna de On, Belize, that would investigate the core capital city of the Postclassic Maya world in parallel terms. This volume's title reflects the complementary relationships of these two books, as the title of the Laguna de On monograph (2000), *In the Realm of Nachan Kan*, referred to an influential leader of the Caribbean polity of Chetumal that was allied with Mayapán. It can be said, however, that even Chetumal was in Kukulcan's realm, which encompassed all of the Maya lowlands in Mayapán's day. This heroic founder of Mayapán's creation saga was central to a great many other late Mesoamerican political capitals, and he cast long shadow of influence. This book originally intended to synthesize the wealth of data that had been published but never fully analyzed by the Carnegie Institution of Washington's Mayapán project. At the time Masson met coauthor Carlos Peraza Lope in 1998, his INAH-Mayapán project was only beginning to change the way that the public and academic communities perceived this incredibly important ancient city. At the instigation of Bruce H. Dahlin, we found ourselves working together as collaborators in 2001 on an extensive project in the settlement zone and realized that no synthesis of Mayapán would be complete until this effort had reached a culmination point.

This book draws on findings of the Carnegie, INAH (Instituto Nacional de Antropologia e Historia), and PEMY (Proyecto Económico de Mayapán) projects, although we realize that understanding the complexities of this city is an ongoing process, and any synthesis is only valid with respect to a particular point in time.

During the first PEMY season in 2001, when Masson, Timothy Hare, Josalyn Ferguson, and Bradley Russell began to walk the surface of the urban landscape, the overwhelming richness of the record struck us. We mused that the site was a great green dragon, covered with forest, and that the tiny spears of our survey instruments and artifact collections would never slay this beast—nor did we harbor such an imperial intent. The dents that we made, however, would bleed morsels of information on which we could hungrily feed in order to reconstruct slices of ancient city life. These romantic musings of a skeleton crew of newcomers to northern Yucatán may seem whimsical, but they illustrate that from the beginning, the historical importance and vastness of this special place awed us. We knew that working there was a privilege. While surveying that first year in the cleared, newly burned milpas of the settlement zone, it became apparent to us how Mayapán in many ways resembled Pompeii without the ash cover. In such clearings, one can read the surface easily to determine the outlines of buildings, rooms, furnishings, activity areas, and workshops. Almost no soil has accumulated since the city's rapid abandonment around AD 1448. We had been accustomed to working in the more tropical area of Belize, where soil accumulation is greater, and studying Mayapán was like working at a Postclassic Belize site that had been completely excavated to a depth of twenty centimeters with all of the artifacts left in place.

Our enchantment with this research was further enhanced by the charm of the host population of Telchaquillo, Yucatán, who speak Yucatec Maya all day long unless prompted to switch to Spanish by members of the archaeological team. Although Carlos Peraza and his team had long appreciated the wellspring of local knowledge, the norteamericanos quickly learned that it would be our workers who exposed us to the extensive secrets of the forested settlement zone, given their lifetimes spent reading this landscape in the daily course of extracting a living. The special tutelage offered by "los dos Fernandos"—Fernando Mena and Fernando Flores—took our knowledge to unanticipated depths, and they have helped us to recruit, lead, and inspire crews of their townspeople for over a decade. Don Fernando Mena has the added distinction of having worked for Tatiana Proskouriakoff at the site when he was twelve years old and Don Fernando Flores is only person we know who successfully hunted a deer with a single rock. Their skills in the milpa and the *monte*, surveying, excavation, and architectural restoration are superior, even by Yucatecan standards, and their institutional memory bridges the traditional ways of the mid-twentieth century with the past. Don Pancho Uc, owner of Itzmal Ch'en, also knew members of the Carnegie project, and his gracious invitation to work at the ceremonial group on his property was the inception of our 2008–2009 investigations.

Many institutions and individuals have contributed in important ways to this book. We are grateful to the funding institutions that shared our conviction that Mayapán was a site of legacy status, including the University at Albany—SUNY, the Institute for Mesoamerican Studies, the Foundation for the Advancement of Mesoamerican Studies, the National Science Foundation, and National Geographic's Committee for Research and Exploration. The Consejo de Arqueología of INAH has paved the way for this research by providing permits and forcing us to diligently take stock of our progress in annual reports sometimes reaching over one thousand pages in length. These informes are now available online at http://www.albany.edu/mayapan, and we thank Sarah Taylor and Sloan Tash for their creative efforts in implementing this resource. The Peabody Museum of Archaeology and Ethnology at Harvard University, thanks to Patricia Kervich, gave us permission to utilize William R. Bullard, Jr.'s unpublished maps of vast tracts of houselot walls, which greatly augmented the quality of our data. The much-appreciated artistic and graphical contributions of Bradley Russell, Anne Deane, Wilberth Cruz Alvarado, Luis Góngora, and Kendra Farstad are well represented in the figures of this book.

Research at Mayapán would not have been possible without our codirectors, Timothy Hare and Bradley Russell, who have dedicated the past thirteen years of their lives to this project and whose current efforts on the Mayapán LiDAR Project will take these investigations to the next level. Clifford Brown also offered gracious assistance and wisdom during our first three years at the site. The quality of the results of any research project lies in its human resources, and without the contributions of our professional Yucatecan staff, especially Pedro Delgado Kú, Bárbara Escamilla Ojeda, Wilberth Cruz Alvarado, and Luis Flores Cobá, we would have faltered. Other professionals and students have lent their talents to our field and lab studies and authored chapters of our INAH reports, including Caroline Antonelli, Andrew Clark, Georgina Delgado Sánchez, Miguel Delgado Kú, Antonina Delu, Jerry Ek, Josalyn Ferguson, Elizabeth France, Karime Gazdik, Robert Hutchinson, Betsy Kohut, Gina LaSalla, Jared Latimer, Meghan McCarthy, Yonny Mex, Juliana Novic, Travis Ormsby, Elizabeth Paris, Amanda Schreiner, Stanley Serafin, Yuko Shiratori, Scott Speal, Elvira and Pilar Várguez, Nicolas Várguez, and Jonathan White. We are grateful for their time and willingness to bleed and sweat for this project and to complete the intellectual mission at all costs. Work at the site is not easy, and ticks, sharp boulders, daily temperatures exceeding

100° F, and waves of feverish intestinal bugs have made our staff members pay many a personal penalty.

For Bruce Dahlin, simple words of thanks are not enough. His Pakbeh Regional Economy Project, centered at the city of Chunchucmil, was the simultaneous sister project to Mayapán, with all of the staff visits, productive arguments, laughter, and parallel experiences that foster familial ties among investigators of ancient urbanism within a single region. Bruce also participated in our work and spent several weeks at Mayapán with Timothy Beach, Sheryl Luzzader-Beach, Richard Terry, and Clifford Brown in order to study the agrarian potential of the city. He was responsible for focusing our thinking on marketplaces and market economy.

The University Press of Colorado has our gratitude for their patience and encouragement with this long-term effort. Editors Darrin Pratt and Jessica d'Arbonne have been adept and nurturing handlers, and in our case, this was just the right approach. We are grateful to one anonymous reviewer and owe a great debt to Prudence Rice for a review that significantly transformed this book. As a consequence of her input, we have strived for greater clarity in supporting our arguments, and we have taken this opportunity to respond to the chapters of her 2012 University Press of Colorado book *The Kowoj: Identity, Migration, and Geopolitics in Late Postclassic Petén, Guatemala* (coedited with Don Rice). We agree with her that the understanding of both Zacpetén and Mayapán is enhanced by consideration of the data from both Postclassic sites. Like Laguna de On, the Kowoj site of Zacpetén was in the distant reaches of Mayapán's sphere of influence, with the added richness of a documentary record that outlines explicit historical relationships of the center and the periphery. Other individuals have long encouraged and inspired our research in the Postclassic and at Mayapán, including Anthony Andrews, Alfredo Barrera Rubio, Judith Gallegos Gómora, Fernando Robles Castellanos, David Freidel, Kenneth Hirth, Patricia McAnany, Jeremy Sabloff, Payson Sheets, Michael E. Smith, and Gabriela Vail.

Working at Mayapán and the process of writing this book has transformed us. We are reminded of Ian Hodder's remark in his 1990 book *The Domestication of Europe*, which states on page 20, "Çatalhüyük and I, we bring each other into existence." This sentiment is probably broadly shared by those who have invested the prime years of their careers immersed in reconstructing the lifeways of an ancient place. Our studies have defined us as scholars, underwritten many successes that we might claim, and our knowledge base has grown as we have sought to understand this city in the greater context of premodern urban studies. These experiences have also had profound effects on our families, mostly good (we hope). We thank our spouses, Robert Rosenswig and Veronica Cruz Flores, and dedicate this book to our children.

At the same time, it is our hope that we have returned new life to ancient Mayapán for the readers of this book and that we have reframed longstanding denigrating assumptions about this city and its society. One prominent Mayanist approached us soon after Carlos began restoring the principal edifices of the monumental center to their original glory and stated that it was now obvious that Mayapán had been an important site. The cosmetic reconstitution of the former ruins brought to light the aesthetic qualities of its murals, sculptures, and architecture. Prior to this point, the rubble buildings had been emblematic of a view of a degenerate civilization. This book adds fuel to the new momentum of scholarly interest in Mayapán, which for us represents one of the great urban cities in world archaeology. Our joint work in the settlement zone reveals commonalities and differences with other places and other times in the planning, organization, and experiences of ancient urban life.

KUKULCAN'S REALM

Archaeological Investigations of an Ancient Urban Place

MARILYN A. MASSON AND
CARLOS PERAZA LOPE

This book presents new perspectives on the complexity of ancient urban life at the last regional political capital in late Maya history at Mayapán, Yucatán, Mexico. This city was the largest urban center of the Postclassic Maya world for about 250 years; its apogee dates from around AD 1200–1450. Analysis of archaeological assemblages of dwellings and public buildings at ancient cities like Mayapán advance historical and comparative anthropology's contributions to understanding urban life in the premodern world. City dwellers from lowly to exalted social ranks in world history shared important experiences and sought to resolve parallel problems. They contended with the advantages and disadvantages of congested living that impacted health and hygiene, food supply, economic codependency, social and economic opportunities and constraints, and the need for monetary units and services. Like populations today, residents of premodern cities navigated through state sanctions on individual liberties, challenges to identity in a pluralistic social landscape, the allure of living in a cosmopolitan and prestigious place, and, for some, the pull of hometown connections in the countryside. Comparative research on ancient urbanism has long been a central focus of anthropological archaeology, and innovative new studies of individual cities or regions continually refresh this topic (e.g., Nichols and Charlton 1997; Sanders, Mastache, and Cobean 2003; Storey 2006; Stone 2007a; Marcus and Sabloff 2008). An emphasis on typological or demographic classifications hinders the investigation of ancient cities, and the Maya area has been no exception. In contrast, a functional definition of urbanism requires that a central place host activities and institutions on behalf of its

DOI: 10.5876/9781607323204.c001

hinterlands; functions can be administrative, religious, economic, or a combination of these, and urban centers can range in size from small to large (Hirth 2003a; Smith 2005, 2008:9). Mayapán is one ancient center that combined multiple urban functions and also fits conventional Western expectations of crowded urban life in the preindustrial world. Mayapán's profound influence in the hinterlands is reflected in surges of economic and religious life and activity timed with the city's thirteenth-century rise to power (Masson 2000). Hinterland elites emulated social and political conventions at secondary centers such as Caye Coco (Rosenswig and Masson 2002) or such practices were transmitted directly by diasporas of influential ethnic groups that departed the city at various points in Mayapán's relatively brief history (Rice and Rice 2009).

It is our hope that this book will contribute toward expanding existing models of Maya state organization through time and that our colleagues will find this investigation of Mayapán's urban patterns to represent a useful and relevant case study. There has been a tendency for Postclassic Maya society to be considered a world apart from its Classic-era predecessors. Here we add weight to the case against longstanding erroneous and dismissive characterizations of the confederacy of Mayapán that have lingered since the era of the Carnegie Institution of Washington's (CIW) Mayapán project in the 1950s. Potent new data reveal the complexity of the city's urban organization, particularly with respect to integrating principles of planning and administration as well as the economic foundations of city life. While the field of Maya studies has come to recognize Mayapán as an important historical landmark, the evidence in support of this accreditation has yet to be amassed in a single volume. This book provides much new information, although it is far from comprehensive. Ideally it will rekindle interest in this late capital city that will inspire future investigations.

URBAN COMPLEXITY, POLITICAL ECONOMY, AND HOUSEHOLD ARCHAEOLOGY

Evaluating the complexity of ancient states has long driven scientific inquiries into cultural evolution and remains a top priority for current research as new, sophisticated data and methods topple longstanding monolithic characterizations of ancient cities and their regions (Kowalewski 1990:39; Pyburn 1997:156; M. Smith 2007:17; Chase et al. 2011). Documenting the complexity of the city of Mayapán sheds light on the regional Postclassic domain that this capital governed or influenced. Our theoretical approach may be characterized as "empirical urban theory," which Michael E. Smith (2011a:171–72) advocates as a useful tool for asking research questions more closely bound to data compared to higher level theories that generate abstract ideas—often from an ideological viewpoint—about ancient civilizations in general. Smith (2011a:169). proposes empirical urban theory as an archaeological adaptation of middle-range theory (unlike Lewis R. Binford's use of the term) that has been used in other social science disciplines. Some of the more sophisticated recent studies of ancient cities have been employing this type of theory without defining it as an explicit research strategy, including those that consider the relationships between residents and the built environment, the materialization of power in monumentality, planning principles, and other examples provided by Smith (2011a). We have been hesitant to unite our investigations of the ancient city under a single approach, as diverse data are suitable for different frameworks for understanding urban life.

In this book's chapters, we characterize the patterned diversity of everyday life in terms of labor specialization, affluence, social identity, and religious practice within the urban environs. A consideration of top-down strategies evinced by monumental buildings and art is complemented by a tandem commitment to investigating bottom-up perspectives offered by household archaeology. Working down the social scale from the archaeology of governing elites and upward from the commoner labor force has led us to conclude that these realms are difficult to fully separate and conceptualize as partitioned spheres of interaction and activity. This conclusion, one of our primary findings, is in line with reports from other late Mesoamerican cities (M. Smith 2002; Cyphers and Hirth 2000). An interrelated set of societal institutions at the city underscores its complexity by governmental design that was affirmed in the daily routines and economic strategies of subject populations who resided at the city and its confederated towns and in its more distant allied trading territories (figure 1.1).

Some theoretical approaches to the archaeology of urbanism have particularly influenced the questions that we ask here of Mayapán's data. Foremost is an archaeological political economy approach, which by definition calls for the investigation of linkages of political officials, economic foundations of power, and extractive strategies that funneled the fruits of commoner labor into the needy reserves of the governing class. Implicit in an archaeological political economy approach is the importance of household archaeology to this line of inquiry (Masson 2002; Masson and Freidel 2002; M. Smith 2004:77). The processes of surplus extraction through such mechanisms as tribute, taxation, or commerce can vary in the degree to which they fulfill top-down preroga-

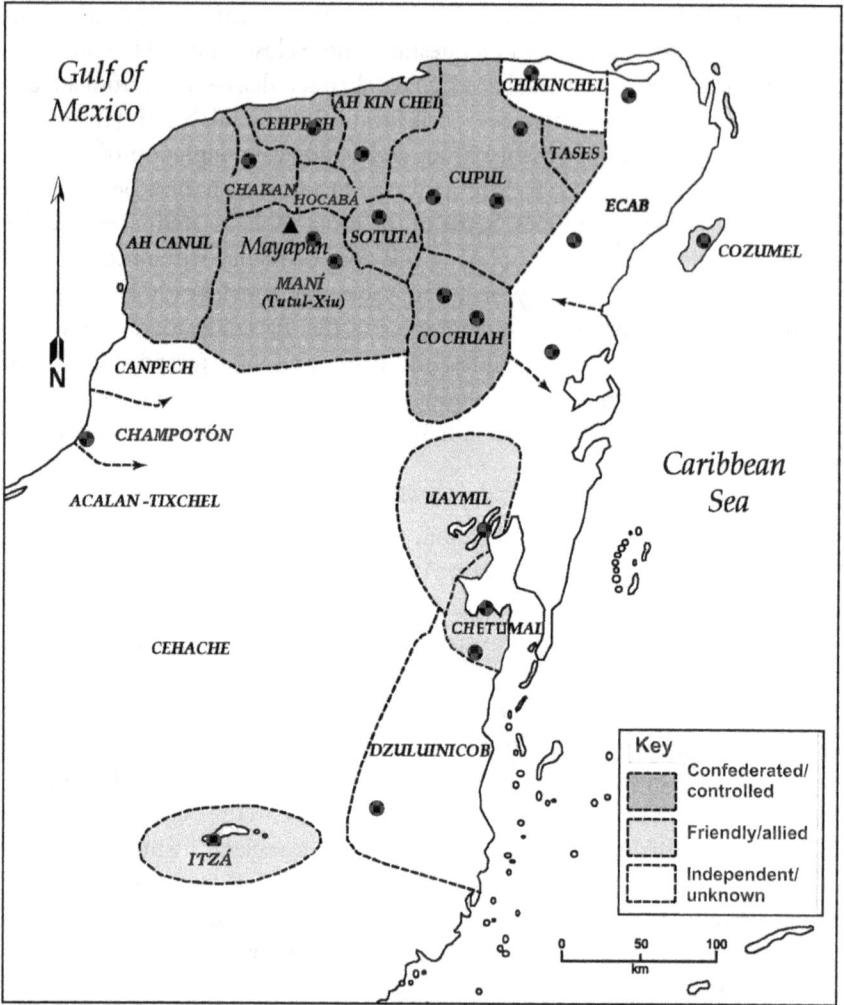

FIGURE I.I. *Polities and territories contemporary with Mayapán. The Mayapán confederacy was comprised of polities of the northwestern portion of the Yucatán under the city's direct control. Other polities to the east and south were closely allied and may not have been under tight control while others were clearly independent. Map by Bradley Russell, compiled from Roys (1962), Jones (1989), and A. Andrews (1993).*

tives. Grounding the analysis of ancient political economies in household archaeology permits the evaluation of the degree of surplus production and its relationship to household wealth and thus provides a commoner perspective on economic life, obligations, and strategies for negotiating household burdens (Hutson, Dahlin, and Mazeau 2012). We do not define a "domestic economy" at Mayapán as separate from a "political economy" (e.g., D'Altroy and Hastorf 2001:4), as our data reveal that these realms cannot be analytically separated due to the interpenetrating effects of urban life and regional economic exchange (Kepecs, Feinman, and Boucher 1994; Kepecs 2003). Eric Wolf (1982:19) recognized long ago that households are embedded in community, polity, and regional frameworks. The connections of domestic economies to regional market systems, as well as to high-level elite activities, have been broadly recognized across Mesoamerica (e.g., Sheets 2000; M. Smith 2002; Feinman and Nicholas 2000; Smith and Berdan 2003a). In contrast, the "domestic mode of production" defined by Marshall Sahlins (1972) characterizes a generalized and autonomous existence geared toward meeting the needs of household residents, and the term best applies to nonmarket societies. Terence N. D'Altroy and Christine Anne Hastorf (2001:9–11) highlight important considerations for the study of household economic activities that include linkages to larger social groups in which domestic units are embedded. They also advocate an analysis of labor allocation across gender lines, the potential for pooling resources or labor, and, as we emphasize in this book, household economic participation in production and consumption relationships with one or more communities.

Our emphasis on dwelling assemblages is due to the fact that households represent the fundamental social and economic building blocks of society, as has long been acknowledged in Maya settlement archaeology (e.g., A. Smith 1962; Rathje 1983; Ashmore 1981; Wilk and Ashmore 1988). Newer to the field is the quest to reconstruct diverse household strategies and lifeways within larger settlement units ranging from villages to regions (e.g., Levi 2002; Yaeger and Robin 2004; Scarborough, Valdez, and Dunning 2003; D. Chase and A. Chase 2004; Lohse and Valdez 2004; Rice and Rice 2009). In many ways, household archaeology has come into its own, and sub-elite domestic units are no longer viewed as homogenous or constant (M. Smith 1994, 2002; Tringham 1996). In the Maya area, the study of occupational heterogeneity has promoted the recognition of the importance of household investigations (Becker 1973; Chase, Chase, and Haviland 1990; Haviland 1985; Shafer and Hester 1983; King 1994; McAnany 1989). Complexity and variation, particularly in the agrarian base, is now widely reflected across the region (Kepecs and

Boucher 1996; Fedick 1996; Sheets 2000; Scarborough, Valdez, and Dunning 2003; Lohse and Valdez 2004; Alexander 2005; Robin 2006; Chase, Chase, and Haviland 2011; Dunning, Beach, and Luzadder-Beach n.d.). More assessments of the degree to which Maya domestic units were enmeshed in regional and interregional commerce through all periods are needed, given the potential for regional variation (Kepecs 2003; Berdan et al. 2003; Masson and Freidel 2012). Diverse home production is an integral part of the formation and maintenance of regional market dependencies (Hirth 1998; Stark and Garraty 2010). In Yucatán, polities clearly specialized in specific products—salt, fish, and copal in Chikinchel, cacao in Cupul and Ichmul, and wax and honey at Tiquibalón and Cozumel Island, for example (chapter 5; Piña Chan 1978:38–40; Freidel and Sabloff 1984:190). Beyond social and economic considerations, elite residences can also serve political and religious functions in the neighborhoods in which they are embedded, as we suggest in chapters 3 and 4 (Hare and Masson 2012).

Beyond the household, neighborhoods represent another important analytical unit at ancient cities, but these can be harder to isolate archaeologically in the absence of walls or other clear features of neighborhood division (M. Smith 2011b; Arnauld, Manzanilla, and Smith 2012). The identification of residential zone units at Mayapán holds promise, as gauged by spatial clustering and shared houselot boundary walls; such efforts have just begun, as houselot walls are not yet fully mapped for the city (chapter 4; Brown 1999; Hare and Masson 2012). Our survey of portions of neighborhoods in sizeable cleared milpa fields across Mayapán has failed to reveal conclusive evidence of socially distinct enclaves (chapter 5). In some cases peculiar house styles tend to cluster but do not share other distinctive attributes such as greater quantities of atypical pottery (chapter 5; Masson and Peraza Lope 2010). But three neighborhoods have been discerned at the city: downtown Mayapán, in which the largest palaces frame the monumental center; a second zone of concentrated elite residences next to the city's primary market plaza; and a crafts barrio located within the downtown zone, just to the west of the site center (chapter 4). Most residential zones that we have surveyed lack distinctiveness and conform to site-wide typical patterns in house form. Atypical dwellings, when found, are amid more traditional Mayapán houses. Our initial analysis of larger residential zones compared composite settlement characteristics of individual milpa samples, but this approach masked considerable variation at individual houselot units within these mapped areas. This realization, coupled with a lack of clear distinctions among household pottery assemblages (Masson and Peraza Lope 2010), led us to designate the dwelling over the neighborhood as our primary unit of analysis.

Adopting an archaeological political economy approach causes us to skirt, but not completely avoid, the allure of the ritual economy approach that currently enjoys popularity (e.g., Wells 2006; McAnany and Wells 2008; McAnany 2010). These authors demonstrate the exceptional importance of the ritual dimensions driving ancient Maya production economies, yet it is our view that production for ritual existed within a continuous matrix of enmeshed economic activities that included distinctly secular realms. Succinctly put, overlap was partial across the sacred and mundane fields of activity (chapter 9). A limited number of specialized, highly skilled artisans met the particular needs of high art and religion at Mayapán, as is observed at earlier Maya cities, and these top-down activities served key purposes in achieving an articulated economy. Loftily symbolic luxury goods were encoded with tangible values, and this process was directly tied to the use of shell, greenstone, cloth, and cacao beans as currencies for the exchange of staple and wealth goods in everyday commerce (Freidel and Reilly 2010; Feinman and Garraty 2010:176; Masson and Freidel 2012).

Temples, for example, were key institutions of consumption. Activities sponsored at these edifices stimulated the production and acquisition of all manner of goods, including ordinary pots and foodstuffs for celebratory meals, common forms of knives and projectiles used in sacrifice and ceremony, and special paraphernalia such as deity effigy censers (Landa 1941:92, 106, 141, 158). Commoners at the city made all of these items, which were consumed by patrons and their guests at events held at temples, colonnaded halls, and other civic-ritual buildings. Except for the special paraphernalia, these inventories of foodstuffs and tools were also used in daily life for mundane occasions at ordinary houses where they were produced. Calendrical ceremonies and rites of passage called for the consumption of all of the valuable and useful goods at Mayapán, and in effect, this contributed to the reification of these goods. The affirmation of the sacred qualities of life's staples is also commemorated in monumental art (chapters 2, 3). These observations fit well within the ritual economy paradigm, and there is no denying that a devout citizenry undertook the activities of daily life through the lens of religious beliefs propagated by the Mayapán state. There is room to consider, however, that some portion of staple products and a significant number of valuables were available through mundane market transactions. It is also true that a system of norms with a religious foundation bound some practices associated with market commerce (Freidel 1981; Freidel and Sabloff 1984), but as we discuss in chapter 6, pilgrimage market fairs were but one form of market exchange (Masson and Freidel 2012).

IN THE FOOTSTEPS OF V. GORDON CHILDE

Our study owes a profound intellectual debt to V. Gordon Childe's work on the urban revolution (Childe 1936, 1950, 1956). Mayapán's status as a secondary state means that our research is more concerned with the specific operations of a late state polity rather than the transformations associated with the emergence of a primary state. The latter topic has been an overriding concern in evolutionary anthropology. Some political structures at Mayapán were innovative, if not revolutionary, even if they can be historically understood and explained in terms of predecessors such as Chichén Itzá. The phenomenon of urban life emerged early in the Maya area—around 1,500 years prior to Mayapán at the metropolis of Late Preclassic era El Mirador—and continued through the Classic Period where networks of cities home to populations 10,000–100,000 strong crisscrossed the lowland Maya landscape (Chase, Chase, and Haviland 1990; Chase et al. 2011; D. Rice 2006). We share Childe's interest in the topics of urban social and economic diversity, in particular the mutual dependencies fostered by the fabric of city life.

Childe highlighted the importance of occupational specialization and its correlate, urban interdependency. This connectedness represents a critical variable for evaluating complexity within cities and their larger regional contexts. Even a cursory read of the sweeping historical treatise of Fernand Braudel (1981) or selections of Contact Period Maya ethnohistorical documents reveals the resounding effects on households wrought by changes in regional political and ecological climates. Connectedness, or connectivity, as Michael Smith (1994:144) phrases it, exposes the linkages of domestic units to one another through nonlocal economic and political institutions. On a more conceptual level, arguments for "entanglement" tie a range of routine daily activities to the underpinnings of *costumbre*, rooted in social identity and religious beliefs (McAnany 2010). Gary M. Feinman and Christopher P. Garraty (2010) have recently argued that a significant degree of embeddedness of socioeconomic institutions is not limited to preindustrial societies. As Jeremy A. Sabloff (2007:21) has recently surmised, "the breadth and interconnectedness of Mesoamerican polities in the Late Postclassic is undeniable," and this regional articulation is observed in ideological exchanges of high art and mythology and the commercial realm (Milbrath and Peraza Lope 2003a; Smith and Berdan 2003a; Sabloff 2007:21; Barrera Rubio and Peraza Lope 2004; Masson and Peraza Lope 2007). Close ties between the Maya area and central Mexico date to at least the Terminal Classic period at Chichén Itzá in Yucatán (Kepecs, Feinman, and Boucher 1994; Kepecs 2007), and it is arguable that external exchange was more important for that great city than for Mayapán (Braswell

2010), which seems to have consolidated some of its important trade networks to an area that lies within the expansive Maya realm (chapter 6).

Our assessments of codependency in chapter 6 document the quantities of goods that were made at the city's dwellings or acquired through exchange from destinations across the Maya lowlands and highlands. Despite inter-regional connections emphasized in studies of Mayapán's art, research in the settlement zone at Mayapán reveals as much about the importance of regional dependencies within the Maya area than beyond it—in part because this study is limited to nonperishable artifacts and also due to the fact that such exchanges were of greatest importance to the city's commoners. Elsewhere in the Maya area, codependency has been analyzed at various scales—for example, between small settlements outside of major centers in a region (Scarborough and Valdez 2009), within large centers, and between these nodes and their hinterlands via market exchange (West 2002; Masson and Freidel 2012).

The concept of heterogeneity provides a useful framework for evaluating societal complexity (McGuire 1983), particularly for craft production (chapter 6). It is relatively simple to document heterogeneity in terms of evidence for the spatial segregation of manufacturing stages or products (M. Smith 1994; Berdan 1988). Other straightforward archaeological reflections of complexity are found in the number of settlement units within a regional system, and more importantly, in the segmentation of social and functional space within a site or residential group (Kent 1990a, 1990b). At Mayapán, segmentation is manifested in separate constructed spaces for living, storage, entertaining, cooking, animal raising, and ritual within elite domestic groups, and at the site level in differen-tiated spaces for agriculture, commerce, education (possibly), ritual, water collection and socializing, houselot and city wall boundaries, workshop buildings, and other features (chapters 3–5). A proliferation of types of ritual buildings at this city is also a correlate of religious complexity (chapter 2; Proskouriakoff 1962a); Harry E. D. Pollock (1962:15) tallied over 100 such edifices.

MAYAPÁN AND MESOAMERICAN URBANISM

Three case studies in Mesoamerican political economy have used partic-ularly innovative approaches that have guided our investigations. Michael Smith's examination of household activities before and after the formation of the Aztec empire has pioneered key methods for assessing wealth (Smith and Heath-Smith 1994; M. Smith 1987, 1999). Our analyses also emulate parallel queries made at the Epiclassic center of Xochicalco in quantitatively compar-ing commoner and elite wealth variation and the relationship of affluence to craft production and market exchange (Hirth 1998; Cyphers and Hirth 2000). Research at Xochicalco also fostered Kenneth G. Hirth's (2003a) model of segmental urbanism that interprets an array of outlying elite architecture as the seats of subject polities (*altepetl*) of the Xochicalco state. Leaders of these annexed territories maintained a residence in the urban center. This model may have interesting parallels to the Mayapán confederacy, in which lords of affiliated polities lived at least part of the time in the city, and we attribute replicated civic-ceremonial architecture to this sector of governing elites (chapters 3, 4). Research at the Early Classic center of Chunchucmil, a unique Classic-era Maya city that specialized in commercial exchange, has motivated and emboldened our efforts in reconstructing a market economy. The differences, as well as the striking parallels in residential zone organization and trade observed at Chunchucmil and Mayapán, serve as a testimony to the diversity and complexity of cities within the Maya region (Dahlin 2009; Dahlin et al. 2010; Hutson, Dahlin, and Mazeau 2012).

Characterizations of Maya cities of the Classic Period prior to Chichén Itzá and Mayapán have been plagued by a lack of consensus, in part due to paradigmatic disagreement, but also due to real variation in the size and importance of specific places across the lowlands, as should be expected for ancient cities (Marcus 1983). Characterizations of all Maya cities as "regal-ritual," weak, or undifferentiated (Sanders and Webster 1988; Webster and Sanders 2001; Ball 1993; Inomata 2001) are no longer tenable due to evidence that the largest Maya cities were functionally and economically diverse, covered extensive areas with large-scale landscape modifications, and some were home to enormous populations of 50,000 to 100,000 or more (Folan 1992; Haviland 1992; Moholy-Nagy 1997; Chase, Chase, and Haviland 1990; A. Chase 1998; A. Chase and D. Chase 2004; A. Chase et al. 2011; Sabloff 2003; Dahlin and Ardren 2002 et al. 2010; D. Rice 2006; Masson and Freidel 2012). Settlements in the Maya countryside also exhibit social and functional diversity (Scarborough, Valdez, and Dunning 2003; Iannone and Connell 2003; Lohse and Valdez 2004; Yaeger and Robin 2004). Impediments to recognizing the complexity of Maya states in general (Pyburn 2008; A. Chase et al. 2011), including Mayapán, trace their origins to Betty Meggers's (1954) assertions in her "Law of Environmental Limitation on Culture," which held that tropical environments in general impose limiting factors on the evolution of civilizations (Sanders 1962, 1973; Sanders and Price 1968; Puleston 1982). The erroneous foundations of this position have been overturned in New World archaeology to the extent that it has become part of the public discussion as exemplified in science writer Charles Mann's (2005) bestseller *1491*.

Mayapán has generally been overlooked as a case study useful for building models about Maya urbanism due to two flawed assumptions about the city: first, that Postclassic society was a devolved and thus unproductive—even unworthy—civilization for comparative study; and second, that Mayapán and its larger societal context were fundamentally different from earlier Maya history due to the importance of mercantile commerce over theocratic political structures of the past. While Jeremy Sabloff and William L. Rathje's (1975) mercantile model illuminated key differences that helped to explain the shift away from investment in monuments of monarchical power, many remaining threads of continuity and historically informed transformations merit deeper analysis. For example, market institutions were likely amplified rather than invented in the centuries following the collapse of Classic-era southern monarchies (West 2002; Braswell 2010; Masson and Freidel 2012, 2013). The study of Maya religion represents a general exception, as it has long taken into account the material indicators of belief systems manifested throughout the Formative, Classic, Postclassic, and Contact Periods, and in some instances, persist among traditional Maya societies today (e.g., J. Thompson 1970; Taube 1992; Freidel, Schele, and Parker 1993).

ILLUMINATING THE DARK AGES

This investigation into urban life finds general inspiration in selected works from historical urban geography, as have some other recent works in Meso-american archaeology (M. Smith 2005, 2007, 2011b; Russell 2008a). Kevin Lynch's (1960) definition of urban landscapes in conceptual and functional terms in his book *The Image of the City* has many applications for the reconstruction of Mayapán's landscape. Identifying focal nodes, roads, gates, and edges has suggested to us ways that residents and visitors navigated and perceived the city via meaningfully connected features or viewsheds that lent structure to the city's morass of stone-encircled house groups. Although our work does not delve deeply into the cognitive effects of monumental landmarks and other features contributing to perception and urban worldview, we acknowledge their probable importance for triggering and generating social memory (e.g., Alcock 2002:28–30; Moore 2005). Such processes are not accidental; and Mayapán's defining features represent some of the best evidence for top-down strategies linked to state-making planning and administration. Susan Alcock (2002:39) eloquently characterizes this phenomenon, which broadly applies to ancient political capitals: "The victorious power's own sense of history is transformed to reflect success and its consequences, while central authorities re-inscribe provincial memories in order either to undercut opposition or encourage compliance." Cultivating a sense of state identity is potentially fraught with dialectical obstacles, especially when residents are frequently replenished with new arrivals from diverse countryside locales. The effectiveness of efforts to grow allegiance to polity over the roots of hometown loyalty can be variable but is often successful through time (e.g., Oudijk 2002; Janusek 2002; Kristan-Graham 2001).

Regional historical syntheses such as those of Josiah Cox Russell (1972) and Norman J. G. Pounds (1973) consider the institutions of town and city life in the late medieval landscapes of Europe north of the Alps in terms that provoke our thinking about parallels in urban life (chapters 6, 8, 9). Such works also attest to considerable geographic variation within a given century and reinforce the fact that life at Mayapán may have been atypical for the Postclassic peninsula in a myriad of ways. Informed by more detailed history than other preindustrial states, these studies reconstruct changing variables such as city size; the relative authority of political, religious, and merchant sectors; economic differentiation and affluence; residential density; and societal implications of amplifying scales of regional commerce. Susan Kepecs's comparisons of Postclassic Maya mercantilism to emerging commercial institutions in Europe in the century prior to the Black Death have drawn on evocative patterns detailed by Janet Abu-Lughod and Fernand Braudel (Kepecs 2003; Abu-Lughod 1989; Braudel 1981). Other analogies to medieval Europe, particularly the feudal estate system (Adams and Smith 1981), have carried little weight in Maya archaeology due to fundamental differences in the specifics and the use of the term *feudal* for the Maya area. But some comparisons that R. E. W. Adams and W. D. Smith (1981) made regarding proprietary hierarchical class relationships, horizontal family obligations, and elite authority over land use remain worthy of consideration. The fact that these authors did not consider the contributions of merchants, craftspeople, and other free laborers in both societies is unfortunate (Pirenne 1925:103; Dyer 1989:11–25), as their analysis primarily focused on the relationships between high elites and agrarian peasants. A closer look at late medieval economies indicates that relationships between social groups and land were variable and not limited to feudal estates (Pounds 1973:353–54, 370, 375, 403). Aside from the specific details of feudal estates and Christianity, the growth of city life in northern Europe from the thirteenth through fifteenth centuries AD presents some interesting parallels with those of the Postclassic Maya in the realm of the "structures of daily life" (Braudel 1981). Town and city life drove the emergence of socioeconomic diversification and created niches for town-dwelling craftspersons, urban peasants, and merchants operating from local-to-distant scales toward the end of the Middle Ages (Pounds 1973:355, 403–7). Late medieval town life added new options for independence in practice, even if official authority under castle or monastic patronage was asserted (Pounds 1973:344–55). Regional bulk goods exchange and distant luxury exchange linked town and city economies over considerable distances, although history reveals significant regional variability in the directions and quantities of trade (Pounds 1973:425–27). As we surmise for Mayapán (chapter 6), most towns in fourteenth-century northern Europe strove to grow much of their own food supply, but some degree of food importation was inevitable. Trade was subject to taxation and other forms of political intervention (Pounds 1973:422). Complex economic institutions south of the Alps, such as those of Venice, are much less useful for comparison to late Mesoamerican states.

Full comparisons across the Atlantic among contemporary (thirteenth and fourteenth centuries AD) cities such as Mayapán and larger walled cities north of the Alps await future attention and do not represent a major focus of this book, tantalizing as we find them to be. Here we skirt the edges in questions raised in chapters 8 and 9. We are not the first, however, to wonder about the potential of late medieval-Postclassic Maya cross-cultural comparisons, even while we assume from the outset that key differences existed. Sabloff (2007:25) recently remarked, "With the new data and insights into the Late Postclassic political economy in mind, when you read volume 2 of Fernand Braudel's 1992], important and highly influential . . . volume entitled 'The Wheels of Commerce', you cannot help but be struck by the parallels between Europe and the Maya world and the rich possibilities for future comparative analyses." Beyond the allure of potential Maya-medieval analogies, it is important not to neglect many other preindustrial towns—in northern Europe or beyond— where residents also contended with the challenges, conflicts, and potential opportunities afforded by city life (chapter 9).

MAYAPÁN: A STORIED CITY

Mayapán was one of the most densely nucleated cities in Maya history, and it has long been an easily recognizable urban site, even by conventional standards (Pollock 1962; A. Smith 1962). This city represents one of the best Mesoamerican cities for the study of preindustrial urbanism due to its chronological placement on the threshold of Pre-Columbian and European Contact Period history. Much of the city's walled settlement dates to the Postclassic Period (around AD 1200–1450), which allows for the spatial analysis of a largely contemporaneous distribution of artifacts and architecture (chapter 2). Colonial-era descendants of the city's lords chronicled rich details of social, political, religious, and economic institutions that can be compared to the archaeological record. Diego de Landa was informed that Mayapán fell in K'atun 8 Ahau (AD 1441–1461), only one hundred or so years before the Spanish conquest of Yucatán in 1542. Some accounts were given directly to Spanish writers while others were compiled from indigenous writings (Roys 1962). The archaeological data presented in this book broaden and revise what is known from historical accounts. The name of the city itself is a matter that is occasionally treated in various ethnohistorical documents.

NAMES FOR THE CITY

The city was referred to as "Mayapán" at the time that Landa (1941:26) wrote his *Relación de las cosas de Yucatan*. The name combines the words *Maya* and *pan* (probably derived from the Nahuatl word *pantli*), which may be translated as "the standard or banner of the Maya" (Tozzer 1941:26n137). Banners were emblematic for Maya political capitals from at least the Classic Period forward (Freidel, Schele, and Parker 1993), and the deeper meaning of this term probably signifies the city's status as the capital of the confederacy. The city may also have been known as Zaklaktun or Zaklaktun Mayapán, according to the Chilam Balam of Chumayel, which may mean "the place where white pottery is made" (Roys 1933:81) and could refer to fine examples of Pelé Polychrome or other Buff Polbox group pottery that has a cream-to-buff slip that is not recovered at contemporary sites along the Caribbean coast of Yucatán (R. Smith 1971:231). This name may have originally been Zacal Actun, meaning "white cave" or "white stone building" (Roys 1933:81). The site's numerous cenote cavities in white limestone or the white-plastered public buildings could have easily fit this description. Bradley W. Russell (2008a) argues that this name has Terminal Classic origins in the vicinity of the far eastern Itzmal Ch'en ceremonial group, where earlier pottery is more ubiquitous, even though it is mixed thoroughly with later Postclassic material. Ichpaa Mayapán is another term that may refer to the city, translated by Ralph L. Roys as "walled enclosure." Mayapán was the largest walled city of the Postclassic Maya region. Tancah Mayapán may also refer to the city or one of its districts (Roys 1933, 1962:78). Prudence M. Rice (2004:77) points out that Mayapán could refer to *may* combined with the Nahuatl suffix *apan*, which could stand for "cycle water place." The east coast settlements of Tancah (near Tulum) and Ichpaatun (near Chetumal) are alternative places that may have been referred to as Tancah and Ichpaa Mayapán (Jones 1989). Notably, Tulum and Ichpaatun, like Mayapán, were walled towns, and both were within allied territories of the Mayapán confederacy (Roys 1962).

ENVIRONS

Mayapán is located in a seemingly inhospitable inland location near the center of the northwestern part of the peninsula on the extensive northern plain of Yucatán (figure 1.1). Aside from certain coastal strips, this area is the driest portion of the Maya lowlands, with an average of 1 meter of rainfall per year, amenable to the growth of desert plants like henequen and Standley cactus (*Cereus yucatanensis*). The latter species is concentrated in remnant stands within Mayapán (Brown 1999:255) and may have been cultivated for its edible fruit and its interior wooden branches that make excellent arrow shafts. Telchaquillo resident Fernando Flores demonstrated to members of our project in 2001 his inherited knowledge of the simple process of extracting straight wooden shafts from these cacti. Carnegie investigators lamented the heat of the city (e.g., Proskouriakoff 1955:84), which exceeds 100 degrees Fahrenheit from March through the summer months. The forest consists of many dry scrub species, and residents of the ancient city derived their water from numerous cenotes in the area. Mayapán is near the brim of the Chicxulub crater that is marked by a ring of such subterranean depressions, known as the "ring of cenotes" (Brown 1999:157; Brown et al. 2006). The city was probably founded in this location for historical reasons that have been lost to us, as many other similar localities exist with multiple cenotes and cultivable land that would have been suitable for founding a political capital. Like the founders of Chichén Itzá, the lords of Mayapán probably chose an inland location favorably situated within a network of key towns and overland exchange routes (Piña Chan 1978:39) despite the importance of maritime trading for both of these political capitals. Sites nearer to the coast have poorer options for agriculture and fresh water (Dahlin and Ardren 2002), but closer proximity would have been possible, as modern Mérida (the site of ancient Tihó) and Classic era Dzibilchaltun are both within 15–20 kilometers from the sea.

EXPLORATION AND RESEARCH AT MAYAPÁN

The chapters of this book draw on our joint investigations at Mayapán, including Carlos Peraza Lope's Instituto Nacional de Antropología e Historia

FIGURE 1.2. *The Temple of Kukulcan. Illustration by Luis Góngora, courtesy of Carlos Peraza Lope.*

(INAH)-Mayapán Project at the site's monumental center (1996–present) and our combined Economic Foundations of Mayapán Project (Proyecto Económico de Mayapán, or PEMY) (2001–present). This latter effort primarily undertook household archaeology in the settlement zone outside of the monumental center in order to evaluate the economic relationships of the noble and commoner social classes. Our studies have had the luxury of building on the legacies of former Mayapán projects, especially the CIW seasons from 1949 to 1955 (Pollock 1962:iii; Pollock et al. 1962; R. Smith 1971) and Clifford T. Brown's (1999) doctoral dissertation research on the city's social organization. In the ensuing chapters we consider the findings of the INAH, PEMY, and Carnegie Mayapán projects.

Initial explorations of Mayapán produced illustrations of the Temple of Kukulcan, the site's principal pyramid, as well as the Round Temple (Templo Redondo) (figures 1.2–1.5). In 1841, John L. Stephens and Frederick Catherwood (Stephens 1843:1:133) described the site center. They also examined and reported the city wall (Stephens [1843] 1963; Pollock 1962:2). Charles Brasseur de Bourbourg (1867:234–49) later described the center, as did Augustus le Plongeon (1882) in 1881, Antonio García Cubas in 1885, and Carl Sapper in 1897 (Pollock 1962:2–3; P. Delgado Kú 2004:18). Other notable Mayanists who visited the city include Sylvanus Morley and Thomas Gann,

FIGURE 1.3. *The Temple of Kukulcan (Q-162), with the Hall of the Sun Disks (Q-161) in the foreground.*

FIGURE 1.4. *View of Mayapán's Round Temple Q-152 and associated colonnaded halls.*

FIGURE 1.5. *Mayapán's Round Temple Q-152 and associated colonnaded halls.*

and Lawrence Roys initially performed more detailed architectural studies (L. Roys 1941; Pollock 1962:3). The CIW study of E. Wyllys Andrews IV and R. T. Patton in 1938 has remained unpublished (Andrews and Patton n.d.), but it was useful to subsequent Carnegie efforts in mapping and exploring the city wall (Pollock 1962:3). Andrews also briefly reported some of his observations at Mayapán (E. Andrews 1942:261–63, 1943:81–82; Pollock 1962:4). G. W. Brainerd excavated a few test pits at the site in 1942 in order to gather pottery samples for his regional ceramic monograph (Brainerd 1958; Pollock 1962:4).

The Carnegie project was methodologically and theoretically innovative for American archaeology of the 1950s due to its emphasis on settlement and household archaeology (figure 1.6, A. Smith 1962:169; Pollock 1954). The program of research was designed to respond to critiques leveled at more conventional Maya projects that focused on monumental architecture and the recovery of descriptive historical data (Pollock 1951; A. Smith 1962; Brown 1999:102–3). As a consequence of this effort, Mayapán remains one of the best-mapped Mesoamerican cities thanks to the efforts of the Carnegie and surveyor Morris R. Jones (1952, 1962), newly augmented by Bradley W. Russell's multiyear mapping efforts beyond the Great Wall. (figure 1.6). In 2013

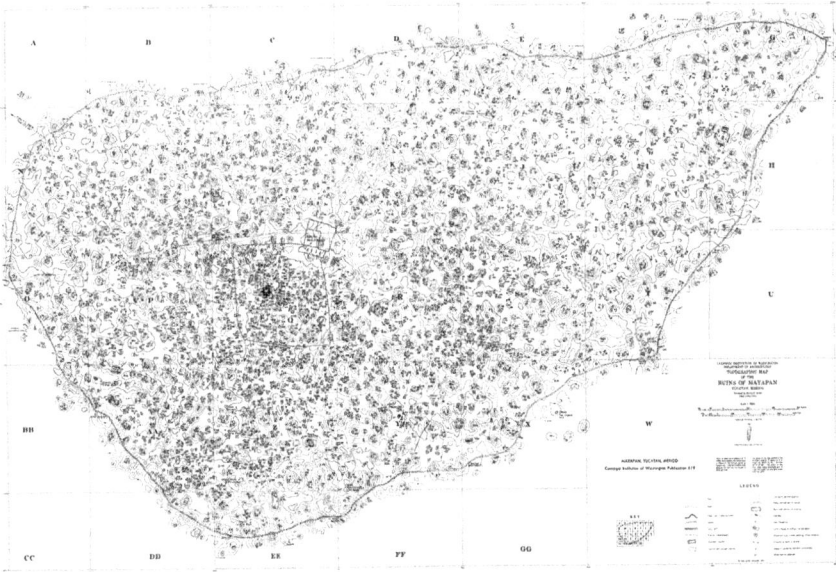

FIGURE 1.6. *Morris Jones's (1962) map of the walled portion of Mayapán.*

a LiDAR remote sensing project, directed by Timothy S. Hare and codirected by the authors and Bradley Russell, will begin to fully document the surface features of the city and a 40-kilometer-square area of its environs.

The bulk of the Carnegie fieldwork took place between 1949 and 1954 under the direction of Harry E. D. Pollock. Mayapán was the last large-scale program of study for the Carnegie's archaeological division, and a team of exceptionally accomplished Mayanists took charge of the research, including Pollock, Tatiana Proskouriakoff, A. Ledyard Smith, Karl Ruppert, William R. Bullard, Jr., Edwin W. Shook, Robert E. Smith, Gustav Strömsvik, and their graduate students who authored the CIW *Current Reports* (Masson 2009; Weeks 2009). Two seminal publications were produced, including a summary report (Pollock et al. 1962) and a ceramic monograph (R. Smith 1971); the annual *Current Reports* have much detailed information from specific investigations and have recently been republished and amassed together for the first time in a single volume (Weeks 2009).

Although the Carnegie work at Mayapán was of exceptional quality and broke the mold in terms of research questions pertaining to settlement and Postclassic Period archaeology for its day (Brown 1999:103–8), it was a difficult project for the investigators. As the fieldwork unfolded, Harry Pollock and his team were aware that this would probably be the last big investment in archaeology for the Carnegie's Division of Historical Research (Solomon 2002). World War II had disrupted the momentum of the archaeological team, and the strong sense of camaraderie was eroding (Solomon 2002:123–25). Mayapán is a difficult place to work. For example, Pollock (1962:1–2) stated, "Present day vegetation . . . is . . . thorny, difficult of passage, offering limited shade, and generally inhospitable to one accustomed to . . . a more temperate climate." He added, "Soil is so sparse that one often has the impression of viewing more rock than earth" and "To make this rocky, shadeless plain even less friendly to the use of man, there is almost no surface water." Travel from Mérida was difficult during the 1950s, and accommodations in Telchaquillo were stark in comparison to earlier team housing at southern Maya sites. The project marked the decline of the archaeology program, and in a parallel fashion, Carnegie investigators outspokenly expressed their dismal regard of Mayapán and the aesthetics and accomplishments of the Postclassic Maya society that it represented (A. Smith 1962:269; Pollock 1962:17; Proskouriakoff 1962b:330). It is worth pondering how the morale and comfort of the research team affected the lens through which its members viewed the site. Nonetheless, the team maintained a high level of professionalism when it came to the duties of fieldwork and publication. Long before it was required, the team restored several of the buildings at which they worked (P. Delgado Kú 2004:23), including Structures Q-71 (Venus Temple), Q-82 (Temple of the Warriors), Q-126 (The Observatory), and Q-151 (Hall of the Chac Masks).

Starting in 1996, the INAH project, supported by the government of the State of Yucatán, the Patronato de las Unidades de Servicios Culturales y Turísticos (CULTUR), and the Secretaría de Desarollo Social (SEDESOL), undertook major excavations and restoration work in the site center. Carlos Peraza Lope directed this work, assisted over many years by field directors Pedro Delgado Kú and Bárbara del C. Escamilla Ojeda. Other field archaeologists whose contributions were especially significant include Miguel Angél Delgado Kú and Mario Garrido Euán (P. Delgado Kú 2004:26) as well as ceramicists Wilberth Cruz Alvarado and Luis Flores Cobá. INAH owns the central portion of Square Q in which the monumental zone is concentrated, and this area is open for tourism and has been targeted for excavation and restoration. Square Q is only one of twenty-six 500-x-500-meter grid squares that cover the walled portion of the city, and dozens of local farmers and ranchers privately own the remainder of the settlement. INAH investigated and restored a total of sixty-seven structures between 1996 and 2000 alone (P. Delgado Kú 2004:27). The project has continued, at a slower pace, to this day. This work has been reported in a large suite of technical reports prepared for INAH (Peraza Lope et al. 1997, 1999a, 1999b, 1999c, 2003; Peraza Lope, Delgado Kú, and Escamilla Ojeda 2002, 2003; Peraza Lope, Escarela Rodríguez, and Delgado Kú 2004) and has been the foundation of four dissertation-length Licenciatura theses by graduates of the Universidad Autónoma de Yucatán. These theses analyze the details of the city's monumental architecture, obsidian industry, mural traditions, and pottery (P. Delgado Kú 2004; Escamilla Ojeda 2004; M. Delgado Kú 2009; Cruz Alvarado 2010).

Fortunately for our purposes, the fastidious standards of reporting by members of the Carnegie team in the *Current Reports* series, including inventories and photographs of artifacts recovered, have permitted us to compile assemblages of materials from specific contexts and fold these data into newer results, particularly with respect to ceramic, stucco, and stone sculptures (chapter 7). Although the Carnegie project sampled many dwellings, methods often involved the trenching of central axes or other features that were likely to yield offerings or burials, as was customary for the archaeology of the 1950s. These data remain a valuable asset because of the costs of research today and newer regulations about partial architectural exploration that make such a large sample of these types of features difficult to obtain. Our own investigations of dwellings have been complementary to prior efforts and employed three modern methods: midden sampling with test pits, screening of all excavated deposits to obtain systematic samples of materials, and full horizontal exposure.

Clifford T. Brown was the first scholar to return to fieldwork at Mayapán following the Carnegie project. His investigations in the 1990s formed the basis of his comprehensive and insightful dissertation on social organization at the city (Brown 1999). He identified key differences in artifact assemblages among domestic groups and demonstrated the importance of cenotes as resources not just for water but as features critical for defining the landscape and social units of the city (Brown 1999, 2005, 2006). Brown's work at Mayapán's houselots paved the way for the investigations of the PEMY project, and we are indebted to him for his help in the field during the early years of our study. His fractal model (Brown 1999; Brown and Witschey 2003) characterizes the organic principles of the city's array of dwellings across the site. This model merits consideration in any subsequent assessments of residential growth and development at the site. Brown also oversaw a valuable survey in Mayapán's hinterlands that has located several contemporary and earlier sites (Brown et al. 2006).

The PEMY project owes its inception to Bruce H. Dahlin, who simply asked Marilyn A. Masson, "Why not perform a study of the economy of Mayapán's dwellings?" during a casual conversation at the 1999 Society for American Archaeology Meeting. His encouragement and direct contributions to questions of the city's economy and ecology helped to launch and sustain this project. The PEMY project performed six field seasons from 2001 to 2009 (figure 1.7). All of the architecture in thirty-six cleared milpa fields (encompassing 52.99 hectares) was fully mapped and has been entered into a GIS database (Hare 2008a, 2008b). A surface survey of all of these milpas was performed and 131 systematic surface collections were collected, primarily from domestic refuse zones (Masson et al. 2008; Masson, Delu, and Peraza Lope 2008). The project also completed 189 test pits, 63 of which were near structures outside the city wall (Russell 2008a, 2008b). Nine domestic buildings have been fully excavated, including eight dwellings and one workshop structure located in a residential area (Masson, Peraza Lope, and Hare 2008; Masson et al. 2012). A colonnaded hall and a temple of the outlying Itzmal Ch'en ceremonial group were also fully excavated and restored in 2008–2009 (Masson et al. 2012; Delgado Kú, Escamilla Ojeda, and Peraza Lope 2012a, 2012b).

The recent book *The Kowoj: Identity, Migration, and Geopolitics in Late Postclassic Petén, Guatemala* represents, in many respects, a study of Mayapán from a hinterlands perspective in the Petén Lakes region of Guatemala (Rice and Rice 2009). This work evaluates the results of years of field research on the Postclassic- to Colonial-era settlement of Zacpetén. The Kowoj were one of the important ethnic groups of Mayapán's confederation, closely tied to the Xiu of western Yucatán who, along with the (Itza-affiliated) Cocom, dominated the governmental affairs of the city (P. Rice 2009a, 2009b; Milbrath 2009; Milbrath and Peraza Lope 2009). Members of the Kowoj group probably left Mayapán just before AD 1400 and resettled (or joined allies and family) after a major political upheaval (chapter 8), according to correlating lines of evidence in historical documents and archaeology (variously interpreted by Jones 1998; P. Rice 2009a; P. Rice 2009c:82). Parallels in architecture, religious ritual, and a specific type of pottery at Mayapán have been tracked archaeologically at Zacpetén, and these patterns support the model that Kowoj ethnogenesis in the Petén region arose from Mayapán roots (Pugh 2002; P. Rice 2009a:15, 2009b; Pugh and Rice 2009a:94, 112). Many references in *The Kowoj* cite specific findings of our study at Mayapán, particularly Prudence M. Rice's interpretations of the similarity of Zacpetén's Chompoxte Red-on-Cream pottery slip color and decoration and Mayapán's Tecoh Red-on-Buff and Pelé

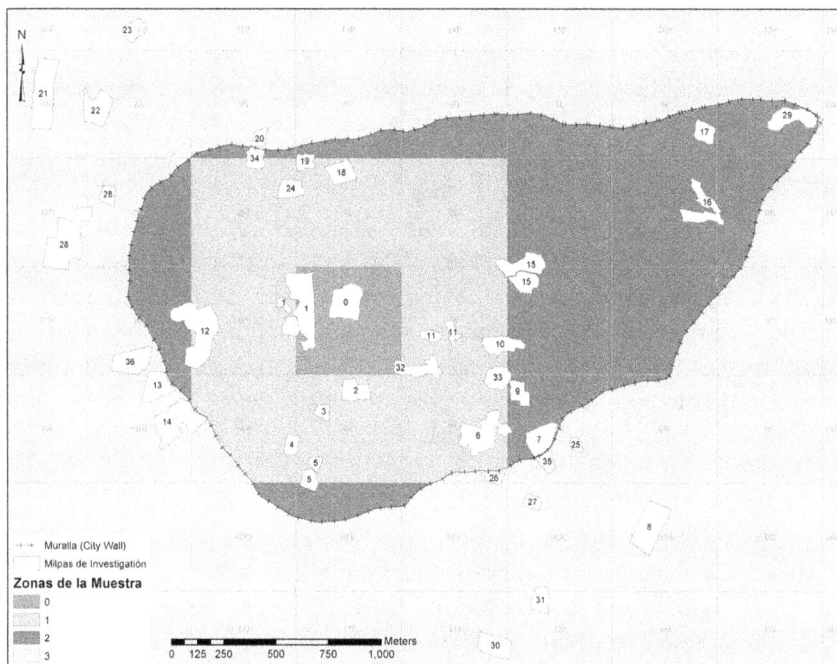

FIGURE 1.7. *Cleared milpa fields at Mayapán that have been fully mapped and surface collected by the PEMY project.*

Polychrome vessels, which were recovered in abundance at elite Residence Y-45a, perhaps a Kowoj dwelling (P. Rice 2009a:15, 2009d:37, 49; Pugh and Rice 2009a:92; Rice and Cecil 2009:242). We evaluate some of these interpretations in chapters 3, 5, and 6, along with other lines of evidence for social diversity in Mayapán's dwellings.

MAYAPÁN'S PLACE IN MAYA RESEARCH

As one of the last great centers of commercial, political, and religious centralization in the Maya area prior to the arrival of Europeans to the New World, Mayapán is different in a number of important ways from most of its better-known Classic-era predecessor kingdoms in the Maya region. These differences include its temporal placement within the Postclassic Period, its unique position as an unrivalled political capital in the Maya realm, and its highly nucleated, dense, walled settlement.

DECADENCE

The city dates to the Postclassic Period, a temporal interval from AD 1100 to AD 1500 that has received comparatively little scholarly attention and recognition relative to its Classic and Preclassic antecedents. Postclassic Period scholarship has labored long and hard in the trenches over the past thirty years to overturn branding of this era as "degenerate" (Pollock 1962:16), "the death of a civilization," or the "dramatic culmination of a long process of cultural decay" (Proskouriakoff 1955:88). Harry Pollock's (1962:17) summary statement at the end of his introduction to the impressive Carnegie project report offers, "Looking at the results of the work as a whole, I think that it has been worthwhile, even though we were dealing with a degenerate civilization, devoid of great art, that to all intents and purposes reached a dead end in the Spanish Conquest."

REFRAMING THE DEGENERATE MODEL

Important works that treat Postclassic Maya society in its proper anthropological context and emphasize its accomplishments over its supposed shortcomings with respect to the Classic Period have emerged since the 1970s (Carmack and Wallace 1977; Freidel 1981; Freidel and Sabloff 1984; A. Chase and Rice 1985a, 1985b; D. Chase 1985a, 1985b; Rice and Rice 1985; Freidel 1985; Pendergast 1986, 1993; D. Rice 1986; P. Rice 1987; Robles Castellanos and Andrews 1986; Sabloff and Andrews 1986; Fox 1987; Chase and Chase 1988; Graham 1991; Jones 1989, 1998; Andrews 1993; Alexander 2005; Restall 2001; Masson 2000; Kepecs 2003; Smith and Berdan 2003a; Sabloff 2007; Pugh 2001, 2002; Rice and Rice 2009; Paris 2012). For recent summaries of this transformation in scholarly thinking, see Sabloff (2007) and P. Rice (2009a). Many of these works draw on the ethnohistory and archaeology of Maya settlements that continued to be occupied during the transformations associated with the Contact and Colonial Periods of the sixteenth and seventeenth centuries, the topic of an eloquent recent synthesis by Elizabeth Graham (2011). A world-systems perspective has been employed to consider the political, economic, and ideological interactions of the entire Postclassic Mesoamerican world that helped to put the Maya area, along with many other regions, into comparative context (Smith and Berdan 2003a; Kepecs and Kohl 2003).

What about Mayapán and Postclassic Period archaeology in general initially provoked derogatory assessment? The traditional list is short and has been well-refuted: the architecture is smaller, the ruins are less well preserved, fewer hieroglyphic records are carved in stone, the aesthetics are judged to be poorer, the long count was no longer used to reckon linear time, and the institution of divine kingship was eroded—and with it the practice of interring rulers in lavish tombs and recording lengthy dynastic records. The size and quality of buildings, construction materials, and the media of art and writing are perhaps most easily dismissed. As much Postclassic Maya architecture was built anew, it lacks the size contributed by larger, earlier building foundations. It also true, however, that massive buildings were not desired in this period, as is generally the case for secondary states (Rathje 1975). The heavy use of stucco would have made these structures glorious in their day, but this medium is especially vulnerable to erosional annual rains. Poorer ruins do not a poorer civilization make, and it has been argued that it is unfair to judge a society by the endurance power of building styles (Webb 1964; Sabloff 2007:16). A preference for mural programs and bark paper books also resulted in poor preservation and recovery in the present day, made worse by Friar Diego de Landa's religious inquisition in which 400 codex books were collected and burned in a single day. Miguel Delgado Kú's (2009) thesis reveals that murals covered the interior rooms of most of the monumental edifices of Mayapán's epicentral plazas. Columns of temples and halls were routinely stuccoed and painted multiple times or sculpted into images of gods or dynasts (Peraza Lope 1999; Milbrath and Peraza Lope 2003a). A confederacy-style council government that replaced divine kingship also disseminated wealth across a plethora of noble families, whose chief monumental investment tended to be in colonnaded halls. Dynasts no longer commissioned funerary monuments to celebrate their deaths, although temples proliferated in number to commemorate a complex polytheistic set of deities and calendrical ceremonies that attest to an amplified religious bureaucracy (Masson, Hare, and Peraza Lope 2006). Principal temples such as the Temple of Kukulcan, the Temple of the Painted Niches, the Round Temple (Q-152), and burial shaft temples that include the Fisherman Temple and the Crematory exemplify Mayapán's mythological charter while secondary temples are located in surrounding groups along with colonnaded halls that frame the city's monumental center (Proskouriakoff 1962a; chapter 2). Portraits of dynasts and ancestral gods were created at Mayapán at secondary temples, halls, shrines, and oratories. In fact, most of these edifices have remnants of modeled plaster or stone portraits of such personages. Credit and acclaim for revered dynasts was abundant, but the numbers of important players increased, diluting the impact of any single governor.

MERCANTILE MODEL

What did nobles do with wealth, given the ethnohistorical and archaeological evidence for maximal commercial development during this period? Sabloff and Rathje proposed a rise in the power of the mercantile sector and with it the implication that wealth (proceeds from commercial exchanges) was reinvested into trading ventures and pursuits other than monumental construction (Sabloff and Rathje 1975; Rathje 1975). Specifically, merchant elites tended to keep their "capital liquid" (Sabloff 2007:17). This model most easily fits what is known for regional merchants who trafficked high-value items along seaborne routes of the Gulf and Caribbean coasts of the Yucatán Peninsula as far as Xicalanco, Tabasco, and Naco or Nito in Honduras. Such far-ranging ventures were a privilege reserved for members of the noble class, although such individuals would have also been active within smaller trade circuits such as northern Yucatán. A nested set of vendors and merchants, operating over shorter geographic distances within polities or cities, handled local trading activities (chapter 6). Sabloff and Rathje proposed a mercantile transformation to explain Classic to Postclassic societal differences. Masson (2000) has been one promoter of this view, but she has recently tempered this interpretation as a matter of degree (Masson and Freidel 2012, 2013). Sabloff and Rathje's research had the effect of setting the Postclassic Maya Period apart—perhaps too much so—from earlier Maya traditions. Commercial development in this period has even led to its characterization as one of Mexicanization and the implicit assumption that the Classic Maya, by definition, engaged in little commerce of relevance. More recently, the question of commerce and market exchange has been reopened for the Classic Period, and, by extension, to the dawn of Maya states during the Late Preclassic era (A. Chase and D. Chase 2004; Dahlin et al. 2010; Masson and Freidel 2012). For some scholars, the time depth of market exchange was always suspected (e.g., Fry 2003; Culbert 2003; Moholy-Nagy 2003). We favor the interpretation that commercial exchange was amplified during the Postclassic Period, but that the Postclassic Maya did not invent it. An amplification occurred in scale—specifically in the matter of regular exchanges and dependencies across the Maya area among coastal and inland zones, among the Maya lowlands and highlands, and among major towns and trading centers at the margins of the Maya area. While maritime trade networks were advantageous for the movement of goods to the boundaries of the Maya area (Sabloff and Rathje 1975), overland routes never ceased in importance (Roys 1957; Piña Chan 1978). From a household perspective, greater quantities of nonlocal goods used in daily life, such as obsidian or Gulf Coast Matillas Fine Orange pottery that could be purchased at the city market, reflect the impact of trade (Rathje, Gregory, and Wiseman 1978; P. Rice 1987; Masson 2000). Earlier sites such as Tikal and Chunchucmil were similar to Mayapán in terms of the volume of trade goods reaching ordinary households, but such access varies markedly between sites located within different political alliance networks (Braswell 2010; Masson and Freidel 2012, 2013; Hutson, Dahlin, and Mazeau 2012). This unevenness at Classic Period sites contrasts with the Postclassic, where even small sites like Laguna de On or Caye Coco had obsidian blade to chert tool ratios of 2:1 or 3:1 (Masson, Hare, and Peraza Lope 2006:201). The evidence for a Postclassic commercial amplification lies in a consistently high level of regional trade goods at households irrespective of site size, location, or political significance in the Postclassic Maya world.

The well-developed marketing institutions of the Postclassic Period are also indicated by extensive Contact Period accounts of these systems, including monies and prices, tiered market and merchant hierarchies and functions, trading regulations, and officials who presided over marketplaces (chapter 6). Greater time depth for these types of systems has been demonstrated prior to Mayapán at Chichén Itzá (Kepecs, Feinman, and Boucher 1994). It is probable that marketing systems were foundational to the stability of Classic and Late Preclassic Maya kingdoms as well. The archaeological correlates of production heterogeneity and widespread distributions of valuables across social status lines are similar among Classic Period sites and Mayapán (Masson and Freidel 2012, 2013). The issue of earlier market systems is not central to the pages of this book, which focuses on the specific aspects of a known market society on the temporal threshold of European arrival. It is our hope, however, that documenting the material signatures of market processes on the household archaeology at Mayapán will make possible better comparisons for investigators working in different regions and time periods of Mesoamerica.

A PRIMATE CITY

Mayapán is distinguished by its status as a single, dominant political center in the Maya lowlands region, an area that extended across parts of the modern nations of Mexico, Guatemala, Belize, and Honduras. In this realm, it had no rivals of equivalent size or power, as its population exceeded all other settlements by an order of magnitude (M. Smith 2005). When the entire Maya area is considered, including the Guatemalan highlands, only one political capital approaches Mayapán's significance—the K'ich'ean center of Utatlán/K'umarcaj in Guatemala (chapter 2; Carmack 1977; Carmack and Wallace

1977; Wallace 1977). In contrast, during the preceding Classic Period, multiple competitor kingdoms arrayed in mosaic alliance networks dotted the Maya realm. Power plays of the most influential central places in this realm, such as Calakmul, Tikal, Caracol, Copán, and Palenque, created a competitive atmosphere (Martin and Grube 2008). Relatively speaking, Mayapán was regionally more important in its day than individual centers of the Classic Period—it was the literal center of the Maya realm of its time. Similarly, Chichén Itzá was likely unrivalled in the ninth and tenth centuries AD. It is unfortunate that regional Postclassic archaeology in northern Yucatán has not yet documented the network of towns and secondary centers of Mayapán's era. The fact that some modern towns are the probable sites of Postclassic centers complicates this task. For example, the post-Mayapán Cocom province of Sotuta had as its seat the town of Tibolon, which is visible as a small place on modern maps just outside of the modern town of Sotuta (Tozzer 1941:37n178). In such places, it is possible that Postclassic settlement has not been completely obliterated by later development. Recent survey work by Brown and his colleagues (2006) also reveals an ancient landscape dotted with towns in the Mayapán area.

POPULATION

The settlement of the city of Mayapán is dense and concentrates within the Great Wall (9.1 kilometer circumference). A recent survey outside the city wall reports additional settlement to a distance of around 500 meters in all directions—this work reveals that Mayapán was home to a total population of 15,000–17,000 souls (Russell 2008a). House counts at the site may have been underestimated, which prompted Brown (1999:149, 189) to offer a similar population range for the zone inside the wall alone. If both Brown and Russell are correct, then the city's population may have approached 20,000 (see also Proskouriakoff 1955:85). The nucleation of Mayapán's settlement is unlike the more spatially dispersed sprawling metropoli of prior centuries (e.g., Folan 1983; Tourtellot and Sabloff 1994; Cobos 2004; Chase et al. 2011; M. Smith 2011b). The walled settlement would have housed an average of 33 people per hectare, based on conservative dwelling counts and an average of 5.6 persons per dwelling. But densities varied within Mayapán, and this figure would have been higher in the downtown area compared to neighborhoods closer to the city wall. Some neighborhoods had 77–126 people per hectare (chapter 5). Classic-era northern Maya cities such as Sayil and Chunchucmil housed an estimated 20–23 people per hectare, a figure higher than some of largest southern cities that exhibit lower densities (Barnhart 2001). As for earlier Maya societies, warfare was a defining characteristic of the Postclassic Period, but in the case of Mayapán, this concern permeated life of a dense urban character within the refuge offered by one of the largest city walls reported for a Maya site. The ruined wall foundations presently reach up to 2 meters in height, and they were probably higher in the past. Stone parapets lined the interior of the wall in places (Shook 1952:9). The wall is penetrated by twelve gates, including seven elaborate entrances, some vaulted.

KUKULCAN'S REALM

Mayapán is said to have been founded by a priest and statesman, the charismatic deified figure of Kukulcan, or the Feathered Serpent. If such a personage existed in the flesh, he was represented several times by individuals claiming the name. Kukulcan is credited with leadership at Tula, departure and exile from Tula, and founding the key centers of Cholula, Chichén Itzá, and Mayapán, among others (Ringle 2004). This personage at Mayapán was Ah Nacxit Kukulcan, probably also known as Hunac Ceel, who defeated Chichén Itzá (Tozzer 1941:34n172). Accounts of Hunac Ceel, who may have been cast to his death in the cenote at Chichén Itzá (Tozzer 1941:183n956), are contradictory and have long confounded ethnohistorians. Foundation myths involving Kukulcan/Quetzalcoatl were broadly claimed at Mesoamerican sites as indicated by art at sites like Xochicalco and Uxmal that include massive Feathered Serpent facades (Hirth 1989; Kowalski 2008). Many fine publications analyze Feathered Serpent mythology that is chronicled in documentary accounts, monumental art, and religious ritual and paraphernalia (Carrasco 1982; Ringle, Gallareta Negrón, and Bey 1998; Ringle 2004; Bey and Ringle 2007; Pohl 2003a, 2003b). Whether he was a living personage or not, Kukulcan represented a visionary statesman credited with founding a civil, urban society at Mayapán. That society—his realm and the realm of those who adapted and perpetuated his charter in subsequent generations—is the subject of this book. Carlos Peraza Lope has spent nineteen years investigating the monumental vestiges of the lords and priests that carried on Kukulcan's legacy at Mayapán. Together we have dedicated the past fourteen years to gather a more complete picture of urban life from the city at large—for the ranks of the realm itself reflect the best measures of the effects of governance.

This book evaluates the evidence for a high degree of integration of political, social, economic, and ideological institutions at the political capital of Mayapán and, by extension, throughout portions of its confederacy. Of key interest is the middle ground, where linkages occurred among the governing class and the governed. We endeavor to consider both top-down, idealized strategies for state-making as well as bottom-up perspectives reconstructed from the material realities of household activities. From the beginning of our research at Mayapán, we anticipated that no simple, monolithic models would emerge from our research, as might be expected for any archaeological investigations of a city—especially a capital of a late-stage secondary state with ample and far-reaching ties. Many of the cumulative developments of the *longue durée* of Maya civilization resided in the social memory of Mayapán's residents, and this historical reservoir merged with a new cosmopolitan world context that brought an influx of goods, ideas, and exotic newcomers into the urban zone (Smith and Berdan 2003a). As Harry Pollock concluded at the end of the Carnegie Mayapán project, the city was a place with diverse social constituents and influences that meshed with the unifying efforts of the confederacy's governors. It is these pluralistic signatures that we unveil in the analyses of monuments, settlement, artifacts, and art in the ensuing chapters. Despite clear variation, patterns do emerge at analytical scales varying from the most general to the most specific. At best, we have succeeded in making Mayapán an archaeological case study of significance to anthropological archaeologists in the Maya area, in Mesoamerica, and beyond.

CHAPTERS OF THIS VOLUME

As Mayapán fell only decades before the arrival of the Europeans, we take advantage of the opportunity to employ the direct historical approach and vet ethnohistorical accounts with the archaeological record for details of political history and religious practice (chapters 2, 7, 8). Information on the political organization of the city is rich. Efforts to correlate names and events with archaeological chronology perpetually strive for greater accuracy, although few works today can approximate the epic insights on Mayapán and contemporary towns provided by Roys (1957, 1962, 1972). We review a cross section of most pertinent diachronic and synchronic documentary descriptions of the development and operation of the confederacy of Mayapán, as well as our archaeological chronology for the city, in chapter 2. The environs of Mayapán were occupied from the Late Preclassic period (350 BC–AD 250) forward, and the area was populous during the Terminal Classic Period from around AD 800–1000. But settlement in the vicinity of the city prior to the Postclassic Period was dispersed near the margins of the city wall or beyond it, and there is little evidence for a coherent town that would have served as a direct precursor to the Postclassic capital (chapter 4; Peraza Lope et al. 2006). The modern town of Telchaquillo, located 1 kilometer north of Mayapán's epicenter, has Classic-era mounded architecture and residential architecture, and it is likely that this was the center of political activity prior to Mayapán's founding; a survey indicates that other clusters of Terminal Classic settlement exist beyond 500 meters of the city wall in several directions (Russell 2008a).

Influential players in the polity's council government built and used enduring monumental symbols in the form of the site center's temples, colonnaded halls, and supporting ritual buildings. The varied architectural and artistic programs of the site center reflect dynamic visions of the foundational charters of the Mayapán state as expressed through creation mythology (Pugh 2001; Milbrath and Peraza Lope 2003a, 2003b; Milbrath, Peraza Lope, and Kelgado Kú 2010; Barrera Rubio and Peraza Lope 2004; M. Delgado Kú 2009). Layers of political strategies for legitimation—ranging from divine birth to supernatural communication and sanction to state terror—are revealed from analyses of monumental center features. Chapter 2 highlights the most important public art at the site center, and in chapter 3 we zoom in on three case studies of focal architecture in the settlement zone that have been investigated in our collaborative research, including the Itzmal Ch'en Temple H-17 and Hall H-15, which form two of six major edifices of this outlying ceremonial group, and secondary elite Residence Y-45a. These edifices provide examples of peripheral groups where activities were closely synchronized with those of the center. Following the presentation of these examples, we zoom out to a broader scale and extend our knowledge of these cases to similar features across the city's landscape.

Considering the strategic placement of focal nodes such as Itzmal Ch'en has assisted us in identifying important planning principles of the urban zone. Chapters 3 and 4 present our argument that such groups facilitated administrative reach into the urban neighborhoods, yet at the same time we are doubtful that they were perceived as hegemonic symbols of state control. On the contrary, they were probably perceived as place markers, not unlike the way that smaller cathedrals or chapels defined multifunctional plaza spaces, intersections, and navigational referents in larger medieval towns and cities that also possessed a central cathedral and principle town square (Pounds 1973:347). On a general level, monumental plazas served similar functions broadly for historical and ancient cities (Lynch 1960; Rapoport 1990). Like cenotes, outlying ceremonial plazas were landmarks with a sacred aura; but unlike them, citizens of the city who had the means to sponsor the construction of civic-ceremonial buildings chose their location. Outlying focal architecture would have had its own particular history and set of sponsors and perhaps were dedicated to specific patron gods. Such groups would also have differentiated and defined the residential zone. Monuments shaped the perception of the city's built environment for residents and other pedestrians who navigated their way through the urban mazeway of houselots (Lynch 1960). Loosely following Lynch's nomenclature for functional attributes of city landscapes, chapter 4 summarizes our improved understanding of the lanes that traversed the city and its neighborhoods and open spaces that could have served as commons areas and marketplaces. The nuts and bolts of administrative duties such as tribute collection, organizing labor for festivals, coordinating military service, and the like were probably performed by secondary officials living in the city's residential zones, as documentary accounts suggest. In chapter 4 we also consider the distribution of elite palaces and secondary residences and the implications of these data for social differentiation of the residential zone. Overall, evidence for planning at Mayapán is greater than previously suggested, and we argue that the activities of the residential populace were well articulated with the objectives of the city's governing elites.

Dwellings were the essential units that comprised Mayapán's neighborhoods, society, and economy, and we fully explore their spatial and metric characteristics in chapter 5. Inspired by John W. Janusek's (2004) approach to studying the articulation of state and hometown identities in the multiethnic landscape of Tiwanaku, at Mayapán we also track integrative and transformative material signatures of polity. A diverse citizenry filtered emblematic state norms at the household level, yet overall, the city's residents adopted relatively homogenous styles of domestic architecture and styles of pottery and tools. Mayapán is unusual in terms of its standard house type with highly specific features, and this dwelling form is scarcely observed in allied territories (Freidel and Sabloff 1984). As might be expected for any large ancient city, idiosyncratic variations in domestic architecture are also detected archaeologically, but these are few in number and tend to cluster, perhaps indicating ethnic or other social distinctions. House form is only sometimes an indicator of state-encouraged emblematic style (Aldenderfer and Stanish 1993:7) Beyond form, other variables, including house size, orientation, the number of houses per group, and the size distribution of houselots, represent an insightful set of indices that aid us in characterizing urban life across the residential zones (chapter 5). Houselot analysis has been pursued at Mayapán since Bullard began to document domestic enclosures as part of the Carnegie project (Bullard 1952, 1953, 1954). The term *houselot* refers to a dwelling or set of dwellings and their yard spaces most often defined by encircling boulder walls, or *albarradas*, at Mayapán. Rare at Maya sites, the houselot boundary wall tradition provides special analytical opportunities to assess emically defined social space (chapter 5).

The economic organization of the city, the topic of chapter 6, considers production and consumption patterns reflected in the assemblages of residences and public buildings investigated by the INAH (1996–2004) and PEMY (2001–2009) projects. Readers of this book will hopefully receive our extended treatment of this topic with the patience it deserves, considering the fact that it represents the major thrust of our collaborative research over the past decade under the auspices of a project titled "The Economic Foundations of Mayapán." The analyses of artifact frequency distributions is used to determine the importance of local and regional scale market exchange for ordinary residents, as measured in the quantities of nonlocal finished goods, nonlocal raw materials (for household industries), locally made valuables, and the scale of surplus production destined for exchange. Detailed data in chapter 6 supports the argument that occupational specialization was well developed at Mayapán, and accordingly, that households at the city were quite dependent on one another and on regional market exchange for the materials used in everyday life. Some residents opted to perform part-time craft production of mundane items while other craftspeople were highly skilled artisans who made the most sacred or valuable of objects. Other residents processed surplus food and engaged in general service activities. Some dwellings were homes to farmers while other edifices housed men who were perhaps performing temporary obligatory service to the state. The quantity of valuable possessions reflects the degree of wealth obtained by commoner and noble classes (chapter 6), and this line of inquiry addresses a key aspect of urban life: How prosperous were ordinary residents, and what kind of variation is observed? We conclude that crafting families, who presumably engaged in some degree of trade in the city's marketplace, were the wealthiest commoners. Other ordinary residential groups that did not engage in crafting tended to have fewer valuable goods. Evidence suggests that some commoners were poor, especially at briefly occupied dwellings in the periphery of the walled settlement. In this regard, Mayapán's commoner affluence cannot be simply characterized, and it meets expectations for a populous urban landscape in terms of variable wealth below the elite sector. New migrants or transitory sectors of the population might be expected to have lower wealth than established urban families.

Religion was an important industry at Mayapán, although one that is difficult to separate from politics, as discussed in chapter 2. By all accounts, parallel sets of hierarchically organized officials populated the political ranks as well as the priesthood during the Postclassic Period (Landa 1941:27; Carmack

1981a:16; Restall 2001:table 11.3). Sons of the nobility tended to find their life's work in political, priestly, or military posts, and some noblemen engaged in long-distance trading. High-ranking priests meddled transparently in Mayapán's political affairs, and there is little doubt that countless calendrically and spatially coordinated ritual observances provided a critical adhesive that helped to bind together the factions of the confederacy. Despite evidence for an amplified religious bureaucracy compared to the Classic Period (chapter 2), religion at Mayapán and its lowland contemporaries has routinely been characterized as decentralized (Proskouriakoff 1955:88, 1962b:136; J. Thompson 1957:624; Pollock 1962:17)—a claim that is oddly linked to the potential portability of deity effigy censer vessels that tend to be ubiquitous in contexts dating to the last half of the Postclassic period. We refute this assertion in chapters 3, 5, and 7, based on the paucity of ritual objects and features at ordinary houses and their concentration at civic-ceremonial edifices and elite residences. Evidence for household shrines and altars at Mayapán is also minimal for commoner dwellings. One might facetiously point out that evidence is greater for religious decentralization in the Classic Period given the frequency of domestic funerary shrines and the close association of caches and burials (e.g., Becker 2003; McAnany 1995). Although Mayapán's commoner houses, including affluent examples, have funerary features, these tend to be compartments within dwellings or simple graves in front of or alongside house groups, and private funerary temples are absent for sub-elite contexts. But we do not doubt that residents of Mayapán were devout and that they practiced ritual at the domestic scale, perhaps with a suite of perishable materials. Many Mesoamerican cultures through space and time widely shared this characteristic. It is interesting that Mayapán's figurines—mostly female—are scarce in commoner houses and thus do not reflect their common use in domestic ritual, as has been argued for contemporary regions in central Mexico (M. Smith 2002; Masson and Peraza Lope 2012).

Effigy censer ceramic sculptures, along with stone and plaster portraits, represent the most direct material icons of religious practice at the city. Chapters 3 and 7 present the results of a contextual analysis of sculptures of these media at edifices investigated by the Carnegie, INAH, and PEMY projects. This analysis represents a comprehensive attempt to analyze the entire corpus of sculptures per context. Masson (2000:tables 6.1, 6.2) analyzed an array of stone and stucco sculptures published by Proskouriakoff (1962a). Chapter 7 expands this study to include ceramic effigies and other portraits reported in the Carnegie *Current Reports* (Weeks 2009), Robert Smith's (1971) ceramic monograph, and new finds by Peraza Lope and the INAH team. The distributions reveal two important patterns. First, most edifices were used on multiple occasions that involved the invocation or propitiation of different patron gods. Second, despite this varied use, some civic-ceremonial structures had concentrations of specific, clearly identifiable Maya gods while others exhibited a focus on individualistic, unique entities that may have represented the apotheosized ancestors of particular lineages. Chapter 7 builds on J. Eric S. Thompson's (1957) deity classifications for Mayapán with the advantage of a larger, more varied sample of effigy ceramics and other sculptures found by the INAH project.

Mayapán rose and fell rather quickly for an ancient state. The center and the settlement zone were probably up and running by AD 1200. The city staggered to its knees during the fourteenth century, briefly recovered, but then suffered collapse and abandonment by around AD 1448. The apogee of the city may have lasted for a brief 150-year (or so) interval, yet its full sequence of occupation and political capital status endured around 270–300 years. Chapter 8 reviews the tumultuous documentary history on the travails of Mayapán, especially during the final one hundred years prior to collapse. The accounts are inexact and chronologically insecure, but we consider Roys' thoughtful interpretations alongside new archaeological and paleoenvironmental evidence that lends credibility to the retrospective histories. In the tale of the prolonged decline of Mayapán we read in the subtext a baseline of resiliency and strength. The city was capable of withstanding a battery of hardships for an extended period of time. Given the impacts of climatic disasters to the food supply, we also infer a reasonably flexible market economy that moved food across the peninsula from east to west in times of shortages, as was the case for many preindustrial states (chapters 7, 8). When the city's end finally came, it is clear that options for recovery were dismal, and the collapse of the confederation and the great urban center are best understood as the culmination of a long series of disasters that may have been difficult for any ancient state to overcome. Much has been made of the balkanized Postclassic Maya landscape at the time of Spanish contact, but as summarized in chapter 8, the plagues of the Mayapán provinces did not desist with the city's fall, as drought, hunger, epidemic, and warfare cycles ravaged the land until the eve of European arrival. When peace may have finally been achieved, and with it the stability upon which a new era of centralization may have been possible, the onset of the Colonial era truncated such options.

The separation of political, social, economic, and religious institutions into different chapters of this book is counterintuitive to our fundamental premise that Mayapán's organizational systems were profoundly integrated, as we claim in the book's concluding chapter (chapter 9). The city's political economy was founded on complementary and overlapping exchange systems involving gifting, tribute, corvée labor, and the marketplace. As a productive place, Mayapán and its craftspeople made various combinations of pots, shell objects, stone tools, obsidian blades, and luxury or restricted goods like copper ornaments or ceramic effigies. Generalists also resided at the capital, presumably farming and raising game and fowl and performing service duties as required. While the full occupational diversity of the city has likely yet to be documented, it is clear to us that households at Mayapán depended on local and regional trade for the material needs of daily life. The city also imported much of its own raw material sources.

The noble class at Mayapán had a vested interest in the production and consumption of the essentials (real or perceived) of daily life and in the mechanisms for their circulation. The valuation of goods originated in the symbolic realm of prestigious social display; currency units were as easily worn as jewels as traded in strands or jars for corn, cloth, services, or any other desirable. The social fabric was literally conjoined by a network of houselot walls that grouped clusters of relatives and neighbors together in neighborhoods that were probably named according to the nearest cenote or outlying ceremonial group (Brown 2005, 2006). Walls, gates, lanes, and monuments also articulated neighborhoods and facilitated pedestrian thoroughfares that traversed the small worlds of neighborhood life. Overseer houses did the governors' bidding in the barrios by tapping the productive energies of residents for contributions of labor and taxes. Ward leaders also coordinated festivals, ceremonies, processions, and proclamations that beckoned neighborhood families toward a sense of citywide social identity. Priests and politicos contributed to the monumental landscape across the city. Replicated architectural arrangements and parallel artistic objects testify to great coordination among center and periphery that we attribute to governmental decree and strategic urban planning. A plethora of gods at public buildings parallels what we know from documentary sources: calendrical ceremonies were frequent and complex. The archaeology of the city now documents the layers of ritual practice at individual buildings and an undeniable concentration of ritual paraphernalia use at elite residences or civic-ceremonial edifices (chapters 3, 7).

Our advancement of an integrated and complex model of Postclassic Mayapán society directly challenges prior characterizations of this period as inherently weak and decentralized. In a very real sense, Mayapán and its contemporaries have often been assessed retrospectively—from the scattered political landscape of townships (*cahob*) encountered one hundred years after the city's fall by Spanish chroniclers (Restall 2001). Judging Mayapán by its collapse and post-collapse periods is akin to judging Tikal by its degree of political coalescence during the ninth and tenth centuries—that is, during the time of its disintegration. The fractious rivalry that led to the Xiu aggression on the Cocom that terminated the confederacy during K'atun 8 Ahau (AD 1441–1461) has been used to characterize Mayapán as fundamentally weak and decentralized despite the fact that the polity held together for at least two and a half centuries and survived episodic bouts of pestilence and the correlating rocky political aftermaths. The tenacity demonstrated by Mayapán during troubled times reflects to us the wiry resiliency of the Mayapán state. Many ancient states are functionally managed by potentially divisive forces from among the roster of politicians, military captains, or priests. Factionalism at Mayapán was not unique.

Deriving models of Mayapán from the political scramble leading to its fall and the ensuing regional balkanization of the Contact Period is a good example of an inappropriate application of the direct historical approach. Long-term state cycles have a dynamic quality (Marcus 1993) and a conjunction of external and internal forces collided in the "segmented century" that followed the city's abandonment, resulting in a fragmented, decentralized realm (Restall 2001). Even centralized periods, including the height of the K'iche' empire at Utatlán, have been characterized as *segmentary*, a term that refers to component parts of a unitary government tied to a political capital (Fox 1987). John W. Fox's detailed investigation into the social, political, and ideological makeup of Utatlán's confederation is invaluable, but the segmentary state model emphasizes the trees (corporate groups) over the forest (empire).

Religious institutions were also critical for cementing Maya geopolitics (P. Rice 2004). Towns across Yucatán rotated the burden of responsibility for festivities and ritual observances associated with each 20-year k'atun of the 13 k'atun cycle of 256 or so years, referred to as the *may* cycle. Alfred M. Tozzer (1941:38) describes k'atun stones being "set" at these various towns, and multiple towns were sometimes accorded this honor for a particular k'atun (P. Rice 2004:78; P. Rice 2009d). A number of large and enigmatic stone drum altars populate the edges of Mayapán's Main Plaza and North Plaza that may be related to such procedures. Political geography was closely bound to passages of calendrical intervals. This time and space matrix was affirmed through territorial, ritualized circumambulation and a variety of pageants, pilgrimages, and celebrations (P. Rice 2004). Prudence Rice (2004) has argued for great time depth for may-oriented monumental construction and shifts in politico-geographic power and prestige. Given the importance of this institution in the Postclassic and Contact Periods, the probability of deep historical roots is strong. An open question is the degree to which shifting may burdens correlate with shifting centers of political power, as the may model suggests periodic willful abdication of power by dynastic centers so that others could assume the cycle's burden (P. Rice 2004:270). Even if this was the ideal scenario, it is easy to imagine how self-interested political agents might have worked around expectations of power concession. Intriguing, however, is that the duration of Mayapán as a political capital falls quite close to the may interval of 256 years—according to both archaeological and ethnohistorical evidence; at the minimum, this fact would have been convenient to later purposes of mythical history. The proposition that may and k'atun cycles influenced politically motivated construction surges at monumental centers is quite compelling (Milbrath and Peraza Lope 2003a, 2009; P. Rice 2004; P. Rice 2009d:31), and it is noteworthy that archaeological periods such as the Early Classic and Late Classic mark transitions in material culture that also approximate the length of may cycles (P. Rice 2004:53–54, 83).

The chapters of this book step back in time and precede the protohistoric slump in the cycle—when integrative political, religious, and economic institutions bound the confederated units into a polity that amounted to an entity much more powerful and complex than the sum of its parts. It is not our intent to paint a utopian view of Mayapán or any other ancient city. Urban places, then and now, were arenas where dialectical struggles played themselves out in contexts that would have ranged at Mayapán from political meetings at the resplendent Hall of Kings (Q-163), to the daily gatherings of women at the waterhole of Itzmal Ch'en. Mayapán had its critics, its simmering internal resentments, its enraptured priests, its enlightened statesmen, its thuggish war captains, its cagey entrepreneurs, its coerced or enslaved laborers, and more. But in this regard the political capital would have been on par with many ancient cities of similar size and regional significance. The earnest objective of this book is not to reify Mayapán but to place this settlement on the list of complex and important ancient cities that contribute to ongoing anthropological goals of obtaining insight through comparative analysis of ancient urban life.

2

Politics and Monumental
Legacies

"He shall declare his lordship. Perhaps not
merely [or in vain?] did he raise himself
to chieftainship, to priesthood, likewise to
captaincy, during his reign, on his throne,
on his mat."

—Roys (1962:44), in reference
to a Mayapán lord of K'atun
9 Ahau, AD 1303–1323

CARLOS PERAZA LOPE AND
MARILYN A. MASSON

The topic of Postclassic Maya political structure has
been studied extensively. Contact Period documentary
accounts offer intriguing details and scholarly attention has focused on the changes that contrast political systems of this period with those of earlier Maya
intervals (e.g., Roys 1957; Schele and Freidel 1990; Fox
1987; Schele and Mathews 1998; Jones 1998; Masson
2001a; Masson 2001b; Masson, Hare, and Peraza Lope
2006; Ringle and Bey 2001; Ringle 2004; Restall 2001;
Sabloff 2007). This chapter provides an overview of historical and archaeological data that reflect aspects of
Mayapán's modes of governance. As a result of recent
research, the city's political organization can now be
viewed more diachronically. Here we consider new
findings within the framework of the foundation of the
political capital and the rise to power of the Mayapán
state. Archaeological chronology building has contributed significantly to this inquiry. The city's demise is
treated separately in chapter 8. Complementary studies of monumental architecture art have been undertaken in collaborative research by Carlos Peraza Lope
and Susan Milbrath. In particular, they correlate building programs at Mayapán with the major dynasties of
Mayapán: the Cocom and the Xiu (e.g., Masson 2000;
Milbrath and Peraza Lope 2003a, 2009). Sustained

DOI: 10.5876/9781607323204.c002

39

efforts of the Proyecto Maya Colonial have developed archaeological corre-lates of the Kowoj ethnic group at Mayapán and in the Petén Lakes region (Rice and Rice 2009).

Monumental center art, including mural and sculpture programs, reflects Mayapán's position as a central node for religious pilgrimage, a place where top-ranking officials deliberated in political assemblies and as the seat of a military power of considerable might. The second half of this chapter reviews the highlights of Mayapán's major monumental works and the lasting tes-timonies of propagated state symbolism that they represent. Monumental displays can be read as strategies for power legitimation for many ancient complex societies. Particularly significant cross-cultural patterns include the expression of divine charters through founding creation mythologies and the explicit broadcasting of state terror in programs emphasizing warfare and sac-rifice (e.g., Schele and Freidel 1990; Freidel, Schele, and Parker 1993; Sugiyama 2004; Dickson 2006; Headrick 2007; McAnany 2010). Political art at the site's center also reinvents ancient dynastic and divine claims to power that echo those of the deeper Maya past but with a transformed cosmopolitan flair that also incorporates deities and creation myths from the broader Mesoamerican world, especially central Mexico (J. Thompson 1957; Proskouriakoff 1962a; Milbrath and Peraza Lope 2003a; Barrera Rubio and Peraza Lope 2004; M. Delgado Kú 2009). Warfare was an instrumental device for the development and maintenance of the Mayapán state, and it was closely linked to the prac-tice of captive sacrifice and a slave trade industry. The site's sacrificial burial shaft temples and the façade of the early Temple of Kukulcan glorify this institutionalized violence. The art programs of the epicenter reviewed in this chapter were the nucleus of a larger, site-wide array of features that fostered ritual and administrative leadership at the city. Chapters 3 and 4 elaborate on outlying ceremonial groups and other features that organized the cityscape and chapter 7 analyzes and compares the ritual furnishings across the city in the form of stone, plaster, and ceramic sculptural art.

In subsequent chapters we argue that governing elites were institutionally and spatially linked to the supporting population through the strategic con-struction and operation of symbolic and functional nodes in the form of elite residences or civic-ceremonial groups in the settlement zone. This articulation encompassed social, practical, and ideological realms. Outlying focal points replicated the functions of monumental facilities in the site center. In this chapter, we review the art and architecture of the central monumental plazas that provide a key frame of reference for understanding facilities in the city's neighborhoods that we discuss in subsequent chapters. Recent investigations at outlying focal nodes such as the Itzmal Ch'en group and secondary elite House Y-45a allow for a full reconstruction of the activities at such localities (chapter 3).

House Y-45a has also been interpreted as the dwelling of a member of the Kowoj ethnic group, perhaps a subgroup of the Xiu who were of great political significance in Mayapán's affairs (P. Rice 2009b, 2009c). The Kowoj were also said to have been charged with guarding one of Mayapán's eastern gates, perhaps even Gate H, near to the Itzmal Ch'en group. Throughout this book, we engage this argument for Kowoj political affiliations at Mayapán as it intersects with various categories of data that we present and analyze.

POLITICS AT THE CITY

Late Postclassic Maya political organization, like much of the ancient world, was dynamic. Mayapán dominated the affairs of its confederacy and allies from at least the thirteenth through the mid-fifteenth centuries AD. Construction of the city's monumental center buildings began during the twelfth century, wars plagued the polity in the fourteenth century, and factional disputes aggravated by external factors led to its primary abandonment by AD 1441–1461 (K'atun 8 Ahau).

The Confederacy and Its Allied Territories

During Mayapán's apogee, much of the northern peninsula was united (figure 1.1). The confederacy included the territories of Ah Canul, Cupul, Tases, Cochuah, and probably more polities not mentioned in historical accounts, including northwestern provinces occupied from the Postclassic through to the present day, such as Mani, Sotuta, and many others (Pollock 1962:11). Mayapán was also allied with polities to the east along the Caribbean coast (Uaymil, Cozumel, Chetumal) and with the Petén Lakes region (Pollock 1962:11–12; Roys 1962:32; Ringle and Bey 2001; Pugh 2002; Rice and Rice 2009). Internal frontiers existed that were at times more autonomous or had shifting, contested alliances (Rice and Rice 2004:139; Alexander 2005). Polities independent from Mayapán include Chikinchel, Ecab, Canpech, and Champotón (Pollock 1962:11). One account notes that Mayapán had a dominion extending to a length of 120 leagues (501 kilometers), which would have covered much of the peninsula (Roys 1962:51). We base figure 1.1, a map of the confederated territories, allies, and independent locations with unknown political relationships to Mayapán, on the sage historical analyses of Ralph L. Roys (1962),

Grant D. Jones (1989), and Anthony P. Andrews (1993). Chikinchel's more tenuous relationships with Mayapán are supported by Susan Kepecs's (1999, 2003) archaeological data; the area was closely affiliated with Chichén Itzá and seems to have prospered before and after Mayapán's domain over the peninsula. This pattern suggests a potential animosity between Chikinchel and Mayapán. Another northern polity, Ah Kin Chel, disputed trade agreements with the Cocom of Sotuta even after Mayapán fell (Landa 1941:40).

In essence, we have little idea of the true extent of Mayapán's confederacy. There has been little Postclassic regional survey in Yucatán. Identifying subject towns or confederated polities within the northern peninsula has its own set of methodological impediments. Strong similarities in material culture exist between Mayapán and its allied trading partners that were neither subjects nor confederated, such as the sites of Cozumel Island (Connor 1983; Peraza Lope 1993) or northern Belize (Masson 2000, 2001b). While decorative differences (incised designs and vessel support shape preferences) can be observed in finer pottery between the east coast and Mayapán, the vast majority of slipped and unslipped sherds are macroscopically indistinguishable from Mayapán's most common type groups (Mama Red, Navula Unslipped) based on slip, paste, vessel form, and rim attributes (Masson and Rosenswig 2005). Lithic tool assemblages exhibit even greater similarity (Masson 2000). The styles of monumental buildings (temples, halls, and shrines) are broadly replicated at sites like Tulum, San Gervasio, and Caye Coco (Rosenswig and Masson 2002), although particular arrangements of these buildings into groups may be more diagnostic (Pugh 2002; Pugh and Rice 2009b). Mayapán house styles have not been ubiquitous at other contemporary settlements (chapter 5). Elite houses at distant political centers such as Tulum do emulate those of Mayapán (A. Smith 1962:178). It is possible that typical Mayapán commoner houses might be useful in delineating the influence of the city, and perhaps its formal confederated territories.

Some sites within the outskirts of Mayapán (figure 2.1) have houses that are variants of those in the city (R. Smith 1954; Ruppert and Smith 1957). A total of ten other Postclassic sites, some with cenotes and temples, identified in surveys by Karl Ruppert and A. Ledyard Smith (1954), are present at distances from 3 to 12 kilometers from Mayapán's wall (table 2.1). Hoal, 3.5–4 kilometers to the north, has a cenote known at the Contact Period to have represented the boundary marker for the province of Maní, in which Mayapán was located. The site has architecture and pottery like those of Mayapán. Figure 2.1 illustrates the locations of sites located beyond 1 kilometer from Mayapán's wall. As prior surveys only generally described locations (table 2.1), some sites'

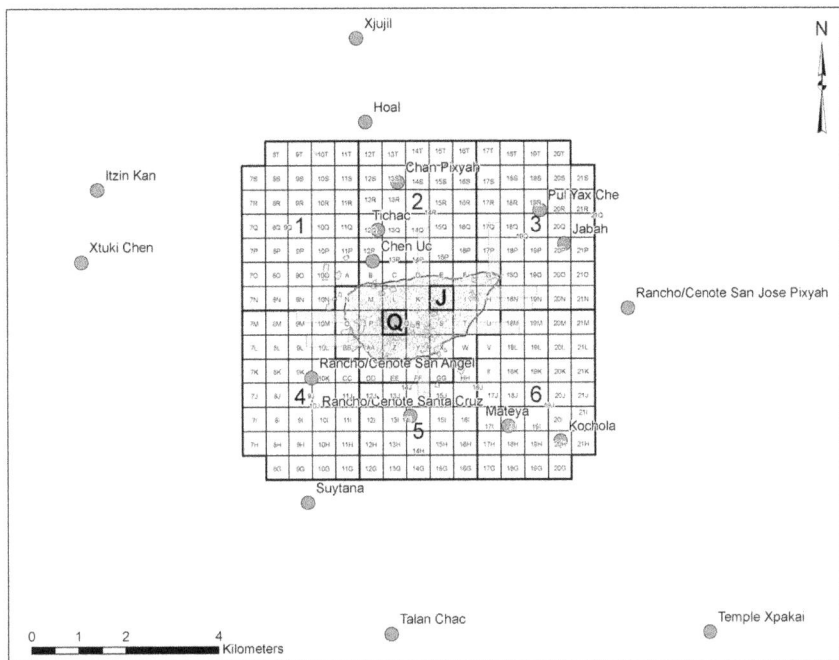

FIGURE 2.1. *Approximate location of settlements with Postclassic occupations near Mayapán. Locations of most of the sites were described in very general terms by Ruppert and Smith (1957); R. Smith (1954) described Santa Cruz and Tichac;. Tichac is modern Telchaquillo, and its principal pyramid dates to the Classic and Postclassic (R. Smith 1954).*

exact coordinates need to be determined (R. Smith 1954; Ruppert and Smith 1954).

One remarkable difference in Mayapán's political landscape compared to that of the Classic Period was the lack of similarly sized, competitive regional capitals. Mayapán dwarfed all lowland rivals by an order of magnitude (M. Smith 2005:419), and we infer that the same was true for Chichén Itzá, although for a time it may have had an influential peer in the polity of Uxmal (Kowalski 2008:252). Ralph Roys's (1957, 1972) analysis of Maya political geography at the time of Spanish contact cannot be outdone, and his efforts stand today as the best summaries of historical sources regarding the Mayapán confederacy, provinces in existence after the city fell, and variation in economic and political organization of these provinces. We learn, for example, that Mayapán's (smaller) peers were headed by regional centers along the peninsula's coasts.

TABLE 2.1 Postclassic sites in Mayapán's vicinity.

Site name, Direction, Type	Description	Source
Itzin Can Northwest Cenote/temple	Located 6 km northwest of Mayapán, large cenote with ample water. A principal radial pyramid similar to the Temple of Kukulcan, 8 m high, no Puuc stones visible. Also present were a colonnade, an elaborate elite Mayapán-style residence, and other dwellings. Classic through Mayapán occupation.	Ruppert and Smith 1957
Tichac (Telchaquillo) North Cenote/temple	Located 1 km north of Mayapán. Pyramid next to cenote has significant Mayapán-era construction as well as earlier layers.	R. Smith 1954
Hoal North Cenote, boundary	Located 3.5–4 km north of Mayapán by northern Maní province boundary, cenote somewhat dry. The cenote itself was the historically named boundary marker for Maní. It has extensive underground passages. Dwellings extend east of the cenote. Site has Mayapán-like buildings and pottery.	Ruppert and Smith 1957
Rancho Santa Cruz South Cenote/temple	Located 1 km south of Mayapán's wall. A 200 × 300 meter area of structures, including eight platforms and a small pyramidal structure that is near to a large jug-shaped cenote, which contains water. Mayapán era and earlier settlement.	R. Smith 1954
Rancho San Angel West Cenote/temple	Located 1–1.2 km southwest of Mayapán. Cenote and temple complex, with some residential settlement. Temple (4–5 m high) has Mayapán effigy censers, columns, and a blank stela.	Masson, personal observation
Jaba Northeast Cenote/temple	Located 1 km west of ruined main house of Hacienda Pixya, 4 km northeast of Mayapán's site center. Has accessible cenote with ample water, extensive houses, no boundary walls, and some stone was taken for the hacienda.	Ruppert and Smith 1957
Ch'en Uc North Settlement with possible cenote	Located between Mayapán and Telchaquillo. Not a compact site, stones robbed by modern use. Houses on altillos, with Mayapán-like architecture. Cenote not reported, but name (Ch'en) implies one.	Ruppert and Smith 1957

continued on next page

TABLE 2.1—*continued*

Site name, Direction, Type	Description	Source
Chan Pixya North Settlement with cenote	Located 2 km north of Mayapán. Cenote is hard to enter due to restricted opening; it has water. Stones probably removed by modern activity, buildings scarce (small site), Postclassic architecture.	Ruppert and Smith 1957
Xjujil North Settlement with cenote	Located 6 km north of Mayapán, good cenote, a number of structures in ruin, but Mayapán dwelling plans identified. No Puuc-style stones visible. Classic through Mayapán-era sherds.	Ruppert and Smith 1957
Xtuki Ch'en Northwest Settlement	Located 6 km northwest of Mayapán, a small site with architecture of Postclassic date, no earlier buildings observed.	Ruppert and Smith 1957
Suytana Southwest Settlement	Located 4–5 km southwest of Mayapán, with poorly preserved structures of Mayapán style. Of interest is an albarrada group of four structures on an altillo. No Puuc stones visible. Sherds mixed Classic and Postclassic Periods.	Ruppert and Smith 1957
Talan Chaac South Settlement	Located 7 km south of Mayapán, no Puuc stones visible. One structure plan was discernible (resembles an atypical Mayapán variant), many structures in ruin. Pottery was not diagnostic.	Ruppert and Smith 1957
Mataya Southeast Settlement	Located 3 km south of Mayapán, two structure plans resemble shrines more than dwellings. No typical Mayapán houses observed. Classic and Postclassic sherds.	Ruppert and Smith 1957

Some of these towns greatly impressed Spaniards making first contact, such as Ecab, which they dubbed "Gran Cayro"; Chauaca was said to be very large (if dispersed); and Cachi had a large market square with permanent stone buildings where officials deliberated over trading disputes (Roys 1972:13, 17, 51; Piña Chan 1978:43). Conil also had a market court (Freidel and Sabloff 1984:191). Sustained archaeological work on the Postclassic or Contact Period has not been performed in these specific towns, but extensive surveys have found many Postclassic sites in parts of the peninsula especially near the northern, eastern, and western coasts (Andrews 1977; Andrews and Vail 1990; Kepecs 1999, 2003; Masson 2000). Coastal towns boasted the most elaborately constructed architecture compared to interior Contact-era sites that Europeans had the occasion to inspect (Roys 1972:19–20). Cozumel's Postclassic sites similarly reveal a populous and prosperous network of settlements (Sabloff and Rathje 1975; Freidel and Sabloff 1984; Robles Castellanos 1986a, 1986b; Peraza Lope 1993), as did sites within the boundaries of the Chikinchel region (Kepecs 1999, 2003). Cobá and El Meco were also important Postclassic centers (Andrews and Robles Castellanos 1986), as was Pole, now known as Playa del Carmen (Márquez Morfín 1982). These studies are examples of a large body of work that has identified Postclassic Maya settlements.

Gauging the monumentality of the highest-ranking towns may never be discernible, however, as modern towns have been built over many of the Contact Period provincial capitals. The bases of razed Prehispanic platforms still impress the informed visitor today, as these are located beneath the foundations of churches built in the sixteenth century at towns like Tecoh, Maní, and others along Yucatán's Ruta de los Conventos. Some of these platforms date to the Classic or Colonial eras, but they may have also been part of Mayapán or post-Mayapán political landscapes. For example, the city of Tihó was emerging as a significant center on the eve of Spanish conquest (P. Rice 2004:80–82), but its plaza and buildings were dismantled in the construction of the original central buildings of Spanish Mérida. (Ligorred 2009). At the minimum, it is described as the "great town" of Tihoo, Ichkansiho (Tozzer 1941:57n279). The largest modern towns that populate Yucatán's countryside today (Sotuta, Mama, Maní, Teabo, Ticul, Tecoh, etc.) existed at Spanish contact and almost certainly have Prehispanic components. Development has taken its toll on Postclassic sites in general across the lowlands, along the east coast "Maya Riviera" (i.e., Xelha, Xcaret), and near the Belize-Mexico border, as exemplified by the modern cities of Chetumal and Corozal. The latter was the site of a political capital of equal significance to Tulum; Santa Rita's beautiful murals and public architecture of Postclassic date have long been destroyed (Chase and Chase 1988). Tulum is largely known for its walled epicenter, but its associated town, presumably beyond the wall, has never been documented. As noted in chapter 1, painted and stucco art in vogue during the Postclassic has been especially vulnerable to destruction, and rare instances of preserved elaborate programs at Tulum and Santa Rita hint at what has been lost (Miller 1982; Gann 1900). Most of Mayapán's murals, which decorated the majority of buildings in the monumental center, have been largely eroded or perhaps were destroyed in the city's final war (M. Delgado Kú 2009:202–18; P. Delgado Kú 2004:108; Peraza Lope et al. 1999a:65). The deterioration and destruction of Postclassic sites should not deter future research; even at Mayapán, these processes have not been uniform, and rich data await discovery. If anything, Postclassic-era research should be accelerated before more damage is incurred.

Roys (1972) and Sergio Quezada (1993) have analyzed Colonial-era politics and reveal variation in political units termed *provinces* by the Spaniards. Emic terms include *batabilob*, which were sometimes located within loosely organized, autonomous territories, and *cuchcabalob*, territories that were more hierarchically organized under the political authority of a *halach uinic* (Roys 1972). The fluid, even segmentary aspects of these entities during the Contact Period has been emphasized (Quezada 1993; Ringle and Bey 2001; Kepecs 2003), but instability is not surprising given the travails of European conquest and the epidemics of the sixteenth century. Similarly, little evidence is seen for residential wards or officials in the Colonial Period (Okoshi-Harada 2012), but bureaucratic complexity was clearly lost through time. It is important not to project the decentralized political landscape of the Contact Period to the Postclassic Period era prior to the fall of Mayapán. The tenuous nature of the available information is reflected in figure 1.1, which reveals the uncertain affiliated status of political territories during the fifteenth and sixteenth centuries AD; boundaries are only approximated (Roys 1962; P. Rice 2004:30–32). Centralized polities after Mayapán's fall, according to Roys's estimation, include Cochuah, Maní, Hocabá, Sotuta, Cehpech, Champotón, Cozumel, Ah Kin Chel, Tases, and Tayasal (Roys 1957; P. Rice 2004:29–32). Prudence M. Rice (2004:33) observes that for the Maya area in general, intersite distances approximate 20–32 kilometers between political centers, or a reasonable day trip for purposes such as commerce or other essential interactions. This metric is not well understood for Mayapán-era Yucatán, but a regular network of large and small towns populate the northern peninsula, many of which predate the arrival of Europeans (Brown et al. 2006).

Mayapán's Largest Maya Contemporary

Parallels in the organization of Mayapán and Utatlán/K'umarcaj are apparent. The Guatemalan highland Postclassic center of Utatlán is the only contemporary political capital that may represent an analog to Mayapán in the Maya area. Both were the capitals of expansionary polities with reasonable territorial reach and both were hierarchically ranked far above their political peers. Leaders of confederated polities held lengthy residency at these political capitals, and the local version of the deity of Quetzalcoatl (Kukulcan at Mayapán, K'ucumatz at Utatlán) was the primary focus of religious patronage for each of them (Carmack 1981a:18), as for many Mesoamerican centers after AD 800 (Carmack 1981a:17; Ringle, Gallareta Negrón, and Bey 1998; Ringle 2004:169). Both cities were densely nucleated and defensible and incorporated art and religious symbols from central Mexican groups with whom they were directly or indirectly in contact (Carmack 1981a:18; Milbrath and Peraza Lope 2003a:29). Carmack observes one key difference: merchants held a relatively minor position at Utatlán compared to Mayapán (Carmack 1981a:18). Utatlán's military emphasis, particularly in hegemonic empire-building in order to dominate access to valuables from the Pacific coast, is interesting, given Mayapán's parallel military potency and its intervention in the affairs of the hinterlands. Some have labeled Mayapán an empire (Russell 2008a), which is technically defined as a state that conquers other polities (Smith and Montiel 2001).

Council Rule

The institution of Maya divine kingship emerged in the Late Preclassic Period and is reflected in courtly art that celebrates the deeds of dynastic individuals (Schele and Freidel 1990; Freidel and Schele 1988; Freidel, Schele, and Parker 1993; Inomata and Houston 2001; Martin and Grube 2008:17). Classic Period hieroglyphic texts legitimize claims of divine status and supernatural power and chronicle political and military prowess. Toward the end of the Classic Period, members of a growing noble class were included to a greater extent in the corpus of art and writing. These inclusionary practices may have been the first steps toward a council-rule government that was developed by the polities of Terminal Classic through Postclassic northern Yucatán (Schele and Freidel 1990:348; Ringle and Bey 2001; Sabloff 2007). Council rule, known as *multepal*, de-emphasized individual sovereigns and is reflected in monumental art that depicts assemblies of high-ranking officials (Ringle and Bey 2001; Ringle 2004). Mayapán was founded by multiple agents who "built houses for the lords only, dividing all the land among them ... giving towns to each one according to the antiquity of his lineage and personal value" (Landa 1941:25–26). We further learn from Diego de Landa (1941:23–26) that Mayapán was initially a planned city that involved resettlement of commoners from confederated towns to provide services.

Colonial Period accounts describe the political organization after the fall of Mayapán among a suite of townships, or *cahcab*, which powerful families ruled. During the Colonial era, the *cah* was the most important entity of political, social, and economic integration; this term referred to a town, its outlying lands, and governed political units (Restall 2001:349) or a township in the general sense of the word. Most influential Colonial Maya family groups (*ch'ibalob*) were descendants of Mayapán's governing council (Restall 2001). Principal men were incorporated into oligarchical councils (*cabildo*) that replicated some pre-Contact principles, and they differed in fundamental ways from the Spanish institution (Restall 2001:364). A *batab* official was appointed to govern towns above the cabildo. Large cabildos had as many as fifty officials, including religious offices.

Council rule also seems reflected in architecture at Cozumel. It is interesting to contemplate whether councils were important at smaller political scales below Mayapán and its confederacy, and we suggest that this was probably the case. The existence of multiple, large house groups and a lack of a single, dominant royal court may provide such an indication. The Early Classic city of Chunchucmil may have been organized by a federation of merchant families, as this city lacked the architectural signatures of political power displayed by its peers (Dahlin and Ardren 2002). A small Postclassic site in Campeche, Isla Civlituk, is interpreted as less centralized, as settlement lacks a specific site center (Alexander 2005:170). This pattern may alternatively represent an oligarchical system headed by town or village leaders (Masson 2001a; Rosenswig and Masson 2002; Ringle and Bey 2001).

Features such as royal tombs and temples dedicated to deceased kings were no longer constructed at Postclassic Maya centers. Multiple colonnaded halls at Mayapán and Chichén Itzá (where they are part of gallery-patio buildings) likely served as meeting halls or council houses for nobles participating in governmental affairs. Colonnade buildings are also associated with temples, altars, and ball courts at the end of radial causeways that extend outward from downtown Chichén Itzá (Cobos 2004:figures 22.3–22.5). A parallel pattern at Mayapán may be indicated by the association of colonnaded halls and temples with at least four major gates in the city wall and an internal portal gate (Strömsvik 1953; Hare and Masson 2012; Russell 2007). Although overt royal glorification is downplayed at Chichén Itzá and Mayapán, divine sanction was sought for major political rites of passage such as accession to office and investiture (Schele and Mathews 1998:254–55; Ringle, Gallareta Negrón, and Bey 1998; Masson 2000:234–38; Ringle 2004; P. Rice 2004, 2009c).

Lords and Kings at Mayapán

The institution of multepal is not extensively mentioned in historical documents, and its time depth remains a topic of study (Restall 2001:387; Ringle and Bey 2001:273–74). Council or mat houses date to earlier sites such as Uxmal or Copán (Ringle and Bey 2001:281). More importantly, council rule masked the tendency for paramounts to dominate political affairs, as exemplified by the fact that late Maya governors were considered the "first among equals." Mayapán's own history was dominated by the actions of the Cocom and Xiu lords, and the Chels also ranked highly among the "three great princely houses" (Landa 1941:40; Roys 1962:60; Restall 2001; Milbrath and Peraza Lope 2003a:31–32, 35). Some fleeting accounts come close to suggesting a Mayapán monarchy. Landa (1941:26) states, "After the departure of Kukulcan, the nobles agreed, in order that the government should endure, that the house of the Cocoms should have the chief power." According to Landa's *Relación de las cosas de Yucatán*, a king at Mayapán had the name or title Cotecpan; Roys (1962:55) points out that this title incorporates the Nahuatl word *tecpan* for "government house" or "palace," which he equates with columned halls (Roys 1962:65). Cotecpan means "man over everyone" (A. Smith 1962:182; Tozzer 1941:24n131). Similarly, the Utatlán confederacy had a supreme ruler, the Aj Pop (Carmack 1977:13). This intriguing reference to a potential king of Mayapán is woefully incomplete and isolated.

For the time being, it is probably best to follow William M. Ringle and George J. Bey III's grounded suggestion that paramount authories dominated, and perhaps ruled, governing councils. After Mayapán fell around AD 1441, its major political families continued to exert significant influence into the Contact Period and are referred to as the "dynamic dozen" in Matthew Restall's (2001) sweeping summary.

Major Dynasties and Ethnic Struggles

The ethnic identity of Mayapán's nobility has been a topic of much consideration (Milbrath and Peraza Lope 2003a, 2009; Masson and Peraza Lope 2010). Cross-culturally, claims of foreign origins commonly buttress elite authority, and Restall (2001:373–75) argues that Postclassic Yucatán elites similarly invoked mythical foreign origins. Restall (2001:373) points out that the use of a Nahuatl name like Xiu is not enough to infer central Mexican identity; such names were common among prominent Contact Period Yucatán families. But clear evidence for sustained contact, including political and economic alliances with port cities like the Gulf Coast Xicalanco (and indirectly, beyond to central Mexico) has long been observed. Many traditions integrated elite culture across Mesoamerica, at least from the Epiclassic Period onward (Diehl and Berlo 1989; Smith and Berdan 2003a; Pohl 2003a, 2003b; Ringle, Gallareta Negrón, and Bey 1998; Ringle 2004; Masson and Peraza Lope 2010).

Diverse social groups occupied Mayapán from localities as distant as southern Campeche or Tabasco, the Petén, and the Caribbean coast, as well as from Yucatán (Landa 1941:32; Tozzer 1941:34n172; Edmonson 1982:9; Masson and

Peraza Lope 2010). Foreign neighborhoods were sometimes established by nonlocal merchants at major trading towns at Spanish contact (Piña Chan 1978:43, 47). Prior efforts to identify ethnic enclaves at Mayapán based on frequencies of imported ceramics, Mexican-style sculptures, mortuary patterns, and foodways have been inconclusive, perhaps due to the small test pit samples for most of the residential zone (Masson and Peraza Lope 2010). More full horizontal investigation of dwellings, such as that undertaken at House Y-45a, is needed to address this question (chapter 3). Two facts confound the task of identifying ethnic signatures. The site in general was outward-looking and many households possessed a few objects of foreign origin or inspiration (Pollock 1962; Masson and Peraza Lope 2010). The Mayapán polity was also successful at promoting an emblematic state style that characterizes many formal artifacts and architectural characteristics (chapter 5).

Ethnohistorical accounts chronicle the names of Mayapán's ruling families (Tozzer 1941:36–37, 40; Ringle and Bey 2001; Restall 2001; Masson 2000). The Cocom and Xiu families vied for paramountcy among this class of governing elites, but the Cocom had greater power and dominated the affairs of the city (Roys 1962:29, 46; Landa 1941:58–59). A rise in Xiu family power marked the final decades, leading ultimately to a war that dismantled the city and its polity (Roys 1962:54–55, 56; Milbrath and Peraza Lope 2009). Hieroglyphic records indicate the antiquity of the Cocom name at Chichén Itzá (Ringle, Gallareta Negrón, and Bey 1998:190–91, 225; Kristan-Graham 2001), and the history of the Xiu traces back to Uxmal's heyday (Kowalski 2003, 2008). The presence of these and other key families at Mayapán indicates that members of ancestral ruling families in the northern lowlands led this city's confederacy.

The Cocom name lingers in Telchaquillo today, but it is not common. For example, Don Fernando Mena of Telchaquillo tells us that his grandmother's name was Cocom. This elder has worked for the Carnegie, INAH, and PEMY projects. Other names echoing those of antiquity held by our workers in Telchaquillo are more common, such as Cauich, Chel, Pech, Cobá, Pat, Chan, Chi, May, and Uc, which is interesting even though direct genealogical ties to the deeper past are not traceable. The Cocom family may have held sway over Mayapán's confederacy for the latter half of the thirteenth and most of the fourteenth centuries (Milbrath and Peraza Lope 2009:602), if not before, given tales linking them to founding events mentioned previously. Landa writes that the leader of this house was the man of "greatest worth" and was from the "most ancient" and "richest" family (Landa 1941:26; Milbrath and Peraza Lope 2003a:33). Milbrath and Peraza Lope (2003a:33–34; 2009:583) expand on the idea that Puuc elements of the city's monumental buildings were linked to members of the Xiu faction (Ringle and Bey 2001:286), along with the city's stelae, given this family's ties to the Puuc region and Uxmal. For example, Hall Q-151's recycled Puuc-style Chac masks may possibly reflect the patronage of Puuc-derived Xiu groups (Ringle and Bey 2001:286). The serpent temples and art programs focused on Kukulcan and art with Mexican influence are attributed to the Cocom faction and their Chichén Itzá roots (Tozzer 1941:24n129; Proskouriakoff 1962a:132, 135).

The Cocom and Xiu at times may have disrupted the governing council. The Cupul and Canul families were allied with the Cocom during the Contact Period and the Chel family was allied with the Xiu at the time of Mayapán's fall (Milbrath and Peraza Lope 2003a:34–35). Tatiana Proskouriakoff (1962a:134) reports thirteen carved and twenty-five plain stelae from Mayapán; Peraza Lope's team has found one other stela in the site center (Milbrath and Peraza Lope 2009) and a new stela was found at Itzmal Ch'en Temple H-17 in 2009 (Delgado Kú, Escamilla Ojeda, and Peraza Lope 2012b). Stelae found regularly near round structures may have had historical content, linking ruling lineages to Kukulcan, the human founder of the city, rather than the deity, according to Proskouriakoff (1962a:136). Other names of Mayapán rulers are known. Hunac Ceel ruled either very early or very late in the site's history (Roys 1962:47). Various Cocom rulers' names are recorded (Roys 1962). The names and deeds of some Mayapán priests are also chronicled, including Ah Kin Cobá (Roys 1962:79); Ah Kin Chel, who was associated with the fall of Mayapán (Roys 1962:35); and Ah Kin May (or Ahau Can Mai). The timing of Tutul Xiu's control of the city is debated (Roys 1962:50), but most sources agree that this probably occurred late in city's history (Milbrath and Peraza Lope 2009). Ah Uitzil Dzul, who is linked to the final depopulation of the city, was a Xiu whom Roys (1962:72, 74–75) equates with Hun Uitzil Chac Tutul Xiu. An individual named Ulumil Ahau was involved in taking the city at its collapse (Roys 1962:74–75). The Kowoj group was affiliated with the Xiu and may even have formed a Xiu subgroup (Jones 1998:11; P. Rice 2009a:10–14). They and other Xiu may have also departed the city just before AD 1400, but migrations were likely multiple, and we know little of how many members of any particular ethnic faction left, remained, or returned to the city (P. Rice 2009a, 2009b). It is clear that Xiu groups were at Mayapán at the time of its fall, and they remained numerous and influential long into the Colonial Period (P. Rice 2009a).

Guardians of the gates of Mayapán included Zulim Chan at the west, Nauat at the south, and Kowoj at the east (Ah Ek was his companion), according to Roys (1962:79); a north guardian is not listed. The ruler at this time was Ah Tapay-Nok Cauich (Cauich with the embroidered mantle), and Hunac Ceel was a "representative" of the office of Ah Mex Cuc, who was later declared a ruler (Roys 1962:79). The four "lineages from heaven"—Zacal Puc, Holtun Balam, Hoch'tun Poot, and Ah Mex Cuc Chan—are listed in passages that make reference to Chichén Itzá. Zacal Puc was a deified ancestor (Roys 1962:79–80). Roys concludes that Hunac Ceel was a member of the Canul clan, who were mercenaries in service of the Cocom of Mayapán at one point in time. One late Cocom ruler was also probably named Kukulcan (Roys 1962:80). The Cocom claimed Itzá descent, at least until the Itzá fell into disrepute during the fourteenth century (Roys 1962:81).

Priests

With the decline of divine kingship—an institution that centralized political and religious authority in a monarch—an expanded bureaucracy emerged of hierarchically ranked priests at sites like Chichén Itzá, Tulum, and Mayapán. Such offices could be hereditary or filled by secondary sons of the nobility, sometimes from infancy (Landa 1941:27). The primary evidence for this lies in proliferation of artistic programs that portray religious practitioners compared to earlier periods; ethnohistorical documents also provide rich details on nested religious hierarchies (Masson 2000:234–47; Masson, Hare, and Peraza Lope 2006:194–97; Ringle, Gallareta Negrón, and Bey 1998; Ringle 2004). If a complex priesthood existed in the Classic Maya era, this theme is de-emphasized in art and writing, although individual ritualists can be found among courtly attendants in carved monuments or polychromes. Mayapán's highest ranking priests held titles of Ah Kin May or Ahau Can May (Landa 1941:27). Prudence Rice (2004:79) suggests that these individuals presided over the 13 k'atun cycle—or *may*, as their name implies—but they also had diverse advisory duties and presided over a religious hierarchy (Landa 1941:27). High priests oversaw the placement of outlying priests in supporting towns and sent representatives to teach "letters" in hinterland regions. Letters presumably included skills in hieroglyphic writing, calendrics, astronomy, and other tools for perpetuating doctrine in the periphery (Roys 1962:50–51, 53, 56).

Political officials shared authority with councils of priests, who also were hierarchically organized and specialized according to ritual responsibilities. One high priest presided over the religious institutions of the state and counseled lords (Landa 1941:27). During the Postclassic and Colonial era in the

Petén Lakes region, political leaders co-governed in certain respects with high-ranking priests (Jones 1998:94; P. Rice 2009d:44). Council members who also shared authority included those individuals who were responsible for each of the 13 k'atuns in the may cycle and distinguished military captains (P. Rice 2009d:44). Earlier versions of tandem political and religious bureaucracies are identified at Chichén Itzá, where priestly officials bestowed political initiates with the rites and regalia of office—and this site is not the only example (Ringle 2004:170–77). As Ringle demonstrates, Epiclassic and Postclassic political officials throughout Mesoamerica received the vestments of governorship from priests, and councils of political and religious authorities helped to administer the affairs of major cities. This system created a complex and complementary system of power-sharing, although paramounts presided over such councils.

Political and religious duties and practices were not well separated in the Postclassic, as governing nobles' authority was founded on religious sanction and priests meddled regularly in political affairs. The collapse of Mayapán was instigated by the actions of one high priest, Ah Xupan, whose political clout also enabled him to help found the post-Mayapán polity of Ah Kin Chel (Tozzer 1941:36n177; Masson, Hare, and Peraza Lope 2006). The prevalence of the twin institutions of priesthood and lordship in late Maya politics is likely due to the growth of the noble class and efforts to achieve greater regional integration by inclusive, complex, ranked institutions. Sons of the Postclassic nobility, as in many ancient states, found occupations in political, religious, or military office or long-distance mercantile activities (Landa 1941).

Given the importance of elite interaction across regions of the Postclassic Mesoamerican world system (Smith and Berdan 2003a), comparisons of Mayapán's political and religious institutions to those of central Mexico are of potential significance. The organizational principles of Cholula reveal some key similarities. A Turquoise House (*Xiuhcalli*), at the city's great square was a facility where six councilors congregated. The two city leaders (Tlalquiach and Aquiyach) were of the Quetzalcoatl priesthood (Ringle 2004:210). Although Cholula was a religious center for the worship of this deity, it was also a political capital, capable of mobilizing military action. Eagle and jaguar knights were commissioned from the priesthood ranks. A captain general who provided oversight for six districts within the city led the secular council of six (Ringle 2004:210). Authority was also split between a priest and a king at Tula 2004:211) and in the Petén Lakes region (Jones 1998).

Mayapán was also a center for the worship of Kukulcan/Quetzalcoatl, for whom the city hosted periodic festivals; after its fall, the town of Maní assumed this role (Roys 1962:63; Tozzer 1941:22n124). Regarding the Maní festivities, Landa (1941:157–58) states, "On the 16th of (the month) Xul, all the priests and lords assembled in Maní, and with them a large multitude from the towns." Roys (1962:63) expresses surprise and doubt that this Xiu stronghold monopolized Kukulcan festivals, which should have been a prerogative of the Cocom, who claimed descendancy from this deity. But this account alludes to the long-term importance of this entity in the Mayapán area and provides a glimpse of the large congregations that gathered for Kukulcan festivities. Mayapán was in fact within the territory of Maní, and as we discuss later, these rites were likely held as part of pilgrimage festivals at Mayapán's Temple of Kukulcan. At this Chic Kaban festival at Maní, Kukulcan was believed to descend from heaven to receive services and offerings on the last day of the five-day event (Landa 1941:158). Although some ceremonies linked to the festival were solemn, comedies were also performed.

OFFICIAL BUREAUCRACY

Ringle and Bey (2001) outline official councils that ranked below batabilob who governed specific townships either independently or beneath a regional authority (halach uinic). Subordinate councils provided oversight for different operations in Contact Period governmental systems. Councils of *ah kulelob* and *ah cuchcabob* could represent *cuchteelob*, or residential wards; such districts were also represented by speakers, or *ah canob* (Ringle and Bey 2001:271). Documents offer lengthy lists of ranked offices within political and religious institutions that imply a well-developed administrative bureaucracy for Mayapán and other Postclassic/Contact Period centers. Beneath the paramounts of Utatlán or in towns in Yucatán, a composite list of appointments held by upper-class males includes duties of receiving guests, speakers or proclaimers, secondary governorships, mat officials, scribes or notaries, district deputies, judges, tribute collectors, military captains, logistical officials, k'atun lords, ball game counselors, territorial administrators, and a variety of specialized priests, singers, and sacrificers (Carmack 1981a:15–17; Restall 2001:table 11.3; Kintz 1983:table 11.1; Love 1994). In Yucatán, the Holpop officer was responsible for festivities along with other administrative duties (Ringle and Bey 2001:271). At Utatlán, three less powerful lords assisted the Ajpop ruler (Carmack 1981a:14–15). At the smaller K'iche' polities of Tamub or Ismachi, the four rulers held lower positions in the regional hierarchy. Below the king, governing nobles held offices of principal men (judges, tribute collectors, military captains, and logistical officials), and priests separately officiated ritual matters, holding titles of priests or sacrificers—Yaqui Winak/Aj Q'uixb or Aj Cajb (Carmack 1981a:16). The Tojil priest was the most highly ranked, and the deity Tojil was the patron god of war for the three confederacies of the Nima K'iche, Ilocab, and Tamub; the K'ucumatz (creator deity) priest was also important (Carmack 1981a:16). Other officials included the ball game counselor (Popol Winak, Pajom Tzalatz), sets of four priests of Tamub, territorial officials for *chinamit* (Utzam), and wall officials known as Aj Tz'alam (Carmack 1981a:17).

The Ah Cuch Cab collected tribute at the level of the residential ward (*cuchteel*), and performed additional duties of organizing conscripted military service and coordinating ceremonies (Roys 1957; Ringle and Bey 2001:271; Quezada 1993:41–42). K'ichean towns were divided into *calpul* social units linked to particular parcels of land. In central Mexico, *calpulli* also formed discrete residential zones and corporate socioeconomic groups (M. Smith 2011b). The deeper similarities of the Maya cuchteel to the K'ichean and Aztec calpulli are poorly known, but they are alike in having formed residential administrative units that pooled resources and service obligations. Another term, *tzucub*, partitioned noble family groups, subject towns, or central towns that served as seats of government (Ringle and Bey 2001:271). Membership in *ch'ibal* groups has recently been scrutinized: these may be analogous to great houses—something more than a patronymic descent group and something less than an all-encompassing corporate group linking members across disparate geographic locations (Ringle and Bey 2001:291–97). Possible evidence for named "houses" of families, affiliates, and their buildings at Chichén Itzá may also support the house society model, at least among elites (Kristan Graham 2001:343, table 12.1).

In Postclassic Yucatán, political offices were complemented by honorary calendrical offices held by priests or lords; some could preside over the beginning of a new 13 k'atun cycle, or may, others were anointed lords of particular 20-year k'atun periods (Love 1994; Rice 2004:79; Rice 2009d:23–25, 44). K'atun office rotations, and perhaps those of shorter calendrical intervals, provided further opportunities for members of local polities to participate in governance (D. Chase 1985a; Masson 2000). The beginning of new may cycles involved an extensive cadre of ritual specialists whose performances are detailed for Contact Period Mérida in 1539 (P. Rice 2004:80–83). Circumambulation of territories was particularly significant for sanctioning political boundaries in terms of sacred geography and ritual (P. Rice 2004). Landa claimed that the Mayapán state was divided among its founding lords, which corresponded at least in theory to thirteen geopolitical units (of unequal size), each of which were associated with one of the thirteen calendrical periods with its own idol and priest (Tozzer 1941:25–26n136). Prominent lords set k'atun stones in confederated town centers and rotated the honorary burden of sponsoring calendrical celebrations (P. Rice 2004:75–76). Prudence Rice (2004) has recently argued for the great time depth of this geopolitical and calendrical system of power-sharing.

Investiture, Pilgrimage

Late Maya political capitals likely sanctioned official positions at subordinate settlements or allied, independent kingdoms. This conferral or investiture bound alliance networks of distant polities together, and it required pilgrimages to important centers to undergo rites of transformation and receive official regalia and holy religious sanction (Ringle, Gallareta Negrón, and Bey 1998; Ringle 2004). Contact-era examples are chronicled in the central Mexican kingdoms of the Mixteca (Byland and Pohl 1994:138–41; Pohl 2003a, 2003b) and Cholula, as well as in the earlier case of Chichén Itzá (Ringle 2004:167–69). Pilgrimages to major sites have long been recognized as important for the Mesoamerica area (Orr 2003; Freidel and Sabloff 1984; Shaw 2001). Complex ritual circuits within larger sites such as Chichén Itzá have been identified (Ringle 2004). Similar to the renowned case of Mixtec Lord 8 Deer's journey to Coixtlahuaca that culminated in his receipt of a nose plug, emblematic of a exalted political authority (Byland and Pohl 1994), the highest ranking lords of the K'ich'ean realm also received nose pieces in elaborate legitimation ceremonies (Carmack and Mondloch 1983:195–96; Carmack 1981a:13). A similar accession ceremony has been suggested for the North Temple scene at Chichén Itzá's main ball court (Villela and Koontz 1993:5). Reference to investiture at Mayapán may be gleaned from Colonial Period records; one governor of this site "ordained his lordships and knighthoods" (Roys 1962:50, citing from the Report of Tekal).

Cosmological Political Divisions

The organization of towns and regions into cosmologically significant divisions, such as four quarters or 13 (k'atun cycle) units, was conceptually important according to numerous Contact Period documentary accounts (e.g., Coe 1965; Carmack 1977, 1981a, 1981b; Fox 1987; P. Rice 2004:44, 2009d:25). Unfortunately, Postclassic settlements exhibit little evidence for quadripartite division, important as it was (Coe 1965), with the exception of radial pyramidal structures like those of Chichén Itzá, Mayapán, and some highland Maya sites (Fox 1987). The principal pyramids at Chichén Itzá and Mayapán are dedicated to Kukulcan (figures 1.2, 1.3). Symbolism across Postclassic Mesoamerica has linked serpents with quadripartite structures and origin myths (P. Rice 1983:317; Schele and Kappelman 2001), including Mayapán, which was formed by the union of four "lineages from heaven" (Tozzer 1941:34n172). Similarly, Chichén Itzá was formed when the "four divisions" came together (Tozzer 1941:21n123).

At Mayapán, four guarded cardinal gates (Roys 1962:79) were especially important among the city's twelve gates. Perfect cardinal correspondences should not be expected on the ground, as revealed by Robert M. Carmack's (1981b:89–92, figures 1, 2) comparisons of the conceptual map of Utatlán (in the Título de Totonicapan) to the archaeological settlement. He found that cardinal principles are revealed in the presence of four main halls around the center's main plaza, but correspondence to the indigenous map is loose. Such divisions may have been more important for ritual and cosmological purposes than for defining social sectors of settlements, as Clifford T. Brown (1999) observes. He suggests that alignments of key focal architecture in the city may indicate quadripartite concepts of city planning. We discuss his model and elaborate on it in chapter 4, along with discussing the full range of features that divide the city's residential zone.

The division of regional political units in Mayapán's domain into thirteen divisions to correspond with the 13 k'atun cycle represented a significant juncture of cosmology and political geography (Roys 1962:64). For the k'atun cycle, each age was celebrated in a different location (shrine, temple, or other edifice) with its prescribed patron god, officiating priest, and accompanying prophecy; Alfred M. Tozzer (1941:26) also reports that the stones were set at different designated towns at k'atun endings. As lords of the confederacy resided at least part time at the center, we might also anticipate that celebration of these rotating burdens also occurred in different parts of the cityscape and throughout the region. Similarly, Diane Z. Chase (1986) finds evidence for rotating burdens of Uayeb (360 solar year ending periods) among upper-status residents at Santa Rita. Masson (2000) argued that the dispersal of turtle sculptures across Mayapán reflects rotated spatial and social responsibilities of calendrical celebrations such as k'atuns. The abundance of these objects at outlying ceremonial groups and the center in Mayapán implies that burdens were exchanged among regional constituents at the city and in their home territories. Proskouriakoff's (1962a) illustration of a Mayapán turtle sculpture engraved with thirteen Ahau faces strongly suggests that these objects were used in such a context (P. Rice 2004:67). It appears to be a Precolumbian version of a k'atun wheel illustrated by Landa (1941:167). At Caye Coco, Belize, an elite residence had a turtle sculpture cache. A cavity in the turtle's carapace had four items that probably symbolized colors associated with the four directions, including a red sherd, a black obsidian blade, a yellow piece of flint, and a green serpentine ax; the turtle itself was white. While the turtle implies a k'atun rite, color directional symbolism was also associated with annual Uayeb rites of the solar year (Tozzer 1941:141nn684, 689). Prudence Rice's (2004, 2009c) model, which holds that regional rotation of ritual burdens of calendrical intervals was an integral component of political geography, is convincing, especially for the Postclassic Period, where references to setting of stones in various communities on k'atun intervals abound. The Paris Codex is also explicit on this point (Love 1994). Prudence Rice (2004, 2009c:26–27, 39–40) discusses this model in full detail as well as the fact that competing calendars were in place during the Contact Period (see also Milbrath and Peraza Lope 2009).

CHRONOLOGY
Confounding Tales of Mayapán's Founding

Efforts to utilize the Books of Chilam Balam for reliable chronological or historical information (e.g., Barrera Vasquez and Morley 1949; Roys 1962:27; Milbrath and Peraza Lope 2003a:36) should be undertaken with considerable skepticism, as Antje Gunsenheimer's (2002) recent analysis shows these documents to be comprised of piecemeal segments contributed by multiple authors over two centuries. Nonetheless, kernels of information may prove to be useful, or even correct, if evaluated with different types of data (e.g., chapter 8, Masson 2000:table 6.8; Milbrath and Peraza Lope 2003a, 2009).

The take-home message about Mayapán's founding is that it was refounded several times as a consequence of political power drives. Recent interpretations of the chronicles by Milbrath and Peraza Lope (2003a:35–36, table 1; 2009:599) argue that recurring founding events occurred with K'atun 8 Ahau (AD 1185–1204), K'atun 13 Ahau (AD 1263–1283), and K'atun 11 Ahau (AD 1283–1303). One stela from the city (Stela 6) has an AD 1283 date, identified by Sylvanus Morley (Pollock 1962:3). Stela 1 and Stela 5 most probably date to earlier k'atuns in AD 1185 and AD 1244, respectively (Pollock 1962:3). These dated monuments constitute the best evidence of the city's establishment as a major capital at least one hundred years prior to K'atun 13 Ahau, ending in AD 1283. Archaeological evidence provides additional support for at least twelfth-century origins (Peraza Lope et al. 2006). Serial founding events likely coincided with episodes of political coalescence and building construction, but such efforts may not coincide well with settlement chronology. Rival Cocom-

Itza and Xiu groups could have competed for prominence by hosting celebrations and erecting buildings during the city's initial decades (Milbrath and Peraza Lope 2003a, 2009). The initial occupation of Mayapán clearly predated the city's heralded "founding" dates (Pollock 1962:10). Gaspar Antonio Chi (in Tozzer 1941:230–31) states that Mayapán fell (in AD 1420) 260 years after its founding, which may reflect a tendency to consider historical cycles in terms of the sacred calendar without concern for accuracy (Roys 1962:65). This claim generally corresponds with our evidence for the onset of monumental building toward the latter part of the twelfth century AD, but the end date falls short of the conventional view of 1441–1461. Landa (1941:37) claims that Mayapán collapsed five hundred years after it was initially established, but he may have referred to an earlier Classic-era monumental center in the vicinity, perhaps Tichac (modern Telchaquillo, 1 kilometer north of Mayapán's center), where the principal pyramid exhibits significant Classic and Postclassic construction (R. Smith 1954). The Xiu and some of their allies may have lingered at Mayapán until K'atun 4 Ahau (AD 1481–1500), when epidemics wrought final, complete abandonment (Roys 1962:73). The dates of Mayapán's fall, like the founding dates, are also contradictory. We explore this issue in chapter 8.

A minor settlement known as Mayapán may have been established in the first half of the eleventh century or even the mid-tenth century AD, prior to Chichén Itzá's fall, according to Tozzer (1941:24n129). Mayapán may have been a small shrine center at this time while Chichén Itzá was declining (Andrews, Andrews, and Robles Castellanos 2003). The Postclassic capital was probably founded in this location for historical reasons, as the generalized natural resources in this vicinity are broadly replicated in this part of the Northern Plains region of Yucatán. Curiously, there is a modern town in Yucatán named Mayapán, located about 22 kilometers to the southeast of the ancient city, but historical connections with the Postclassic political center are unknown.

Ethnohistorians debate the roles of legendary individuals instrumental in founding the city (Tozzer 1941:24n129). Tozzer suggests that Itza captains may have migrated to the Mayapán vicinity during the tenth century, but the League of Mayapán, an allegiance among peers (Uxmal, Mayapán, Chichén Itzá; Barrera Vasquez and Morley 1949:33–35), was likely formed in the twelfth century. In K'atun 13 Ahau (AD 1263–1283), a founding event marked by setting the mats (seats of rulership) in order. Major public architecture at the site center and royal residences may have been amplified or built at this time (Roys 1962:43, 71; Landa 1941:57). These activities were supposedly presided over by Kukulcan, as the political or religious leader who established peace and helped to select the location for the new city. As legend presents the tale, he partitioned the confederated territory among the ruling nobility and named the city (Landa 1941:26). The settlement zone grew incrementally over the next half century (Roys 1962:43).

Mayapán may have risen to power following political treachery. Hunac Ceel, along with his followers, compelled a Chichén Itzá ruler (Chac Xib Chac) to covet and abduct the bride of an Izamal ruler. Political relationships broke down, leaving Chichén Itzá vulnerable to attack (Roys 1962:47), and Mayapán rose due to this opportunity. This occurred in K'atun 8 Ahau, presumably the one starting in 1185, but other interpretations are possible (Roys 1962:56). Chichén Itzá's diminished occupation continued until Spanish contact, under various leadership regimes (Roys 1962:48). The Postclassic settlements of Chichén Itzá and Uxmal may have been members of the Mayapán league, which may have existed prior to the plot of Hunac Ceel. Despite this indication of animosity, founding members of Mayapán are said to have been descendants of Chichén Itzá's nobility, the Cocom/Itza (Roys 1962). Other heroic histories concerning the founding of Mayapán revolve around the mytho-historical personage of Kukulcan (Landa 1941:23–24). The timing of his legendary involvement is unclear, but some experts suggest that his "second coming" was invoked in the mid-thirteenth century, perhaps as a response to political strife (Roys 1962; Masson 2000:259). Like King Arthur of Camelot, his actual existence remains a topic for speculation.

Given that multiple calendars were in use during the early Colonial era, Milbrath and Peraza Lope observe that if the twenty-four-year K'atun (popular in the eighteenth century) has greater antiquity, some founding k'atun events at Mayapán reach as far back as the eleventh century AD and better coincide with the timing of Chichén Itzá's decline (Milbrath and Peraza Lope 2003a:36). Currently little evidence exists for a prosperous political center from around AD 1000 to about AD 1150 in northern Yucatán by the usual gauge of monumental works (Andrews, Andrews, and Robles Castellanos 2003). Even using the alternative calendrical system, very few radiocarbon dates at Mayapán open up the possibility of major construction prior to AD 1100, and given the error ranges for C14 dates, the likelihood is strong that the onset of major construction at this political center was closer to AD 1150 or 1200.

ARCHAEOLOGICAL CHRONOLOGY

Historical information on the timing of Mayapán's origins and rise to power are confounding due to the many versions of when and how this came about. Founding tales probably refer more to specific dynasties and construction programs than to a single, meteoric rise of the capital. Nonetheless, the establishment of the monumental landscape was not gradual, since most of the public buildings seem to have been in place around AD 1200. Only four radiocarbon samples fall solidly within the eleventh century AD, and each of these could as easily date to as late as 1160 or 1190, given the two sigma ranges (figure 2.2). The contexts are also ambivalent (Peraza Lope et al. 2006), as two samples are from charcoal found in early plaza floors or construction fill and are not exempt from the "old charcoal problem" (i.e., the burned material could predate the deposit). A third sample, old copal, is possibly from the later surface of Q-95, but details of its context are unknown. A fourth sample dates pit features that lie beneath a monumental hall, and thus it does not date the architecture itself. For these reasons, we continue to skirt the issue of Mayapán's possible eleventh-century roots, as the evidence is not as strong as for the twelfth century. Indications are stronger in Mayapán's hinterlands of Belize for the origins of Postclassic occupations and pottery sometime in the eleventh century, perhaps close to AD 1100 (Masson 2000; Rosenswig and Masson 2002).

More archaeological research on earlier monumental phases at Mayapán is clearly needed. The chronology of the city has been recently refined with thirty-nine new radiocarbon dates from carbon, copal, wooden cinders, and human remains (figure 2.2; Peraza Lope et al. 2006). Most radiocarbon dates at Mayapán fall between approximately AD 1190 and 1450 (figure 2.2), although our sample is biased toward later activities that left the remains of copal and charcoal in final features. Some structures have as many as seven phases of modification, such as Hall Q-70 (P. Delgado Kú 2004:47).

Unlike many Maya centers, the monumental and residential architecture of Mayapán was not constructed over platforms of earlier periods. Late Preclassic pottery forms 0.4 percent of our test pit sample of 94,725 sherds—Early Classic sherds formed 0.3 percent and Late Classic sherds represented 0.2 percent. This sample includes all test pits and three fully excavated houses within the wall and test units outside of the city wall, where earlier materials were more common, as is indicated by pottery sherd distribution maps (figures 2.3–2.7). Terminal Classic pottery forms 3.8 percent of our total sample of sherds from the settlement zone, and Colonial pottery forms .01 percent. These data are from our 2001–2004 investigations (Peraza Lope et al. 2008:table 15.2). Surface collection results, which sampled more contexts, are equivalent, with Preclassic through Late Classic materials representing 0.1 to 0.3 percent, and Terminal Classic sherds forming 3.5 percent of the sample of 45,567 sherds (Peraza Lope et al. 2008:tables 15.3, 15.4). Ceramic material from the 2008–2009 seasons, totaling 195,686 sherds, yields similar results from seven fully excavated domestic structures and three civic-ceremonial contexts at the Itzmal Ch'en

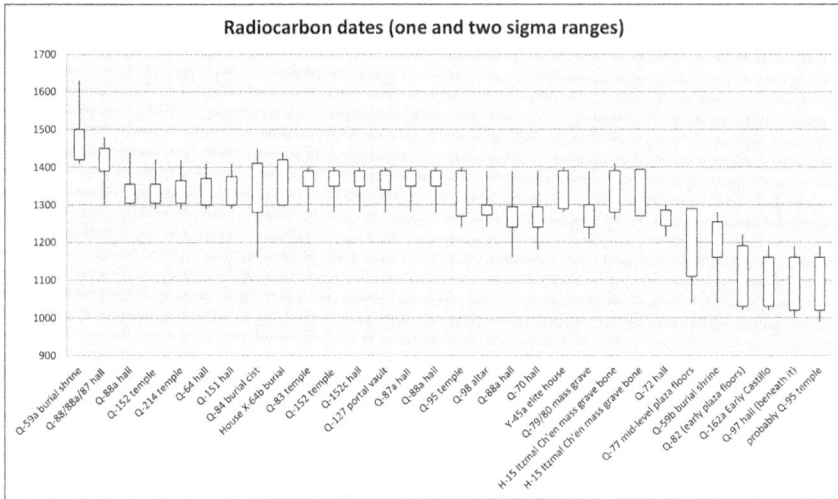

Figure 2.2. *Calibrated radiocarbon dates with results between AD 1000 and 1500 from Mayapán. Full results are reported in Peraza Lope et al. (2006:table 4), with the exception of a new second date for the mass grave next to Hall H-15 (with identical results to the first) that is included in this graph.*

group (Cruz Alvarado et al. 2012). From this sample, Terminal Classic sherds form 2.5 percent of the total sample; occupations in the Itzmal Ch'en area contributed to a higher admixture of Terminal Classic materials—for example, 5.7 percent of the Itzmal Ch'en temple (H-17) sample and 10.6 percent of a lithic workshop building in a nearby residential group (I-57).

The possibility of a Terminal Classic (AD 850–1000) site at the vicinity of Mayapán has been the topic of much analytical deliberation due to the higher quantities of sherds of this era compared to earlier periods and the potential historical links to a previous settlement (figures 2.3–2.7). Harry E. D. Pollock (1962:6) observed, "Not a single Florescent or Early Mexican building . . . has been found, and it seemingly was not until Middle Mexican times (abandonment of Chichén Itzá) or even later that any structure that now survives was erected." This observation has withstood the test of time. A total of 96 percent of the pottery sample from the monumental center and 95 percent of the walled settlement pottery sample dates to this period (P. Delgado Kú 2004:119), as figure 2.3 indicates (Peraza Lope et al. 2008). Nonetheless, Carnegie investigators lacked consensus regarding the importance of Late/ Terminal Classic Maya settlement largely due to the ubiquity of recycled cut stones of the Puuc style. The question continues to prompt disparate views

(Milbrath and Peraza Lope 2003a:8; Peraza Lope et al. 2006). Despite the reuse of Puuc style cut stone blocks in Mayapán's buildings (Proskouriakoff 1962a:92), as well as the fact that one central hall (Q-151, The Hall of the Chac Masks) has two mosaic Chac masks that were brought in from an earlier site, possibly Kabah (Proskouriakoff 1962a:95; Milbrath and Peraza Lope 2003a:11; P. Delgado Kú 2004:111), evidence for a major Terminal Classic city beneath Mayapán has not been forthcoming (Proskouriakoff 1962a:92). No architectural evidence for early buildings of this date has been found in fourteen years of INAH work at the site center (P. Delgado Kú 2004:144), nor in our own PEMY investigations. Most Puuc stones were brought from other sites in the region and were covered in plaster along with local stones, which would have concealed their decorative distinctiveness (P. Delgado Kú 2004:144–45).

There is no doubt, however, that Terminal Classic occupation in the vicinity of Mayapán was widespread given the admixture of sherds in Postclassic deposits. It is doubtful that this earlier settlement was conceived of as the political entity of Mayapán. The distribution of Terminal Classic sherds indicates that settlement of this period corresponds poorly to the heart of the Postclassic city (figures 2.3, 2.4). Rather than concentrating beneath the site center and the densely occupied downtown area around it, Terminal Classic materials are densest near or outside the city wall. It is important to remember that in almost all test pits and surface collections of the INAH, PEMY, and Carnegie projects, where Terminal Classic pottery is found it represents a minority of material that is mixed with greater quantities of Postclassic pottery (Peraza Lope et al. 2006). The large water-bearing Cenotes Itzmal Ch'en and X-Coton clearly attracted earlier settlement (figure 2.4, Russell 2008a). Burials of Late/Terminal Classic age have also been found in the eastern margins of Mayapán's walled enclosure, next to Postclassic Houses F-13b and H-11 (Peraza Lope et al. 2006; Latimer and Delgado Kú 2012). Whole vessels dating to periods prior to the Postclassic have not been recovered at Mayapán (P. Delgado Kú 2004:155), with one exception: Robert E. Smith's (1953) discovery of a Terminal Classic sealed burial cavern within Cenote X-Coton. Partial Terminal Classic vessels were found with two burials at House H-11 (next to the Itzmal Ch'en group), but the house itself was of Postclassic date (Latimer and Delgado Kú 2012). About 500 meters beyond the city wall, Classic Period architecture density increases and buildings are intact, often clustering near major cenotes in the periphery (Russell 2008a). Evidence points to a population of Terminal Classic age in Mayapán's vicinity that was aggregated into multiple, small settlement clusters around major water sources and other agrarian resources. Beyond the city wall, nodal archi-

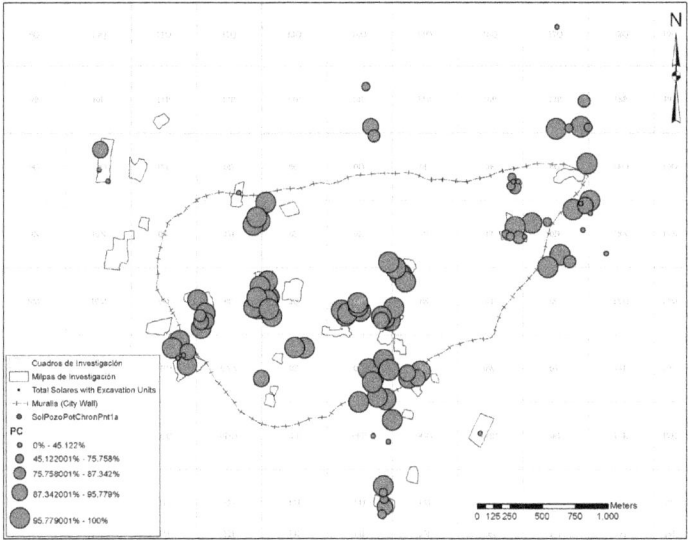

FIGURE 2.3. *Density of Postclassic ceramics in Mayapán test pits. Percentage shown is that of total ceramics per unit. Map by Timothy Hare with data from Peraza Lope et al. (2008).*

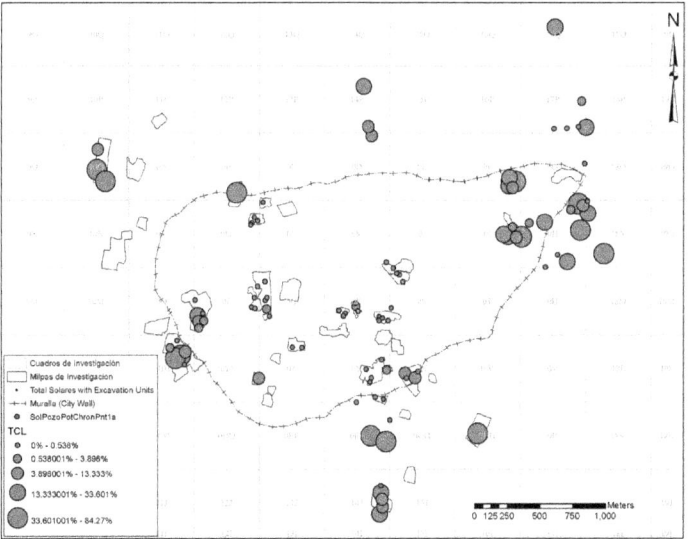

FIGURE 2.4. *Density of Terminal Classic ceramics in Mayapán test pits. Percentage shown is that of total ceramics per unit. Map by Timothy Hare with data from Peraza Lope et al. (2008).*

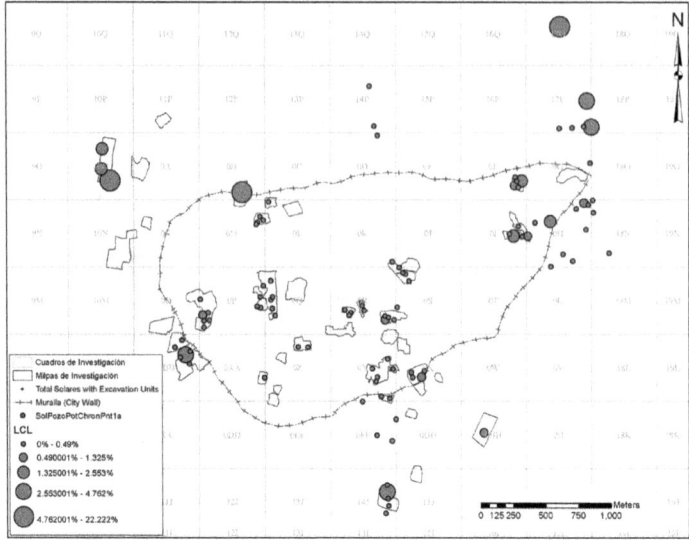

FIGURE 2.5. *Density of Late Classic ceramics in Mayapán test pits. Percentage shown is that of total ceramics per unit. Map by Timothy Hare, with data from Peraza Lope et al. (2008).*

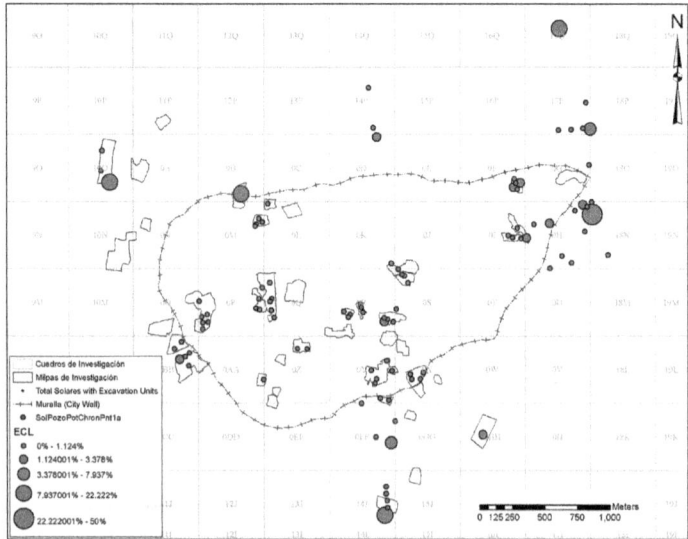

FIGURE 2.6. *Density of Early Classic ceramics in Mayapán test pits. Percentage shown is that of total ceramics per unit. Map by Timothy Hare, with data from Peraza Lope et al. (2008).*

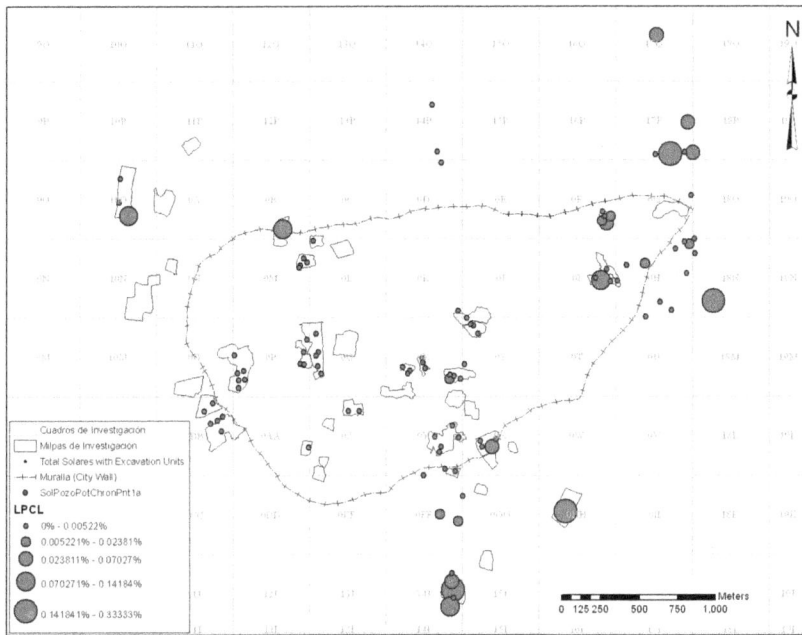

FIGURE 2.7. *Density of Late Preclassic ceramics in Mayapán test pits. Percentage shown is that of total ceramics per unit. Map by Timothy Hare, with data from Peraza Lope et al. (2008).*

tectural features such as shrines and outlying temples have been found that were probably important for dividing and marking Terminal Classic settlement zones in the area (Russell 2008a). These populations were likely linked to a larger town, probably Tichac (modern Telchaquillo), which has at least two standing Classic/Postclassic Period monumental edifices (Roys 1972:180; Proskouriakoff 1962a:92). Other Postclassic sites near Mayapán (figure 2.1) also had significant occupations during the Late or Terminal Classic Periods (Ruppert and Smith 1957).

The most interesting results of the new radiocarbon dates reveal a period of strife and violence that occurred prior to the city's mid-fifteenth-century fall. Between AD 1290 and 1400, two mass graves of descrecrated human remains were deposited in the plaza next to Temple Q-80 in the monumental zone and along the platform of the distant Itzmal Ch'en group (Adams 1953; Peraza Lope et al. 2002; Paris and Russell 2012). Hall Q-88a (the Maize Jaguar building) of the Templo Redondo compound was burned during the same interval (Peraza Lope et al. 1999a). The cinders of its incinerated roof were not removed by Mayapán's inhabitants during the remainder of the site's occupation. Occupants of outlying elite House Y-45a also abandoned their dwelling during this time, taking pains to smash their fine pots in rear rooms, burn offerings, and fill the rooms with rubble before departing (Peraza Lope, Masson, and Delgado Sánchez 2008). These diverse classes of evidence suggest that the city declined in vitality and power at least 50–150 years before its official fall. This fourteenth-century (or late thirteenth-century) strife may correlate with historical accounts of Mayapán in the third Chumayel chronicle, which reports a depopulation of the city in K'atun 1 Ahau (AD 1382–1401) that presages the final downfall (Roys 1962:78). Migrations of groups such as the Kowoj to the Petén Lakes region probably date to this k'atun (Pugh and Rice 2009a:94).

Postclassic ceramic chronology of Mayapán and its contemporaries has been treated in considerable detail elsewhere (R. Smith 1971; Connor 1983; Peraza Lope 1993; Masson 2000; Masson and Rosenswig 2005; Milbrath and Peraza Lope 2003a; Peraza Lope 2005; Peraza Lope et al. 2006; Peraza Lope et al. 2008; Cecil 2009; Cruz Alvarado 2010; Cruz Alvarado et al. 2012) and is not fully described here. The early (Hocabá) and late (Tases) phases of the Mayapán sequence (R. Smith 1971) have caused some confusion. The main utilitarian types and forms of the Mama Red and Navula Unslipped groups continue in both phases (Masson 2000; Peraza Lope et al. 2006; P. Delgado Kú 2004:121). More detailed modal observations are more useful for identifying temporal differences in paste and form for these Postclassic types (Cruz Alvarado 2010, 2012a). The manufacture of Chen Mul Modeled effigy censers in the latter half of the sequence represents the primary phase distinction at Mayapán, and this tradition may have originated in the late thirteenth (Milbrath and Peraza Lope 2003:7) or fourteenth centuries (chapter 8). Stratigraphic comparisons suggest that sherds of the Matillas Fine Orange group may be more ubiquitous in the earlier levels of Mayapán's occupation while Buff Polbox (Tecoh Red-on-Buff, Pelé Polychrome) pottery may be more common in later levels, but overlap throughout the occupation for both ceramic groups is observed (Peraza Lope et al. 2006:170).

Buff Polbox pottery has been of considerable interest to researchers at Zacpetén and other Kowoj settlements due to similarities in surface treatment and decoration shared with Kowoj pottery (Rice and Cecil 2009a; P. Rice 2009e). It is not, however, confined only to late contexts at Mayapán, nor is it found only in isolated locations as claimed (Pugh and Rice 2009a:92). The most decorated type of the Buff Polbox group, Pelé Polychrome, is rare in the settlement zone, and this pottery is of greatest significance for Zacpetén comparisons. We have generally concluded it to be a high-status serving ware for Mayapán, due to its ubiquity at one monumental center hall (Q-88), one elite palace (R-86–90), and one elite house (Y-45). Distribution maps from test pit and surface collection contexts illustrate some tendency for Buff Polbox group pottery (mainly represented by the Tecoh Red-on-Buff type) to occur in slightly higher proportions (but not more than 2 percent of the samples) in clusters near the eastern Gate H, western Gate AA, and in the south central part of the city toward Gate X (figures 2.8, 2.9). The small proportions, however, do not constitute a strong indicator of social enclaves.

General resemblances between Kukula Cream group pottery, especially the Xcanchakan Black-on-Cream type and Terminal Classic Peto Cream pottery have contributed to efforts to divide Mayapán's pottery assemblages into two phases, with Kukula Cream sherds representing the best candidate for an earlier Hocabá phase diagnostic (R. Smith 1971). Like most other rarer Postclassic pottery types, they are recovered in low numbers in lots dominated by Mama Red and Navula Unslipped sherds; they also occur in contexts that have pottery considered to belong to the later Tases phase. A more detailed study has now been completed by Wilberth Cruz Alvarado (2010). In the settlement zone, frequencies are very low, but we do observe slightly higher proportions near to the Itzmal Ch'en cenote in our surface collection and test pit samples, where Terminal Classic pottery is also relatively more ubiquitous. This co-occurrence may lend weight to the Hocabá phase argument, but the higher frequency is marginal—near Itzmal Ch'en these sherds account for 1–3 percent of the sample, and elsewhere they are less than 1 percent.

Archaeologists are still working out the chronological details of northern Yucatán during the interval from AD 1000–1200 (Milbrath and Peraza Lope 2003a, 2009:589; Peraza Lope et al. 2006). Some argue that Chichén Itzá ceramics (Sotuta Complex) lingered for at least a century after AD 1000, although the architecture of this site was completed earlier and not expanded after this date (Andrews, Andrews, and Robles Castellanos 2003). Chichén Itzá was probably occupied in the eleventh and twelfth centuries, although its power waned and new groups may have moved into the site (Milbrath and Peraza Lope 2003a:21). Anthony P. Andrews, E. Wyllys Andrews V, and Fernando Robles Castellanos (2003:152) and Ringle, Gallareta Negrón, and Bey (1998:189–90) are more inclined to view the Postclassic as a single ceramic phase. Recent work at Mayapán and in its hinterlands is in general agreement for a Late Postclassic Period from around AD 1100 to Spanish contact (Masson 2000; Masson and Rosenswig 2005; P. Delgado Kú 2004). In Belize

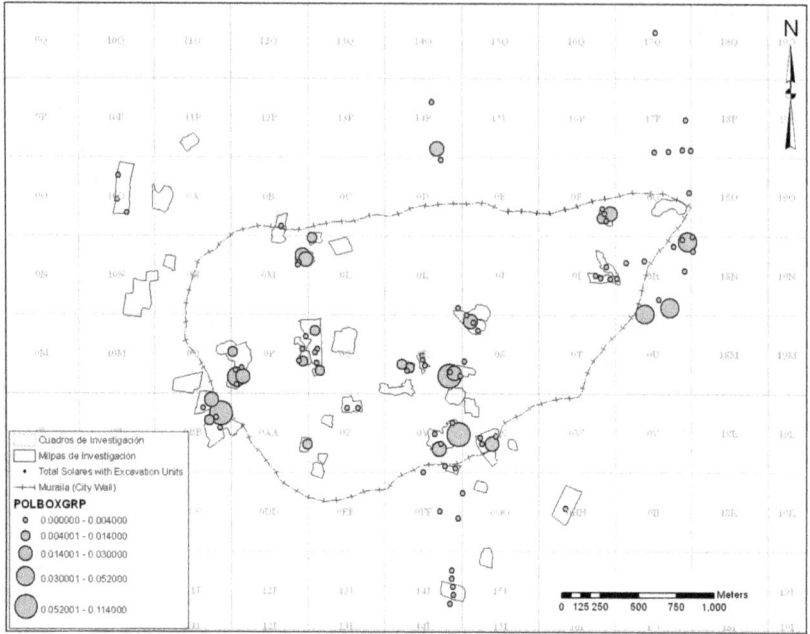

FIGURE 2.8. *Buff Polbox group pottery in Mayapán's test pits (mainly Tecoh Red-on-Buff). Percentage shown is that of total sherds per unit. Map by Timothy Hare, with data from Peraza Lope et al. (2008).*

the sequence is more nuanced, as pottery assemblages can be defined for the Early Postclassic Period (Walker 1990; Graham 1987; Masson and Rosenswig 2005), as can a post-Mayapán set of diagnostics that date to the segmented century beginning around AD 1450 and lasting into the Colonial Period (Graham 1987; Oland 2009). Architectural changes may have greater potential for tracking chronological and historical developments. For example, dance platforms and other features may be earlier, as they emulate the architecture of preceding northern sites (Milbrath and Peraza Lope 2009:593–94).

A fourteenth-century resurgence in the Belize hinterland coincided with the rise in Chen Mul effigy censer use at Mayapán and an increase in site construction and trade at sites across the lowlands (Masson 2000). These efforts may have been part of a revitalization movement originating at Mayapán that emphasized ancient gods, myths, and symbols (Masson 2000), perhaps in response to severe societal and environmental stress (chapter 8). Milbrath and Peraza Lope (2009) make an argument for multiple, smaller scale revivals in

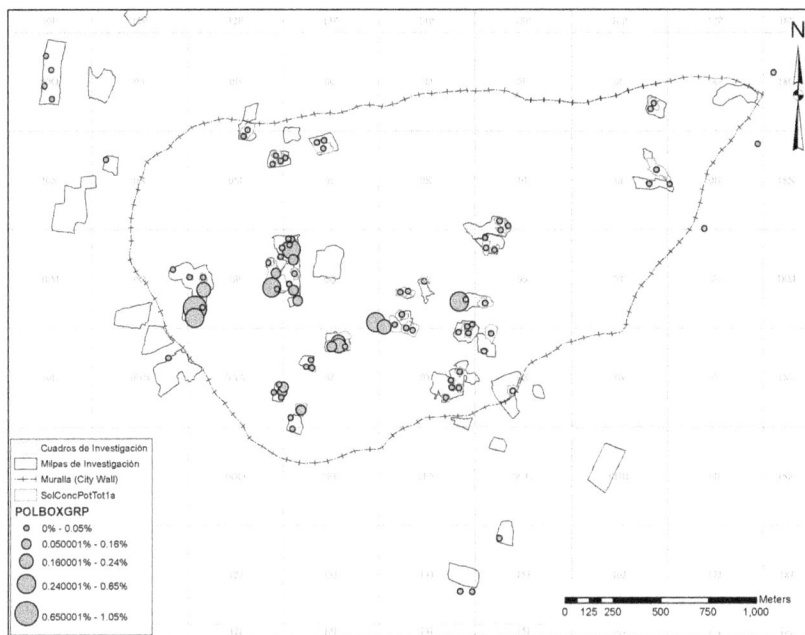

FIGURE 2.9. *Buff Polbox group pottery in Mayapán's surface collections (mainly Tecoh Red-on-Buff). Percentage shown is that of total sherds per unit. Map by Timothy Hare, with data from Peraza Lope et al. (2008).*

building styles and stelae erection throughout Mayapán's history (Milbrath and Peraza Lope 2009:596, 600). It remains difficult to address the timing of such phenomena with the constraints of radiocarbon and ceramic dating, which can provide at best temporal accuracy within a one hundred-year period (Peraza Lope et al. 2006; Milbrath and Peraza Lope 2009:595).

MAYAPÁN'S PUBLIC BUILDINGS

A conventional approach to the study of political organization is to examine the distribution of types of elite architecture, including temples, large residences, and other large buildings of specialized function. Landa (1941:23–26) reveals that an inner enclosure, presumably the monumental center, was constructed first, which contained temples and houses for high priests and lords, followed by a resettlement effort that brought subject peoples from townships that were part of the confederacy to the city. These families built houses outside of the monumental zone, as Landa tells it. This passage hints at the process of founding a political capital, although some details are glossed over. The monumental plazas of the city contain only colonnaded halls and ritual edifices; this zone is ringed by the largest and most elaborate residences, but they are clearly outside of it and a possible remnant of the inner enclosing wall. One possible explanation for this model is that halls were considered emblematic of "big houses," as was the case for Utatlán (Carmack 1981a). Alternatively, the fact that Mayapán's major palaces encircle the monumental zone a short distance away may have constituted sufficient proximity and nucleation to earn this concentric description. Today a rectangular wall surrounds the monumental civic-ceremonial groups. The wall was probably reconfigured from a rounded shape to its current form by ranchers before the Carnegie investigators arrived, but its location may approximate that of the earlier enclosure (Brown 1999). If Landa's account can be believed, the construction of the monumental core was initiated in an organized effort to found a political capital. As many of the monumental zone structures exhibit multiple Postclassic Period modifications (P. Delgado Kú 2004), it is not a simple matter to reconstruct the original appearance of the center.

Types of Buildings and Architectural Groups

Colonnaded hall courtyard groups, sometimes with temples, frame the monumental center (figures 2.10, 2.11). Most public buildings had composite roofs of wooden beams and masonry, which were plastered over (Proskouriakoff 1962a:94–95). The epicenter has twenty-two halls, and at least seven others are found within or near the city wall. Eleven temples are present at the monumental center, including one next to a portal gate that forms an eastern entrance to this zone. There are five general types of temples, including (1) large pyramidal structures housing an upper shrine room or two, (2) burial shaft temples housing an upper shrine room with an ossuary shaft, (3) radial temples (two to four cardinal staircases), (4) round temples, and (5) twin temples (only one exists at Mayapán, T-70). A variant of the first and second types includes the serpent column temples defined by the Carnegie project (e.g., Q-58, Q-143, Q-159, Q-162, and Q-218), which had serpent effigies carved of plaster or limestone at the base of staircase balustrades or columns forming an entranceway to the upper sanctuary (Proskouriakoff 1962a; Pugh 2001). Four more temples are present in strategically important locations in residential zones inside the wall as well as numerous oratories, sanctuaries, shrines, constructed altars, and round columnar altar stones (Proskouriakoff 1962a:91; P. Delgado Kú 2004:135). Small custodial houses (e.g., Q-92, Q-93, Q-67, and

Q-68) are sometimes located next to temples (e.g., Q-95 and Q-58), as indicated in figure 2.10.

The Carnegie project defined oratory buildings as those with temple-like rooms supported by smaller substructures (Proskouriakoff 1962a). Unlike Mayapán's temples, oratories were often used for funerary purposes and were probably ancestral shrines for privileged families. Both oratories and temples tend to have stucco human effigies in front of the altars in their upper buildings. Shrines and altars can be freestanding, adjoined to building bases, or centered on internal benches; sanctuaries are small rooms attached to buildings. It is difficult to know whether Mayapán residents perceived differences among shrines, altars, and sanctuaries, as their associated materials exhibit considerable overlap (Proskouriakoff 1962a:90–91). In general, these features have anthropomorphic stucco sculptures, censers, and/or human bones or skulls (e.g., Adams 1953:149, Proskouriakoff 1962a:90, 100). Sanctuaries were built later in the building sequences at Mayapán's center (P. Delgado Kú 2004:132).

The Main Plaza is dominated by the Temple of Kukulcan at its southern edge (figures 1.3, 2.10); the Round Temple (Templo Redondo) (Q-152) is located along its eastern border; and Hall Q-81 (with Temple Q-80 behind it) defines the northern edge. The western side of this plaza has three colonnaded hall groups (Q-70, Q-72, and Q-54). The North Plaza is formed by the front of Temple Q-80, burial shaft Temple Q-58 to the west, and Hall Q-64 to the north. Additional smaller plazas are observed to the northeast, east, and south—for example, groups including Temple Q-95/Hall Q-97 or Halls Q-87/Q-99, Hall Q-151/Temple Q-153, and Hall Q-142/Temple Q-141 (P. Delgado Kú 2004:99, 107, 111). Other conspicuous groups are also present just south of the Temple of Kukulcan and outside of the Main Plaza (figures 2.10, 2.11). We agree with Gustav Strömsvik (1953:137) and Edwin W. Shook (1955:267) that the main entrance to the monumental zone was through a portal gate (Q-127) located just east of the site center (for a more dubious assessment, see Proskouriakoff 1962a:124).

Proskouriakoff (1962a:91) classified monumental center arrangements into basic ceremonial groups and temple groups. Basic ceremonial groups include a hall, shrine, and oratory and may or may not be spatially linked to temples. Temple assemblages are distinguished by a pyramidal temple with serpent columns that forms a right angle to a colonnaded hall, with a shrine centered on the hall that faces the temple, and an oratory (Proskouriakoff 1962a:91). These elements reveal a high level of standardization in civic-ceremonial groups. Archaeological research has revealed little functional difference between these types of groups.

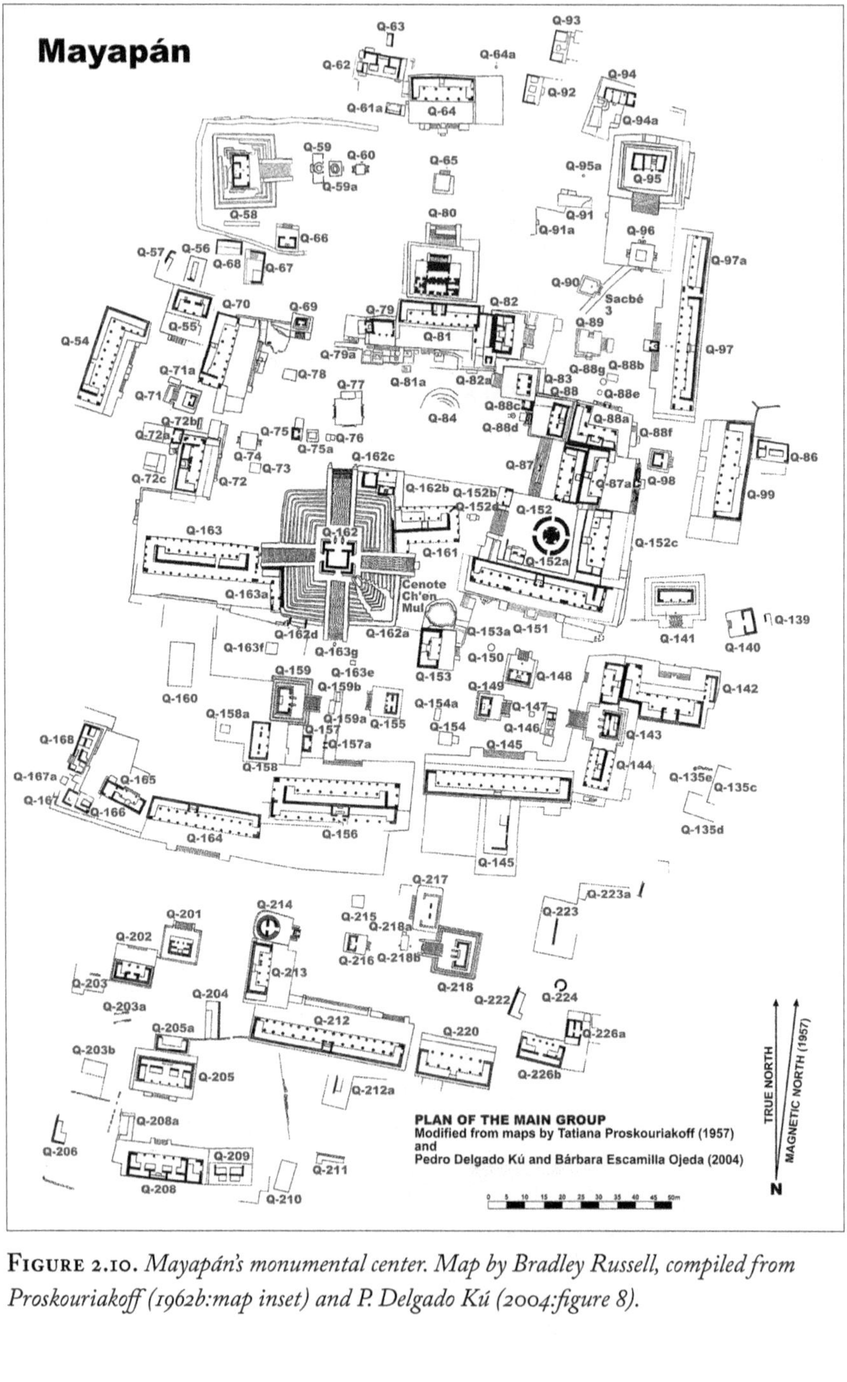

FIGURE 2.10. *Mayapán's monumental center. Map by Bradley Russell, compiled from Proskouriakoff (1962b:map inset) and P. Delgado Kú (2004:figure 8).*

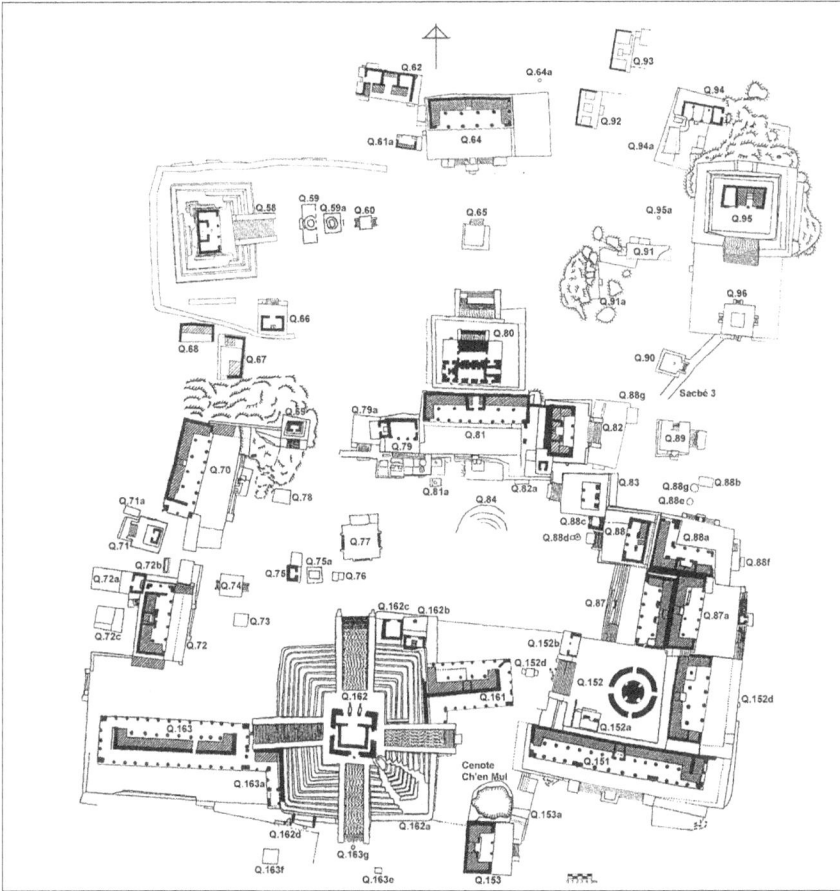

FIGURE 2.11. *The Main Plaza and North Plaza of Mayapán's monumental center, showing the locations of the Temple of Kukulcan (Q-162), Cenote Ch'en Mul, the Round Temple (Q-152), the Hall of the Sun Disks (Q-161), the Hall of Kings (Q-163), the Hall of the Chac Masks (Q-151), the Temple of the Painted Niches (Q-80), burial shaft Temples Q-58 and Q-95, and other associated buildings discussed in the text. Map by Pedro Delgado Kú and Bárbara Escamilla Ojeda.*

REMEMBERING CHICHÉN ITZÁ

Architectural conventions such as radial temples, round temples, and serpent balustrades and columns link Mayapán to Chichén Itzá (Proskouriakoff 1962a; Andrews and Sabloff 1986:433–56; Milbrath and Peraza Lope 2003a:11; Milbrath and Peraza Lope 2009; P. Delgado Kú 2004:153–54, 156). Round

Temple Q-152 shares an alignment with Chichén Itzá's Caracol that faces the sunset in late April and mid-August, marking day intervals (105 and 206) useful for agriculture (Aveni 1980:269; Aveni and Hartung 1978:139–40; Milbrath and Peraza Lope 2003a:12). Equinox orientations are also identified (Milbrath and Peraza Lope 2003a:12; Aveni, Milbrath, and Peraza Lope 2004). The Temple of Kukulcan emulates its analog, the Castillo at Chichén Itzá (Proskouriakoff 1962a:91), in terms of serpent balustrades, nine terraces, four radial staircases, and a primary northern orientation (figures 1.3, 2.10; Milbrath and Peraza Lope 2003a:16). Subtle differences are also identified. Mayapán's Kukulcan temple may have originally had 65 steps per side for a total of 260, a number significant to the ritual calendar, whereas the Chichén Itzá temple stairs commemorate the solar year (Carlson 1982; Milbrath and Peraza Lope 2003a:17). A rattlesnake shadow appears on the Mayapán temple staircase around sunset at the time of the winter solstice, whereas this pattern is present at the Chichén Itzá temple for the equinox (Milbrath and Peraza Lope 2003a:17). The burial shaft temples of Mayapán generally resemble Chichén Itzá's Osario in having a central shaft containing human remains; we outline their differences later in this chapter. Mayapán, along with all of its contemporaries in the Maya lowlands, curiously lacks ball courts, a central feature of public architecture at Chichén Itzá and other Classic Period northern centers. Gallery-patio groups, a hallmark form at Chichén Itzá, include a long frontal colonnaded hall. The hall component continues at Mayapán without the square columned patio enclosure of its predecessor. Variants of Mayapán's public architecture and art have been identified at sites along the east coast of Yucatán (Freidel and Sabloff 1984; Barrera Rubio and Peraza Lope 2004; Milbrath and Peraza Lope 2003a:24–25; P. Delgado Kú 2004:154), at northern Belize sites (Masson 2001a:96; Rosenswig and Masson 2002) in the Petén Lakes (Pugh and Rice 1997, 2009b:143–47; Pugh 2001:253, 2002), and in highland Guatemala (Carmack 1981a).

RECENT INVESTIGATIONS

Many monumental zone buildings have been investigated archaeologically. The Carnegie project performed work at a selection of temples, halls, oratories, and shrines in the site center (Proskouriakoff 1962a; Weeks 2009). Some work involved formal excavation while other buildings had selected features cleared for mapping purposes (Proskouriakoff 1962a). Special features were tested—including dance and monument platforms Q-77, Q-96, and Q-84 (Proskouriakoff 1962a:104, 106, 109)—and plaza floors were trenched (Adams

1953). Peraza Lope commenced the INAH project in 1996 and has fully excavated and restored the majority of temples, halls, associated ancillary buildings, and attendant houses of Mayapán's Main Plaza and the adjacent North Plaza (Peraza Lope et al. 1997, 1999a, 1999b, 1999c, 2003; Peraza Lope, Delgado Kú, and Escamilla Ojeda 2002; Peraza Lope, Escarela Rodríguez, and Delgado Kú 2004). The details of monumental building construction have been fully chronicled in Pedro C. Delgado Kú's (2004) masterful Universidad Autónoma de Yucatán tésis. All mural fragments from the site center have been the subject of a recent synthetic study by Miguel Angél Delgado Kú (2009). Milbrath, Peraza Lope, and Alfredo Barrera Rubio have published a suite of articles on newly discovered art objects and mural programs from the city (e.g., Peraza Lope 1999; Barrera Rubio and Peraza Lope 2004; Milbrath and Peraza Lope 2003a; Milbrath, Peraza Lope, and Delgado Kú 2010).

HIGH ART AT SELECTED MAYAPÁN BUILDINGS

Mayapán was a cosmopolitan world city, and its widespread contacts with other polities in Postclassic Mesoamerica are observed in diverse art styles (Pollock 1962:14; Milbrath and Peraza Lope 2003a:40; Masson 2003a; M. Delgado Kú 2009; Masson and Peraza Lope 2010). Various studies differ in their interpretation of the degree of direct contact between central Mexican Aztec polities, intermediaries in the Gulf Coast region of southwestern Campeche or eastern Tabasco, and Mayapán. This kind of debate often ensues in Mesoamerican archaeology whenever major political art incorporates styles recognized from another region (Chase and Chase 1988; Masson 2003a; Braswell 2003). As Masson and Peraza Lope (2010) point out, Aztec pottery or other trade goods are not found at Mayapán. In the equally distant Postclassic Soconusco region, settlements with close ties to the Aztec empire do have low quantities of Aztec pottery (Voorhies and Gasco 2004:figure 6.10). It is clear, however, that Mayapán was directly or indirectly in contact with central Mexico and that this interchange resulted in a mixture of art of local or international inspiration at the city (Pollock 1962:14; P. Delgado Kú 2004:156; Andrews and Sabloff 1986:433–56; Barrera Rubio and Peraza Lope 2004), although some similarities also date back to Chichén Itzá's apogee (Milbrath and Peraza Lope 2003a:26). Some of Mayapán's most conspicuous public art is reviewed in the remainder of this chapter, including programs at the Kukulcan temple and adjacent Halls Q-161 and Q-163, Temple Q-80, burial shaft Temples Q-58 and Q-95, and the Itzmal Ch'en temple and halls (H-17, H-15, and H-12).

The Temple of Kukulcan

Mayapán's principal pyramid, Q-162 (figures 1.3, 2.10, 2.11) bore the name of Kukulcan (Landa 1941:25). The cosmological and astronomical features of Temple Q-162's architecture, as well as comparisons to Chichén Itzá, have been well studied, and we have reviewed these findings in the previous section (Milbrath and Peraza Lope 2003a:16–19; P. Delgado Kú 2004:74). The temple has nine tiered levels and reaches a height today of 15 meters; its upper room would have added at least 2 meters to this height (P. Delgado Kú 2004:74). Sanctuaries Q-162b and Q-162c were later built at the plaza level in front of the pyramid, to the east of the northern staircase (P. Delgado Kú 2004:79–80). Sanctuaries Q-162d, Q-162e, and Q-162f are located at the rear (south) side of Q-162 (P. Delgado Kú 2004:114–16).

The Cenote Ch'en Mul was of symbolic significance at Mayapán, located to the immediate east of the Temple of Kukulcan (figure 2.11). Together with this temple it represented an ancient Mesoamerican temple-cave complex, and cavernous chambers within Ch'en Mul extend to beneath Round Temple Q-152 (Brown 1999:181; Pugh 2001). Rituals pertaining to the cenote may have taken place at the cenote temple (Q-153), located at the southern edge of its opening. Contrary to Colonial accounts, the cenote was not used to any recognizable extent for sacrifice or offerings (Roys 1962:49). Tests in the Cenote Ch'en Mul performed by Robert E. Smith (1954) yielded only general midden debris, some of which probably washed in from above. The cenote holds small pools of water. "Cenote" Ch'en Chooch on the Morris R. Jones (1962) Carnegie map, located just north of the monumental center, is actually a large sascab mine used for building materials at the site center and was not part of the sacred landscape (A. Smith 1962:213).

The INAH project exposed an earlier phase of the Temple of Kukulcan, Q-162a, at the southeast corner of the building (Peraza Lope et al. 1997; Peraza Lope 1999; Milbrath and Peraza Lope 2003a:19). This early building may not have been radial, as evidence for a north-facing staircase was not found—it was either destroyed or did not exist (Milbrath and Peraza Lope 2003a:18, 2009:592). A stucco frieze on the southeast corner of the interior temple (figure 2.12) illustrates the theme of war. Three scenes in the facade feature skeletonized figures (P. Delgado Kú 2004:79). Rectangular niches rather than heads appear above the torsos of these figures. Peraza Lope and his colleagues observe that skulls would have been placed in these niches (Peraza Lope 1999; Peraza Lope et al. 1999a:82, plates 236–43; Milbrath and Peraza Lope 2003a:18; P. Delgado Kú 2004:77). In one niche, human maxillary bone was found along with an effigy mandible of stucco (Peraza Lope et al. 1999a:82, plate 240; P.

Delgado Kú 2004:79; Serafin and Peraza Lope 2007). On the south, lower side of this façade, the skeletal figure has an attendant. The most striking of these three façade segments is on the east side (figure 2.12), where the hands of the skeletal figure are being pecked at by birds, perhaps vultures (Milbrath and Peraza Lope 2003a:18). An oversized, personified sacrificial knife is aimed at the figure's midsection. These personages stylistically resemble tomb stucco figures from a Postclassic tomb at Zaachila (Flannery 1983:figure 8.26), and they are rendered in an International style that is not characteristic of the Maya area, although a skeletal death god frieze is known from Tonina (Schele and Mathews 1998:figure 7:25). Peraza Lope (1999) interprets these figures as warriors glorified in death or cultic death god figures (Peraza Lope et al. 1999a:80–82), and the entities are similar to personages on pages of the Dresden Codex (Milbrath and Peraza Lope 2003a:18, 2009:592). The façade attests to underpinnings of violence and warfare associated with the early Mayapán state. This militaristic emphasis did not dissipate through time.

As the physical and cosmological center of the Mayapán world, Temple Q-162 was the nexus of a wide range of ritual activities essential to the unity and prosperity of the polity. Smaller art objects attest to the diversity of occasions hosted at the Temple of Kukulcan and its two adjacent halls. Higher proportions of whiskered merchants or warriors are found in this group among the effigy assemblage (chapter 7). Art commemorating females and the site's only Ehecatl (wind god aspect of Kukulcan) effigies also set the Temple of Kukulcan compound apart from other edifices. A nearly life-sized sculpture of a woman grinding maize on a stone metate commemorated the productive contributions of women to society (figure 2.13). This working woman, found by the INAH project, was featured prominently between Q-162's eastern staircase and the Cenote Ch'en Mul. The temple also had slightly more clay figurines than any other monumental edifice, which suggests that the owners left them near the temple as votive offerings, perhaps in the context of processions or pilgrimages (Masson and Peraza Lope 2012).

STELA 1 AND STELA 9

Stela 1, now at the hacienda of Xcanchakan (at a nearby town), features two actors (Figure 2.14), marked by a K'atun bird and a K'atun 10 Ahau date, probably AD 1185 (Pollock 1962:3; Milbrath and Peraza Lope 2003a:39). Its larger protagonist is enthroned above and to the right of a lesser figure, and he is gesturing and speaking, as indicated by a speech scroll emanating from his mouth. This lord appears in the guise of Chac, with a Chac headdress and

FIGURE 2.12. *The stucco façade on an earlier phase of the Temple of Kukulcan (Q-162a) features skeletonized figures, as shown in this example from the building's east face. Note that the birds peck at the figure's hands and a personified knife is located beneath the figure's right arm. Illustration by Anne Deane.*

a reptile eye. A turbaned figure, also wearing a possible Chac mask, extends an offering to this lord. Both figures have headdress miters that Karl A. Taube (1992:figure 14) links to the priesthood and Itzamna, although other entities wear it. A similar theme is observed on Stela 9, found near round Temple Q-126. Like Stela 1, the principal figure is seated on a throne on the right, facing an eroded figure or set of offerings (including a tripod bowl) on the left. Two other fragments (Stelae 5 and 6) have probable dates of AD 1244 and AD 1283 (Pollock 1962:3).

Q-161—HALL OF THE SUN SYMBOLS

Hall Q-161 was a multifunctional building decorated with scenes linked to celestial bodies, astronomy, mythology, and conjuring (Barrera Rubio and Peraza Lope 2004:439; M. Delgado Kú 2009:279–80, 295). Its mural was carefully covered in stucco during antiquity and was not visible during the final occupation of the site; INAH's investigations have uncovered it (Peraza Lope et al. 1997:90). Mayapán's murals in general resemble other International-style murals found broadly across Mesoamerica in localities such as central Mexico, eastern coastal Yucatán, and highland Guatemala (Proskouriakoff 1962a:137;

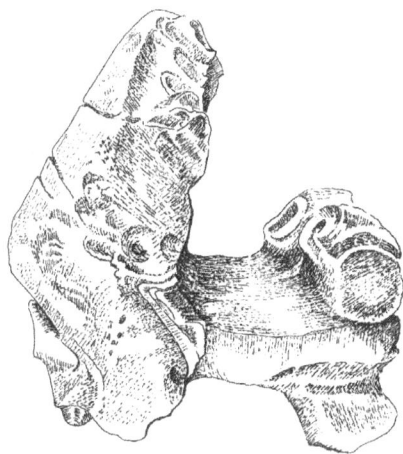

FIGURE 2.13. *A nearly life-sized stone sculpture of a woman working at a grinding stone was recovered at the base of the east staircase of the Temple of Kukulcan. Illustration by Anne Deane.*

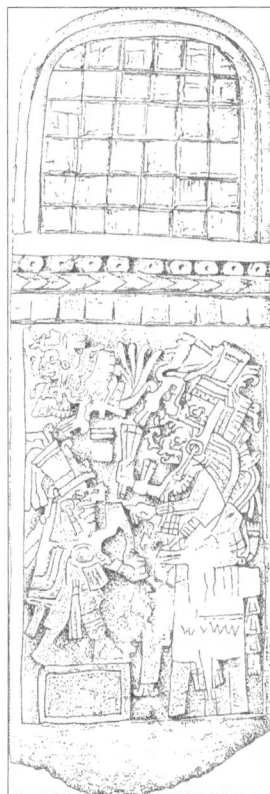

FIGURE 2.14. *Stela 1 from Mayapán. Illustration by Kendra Farstad, from Proskouriakoff (1962a:figure 12a).*

Miller 1982; Barrera Rubio and Peraza Lope 2004; Milbrath and Peraza Lope 2003a:28–29; Masson 2003a). The style of these murals has prompted suggestions that central Mexican artisans painted them (Milbrath and Peraza Lope 2003a:29–30; Milbrath, Peraza Lope, and Delgado Kú 2010:1–2).

The Q-161 mural originally had a series of eight yellow panels outlined in red-painted bands in which a sun disk is the central element (Barrera Rubio and Peraza Lope 2004; M. Delgado Kú 2009:222). The eight panels may be related to the eight solar years in the Venus almanac; star eye symbols descend from the panels' upper frames, also attesting to the importance of Venus (Milbrath and Peraza Lope 2003a:28; Milbrath, Peraza Lope, and Delgado Kú 2010; M. Delgado Kú 2009:295). The descending figures in this Venus almanac could be avatars of the sun (Milbrath, Peraza Lope, and Delgado Kú 2010:3). Alignments from the Round Temple (Q-152) toward Q-161 and the Castillo mark key solar dates and lend credibility to this argument (Aveni, Milbrath, and Peraza Lope 2004; Milbrath, Peraza Lope, and Delgado Kú 2010:3).

From each sun disk at Q-161, a unique descending figure emerges. These personages are scarcely identifiable due to the mural's eroded state (figures 2.15, 2.16). On either side of the sun disks are two religious practitioners who use serpent staffs to help the disk descend (e.g., M. Delgado Kú 2009:226, 276, figure 69). The figures are elaborately dressed in textiles and head gear signifying their elite status, and they likely portray supernatural entities—gods or ancestors—who were called out from sun disk portals at the behest of serpent staff–holding priests. Miguel Delgado Kú (2009:276–78) argues they may represent deities such as the death god, the sun god, or Mayapán founder Hunac Ceel. One figure bears a large ring-shaped ornament in its headdress that is reminiscent of Tlaloc goggles, and another figure carries such an object or it is attached to his clothing (M. Delgado Kú 2009:figures 70, 74).

Of interest to us here are the pair of ritualists flanking each of the solar disks, whose serpent-headed staffs attach to the disks. These priests are clearly responsible for pulling down the disk from the sky band and coaxing the conjured entities to emerge from the sun symbols. Sun priests or Ah Kin May served as primary prophets for the may k'atun cycle, as Prudence Rice (2004:79), points out, but their power would have extended into a variety of political and official affairs, as discussed earlier in this chapter (Landa 1941:27). Another name for such supreme religious authorities according to Landa was Ahau Can May, which incorporates an ancient title for a political lord (Ahau). Might these manipulators of solar disks be sun priests? A second possibility is that they are Feathered Serpent priests, as they wield serpent staffs. The association of priests connected to serpent symbols and solar disk personages is reminiscent of themes in Chichén Itzá's Temple of the Jaguars. The Q-161 panels differ from imagery at Chichén Itzá in that snakes themselves are not being conjured at Mayapán and there are multiple sun disk figures at Mayapán rather than one primary figure (e.g., Schele and Mathews 1998:figure 6:33).

The existence of Feathered Serpent priests at Mayapán merits greater consideration given the importance of this office at Chichén Itzá. Ringle and his colleagues argue that Feathered Serpent priests performed the rites of accession for kings at Chichén Itzá, who are portrayed in sun disks at the Temple of the Jaguar (Ringle et al. 1998; Ringle 2004). They further suggest that high priests were important authorities in Chichén Itzá's governance, along with the king. Grant Jones (1998) has proposed an institution of paired rulership, consisting of a king and a priest, in the Petén Lakes region, a location to which some Itza migrated after Chichén Itzá's fall. Kowoj groups migrated to the Petén

FIGURE 2.15. *One panel from sun disk mural at Hall Q-161, Mayapán. The sun disk at center is flanked by two standing ritual practitioners who extend serpent head staffs to either side of the sun disk.*

from Mayapán later in time (P. Rice 2009d). Source material on Mayapán lacks explicit descriptions of formal paired authorities, nor does it emphasize serpent priests. Only three sculptures at the site may portray ritualists in the service of Kukulcan, wearing conical headdresses with three knots (chapter 7). Sun priests, on the other hand, were powerful, and their reputation endured long into the Colonial Period (Landa 1941:27). An idea of the ominous power of sun priests is provided by Tozzer (1941:27n146), citing a retrospective account as late as 1633, referring to the Izamal ruins: "There dwelt the priest of the Gods and they were revered to such an extent that it was they who were the lords and who punished and rewarded and who were obeyed with great fear . . . the priests were called and are called so at the present day . . . Ab (Ah) Kin."

The practice of conjuring deities who descended to receive offerings was routine for the Contact Period Maya area (Landa 1941:158). The diving god at Tulum may represent such a conjured entity, perhaps even Kukulcan, as described for festivals at Maní following Mayapán's collapse (Masson 2000:221, 231–37; Landa 1941:158).[1] The descending personages represented in the Hall Q-161 panels may portray dynasts who were later commemorated in the city's history or conjured in apotheosized form to sanction political actions in this life. It is hard to know the occasion for which they were conjured by the serpent staff wielders. Linda Schele and Peter Mathews (1998:230, 252) identify a sun disk ancestor on a lintel and mural of the Temple of the Jaguars while Ringle (2004) argues that sun disk figures may be initiates into

FIGURE 2.16. *Close-up of one figure descending from a sun disk panel at Hall Q-161, Mayapán. Reproduced with his permission from M. Delgado Kú (2009:figure 72).*

political office at the behest of Kukulcan priests. It is highly likely that the panels portray conjured patron deities (or apotheosized patron ancestors) who presided over solar-Venus cycles (Milbrath et al. 2010). One other possibility must be reviewed: Might the panels illustrate the simultaneous manifestations of multiple beings? One creation scene on page 48c of the Mixtec Codex Vindobonensis (Byland and Pohl 1994:130, figure 58) shows four versions of a founder-hero, 9 Wind (a version of Quetzalcoatl), descending from the sky. Potentially analogous are the lintel paintings of the Mitla palaces, which depict epic heroes, officials, oracles, and patron deities of three major Oaxacan social groups (Pohl 1999:193). We know that Mayapán was held together by confederated factions who may have rotated the burden of solar or sacred calendrical cycles with the aid of their patron gods. The conjured beings from Mayapán's sun disks could represent some of those gods. The Q-161 panels hold many potential insights into Mayapán's political and religious organization.

Q-163—HALL OF KINGS

Hall Q-163 extends westward from the Temple of Kukulcan. It was named the Hall of Kings due to the recovery of seven nearly life-sized, fragmentary stucco portraits that covered its frontal columns (Proskouriakoff 1962a:95, figure 7p; Peraza Lope et al. 1999a:205–7; Peraza Lope et al. 1999b:photos 420–29; Peraza Lope 1999; Milbrath and Peraza Lope 2003a:26). The historical or mythical entities of the Q-163 portraits may not, however, portray "kings" (figures 2.17–2.19). It is difficult to determine gods from ancestors who became deified in death (Proskouriakoff 1955:87; Masson 2000:224). Ancestors were often portrayed in the guise of gods such as K'awil in Classic Period Maya art (e.g., Looper 1991). We favor the interpretation that deities are represented on the Q-163 columns following Milbrath and Peraza Lope (2003a:26; Peraza Lope 1999:51), who identify the following personages: one deity with fangs, one column with the monstrous clawed feet of Tlatecuhtli (central Mexican earth lord), one Xochipilli, one Xipe Totec (figure 2.19), and one youthful pregnant female goddess (perhaps Tlazolteotl). Three male faces lack distinctive deity face markings, although two of these have whiskers and/or hollow eyes that may signify merchants (figure 2.18). One "merchant" has a bird (Quetzal) headdress that may be linked to martial capacities. Four examples exhibit the miter headdress, including the Xipe Totec, four other males, and one whiskered male.

In central Mexico, portraits of deified rulers or their offices were among the corpus of Aztec and Tlaxcalan Postclassic art. Richard F. Townsend (1979:31–33) describes these statues, or *teixiptla*, which became the focus of community ancestral rituals. Townsend's (1979:34) thoughtful analysis describes the teixiptla as embodiments of communities (of people and perhaps places) and their relationship to the supernatural realm, or the "animating spirits of the universe." In contrast, the cliff carvings of Mexica emperors (now greatly destroyed) on the hill of Chapultepec emphasized historical individuals rather than dynastic offices or symbols (Townsend 1979:33). Townsend points out that deceased Aztec royalty were sometimes portrayed in deity attire. He specifically mentions Xipe Totec as one example, and this entity is the most clearly portrayed personage at Q-163. The columns of Q-163, whether they portray gods or historical persons, probably reference the founding mythology of a paramount and his social group. Although Mayapán's ruling council was hierarchically ranked (Ringle and Bey 2001), the doctrine conveyed in the Q-161 and Q-163 programs is one of relatively equal representation of multiple supernatural players. The lack of individual glorification may be masked, however, by the portrayal of multiple supernaturals who legitimated the heroic histories of a particular paramount dynasty. The fact that the Q-161 mural was covered suggests revisionist history.

Other halls may have had similar stucco portraits to Q-163, suggesting that each hall commemorated the otherworld patrons of its dynasty. Vestiges of plastered columns suggest that stucco portrait figures might have graced the pillars of Q-163's corollary, the Q-161 sun disk panel colonnade (Peraza Lope et al. 1999b; Peraza Lope 1999; P. Delgado Kú 2004:151–52). Behind (south

FIGURE 2.17. *Hypothetical reconstruction of Hall Q-163, the Hall of Kings, showing how sculpted columns may have appeared. Illustration by Luis Góngora, courtesy of Carlos Peraza Lope.*

of) the Temple of Kukulcan, Hall Q-156 was also "decorated with life-sized human figures modeled in high relief stucco on the columns" with the "feet of the figure in place, and a fragment of a well modeled stucco head was found nearby" (Proskouriakoff 1962a:116, figures 7q, r). In fact, portions of anthropomorphic stucco sculptures are relatively common on columns of other halls (P. Delgado Kú 2004:152), and one can envision a resplendent monumental center with stone-roofed, plastered columned buildings filled with art and portraiture visible to pedestrians in the plazas. Within most buildings, colorful, elaborate murals commemorated themes of high culture in myth, history, religion, and astronomical science. Luis Góngora's artistic reconstruction of Hall Q-163 captures the feel of the original appearance of such halls (figure 2.17).

Q-80—TEMPLE OF THE PAINTED NICHES

Temple Q-80 is atypical for Mayapán in that it has seven small interior rooms—some of them vaulted—on all sides of the building (Winters 1955a; P.

FIGURE 2.18. *Stucco portrait of a merchant deity from a column at Hall Q-163. Photo by Bradley Russell.*

FIGURE 2.19. *Stucco portrait of Xipe Totec from a column at Hall Q-163. Photo by Bradley Russell.*

Delgado Kú 2004:90–95). The frontal staircase of the building descends to the north. The north wall of the rear, southern room (Room 1) has a resplendent mural that the Carnegie project found, which depicts five painted effigy temples with built-in niches that represent the doors of these temples (Winters 1955a; Proskouriakoff 1955). This scene, referred to as the Temple of the Serpent Heads mural (M. Delgado Kú 2009), has four reptiles with gaping mouths that are painted between the temples. These reptiles have been linked to the founding mythology of the city (Pugh 2001; Masson 2003a; Milbrath, Peraza Lope, and Delgado Kú 2010:4), perhaps even to Kukulcan, with respect to his role in bringing together four divisions at Chichén Itzá and uniting four lineages from heaven at Mayapán (Masson 2003a). Recent detailed descriptions of this mural are provided by Miguel Delgado Kú (2009:142–55). Timothy W. Pugh (2001) has argued that these reptiles may represent primordial crocodile deities linked to a particular creation flood myth. He also argues that five serpent temples were important to the center's cosmological organization with respect to this origin myth.

Different markings on the bands above the serpents have been variously suggested to imply different mythological places, social entities associated with them (Masson 2003a), or Venus imagery (Milbrath, Peraza Lope, and Delgado Kú 2010:5). Turquoise or *chalchihuitl* symbols indicate Venus symbolism in this program (Milbrath and Peraza Lope 2003a:27) and for the murals of Q-95 and Q-152 (Barrera Rubio and Peraza Lope 2004; M. Delgado Kú 2009:192, 217). Kukulcan is widely linked to myths and movements of the planet Venus. The great square of Cholula, a hub for Feathered Serpent ritual and pilgrimage (Pohl 2003a), contained a Turquoise House. Quetzalcoatl's Temple of Turquoise at Acatlán is also shown in the Codex Nuttall (Nuttall 1975:15; Milbrath and Peraza Lope 2003a:27). Mayapán was obviously the center of Kukulcan veneration in the Maya world, and Feathered Serpent priests at this city may have operated out of a religious edifice similar to those of other Postclassic centers. In Landa's lifetime, Mayapán's Temple of Kukulcan was known to have been named for this entity, and perhaps Q-80 was a Xiuhcalli facility used by politico-religious councilors of esteem. With multiple vaulted rooms, the building is unique at the city, and the fact that it is centrally located across from the Temple of Kukulcan reflects its significance (figures 2.11, 2.20). It is noteworthy that the site's four Venus ceramic censer effigies are concentrated at Shrines Q-79/79a and Hall Q-81 (chapter 7); these structures are adjacent to Temple Q-80.

Other layers of celestial and cosmological symbolism have been well argued for this mural. Barrera Rubio and Peraza Lope (2004:431) suggest that the red paint dominating the upper part of the scene and the black paint at the lower part refer to the sun's daily cycle of rising and setting, drawing on the symbolism of these colors outlined in the Chilam Balam of Chumayel (Roys 1967:64–65; M. Delgado Kú 2009:159). The temples, their niches, and the serpents may signify the temple-cave complex (Barrera Rubio and Peraza Lope 2004:431). Proskouriakoff (1962a:137) was the first to observe that the stylistic conventions of this mural were comparable to those in vogue in contemporary central Mexico. Mural fragments were also found beneath two stucco floors and a thick layer of fill in Temple Q-83, a small edifice immediately east of Q-80 (Peraza Lope et al. 1999b:122–23). It is referred to as the Mural of Substructure Q-83 and shows the feet of human actors, costume regalia, and a serpent band, and it exhibits a style and color scheme that strikingly resemble the Structure 16 and Structure 25 murals of Tulum (M. Delgado Kú 2009:166, 171).

Serpent Temples

Serpent sculptures at Mayapán are not confined to building forms classified as serpent temples by Howard D. Winters (1955b) and Proskouriakoff (1962a). That classification was based on the presence of serpent columns and/or balustrades at five structures: Q-162, Q-218, Q-159, Q-143, and Q-58. Despite these shared features, the buildings differ in some ways, and they also share additional characteristics with temples not classified as serpent temples. For example, Q-162 is the only radial pyramid in this group (figure 2.10). Three other temples had serpent sculptures in their surface rubble: Q-95, Q-82, and H-17. Structure Q-95, which lacks evidence for serpent columns or balustrades, is highly similar to serpent Temple Q-58, with its central mass burial shaft that descends to bedrock from the top of the structure. The size and prominent placement within the site center also distinguish Q-95 and Q-58. The other two structures, classed as an oratory (Q-82) and temple (H-17), similarly possess single upper-room sanctuaries with rear central shrines that are present on the smaller serpent temples (Q-159, Q-143, and Q-218). Miguel Delgado Kú (2009:129) suggests that serpent iconography in various elements of Mayapán's temples is more broadly attributable to parallels with Chichén Itzá. The presence of serpent art reflects the importance of Kukulcan veneration at such edifices as Q-95, Q-82, and H-17, where fragments derive from staircase or upper temple decorative features. Serpent temples as discussed by Pugh (2001) do not represent a complete picture of the sacred, commemorative monumental landscape of Mayapán, although he reveals their special importance.

Stone serpent fragments are generally common at the site center (Masson 2000), as pieces are present at twelve other structures beyond those described in the preceding paragraph, including altars, shrines, and sanctuaries (e.g., Q-71, Q-82a, Q-88b, Q-90, Q-96), halls (Z-50), and monument or dance platforms (Q-84, Q-77).[2] No more than two individual serpents are represented among the fragments of most structures. Temple H-17 at the Itzmal Ch'en group is an exception (chapter 3).

An architectural enclave that may be linked to Kukulcan priests lies in a court formed by the cenote temple (Q-153), Halls Q-151 and Q-145, and Temple Q-143. Near raised Shrine Q-149 in this group, two sculpture heads were found. Each has a human face and a conical headdress with three knots (Proskouriakoff 1962a:96, figure 8c). The headdress and knots are part of Quetzalcoatl regalia across Mesoamerica during the Postclassic (Miller and Taube 1993:141), and this group may have been a focal point for the activities of Feathered Serpent

FIGURE 2.20 *Hypothetical reconstruction of Temple Q-80, the Temple of the Painted Niches, with the summit of the Temple of Kukulcan seen in the background. Illustration by Luis Góngora, courtesy of Carlos Peraza Lope.*

priests. The group's location, adjacent to the Temple of Kukulcan and Cenote Ch'en Mul, makes it a logical locus for activities focused on this deity, although Q-80 may have been a formal facility for this purpose, as suggested previously. Given the importance of this deity, it is logical that multiple ritual groups at the city provide evidence of religious practice in his honor. A third example of a sculpture with this headdress was found at outlying House P-33 (chapter 7).

Winters (1955c:411–12) and Proskouriakoff (1962a:139) identify interesting variants in serpent head iconography at the site. Two examples are particularly distinctive. The head at Structure Q-159 has earth lord riders astride it and at Structure Q-218 a gouged eyeball protrudes from the snake's head. Quetzalcoatl, in his Ehecatl form, is shown with a similar gouged eyeball in the Borgia and other Laud codices (Díaz, Rodgers, and Byland 1993:27), although other deities can share this characteristic (Díaz, Rodgers, and Byland 1993:30, 31, 35). Eyeball gouging was a popular form of sacrifice in Postclassic central Mexico (Díaz, Rodgers, and Byland 1993:62, 63). Proskouriakoff (1962a:136) was the first to link earth monster depictions at Mayapán to the central Mexican deity of Tlatecuhtli.

Burial Shaft Temples Q-58 and Q-95

A central theme of the city center's art and architecture is oriented toward death and sacrifice. Two burial shaft temples represent the most conspicuous of such features (Shook 1954a; Masson and Peraza Lope 2007). Structures Q-58 and Q-95 are located at the northwest and northeast corners of the monumental zone and seem to have marked the boundaries of the ceremonial precinct (figures 2.10, 2.11, 2.21, 2.22). Structure Q-58 reaches a height of 8 meters (Peraza Lope, Delgado Kú, and Escamilla Ojeda 2003:31) and Q-95 is 5 meters tall (P. Delgado Kú 2004:104).

Shafts at Q-58 and Q-95 were planned from the beginning of construction, as they are incorporated into two construction phases at Q-58 and are associated with two ceramic phases at Q-95. Chen Mul effigy censers were present in the upper half of the Q-95 shaft (Shook 1954a). Gustav Strömsvik, of the Carnegie project, was lowered into each of the shafts to investigate them (Shook 1954a:256). The shaft of Q-58, the Crematory, was looted, although a few remains of children and adults were recovered intact at its base (Shook 1954a:256). Over forty adults and subadults were found in the Q-95 shaft (Temple of the Fisherman), along with sacrificed animals and birds, offerings of broken vessels (including effigy censers), metal artifacts, and objects of conch and stone (Shook 1954a:271). Of four such temples, Q-95 is the only one with a sacrificial stone still in place (Shook 1954a:271; Peraza Lope et al. 2003:50), although a stone was present near H-18, in front of the Itzmal Ch'en temple (H-17).

Two other more modest burial shaft shrines were reported at the Cenote X-Coton and the Itzmal Ch'en groups, although these shafts do not extend to bedrock (Shook 1953; Chowning 1956; Masson and Peraza Lope 2007). As smaller examples are only detected through excavation, others probably exist at the site. For example, Temple R-19, in the settlement zone to the east of the monumental center, has never been investigated, but like the X-Coton group and Temple Q-58, it also has three frontal plaza-level altars (one of which is round). Except for H-18, Chen Mul effigy censers were abundant in the shafts. At H-18, the censers were instead concentrated at a nearby plaza-level shrine, H-18a (Chowning 1956:455). The Cenote X-Coton group has a double temple/shrine, T-70 (figure 2.23), that features two separate upper enclosed rooms. This design was implemented late in the construction sequence of the temple (Shook 1953:210–12), which Proskouriakoff (1962a:130) reclassed as a shrine due to its small size. Oratory T-72, next to Temple/Shrine T-70, had a small circular burial shaft, 1 meter deep, in which the cremated human remains of adults, children, and animals were found (Shook 1953:209). It is possible that the human remains in this oratory were funerary rather than sacrificial, although the presence of significant quantities of animal bones and censers, as well as the practice of cremation, are unusual among Mayapán burials (Smith 1962; Masson 2009). A small round shrine at the Itzmal Ch'en group (H-18) also had a burial shaft with (noncremated) interments that were very clearly sacrificial victims (Chowning 1956:446–47). Fifteen individuals were placed in the H-18 burial shaft. The heads were disarticulated from the bodies and some skulls were missing. Except for one adolescent, all were adults. Ann Chowning (1956:447) observed that these individuals were placed in the feature one or two at a time and that they were sacrificed.

Three facts link Shrine H-18 to the Feathered Serpent deity. First, it is round structure, a hallmark of the veneration of this god (Pollock 1936). Second, a conch shell was placed at the base of the shaft beneath the victims; this shell or other large shells are emblematic of Quetzalcoatl/Kukulcan. Third, serpent sculptures represent a large majority of decorative items found at Temple H-17 (chapter 3), the principal edifice of this group. Other shaft temples shared serpent symbolism: Q-58 is a serpent column temple and Q-95 probably portrays Kukulcan on its mural, as we will discuss shortly. Marilyn A. Masson and Peraza Lope (2007) have published a detailed argument for the association of burial shaft temples with creation mythology involving the Feathered Serpent based on the observation that they are regularly associated with round buildings, sets of three altars, or nearby cenotes. Temple Q-58 (a serpent column temple) has two round frontal altars and three altars altogether. Temple T-70, next to Structure T-72 (with a burial shaft) has three altars, one of them round. H-18 is round. Both the H-18 and T-72 groups are next to major cenotes (P. Smith 1953). Only Q-95 lacks any of the associations described for other shaft temples. Other temples that lacked burial shafts are also associated with cenotes and round structures, such as Q-162 and H-17.

At Chichén Itzá, the Osario has a similar burial shaft. The Osario is a serpent temple linked to Cenote Xtoloc (Proskouriakoff 1953:266, 1962a:133; Shook 1954a:254). Its shaft terminates in a subterranean cavern that had a deposit of human bone (E. Thompson 1938:50) that was similar to the remains from the Mayapán temples. These remains were disarticulated and partly charred (like those of T-70), but they were of Terminal Classic age. A square shaft above the cavern descends from the Osario's surface, and it had seven layered interments, each with offerings (E. Thompson 1938). The articulated, stratified burials of this shaft imply reverential treatment, unlike the disarticulated, bone-filled shaft temples of Mayapán or the lower cavern of the Osario (Proskouriakoff

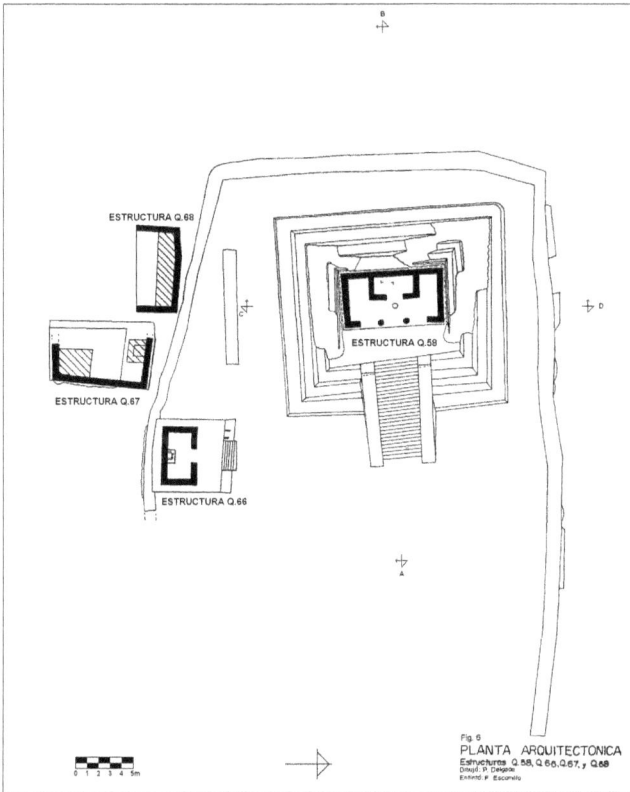

FIGURE 2.21. *Burial shaft Temple Q-58, Oratory Q-66, and custodial house group Q-67/Q-68 (from P. Delgado Kú 2004:figure 63).*

1962a:133). The shaft graves of Osario at Chichén Itzá are contemporary with Mayapán (Proskouriakoff 1962a:133), as offerings included Mama Red tripod vessels, a Navula Unslipped tripod cup, copper bells of Late Postclassic style, Chen Mul effigy censers (E. Thompson 1938:figures 16a–d, 16f, 16g, 16j, 21), and crystal and turquoise ornaments that E. H. Thompson (1938:7) recognized as late. Only one other possible burial shaft temple has been reported in Mesoamerica, from the site of El Tajín. Rex Koontz (2002:115) summarizes the investigations of the Pyramid of the Niches at El Tajín by S. Jeffrey K. Wilkerson (1990:161) and Jürgen K. Brüggemann (1992:77), which had a vertical shaft descending from the upper sanctuary. As bone preserves poorly in this region and no remains were present in the shaft, its use is unknown (Koontz 2002:115).

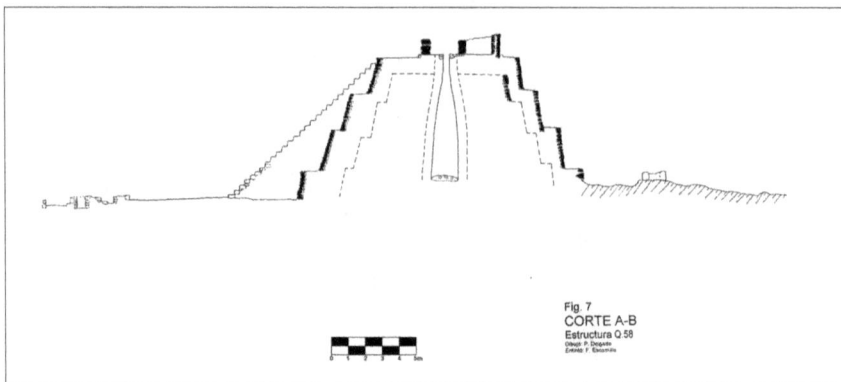

FIGURE 2.22. *Cross-section of burial shaft Temple Q-58 (from P. Delgado Kú 2004:figure 7).*

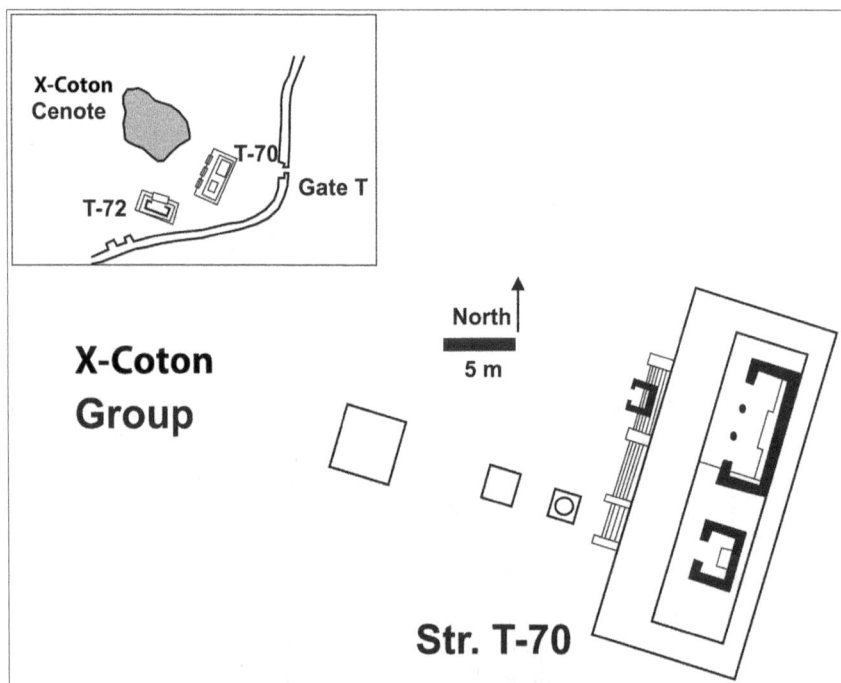

FIGURE 2.23. *Double Temple/Shrine T-70 and Oratory T-72, with cremation burial shaft, next to Cenote X-Coton by Gate T, Mayapán (from Shook 1953:figure 1).*

The Fisherman Mural

Two themes are evident in the art of Temple Q-95 and its associated buildings that form a courtyard at the center's northeast corner. The first is a creation myth that is implied by a mural on top of a bench in Q-95's upper room (figure 2.24). The second theme is that of death, which is related to the first theme of the resurrection and recreation of the human race. The mural displays the watery underworld, populated by three impaled fish, one uninjured fish, a crocodile bound by its limbs, one water serpent, and a central human figure—a.k.a. the Fisherman (Peraza Lope, Delgado Kú, and Escamilla Ojeda 2003:53; Milbrath and Peraza Lope 2003a:28). Detailed studies of this mural have been undertaken by Peraza Lope et al. (2002:287), Barrera Rubio and Peraza Lope (2004), Milbrath and Peraza Lope (2003a), Masson and Peraza Lope (2007) and Miguel Delgado Kú (2009). The serpent is marked with a Venus (chalchihuitl, turquoise) symbol (M. Delgado Kú 2009:192), and importantly, this snake resembles the water Chicchan serpent of the Madrid Codex, which has possible Venus associations (Milbrath and Peraza Lope 2003a:28; Milbrath, Peraza Lope, and Delgado Kú 2010:7). Miguel Delgado Kú (2009:195–96) observes similarities in the portrayal of the protagonist in this mural with the Mixtec codices (particularly the Codex Nuttall) and the Borgia Codex.

The fisherman on the mural may be Kukulcan/Quetzalcoatl. An identifying feature includes the figure's oversized olive shell pectoral (figure 2.24). Kukulcan wears a collar of olive shells on page 4a of the Dresden Codex (Taube 1992:figure 27a). Other associations are significant. The Dresden Kukulcan is identified by the glyph for God H (Taube 1992:60), which in the Classic era is linked to wind (Ik), as are the Classic Water Lily serpent and the Ehecatl manifestation of Quetzalcoatl (Taube 1992:59). Water serpents like the one on the fisherman mural are sometimes linked to wind, and by extension, to Kukulcan. Other interpretations merit consideration. The Venus associations identified by our colleagues are compatible with an identification of Kukulcan, who is often linked to Venus symbolism.

The Aztec myth of the Fifth Sun, the current creation era in which we now live, seems to be commemorated at Temple Q-95. Principal evidence in support of this hypothesis is the pairing of the (probable) Kukulcan figure in the mural with death god imagery, including small Mexican death god sculpture at Q-95 (Milbrath and Peraza Lope 2003a) and a significant quantity of other death god imagery of the Q-95 group (chapter 7). The association with vanquished marine animals is also important. In this myth, Quetzalcoatl (and

Tezcatlipoca) transformed themselves into sea serpents and slew a crocodilian earth monster (Tlatecuhtli) that had been terrorizing the earth, which was at the time covered in water. Quetzalcoatl's next mission was to retrieve the bones of the humans from past creation eras; these bones had been turned into fish (Taube 1993:37–39; M. Smith 2003a:194). In the process of retrieving them, Quetzalcoatl is said to have fallen into a deep pit and the bones became fragmented. The retrieved bones were combined with blood offerings by Aztec gods, and a paste ground from them created the next generation of humans. The deep shaft of Q-95 may represent the underworld pit of this myth, and the deposition of human bones may have been intended to help in reenacting creation events. Perhaps the fish on the mural represent the former humans of the past creation, destined for retrieval by the central figure.

Our *Mexicon* article (Masson and Peraza Lope 2007) was not the first to identify the fisherman mural with this myth; David Stuart (2006:178) presented this argument in his book on Palenque, as a consequence of his discussions with Karl Taube. Gabrielle Vail (2006) also links the crocodile in this image to a central Mexican myth in which a beast of this type is speared by Quetzalcoatl. Milbrath, Peraza Lope, and Delgado Kú (2010:8) point out that myths in the Chilam Balam books also feature a crocodile slain by a Maya personage, Bolon ti ku, after a flood, and it makes sense that the myth would be adapted in ways deemed suitable to the Maya area. Some parallels in the Popul Vuh myth are easily identified, such as where the skeletal object of desired retrieval is a decapitated head. The transformation of the Hero Twins into catfish in the underworld prior to their ultimate victory is another intriguing reference to fish.

Still, the Aztec mythological parallels are quite close, and it is noteworthy that central Mexico, not the Maya area, has a tradition of temples associated with mass sacrifice at Teotihuacan and Tenochtitlan (Sugiyama 2004; López Luján 1998:183–84). In the case of Teotihuacan, mass sacrifice is explicitly associated with the Feathered Serpent Pyramid, among others. Oddly, the only sacrificial burial shaft temples for Mesoamerica are from Mayapán, with the possible exception of the Osario's burial cavern deposit of Terminal Classic age at Chichén Itzá. Although the Bonampak murals indicate the capture and torture of a large number of individuals, and their impending sacrifice is implied (Miller 2000), there is little archaeological evidence of sacrifice of large numbers of people in the Classic Maya Period. Exceptions seem to include dynastic conquest, as at Colha or Cancuen (Hester et al. 1982; Demarest 2013). Maya art illustrates plenty of captives and the sacrifice of individuals in the context of creation myth reenactment or as part of royal funerals (e.g., Freidel,

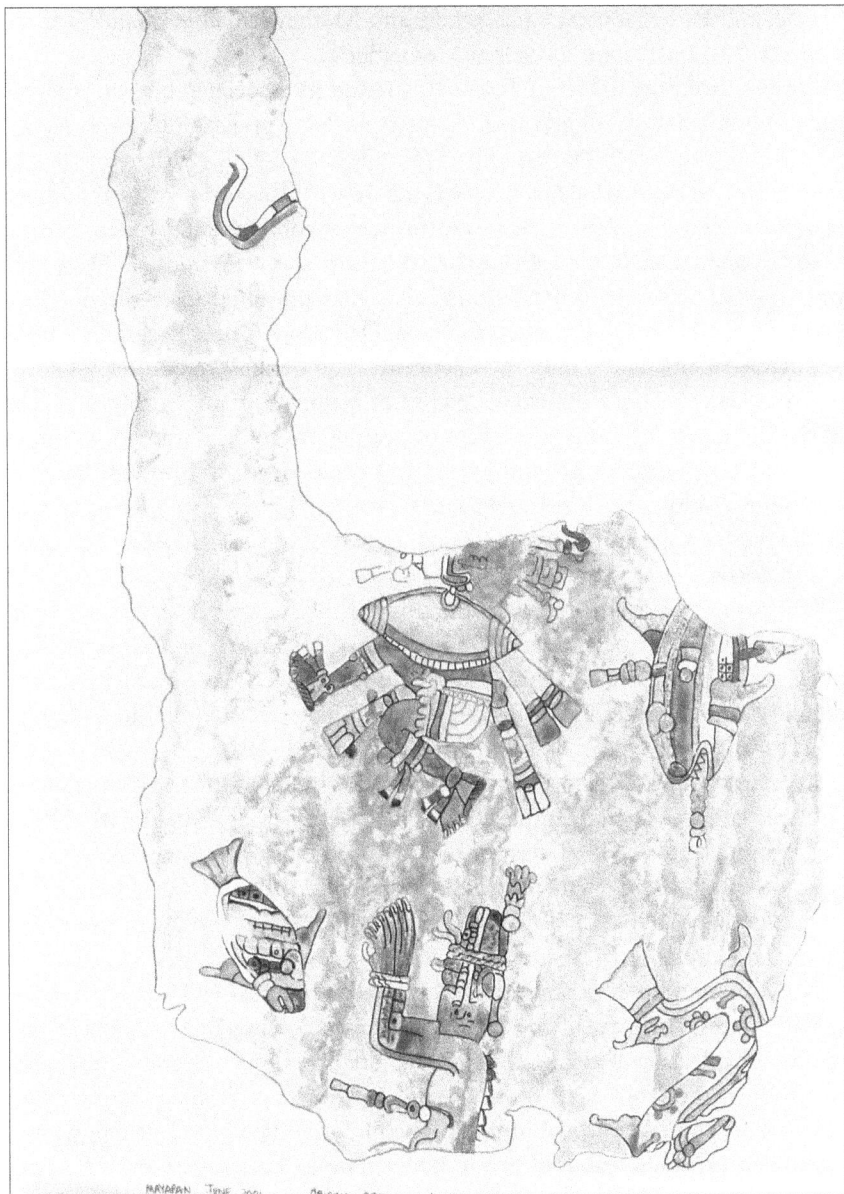

FIGURE 2.24. *Mural on a bench at the top of Temple Q-95, the Temple of the Fisherman, Mayapán. Illustration by Anne Deane.*

Schele, and Parker 1993:237, 314; Schele and Mathews 1998:109), and in these respects, Maya art is not unique in Mesoamerica.

Objects from the debris of Temple Q-95 and its associated buildings reveal the importance of death gods. An Aztec-style death god sculpture was recovered at the temple (Milbrath and Peraza Lope 2003a) along with five skull cup fragments and two skeletal face censers (chapter 7). This is the greatest number of skeletal ceramic objects recovered from any context at Mayapán. Shrine Q-89 (named Death House), in the courtyard space in front of Q-95 and Hall 97/97a, had nine skeletal stone heads that projected from the building from attached stone spikes (Peraza Lope, Delgado Kú, and Escamilla Ojeda 2003:110–11). This is the only such concentration of skull sculptures found at the site. Other than a disarticulated set of human remains within a corner of Shrine Q-89, no unusual objects or features were encountered within it (Peraza Lope, Delgado Kú, and Escamilla Ojeda 2003:107). Shrine Q-89 may represent a skull platform (*tzompantli*), or alternatively, a *tzizimime* shrine. Both types of features have skull iconography in Postclassic Mesoamerica (M. Smith 2003a).

Platform Q-96, immediately to the front of the staircase, also has a skeletal ring sculpture. This performance or gladiatorial platform emphasizes the significance of public ritual in this location. Just to the west of Q-95, more human remains were deposited in an ossuary tomb in a specialized building (Q-94). Clearly, Q-95 was a place associated with death and sacrifice.

Leonardo López Luján (1998:183–84) has documented the sacrifice of probable war captives at the Templo Mayor that were perhaps timed with a Xipe Totec annual ritual. He argues for concepts of dually opposing deities (solar and aquatic) incorporated into this temple's offerings and the timing of its rituals. Perhaps similar duality underlay the construction and use of two major sacrificial temples at Mayapán, Q-95 and Q-58.

Notably, the serpents marking the columns of Temple Q-58 had earth monster attributes with claws (Proskouriakoff 1962a:100, figure 60). Other than this important reference to Tlatecuhtli, the materials at Q-58 reflect a different set of symbols compared to Q-95. Mayapán's magnificent Monkey Scribe effigy censer was found face-down in the soil behind Temple Q-58. This effigy must have been previously housed in the upper temple. Its imagery draws deeply from traditional Maya creation mythology that is quite apart from the Aztec Myth of the Five Suns (Milbrath and Peraza Lope 2003b). Like the Aztecs, the Maya had multiple creation myths. A relatively high proportion of enigmatic male personages are portrayed on other effigy censers from Q-58. These examples lack diagnostic deity attributes and may depict warriors (chapter 7).

It is a shame that so little iconography remains from Q-58, as it is difficult to understand concepts of duality or opposition embodied in the symbolism of Q-58 and Q-95 and the sacrificial rites enacted at them. As this temple was looted prior to the Carnegie project, other diagnostic objects may have been removed (Shook 1954a:255–56).

WARFARE AND SACRIFICE

Activities at burial shaft Temple Q-58 and Q-95 buildings helped to generate terror among the subjects and residents of Mayapán and strengthened political power by demonstrating what state authorities were capable of (Dickson 2006). One account, the *Relación of Chunchuchu*, described a "burning furnace" at Mayapán into which those who committed certain crimes were thrown during the Colonial era (Tozzer 1941:124n576). This intriguing allusion may refer to the occasional use after the city fell, although the materials reported by Shook (1954a) from within Q-95 seem to have been of Prehispanic origin. Accounts of sacrifice are ubiquitous during the Colonial Period (Landa 1941:115–17; Scholes and Roys 1938), but France B. Scholes and Roys pondered whether levels intensified in response to the extreme stress of the impacts of European contact. Although sacrifice was supposedly introduced to Yucatán by the "Mexicans" and performed at the insistence of priests, the Colonial era was rife with continued sacrifices, even Christian-inspired crucifixions, among decentralized townships, if documentary accounts can be believed (Tozzer 1941:115–16n532, 533).

Sacrifice at Mayapán tied this polity to earlier traditions where the enactment of creation mythology called for sacrifice (Freidel, Schele, and Parker 1993). Stanley Serafin and Peraza Lope (2007) argue that dismemberment of individuals, like those next to Templo Redondo, may have been linked to gladiatorial sacrifice and mythological enactment of tearing apart the earth monster, the same myth that may have been significant for rites at Q-95 (Masson and Peraza Lope 2007). Unlike Classic Period Maya art, individual actors responsible for such activities at Mayapán were not acknowledged in lasting artistic works. Another major difference may be the sacrifice of men, women, and children at Mayapán, as only male captives are shown in Classic Period political art. Clearly, some dynastic families were fully annihilated, and women were not spared, similar to Colha (Hester et al. 1982; Massey and Steele 2006) or Yaxuna (Ardren 2002). For Mayapán's burial shaft temples, lords or war chiefs captured individuals of mixed ages and gender, and priests would have performed the sacrifices (Shook 1954a). Heart extraction on the tapered altars at Mayapán would have been one of several sacrificial methods, including gladiatorial sacrifice by tethering victims to ring stones or upright sculpted stones or wooden beams (Tozzer 1941:115; Freidel and Sabloff 1984:153). Arrow sacrifice at Canpech (Campeche) occurred on a wooden platform that supported multiple large sculptures (Freidel and Sabloff 1984:153).

Two possible gladiatorial sacrifice stones with perforations (other than the Q-96 example) for tethering were in front of Hall Q-81 (Winters 1955b:402; Proskouriakoff 1962a:138; Milbrath and Peraza Lope 2003a:16; Serafin and Peraza Lope 2007:245). Tapered sacrificial blocks were also present near the principal pyramid (Q-162) as well as at Temple Q-95 (Milbrath and Peraza Lope 2003a:16; Shook 1954b:98, figure 1a, c). The Totonicapán model map of Utatlán (Carmack 1981b) indicates a platform for gladiatorial sacrifice (*zoquibal*, or place of the obsidian hatchet) that supported a round stone for tethering prisoners, as well as a skull rack altar (*tzumpan*). Circular platform Q-84, located in the city's Main Plaza, may have been a place of sacrifice, as a tapered sacrificial stone was found near it (Shook and Irving 1955:133; Milbrath and Peraza Lope 2003a:15). The Maya codices have several references to captives, sacrifice (decapitation), and trophy heads (Bricker and Bill 1994: 195–99).

Mayapán's monumental center is, among other things, a graveyard where many sacrificial victims were interred. Most human remains at the central buildings were non-funerary (Serafin and Peraza Lope 2007; Serafin 2010). For example, in a passageway between Round Temple Q-152 and Hall Q-152c, cranial and long bones of twenty adults (or near adults) were found in Burial 29 (Peraza Lope et al. 1999a; Milbrath and Peraza Lope 2003a:15; Serafin and Peraza Lope 2007; Serafin 2010:71). Another concentration of human remains (Burial 27) overlay this (Peraza Lope et al. 1999a:197; Serafin 2010:72). Between Q-162 and one of its frontal sanctuaries, nine individuals were interred; all but one skeleton was disarticulated (Peraza Lope et al. 1997; Serafin and Peraza Lope 2007; Serafin 2010:72). Serafin (2010:74) reports that additional non-funerary human remains were recovered in the west plaza of the epicenter. Only a few shrines or off-structure contexts reveal reverential mortuary treatment. The presence of two ground-level mass graves is documented—one next to epicentral Temple Q-80 and the other next to the outlying Itzmal Ch'en ceremonial group (Adams 1953; Peraza Lope, Delgado Kú, and Escamilla Ojeda 2003; Peraza Lope et al. 2006; Paris and Russell 2012). The governors of Mayapán ruled with an iron hand, backed by military might. This strategy was only partly successful. If the mass graves at Q-80 and Itzmal Ch'en reflect Mayapán war casualties, then the consequences of a militaristic state were eventually experienced at home. These desecrated human remains lie in two of the most sacred precincts of the city; their interment with effigy censers sets them apart from other non-funerary remains and implies that the individuals were from Mayapán.

These findings hint at a brutal picture for the underpinnings of power of the Mayapán state. Although sections of the Maya chronicles critique the regimes of this city and their abuses of power, few specific historical details are offered. As summarized by Roys (1962:44), K'atun 9 Ahau (AD 1303–1323) was one of terror, war, adultery, and sin, and K'atun 7 Ahau (AD 1323–1342) was one of corruption and immorality (adultery, indecency). K'atun 5 Ahau (AD 1342–1362) was perverse and without shame; rulers lost political power; fertility was low; and governmental dysfunction is described poetically as "they bite one another, the kokob snakes and the jaguars . . . they are greedy for dominion" (Roys 1962:44) and "he shall bite his master, the tame dog" (Roys 1962:45). Some of this critical commentary may be run-of-the-mill factional propaganda (retrospective or otherwise) that is difficult to distinguish from larger societal unrest. Whatever its origins, this discontent may have culminated in a revolution in K'atun 3 Ahau (AD 1362–1382) in which many rulers were questioned, tortured, deposed, and replaced (Roys 1962:45–46). New archaeological features found at Mayapán lend credibility to these accounts (chapter 8).

We do not know with whom Mayapán may have waged war, but warfare was endemic. Gaspar Antonio Chi reported that vassals served personally in the wars of Mayapán, "of which there were many" (Tozzer 1941:230). External warfare with groups outside of the Maya area seems unlikely due to prohibitive distances. War was probably waged within the Maya lowlands, perhaps aimed at rebellious *batabils* who resisted tributary obligations. Military power would have also supported regional mercantile activities by guaranteeing the safety of merchants, as is common in many ancient states. The objective of obtaining war captives for the slave market was also probably important. Slaves were a key export product from Yucatán into western markets at Xicalanco and beyond (Scholes and Roys 1938; Roys 1972:34–35). In the sixteenth century, the rulers of Hocabá warred with their neighbors in order to capture slaves for sale (Roys 1962:47). Other historical sources are more elusive; under one lord, Tutul Xiu, the land was annexed into the Mayapán state through diplomatic efforts (and modest tribute) instead of by force, yet military conscripted service was expected from subjects (Roys 1962:50). This description sounds more than a little propagandistic, and depending on the source, both Xiu and Cocom rulers can be portrayed as benevolent at different points in time.

SUMMARY

The information on Mayapán's political organization is undeniably rich. Our review of selected sources at the beginning of this chapter demonstrates the bureaucratic complexity of political and religious offices. The view that emerges is one of a sophisticated secondary state that was anything but "degenerate" (chapter 1). The origins of the Mayapán confederacy are shrouded in layered events of dynastic assertion, construction, calendrical celebration, formal (if not necessarily peaceful) rotation of political authority, cycles of centralization, decentralization, and reorganization. We use the term *dynastic* loosely, in the sense that the city's history was diverted repeatedly by the strong hands of powerful hereditary noble corporate groups who vied for paramountcy within the framework of the multepal confederate system.

The archaeological chronology for the city has been refined with the aid of radiocarbon dating, with some hints of early activity in the monumental center in the eleventh (and perhaps tenth) century, prior to the establishment of Mayapán as the political capital. Earlier occupations in the area as far back as the Late Preclassic are indicated by pottery from survey of the environs of Mayapán, but dispersed agrarian settlement clusters characterize most prior periods. Population levels in the periphery rise considerably during the Terminal Classic Period, but Postclassic-era construction activities within or near to the great wall razed earlier architecture.

The art and architecture of the major monumental works in the site center reveal standardized patterns of civic-ceremonial groups, and at the same time we can now discuss a range of art programs sponsored by a pluralistic, dynamically changing set of governing elites. The monumental buildings illustrate the periodic renewal of the city's divine charter as a political capital. Individual factions also celebrated their own leadership entitlements with mural, stucco, or other sculptural art at halls and smaller temples or oratories that portray venerated ancestors and patron gods. Civic-ceremonial edifices were furnished with effigy censers during annual Uayeb rites, k'atun intervals, and other calendrical events (D. Chase 1986, 1988; P. Rice 2009f:300–301). The result is an impressive array of public monuments and art that reveals a blend of emblematic state codes and idiosyncratic decorative elements that broadcasted cosmopolitan elite status. The Temple of Kukulcan began as a war or death god monument, with grisly figures and skulls displayed conspicuously in stucco facades. The importance of this temple, as well as many others at the site, for the veneration of the founding personage of Kukulcan is revealed in serpent or Ehecatl imagery, quadripartite concepts, temple-cenote/cave complexes, and round temples. Monumental art reveals that priests made use of central Mexican Quetzalcoatl myths but also drew on knowledge of creation myths from the deeper Maya past, as suggested by the Monkey Scribe effigy from Temple Q-58. Like many earlier Maya cities, Mayapán's monuments hailed themes of critical importance to the power of its regimes: creation myths, warfare, sacrifice, gods, divine ancestry, cosmology, and the productive activities and food staples that sustained its citizenry.

The multi-entity programs of Halls Q-161 and Q-163 that extend to the east and west from the Temple of Kukulcan do not single out the deeds of individual monarchs but may commemorate the divine mythology of a series of political entities or the supernatural sanction of one or two paramount families. A potential parallel is found in the Mitla lintel paintings that celebrate selected dynasties of Postclassic Oaxaca and their cosmogonies while the palaces in which they were located served as unifying facilities where royals convened to feast, trade, consult oracles, recap history, and negotiate differences with the aid of the paintings (Pohl 1999). Key art programs at Tulum also record events critical to the history of this city's ruling dynasts, some of whom are presented in a cosmological framework involving supernaturals or their impersonators (Miller 1982; Masson 2000, 2003a). The Mitla paintings provide details of selected, multiple players, and by analogy, it is likely that the Mayapán halls similarly recorded mytho-historical heroes of city's nobility. The sculptures, stelae, and columns reveal portraits of venerated personages in stone, stucco, or stelae form; some of these were probably historical individuals. Although much public art focuses on deities—and the Postclassic Period differs from the Classic Period in terms of the emphasis on dynastic figures—it is important to recognize that dynastic art did not disappear altogether at Mayapán. The significance of this tradition is diffused by the fact that sculptures are numerous and spread out at multiple halls and oratories. Additional diverse religious themes derive from murals that emphasize deities and creation myths. The significance of historical art is also obscured by its smaller scale, its eroded state, and the erosion of nearly all of the hieroglyphs on Mayapán's stelae. Chapter 7 considers examples of portraiture of historical individuals more comprehensively.

In the next chapter, we look more closely at examples of civic-ceremonial features located outside of the monumental center at Mayapán. We argue that colonnaded halls and elite residences replicated functions of the edifices of the monumental center, as nobles sometimes hosted political gatherings or religious celebrations in their homes. It is also true that the use of halls varied through time and across space, and we discuss how halls functioned differently from one another. Analyses of halls and elite residences excavated by the

Carnegie and INAH projects are supplemented with new data from our own investigations at the Itzmal Ch'en group and secondary elite Residence Y-45a. Chapter 3 provides detailed comparisons of these edifices, which contribute to our argument in chapter 4 that outlying focal nodes reflect the long arm of Mayapán's governing elites; they were strategic facilities that integrated the settlement zone into urban society as a whole.

NOTES

1. Tozzer (1941:158n804) speculates that there was a temple dedicated to Kukulcan in Maní after the fall of Mayapán. But Landa's passage refers to both the town and province of Maní, and given the fact that Q-162 was named for Kukulcan and that Mayapán was located within the province of Maní, we should entertain the possibility of post-occupational use of the Mayapán temple for this ritual, especially as it involved conjuring the deity. As Tozzer notes, only two such temples within Yucatán bore Kukulcan's name (the other is at Chichén Itzá), and there is no evidence at this point for a significant Postclassic temple in the Colonial town of Maní.

2. Hall Q-161 also has a serpent sculpture, but the sculpture may have tumbled down from Temple Q-162, the Castillo, which lies adjacent to and above the hall.

3

An Outlying Temple, Hall, and Elite Residence

Carlos Peraza Lope and
Marilyn A. Masson

Documenting the complexity of an urban place such as Mayapán relies to an important degree on evidence for specialization and differentiation within the basic institutions of social, political, economic, and religious organization (Kent 1990a, 1990b; Trigger 1968:57). Civic-ceremonial and residential architecture have great potential to reflect functional or social spatial segregation that accompanies occupational diversification and bureaucratic development (Inomata 2001). This chapter examines the details of three examples of differentiated administrative and ritual features in Mayapán's residential zone: an outlying temple, a colonnaded hall, and an elite residence. Architects of these groups took pains to design and build these edifices according to sets of relatively standardized criteria and to distinguish them from one another. Standardization among elite or public buildings is an important criterion for identifying principles of urban planning within an archaeological site (chapter 4; M. Smith 2007, 2008). Our challenge is to reconstruct how differently and by whom these spaces were used. One other point is significant in the analysis of these three types of features that we identify as focal nodes in Mayapán's neighborhoods. Outlying temples and halls replicate characteristics that are concentrated in the monumental zone; a simple inference leads us to conclude that the activities performed at these structures were also replicated. In this respect, they form an intermediate level of facilities within the residential zone (chapter 4). Activities at these buildings would have tied Mayapán's population of 15,000–17,000 people into the administrative and religious affairs of the city's governing elites. Chapter 4 considers the distribution and characteristics of these

DOI: 10.5876/9781607323204.c003

focal nodes and other differentiated spaces such as market plazas, distinct neighborhoods, and streets. Here we set the stage for that site-level analysis by illustrating the diverse yet patterned activities that took place at three different types of buildings.

Our findings discern three significant patterns among temples, halls, and elite residences, following up on our review of monumental art in chapter 2. First, the activities and architecture of outlying temples and halls conform in many ways to top-down conventions, as their characteristics match those found in the site's central monumental groups. Second, on a more specific level, there was room for idiosyncratic variation in details of architectural design, sculpture and effigy assemblages, offerings, and ritual that clearly reflects the imprint of specific patron elite groups that built and used these buildings. Some of this variation may be attributed to ethnic differences, as has been argued for elite House Y-45a by Prudence M. Rice, Timothy W. Pugh, and Leslie G. Cecil (P. Rice 2009c:37, 49; Pugh 2009:176; Rice and Cecil 2009a:245). We consider these claims in our review of the features of House Y-45a, which we infer to have been the home of an overseer within the southern Mayapán neighborhood in which it was embedded. Third, despite the sustained efforts to construct these three distinct types of facilities, significant overlap can be tracked in the activities performed at them, particularly among halls and elite residences. On one level this overlap attests to fuzzy boundaries among the differentiated facilities that we interpret as evidence for complexity and functional diversity. On the other hand, these comparisons allow us to identify elite residences as a third type of civic-ceremonial node that helped to articulate neighborhood commoners to city government and cement inter-elite ties through ceremonies, feasts, and other sociopolitical gatherings.

The use of ritual paraphernalia was important at elite residences, although the ubiquity of ritual objects is much higher at the largest palaces compared to secondary elite dwellings. A quantitative comparison of censer distribution at public buildings and elite and commoner residences overturns the old Carnegie project model of decentralization of religious practice during the Postclassic Period, which was said to be commonplace at the household level (Thompson and Thompson 1955:238–42; Proskouriakoff 1955:88, 1962b:136; J. Thompson 1957:624; Pollock 1962:17). Carnegie investigators drew this conclusion based on a biased sample geared toward higher status residences as well as altars, shrines, caches, and tombs that are rare at the site's majority of commoner dwellings (chapter 5). The concentration of ritual at the homes of Mayapán's most prosperous lords and priests supports the argument that integrative activities were staged at these localities that helped to hold Mayapán's society together. In chapter 7 we fully assess the variation in ritual objects at different contexts.

We begin with an overview of interpretations of colonnaded halls, which represent the most enigmatic of civic-ceremonial architectural categories at Mayapán (Shook and Irving 1955:127). By contrast, the functions of temples and elite residences have never been particularly problematic to ascertain. In a very real sense, halls lie functionally between temples and residences, as their features replicate aspects of both. We reiterate, however, that Mayapán's elites felt that the purpose of halls was sufficiently distinct that they took pains to construct them according to a clearly recognizable architectural plan, with minor variations (Proskouriakoff 1962a).

THE FUNCTION OF HALLS

Halls were probably built and operated by noble members of Mayapán's confederacy (Proskouriakoff 1962a:90; Freidel and Sabloff 1984:182; D. Chase 1992; Ringle and Bey 2001:289). The function of Mayapán's colonnaded halls has been debated since the Carnegie project of the 1950s. These edifices are intriguing in their potential to represent civic facilities for political meeting and deliberation. Middens have been found in the general vicinity of some halls that open up the possibility of part-time occupation or large-scale, short-term consumption activities such as feasts. The dense nature of some of this material (behind Halls Q-97 and Q-99, for example) originally raised the question of hall occupation (Shook and Irving 1955:134). Debris from feasting may also be represented by broken pottery, such as the pottery "dump" at the juncture of Hall Q-151 and Temple Q-152 (Shook and Irving 1955:145).

Rituals performed at Mayapán's different halls exhibit patterned variation. Some halls have unique offerings or ritual debris, specific sculptures, or murals; but similar furnishings are also found in altar caches and anthropomorphic sculpted columns or altar figures (chapters 2, 7). A comprehensive examination of effigies at halls and other building types is provided in chapter 7, and in the section below we provide examples of varying hall artifact assemblages.

The defining attributes of colonnaded halls include their elongated rectangular form and the presence of a row of stacked, plastered stone columns that formed a multiple entranceway to the frontal room (Shook and Irving 1955:128; Proskouriakoff 1962a). Halls also had flat beam, mortar, and stone roofs (figure 2.17). Major halls have two parallel rectangular rooms, including the colonnaded entrance room and a rear room that features a long low bench (figures 2.10, 2.11). Central altars are generally present on this bench in the form of recessed, raised, or projecting altars, or a small sanctuary. Some halls have one or two transverse structures located at either end, and more rare examples, such as Q-163 and Q-156, have back-to-back galleries divided by a central wall and face two directions (Proskouriakoff 1962a). While temples, oratories, and elite residences also often have columns marking the frontal doorway, the long rectangular shape is particularly diagnostic of halls, as is the general expectation that their frontal rooms have three or more columns.

Tatiana Proskouriakoff (1962a:90) tabulates twenty-one halls in Mayapán's main group of the monumental center, and five others were counted elsewhere at the site at the time of her analysis. Survey continues to identify more halls in the settlement zone (chapter 4; Russell 2007). Of the twenty-one, she argues that thirteen stand independently and may have been linked to factions of the confederacy. They are found in architectural association with other halls, oratories, or temples (chapter 2; Proskouriakoff 1962a). The lack of partitioned rooms and abundant grinding stones suggests that they were not residential. In contrast, high-status residences have multiple shorter room divisions in which self-standing rectangular benches are located; residences also have burial features within or around them. Unlike halls, residences are located within courtyards that are formed by other dwelling structures, kitchens, and outbuildings.

Edwin W. Shook and William N. Irving (1955) first contended with the issue of hall function, and they listed possibilities that were later considered in the chapters of Harry E. D. Pollock, Ralph L. Roys, Proskouriakoff, and A. Ledyard Smith's (1962) report. The options they listed included palaces, young men's houses (*telpuchcalli*), and meeting halls for governmental affairs, and they suggest that hall functions changed through time from secular to religious purposes (Shook and Irving 1955:134–35). Proskouriakoff suggested that halls were sometimes used as young men's houses. Alternatively, she proposed that they may have served as seats of political and religious families for members of the city's confederacy (Proskouriakoff 1962a:89; see also D. Chase 1992:128–31). Proskouriakoff (1962a:89) observed that the central Mexican young men's houses or "bachelor's halls" were dispersed around Tenochtitlan and were not listed among Sacred Precinct edifices. This pattern differs from Mayapán, where the majority of halls concentrate at the site center. A. Ledyard Smith (1962:223) also struggled with the functional classification of halls; he proposed that they were ritual edifices and that custodial houses located behind some halls served as retreats for individuals organizing ritual celebrations. He was open to the idea that halls sometimes housed young men or served as places for education or religious training (A. Smith 1962:267). But Smith suggested that Structures Q-116 and Z-146 were better matches for Diego de Landa's (1941:181) description of young men's houses. These edifices are large buildings that are unique at Mayapán, as they were open on all sides. Building Q-116 may have been a school, or *calmecac* (A. Smith 1962:223), but it has never been investigated. Colonnaded halls could have housed visiting merchants, their entourages, or their goods, as suggested for Cozumel (Freidel and Sabloff 1984:157), although merchants in Yucatán also paid to stay at inns during their travels (Tozzer 1941:97n424, 231).

The lack of burials distinguishes halls from elite residences, with a few exceptions. Carlos Peraza Lope, Pedro Delgado Kú, and Bárbara del C. Escamilla Ojeda (2002:113) report graves in the plaza just to the west of Hall Q-72. One was a primary seated interment (Burial 30), and the other consisted of a skull and long bones (Burial 31). A third was found along the north side of the structure's base (Burial 32) in which two individuals were present, but one had an obsidian projectile point embedded in its ribs (Peraza Lope, Delgado Kú, and Escamilla Ojeda 2002:114). No grave offerings were present in these simple graves except for a few obsidian blades that may or may not be associated. It is difficult to know whether these were sacrificial victims or not. Two possible cemetery zones have been associated with custodial houses, defined as small houses next to major temples or halls. These examples include burials near Q-67 and Q-68 and also near Q-92 and Q-93 (Peraza Lope, Delgado Kú, and Escamilla Ojeda 2003:71–77; Serafin 2010:67). Colonnaded Halls Q-152c and Q-54 had burials within them (Serafin 2010:71). But the Q-152c example (Burial 28) was beneath construction fill and close to bedrock. It was near the corner of the frontal terrace rather than being centrally located and predates the hall (Peraza Lope et al. 1999a:175–77). Burial 57 was in front of the altar of Hall Q-54 at a depth of only 55 centimeters below the floor, and it is a better candidate for a funerary feature (Peraza Lope, Escarela Rodríguez, and Delgado Kú 2004:68). Shrine burials at Mayapán represent funerary rituals rather than sacrifices (Serafin and Peraza Lope 2007). In Shrine Q-88c, human remains, mostly crania of at least nine individuals, were placed beneath the floor. Stanley Serafin and Peraza Lope (2007:238) note that this feature may reflect reverential post-mortem treatment of the type accorded to the Cocom family (Landa 1941). Shrines associated with colonnaded hall groups may have housed the remains of revered ancestors of the social factions who built and used the groups. Examples of such shrines include Q-69, associated with Hall Q-70 and facing Hall Q-54 (figure 2.10).

At Utatlán/K'umarcaj, high-ranking lineages were each associated with a long, rectangular structure, or "big house" (*nim ja*); these are displayed on the Totonicapan map of the site center (Carmack 1981a:89). Some of these buildings had more specific names. Lineage groups that built and used these edifices at Utatlán were sometimes also called nim ja, underscoring the fact that the edifices were seats of political power that embodied the factions who built and used them (Carmack 1981a:89). These buildings represent probable analogs to Mayapán's colonnaded halls, although they lacked stone columns. In the settlement zone of Utatlán, residential settlement units were headed by secondary leaders who answered to the lords of the town. These residential unit authorities were referred to as the Chuch Kajaw/mofa, and their duties were religious as well as political (Carmack 1981a:12). Events at Utatlán's nim ja included ceremonies, lecturing, bride-price bestowal, feasting, and marriage events (Carmack 1981a:11). The list of activities reveals the use of these structures for ritual, political, and social events.

By analogy, the Mayapán colonnaded halls probably functioned similarly. As chapter 2 details, some Postclassic towns were also organized into residential wards headed by secondary authorities (Ah Cuch Cab). These two tiers of administration are of great potential significance for discerning the use of halls versus secondary elite residences. Halls may have hosted higher level activities performed by governing nobles of the city's confederacy while neighborhoods may have been administered more often from the more ubiquitous secondary elite residences. These activities would have been complementary and were presumably coordinated and articulated through communication among top-ranking and secondary officials. Complicating this distinction are Mayapán's largest elite palaces, which overlap with hall assemblages more than smaller elite dwellings. It is reasonable to assume that residents of the major palaces of Mayapán were not secondary administrative officials whose domain was limited to a residential zone. Despite the rich documentary information for Utatlán, Mayapán, and Contact Period towns in general, it is difficult to fully separate material assemblages of halls and elite residences, as Dwight T. Wallace reported many years ago (Wallace 1977). A significant ceremonial component is also attributed to an elite residence with hall-like characteristics at Structure 719 at Zacpetén (Pugh et al. 2009:193, 207–11).

ACTIVITIES AT HALLS AND ELITE RESIDENCES

Proskouriakoff (1962a:89–90) highlighted the fact that colonnaded halls and the largest elite palaces at Mayapán overlapped in function and that they were nodal localities for political meetings, religious celebration, associated feasting, or other purposes. Additional work confirms this pattern based on analysis of architectural space, offerings, altars, and art objects (Masson and Peraza Lope 2004). The site's most important elites conducted similar rituals and administrative activities at their residences to those occurring at halls, as argued for contemporary sites at Cozumel (Freidel and Sabloff 1984:31, 41) and at Santa Rita (D. Chase 1986). An exception is reported from Buena Vista (Cozumel), where halls lacked a ritual focus (Freidel and Sabloff 1984:172), which illustrates that the use of these buildings is not simply characterized across a single site or within a region.

Differences among Mayapán's halls are clearly observed in pottery assemblages. Halls at some of the larger groups likely served different functions. This pattern is particularly true for the Templo Redondo complex, where halls are clustered in a unique back-to-back configuration atop a shared platform (figure 2.11). A small "hall" at the northern end of the platform, Q-88a (Peraza Lope et al. 1999a:41–45), was burned upon abandonment, and the artifacts found on its floor represent unique or rare possessions. Nineteen complete serving, storage, and cooking vessels were present on the floor, including seven Pelé Polychrome dishes with fish designs (Peraza Lope et al. 1999a:45). Pelé Polychrome vessels may represent a special category of elite serving vessels that were circulated through gifting and were used primarily for political events, including feasts (Smith et al. 2003). Other Mesoamerican sites report the limited distribution of very rare types of vessels, which represent a minor quantity of the assemblages of ancient cities and individual contexts (e.g., Culbert 2003).

Whole vessels of this rare type were found at two other elite contexts, including a single dish from Palace group R-86–90 and a concentration at House Y-45a (Proskouriakoff and Temple 1955; Peraza Lope et al. 2008). At Y-45a, in addition to two fish dishes, several painted and modeled turkey effigy jars of the Pelé Polychrome type were also present (figures 3.1, 3.2). The fish design depicted in figure 3.1 exhibits teeth like the shark in the fisherman mural (figure 2.24), although many fish species have sharp teeth. Pelé Polychrome vessels may identify edifices used by the Kowoj ethnic group, as they share similarities with Chompoxte Red-on-Cream pottery at Zacpetén and Topoxté. We explore this ethnic interpretation in greater detail later in this chapter. A small glyph-inscribed stone jaguar was also found at Hall Q-88a, with day signs Lamat, Chuen, and Etz'nab and a 3 Ahau date, probably the K'atun ending in AD 1382 (Milbrath and Peraza Lope 2003a:40). Hall Q-88a has an assemblage unlike other halls investigated at the site. The quantity of fancy serving vessels suggests that it may have been a residence or perhaps a storage facility for other ritual edifices of the Round Temple (Templo Redondo) (Q-152) group, with which it shares a platform. In fact, it lacks the characteristic elongate

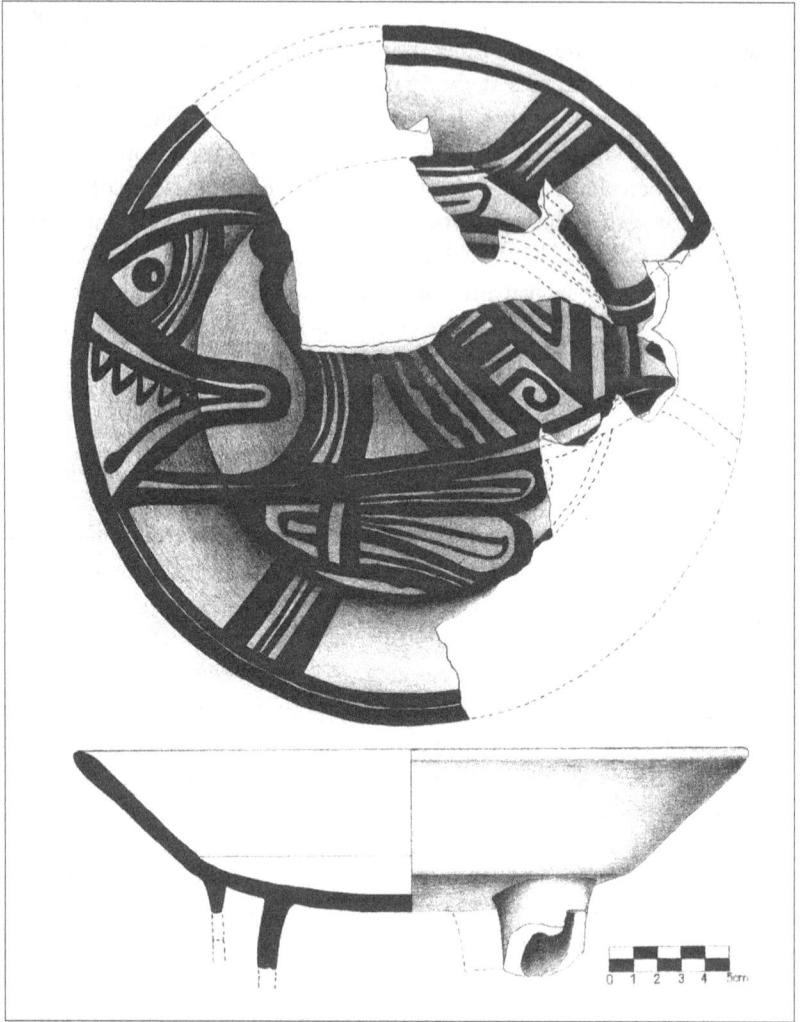

FIGURE 3.1. *Pelé Polychrome dish from elite Residence Y-45a with a painted fish design. Illustration by Wilberth Cruz Alvarado.*

rectangular shape and long gallery. Structure Q-88a is an L-shaped building, and although it has a central shrine room, it is atypical for a hall (figure 2.11). In addition to the seven Pelé Polychrome dishes, Q-88a had two other dishes (one Kukula Cream, one Mama Red), four jars (two Navula Unslipped, one Tecoh Red-on-Buff, one Buff Polbox), four basins, and one non-effigy ped-

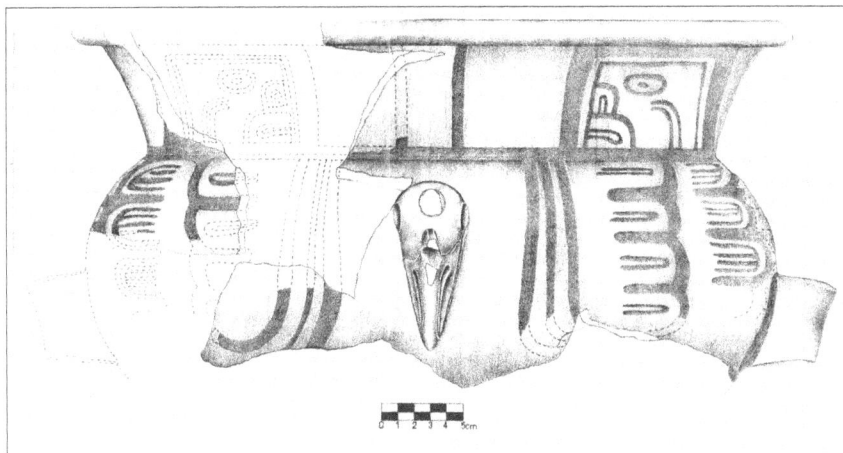

FIGURE 3.2. *Pelé Polychrome vessel from elite Residence Y-45a with a painted and modeled turkey. (Note the Ahau glyph on the rim.) Illustrated by Wilberth Cruz Alvarado.*

estal censer (Navula Unslipped), and one Mama Red miniature tripod bowl (Peraza Lope et al. 1997).

Other halls were associated with different surface materials. In contrast to Structure Q-88a, Hall Q-152c had very few materials recovered from it, although ceramic drums were among the vessels present (Peraza Lope et al. 1999a). Table 3.1 illustrates Ch'en Mul effigy censer sherd percentages from selected structures investigated by the Carnegie and INAH projects. Hall Q-151 is conspicuous for the presence of two Puuc-style mosaic stone masks (chapter 2) and a large quantity of broken Chen Mul Modeled effigy censers and other debris on its floor (Shook and Irving 1955; Peraza Lope et al. 1997). Hall Q-81 was also covered with many broken effigy censers (Winters 1955b; Peraza Lope et al. 1997). Two elite dwellings also exhibit particularly high effigy censer proportions (Q-208 and K-67a; table 3.1). No censers were found at Halls Q-72, Q-152c, and Q-87 (Peraza Lope et al. 1997, 1999a). Similarly, elite Residence Q-244b had few censers (chapter 7). But elite Residences R-86–90 and Q-208 had ubiquitous censer fragments, some of them in burial contexts, and these are the only two high-status dwellings from which Xipe Totec effigy censer fragments were found (Proskouriakoff and Temple 1955; J. Thompson 1954, 1957:625).

Other halls and elite residences shared types of specialized vessels, including tripod cache cups, stucco anthropomorphic altar figures, and stone or ceramic turtles. For example, stucco altar figures were found at Palace R-87

TABLE 3.1 Frequencies of human effigy sherds from selected halls and elite residences (percentage of effigies of the total number of sherds per context). Data are compiled from lot lists in the Carnegie Institution of Washington's *Current Report* series (sources provided in table 7.22, data now available in Masson 2009). Q-88a data are courtesy of Carlos Peraza Lope.

Structure	Human effigy (%)
Hall Q-81 surface	87.0
Hall Q-151 surface	82.4
Hall Q-97 surface	55.4
Hall Q-152c surface	52.7
Hall Q-87a	38.0
Hall Q-88a	37.7
Hall Q-213 midden upper	35.7
Hall Q-72	35.6
Hall Q-64	26.5
Residence Q-208	69.6
Residence K-67a (2 room)	64.0
Residence R-86 group all	48.9
Residence A-1 (shrine w/small house)	28.1
Residence K-52a (4 bench)	26.5
Residence Q-62 (4-room dwelling)	23.0
Residence S-133b (4-room dwelling)	17.5
Residence Q-244b (6-room dwelling)	12.0

and Halls Q-97 and Q-151 (Proskouriakoff and Temple 1955:figure 21a; Shook and Irving 1955:131). These materials are also commonly found at oratories, shrines, and temples (chapter 7) and are thus not particularly diagnostic to building type. Calendrical ceremonies were celebrated at both halls and residences but are not limited to these edifices (Masson 2000:table 6.2). A stone turtle at the R-87 palace dwelling was inscribed with a K'atun 10 Ahau and a K'atun 8 Ahau date, and another turtle without dates was also found there (Proskouriakoff and Temple 1955:298, figure 21i, h). The placement of small numbers of jade and shell beads in cache vessels was common at elite residences and halls and other ritual structures (chapter 7).

Except for individual cases such as Q-88a and Y-45a, halls and residences in general are not distinguished by their quantities of uncommon pottery types,

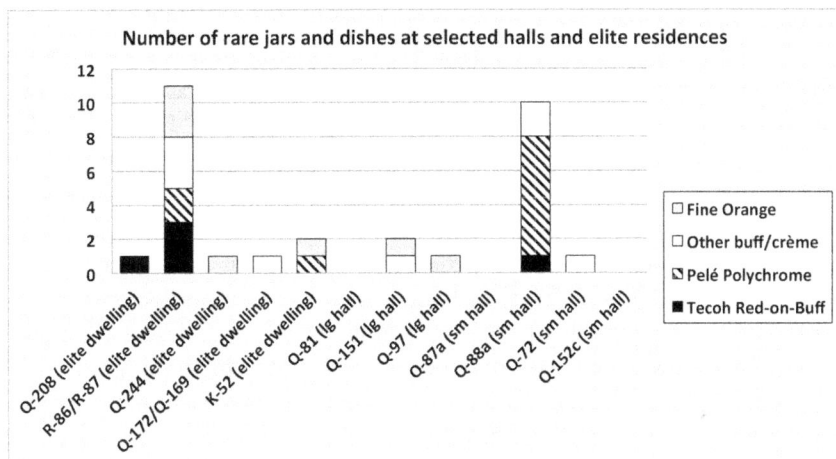

Number of rare jars and dishes at selected halls and elite residences

Legend:
- Fine Orange
- Other buff/crème
- Pelé Polychrome
- Tecoh Red-on-Buff

x-axis labels: Q-208 (elite dwelling), R-86/R-87 (elite dwelling), Q-244 (elite dwelling), Q-172/Q-169 (elite dwelling), K-52 (elite dwelling), Q-81 (lg hall), Q-151 (lg hall), Q-97 (lg hall), Q-87a (sm hall), Q-88a (sm hall), Q-72 (sm hall), Q-152c (sm hall)

FIGURE 3.3. *Rare pottery at selected halls and residences, Mayapán. Data taken from the Carnegie Institution of Washington's Current Reports (see table 7.22 for citations per structure, also Masson 2009) and from Peraza Lope et al. (1999a, for Q-88a).*

including Matillas Fine Orange, Buff Polbox, and Kukula Cream (figure 3.3). Decorated (painted or modeled) Mama Red and Palmul Incised pottery also tends to be rare and does not concentrate in elite contexts (Hare and Masson 2010). The results presented in figure 3.3 in part reflect the scale of excavation per structure, which was greatest at palace group R-86 and Hall Q-88; and the quantity of partially reconstructible non-effigy vessels at Y-45a exceeds those for any other structure yet investigated at the site. But other fully excavated contexts yield low quantities. Only 1 Pelé Polychrome sherd was recovered from full excavations of four features at Itzmal Ch'en: Temple H-17, Hall H-15, House H-11, and the Hall H-15 mass grave (Cruz Alvarado et al. 2012). Buff Polbox group and Tecoh Red-on-Buff types amount to 0.008 percent of the Temple H-17 sherd assemblage (99 total sherds out of a Postclassic sample of 46,738). Similarly, Altar H-17a, in front of the temple, had only 3 sherds of Tecoh Red-on-Buff (of 1,490 Postclassic sherds) and Hall H-15 had 35 Buff Polbox sherds and 64 Tecoh Red-on-Buff sherds (or 0.6 percent of a Postclassic sample of 8,549). If Buff Polbox, Tecoh Red-on-Buff, or Pelé Polychrome pottery represent ethnic markers, then the signal is weak Itzmal Ch'en. Elsewhere at the site, frequencies of these types are higher (figures 2.8, 2.9).

Ritual vessels, including tripod or pedestal cache cups (effigy and non-effigy), non-effigy appliqué censers, and rarer ladle censers are found in both contexts. In a sample of sixty excavated contexts of the PEMY project (test pits and fully excavated structures) with samples of 97 or more sherds, non-effigy censers were quite rare. Forty-three of these contexts lacked non-effigy sherds and the remainder had between 1 and 38 sherds of this vessel form. Fully investigated Y-45a had 12 sherds of the combined types of Cehac-Hunacti Composite, Cehac Painted, and Huhi Impressed, and it also had 13 sherds of Acansip Painted (small cups or cylinders usually used as cache vessels). Numbers were greater at Itzmal Ch'en; Hall H-15 had 711 non-effigy censer sherds and Temple H-17 had 311, although their proportions were low compared to effigy censers (the latter numbered 17,586 and 26,826, respectively). These low frequencies may be misleading due to the limitations of fragmentary sherd analysis. Composite censers are only identifiable from a small portion of the vessel that has applique decorative elements. Some decorated composite vessels were made in jar form, and their body sherds are not distinguishable from ordinary ollas used at the city. Complicating this matter further is the fact that vases attached to effigy censers sometimes had the same rosette or banded motifs that are found on non-effigy vessels.

Differences in the surface assemblages of some halls and elite residences may attest to the final circumstances of use or abandonment rituals rather than to overall function, and some odd materials may postdate the city's abandonment (Shook and Irving 1955:145). Hall Q-88a was burned, and its serving vessel assemblage was found intact beneath the cinders of its thatched roof. House Y-45a and Palace R-86–90 were systematically abandoned. Residents of Y-45a took the time to smash their fancy vessels on a rear room bench and cover them with fill (as described later in this chapter), and residents of the R-86 group may have cached their Chen Mul effigies in a tomb upon departure (Proskouriakoff and Temple 1955:327). Other dense floor assemblages at Mayapán, such as the effigy incense burners covering Hall Q-81 (Winters 1955b), may also pertain to rites of abandonment or destruction, as we discuss for Temple H-17 and Hall H-15 later in this chapter. Terminal events at Mayapán probably led to the destruction, disposal, or caching of effigies housed within public buildings and elite residences, as considered more fully in chapter 8.

Interesting patterns are revealed in the spatial distribution of specific deity effigies (chapter 7). Examples thought by J. Eric S. Thompson (1957) to have been indigenous in origin, including merchant god, diving god, youthful/ maize god, Chac, Itzamna, whiskered deity, and old god faces, are found in both residential and hall contexts. Large censer collections at the R-86 palace group and the Q-81 hall show equal diversity, with eight deities each (chapter

7). Effigies thought to be of Mexican inspiration by J. Thompson are present at both residential and hall contexts, although they are not evenly distributed. Xipe Totec faces are only found in residential contexts, but a female figure that Thompson identified as Tlazolteotl is found in both context types, and all other Mexican god identifications are singular occurrences (chapter 7; Masson and Peraza Lope 2010). Some concentrations of deities are observed. Chac and Itzamna are numerous at the R-86 palace group; Itzamna and the youthful/maize god are present in relatively high quantities at the Q-81 hall; and all but one Xipe Totec representation was found at the Q-208 elite dwelling, associated with a multiple child burial (J. Thompson 1954). The Xipe Totec deposit may reflect a special, unique event. The most common pattern is the use of diverse censers at most locations, and the majority of deities have their origins in the Maya area. A focus on particular patron deities is indicated at a few contexts (chapter 7).

The proportion of ritual pottery sherds is very low compared to pottery used for everyday tasks in the fully excavated contexts of the PEMY project (table 3.2). Ritual pottery sherds include effigy and non-effigy ceramics, although we have demonstrated that the latter are uncommon in our contexts. Slipped sherds in table 3.2 are largely made up of Mama Red jars, bowls, and dishes, and unslipped (non-effigy) sherds consist of a majority of Navula Unslipped or Yacman Striated jars, as well as low numbers of bowls or basins (Cruz Alvarado et al. 2012; Cruz Alvarado 2012a). The sherds are tabulated according to the total square meters of excavation and the total estimated volume of excavation units (cubic meters) in table 3.3. The table reveals many interesting patterns, some of which are relevant to our comparisons in this chapter. Very high quantities of ceramic sherds at Houses Q-40a and Q-176 reflect the fact that these were pottery workshops and ubiquitous ritual sherds at Q-40 are due to the fact that it was an effigy censer manufacturing locale (chapter 6). Low quantities of sherds at I-57 and X-43 make sense as the former edifice was dedicated to stone tool making, and the latter was not occupied for long.

Pertinent to this discussion are the low quantities of ritual pottery at Hall H-15 (25.3 sherds per cubic meter) compared to the mass grave (H-15Z/E) that has 503.7 ritual pottery sherds per cubic meter (table 3.3). This pattern likely indicates the removal of materials from this hall (and probably from other Itzmal Ch'en ceremonial buildings) for placement in the mass grave that is adjacent to this building (H-15Z/E). The human bones in the grave were desecrated by chopping and burning and numerous smashed effigy censers were broken amidst the human remains (Vidal Guzmán 2011; Paris and Russell 2012). Except for the mass grave, Temple H-17 exhibits the highest

TABLE 3.2 Percentages of common types of Mama Red, Navula Unslipped (undecorated), and Yacman Striated in all PEMY contexts, including fully excavated buildings, listed by number below, as well as composite test pits and surface collection results. Percentages shown are of total sherds per structure or per sample.

Structure	Mama Red (percent)	Navula Unslipped (percent)	Yacman Striated (percent)
Q-40	40	14	36
L-28	39	21	36
I-57	37	32	29
Q-39	34	14	47
Q-176	34	10	51
X-43	32	44	16
H-11	29	10	25
Y-45a	29	29	19
I-55	27	11	56
H-15	25	15	8
H-17	17	8	14
H-17a	13	7	7
H-15Z/E	11	5	4
All test pits	36	21	30
All surface collections	35	31	29

quantity of ritual sherds of all contexts listed (85.1 per cubic meter) and elite House Y-45 has significantly more ritual sherds (11.6 per cubic meter) than commoner Houses Q-176, L-28, I-55, and X-43. This pattern is important, especially considering that volume estimates tend to be deflated for larger elite residences, temples, and halls due to the amount of fallen construction rubble that contains fewer artifacts and lowers artifact density calculations. Frequencies per square meter assist in checking this potential bias (table 3.3). Results by this index parallel those by volume, with highest ritual pottery densities at Temple H-17 (46.4 per square meter), followed by Hall H-15 and elite House Y-45a (6.7 and 5.4 per cubic meter, respectively), and almost nonexistent quantities at five commoner houses where pottery was not made (below 0.5 per cubic meter).

Our data on fully excavated contexts thus reveal that ritual artifacts and features are concentrated at public buildings and are scarce at ordinary houselots. This finding applies more generally across the city at contexts that we have investigated with surface collection or test pits and also in the results of the Carnegie investigations, contrary to their interpretations. The claim that religious practice involving the use of censers and other ritual paraphernalia was a common household occurrence in the Postclassic Period must be refuted due to the scarcity of effigy ceramics at houselots tested across the site. Sixty-one contexts investigated by the Carnegie project lacked Chen Mul effigy pottery (Masson 2009). In a sample of forty-four excavated contexts of the PEMY project where at least 97 sherds were recovered, 60 percent of the contexts had less than 2 percent effigy or non-effigy censers (figures 3.4, 3.5). Itzmal Ch'en contexts contrast with the rest of the PEMY sample with Chen Mul effigy percentages of 61 percent and higher (figure 3.4); elite House Y-45a had 10 percent, more than all of the other houses in the sample. These proportions illustrate our argument that ritual paraphernalia was concentrated at civic-ceremonial buildings and elite residences. Similarly, at Zacpetén, effigy censers were not recovered at four excavated structures in contrast to Structure 719, a dwelling that had a civic-ceremonial dimension (Pugh, Rice, and Cecil 2009:210). Effigy censers were not recovered at ordinary houses at the secondary Postclassic center of Caye Coco, and the pattern of their spatial concentration at highly specific localities is widely reported from hinterland sites (Russell 2000; Milbrath et al. 2008:107).

On a more mundane level, debris in and around halls and temples indicates the occasional use of common food preparation and serving vessels, including Navula Unslipped, Yacman Striated, and Mama Red types. Mama Red sherds formed 27–40 percent of all residential contexts and 11–25 percent of civic-ceremonial contexts in our sample (table 3.2), including all test pits, surface collections, and fully excavated buildings (Peraza Lope et al. 2008; Cruz Alvarado et al. 2012). Navula Unslipped (undecorated types) form 10–44 percent of dwelling sherd assemblages and Yacman Striated formed 16–45 percent (table 3.2). Proportions of Yacman Striated in fully excavated ceremonial buildings and Y-45a are lower, ranging from 4 to 16 percent. Undecorated Navula vessels are low for the Itzmal Ch'en contexts (5–8 percent) compared to all residences, including Y-45a.

The greater abundance of ordinary vessels at residences is also indicated in table 3.3; non-pottery workshop Houses I-55, Q-39, and H-11, for example, have sherd densities ranging from 118 to 186 slipped sherds and 119–224 unslipped sherds per cubic meter. These quantities are far greater than Temple H-17's density of 30 slipped and 21 unslipped sherds per cubic meter (Hall H-15's densities are even lower). Using a subset of the ceramic assemblage

TABLE 3.3 Slipped, unslipped, ritual (effigy censers and decorated braziers), and total Postclassic Period sherds per square meter and by volume of excavation at fully excavated buildings of the PEMY project.

Structure	Slipped total	Number/ square meter	Number/ excavation volume	Structure	Unslipped total	Number/ square meter	Number/ excavation volume
I-55	8817	44.98	186.2	I-55	10,648	54.33	224.9
H-11	4238	31.79	118.1	H-11	4299	32.25	119.8
L-28	1104	5.21	36.3	L-28	1573	7.42	51.7
X-43	494	1.96	26.6	X-43	921	3.65	49.5
Y-45 elite	9584	25.49	54.4	Y-45 elite	10993	29.24	62.4
H-15	3157	6.64	25.0	H-15	2219	4.67	17.6
H-15Z/E	3201	79.53	111.7	H-15Z/E	1699	42.21	59.3
H-17	9859	16.39	30.0	H-17	7134	11.86	21.7
Q-40	12335	139.38	567.4	Q-40	8718	98.51	401.0
I-57	491	6.80	26.0	I-57	582	8.06	30.8
Q-39	5536	46.13	161.7	Q-39	5674	47.28	165.8
Q-176	15340	112.79	463.9	Q-176	14805	108.86	447.7

Structure	Ritual total	Number/ square meter	Number/ excavation volume	Structure	Grand total	Number/ square meter	Number/ excavation volume
I-55	22	0.11	.5	I-55	19487	99.42	411.6
H-11	61	0.46	1.7	H-11	8598	64.50	239.6
L-28	19	0.09	.6	L-28	2696	12.72	88.6
X-43	112	0.44	6.0	X-43	1527	6.06	82.1
Y-45 elite	2039	5.42	11.6	Y-45 elite	22616	60.15	128.4
H-15	3196	6.72	25.3	H-15	8572	18.03	67.8
H-15Z/E	14437	358.68	503.7	H-15Z/E	19337	480.42	674.7
H-17	27928	46.42	85.1	H-17	44921	74.66	136.9
Q-40	888	10.03	40.8	Q-40	21941	247.92	1009.3
I-57	3	0.04	.2	I-57	1076	14.89	56.9
Q-39	300	2.50	8.8	Q-39	11510	95.92	336.2
Q-176	243	1.79	7.3	Q-176	30388	223.44	919.0

Estimated volume of excavated units at these buildings is as follows (in cubic meters): I-55 was 47.4, H-11 was 35.9, L-28 was 30.4, X-43 was 18.6, Y-45a was 176.1, H-15 was 126.4, H-15 Z/E (mass grave) was 28.7, H-17 was 328.2, Q-40 was 21.7, I-57 was 18.9, Q-39 was 34.2, and Q-176 was 33.1.

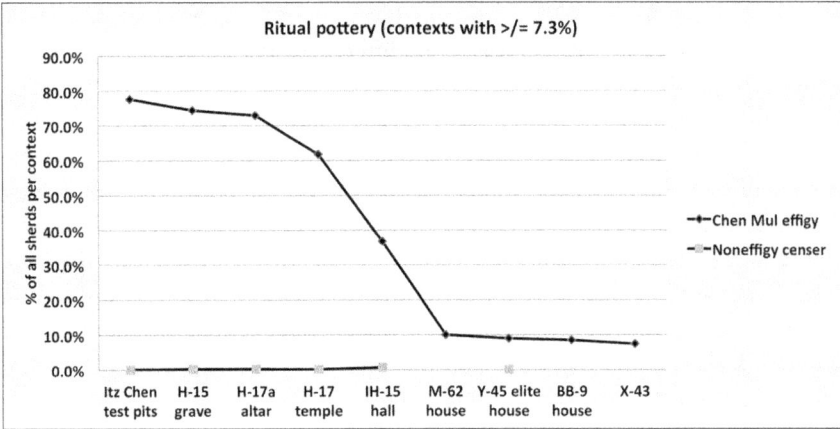

FIGURE 3.4. *Ritual pottery concentrates at civic-ceremonial buildings and elite residences at Mayapán. The graph illustrates excavated contexts of the PEMY project with higher proportions of ritual pottery (effigy and non-effigy); selected contexts in figures 3.4 and 3.5 are limited to those where 96 or more sherds were recovered.*

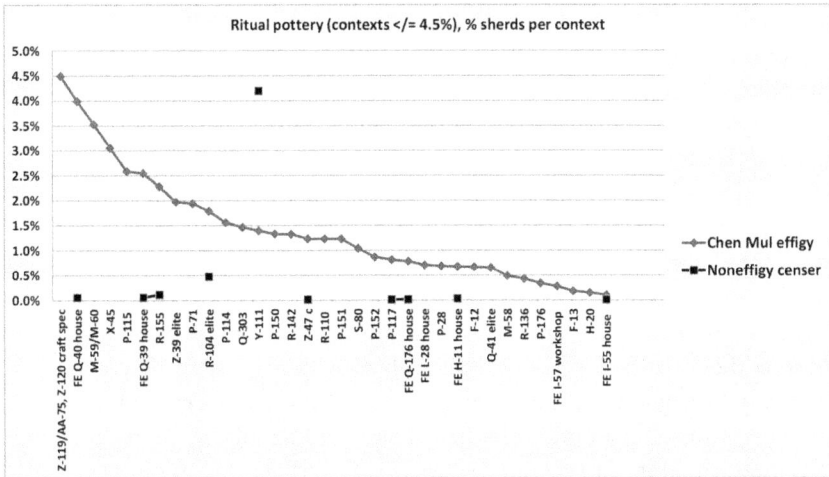

FIGURE 3.5. *Ritual pottery is scarce in a majority of domestic contexts. Excavated contexts of the PEMY project with proportions of ritual pottery below 5 percent (effigy and non-effigy). Percentage shown is that of all sherds per context.*

for which vessel form could be identified from rim sherds or other diagnostic fragments, we can identify some activity differences at Temple H-17, its frontal altar H-17a, Hall H-15, and the H-15 mass grave (table 3.4). These ritual buildings tend to have relatively high proportions of slipped serving dishes relative to jars, as illustrated by ratios that are four to seven times higher than commoner Houses I-55, H-11, L-28 and X-43, but this pattern is complicated by nearly equivalent ratios at affluent commoner houses and pottery workshops (table 3.4). At the minimum, these results suggest that festive meals may have taken place at the affluent House Q-39, and perhaps Q-176 or Q-40, although occupants of Q-176 may have produced dishes. The recovery of a large set of whole vessels at Y-45a potentially invalidates its low dish to jar sherd ratios in table 3.4, although jars form a large majority of this dwelling's reconstructible vessels (table 3.5). Using sherds to compare form frequencies is of limited accuracy due to the correlation of vessel size to the number of sherds. But the size ranges of bowls and jars do not appear to differ according to context in a way that would affect the reliability of relative ratios at this site. The dish to jar ratio is not necessarily the most important indicator of festive celebrations, given the importance of highly decorated jars at Y-45a (table 3.5).

From these data we may infer overlapping use of nonritual pottery at public buildings and residences, with civic-ceremonial contexts tending to have lower overall frequencies and greater relative ratios of dishes to jars, with some exceptions among commoner residences. At Xochicalco, ceramic assemblages also overlapped among residential and public buildings, indicating that a stringent separation in activities was not observed (Cyphers and Hirth 2000). Meal preparation for events in public buildings seems to have taken place at or near public buildings at Xochicalco and Mayapán. Similarly, ordinary pottery represented the bulk of vessels used in political activities at Aztec sites (M. Smith 2002:111; Smith, Wharton, and Olson 2003). Analysis of faunal remains suggests that animals consumed at monumental buildings were brought to those edifices in their entirety (either alive or dead), where they were subsequently butchered and prepared as food (Masson and Peraza Lope 2013). Pottery assemblages around colonnaded halls and temples contain a full range of storage, cooking, and serving vessels that is perhaps due to onsite preparatory and consumptive activities. Metates are sometimes found at colonnaded halls, for example, at Itzmal Ch'en Hall H-15, at Hall Q-81, and between Q-81 and Temple Q-80 (Peraza Lope et al. 1997:198–99; Delgado Kú, Escamilla Ojeda, and Peraza Lope 2012a). Fifty-three metates were found in monumental center buildings by the INAH-Mayapán project during the 1999–2000 season (Peraza Lope, Delgado Kú, and Escamilla Ojeda 2003:120). While they

TABLE 3.4 Ratios of dishes and bowls to jars at fully excavated contexts of the PEMY project, including all vessels (left) and slipped vessels only (right). Vessel form data is from rim sherds and other diagnostic sherd fragments (Masson et al. 2012:appendices B1, B2).

All bowls and dishes/jar ratio slipped and unslipped	Structure	All slipped bowls and dishes to slipped jar ratio	Structure
0.1	Hall H-15	0.2	Commoner X-43
0.1	Commoner X-43	0.3	Commoner L-28
0.2	Mass grave H-15	0.3	Elite Y-45
0.2	Commoner H-11	0.3	Workshop I-57
0.2	Commoner L-28	0.4	Commoner H-11
0.2	Elite Y-45	0.6	Craft specialist I-55
0.2	Craft specialist Q-176	2.8	Hall H-15
0.8	Temple H-17	3.6	Mass grave H-15
0.9	Shrine H-17a	3.6	Craft specialist Q-39
1.0	Craft specialist Q-39	3.7	Craft specialist Q-176
1.6	Craft specialist I-55	3.7	Craft specialist Q-40
2.0	Workshop I-57	4.1	Temple H-17
4.4	Craft specialist Q-40	5.6	Shrine H-17a
0.3	Average	0.9	Average
0.7	St dev	1.2	St dev

are sometimes reused in fill or wall construction, in other instances they were located on or around buildings in a manner that suggests use.

In chapter 7 we document parallel inventories of stone, bone, and shell tools and debris on or around halls, temples, and residences. Like pottery, the principal difference is the lower ubiquity of these materials at civic-ceremonial contexts. Some of these artifacts may derive from the informal use of plaza space by visitors or residents of the neighborhood. The cenote at Itzmal Ch'en, as a water source, would have drawn daily traffic, and the ceremonial group was a landmark for pedestrians entering the city from Gates G and H. The plaza may have been relatively vacant between periodic meetings, ceremonies, and other formal gatherings, and it might have served as a public square, used for the purposes of casual social life.

Other seemingly ordinary debris may originate from festive celebrations held at such groups. Ceremonious events were provisioned by a large stock of

TABLE 3.5 Reconstructible vessel fragments from elite House Y-45a.

Form and type: variety classification	Grid square of horizontal excavation	Room number
Jar Buff Polbox: Polbox	3-G, 4-G	2
Jar Buff Polbox: Polbox	3-G	2
Jar Buff Polbox: Polbox	4-G	2
Jar Buff Polbox: Polbox	4-G	2
Jar Buff Polbox: Polbox (fragment)	3-G, 4-G	2
Jar Buff Polbox: Polbox (fragment)	4-G	2
Jar Buff Polbox: Polbox (fragment)	3-G	2
Jar Buff Polbox: Polbox (fragment)	3-F	Passageway
Jar Tecoh Red-on-Buff: Tecoh (fragment)	4-G	2
Jar Tecoh Red-on-Buff: Tecoh (fragment)	4-G	2
Jar Tecoh Red-on-Buff: Tecoh (semicomplete, base missing)	4-G	2
Jar Tecoh Red-on-Buff: Tecoh (semicomplete, base missing)	3-G, 4-G	2
Jar Tecoh Red-on-Buff: Tecoh (semicomplete, rim missing)	3-G	2
Jar Tecoh Red-on-Buff: Tecoh	4-G	2
Effigy jar Tecoh Red-on-Buff: Tecoh	2-D, 3-D	1
Jar Tecoh Red-on-Buff: Tecoh	3-H	2
Jar Tecoh Red-on-Buff: Tecoh	3-G, 4-G	2
Dish Tecoh Red-on-Buff: Tecoh (fragment)	1-F	Passageway (outside of entrance)
Jar Pelé Polychrome: Pelé	3-G, 4-H	2
Tripod dish Pelé Polychrome: Pelé (semicomplete)	3-D, 4-D	1
Jar Mama Red: Black-on-Red (fragment, Jar Katún 8 Ahau)	3-D, 4-D, 3-E	1
Tripod jar Mama Red: Mama	4-C	5
Tripod jar Mama Red: Mama	4-D	1
Tripod dish Mama Red: Mama	3-I	3
Jar Trapiche Pink: Trapiche	3-G, 4-G	2
Tripod cup Cehac Painted: Cehac	3-I	3
Very large jar Kanasín Red/Unslipped: Kanasín	4-E	1

local supplies, including plant and animal foods and everyday pots and tools, as Contact Period accounts indicate. Special objects were also commissioned locally from sculptors working in clay, stone, or stucco. Gifting associated with specific rites required ritual sponsors to accumulate shell ornaments, cotton mantles, and other valuables for bestowal on those who attended the ceremonies (e.g., Landa 1941:106). The economic dimensions of public life had real economic consequences for household activities. To illustrate this point, the following material objects were essential for different steps of a rite of passage overseen by priests in Landa's (1941:105–6) account: mats, priestly garments, brilliantly colored feather jackets, loose feathers (beautiful), cotton ribbons, white cloth and linen, cotton mantles, serpent aspergillum (staff of wood or pottery), water vessel, flowers and cacao, bone armament, beads, stone knife, tobacco, wine (*balche*), deity effigies, shell ornaments (tokens of girls' purity), and much food and drink for the ensuing feast. These expenses were paid for by the patron who hosted the event. As Landa's account illustrates, formal activities at the outlying Itzmal Ch'en group would have stimulated production of specialty ceramic, stone, and stucco sculptures; knives for sacrifices and offerings; and shell ornaments or other valuables given as gifts. They also called for production of tamales, the delivery of game and fowl for consumption at ritual feasts, and a range of pottery vessels for cooking and serving meals. The production and consumption activities for such events represent the ritual dimensions of economy as outlined by Patricia A. McAnany (2010:200–6), who points out that households devote a significant proportion of their surplus production to ritual obligations in a variety of ethnographic cases. Although we do not argue that the majority of household surpluses at Mayapán were commissioned for ritual economies, we acknowledge that this process would have been significant.

The symbolic importance of the economic foundations of daily life is evident in certain sculptures and offerings at Mayapán. Seven examples in public contexts illustrate the reverence of daily labors. In chapter 2, we discussed a sculpture of a woman grinding at a metate placed next to the eastern staircase of the Temple of Kukulcan (figure 2.13). Other instances similarly celebrate the tools used for productive activities. The INAH team discovered three manos with a secondary long bone and crania in a plaza burial near to Temple Q-80 (Burial 24, Cuadro 20-M; Peraza Lope et al. 1997:190, photo 306). A mano was cached in a bedrock cavity beneath the plaza floor adjacent to the rear (west) foundation of Temple Q-58 (Peraza Lope, Delgado Kú, and Escamilla Ojeda 2003:27; Peraza Lope et al. 2003:photo 65). Elsewhere, a mano, two conical chert pestles, one other chert pestle, and two chert polishers, along with a conch shell trumpet, two jade beads, a chert knife, a bone awl, and other chert tool/debris fragments formed a cache in a bedrock cavity beneath the plaza floor at Hall Q-72, inspiring the investigators to name it "La Casa del Albañil," or House of the Masons (Peraza Lope et al. 1999a:101). Finds that seem to reflect pride in craftsmanship and subsistence staple production are also observed in the settlement zone. In two recent investigations, one potter and the child of a potting family were interred with the tools of this trade at Residences Q-40a and Q-176a (M. Delgado Kú 2012b; Russell, Hutchinson, and Delgado Kú 2012; Cruz Alvarado et al. 2012:figure 15.15). Staple foods were also given a place in ceremonial offerings. A cache at the Itzmal Ch'en temple (H-17) included a turkey sculpture, and this fowl was the second most important staple animal food at the city, after white tailed-deer (Masson and Peraza Lope 2008). In chapter 6, we review examples of using deer bones as funerary offerings, which we infer to be related to the symbiotic relationship at Mayapán between deer raised in captivity and their human caretakers (Masson and Peraza Lope 2008).

ART AT ITZMAL CH'EN TEMPLE H-17 AND HALL H-15

The Itzmal Ch'en ceremonial group illustrates the tendency for outlying groups to conform to citywide emblematic conventions of architectural form and religious practice. Temple H-17 and Hall H-15 also reveal that individual groups exhibit unique design elements or religious art that reflects the choices or obligations of their patrons.

The Itzmal Ch'en group is the largest of the outlying administrative features at Mayapán, located 1.9 kilometers east of the Main Plaza. The limited work Carnegie investigators performed at Itzmal Ch'en involved clearing part of the upper room of the temple (D. Thompson 1955) and exposing a round shrine (with a burial shaft) and altar in the center of the plaza, H-18/H-18a (Chowning 1956). Proskouriakoff (1962a:figure 1) mapped the group and cleared a few architectural features for clarification, and she illustrated the group's sacrificial stone on which a prowling jaguar is carved (Proskouriakoff 1962a:127, 138). This cenote group has remained sacred ground to the present day. At the time of the Carnegie project, Telchaquillo residents conducted Ch'a Chaak rain ceremonies there (Proskouriakoff 1962a:129), and this practice continued until around 2003. During our 2009 investigations, Itzmal Ch'en landowner Don Pancho Uc invited a *h'men* ritualist from Mérida to bless the ceremonial group, so that malevolent spirits potentially evoked by the excavations would do no harm.

A major city wall gate (Gate H) is located just 125 meters east of the Itzmal Ch'en group. Roys (1962:79) revealed that one of Mayapán's eastern gates was under the guardianship of the Kowoj faction along with their "companion" Ah Ek. In the eastern Petén Lakes region of Guatemala, Mayapán-style temples and halls are emulated in the homeland of the Kowoj, who are said to have migrated there from Mayapán (Jones 1998; Pugh 2002; P. Rice 2009a:15; P. Rice 2009c). Given the paucity of Pelé Polychrome sherds at Itzmal Ch'en, it is possible that the Kowoj were guardians of a different eastern gate, perhaps Gate G or Gate T. Bradley W. Russell (2007, 2008a) discovered and mapped a basic ceremonial group located outside the city wall just 100 meters northeast of Gate G. Such a facility might well have hosted activities linked to gate oversight.

We fully excavated the largest colonnaded hall from this group (H-15) and the Itzmal Ch'en temple (H-17) in 2008 and 2009 as well as a nearby dwelling (H-11) and two craft production localities that are within 50–100 meters of the group, including House I-55a and a lithic workshop building, I-57 (Delgado Kú, Escamilla Ojeda, and Peraza Lope 2012a, 2012b; Latimer and Delgado Kú 2012; Hutchinson and Delgado Kú 2012; Kohut et al. 2012). In 2003 we also conducted test pits at three other nearby structures—H-20, H-24, and I-56—and behind three structures of the ceremonial group (Masson, Delu, et al. 2008). Activities performed at the houses near Itzmal Ch'en included craft production and ordinary domestic activities; evidence for ritual specialization was not found. No elaborate residence is located in this part of the city, and we infer that the high-status patrons of the Itzmal Ch'en group resided closer to the central portion of the city, where elite dwellings tend to concentrate (chapter 4). The human remains of a mass grave of burned and chopped bones and effigy incense burners at the southwest corner of the group's platform (next to H-15) are probably those of the group's elite patrons (Paris and Russell 2012; Serafin, Russell, and Delgado Kú 2012). Our investigations of Hall H-15 and Temple H-17 screened all deposits with 1/4" hardware cloth, which allows for more detailed analysis of material assemblages compared to prior work.

Proskouriakoff (1962a:127) identified blended architectural features at Temple H-17. In one respect, its frontal shrine and altars are like those of serpent column temples, but its upper room has more of an oratory plan, with interior columns and benches (figure 3.6). A more typical oratory is also present in the group, H-14 (Proskouriakoff 1962a:128). In its final form, Temple H-17 measures 8 meters high × 26.5 meters long × 19.5 meters wide (Delgado Kú, Escamilla Ojeda, and Peraza Lope 2012a); the stone roof of the upper room would have added more height. Volumetrically, it is the second largest

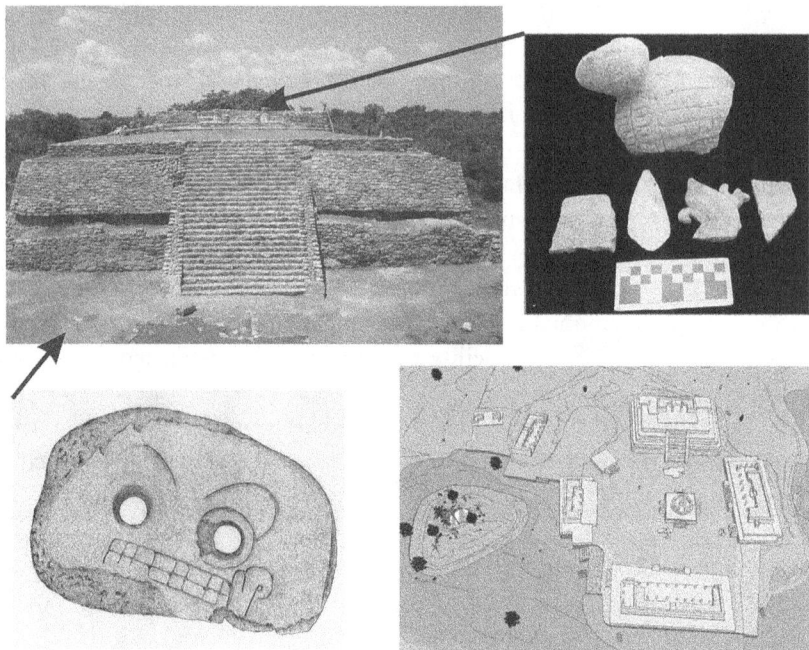

Figure 3.6. *Itzmal Ch'en group. Top left: Itzmal Ch'en Temple H-17 and frontal altar H-17a, restored by our project in 2009 (photo by Pedro Delgado Kú). Top right: Offering at Temple H-17, including a turkey sculpture. Bottom left: A death god stela found on front of Temple H-17, west of altar H-17a. Bottom right: A reconstructed view of the Itzmal Ch'en group and cenote (illustration by Bradley Russell).*

temple at Mayapán and one of the largest Postclassic Maya temples yet documented. Buildings of the Itzmal Ch'en group were constructed in several episodes. Two major phases were discerned at Shrine H-18 by Ann Chowning (1956) and three are identified at Hall H-15 and Temple H-17 (Delgado Kú, Escamilla Ojeda, and Peraza Lope 2012a, 2012b).

Forty stone sculpture fragments were found in 2009 in the vicinity of Temple H-17 and its frontal altar complex, H-17a (Cruz Alvarado 2012b). The majority (N = 12) were serpent effigies (figure 3.7). Human deities were also represented, including male deities emerging from a turtle or shell, as well as a pregnant monkey effigy, turtles (N = 3), birds (N = 2), and various fragments of human limbs or geometric elements (figure 3.8, Cruz Alvarado 2012b). Some of the anthropomorphic examples in figure 3.8 appear crudely rendered in their current state, but it is important to remember that these represent only

FIGURE 3.7. *Examples of serpent sculptures from Temple H-17, Itzmal Ch'en, 2009 season. Photos by Caroline Antonelli.*

the interior canvases of more elaborate pieces. For example, one side of the pregnant monkey effigy's (figure 3.8, top center) cape had preserved remnants of smooth and polished stucco and detailed painted feathered designs. Pieces like this one were embellished with stucco and paint while others were beautifully carved from stone (e.g., figure 3.8, top left).

The diversity of sculpture types from the temple indicates a varied program of religious activities through time. Some sculptures likely formed part of the upper façade; others may have been installed inside the upper temple or in two niches on the edifice's western side; and additional sculptures were placed or buried on the later plaza floors around its base. Small animal sculptures are also regularly recovered at the monumental center (P. Delgado Kú 2004:153). The preponderance of serpents is the primary pattern for Temple H-17 (figures 3.7, 3.8), suggesting that rites dedicated to Kukulcan were especially important at this group. The presence of a round shrine (H-18) in the middle of this plaza also points to the significance of Kukulcan's wind god aspect.

Hall H-15 was much embellished in its day (figure 3.9). Cut geometric stones (recycled Puuc style) had been integrated into its roof façade and sculptures of animals emerged from its basal wall. These latter sculptures had fallen onto the plaza floor and included a dog, a serpent head, a jaguar, and a turtle, all with tenons that had enabled them to project from the architecture (figure 3.10). Several fragments of large stone human sculptures were found along with a large serpent head, which was found on the floor of the western transverse room of the hall. This serpent head differs from most at Mayapán in its vertical orientation that portrays the snake head in a rising position (figure 3.10). The hall was probably intentionally destroyed, as a zone of burned floor materials was encountered in the eastern interior room.

Both Temple H-17 and Hall H-15 were ritually abandoned with effigy censer rituals. Nine smashed censer concentrations were placed at the temple—five within the upper room and four in front of the building on either side of the staircase on the plaza floor (figures 3.11, 3.12). Three censer offerings were on the floor of the hall. In one concentration at each building, a crude piece of greenstone was placed; a recycled chisel (perhaps a former ax) was placed at Hall H-15 and a piece of raw material was placed at Temple H-17. This parallel set of materials suggests the simultaneous symbolic termination of both buildings. None of the concentrations contained a fully reconstructible effigy censer, indicating that the vessels had been broken, mixed, and then deposited in discrete piles. Future analysis will determine whether refits can be made between concentrations or with the effigies of the Itzmal Ch'en mass grave. A tally of noses from censer faces indicates that a minimum of fifteen effigies are represented in the Temple H-17 concentrations. The fragments are not diagnostic to specific deities. Censer assemblages have also been well documented from Zacpetén buildings—for example, at Structure 602 (Pugh and Rice 2009b:147). Some differences exist in the Structure 602 deposit and those of Itzmal Ch'en. Unlike H-17 and H-15, at Zacpetén partially reconstructible

7-D 5203 **4-I 5101** **4-Y 5338**

12-K 5276

4-N 5319 **7-D 8050**

11-C 5100

FIGURE 3.8. *Examples of anthropomorphic and turtle sculptures from Temple H-17, Itzmal Ch'en, 2009 season. Photos by Caroline Antonelli. Top row, ring sculptures (left to right): deity emerging from turtle mouth with offerings, pregnant female monkey, old god holding offering. Bottom row (left to right): human–bird figure, old god face possibly emerging from a shell, hand fragment of human portrait figure (top), turtle (bottom). The sculptures had remnants of plastered, painted surfaces.*

FIGURE 3.9. *Hall H-15 of the Itzmal Ch'en group, as seen from the top of Temple H-17. The hall was excavated and restored in 2008 by the PEMY project. Photo by Pedro Delgado Kú.*

censers were present along with a mixture of other types of non-censer vessels. The Zacpetén deposit is not considered to represent a termination event (Pugh and Rice 2009b:150).

More formal offerings were also found at the hall and temple. Behind the altar on the floor of the upper room of the temple (figure 3.6), a turkey sculpture was found, along with a bifacial knife, brightly painted effigy censer fragments (vegetation scrolls), and a plain sherd (Delgado Kú, Escamilla Ojeda, and Peraza Lope 2012b). A polychrome Itzamna effigy cup was cached (figures 3.12, 3.13) within the altar of Hall H-15 (Delgado Kú, Escamilla Ojeda, and Peraza Lope 2012a).

The Itzmal Ch'en group shares some symbolic features and artifacts with the site center. The rectangular base of Temple H-17 is like that of some central temples, but the broad and elongated foundation of this temple, combined with its height, makes it stand out from many other examples at the site (Delgado Kú, Escamilla Ojeda, and Peraza Lope 2012b). Aspects of the hall's architectural layout and upper molding resemble halls in the site center, but rounded stones forming the corners are unique among halls at the site (Delgado Kú, Escamilla Ojeda, and Peraza Lope 2012a). Circular shrines and

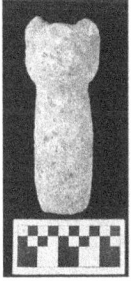

4-I 4034

5-J 4135

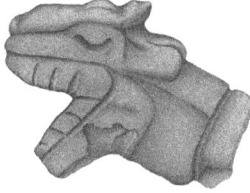

6-I 4047

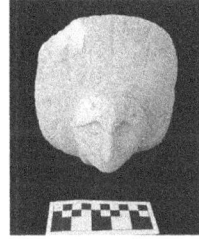

6-K 4171

16-I 4175

FIGURE 3.10. *Examples of sculptures from Hall H-15. Top: dog, jaguar. Center: serpent, human face emerging from turtle. Bottom: serpent. Illustrations by Wilberth Cruz Alvarado, photos by Caroline Antonelli.*

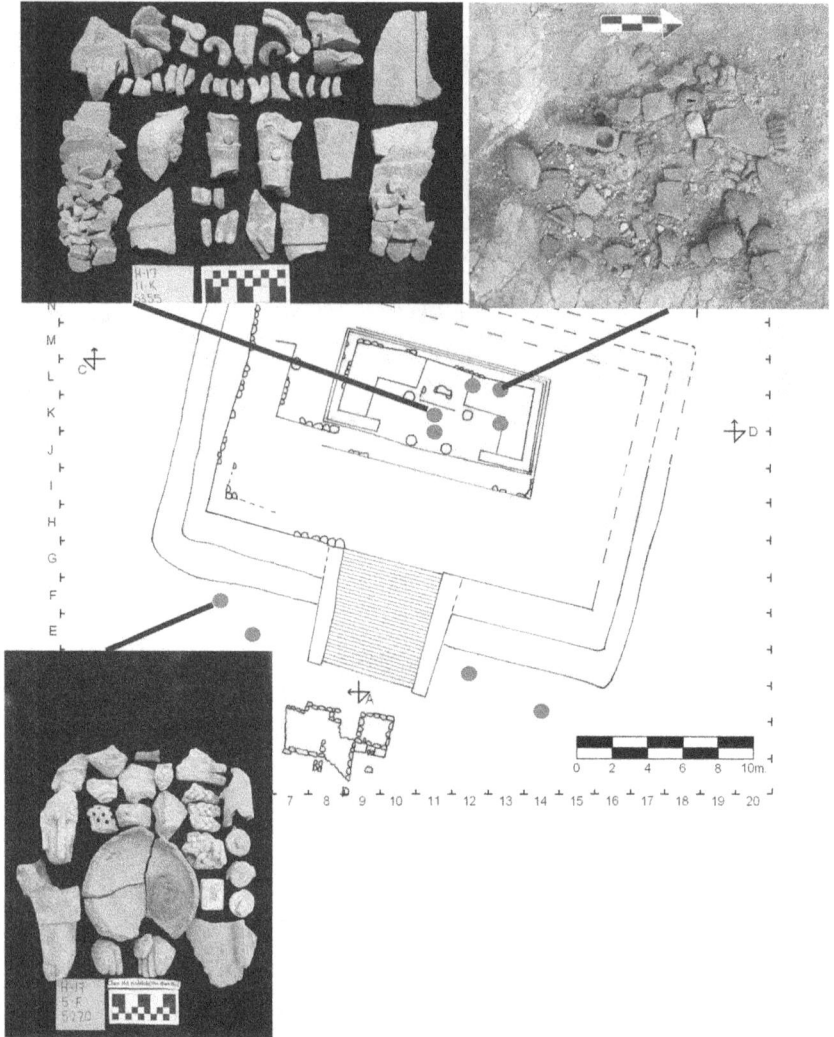

FIGURE 3.11. *Dots indicate the locations of nine smashed effigy censer offerings on the floor of Temple H-17. The photos illustrate examples of sherd fragments in the concentrations. A small piece of greenstone raw material is shown within one of the concentrations (upper right).*

burial shafts like those of H-18 occur elsewhere at the site but not in combination (Proskouriakoff 1962a). The H-18a earth lord altar differs from other representations of Tlatecuhtli at the city, which occur as smaller stone sculptures

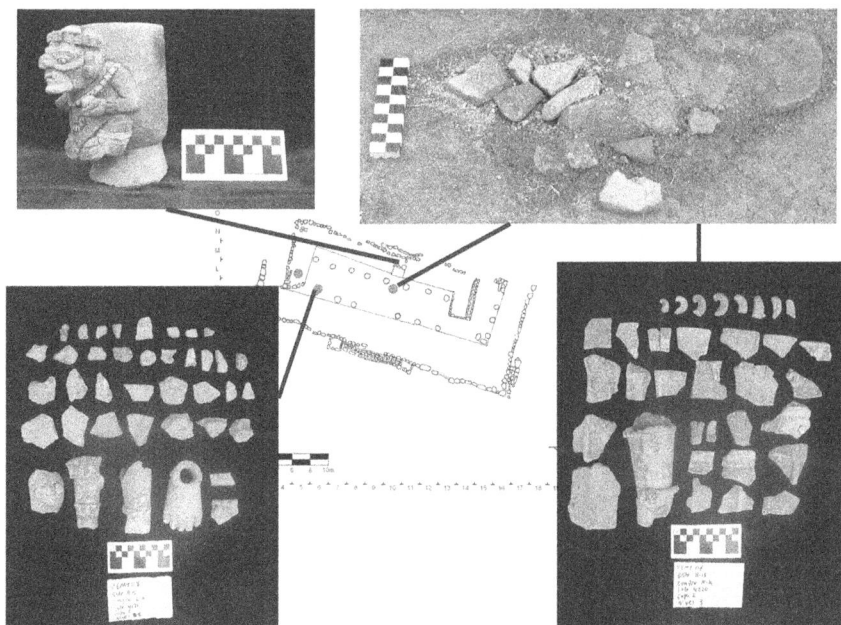

FIGURE 3.12. *Dots indicate the locations of three smashed effigy censer offerings on the floor of Hall H-15. The photos illustrate examples of sherd fragments in the concentrations. A small piece of reworked greenstone is shown within one of the concentrations (upper right), and the Itzamna effigy is from the hall's altar cache (upper left).*

or are in the form of serpent riders (chapter 2; Proskouriakoff 1962a; Taube 1992:128; Milbrath and Peraza Lope 2003a:26). The recovery of an Itzamna effigy censer at Hall H-15 links this structure with one of the most common gods represented in Postclassic Maya ceramics and codices (chapter 7). Unique for Mayapán is the tabletop stone altar in the interior upper room of Temple H-17. It is supported by small seated stucco figures (D. Thompson 1955) that resemble many other such human altar sculptures found at a variety of ritual building types at the city. Although the idea of a table altar with anthropomorphic supports is reminiscent of Chichén Itzá's Temple of the Jaguars, the style of the Itzmal Ch'en figures is dissimilar to the earlier site. The prowling jaguar sculpted on the sacrificial stone at Itzmal Ch'en does resemble those at the Temple of the Jaguars and other buildings at Chichén Itzá. One small monkey sculpture was found at Itzmal Ch'en Temple H-17 (figure 3.8). David A. Freidel and Jeremy A. Sabloff (1984:156) observe that monkeys are sometimes

FIGURE 3.13. *Itzamna offering vessel from the altar of Hall H-15, PEMY project, 2008. Photo by Bradley Russell.*

an attribute of the goddess Ixchel (Tozzer 1941:10) in their discussion of a leaping monkey stucco façade at San Gervasio. A new stela found in front of the temple, just west of Shrine H-17a, on the plaza floor, is carved with a large, crude rendition of the death god; no other stela at Mayapán shares its style or appearance (figure 3.6). Clearly those who commissioned the art and architecture of the Itzmal Ch'en group had the leeway to innovate, and these patrons tapped into a diverse array of ritual knowledge in the Postclassic Mesoamerican world. Itzmal Ch'en, like the site center, was cosmopolitan. The symbolic objects and features of this group accumulated through time as the facility was used and renovated. They reflect a number of diverse ritual activities and pluralistic themes of religious practice.

ELITE RESIDENCE Y-45A

Residence Y-45a is an eight-room building located on an *altillo*, or knoll (figures 3.14, 3.15). The dwelling forms a group with a smaller structure (Y-45b), which may represent a secondary house or ancillary building, and a small family shrine (Y-45c). Full investigations of this structure in 2003 (Peraza Lope, Masson, and Delgado Sánchez 2008) revealed that it was much bigger and more complex than it appeared to be at the surface. It is 23 meters long and 12 meters wide. Mapping of this residence by Morris R. Jones (1962) and as part of our 2002 survey (Hare 2008a) detected only the upper long gallery rooms and benches. The upper level has characteristics that we described previously as typical for elite residences (figures 3.14, 3.15). Frontal Room 6 is a long gallery of 19 × 3 meters (Figure 3.16). A parallel rear room of nearly equal dimensions (Room 7) has five benches (figures 3.15, 3.16). Two transverse rooms are present at either end (Rooms 5 and 8), which are lower than the upper gallery rooms on a modified contour of the altillo (figure 3.16). Room 8 may have been a kitchen; it faces east, from which the breeze comes at Mayapán, and the structures' middens were located below it at the base of the altillo. One Mama Red tripod jar was left in place on the floor of Room 5. During excavation, we exposed a lower rear level of this house that contained four rooms, as shown in figure 3.16. The rooms had been filled in with soil and rocks to the level of the surrounding altillo, concealing the entire lower tier. It is unlikely that the fill is due to roof collapse, as the walls of the rooms reach nearly two meters; roof fill would have not reached the altillo's surface, and there was a large quantity of soil and smaller rocks that are uncharacteristic of roofing material. Also, at least three distinct layers of offerings were discerned in the fill of Room 2 and its passageway. We determined that the rooms had been filled intentionally with debris after a series of termination rituals that took place in Rooms 1 and 2.

This split-level design is unique for houses that have been investigated at Mayapán. Room 1 is a bench room on the western end of the lower level that may have been used for formally receiving guests (figure 3.16). Room 2, a shrine room, was especially unique for the site, as its approach was delineated by a finely built stone passageway of four meters in length, with foundation walls that reached nearly two meters (1.89 meters) in height (figure 3.16). At the end of the passageway, Room 2 was located at a right angle to the east. A stone window was present at the rear of Room 2 that connected it to Room 3 (figure 3.16). The function of smaller, square Rooms 3 and 4 is less clear. They were fully enclosed and lacked entrances. Room 3 may have been a concealed locality for ritualists to speak through talking idols in Room 2, as suggested for Cozumel features (Freidel and Sabloff 1984), or it may have served as a storeroom or both. Indications of Room 3's ritual importance include the recovery of two miniature vessels in its fill, a small tripod cup and bowl;

FIGURE 3.14. *View of upper rooms of elite House Y-45a during excavation. A possible uncarved stela was present on the central bench.*

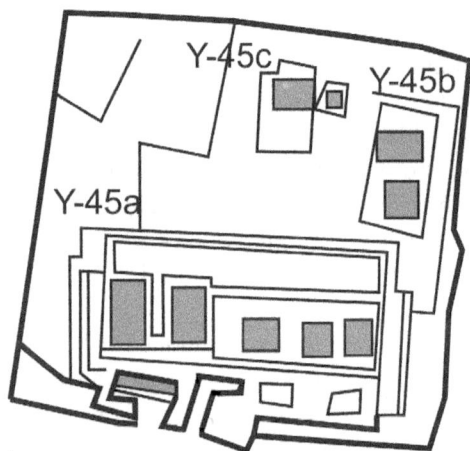

FIGURE 3.15. *Plan map of elite House Y-45a, secondary House Y-45b, and Shrine Y-45c.*

8 meters

these are commonly used for offerings or caches at the site (figure 3.17). Room 4, completely self-contained, was a probable storeroom. Neither Room 3 nor Room 4 had concentrations of smashed vessels or burned offerings, but they were likely infilled at the same time as Rooms 1 and 2.

FIGURE 3.16. *Map of elite Residence Y-45a and photos of its rear lower-level rooms: (A) Room 1 with stucco bench, (B) passageway to Room 2 (note the stair cut into bedrock), (C) Room 2 with burned offering in fill during excavation (note window to Room 3 at rear), (D) Room 3, and (E) Room 4.*

In Room 1, vessels were smashed over a plaster bench and on the floor in front of it, including reconstructible vessels of Mama Red: Black-on-Red type, Pelé Polychrome, Tecoh Red-on-Buff, Buff Polbox, and an extremely large stucco-covered Kanasín Red/Unslipped jar (figures 3.17–3.19). The rear half of the passageway and Room 2 had multiple smashed pottery concentrations and burned organic offerings in at least three different levels in the soil, indicating that the infilling of this room was intentional. Effigy censer fragments were concentrated in the passageway, and these included cacao pod adornos that are sometimes worn or held by effigies (chapter 7). Three ceramic cacao pods were in the passageway, and an additional two were in Room 2. Three others were found in various lots at Y-45a. Cacao pod adornos do not generally concentrate at Mayapán buildings, and we infer that they were of special symbolic significance to the activities at the group. No effigy faces were recovered, and the censer fragments did not represent reconstructible vessels. These vessels were likely broken else-

FIGURE 3.17. *Reconstructible vessels from elite House Y-45a. Most of the vessels were smashed on the floors of Rooms 1 and 2, with the exception of the tripod jar at the far left (Room 5) and the miniature tripod bowl and tripod cup in the front (Room 3). Note the extremely large stucco-covered jar of the type Kanasín Red/Unslipped. Vessels were identified and reconstructed by Wilberth Cruz Alvarado and Luis Flores Cobá. Photo by Bradley Russell.*

where, with only fragments brought to the passageway for deposition. The only effigy head was that of a rodent that was part of a figurine or vessel appliqué.

A total of twenty-seven reconstructible partial vessels from Y-45a are listed in table 3.5 (figures 3.17–3.19). Although the quantities of smashed vessel sherds were higher in Room 1, covering most of the bench and floor and piled in concentrations that were 30 centimeters deep in places, table 3.5 illustrates that reconstructible vessels were more abundant in Room 2. Reconstruction efforts by Wilberth A. Cruz Alvarado and Luis Flores Cobá indicate that some vessels were incomplete at the time of their breakage in the Y-45a rooms. Twenty of the vessels are classified as Buff Polbox group pottery, including

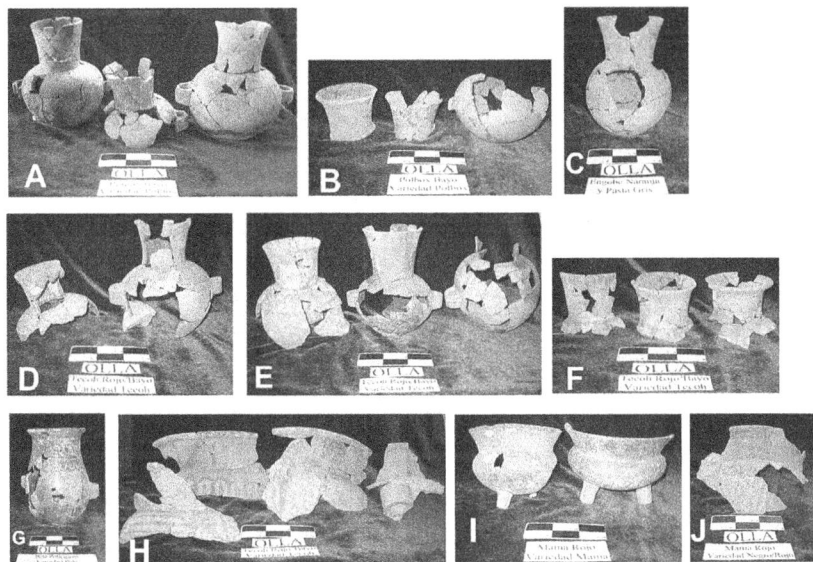

FIGURE 3.18. *Jars of Buff Polbox (A, B), unknown type (C), Tecoh Red-on-Buff (D, E, F), Pelé Polychrome (G, H), and Mama Red (I, J) types from elite House Y-45a. All examples are from Room 1, Room 2, or the passageway to Room 2, with the exception of the tripod jar shown in photo I at left (Room 5). Photos by Bradley Russell.*

Tecoh Red-on-Buff or Pelé Polychrome (table 3.5). The polychromes include a turkey effigy jar (figures 3.2, 3.18h) and a painted fish dish (figures 3.1, 3.19); other Tecoh Red-on-Buff jars are also decorated with red paint (figure 3.18e, f). One jar from Room 2 may represent Trapiche Pink (figure 3.18c), a type from the Petén Lakes area of Guatemala (P. Rice, personal communication to Carlos Peraza Lope, 2004). Why were partial vessels brought to Y-45's rooms for breakage? As the entire structure was excavated, we can be certain that the remainder of the vessels were not placed in another room of the house. We also tested two areas of a rich midden deposit to the east of the altillo within the Y-45 group albarrada, and we did not recover significant quantities of the rare types of vessels found in the rear rooms.

Of the four Mama Red vessels, one has an Ahau face painted on the rim (figure 3.20), as does the turkey effigy vessel shown in figure 3.2. Calendrical motifs are part of the decorative inventory of Kowoj pottery at Zacpetén, including Ahau glyphs (Rice and Cecil 2009a:245; Cecil 2009:233). Other

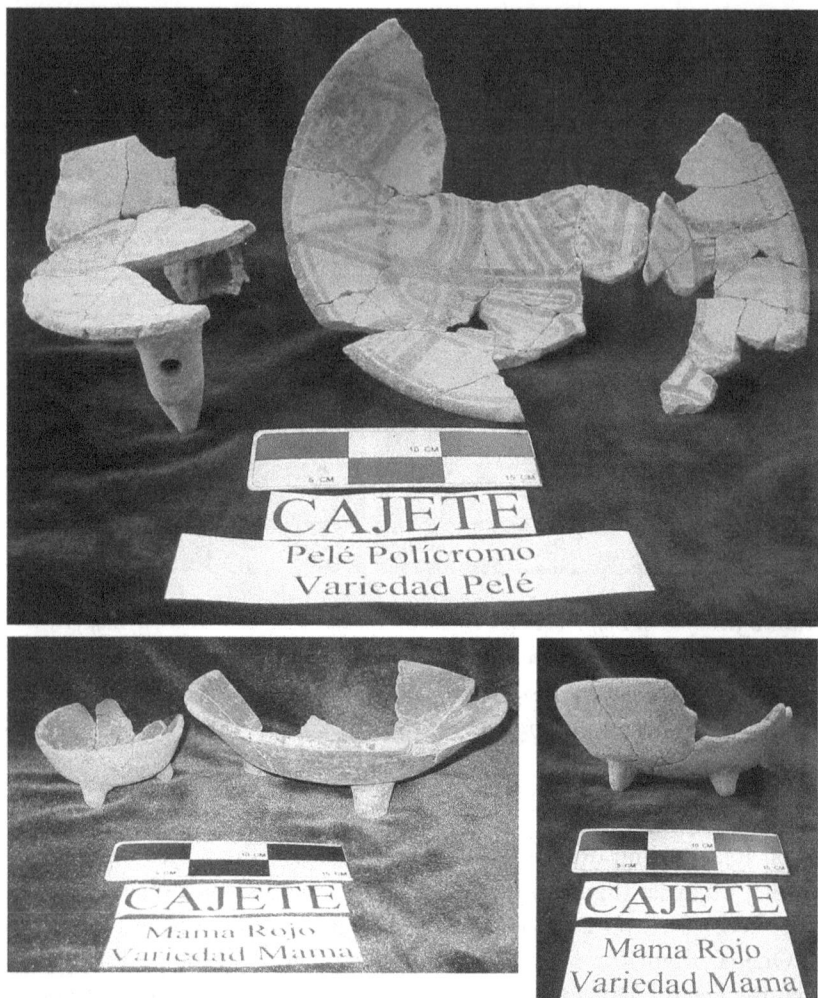

FIGURE 3.19. *Reconstructible dishes from elite House Y-45a. All vessels were broken in Rooms 1 and 2, except for the miniature tripod Mama Red dish (bottom left). Note the effigy supports on the Pelé Polychrome dish at top, which is characteristic of these vessels. Photos by Bradley Russell.*

calendrical signs are known from this area on Chompoxté Red-on-Cream vessels, including Lamat year-bearer glyphs (Rice and Cecil 2009:247, figure 11.3a, b), and one of the Tecoh Red-on-Buff jars from Y-45a also has this symbol (figure 3.20). The presence of these three glyphs on the Y-45a vessels repre-

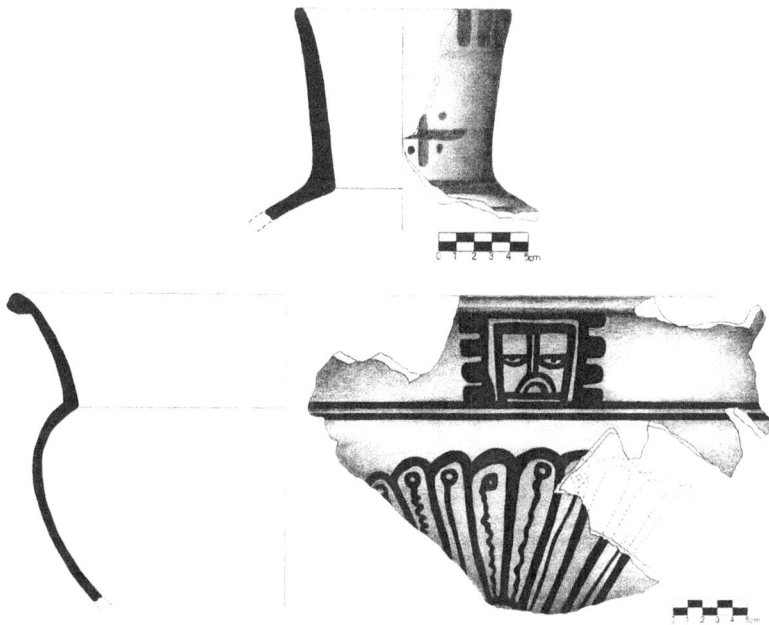

FIGURE 3.20. *Partial vessels with glyphs from elite House Y-45a. Top example has a painted Lamat glyph on the neck of a Tecoh Red-on-Buff jar. Bottom example is a Mama Red: Variety Black-on-Red vessel with an Ahau glyph on the neck. Figure 3.2 illustrates an Ahau glyph on another vessel from the structure. Illustrations by Wilberth Cruz Alvarado.*

sents intriguing evidence in support of these investigators' suggestion that this Mayapán house was occupied by members of the Kowoj faction. These glyphs are exceedingly rare on Mayapán pottery. We initially thought that the eight dot-like designs next to the Ahau face on the Y-45a Mama Red jar represented a pseudo-glyphic reference to K'atun 8 Ahau. But this date is properly written as a bar and three dots. Taking into consideration our radiocarbon results that indicate Y-45a's abandonment before 1400—earlier than K'atun 8 Ahau in 1441–1461—we view the dots as decorative rather than calendrical.

The similarities of Kowoj Chompoxté Red-on-Cream pottery to Tecoh Red-on-Buff and Pelé Polychrome pottery have been outlined in detail by Rice and her colleagues (P. Rice 2009c:37; Pugh and Rice 2009a:92; Rice and Cecil 2009a:242–51). There are additional similarities and differences worth mentioning for the purposes of ongoing comparisons. The tendency to decorate the interiors rather than exteriors of dishes and the exterior of jars is shared by both sites (P. Rice 2009e:218; Rice and Cecil 2009a:242). Some differences might be expected given the great distances between Yucatán and the Petén. Unlike Chompoxté Red-on-Cream, Pelé Polychrome vessels tend to have black painted designs instead of red ones, although some Tecoh Red-on-Buff vessels do have red painted decorations (figure 3.18e, f). Fish designs are popular on Pelé dishes at Mayapán, but examples of this theme are not published for the Zacpetén and Topoxté area. Pelé dishes also have zoomorphic effigy supports, which are not listed as diagnostics for the Kowoj by Rice and Cecil (2009). Modeled pots with turkeys, such as the example from Y-45a, are also not reported from the Petén. Non-effigy censers often have spikes in Zacpetén examples (P. Rice 2009f:286–88) but are rare at Mayapán; and small cache bowls with side handles reported from Zacpetén are unlike Mayapán's more common miniature tripod cups, bowls, and vases, although the practice of putting beads of shell and jade in them is shared at both sites (P. Rice 2009f:290).

In summary, Structure Y-45a contributes in important ways to the study of complexity at Mayapán by revealing a high level of segregation of social space. The unique features of this building indicate that simple classifications of residential form and function do not always hold up when full excavations are undertaken. Some of the idiosyncratic variation in building design and artifact assemblages of the sort revealed by this structure may be attributable to ethnic associations. The rooms of Y-45a also point to functions performed in a residential zone by occupants of a secondary elite residence. A frontal gallery on the upper level of the structure provided a suitable space for hosting gatherings. A rear bench room may have emphasized the authority of the head of household and provided a staging ground for formal transactions with subordinates (e.g., Inomata 2001). Given the historical descriptions of the activities of mid-level administrators in Contact Period Maya society (chapter 2), it is possible that officials used Room 1 to receive tribute and negotiate other demands for service to the state. Surplus may have been stored in Room 4 or elsewhere at the building. Cacao, a primary currency of the Postclassic Period, may have been collected as tribute at Y-45a, and the importance of this item was underscored by a rare concentration of effigy adorno cacao pods at the house. Authority at the house may have been buttressed by the maintenance of a shrine room in which a communicating idol may have been housed, as suggested by the passageway, Room 2, and the window between Rooms 2 and 3. The upper rooms were used for conventional purposes of living and entertaining, as is observed at many elite residences at Mayapán. The exercise of secular and religious authority, clearly spatially separated by Room 1 and Room 2, imply additional duties for a probable intermediary administrator in this part of the city. Alfred M. Tozzer (1941:n.859) points out that a possible cacao deity was also a god of merchants. Given the diversity of fancy pottery at this structure that indicates the wealth of its residents, it is also possible that they were engaged in distant commercial exchange. This occupation was common for members of Mayapán's nobility, and if their ties to the Petén were strong, they would have had advantageous connections for north-south trade.

IN SUM

Outlying colonnaded halls, temples, and elite residences were key focal nodes for political and religious integration in the city. In some cases the symbolic objects and features of these buildings overlapped. The matching offerings of broken Chen Mul effigies and greenstone objects on the floors of Hall H-15 and Temple H-17 provide an apt illustration of parallel, contemporary rites. Overlap is also observed in events held at halls and elite residences at Mayapán that parallels patterns documented for Utatlán and Zacpetén (Wallace 1977; Pugh et al. 2009:207). But this statement cannot be easily generalized, given evidence for variation in activities among halls and elite residences (Pugh, Rice, and Cecil 2009:207). The patrons of Mayapán's colonnaded halls were among the same individuals who inhabited its loftiest palaces. Long columned gallery rooms at elite homes such as R-86, R-87, and Y-45a may have been used for gatherings, feasts, and calendrical celebrations in a similar manner to the rites of some halls and temples. Proskouriakoff and Charles R. Temple (1955:294; A. Smith 1962:figure 6) note that the gallery of R-86 is 4 meters wide and 22 meters long, with 3-meter spaces between massive columns; and an adjacent palatial dwelling, R-87, has a frontal columned room that is nearly as spacious (17 meters × 4 meters). Secondary elite House Y-45a lacks columns but has a frontal gallery of a size close to that of R-86. Such spaces resemble those provided by colonnaded halls.

Halls differ in symbolic emphasis. The specific mural and columnar art of certain resplendent monumental halls was outlined in chapter 2. Some halls like Q-64 (La Sala de los Incensarios) were littered with effigy censers (Peraza Lope, Delgado Kú, and Escamilla Ojeda 2003:18), some had carefully smashed concentrations of censers (H-15), and others had rich polychrome serving ware assemblages (Q-88a) while additional examples were more devoid of materials (Q-152c). Altars at halls often had paired ceramic vessel offerings of Navula Unslipped or Acansip Painted tripod or cylindrical vessels, which regularly contained a shell ornament/bead and jade bead offering.

Paired vessel offerings and censers have been linked to calendrical ceremonies (Chase and Chase 1988:85; P. Rice 2009f:300–1; Milbrath et al. 2008; Milbrath and Peraza Lope 2009, 2013), but single offerings such as H-15's Itzamna vase were also important.

Chapter 7 explores greater variation in the identity of effigy sculptures of different hall and temple groups at Mayapán. The diversity of sculptures at Hall H-15 and Temple H-17 of Itzmal Ch'en reflects a plurality that is attributable to long-term use and a range of ritual practices at this group. Outlying ceremonial groups like Itzmal Ch'en may have hosted a greater variety of events than at the site center, which had more numerous specialized buildings and groups. It is still unclear who constructed and used the Itzmal Ch'en group. This question is difficult to answer since no large elite palaces are found near Itzmal Ch'en. Houses in the neighborhood were engaged in a full range of work activities, like those found in other parts of the city; some were generalized and presumably engaged in agrarian production and custodial activities (H-11) while others produced surplus quantities of fine or mundane craft objects (I-55a and I-57), as documented in chapter 6. The Itzmal Ch'en group likely served more than the neighborhood in which it was embedded, as the rich symbolic array of materials is well linked to the art and ritual of the site center. Outlying focal groups were probably incorporated into site-level celebrations, perhaps on a rotating calendrical basis. They would have been landmarks and may have been of key significance to quadripartite division or other cosmological concepts (chapter 4). Turtle sculptures and censers (among other objects) probably reflect rotating calendrical celebrations that took place at geographic subdivisions of towns, polities, and territories (Masson 2000; P. Rice 2004; P. Rice 2009c:23–25). Although the buildings of Itzmal Ch'en exhibit idiosyncratic design elements, their functions and general assemblages mimic the style and content of the site center. An emphasis on Kukulcan inferred from the prevalence of serpent sculptures and a round shrine also links this group to the major founding deity of Mayapán. While the Itzmal Ch'en group may have been a site-level facility, it undoubtedly served as an important defining entity for the surrounding residential zone. It would have been a landmark in the cityscape and perhaps a public square for local and visiting pedestrians. As a public water source, it would have been imbued with both sacred and mundane attributes (Brown 1999, 2005, 2006, 2008).

The political economy of Mayapán linked rather than segregated domestic, craft, and ritual institutions and practices. It is possible that ordinary goods used at ceremonial groups were purchased in the marketplace, as suggested for Aztec sites (Smith, Wharton, and Olson 2003). We develop this argument further in the analysis of artifacts in chapter 6. The next chapter considers evidence for the structuring principles of the Mayapán settlement that are observed in the distribution of roads, cenotes, public plazas, and nodal architecture of the city.

4

The Urban Cityscape

Timothy S. Hare,
Marilyn A. Masson, and
Carlos Peraza Lope

New analyses of Mayapán's urban form and layout reveal principles of the organization and articulation of the city's residential and public districts. Chapter 3 addressed the activities performed at specific outlying nodes in the cityscape, and in this chapter we consider the full array of special function features that reveal differentiation and division of the settlement zone, including a market plaza and other open spaces, temples and halls outside of the epicenter, elite residences, principal wells (cenotes), and stone-marked pedestrian pathways. We argue that these features indicate degrees of formal planning and the distribution of mid-level institutions in the settlement zone. From these localities, activities were staged that linked governing elites to residents of the city's neighborhoods. Like many of its predecessors, Mayapán has been poorly credited with any degree of urban planning or administrative complexity despite rich ethnohistorical descriptions to the contrary. Given the lingering effects of characterization of the Postclassic Period as weak and decentralized compared to its Classic-era predecessors (chapter 1), it is understandable that recognizing the importance and sophistication of this city has been a slow process. As Classic Maya cities have sometimes been classified as politically and economically weak (e.g., Sanders and Webster 1988; Hendon 1991; Webster and Sanders 2001; Inomata 2001; Foias 2002), it is logical that a state considered to be devolved from the Classic would by implication be accorded even greater frailty. Opinion has been divided, however, with some clear arguments advanced for significant Classic Maya city size and complexity (Chase, Chase, and Haviland 1990:500–3, 2011; Haviland 1992:937; Folan 1992; Fry 2003; Sharer and Golden 2004:26).

DOI: 10.5876/9781607323204.c004

Recognizing the complexity of urban organization and patterns of occupational diversity at Mayapán is an effort that runs parallel to inquiries that have targeted Classic Period kingdoms. Beyond the walled perimeter, Russell (2008a) has identified additional administrative nodes in the form of outlying temples, halls, and elite residences as well as specialized zones for agriculture, raising game, and producing lime. This chapter presents some emerging data that suggest a significant degree of organization and differentiation of Mayapán's walled settlement that structured its nucleated mazeway of thousands of houses.

The presence or absence of an orthogonal layout is not the only criterion by which urban form and the degree of planning should be evaluated and compared (M. Smith 2007, 2008). Many ancient cities can exhibit orthogonal principles within their monumental centers, even if the remainder of the residential zone is more loosely organized (M. Smith 2007:17–18). Single attributes such as population size, density, or type are also of limited utility for defining a place as urban. The functions that cities provided for their hinterlands are arguably the most important characteristic (M. Smith 2007; Hirth 2003a, 2003b). Mayapán meets Michael E. Smith's (2007) updated functional definition of urbanism as it exerted religious, political, and economic influence on its hinterland (Freidel and Sabloff 1984; Masson 2000; Rice and Rice 2009). We have discussed Mayapán's position as a political and religious center in chapter 2, and economic data for the city are provided in chapter 6. But it is at hinterland localities such as Laguna de On that the influence of a regional center is best measured, and the footprint of Mayapán's rise to power was evident in the thirteenth- to fifteenth-century prosperity of this small hamlet (Masson 2000).

On a regional scale, functional differentiation among settlements can be gauged at both horizontal and vertical scales (chapter 2; Kowalewski 1990; Crumley 1995). In the Maya area, the largest centers were diverse places of consumption and production (e.g., Becker 1973; Fry 2003; Chase et al. 2011), and smaller towns and villages tended to specialize in the surplus production of local resources, including agricultural or forest products, marine resources, chert, or clay for pottery making (Hester and Shafer 1984; McKillop 1996; Mock 1994; King 2000; Graham 2002; Scarborough, Valdez, and Dunning 2003; Fry 2003; Masson 2003b; McAnany 2004). Surplus production was undertaken alongside more generalized household economies that balanced potential risks (Dunning et al. 2003), but evidence is clear that domestic units were not autonomous in acquiring all of their raw materials and manufacturing craft goods (Masson and Freidel 2012). Exceptions are known where some towns focused on levels of craft production or market exchange that far exceeded the norm (Shafer and Hester 1983; Dahlin and Ardren 2002). At the market center of Chunchucmil, monumental architecture typical of Maya political capitals is absent, and this city was located in an environment that would have not permitted it to grow its own food (Dahlin and Ardren 2002). Where production took place within cities such as Tikal or Mayapán, raw material for some objects such as stone tools or shell ornaments was imported to the center, where it was converted to more valuable finished goods (Fedick 1991; Moholy-Nagy 2003; chapter 6). Variation in local and exchange economies that attests to regional functional differentiation among sites is observed within the Classic, Postclassic, and Contact Periods (Piña Chan 1978; Freidel 1978, 1981; Masson and Freidel 2012). At the smaller scale of individual sites, public spaces, monuments, and households, productive activities are also functionally differentiated, as we demonstrate in this chapter and in chapter 6.

Activities of the members of the Mayapán confederation may be reflected archaeologically by important focal architectural groups—neighborhood temples, halls, and outlying elite residences that are distributed regularly across much of the city (chapter 3, figure 4.1). Diego de Landa's (1941:62–64) account states that the lords of the confederated towns each built a residence at Mayapán. These edifices may correspond to colonnaded halls, elite residences, or both, recalling that halls for Utatlán were referred to as the houses of lineages (Carmack 1981a). Mayapán's smaller temples and outlying ceremonial groups were also likely built by members of the governing nobility (chapter 3).

Within the city, strategic facilities performed the following functions: (1) coordinate the administration of residential zones, (2) replicate features of the site's monumental zone within its residential neighborhoods to foster integration, (3) designate spaces of the city for specialized functions used by residents and visitors, and (4) direct the pedestrian traffic of residents and visitors to key nodes of activity and resources. It is important to keep in mind that functional features in the landscape, such as the city wall, cenotes, or other edges or nodes, may have had practical as well as symbolic importance (e.g., R. Fletcher 2000–2001:10; Erickson 2009:233; Russell 2013). The cohesion of socioeconomic subdivisions of Mayapán, whether spatially clustered or not, was important for achieving city unity. We envision a dialectical relationship between such subunits and the political capital as a whole. The resolution of opposing attractions of hometown identities (and other social groups) and polity scale unity would have been an ongoing priority for the governors of the confederacy. This problem was not unique to Mayapán and was often resolved by investment in inter-elite cultural interaction (e.g., Oudijk 2002; Pohl 2003b;

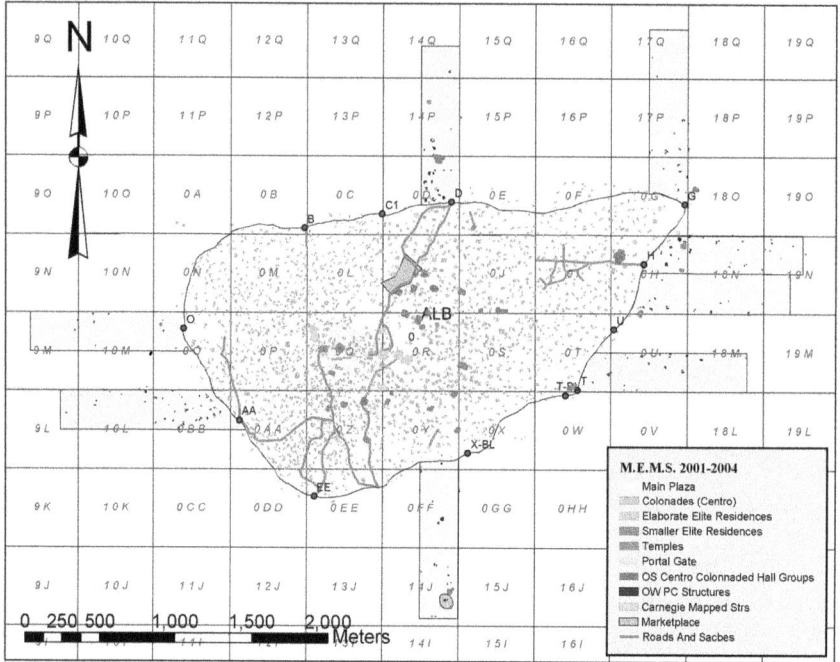

FIGURE 4.1. *Focal nodes and roadways that helped define Mayapán's cityscape. Map by Bradley Russell.*

Janusek 2004). Social subunits of the residential zone may have been large, representing settlers or descendants of *cahob* (hometowns) of the confederacy (chapter 2; Restall 2001), migrant groups to the city (Roys 1962), or smaller entities at the scale of isolated houselots or houselot clusters (Brown 1999). Identity politics may also have included occupational specialists such as those who lived in Mayapán's downtown crafts neighborhood (chapter 6).

The dynamic model of Maya states productively highlights the cyclic nature of centralization and decentralization (e.g., Marcus 1993; Iannone 2002). Within this long-term trajectory, the apogee of Mayapán represents an era of significant centralization in which its governors institutionally bound together potentially fractious segments within the city, across the northwest Yucatán confederacy, and among more distant allies in the Caribbean and Gulf coastal regions. Kenneth G. Hirth's (2003b) model of segmental urbanism identifies the presence of political, social, and territorial subunits of Xochicalco and its hinterlands in a way that is relevant to our examination of Mayapán. He proposes that hinterland geopolitical units (*altepetl*) within Xochicalco's domain were articulated with the center by representatives who occupied and operated key architectural facilities for administrative purposes within the city's urban landscape. Although the term *segmentary* is sometimes used to describe decentralized societies comprised of autonomous lineages (Iannone 2002; Fox 1987), it can also refer to the existence of similar, replicated units (Brown 1999). These specific meanings differ from the concept of segmental urbanism. At Xochicalco, architectural facilities of altepetl that belonged to the centralized polity represented secondary seats of authority within the urban capital that served to integrate the subunits with which they were associated—and in our view, this situation was analogous to Mayapán. While the spatial boundaries of social subunits may be difficult to identify archaeologically at Mayapán, as for many ancient cities (M. Smith 2010a; Hare and Masson 2012), ethnohistorical records explicitly describe neighborhoods or wards (Roys 1962; Piña Chan 1978). The centralization of lineages and larger corporate units at capitals like Mayapán (or Utatlán) represents a unitary state that is more than the sum of its parts—in other words, a confederated state (Blanton 1976). The problem, even at Utatlán, has been an emphasis on segmentary components rather than the clear fact of their centralization at political capital, an approach that focuses on the trees rather than the forest. Robert M. Carmack and Dwight T. Wallace (1977:109) applied the term of *segmentary-centrism* to K'ich'ean political cal structure to overcome the weaker implications of a segmentary model.

Territorial subunits within Mayapán's urban zone were referred to as *cuchteel* (ward or barrio). These economic and political units were officiated by a ward leader or Ah Cuch Cab (Roys 1957; Ringle and Bey 2001:271; Quezada 1993:41–42), and they have general analogs in the residential administrative divisions of central Mexico (Hirth 2003b:295; Cowgill, Altschul, and Sload 1984), highland Guatemala (Carmack 1981a), and early Colonial Yucatán (Roys 1957; Restall 2001). It is not known whether the cuchteel at Mayapán also represented social groups that shared hometown affiliations from the confederated territories, or whether they were primarily units for administrative convenience.

THE MAYAPÁN SETTLEMENT

The majority of structures in the walled (4.2 square kilometers) portion of the city were mapped by Morris R. Jones (1952, 1962) and his team. Close inspection of Jones's map, combined with our survey efforts, has revealed features that help to define portions of the city (figure 4.1). The density of settlement sets this site apart from other, earlier Maya centers. PEMY project research (2001–2009) mapped sections of the city in greater detail using modern survey technology (figure 1.7, Hare 2008a). The great wall, with a 9.1 kilometer circumference, encloses a large portion of the site's settlement (Shook 1952:8). Parapets have been documented at some locations on the 1.5–2-meter-high ruins of the wall, which stood higher prior to the final battle at Mayapán (Shook 1952:9). Twelve ancient gates existed and seven of these (Gates G; H; D; T; a second, blocked Gate T; O; and EE) are finely constructed with porticos and columns (Shook 1952). There was probably an inner enclosure around the monumental center that ranching activities reshaped prior to twentieth-century scientific investigations (Tozzer 1941:23–26; Brown 1999). The rectangular ranch wall now encloses much of the original monumental center (figure 1.6). The Carnegie project map recorded approximately 4,100 buildings within or adjacent to the city wall—just over half of these were identified as residences (A. Smith 1962).

Mapping efforts by Clifford T. Brown (1999:149–50) and the PEMY project have uncovered more structures within groups than are recorded on the Carnegie map—including house-sized alignments that may represent additional dwellings (Hare 2008a; chapter 4). The city's settlement also expands, in lower densities, beyond the city wall to a distance of 500 meters (Russell 2008a, 2008b). As reviewed in chapter 1, Russell estimates the city's population to have been between 15,000 and 17,000 people. Many residential groups at Mayapán are enclosed by houselot walls, known locally as *albarradas* (Brown 1999; Bullard 1952, 1953, 1954; A. Smith 1962:208–9). This unusual characteristic for a Maya city is observed at some other northern sites, such as Chunchucmil (Dahlin and Ardren 2002), Dzibilchaltun (Kurjack 1974), and Cobá (L. Fletcher 1983; Fletcher and Kintz 1983). Brown (1999:78–79) expanded the study of these features to identify larger social units termed *houselot clusters*—these consist of residential groups that share dividing walls. Chapter 5 presents an updated analysis of an expanded sample of mapped albarrada residential groups at the city. These houselot walls are also relevant for this chapter's questions on site organization, as spaces between these enclosures formed lanes and guided pedestrian traffic.

Prior analyses of Mayapán's settlement characteristics have achieved no consensus. Two models, derived from ethnohistory and archaeology, characterize the city as either concentrically organized, with elite, ritual, and administrative features nucleated around the epicenter (Landa 1941:23–26), or alternatively, structured into distinct neighborhoods administered by outlying elites (D. Chase 1992). Aspects of both of these models have been verified. Elite architecture, including residences, clusters near the epicenter (A. Smith

1962:206), yet outlying halls, temples, and secondary elite homes also punctuate key points in the urban cityscape. In this respect, Mayapán is comparable to some earlier Maya cities, such as Seibal or Dzibilchaltun (Tourtellot and Sabloff 1999:74; Kurjack 1974:89). Classifications of groups with temples, halls, and oratories by Tatiana Proskouriakoff (1962a) and others (Ringle and Bey 2001; Pugh 2003; D. Chase 1992) provide archaeological support for documentary descriptions of confederacy government at Mayapán, as they represent multiple, functionally similar facilities that were likely operated by ruling families of the site's governing council.

A. Ledyard Smith (1962:265) stated that there was a "minimum of city planning at Mayapan," which he attributed to the irregular terrain. William R. Bullard, Jr. (1954:238) also concluded that Mayapán houses were scattered and not organized according to a formal city plan. Based on a statistical study of digitized portions of a subset of the Carnegie site map, Clifford Brown (1999:174–77) argues that the site's settlement was self-similar and consisted of replicated kin units on different scales. While he acknowledges that the civic-ceremonial architecture conforms to cosmological principles (Brown 1999:190, 588), the residential features are fractal, chaotic, mathematically unpredictable, and nonlinear; and evidence for wards or barrios as described in Colonial accounts is "weak" (Brown 1999:148). In summary, he argues, "The evidence for an administrative and bureaucratic type of government is virtually nil" at Mayapán (Brown 1999:585), and he views the site's political structure as segmentary and galactic.

As Michael Smith (2010b) notes, even residential zones are planned by generative, bottom-up processes by their occupants; but we are concerned here with planning principles that would have originated from elites to fulfill the needs of administering and defining the urban landscape. Following some of Michael Smith's (2007) criteria, we observe evidence for a degree of planning while refraining from typifying the entire settlement as either planned or unplanned. Planning elements can include the formality of monumental buildings constructed or arrayed according to recognizable, standardized principles (M. Smith 2007:8). Access and visibility also attest to planning principles. Mayapán's largest monumental buildings would have been visible from the city gates and would have served as landmarks for navigation. For example, in the 1950s, the site was less covered by forest and Edwin W. Shook (1952:15) was able to view the central Temple of Kukulcan from western Gate O. Outlying groups were open, and pedestrians may have had easy access to these plazas. Replicated architectural features attest to the use of standardized plans by having a limited number of orientations and parallel functions (M. Smith

2007:25, 29). These urban features were symbolic of three levels of meaning described by Michael Smith (2007:35–37), based on Amos Rapoport's (1988) classification: high level (cosmological, religious), middle level (status and other identities, monumentality, sacred space), and low level (landmarks, navigation tools, access, and other personal experiences of landscape). Timothy W. Pugh (2001) has offered an interpretation of high-level cosmological symbolism for Mayapán's epicenter that emphasizes serpent temples, a cenote/cave complex, and creation mythology involving an epic flood and crocodilian supernaturals. Such high-level cosmological symbolism can function separately from other, more mundane organizational principles of dividing the site (M. Smith 2007:30). Our facility-based approach to identify planning principles in Mayapán's settlement zone considers primarily middle-level and low-level categories of meaning.

For Postclassic- and Contact-era Maya communities, an example of high-level meaning is the conceptual division of settlements into quadripartite sectors (Coe 1965; Carmack 1977, 1981a; Fox 1987), including Mayapán (Roys 1962:37, 78). But material correlates of this principle have been difficult to recognize in residential zones, which lack clear divisions such as straight walls or roads (Brown 1999:67–73). Beyond settlement boundaries, quadripartite principles were applied to other features. For example, Prudence M. Rice (2004:279) recalls that four principal roads entered the town of Mama. At Mayapán, at least two major historical roads cross through the city's north, south, and eastern walls, and one principal road enters from the west. These were mapped by Morris Jones (1962) and Bullard (1952, 1954) and generally adhere to cardinal principles as they loosely align east-west or north-south but are off by a few degrees.

Brown (1999:67) offers a compelling suggestion that the four conceptual divisions of Mayapán may be represented by axes drawn from four major cardinal gates through the site's epicentral pyramidal structure (Q-162). Although the chronicles refer to principal cardinal gates and their named lineage head guardians (Roys 1962:79), identifying the correlates of four cardinal gates is difficult, as the city has twelve gates of differing size, elaboration, and probable significance (Shook 1952; Brown 1999:66). But major gates in cardinal positions along the wall may have had greater symbolic import.

We assume that multiple symbols of directionality may exist at Mayapán as a consequence of cumulative processes of rituals, shrine construction, and other ceremonies sponsored by a series of governing elites through time. The location of external shrines, as well as nearby temple/cenote complexes, may help with identifying quadripartite and other key features of landscape conceptualization

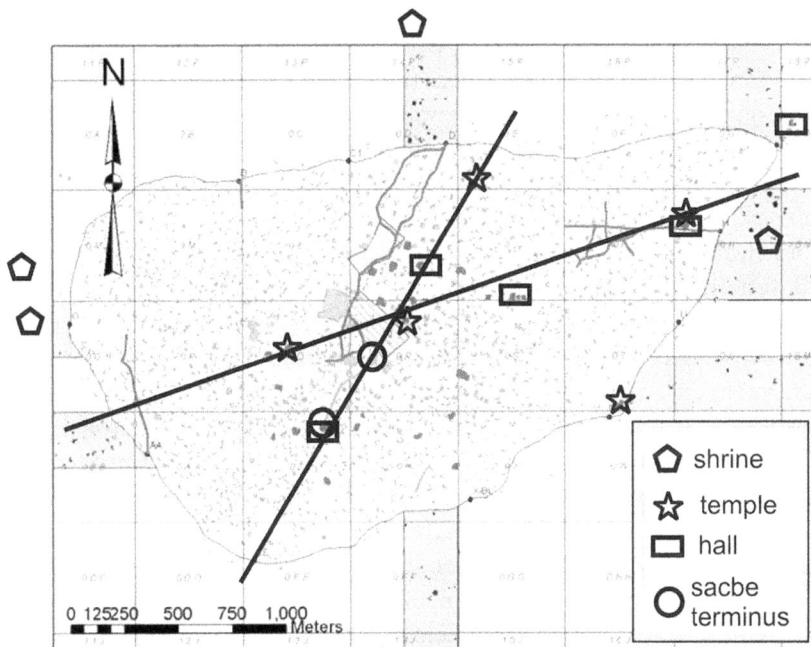

FIGURE 4.2. *Location of outer shrines, temples, halls, and terminal groups of the major sacbe at Mayapán. Lines indicate potentially important alignments of three or more focal features. Many more alignments of fewer features can be drawn. The only gate in the city wall included in the alignments shown here is in Square EE, at the bottom of the map. Base map of Mayapán by Bradley Russell.*

and definition. Uayeb ceremonies were particularly concerned with setting up directional shrines, or Acantun (Tozzer 1941:138n639; D. Chase 1985a, 1986; P. Rice 2004:21), but quadripartite imagery was integral to many aspects of the ancient Maya worldview (P. Rice 2004:76). Russell (2008a:657, figures 9.5–9.7) identified three shrines located in cardinal points within 300 meters of the city wall's exterior—to the east, north, and west—and he suggested that they may have been calendrical boundary markers (figure 4.2). Additional shrines may be found beyond the boundaries of Russell's 250-meter-wide transects—for example, one was found in Milpa 28a (west of the wall) that was covered with Matillas Fine Orange pottery sherds (figure 4.2; Masson, Delu, and Peraza Lope 2008:441). An outer set of ceremonial complexes is documented at a distance of 800–1,200 meters from the wall, where temple/cenote groups of

Postclassic age are present in at least three general cardinal directions (figure 2.1), including localities referred to today as Rancho San Angél (to the west), Santa Cruz (to the south), and Tichac (modern Telchaquillo). Like the smaller set of shrines closer to Mayapán's wall, these settlements and their temple/cenote groups may have been part of the symbolic regional landscape.

Key features within Mayapán's walls, including gates, elevated pathways (*sacbeob*), and monumental buildings, are aligned on axes that may have conceptually divided the city into northern and southern halves, as well as eastern and western halves (figures 4.1, 4.2). Figure 4.2 illustrates those axes that intersect with or pass near three or more features. Stone lanes formed by passageways between albarrada houselot enclosures tend to parallel these axes of key features (figure 4.1). Many more axes can be drawn among sets of three aligned features, but it is difficult to know which of these may have been significant to Mayapán's residents. Important Postclassic political centers were referred to with profound symbolic terminology, such as the "crossroads of the country" or the "navel of the world," particularly with respect to monuments integral to the 13 K'atun may cycle (P. Rice (2004:78). Unraveling the correspondence of specific sacred buildings with ceremonies corresponding to these divisions of time is difficult based on the archaeological record alone.

One primary north/northeast-to-south/southwest axis appears particularly important (figure 4.2). It extends southward from Temple E-11, near Gate D, through a number of features until it reaches Gate EE. A number of special buildings and facilities are along this axis or to its immediate west. To the south of Temple E-11 lies the open space of the city's probable central marketplace. Below this large plaza the alignment of features includes a cluster of the three most resplendent palaces at Mayapán near the only portal gate to the monumental center. The middle palace group in this cluster of palaces forms the northern terminus of the site's principal sacbe, which terminates at ceremonial group Z-50; the sacbe itself continues this axis (figures 4.1, 4.2). A nearly straight path is further traced from Z-50 southward to Gate EE. Heading toward Temple R-19b and the site's major pyramid (Q-162) from the east is another axis partly followed by a major stone lane that originates at the Itzmal Ch'en cenote near Gate H. As Bullard (1952, 1954) observed, this is the longest stone lane at the city independent of houselot enclosures, and it is also the straightest. The full details of Mayapán's pedestrian pathways are presented later in this chapter. They were important routes that connected gates, cenotes, major and minor commons spaces or market plazas, outlying architectural landmarks, and the site center. These features differentiated the urban landscape and exhibit a significant degree of planning and administration.

MAYAPÁN'S DIFFERENTIATED AND ADMINISTERED CITYSCAPE

Mayapán's organization can be envisioned as the cumulative result of settlement processes. Five processes merit special consideration: (1) initial settlement cluster formation by migrants from confederated towns, (2) governance of residential zones by officials of these towns or other appointees, (3) unequal development, (4) economic opportunities, and (5) the influence of natural and constructed facilities. The first of these processes is derived from Landa's (1941:23–26) account that supporting populations were resettled to the city to provide services. The possibility is strong that residential zones were initially composed of social segments that originated from confederated towns. Such a founding populous could have included overseers, servants, merchants, farmers, and craftspeople. Through time, links between settlement zone officials and hometown affiliations of neighborhood residents may have been diffused as the population diversified as a consequence of migration, and some residents who were born in the city may have identified more strongly with the urban capital. Ethnic enclaves have only rarely been identified in the archaeology of Mesoamerica, and in those cases, ethnic groups were from distant regions (Millon 1976; Santley et al. 1987). Mayapán's migration from within peninsular Yucatán may not have involved groups with highly distinctive material culture (Masson and Peraza Lope 2010). More work is needed to determine specific technological or stylistic attributes of Mayapán's contemporaries in Yucatán that can be used to identify such groups within the city. Subtle attributes of paste, slip, and form of east coast pottery, as defined at Cozumel (Connor 1984; Peraza Lope 1993), are useful for documenting these imports at Mayapán, but they are quite rare and not widely distributed. New sourcing data on east coast Payil Red and Navula Unslipped pottery shows some promise for distinstinguishing these materials from similar pots made at Mayapán (Cecil 2012). Gulf Coast Matillas Fine Orange pottery is distinctive and also infrequent, but its wide distribution suggests marketplace access; for this reason it is not a good ethnic marker (chapter 6). Certain decorative attributes of Pelé Polychrome, as discussed in chapter 3, may signify relationships to the Petén Lakes Kowoj Maya (Rice and Rice 2009).

Officials originally appointed to administer residential zones would logically have shared hometown affiliations with settlers brought to the city, but we do not know the degree to which such subunits were sustained through time. The longer term evolution of Mayapán's administrative strategies would have contended with the bipolar influences of polity versus hometown loyalties. We know from historical accounts that factional social identity remained strong throughout the city's history, and one manifestation of subunit cohesion may have been close-knit neighborhoods. Despite these fractious stakeholders, the Mayapán polity remained intact for just over 250 years (chapter 2).

A third consideration that is useful for interpreting Mayapán's settlement organization is that political subunits of the confederation were of unequal strength and importance (chapter 2; Restall 2001). Likewise, there is no reason to expect that residential zones of the city were evenly developed, either due to their affiliation with leaders of varying political clout or other hierarchical processes affecting colonization and opportunities for wealth (McAnany 1995). The oldest residential zones—those originally settled—were probably affiliated with major political groups of northwest Yucatán and may have been more invested in the confederated government during times of stability. This inference is drawn from Landa's account that jurisdiction over towns and lands was divided among the lords of the confederacy "according to the antiquity of his lineage and his personal value" (Landa 1941:23–26). At other Mesoamerican cities, uneven neighborhood development is observed in terms of the presence or absence of public architecture (Mastache, Cobean, and Healan 2002:173; Cowgill, Altschul, and Sload 1984). Similarly, the western fourth of Mayapán contrasts with zones to the east, as it lacks elite or public architecture (figure 4.1).

Some neighborhoods might have been formed or filled in later due to the attractive forces of urban commerce that fostered entrepreneurial opportunities or obligatory duties. These processes represent our fourth consideration of principles contributing to settlement form. Through the 250 or so years of Mayapán's history, some residential zones would have been populated by families who did not share mutual ties to places of origin. Our primary evidence for this observation lies in the proximal juxtaposition of typical and atypical house forms, houses engaged in surplus crafting that are adjacent to houses that were not, and houses with high proportions of valuable trade goods alongside those with diminished quantities (chapters 5, 6). Although most residential zones exhibit this diversity, there is one locality where surplus crafting houses are densely clustered: Milpa 1, to the immediate west of the monumental center (chapters 5, 6). Extensive clusters of craft specialists are relatively rare at Mesoamerican sites but are known from Otumba, Teotihuacan, and Colha (T. Charlton 1994; Charlton, Nichols, and Charlton 2000; Millon 1976; Manzanilla 1996; Shafer and Hester 1983).

The influence of infrastructural elements represents a fifth consideration that influenced settlement patterns. Such facilities include marketplaces, roads, monumental buildings, gates, and water sources that would have differentiated the urban zone. Brown (2005, 2006) demonstrates the importance of cenotes for socio-spatial identity at Mayapán, and it is probable that cenotes were significant at multiple scales, including lineage, neighborhood, larger intra-city residential units, and for the site as a whole. As Brown observes, cenotes have heterogenous attributes such as size, water, access, formation history, and the presence or absence of caves. Certain cenotes would have been more important than others for specific purposes, and the location of large cenotes and those that represented good water sources were especially important. Access roads, temple groups, and nearby gates would have enhanced their value to the city's residents at all of the levels outlined by Rapoport (1990). In the absence of clear boundary markers for settlement zones of the city, focal nodes that conjoined anthropogenic and natural resources have good potential for identifying vicinities of special importance to the city's residents. We consider it likely that these nodes served as neighborhood as well as citywide landscape markers.

In the remainder of this chapter, we review the evidence for focal features and their connectedness. Each type of focal feature is considered individually, including market spaces, outlying public architecture, and elite residences. Roads and cenotes are discussed together, as their relationship appears explicit.

SETTLEMENT DATA

Three new kinds of mapping data shed light on the organization of Mayapán. The first data set is from a digitized GIS version of Morris Jones's (1962) Mayapán site map created by Timothy S. Hare. This resource permits new observations on the distribution and location of elite features in the settlement zone.

The second data set includes maps of thirty-six modern, cleared agricultural fields created by the PEMY project from 2001 to 2003 (figure 1.7; Hare 2008a). Twenty-one of these milpa fields are from within the city wall and are of greatest importance to this study. Our mapped milpa data includes many features mapped by Jones (1962), but the new information contains greater detail and is more accurate (Hare 2008a). The Jones map is useful for identifying the structures and navigating the city, but it varies widely in the accuracy of the size, number, orientation, location, and details of architectural features. The PEMY map data is supplemented with additional information collected on features and stone-lined lanes from areas outside of the mapped fields (Hare 2008a).

The third major data set is from previously unpublished maps created by Bullard (figure 4.3). We located these maps in Carnegie project archival

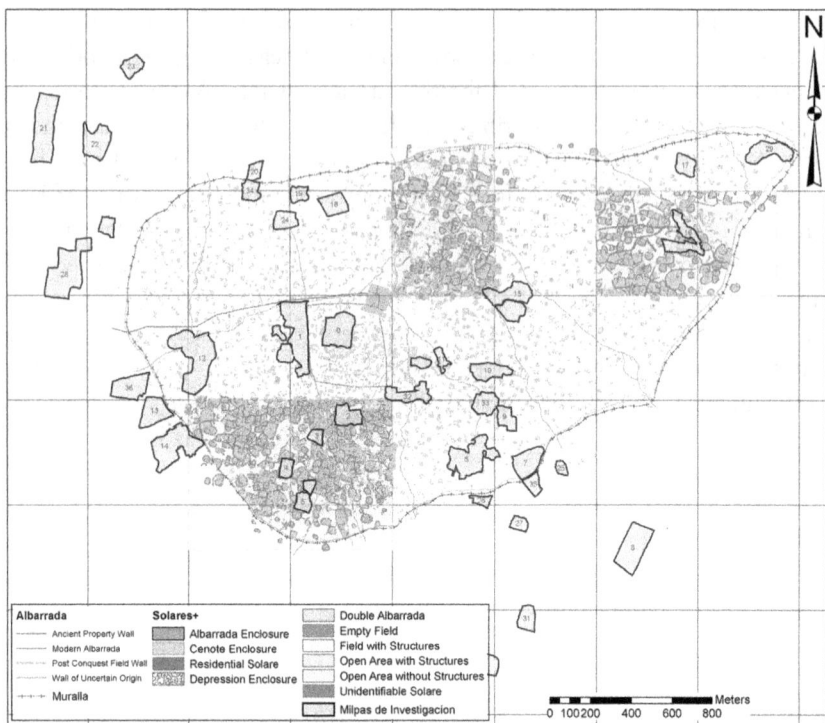

FIGURE 4.3 *Map of Mayapán showing areas with mapped albarradas, including those mapped by William Bullard (shaded squares), and irregular milpa sample units from the PEMY project. Map by Timothy Hare, using Bullard's archival map from Harvard's Peabody Museum.*

records at the Peabody Museum of Archaeology and Ethnology at Harvard University, and we use them here with the Peabody's permission. Bullard's (1952, 1954; A. Smith 1962:figure 1) work on documenting houselot walls and searching for stone-lined pedestrian pathways through Mayapán is well known, but the only published maps of his efforts are from Squares H and I (A. Smith 1962:figure 1). Squares H and I had the longest segments of lanes found at Mayapán, and these were viewed as atypical for the site. As it turns out, Bullard also recorded all of the albarrada walls present in Squares D/K, AA/DD, and Z/EE, which he mentioned in an early publication (Bullard 1952:36). We located his penciled recordings of these walled spaces on an early version of Jones's map in the Peabody archives. Hare (2008b) digitized this information. The twenty-two PEMY milpa localities have similarly mapped data of all walled features, but the milpa sample areas are of irregular shape. In contrast, the large, contiguous areas of Bullard's 500 × 500 meter squares offer improved analytical opportunities. Bullard's data also covers areas where we have the least mapped milpa samples. His information has enabled us to reconstruct longer pedestrian pathways between houselots from major city gates toward destinations in the city's interior. There are some limitations to the Bullard data. We have less confidence in the types, dimensions, and shapes of walled areas than in our own data mapped with newer survey technologies.

MARKET SPACES

Mayapán's Main Plaza, defined by the quadrangular space between the site's main pyramid (Q-162, the Temple of Kukulcan) and Hall Q-81/Temple Q-80, is quite small, and an even smaller plaza exists to the north, between Q-80 and Hall Q-64. This area is too small to have served as a major marketplace. Bullard's maps of houselot walls reveal a large, rectangular plaza (250 × 150 meters) in Square K, located approximately midway between Mayapán's monumental center and a major northern gate in the city wall, Gate D (figure 4.4). Other open spaces exist within the settlement zone that may represent market spaces that served nearby residential zones. These are more difficult to interpret as market spaces, as they could have served as general purpose "commons" areas that were used for a variety of purposes, including commercial activities (Dahlin et al. 2010:206). One example of an open area is near Gate H, by the Itzmal Ch'en group (figure 4.5). Other relatively empty spaces are located near city gates (e.g., Gate B) and are also within the heart of the walled settlement, as the structure density map indicates (figure 4.6). It is reasonable to infer that local neighborhood market plazas may have served nearby residents with a smaller range of goods and that the city also maintained a larger, central market plaza that hosted visiting merchants who sold more nonlocal or non-regional items to each other and citizens of the political capital. A similar nested system of market exchange has also been proposed for Tikal (Fry 2003).

The Square K plaza is different from other open spaces at Mayapán in terms of its large size, rectangular shape, and internal features (figure 4.4). This space is oriented northeast-southwest, essentially on an axis that aligns the site center to Gate D. It is devoid of houselot walls or dwellings. An extension of the Square K marketplace may be present in Square R (figure 4.6), which has no mapped houses. The combined Square K and R spaces form a large L-shape near the city's center (figure 4.6). One expectation of marketplaces

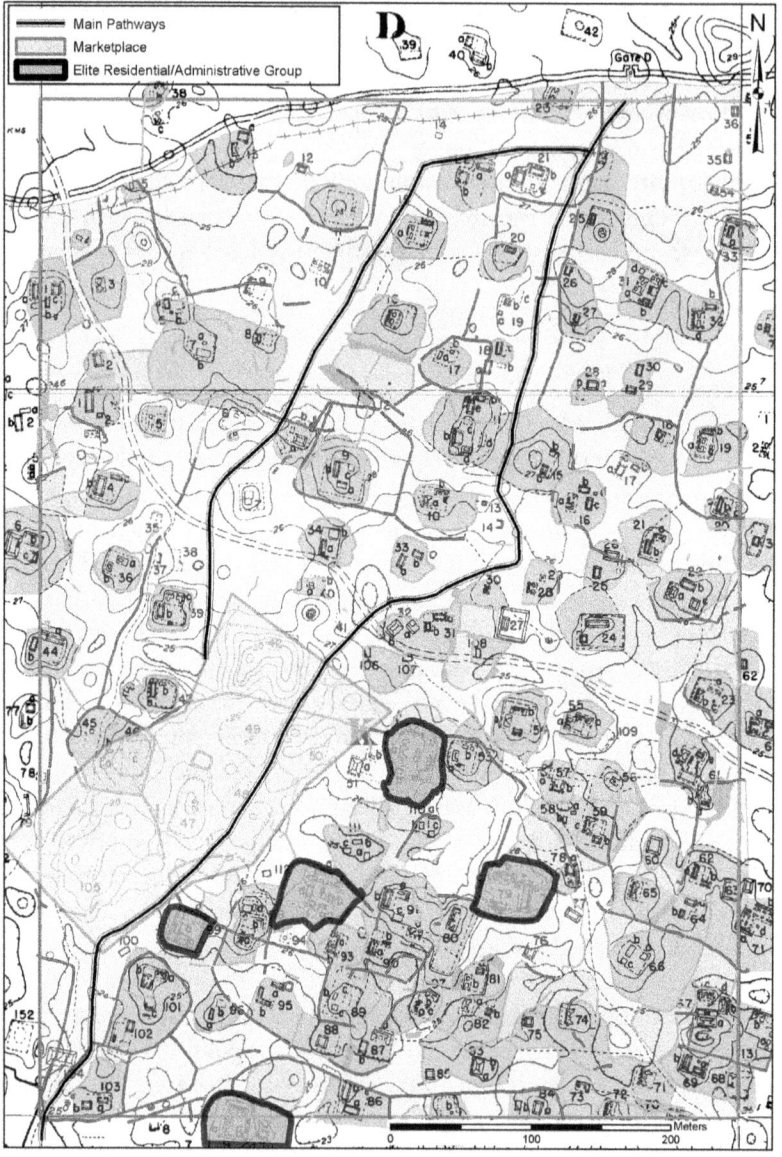

FIGURE 4.4. *The gray-shaded rectangular space indicates a probable marketplace in Square K. A concentration of elite and public buildings is found to the east of the plaza. Pathways between houselots are traced from this area to Gate D. Note the large platform K-42 at the north end of the marketplace. Map by Timothy Hare from Bullard's archival map, courtesy of the Peabody Museum.*

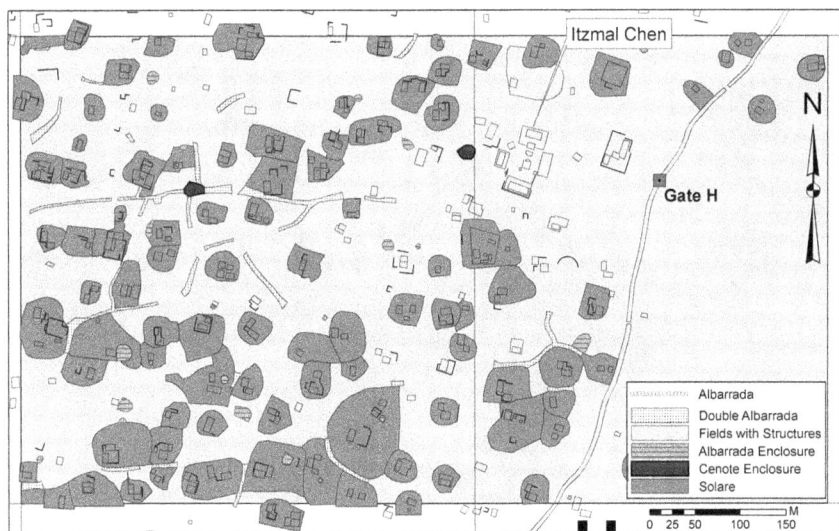

FIGURE 4.5. *The map illustrates an open space between the Itzmal Ch'en ceremonial group and Gate H as well as enclosed houselot spaces, enclosed field spaces, and independent stone lanes. Map by Timothy Hare from A. Smith (1962:figure 1).*

is the presence of nonresidential alignments or architecture that may have served as stall foundations or other market buildings. These types of alignments led Karl Ruppert (1943:230) to suggest a market space in the Group of One-Thousand Columns at Chichén Itzá and Tourtellot and Sabloff (1994) to propose the same for the Mirador Flats area of Sayil. Bruce H. Dahlin's recent work (Dahlin et al. 2005, 2007) identifies similar features in an ancient marketplace at Chunchucmil. Such alignments are present in the Square K plaza and have not yet been observed elsewhere at the site (figure 4.4). Smaller, more asymmetrical open spaces within the city lack evidence for nonresidential alignments.

Structures K-40, K-41, K-47, K-48, K-49, K-50, and K-105 represent examples of such alignments in the Square K plaza (figure 4.4). All of these structures (except K-49) are shown as dashed lines on the Jones map, suggesting that some of these were modifications of natural contours or that they were generally ephemeral (unlike almost all of the houses mapped at the city). The K-49 feature consists of two small bench-sized features in the center of the field. Anomalous Structure K-42 is of particular interest (figure 4.4). Located at the north edge of the plaza, this massive building faces south across the

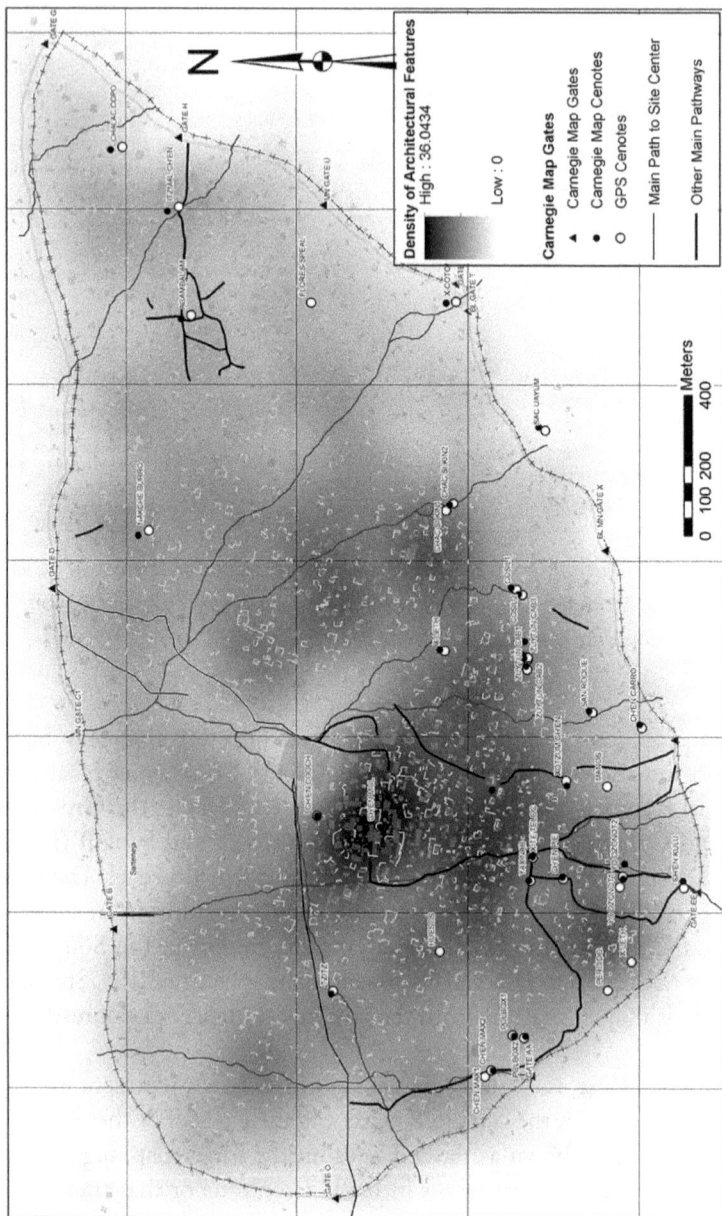

FIGURE 4.6. *The map illustrates structure density at Mayapán, cenote locations, and empty spaces, including the plaza areas in Squares K and R. Historical trails are shown in gray and known ancient stone-lined pathways, or sacbeob, are shown in black. In some cases they coincide, especially in the southern and western parts of the city. Map by Timothy Hare.*

open space and dominates the landscape of this area. It appears to be a large constructed platform over a modified hillock that rises 3–4 meters above the surrounding terrain. Its basal contour (at least 50 × 45 meters) was modified into a C-shaped platform, with a depression within the three interior sides of the building large enough to hold a truck. It has no visible upper rooms or wall divisions. This form is unlike any other edifice at the city. The lack of surface features is also dissimilar to Mayapán's residences; all other buildings of this size have clear surface remains of upper benches and room divisions. It was clearly a central feature of the plaza, as it slopes southward toward the open space and the ground-level alignments. A small shrine is located along the western edge of the plaza (K-51). Except for the K-42 platform, the ground is low and relatively flat throughout the plaza, and all other alignment structures are without substantial elevation.

Román Piña Chan (1978:43) describes a facility for Contact Period Yucatecan towns that he refers to as a "House of Commerce" within a marketplace, where merchants brought their commodities for sale to elites. Unfortunately, he cites an early version of Landa's account, and we have been unable to locate the original passage (Rosado Escalante and Ontiveros 1938). Similar market oversight is reported, however, at the Contact Period market of Cachi, where a building at one end of the marketplace housed inspectors of weights and measures; Piña Chan (1978:40) cites Gonzalo Fernández de Oviedo y Valdés's (1853) account for this. K-42 is a possible facility for these types of market oversight. The market at Chauaca had permanent thatch roof buildings (Piña Chan 1978:43), and the alignments (and K-42) in the Square K plaza may be remnants of similar facilities. The lack of surface features at K-42, which is unique for an edifice of this size at the site, implies that it supported a large pole and thatch superstructure. The Square R plaza also has low alignment features of a range of sizes (R-63, R-64, R-114). The north end of the Square R space is marked by two parallel rows of altars aligned north to south, including R-1, R-2, and R-3 that form the western row and diminutive Structures R-7, R-5, and R-4 that form the eastern row. The rows are approximately 90 meters apart. Contact Period commercial activities were sometimes linked to religious pilgrimage shrines, and this practice was also probably true for Mayapán (Freidel 1981; Freidel and Sabloff 1984). The presence of shrines in the Square R space implies an association of ritual with potential commercial activities nearby in Square K. Near the Square K and Square R plazas, a unique concentration of elite residences and public buildings affirms the significance of this area of the city, as discussed later in this chapter.

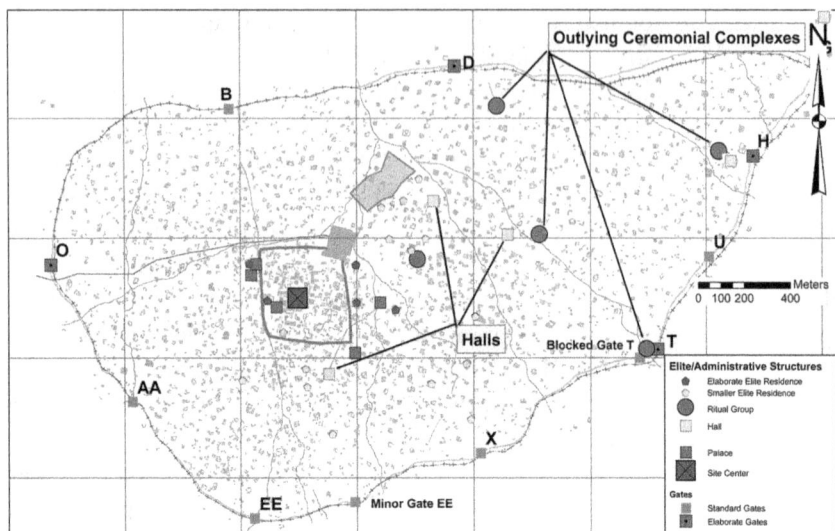

FIGURE 4.7. *Location of outlying halls and temples in Mayapán's settlement zone.*

OUTLYING HALLS AND TEMPLES

Outlying halls and temples, as well as the hall group termini of the site's principal sacbe, are distributed in striking regularity in the walled settlement zone to the east of the site center (figure 4.7). Carnegie archaeologists described four outlying ceremonial complexes, including the Itzmal Ch'en group by Gate H, the X-Coton group by Gate T, Temple E-11 (with a small sacbe) by Gate D, and a hall and oratory complex (J-109–111 group) in the east central part of the city (Proskouriakoff 1962a:127–31; A. Smith 1962:204–5). Temple R-19b, which is associated with an oratory (R-19a), should be added to this list. Like X-Coton Temple T-70, R-19b faces west while E-11 and H-17 of Itzmal Ch'en face south. Other focal nodes contain additional halls outside of the site center, including Halls K-79 and Z-50c, the southern terminus of the largest sacbe (A. Smith 1962:203, 223), as well as Hall 18-O-1, recently discovered outside the wall near Gate G (Russell 2007), and possibly another hall (J-122b) near J-111. These administrative nodes seem relatively "vacant" in the sense that elites did not reside nearby, and their official use was probably periodically timed with calendrical events (chapter 3; P. Rice 2004, 2009c; Freidel and Sabloff 1984:161). Two possible men's houses or schools (*calmecac*) were observed by A. Smith (1962:181), including Q-116 and Z-146—both of these structures are described as large, columned, and open on all sides. Although Aztec ethnohistorical sources describe structures where young, unmarried men lived—and these may have existed at Mayapán (Proskouriakoff 1962a:89–90)—this usage is difficult to distinguish archaeologically from features that served as periodic guest houses for visitors, feasting, and conferral (chapter 3).

The J-111 hall/oratory group and the R-19b temple help to form a potentially significant axis and pedestrian route that extends from the Itzmal Ch'en group to the site center (Russell 2008a). A major north/northeast-south/southwest axis, described previously in this chapter, is formed by an alignment that connects Gate EE, the southern and northern termini of the site's main sacbe (hall group Z-50 and palace group R-95–98), Temples R-19b and E-11, elite residential group R-20–23, and Hall K-79.

Temple R-19b is centrally located within the walled portion of Mayapán's settlement (figure 4.7); the other three outlying temple groups mark major gates along the city wall. The R-19b group is part of the Square R plaza, and it is close to elite dwelling group R-20–23 and a suite of other east central features, including the R-9 elite dwelling, the Square K marketplace and adjacent elite neighborhood, and Hall K-79. It is unique among the outlying temple groups in its close proximity to elite dwellings. The location of outlying temples at the city strategically coincides with clusters of other features, including entrances, throroughfares, cenotes, and in at least two cases (E-11 and R-19b), proximity to the Square K plaza.

The hall found by Russell outside of the wall is spatially associated with a fourth gate (Gate G). The east central area within Mayapán is also punctuated by the J-111 hall/oratory group and another possible hall, J-122. The axis that extends toward the site center from the Itzmal Ch'en group aligns the J-111 group, Temple R-19b, the northern terminus of the largest sacbe (R-95), and the eastern portal gate (Q-127) to the site center (Russell 2008a:figure 9.21; Hare and Masson 2012). This axis splits the walled settlement zone to the east of the monumental center into northern and southern halves of nearly equal size (figure 4.6). To the west of the site center, an old road that was reused during the hacienda era extends from the vicinity of western Gate O to the northern edge of the site center and splits this part of the settlement into nearly equivalent north and south halves (figure 4.6).

As argued in chapter 3, outlying halls and temples represented important focus points for neighborhoods of the city. It is probable that secondary nobility (religious and secular officials) hosted ceremonies, feasts, and other congregations associated with these features. Justine M. Shaw (2001) argues that outlying temples may have helped to define ancient Maya cityscapes and that they guided pedestrian traffic through neighborhoods. Shaw suggests that landmarks, open spaces, and formal plazas were as important as raised roads. Mayapán's landscape was similarly populated with cues for wayfinding (Lynch 1960). Specific pathways traced at the city in the form of stone lanes provide further support for the role of elite halls, temples, and palaces as important practical and symbolic landmarks. These pathways are described later in this chapter.

ELITE RESIDENCES

The site's monumental center differs from Classic Period epicenters in that the main plazas lack palaces and are instead lined by architectural groups that include halls, temples, oratories, and shrines (Proskouriakoff 1962a:89, 99; Brown 1999:586–87). But the largest and most elaborate elite residences at Mayapán cluster around the eastern and western margins of the site center, and at least three of these could be termed palaces (figures 4.1, 4.2; 1952:196). We define two tiers of elite residences, based on criteria of size and elaboration (Hirth 1993a, 1993b). Table 4.1 lists elite residences identified by A. Smith (1962:218) and our own survey efforts. Some of Smith's "elite" residences were classified as such according to funerary offerings, although their surface architecture is indistinguishable from typical Mayapán commoner houses. These examples are excluded in our discussion of high-status residences in this chapter. More elite residences may be identified in future survey and excavation at Mayapán, as the Jones (1962) site map varies in the accuracy of size and surface details of architecture (Hare 2008a, 2008b).

Group R-85–91, excavated by Proskouriakoff and Charles R. Temple (1955), and group R-95–98 (northern sacbe terminus) each have vaulted tunnels that fully pass underneath their elevated basal platforms; only two such tunnels are known at Mayapán (figure 4.8). A third group, R-102–107, is atop one of the tallest basal platforms at Mayapán. It was built upon a tall natural hillock (or *altillo*) and is exceptionally large and complex (figure 4.8). These three groups are clustered together, aligned east-west, just to the east of the site center and its principal portal gate entrance (Structure Q-127, Strömsvik 1953).

Ten Tier 1 elite residences are recognized thus far based on size and elaboration (table 4.1, figure 4.1). In addition to the three palaces just described, five other large residential groups are clustered around the edges of the monumental zone (figure 4.1), including groups Q-208, Q-244, Q-41, Q-42, and Q-169 (J. Thompson 1954; Thompson and Thompson 1955; Smith and Ruppert 1956).

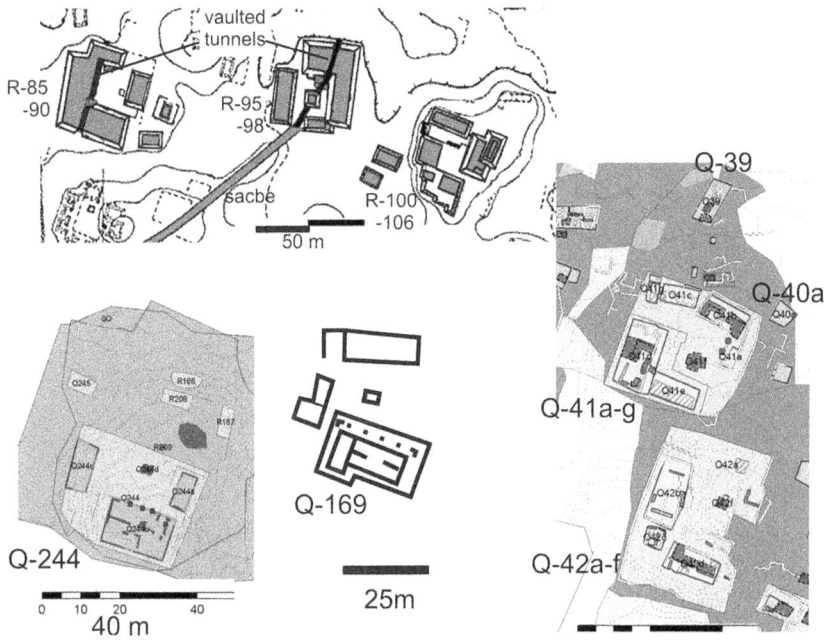

FIGURE 4.8. *Examples of Tier 1 elite residences identified at Mayapán. Groups R-85–90, R-95–98, R-102–107, and Q-169 modified from Jones (1962). Groups Q-244, Q-41, and Q-42 mapped by Timothy Hare.*

Structures Q-41, Q-42, and Q-169 are located on the western side of the site's monumental plazas; Q-208 is south of the Main Plaza; and Q-244 is located southeast of the center (figure 4.8). Two other Tier 1 elite residences include K-52, located northeast of the site center near the Square K marketplace, and group R-20–23, which is located to the east of the site center and near Temple R-19b, also close to the Square K marketplace (figures 4.1, 4.4). Group R-20–23 and Temple R-19b are located only 200 meters north/northeast of the northern sacbe terminus and the three-palace cluster mentioned previously and are near the Square R plaza.

Mayapán's only cluster of elite residential groups beyond the margins of the site center is found east of the Square K marketplace. Secondary elite groups R-9, K-99, and K-92, along with Tier 1 dwellings R-20–23 and K-52, are found in this neighborhood (figures 4.1, 4.4). A hall group, K-79, is also within this cluster, located 100 meters east of residential group K-92 (figure 4.7). There is a small attendant house within the K-79 hall group (A. Smith 1962:207).

TABLE 4.1 Elite residences at Mayapán listed by A. Smith (1962:218) as well as additional newly recognized examples.

Classification	Group	Area of largest structure in group	Total area of all structures in group	Location at site	Distance from Castillo (meters)
Tier 1 elite palaces	R-85–91	572.5	1,466.9	E/near site center near portal vault	282.0
	R-96–98	470.6	1,149.4	E/near site center near portal vault	368.0
	R-102–107	309.9	1,078.1	E/near site center near portal vault	444.0
Tier 1 elite residences	Q-41	187.9	1,745.7	W/near site center	173.0
	Q-42	152.9	2,187.6	W/near site center	154.0
	Q-244	183.8	1,277.7	SE/near site center	352.0
	Q-208	273.8		SW/site center	228.0
	Q-169/171	225.2	400.4	W/site center	138.0
	R-20–23	413.0	532.1	E of site center by Temple R-19/Square K marketplace	494.0
	K-52	—	670.4	NE of site center by Square K marketplace	652.0

Classification	Group	Area of largest structure in group	Total area of all structures in group	Location at site	Distance from Castillo (meters)
Tier 2 elite residences	Q-119a	282.2	398.2	NE/near site center	254.0
	Z-152	128.1	261.2	S of site center	657.0
	Z-39	119.1	1,229.9	S of site center by southern sacbe terminus	395.0
	Y-24?	102.8	198.2	SE of site center near cenote	719.2
	Y-45	177.3	1,068.4	SE of site center	926.0
	Y-41?	105.8	335.9	E of site center	785.0
	R-100	82.6	1,121.0	E/near center (by Palace R-102–107)	418.0
	S-133	151.7	593.8	E of site center	800.0
	K-92	201.1	403.2	NE of site center by Square K marketplace	552.0
	K-99	119.0	268.2	NE of site center by Square K marketplace	560.0
	R-9	81.6	208.0	E of site center by Square K marketplace	428.0
"Elite" according to funerary features (A. Smith 1962)	U-2b	Lack surface characteristics of size and elaboration of residences listed above.			
	Y-1b	Lack surface characteristics of size and elaboration of residences listed above.			
	R-127	Lack surface characteristics of size and elaboration of residences listed above.			
	Y-2d	Lack surface characteristics of size and elaboration of residences listed above.			
	Z-4	Lack surface characteristics of size and elaboration of residences listed above.			

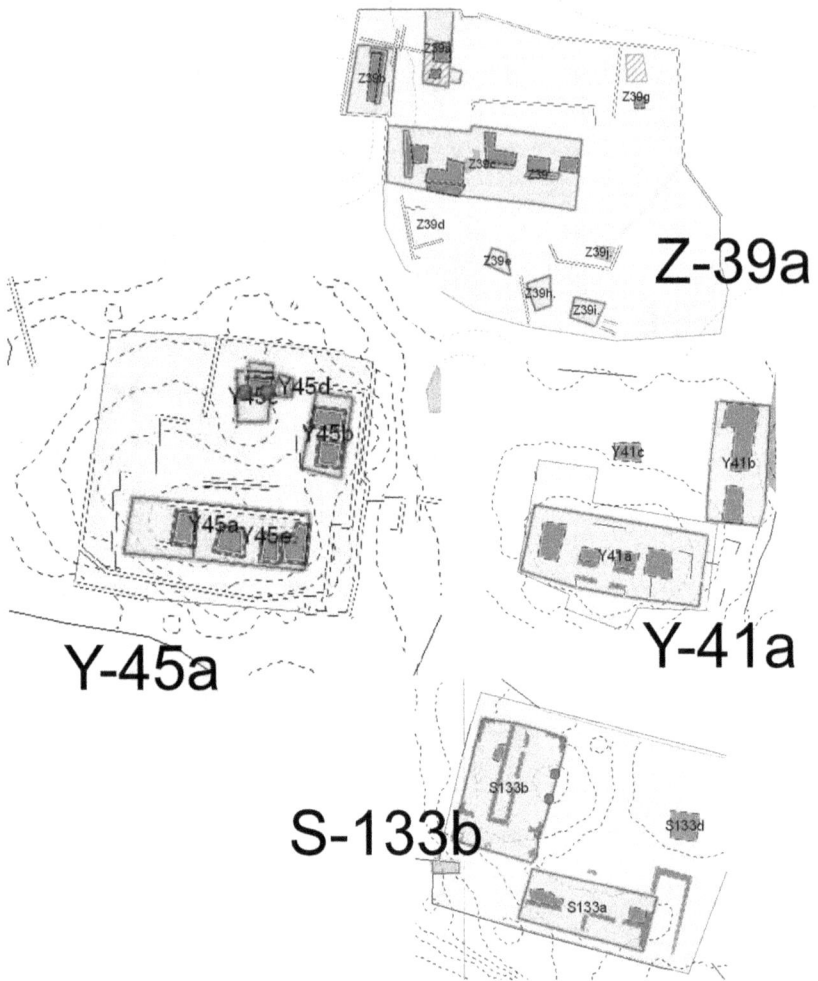

FIGURE 4.9. *Surface characteristics of secondary elite residences identified at Mayapán, mapped by Timothy Hare. For a full view of Y-45a's lower tier of rooms, which do not appear on this surface map, see figure 3.15.*

This group of houses and the hall gives the appearance of an elite marketplace neighborhood at Mayapán. But this zone's link to the site center is blended by the regular occurrence of significant architectural groups between the cluster and the monumental zone, including elite House Q-119, the three-palace cluster to the east of the center, and Temple R-19b (figure 4.7). In general, the zone between the (Square K) marketplace and the site center was a hot spot for elite activities, and by implication, northern Gate D (just beyond the Square K plaza) was an especially important entrance to the city.

Other individual elite dwellings are located near key features. Secondary elite Residence Q-119 is located on the eastern margin of the site center, and it is just to the north of the three-palace cluster (figure 4.1). Secondary elite House R-100 is adjacent to one of these palaces (R-102–107), placed at the base of the tall hill on which the palace rests (figure 4.8), and was probably part of this group. Elite Residence Z-39 is near to the southern sacbe terminus (Z-50 hall group). Other examples of Tier 2 residences are dispersed as relative isolates in the settlement zone (figure 4.1), including Y-45a, Y-41, S-133, and Z-152, although a pattern of pairing may be evident in the relative proximity of Z-39 and Z-152 (250 meters apart) and Y-41 and Y-45a (200 meters apart). Two of the structures listed in table 4.1 are possibly Tier 2 elite residences but need further investigation: Y-41 displays surface similarities to Y-45a. The map of its altillo indicates a rear rectangular shape that may represent lower infilled rooms like those of Y-45a (chapter 3). Structure Y-24a's elite status is also suspected but is unconfirmed. Examples of Tier 2 dwellings are illustrated in figure 4.9.

The proximity of Tier 2 elite dwellings to cenotes varies. Structure Z-152 is adjacent to Cenote Xot Zum Ch'en while Y-41 is about 150 meters from Cenote Chac Si Kin. A. Smith (1962:219) suggested that Structure Y-24a represented an elaborate house. Although no detailed plan of it was published, he mentions that it had four masonry columns that supported a thatched roof in the frontal room. Groups Y-24 and Y-45 are located nearly equidistantly (about 100 meters) from Cenote Cosil, and Cenote Zuytun Cab is also located 100 meters from Y-24. It is interesting that the Square R three-palace cluster and some other Tier 1 and Tier 2 elite residences in Squares Q, R, and K are not located near cenotes, yet these are some of the largest elite houses at Mayapán. Other factors such as proximity to the site center, the marketplace, and the route from Major Gate D to the center were perhaps more important. These families were obviously able to obtain water from more distant cenotes, probably with the aid of servants.

The elite dwellings identified thus far at Mayapán attest to the previously noted pattern of upper-status feature dispersion throughout the city's neighborhoods that Diane Z. Chase (1986, 1992) argued represent a "barrio" model of site organization. This model contradicts Landa's 1941:62–64) claim that the city's nobility dwelt only in the site center. It is also known that there is no consistent relationship between cenotes and high-status elite dwellings (A. Smith 1962) despite Landa's (1941:62–64) statement that "the wells, if there were few of them, were near to the houses of the lords." It is difficult to evaluate why he felt that wells were scarce, as twenty-seven well-known examples are shown in figure 4.6. In Colonial-era towns, palaces and cenotes were more closely associated (Restall 2001). Aspects of both Landa's and Diane Chase's models seem to be correct for Mayapán. Most of the Tier 1 residences are in fact within a 400-meter circumference of the site center (figure 4.1), with two exceptions in the market vicinity. These large groups were probably the homes of the city's most influential governors, or the "lords and priests" referred to by Landa. Tier 2 elite residences, perhaps occupied by "the richest and those who were held in highest estimation"—after the lords and priests—can be found in neighborhoods farther from the site center, and these probably housed secondary officials or lower ranking council members, some of whom would have served as administrators for neighborhood affairs (chapter 2). Diane Chase (1986:376) presented ethnohistoric and archaeological evidence attesting to the practice of rotating ritual-political activities at dispersed elite residences in the barrios of Postclassic Maya sites. Although elite residences are not found in all parts of Mayapán thus far, they are regularly distributed across parts of the east central and south/southeast central portions of the city (Squares Q, K, R, S, Y, and Z, figure 4.1).

The proximity of some high-status houses to the Square K plaza implies that long-distance merchants of noble birth may have occupied them. Smaller, outlying elite dwellings like Y-45a would have been occupied by mid-level officials or neighborhood priests. These residents were also probably engaged in trading activities, given the diverse nonlocal goods, a storeroom, and ubiquity of cacao pod effigies at House Y-45a (chapters 3, 6). Excavations are needed to determine the variation in production and exchange activities of Mayapán's elites in order to compare them to their Classic-era counterparts (McAnany 1995; Hendon 1992, 1996). Ironically, elite houses are poorly studied at Mayapán compared to commoner houses; Y-45a remains the only fully investigated secondary elite residence at the city to date. A range of part-time occupations of elites and commoners is described in Contact Period accounts, and we can anticipate diverse and variable activities (chapter 5). Investigation of these structures is also important for a fuller reconstruction of administrative duties. The presence of a throne-like receiving room and an elaborate bench at Y-45a, along with at least one rear storeroom, suggests oversight. The elaborate passageway and shrine room of this edifice points to religious obligations as well (chapter 3).

All of the elite dwellings identified thus far (except for one) are at least 300 meters from the interior edge of the city wall—the exception is Y-45a, located 140 meters from the wall. Dwelling safely within the urban zone may have been advantageous. Onsite administration of the city gates was clearly not the responsibility of important elites. As Smith and Ruppert claimed to have examined each building at Mayapán, square by square, it is unlikely that they missed any other Tier 1 elite houses (Ruppert and Smith 1952, 1954; Smith and Ruppert 1953, 1956; A. Smith 1962:173). Nonetheless, they failed to identify some Tier 2 dwellings that we located (table 4.1), and the infilling of rooms, as at Y-45a, makes surface mapping only partially reliable for this task. Future work will likely reveal more Tier 2 structures. Thus far, no elite features of any kind (dwellings, halls, and temples) have been found in the western fourth of the city (Squares N, M, O, P, BB, AA, and DD), nor, for that matter, in Square L (north of the site center) or squares that encompass the city wall—C, F, G, X, and EE (figure 4.1). Neighborhoods of commoners may have existed in these areas that were more loosely organized or affiliated with spatially disembedded administrators. Although elite residences were not located near the wall or gates, four gates were marked by nearby outlying ceremonial groups or temples: Gates D (Temple E-11), T (Cenote X-Coton group), H (Cenote Itzmal Ch'en group), and G (Hall 18-O-1). A. Smith (1962:208) suggested that House H-24 was occupied by local elites near to Itzmal Ch'en, but our inspection of this structure reveals it to be a typical commoner type dwelling of unimpressive size and complexity. Activities at public architecture near city gates were likely overseen by officials residing elsewhere in the city. A large, simple structure (G-17) located in Milpa 29 by Gate G may represent a sleeping facility for guards (chapter 5). Focal architectural groups with temples and/or halls provide further evidence of barrio integration with the site center.

THE STREETS OF MAYAPÁN
MAJOR AVENUE

Our inspection of Bullard's map of Squares K and D indicates two relatively straight potential pedestrian paths from Gate D to the Square K plaza. These routes would not have crossed albarrada houselot walls (figure 4.4). The Square K plaza and its adjacent elite residential district were situated along an axis between Gate D and the site center, and these features would have marked a major pedestrian route. Although fully mapped sectors are not yet available below Square K, the southern end of the market plaza is aligned with a set of highly conspicuous features to its south that fill the space between the plaza and the site center (figures 4.1, 4.2). Continuing south from the Square K plaza, one would have entered another empty, quadrangular space (the Square R plaza). Notably, outlying Temple R-19b is located at the northeastern edge of the Square R space (figure 4.7). Two of the houses within the cluster of seven elite groups by the Square K plaza are also near to Temple R-19b (groups R-9 and R-20–23).

Pedestrians walking due south of the Square K plaza would have crossed a space relatively void of residences in Square R, and rows of aligned altar/shrine structures (listed previously) may have marked a formal pathway. Individuals headed toward the site center could have turned west upon nearing the east-west alignment of the site's three palaces (R-85–90, R-95–97, and R-102–107) and entered the center through the monumental zone's only interior portal gate (Q-127), but alternatives are possible. A row of shrines is also represented by Structures Q-3, 4, 5, 6, 10, and perhaps Q-11, and these are near Q-116, a curious, anomalous building. A. Smith (1962:223) suggested that this open building with columns on all sides might have served as a school. Alternatively, it may have been a house of commerce such as that described by Piña Chan (1978:43). Pedestrians passing by Q-116 would likely have continued south to the the portal gate (Q-127) group, where they would have turned west to enter the monumental zone.

The portal gate (Q-127) would have been conspicuous, as it is part of a group that includes one of the site's four round structures (Q-126) and a large colonnaded hall (Q-129). The significance of this portal gate has been little emphasized since Shook (1955:267) described it as "the most elaborate and formal entrance to the ceremonial center of Mayapán" and the "principal eastern avenue of approach to the heart of the city," following Gustav Strömsvik's (1953) early investigations. Thanks in part to Bullard's maps of Squares D and K, we have documented probable street segments of the hypothesized route, and as discussed at length in the previous sections of this chapter, the routes are punctuated by key architectural nodes. The locations of pathways that we identify in Squares D, K, R, and Q are hypothetical, but they represent the most direct and efficient connections between key features.

Other hints about Mayapán's ancient road system are provided by a system of historical dirt roads through the city in use during the 1950s and mapped by Morris Jones (1962). In three places, these roads correspond well with vestiges of ancient pathways in our surveyed areas of the site, as shown in figure 4.6, on a north-south route near the western margin of the city, along another north-south route near to Gate B, and along a historical north-south route to Chapab (according to Jones 1962) that parallels the western margin of the site center and exits the city wall through southern Gate EE. In figure 4.6, historical trails are delineated in light gray and the stone-lined ancient pathways that we have mapped at Mayapán are indicated in black. Ancient pathways at the site are indicated by stone lanes, broad trails of flat bedrock, or both. Comparisons reveal areas of overlap and suggest that some of the trails of the 1950s were in use during the Mayapán era. Full mapping of the site will permit a more complete comparison. It is noteworthy that the historical trails, if ancient, lend a more orthogonal, gridded quality to the city street system, especially in the western part of the site, as the streets are nearly north-south in orientation and are bisected east-west by another old trail. The trails of the eastern portion of the site are consistent in their northwest-southeast orientation. Figure 4.6 also indicates that the north-south trails are relatively regularly spaced from east to west. Some, but not all, utilize ancient gates of Mayapán's city wall. The majority of those that do not utilize the ancient gates cross the wall near the gates. Perhaps the breadth of carts made the narrow gates impractical in the Colonial era and beyond.

It is notable that the R-95–98 palace is linked to a southern hall compound Z-50 by the site's principal sacbe (figure 4.2), which continues in the same northeast-southwest direction as the pedestrian pathway that we identify from Gate D to the center. Visitors not bound for the center may have traveled along this sacbe to the hall compound at its southern terminus and beyond. The R-95–98 palace is thus situated at the intersection of two of the city's primary roads: the route from Gate D to the site center to its north and the major sacbe extending to the south. The road that heads from Itzmal Ch'en toward the site center also probably led to this juncture. It is perhaps noteworthy that the Gate D route and the site's principal sacbe nearly bisect Mayapán into two almost equal eastern and western segments. Similarly, the east-west lane that heads inward from Itzmal Ch'en and the east-west historical (and probably ancient) trail that heads inward from the Gate O vicinity, divided the northern and southern sectors of the city. The full extent of the route from Itzmal Ch'en to downtown awaits ground documentation. These effects are illustrated graphically in figure 4.2. In addition to major routes, winding lanes used for neighborhood purposes divided much of the city.

OTHER ROADS FROM CITY GATES

The Gate D route expands on Bullard's published work on pedestrian lanes at Mayapán. He was especially interested in identifying parallel alignments of stone walls independent of houselot walls (Bullard 1953, 1954; A. Smith 1962:209–10, figure 1). He discovered the longest segments of lanes heading from inside Gate H near Itzmal Ch'en toward the site's interior (A. Smith 1954:244). This set of lanes is part of a matrix of other shorter segments and represents the most well defined set of pathways at Mayapán (figures 4.1, 4.3, 4.5). Bullard (1954:244) presumed that many of the streets through Mayapán were likely simple trails through residential areas, and some lanes are formed by spaces left between sets of houselot walls that define residential *solares* (enclosures). Only a few pathways were formed by parallel sets of lanes independent of houselot property walls (Bullard 1952:39. A. Smith (1962:210), discussing the Mayapán road system, concluded, "There does not seem to be any organized system of paths or streets—just confusion." Bullard and A. Smith were mostly concerned with searching for straight roads that were independent of houselot walls, perhaps due to the fact that an example was found in Squares H and I. But relatively direct pathways formed through houselot walls were also important for linking features together. Intervening open spaces and the use of flat bedrock roads were additional key attributes of pedestrian routes. Mayapán's lattice of interlocking solares, field walls, and pens may have added additional security that inhibited visitors from arriving at the site center except by prescribed routes, as suggested for Chunchucmil (Dahlin and Ardren 2002).

Four other ancient routes are identified thus far beyond those already discussed that originate at Gate D and Gate H (the Itzmal Ch'en vicinity). We traced the four potential pathways through houselot walls and open spaces northward from Major and Minor Gates EE and Minor Gate AA toward the center (figure 4.1). Pavement routes were not simply fortuitous in relying on bedrock naturally exposed by erosion. In some cases it is probable that level strips of bedrock were cleared of soil for the purpose of path making. The conjunction of sections of parallel stone lanes and exposed bedrock suggests that some path trajectories were strategic and that bedrock was intentionally cleared. Bullard (1954:243) excavated in a lane of parallel stones near to Itzmal Ch'en (by Structure I-54) and discovered a broad flat stretch of bedrock within them. The neglected surface had been covered by soil since the abandonment of the city. Excavation at Mayapán regularly reveals the modification of bedrock. At times it was scraped clean to provide a patio surface for dwelling groups. Bedrock cavities near houses were often filled in with soil and rocks to create a level surface (e.g., Hutchinson and Delgado Kú 2012; Kohut et al. 2012). The placement of burials into bedrock cavities and the fact that they do not intrude into one another also reveals an intimate knowledge of bedrock and its characteristics (e.g., Latimer and Delgado Kú 2012). The search for bedrock streets at Mayapán merits sustained scientific attention and will require excavation in places where surfaces have been buried.

Pathways are more difficult to identify in areas of dense forest, but parallel lane segments hint at their existence (Hare 2008a). Once the albarrada alignments of the site are fully mapped during the 2013 Mayapán LiDAR Project, all of the stone-lined routes from the gates toward the center will be traced. Currently we are limited to mapped sectors. Some lanes would have been less significant for visitors and would have served the needs of residential zones, as is the case for many cities in world history.

Paths from Minor and Major Gates EE

The paths northward from Minor Gate EE cross a zone of relatively open space where only a few houselot walls are present near the wall in the northeastern portion of Square EE (figures 4.1, 4.6, 5.1). One potential path could have veered west along the wall before turning north and intersecting with a historical trail to Chapab (just north of Structure EE-173). Further north, before reaching the monumental center, this historical trail passes an open space that contains two cenotes (Yax-nab and X-te Toloc). Brown (1999:525–34) observes that cenote names are used to designate places today and that this tradition probably has great antiquity. An alternative trail north from Minor Gate EE heads more directly north-northwest and would have reached Cenote Xot Zum Ch'en (the slight westward zag of the stone lane is at the cenote) before continuing northward to group Z-50, the southern terminus of the site's main sacbe. The sacbe would have directed pedestrians to palace group R-86–90, located just east of the center's portal gate.

Northward from Major Gate EE, there were two alternatives for pedestrians headed toward the site center (figures 4.6, 5.1). Both paths would have encountered Cenote Ch'en Kulu, located just inside the gate. One path directly overlays a historical trail to Chapab shown on the Jones 1962 map and heads directly toward the monumental center's western margin. It passes by Cenote Yo Dzonot (the first westward zag in the trail) and also reaches the location where Cenotes Yax-nab and X-te Toloc are located in Square Z before heading further north to the site center. The alternative route turns west at Cenote Ch'en Kulu, then heads northeast to Cenote Ch'en Pie, followed by the Cenote Yax-nab and X-te Toloc locality, which appears to have been a major intersection. This route ultimately joins the historical trail to Chapab. Although we did not anticipate finding cenote landmarks on these trails and simply sought to trace clear walkways from the gates toward the site center, it makes sense that these important landscape features and critical resources were incorporated into Mayapán's roads.

Path from Minor Gate AA

Two other pathways are identified in Squares AA and DD that extend into the city from Minor Gate AA (figures 4.6, 5.1). One path follows the interior of the city wall in a southeast direction before turning east, then northeast toward the Cenote Yax-nab and X-te Toloc location. This path would then have joined the historical trail to Chapab that also coincides with paths from Major and Minor Gates EE. Upon entering the city at Minor Gate AA, two cenotes would have been accessible to pedestrians using this path—going to Cenotes Polbox and Ch'en Max would have involved only a minor detour before proceeding inward to the city.

A second path heads directly northward a short distance from Minor Gate AA to Cenote Ch'en Max. It directly overlays another historical trail mapped by Jones (1962) that extends from Minor Gate AA northward. Although the historical trail goes all the way to the north part of the city wall and beyond, to the town of Telchaquillo, it does not cross the wall near any ancient gate (figure 4.6). Much of this trail remains in forest, but sections of it have been detected archaeologically in our work in Milpa 12 (mapped by the PEMY project) that covers portions of grid Square P (figure 4.6). This historical trail crosses another old east-west road that links Hacienda Xcanchakan (through an opening near western Gate O) with the site center. Just north of this inter- section, the north-south trail is delineated by an ancient lane of parallel stone walls that are independent of houselots in the northwest corner of Square P. This latter characteristic strongly suggests the trail's antiquity. Following the trajectory of this historical route from the stone lane southward through Milpa 12 to the southwest corner of Square P, it does not cross any houselot groups and is easily recognized by broad, flat segments of exposed bedrock that formed a natural pavement.

It was fortuitous that we were able to extend a potential trail from Bullard's Square AA map with the survey data from Milpa 12 in Square P and the historical trail mapped by Jones (1962). Cenote Ch'en Max is the only doc- umented water source on the entire extent of the trail from Square AA to the north wall. Sections of the historical east-west trail from Xcanchakan to Mayapán's center may be of greater antiquity as well (figure 4.6). A. Smith (1962:210) observes, "A fairly straight route could be followed from the large gate (Gate O) in Square O to the main group without crossing property walls," but no evidence (i.e., parallel lanes independent of houselot walls) indicating a definite road or street was found by the Carnegie team. The exact location of this route was not published by Smith or Bullard, but it may coincide with portions of the Xcanchakan road that are currently in use.

TIMOTHY S. HARE, MARILYN A. MASSON, AND CARLOS PERAZA LOPE

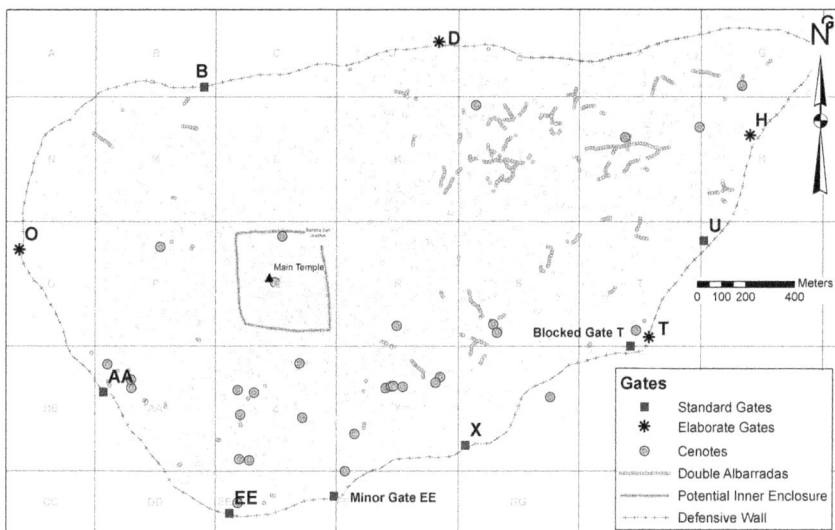

FIGURE 4.10. *Other short lane segments identified in survey of portions of Mayapán's settlement zone—these features are shorter than the pathways identified in figure 4.1. Map by Timothy Hare.*

PATH FROM MINOR GATE B

One final pedestrian pathway can be proposed from our investigations. It extends southward from Minor Gate B, located by the north part of the city wall. Like the pathways just described from Gate AA, it also follows a historical trail marked by sections of broad, flat, exposed bedrock (figure 4.1, 4.6). After entering Minor Gate B, pedestrians would have turned east for a few meters before encountering the trail that extends due southward. Oddly, the historical trail cuts through Mayapán's wall only about 120 meters east of Minor Gate B. As the trail does not cross through houselot walls and is marked by natural bedrock pavement similar to that which we observed in Milpa 12, we infer its antiquity. We marked this path as far as our mapping in Milpas 19 and 24 permitted. The route indicated on the Carnegie map continues all the way to the western margin of the site center and forms part of the trail to Chapab that joins up with four proposed pathways from Minor and Major Gates EE and Minor Gate AA. There are no documented water sources along the trail that extends southward from Minor Gate B.

Our survey team searched for additional lanes at Mayapán. This search was conducted with the help of local assistants—notably, Fernando Flores of

Telchaquillo, who remembered many lane segments that he had spotted in the forest (Hare, Ormsby, and Speal 2002). We identified eight additional segments of semi-linear lanes formed by spaces between houselot walls (figure 4.10). The average length is 33.1 meters, with lengths extending from 5.9 to 96.8 meters. They do not appear spatially clustered, nor do they concentrate in areas of especially light or heavy settlement density. Some routes may have simply served the needs of pedestrian traffic within the neighborhoods where they are found.

NAVIGATING THE MAZE

In contrast to prior assumptions that Mayapán's network of streets was confusing, we suggest that the mazeway of pedestrian lanes was coherently perceived and used. Carnegie scholars expected Mayapán's streets to be well marked by permanent features such as nonresidential stone lanes, which was only sometimes the case. Bullard was correct in proposing that the main streets of Mayapán were trails through open spaces between houselot walls (Bullard 1954:244; A. Smith 1962:210), but the significance of these trails may have been underestimated. Some routes directed travelers heading inward from the city gates toward features of interest such as interior temples, halls, sacbeob, cenotes, the central marketplace, and the site center. These lanes also connected various neighborhoods. Water sources were key features of the Mayapán landscape, as Brown (1999:541, 2005, 2006) has emphasized. The pathways described here indicate that certain cenotes may have served as navigation points as well as destinations of practical and symbolic importance (Brown 1999:541, 2005, 2006). The public nature of Mayapán's cenotes has been previously observed (A. Smith 1962:210, 265; Brown 1999:72). Although they are sometimes encircled by their own walls, they are not contained within the solares of house groups. Cenote Acanbalam, near to Itzmal Ch'en, is at the juncture of four lanes (A. Smith 1962:210). Although dense residential zones in the southern portion of the city had plentiful access to cenotes, this was not true for the entire city. Some paths, such as the one descending from Gate B, do not coincide with cenotes. As figure 4.6 indicates, some dense residential areas formed in areas without close access to cenotes, and some neighborhoods of lesser density were near cenotes.

DISCUSSION

The spatial organization of Mayapán manifests greater complexity than previously recognized (figure 4.1). The city is not simply an aggregation of residences extending outward from an elite precinct. A concentration of temples, halls, and the largest residential groups around the monumental center reflects a clear nucleus that has long been recognized (Landa 1941:23–26; Jones 1962; Proskouriakoff 1962a). Some elite residential groups and features, however, are found well beyond the Main Plaza (A. Smith 1962:264–65; Proskouriakoff 1962a; D. Chase 1992:128, 130, figure 8.4). Diane Chase's emphasis on the presence of outlying elites at Mayapán is refined in our closer examination of the size and elaboration of elite residences. The site's seven largest elite dwelling groups are found on the east and west margins of the epicenter. Some secondary noble residences are distributed as isolates or pairs through parts of the city east and south of the Main Plaza and in a cluster of such dwellings next to the probable central marketplace.

Newly identified pedestrian pathways extend from the city's gates toward its ceremonial core as well as to functionally distinct market and cenote spaces. These routes are visible as trails between houselot walls or independent lanes, over bedrock pavements, and through open spaces. The routes connect features such as cenotes, a marketplace, and civic-ceremonial groups. Prominent outlying elite architectural compounds are commonly identified at other primary Mesoamerican centers—for example, at Cobá, Uxmal, Chichén Itzá, Xochicalco, and Monte Alban (Blanton 1978; Folan 1983:53; Ringle and Bey 2001; Cobos and Winemiller 2001; Cobos 2004; Kristan-Graham 2001; Hirth 2003b:303). The identity of outlying elites is an important question for cities, as they can represent diverse social groups linked to home communities who arrived at the city at various points in time (Janusek 2002:52–55). The argument that some of these outlying elite houses were likely the homes of neighborhood officials is highly compelling (Folan 1983:53; Cowgill, Altschul, and Sload 1984:175; Millon 1976:25; D. Chase 1992; Mastache, Cobean, and Healan 2002:171). Outer temples and halls may have been nodes for elite interaction, hospitality, calendrical celebrations, and religious pilgrimage (Wallace 1977; Freidel and Sabloff 1984:41; D. Chase 1986; Freidel 1981; Masson and Peraza Lope 2004). Barrio temples have been identified and discussed for Teotihuacan (Cowgill, Altschul, and Sload 1984) and Tula (Mastache, Cobean, and Healan 2002), and implicit in this term is their role as focal points for neighborhood units in which they were embedded. Temples also demarcated urban zones at Sayil (Carmean, Dunning, and Kowalski 2004). The presence of replicated features in a settlement zone implies a strategic purpose of overall site integration (D. Chase 1986:364).

Neighborhoods are difficult to identify archaeologically, and a variety of other fluid or formal city subunits may have also been integrated by the activities at nodal facilities. The relationship of focal architecture with neighborhoods or districts at Mayapán is unclear, as there is no distinct evidence of spatial clustering or other meaningful residential divisions or aggregations (e.g., M. Smith 2010a:145). But Brown (1999, 2005, 2006) makes a good case for major cenotes as profound markers for social groups at Mayapán, and clusters of public architecture that include cenotes such as Itzmal Ch'en are good candidates for neighborhood or district symbols. A more complete analysis of neighborhood divisions will be feasible once Mayapán's networks of lanes are mapped. It is reasonable to suppose that outlying elite houses, temples, and halls served to connected the daily activities of ritual and economic life in Mayapán's settlement zone to the administrative goals of the site's government. The case for residential zone administration is strong from Contact-era accounts (chapter 2).

It is important to note that residential zones vary in their characteristics. Focal architecture is not found in all areas of the site, as the western fourth of the city lacks them. Similarly, George L. Cowgill (2007:279) observes that Teotihuacan's outlying "three-pyramid complexes" tend to concentrate in the site's northwestern quadrant, prompting him to doubt that they functioned primarily at the barrio level. Variation may have existed in the degree of settlement organization and significance, and smaller elite residences may have administered poorer or less influential residential areas of the city. Nodal features at Mayapán and earlier sites also served purposes beyond the neighborhood scale as landmarks and nodes of polity-wide ritual circuits. Four outlying rubble step pyramids are thought to represent boundary markers for Sayil (Tourtellot and Sabloff 1999:75) while other temples may delineate urban zones (Carmean, Dunning, and Kowalski 2004:435). From Russell's 2008a surveys and our own PEMY mapping, we have located shrine structures at some of the cardinal points outside Mayapán's city walls that are candidates for Uayeb or other rites that used quadripartite settlement markers (figure 4.2, Russell 2008a).

Artifacts or house styles tend to be poor indicators of neighborhood-scale social identity at Mayapán despite evidence for much variation in economic activities at individual dwellings (chapters 3, 5). The distinctiveness of House Y-45a's pottery and architecture (chapter 3) contrasts with other houses investigated at the city, and it is probable that continued extensive work at individual dwellings will reveal more socially contrastive assemblages. It is clear, however, that Mayapán commoner houses exhibit much overlap in material inventories (chapters 5, 6), and diversity may be more marked at elite dwellings.

At least three important neighborhoods at Mayapán are distinguished by high social status or occupation. These zones loosely conform to Kevin Lynch's

(1960:103) expectation for districts as "an area of homogenous character, recognized by clues that are homogenous throughout the district, and are discontinuous elsewhere." The Tier 1 elite residences that bracket the monumental center represent a key component of epicentral Mayapán, which was the center for civic-ceremonial activities and activities of top-ranking nobles and priests. A second cluster of elite residences, as well as a hall group and a temple group to the east and southeast of the Square K marketplace, also points to an upscale neighborhood between the epicenter and Gate D. A third neighborhood, discussed in greater detail in chapters 5 and 6, is defined as a crafts barrio due to its concentration of households engaged in high levels of surplus production of shell, stone, and pottery objects. The crafts barrio (Milpa 1) extends along the western edge of the monumental zone and contains two of the Tier 1 residences. This concentration of crafting households is unique thus far for the site, and this zone was probably an important part of downtown Mayapán. The concentration of wealthy residents and the need for consumed goods in the epicenter were probably important factors that drew crafting households to this part of the city.

Key members of the confederacy were probably responsible for building and operating the major public buildings of the city, in a manner similar to that proposed for the organization of other late Mesoamerican cities (Hirth 2003b; M. Smith 2008). Like the Aztec altepetl, the Maya *cah* was a pervasive sociopolitical unit, comprised of leaders housed in a capital town, members of the nobility, supporters, and landholdings. Both of these organizational units had fluid geospatial territories as a consequence of dynamic, shifting politics, especially in the Colonial Period. For Mayapán, resident elites likely helped draw settlers to the city from their outlying cahob to provide services (Landa 1941:23–26). Once settled at Mayapán, the labor and service sector required organization for the extraction of obligations of work, military service, tribute, and ritual. The manner in which this was accomplished was likely to have been complicated and variable, given the citizenry's diverse origins and agendas (Canuto and Fash 2004:58–59). The founding of neighborhoods from outlying townships was but one factor in their ultimate composition and appearance in the archaeological record. The identity of neighborhood administrators and residents would have shifted with political climates and the emergence of new opportunities presented to those born in the urban environment. While top-down processes were probably instrumental to the founding and initial settlement of the city, we can expect that bottom-up processes increased in importance through time within the residential zone, especially with respect to dwelling group characteristics and composition (M. Smith 2010a:150–51).

For many Postclassic Mesoamerican states, a dialectic existed between polity identity and the pull of hometown or ethnic origins (Oudijk 2002; Pohl 2003b; M. Smith 2008:11). Intermarriage, pilgrimage, ritual calendrical cycles, investiture, and other activities promoted unity, at least for elite culture. The degree to which polity scale identity was embraced by commoners is a topic of considerable interest in Mesoamerican archaeology. Commoner dwellings and material assemblages at Mayapán suggest that polity scale identity was widely embraced in the settlement zone (chapters 5, 6). To the contrary, in Colonial Yucatán the cah was the single most important framework for social identity, although during this time there was no regional political capital that was working to centralize the cahob (Restall 2001).

While residential units may be highly replicated across Mayapán's landscape, as Brown (1999) demonstrates, this observation cannot be used to dismiss a higher level of organization of such units at the scale of the city. Other patterns of settlement reflect a significant degree of planning and administrative oversight than has been previously recognized. The replication of focal architecture, in our view, reflects an integrated elite political and religious bureaucracy rather than autonomous segments.

All "replicated" symbols are not identical. Temples differ in their orientation, numbers of staircases, decoration, architectural design, associated shrines or sanctuaries, and other buildings (chapter 2; Proskouriakoff 1962a; Pugh 2001, 2002; P. Delgado Kú 2004). Different decisions guided the construction of the Itzmal Ch'en and X-Coton outlying ceremonial groups. The temple at the former group is associated with three halls, an oratory, a circular shrine, and an attendant house; the latter has a double shrine/temple, an oratory, and a small shrine that is actually within the cenote. On a more general level, these two groups share attributes such as the presence of temples, cenotes, and a burial shaft in at least one building of the group—and these features are also shared with the suite of temples found at the site's monumental center in Square Q (chapter 2). On the other hand, unusual features exist at Itzmal Ch'en that may express idiosyncratic identity, including a high number of reutilized Terminal Classic mosaic mask sculpture fragments, a unique sacrificial stone carved with a prowling jaguar (Proskouriakoff 1962a:figure 10x), and a stone table supported by plaster sculptures (E. Thompson 1955). At major regional capitals, multiple dimensions of social identity should be expected, even within the same architectural and artifact assemblages. For example, John W. Janusek's (2002, 2004) study of Tiwanaku tracks patterns of incorporative versus transformative state strategies in artifact styles through time. At Mayapán, emblematic architectural conventions and certain ceramics (especially Ch'en

Mul effigy and Navula Unslipped non-effigy censers), as well as commoner house styles, reflect widespread adoption of symbols of polity scale identity (chapter 5). These powerful signatures are found alongside idiosyncratic variations in artifacts, art, and domestic and public architecture that likely reflect the identities of social subgroups (Masson and Peraza Lope 2010).

The notions of homogeneity and chaos with respect to Mayapán's settlement organization must be reconsidered given new evidence for signs of logistical and symbolic planning. Recent studies of other lowland Maya cities of the Classic Period suggest that radial or linear roads, represented by elevated pathways, indicate urban planning and political or economic integration despite the fact that orthogonal, gridded patterns are not observed (Chase, Chase, and Haviland 1990:500; A. Chase 1998; Folan 1992; Shaw 2001; Cobos 2004). Visual cues that lend structure to an urban environment can take a variety of forms, and focal architecture is critical for wayfinding (Lynch 1960:3–4). The degree of planning, and even the function of cities themselves, is likely to have exhibited considerable variation among central places (Marcus 1983:195; Dahlin and Ardren 2002). The dichotomy of planned versus unplanned cities is a false one imposed by investigators (M. Smith 2007:6), and various plans can be imposed on a city's landscape by multiple factions through time (M. Smith 2007:6).

While Michael Smith (2008:8, 2010a) favors the notion that epicenters reflect planning, in contrast to residential zones at most Mesoamerican cities, we argue here that planning principles can now be observed outside of Mayapán's epicenter. A system of pedestrian pathways, by which individuals navigated the city using landmarks such as market plazas, interior and gate temples or hall groups, and cenotes, also attests to a degree of organizational complexity that has not previously been recognized. In addition, the antiquity of at least portions of historical trails across Mayapán adds a semblance of semi-orthogonality, as these tend to cross the city in axes that trend east-west and north-south. Such structure was not accidental but compatible with the terrain and technology for facilitating the hustle and bustle of urban life. Michael Smith's (2007:8) criteria of "coordination among the buildings" is one measure by which the degree of planning in urban form can be assessed; this refers to a pattern whereby "individual architectural features appear to have been arranged and constructed in reference to one another." For example, they may be oriented in the same direction or oriented toward focal features (M. Smith 2007:8). Replication of public architecture across a settlement is one useful way to identify residential subdivisions at Maya sites (D. Chase 1986:364).

Mayapán's civic-ceremonial groups exhibit a high degree of replication and spatial linkages (Proskouriakoff 1962a). They tend to articulate with pathways and cluster with other key features of the site such as the gates or cenotes. Lines of sight would have been important at this city, especially from the gates to the epicenter (Shook 1952:15). Visibility represents another important facet of coordination of features (M. Smith 2007:23–24). The Temple of Kukulcan and Temple H-17 of the Itzmal Ch'en group, nearly 2 kilometers apart, are mutually visible, at least from their summits. The replication of epi-central monuments in outlying groups like Itzmal Ch'en conforms to another planning principle described by Michael Smith—that of "standardization" (M. Smith 2007:25; Delgado Kú, Escamilla Ojeda, and Peraza Lope 2012a, 2012b).

Economic patterns, attested to by artifact distributions, can shed light on the heterogeneity and integration of Mayapán (chapter 6; Masson and Freidel 2013). The regular distribution of lithic workshops throughout Mayapán's neighborhoods parallels a pattern observed at Xochicalco (Hirth 1993b) and suggests that neighborhood economies were one important aspect of city pro-visioning (chapter 6).

While defining the boundaries of specific barrios is not possible at Mayapán using current data, we hypothesize that outlying architectural groups may have coordinated activities linked to socioeconomic residential zones within the city (Hare and Masson 2012). In this chapter we have demonstrated the complexity of the urban settlement zone. Neighborhoods had unequal status, and some were occupied primarily by members of the commoner class. One area was a market and elite residential district; other zones were less densely inhabited but housed key landmarks and outlying ritual nodes for the city. Proximity to water and the size of domestic solares are factors that do not cor-relate neatly to residential density. Social factors, including norms and status, were compounded considerations that affected settlement growth and dis-tribution through time. Water access was one primary need that would have motivated and guided daily traffic on city lanes through Mayapán. Chapter 5 examines residential density, which is greater near the site center, but complex patterning defies a simple generalization. Mayapán was a garden city with many open or enclosed nonresidential spaces for cultivation or informal use (Killion 1992a, 1992b; Chase and Chase 1998; M. Smith 2011b).

Lynch (1960:8) long ago pointed out that "environmental images," created by interactions between humans and the environment, can simultaneously embody unique and recognizable meanings to the observer. Focal nodes dis-cussed in this chapter for Mayapán have high degrees of "imageability," or the capacity of a physical object to evoke an image in the observer that is legible and consistently understood (Lynch 1960:9). We have identified at least four of Lynch's (1960:45) five types of city images, including paths, edges, nodes, and landmarks, which may overlap for a particular feature. More difficult to identify are his fifth type—districts—which may be implied by the others at Mayapán. The city wall provides a clear edge, and full mapping is needed to see whether interior streets also functioned as edges. Paths, nodes, and landmarks tend to occur in conjunctions of pedestrian lanes, cenotes, gates, and outlying monumental architecture—some of which are clearly spatially linked to the city wall. The most effective landmarks occur at junctions (Lynch 1960:81). Paths in particular rely strongly on landmarks for their continued use, and ethnoarchaeological studies reveal the degree to which landscapes within and between settlements were symbolically imbued (Snead, Erickson, and Darling 2006). City images may vary in scale, and it is probable that we have only identified the most conspicuous of those at Mayapán. As Lynch (1960:101) remarked, "A landmark is not necessarily a large object; it may be a doorknob as well as a dome." Lynch's approach to the organization of the city anticipated landscape approaches to archaeology that have been making important contributions to research for some time (e.g., Haviland 1970; Folan 1983; Kristan-Graham 2001; Pugh 2002; Snead, Erickson, and Darling 2006; M. Smith 2007; Chase et al. 2011). Most comprehensive settlement analyses of ancient cities in Mesoamerica have considered some of the aspects reviewed in this chapter for Mayapán.

The architectural nodes distributed in the barrios of Mayapán reflect the practical facilities of its confederacy government. At its height, Mayapán was held together by an efficient governmental council linked to the settlement zone by secondary overseers. The city's residential zones were at least partly populated by occupants with hometown affinities from various towns of the confederacy. A plethora of religious ceremonies that stimulated the construction of shrines and larger monuments is implied by the distribution of religious features that punctuate the city landscape. At least some of these features were probably tied to political status and the hosting of annual, k'atun, or may cycle events (P. Rice 2004). This type of ceremonial transfer of power is argued to have united members of the Kowoj polity in the Petén Lakes, where public buildings at Zacpetén are attributed to specific elite groups (P. Rice 2009c; Pugh and Rice 2009a, 2009b:165). The formation of Mayapán was a cumulative process, the end result of top-down and bottom-up processes and agendas that were at times complementary and at times competitive. Like many cities, it was "the product of many builders who are constantly modifying the structure for reasons of their own" (Lynch (1960:2). The next two chapters of this book focus on bottom-up processes and provide details of our analysis of residential settlement and material assemblages.

5

The Social Mosaic

MARILYN A. MASSON,
TIMOTHY S. HARE, AND
CARLOS PERAZA LOPE

This chapter assesses dimensions of social organization from the perspective of Mayapán's dwellings. We assess dwelling style and size as well as patterned configurations of dwelling groups, benches, orientation, *albarrada* enclosures, and special function buildings. Data is primarily derived from mapping efforts within the milpa areas studied at Mayapán (figure 1.7), and thus, the patterns reflect surface observations. These findings contribute toward identifying social differences such as wealth, status, and ethnicity across the urban landscape. Wealth and status tend to vary along a continuum in the archaeology of complex societies (chapter 3; M. Smith 1987:318, 327). House size and elaboration are markers of elites (Hirth 1993b:123), and most commoner dwellings at Mayapán are easily identified. Nonetheless, as observed elsewhere, the status of some residences is not obvious, as they fit into the middle of a continuum of variation (Hirth 1993b:122). Greater segmentation and specialization of social space, as well as special function buildings, represent additional cross-cultural correlates of status (Kent 1990a:137; Hirth 1993b:123), although this is not always the case (Alexander 1999a:89, 92). Ideally, quality, quantity, and diversity of household materials and architecture are evaluated together to assess wealth variation (M. Smith 1987; Hirth 1993b:125). The assessment of surface architecture represents an initial effort to evaluate complexity and variation in the residential zone.

Household artifact and architectural data are often the result of a generation or more of occupation. Cumulative assemblages represent a "household series" (Hirth 1993a:25; M. Smith 1992). At Mayapán, settlement features reflect facilities in use during the city's

DOI: 10.5876/9781607323204.c005

maximal occupation in the thirteenth or fourteenth centuries AD. All of the structures examined within the city wall since the Carnegie project of the 1950s date to the Late Postclassic Period. Postclassic Period pottery of the Hocabá/ Tases phases forms the vast majority of our test pit (95.4 percent) and surface collection (96 percent) samples (figure 2.3). The ceramic database from surface collections and test pits is large at Mayapán (N = 140,292), as is the sample size of units of analysis. A total of seventy-two test pits (1 × 2 meters or 1 × 1 meter) and a total of seventy-nine surface collections (28.2 square meters) provide samples from a total of 119 houselots or other types of architectural groupings. This count of units is from sample areas within or close to the city wall. Bradley W. Russell (2008a) investigated additional contexts beyond the city wall that are not considered in this chapter. As figure 2.4 indicates, Terminal Classic settlement density was higher around the edges of Mayapán's city wall rather than in the monumental center and the central part of the Postclassic city. As almost no intact Terminal Classic architecture has been found within the city walls (chapter 2), the analysis of surface features within this boundary can be conducted with a high level of certainty that results pertain to the Postclassic Period.

SOCIAL IDENTITY AND HOUSEHOLD ARCHAEOLOGY

Social identity, including ethnicity, class, and wealth, are important considerations for household archaeology at Mesoamerican sites. Diverse social identity at Mayapán has long been surmised, based on documentary accounts of the city's Gulf Coast residents and analyses of Mexican-Mayan artistic elements in the site's central mural and sculptural programs (e.g., chapter 2, chapter 3; Pollock 1962:14; Proskouriakoff 1962a; Milbrath and Peraza Lope 2003a). The search for ethnicity in the archaeological record is fraught with methodological obstacles, and in many cases, evidence for group distinctiveness can be contested or is simply not conclusive (Shennan 1989). It is hard to predict how style will act within a given society, as considerable variation is observed cross-culturally (Dietler and Herbich 1998:242).

Despite these caveats, Mayapán evinces a clear normative dwelling style, to the extent that examples of Mayapán-style houses can be identified at contemporary Postclassic sites (Ruppert and Smith 1957; Rosenswig and Masson 2002; Freidel and Sabloff 1984:181). On a general level, residents adopted city-wide conventions in houses, pottery vessels, and stone tools. The construction of relatively standardized masonry houses may have been a symbol of commitment to community, as argued for Cozumel (Freidel and Sabloff 1984:181).

Closer examination reveals dimensions of idiosyncratic variation even within "typical" Mayapán houses (A. Smith 1962). Builders had leeway to innovate within certain parameters, such as the number and shape of benches, house size, number of houses or ancillary buildings, and houselot size. The dialectic between polity-wide styles on one hand and the more personal expression of hometown (or smaller) social group affiliations on the other is a phenomenon that can be studied for many ancient states (Janusek 2002:54–55). For example, Laura Levi (2002:136) observes evidence at the household scale of efforts to balance authoritarian influences of polity with local choices regarding architectural composition and form. Most of Mayapán's residents would have come from *cahob* in northwest Yucatán, where many descendant towns until recently constructed traditional Yucatecan houses. It may be unreasonable to expect dissimilarity among ancestral families from these towns who lived at Mayapán, as like today, notions of *costumbre* may have been broadly shared across the northwestern part of the peninsula.

Some ethnohistorical sources clearly describe ethnic enclaves, although not at Mayapán. For example, the lord of the Acalan (Gulf Coast) polity had an agent in Nito (Honduras) who occupied a "neighborhood populated with subjects and servants" (Piña Chan 1978:43, 47). Full excavation of dwellings and comprehensive artifact recovery represents the most effective approach for identifying ethnic affiliations at Mayapán, as at other sites (Santley et al. 1987; Stanish 1989; Meskell 1999). Surface architectural features of the type analyzed in this chapter tend to be less diagnostic of social subgroups. Although we identify atypical house plans in this chapter, test pits next to these features did not reveal unusual artifact types (Masson and Peraza Lope 2010). Until more atypical dwellings are fully investigated, their affiliations cannot be fully gauged. Cross-culturally, storerooms, atypical house plans, foreign cult items, and architectural patterns have been particularly useful for identifying the presence of foreigners (Trigger 1968:63; Stanish 1989:12; Tourtellot and Gonzalez 2004:63–64). The lower rooms (including storerooms) of Y-45a may represent an example of such distinctiveness (chapter 3)—unfortunately, they were not visible at the surface, and such details for other structures may be absent in our mapping data. The potential for social distinctiveness at elite houses may be greater than for commoner dwellings.

The social structure of Postclassic Maya society is well described in ethnohistorical accounts (Brown 1999) and is only briefly reviewed here. At Spanish contact, individual identity was strongly rooted in the *cah*, a birthplace settlement, where the majority of social ties were located (chapter 2; Restall 2001). It is probable that this identity has great time depth and that some residents of Mayapán wrestled with hometown loyalties alongside the influences of living in a large urban place. Maya society at contact had two primary social classes: nobles (*almehen*) and commoners (*macehual*), although wealth varied considerably within these sectors. From our own mapped milpa samples, the identification of elite versus commoner dwellings has been relatively straightforward, but we are doubtful that these distinctions can be made from the Carnegie map made by Morris R. Jones (1962). Matthew Restall (2001) detects eight levels of social status in the Colonial Period that nuance the two-class model—four within the noble sector and four within the commoner sector that may have pre-contact precedents. Social power derived from class, *ch'ibal* (family group) membership, wealth, and also a family's participation in the Contact-era *cabildo*, or community governing council, according to Restall. Slaves (female, *munach*, and male, *pentac*) represent a third social class that dates at least to the Postclassic era, but slave residences are difficult to identify archaeologically given that slaves sometimes lived and worked in the households of their captors (Scholes and Roys 1938). Warfare was often performed for the purpose of raiding for captives, some of whom were sacrificed and others were enslaved (Scholes and Roys 1938). Some were also exported for profit to central Mexico. Restall (2001:359) argues that male slaves were more common and that they labored in agriculture and fishing.

RESIDENTIAL PATTERNS

Some questions of occupational intensity, work specialization, or religious practice can be addressed from surface settlement data. Others are more difficult to answer. The issue of short-term or temporary occupation is significant for the analysis of Mayapán dwellings. Fortunately, test pits and surface collection indirectly reflect occupational intensity, as we discuss later in this chapter. Some houses near the wall were inhabited very briefly.

Another consideration of temporary occupation is the fact that visitors to the site, particularly traders, would have sought temporary shelter. Professional merchants were known as *ppolom* and traveling merchants were *ah ppolom yoc*. Some merchants paid to stay at local inns during their travels (Piña Chan 1978:43, 47), although it is not known whether such establishments would have differed from typical house groups with sleeping huts available for guests. Public buildings might have also been used to house visiting merchants (Freidel and Sabloff 1984:157). Alternatively, merchants may have stayed with family members who resided at the site. At Cozumel, upper-status dwellings were spatially associated with religious, political, and commercial facilities.

David A. Freidel and Jeremy A. Sabloff 1984:136–38, 141) observe that a probable merchant family compound was linked to an agglutinated set of platforms that may have been used for storage or other specialized commercial activities at the household level. Merchant activities were one option for income diversification for large family groups (Freidel and Sabloff 1984:181).

Another important question that has pervaded Postclassic settlement studies concerns the distribution of religious features. Mayapán was generally characterized as having widespread religious practice at the household scale (Pollock 1962:17; Proskouriakoff 1962a:136; J. Thompson 1957:624). This view derived from the fact that dwelling investigations were biased toward more elaborate examples (A. Smith 1962). In the areas that we have mapped, ritual architecture such as oratories or household altars is exceptionally scarce at ordinary Mayapán house groups. Similarly, effigy incense burners are rare in commoner contexts (table 3.3). At Cozumel, religious buildings were located at strategic locations within settlements or between them, suggesting that ideological activities were not strongly associated with households on the island (Freidel and Sabloff 1984:183–84). Freidel and Sabloff suggest that this pattern confirms the statements of documentary sources that priests were responsible for the majority of rituals. The principal deity of merchants was Ek Chuah, and Freidel and Sabloff (1984) argue that shrine pilgrimage was an important aspect of traveling merchant activities. Host communities at Cozumel constructed special shrines at a comfortable distance from settlements for pilgrimage and trade circuits.

The settlement variables analyzed in this chapter follow important prior studies on social organization at the city. Clifford T. Brown (1999:124) defined a useful hierarchy of units for the site, including features, dwellings, groups, houselots, houselot clusters, barrios, and the site. Brown (1999:143) suggests that houselot clusters, consisting of adjacent *solares* (enclosures) that shared albarrada walls, might represent a particularly important socioeconomic unit for Mayapán. Figure 5.1 illustrates a concentration of large clusters of houselots that share albarrada walls in Squares AA and EE of the site, and it was this locality that Brown referred to in defining this pattern. Pedestrian thoroughfares are traced between these clusters (chapter 4). It is not known how closely these residential clusters correspond to emically defined nuclear or extended families. Neighborhoods (*china*) or administrative wards (*cuchteel*) were divisions present in larger towns (Roys 1957:7), but these units were probably larger than the houselot clusters identified by Brown. Clusters of residences are also observed at Cobá, (Kintz 1983:181).

Such nucleation would have had serious implications for sanitation, yet osteological markers reveal that Mayapán infectious disease rates were similar to

FIGURE 5.1. *Clusters of houselots in map of Squares AA, Z, and EE of the Mayapán settlement zone. Black lines trace pedestrian pathways through houselot enclosure walls from the city wall toward the center. Also note partly enclosed fields, field walls, and open spaces.*

other, more dispersed Maya cities (Serafin 2010). A. Ledyard Smith (1962:267) also considered the problem of city hygiene, and he pondered the role of buzzards and pigs in eliminating organic debris. But peccaries were not particularly abundant at Mayapán (Masson and Peraza Lope 2008). Some form of composting and burning is implicated by the rich, black earth anthropogenic soil found in the denser residential zones of Mayapán (Brown 1999). In residential solares near the site center, this layer of soil can be 30 centimeters to 1 meter deep. Farmers today covet this soil for its productivity.

We take this opportunity to revisit some of the original questions asked of Mayapán by A. Smith (1962) by considering the frequency and distribution of ten specific attributes of the city's dwellings:

1) structure density
2) dwelling form
3) dwelling group characteristics
4) house bench shapes
5) house group orientations
6) shrines, kitchens, and enclosed bench structures

MARILYN A. MASSON, TIMOTHY S. HARE, AND CARLOS PERAZA LOPE

7) dwelling size
8) domestic solares
9) other enclosed spaces
10) burials

Burials and pottery have been subjected to special studies by our colleagues, and we do not treat them in lengthy detail in this chapter (Serafin 2010; Peraza Lope et al. 2008; Cruz Alvarado et al. 2012).

STRUCTURE DENSITY

The variable relationship between dwelling density and cenotes across the walled settlement zone was described in chapter 4 (figure 4.6). To the south of the site center, densely packed residents lived near multiple water sources, but this benefit was not uniformly enjoyed across the site. Distances to cenotes from most houses were not particularly prohibitive, as water was within 250 meters for many occupants and within 500 meters for nearly everyone inside of the wall (Russell 2008a). It is important to consider the fact that cenotes varied in terms of size, accessibility, and quantity of water (Brown 1999:73, 2005, 2006). Such variables would have inconvenienced certain residents. On the other hand, we have not recorded all of the cenotes and caves at Mayapán, and new examples have been shown to us by landowners during every archaeological season (Brown 2006, 2008; Hare, Ormsby, and Speal 2002). For example, Don Pancho Uc (owner of Itzmal Ch'en) and his fellow ranchers sealed entrances to water-bearing caves during the Carnegie era to protect cattle from bats (A. Smith 1962:211; Don Uc, personal communication to Masson, 2008). Settlement density is also related to factors other than water sources: certain areas of Mayapán that lack known cenotes (e.g., Squares L, M, and R) exhibit a density that approximates that of squares that have cenotes (such as Square Y), and some areas with cenotes (e.g., Square G) are sparsely settled (figure 4.6). As Squares K and R have a concentration of elite residences and features, the lack of numerous nearby cenotes is especially interesting and perhaps attests to nobles' ability to rely on domestic servants for provisioning.

The length of a neighborhood's occupation is one factor that likely influenced settlement density at the city. Family groups that endured beyond one generation had longer developmental cycles (Haviland and Moholy-Nagy 1992), and additional homes would likely have been built within or adjacent to parent solares where space permitted. The quantity of artifacts present provides one reflection of occupational duration. Occupational intensity is another factor that may reflect settlement density. Houselots and other groups that engaged in specialized activities to a greater degree, such as ritual ceremonies, feasting, market exchange, and certain forms of crafting, might be expected to generate a higher quantity of trash than their contemporaries in other parts of the site. Larger families living under the roofs of single dwellings might also generate more trash than smaller units. Dwelling and house group size are also indicative of larger family groups and may identify more affluent residences (Hirth 1993b). Some dwellings with lower structure and artifact density at Mayapán were occupied for less time—for example, House X-43, adjacent to the southeast portion of the city wall. A radiocarbon date from a burial in this field dates to the latter half of the site's occupation (Peraza Lope et al. 2006:table 1) and House X-43 (figure 5.2) had very low artifact densities. Test pits from similar structures nearer to the site center had ten times more pottery (Masson and Peraza Lope 2005). This structure was not inhabited for long.

We determined that the structure density, structure size, and artifact density of residential groups and surveyed fields are positively spatially autocorrelated, by using a multivariate test of spatial correlation to assess the relationships among the variables. Spatial autocorrelation is an appropriate method with which to analyze these variables (Fotheringham, Brunsdon, and Charlton 2000:202–9; Kaluzny et al. 1998:124–27; Kvamme 1990). It measures the extent to which data values in neighboring spatial units vary together. Performing these tests was deemed necessary before analyzing the spatial distribution of these variables, as they had the potential to independently reflect different patterns within the Mayapán settlement and undermine the validity of many statistical techniques. Positive spatial autocorrelation indicates that similar values are more spatially clustered than predicted by the assumption of randomness and negative spatial autocorrelation indicates that similar values are more dispersed. When spatial autocorrelation is found, the data set contradicts the standard statistical assumption of the independence of observations (Anselin and Bera 1998; Lee and Wong 2001:136). We tested for the presence of spatial autocorrelation using Moran's I, a standard test of spatial autocorrelation (Anselin 2003). The Moran's I statistic for structure density, structure size, and artifact density are 0.1906, 0.3339, and 0.1384, respectively, and all are significant at the 0.05 level. These results indicate that all variables are positively spatially autocorrelated, hence necessitating the use of a spatial measure of correlation between the variables.

The Multivariate Moran is a bivariate measure of spatial correlation that assesses the relationship between the spatial distributions of pairs of variables (Anselin et al. 2002). The Multivariate Moran correlation between artifact density and the density of structures by residential group is 0.2693 and is sig-

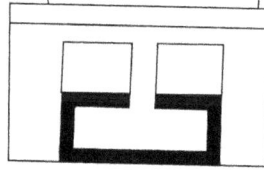

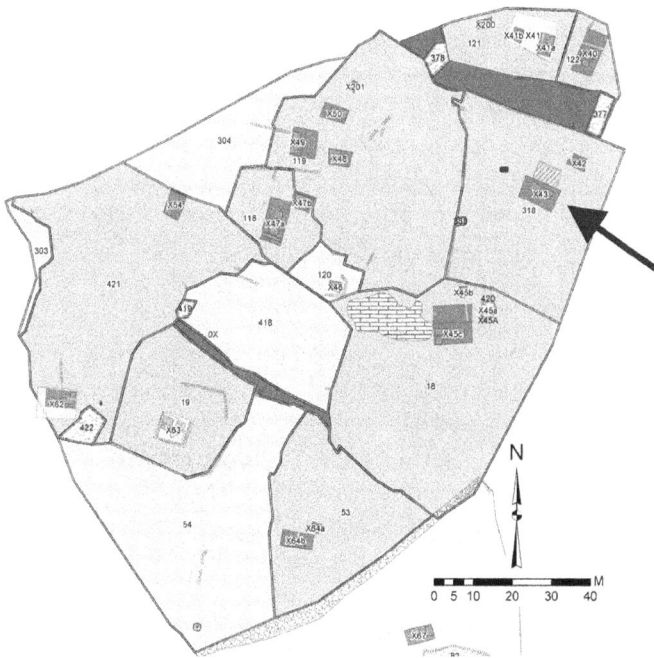

FIGURE 5.2. *House X-43, a typical style, is an isolated commoner house next to the southeast side of the city wall, with two benches and a rear room. Top right: plan drawing. Top left: frontal, southward view. Bottom: X-43 and its neighbors (Milpa 7), with two lane segments (dark gray), walled houselot enclosures (medium gray), enclosed or open fields and small pens (light gray), and sascabera depression (brick shading). House X-43 had low quantities of occupational debris.*

nificant at the 0.01 level. The Multivariate Moran correlation between artifact density and the area of structures by residential group is 0.3142 and is significant at the 0.01 level. These results indicate the artifact density is strongly positively spatially correlated with both structure density and structure area.

Frequency distributions of these variables are graphed separately in our milpa samples in figures 5.3–5.6 using surface collection artifact data. These maps illustrate that there are fewer houses and ceramics toward the wall of the city and that larger houses are more common near the center. These gross level metrics reflect averages for each milpa field, although we reveal in this chapter that variation exists within the city's neighborhoods in terms of structure size and function. Based on these observations, we argue that Mayapán expanded outward from the site center over time; many houselots nearer to the city wall were constructed and occupied for less time than those closer to the monumental zone. This pattern varies according to location. Residential areas close to major cenotes along the eastern part of the city wall illustrate some higher densities, but these are not equivalent to those in the central part of the city. Key resources, like large cenotes, were thus important in settlement decisions through time, even prior to the Postclassic Period (figures 2.4–2.7; Russell 2008a).

DWELLING FORM

The typical Mayapán dwelling form has one or two parallel longitudinal rooms, interior benches, and a frontal patio (A. Smith 1962:217), as observed at Structure X-43 (figure 5.2). The two-room house form fits Diego de Landa's (1941:130) description of houses that had rear sleeping rooms. Mayapán's one- and two-room rectangular houses with benches represent a distinctive pattern that differs from earlier sites in the region, such as those from the Puuc area, Dzibilchaltun, and Chichén Itzá that have alignments of room blocks or apsidal configurations (A. Smith 1962:figure 10; Kurjack 1974). Sleeping facilities other than stone benches are known from the Contact Period—for example, hammocks were in use at Cozumel when the Spanish first visited (Freidel and Sabloff 1984:16). Identifying dwellings for some sites can be difficult without excavation (A. Smith 1962:211; Freidel and Sabloff 1984:9), although benches make this easier at Mayapán. We observe that a frontal stone-lined veranda is not always visible from the surface, even in shallow soils where it should appear. The feature is not present at all of the Mayapán houses. Some verandas may have been constructed from perishable posts. This style of house is rare in the Yucatán Peninsula at earlier sites, and it is only occasionally observed

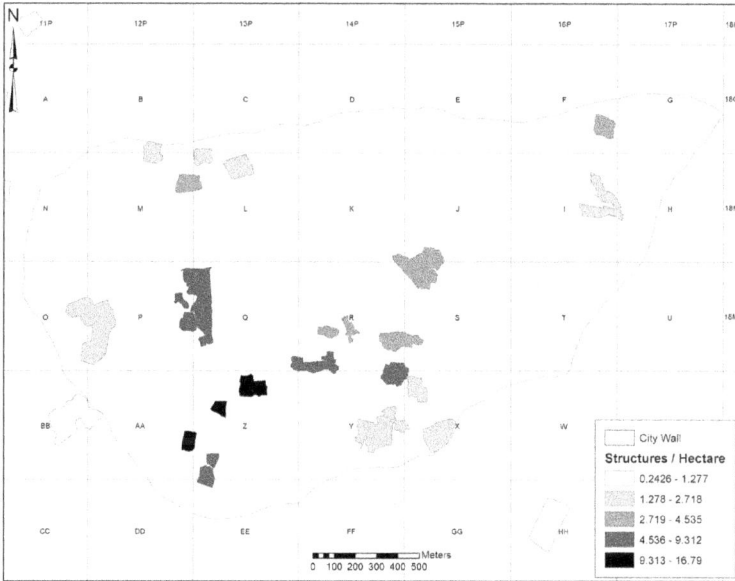

FIGURE 5.3. *Number of structures per hectare in Mayapán milpas surveyed by the PEMY project.*

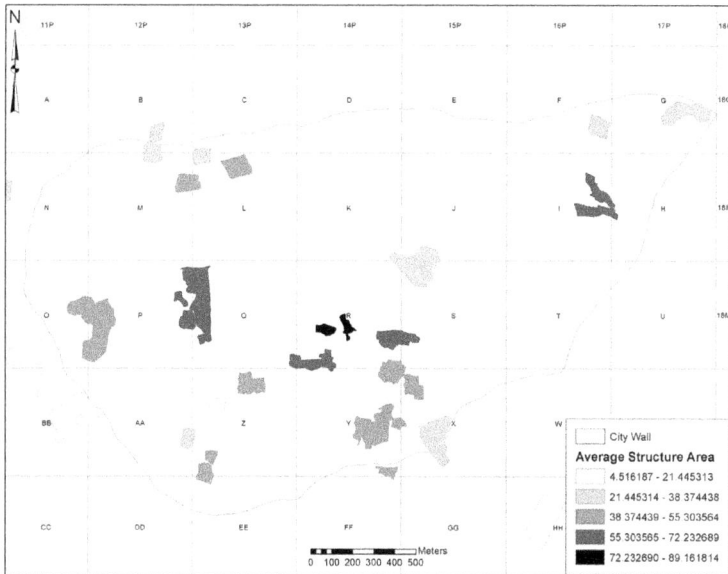

FIGURE 5.4. *Average structure area in Mayapán milpas surveyed by the PEMY project.*

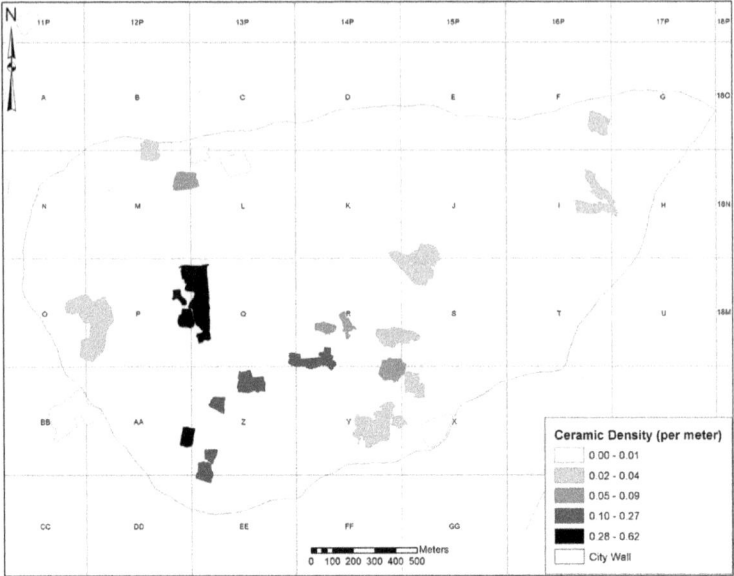

FIGURE 5.5. *Density of ceramics by residential group in Mayapán milpas surveyed by the PEMY project.*

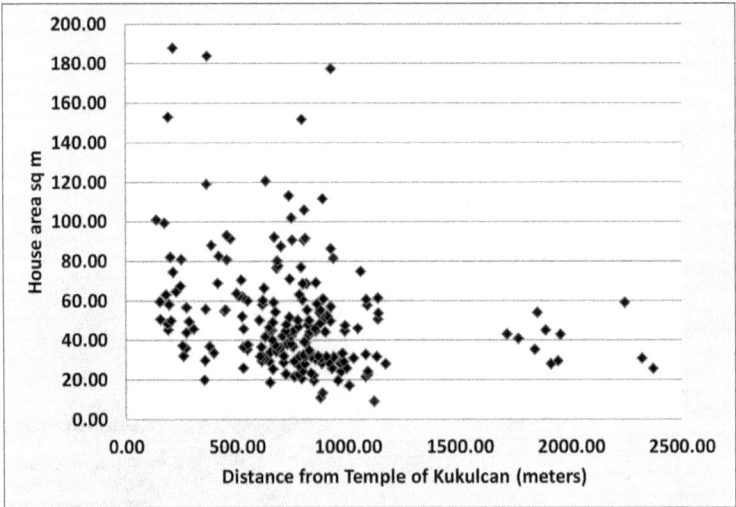

FIGURE 5.6. *Plot of house sizes against distance from the Temple of Kukulcan indicates that no large houses are beyond 1,000 meters from this monumental center edifice.*

at contemporary settlements such as Tulum and Cozumel (A. Smith 1962:231; Freidel and Sabloff 1984).

Other dwelling forms deviate from this plan. These include large square alignments, rectangular alignments, massive platforms, and bi-directional structures that are described in greater detail in this chapter. Table 5.1 lists additional low-frequency anomalies that may represent dwellings but are not described further in this chapter. These unusual types include long and narrow structures and commoner houses with rear self-standing or bench altars. They are primarily found near the site center, where structure form diversity is higher. Before describing typical and atypical houses, it is worth considering the number of rooms, as this is one diagnostic criteria of the dwelling typology.

The number of rooms can be determined for a total of 197 (of 221) structures in the mapped milpa sample. Of these, 32 percent have one room, 54.8 percent have two rooms, 9.1 percent have three rooms, 3.0 percent have four rooms, 5 percent have six rooms, and .5 percent have eight rooms. Benches are sometimes located so close to the rear wall that a rear room cannot be inferred from surface mapping data. Freidel and Sabloff (1984) point out a contrast between Mayapán and Cozumel: the majority of dwellings at Cozumel are single room structures (Freidel and Sabloff 1984). Our data reveal, however, that single room dwellings are also common at Mayapán. In fact, A. Smith (1962:217) notes that only fifty structures of 2,100 dwellings identified in his survey had two rooms.

Structures that we identified as dwellings in our milpa maps were classified according to the following working typology:

1) elite three or four room houses (N = 11)
2) big versions of typical commoner houses (N = 3)
3) typical commoner houses with one or two rooms and benches (N = 155)
4) a long, narrow structure (N = 1)
5) house-sized alignments of similar size and shape to houses but without benches (N = 19)
6) house-sized alignments with internal room divisions (N = 21)
7) a typical commoner house variant with a long rear bench (N = 1)
8) a typical commoner house with a rear altar (N = 1)
9) houses with front and back entrances (N = 4)
10) large square houses without benches (N = 2)
11) large square houses with benches (N = 3)
12) house-sized platforms (N = 3)

For the purposes of this study, the "typical" commoner house refers to the one- or two-room house with benches described by A. Smith (1962:217).

TABLE 5.1 House types in mapped milpa samples

Milpa	Elite 3–4 room	Big typical commoner	Typical commoner	Long house	House-like alignment	House-like alignment with room divisions	Commoner long rear bench	Commoner rear altar	House front and back entrance	Large square no benches	Large square with benches	Platform House size	Total
1	3	1	19	1	3	1	–	–	–	–	–	–	28
2	1	–	1	–	–	–	1	1	–	–	–	–	4
3	–	–	1	–	–	1	–	–	–	–	–	–	2
4	–	–	7	–	2	–	–	–	–	–	–	–	9
5	–	–	4	–	–	1	–	–	–	–	–	–	5
6	2	–	11	–	–	2	–	–	–	–	–	–	15
7	–	–	10	–	–	–	–	–	–	–	–	–	10
8	–	–	–	–	–	2	–	–	–	–	–	–	2
9	–	–	6	–	–	–	–	–	–	–	–	–	6
10	1	1	6	–	–	–	–	–	–	–	–	–	8
11	1	–	4	–	1	1	–	–	1	–	–	–	8
12	–	–	18	–	–	–	–	–	–	2	2	2	24
13	–	–	3	–	–	–	–	–	–	–	–	–	3
14	–	–	1	–	–	–	–	–	–	–	–	–	1
15	1	–	8	–	1	6	–	–	–	–	1	–	17
16	–	–	1	–	–	1	–	–	–	–	–	–	2
17	–	–	4	–	–	–	–	–	–	–	–	–	4

Milpa	Elite 3–4 room	Big typical commoner	Typical commoner	Long house	House-like alignment	House-like alignment with room divisions	Commoner long rear bench	Commoner rear altar	House front and back entrance	Large square no benches	Large square with benches	Platform House size	Total
18	–	–	4	–	–	–	–	–	–	–	–	–	4
19	–	–	4	–	–	–	–	–	–	–	–	–	4
20	–	–	–	–	–	–	–	–	–	–	–	1	1
21	–	–	1	–	3	–	–	–	–	–	–	–	4
22	–	–	–	–	1	–	–	–	–	–	–	–	1
23	–	–	–	–	1	–	–	–	–	–	–	–	1
24	–	–	6	–	1	–	–	–	–	–	–	–	7
26	–	–	1	–	–	–	–	–	–	–	–	–	1
28	–	–	–	–	2	1	–	–	–	–	–	–	3
29	–	–	2	–	1	1	–	–	–	–	–	–	4
30	–	–	1	–	–	–	–	–	–	–	–	–	1
31	–	–	2	–	–	–	–	–	–	–	–	–	2
32	1	–	9	–	–	2	–	–	–	–	–	–	12
33	1	1	9	–	2	1	–	–	–	–	–	–	14
34	–	–	3	–	1	–	–	–	–	–	–	–	4
35	–	–	1	–	–	1	–	–	–	–	–	–	1
36	–	–	8	–	–	1	–	–	–	–	–	–	9
Total	11	3	155	1	19	21	1	1	1	2	3	3	221

Typical (large and average size) commoner houses form 71.5 percent of our sample and house-like alignments (with or without discernible room divisions) exhibit considerable specific variation and comprise 18.1 percent of the sample. Atypical house forms, by definition, are rare at the site. House-like alignments could represent unfinished or poorly preserved typical dwellings, although often the internal room divisions varied from typical patterns—for example, by dividing internal space in a direction perpendicular to the long axis. Table 5.1 indicates the distribution of these houses in mapped milpas at the site. More details on selected dwelling forms are provided in subsequent paragraphs.

Typical Commoner Houses

Typical commoner houses form the majority of types (N = 155) recognized in the sample of 221 dwellings (figure 5.7, table 5.1). Many of these houses show little evidence of having had two rooms. Rear exits are also uncommon (A. Smith 1962:217). An examination of some of Smith's (1962: figure 5c, e, f) structure maps suggests that the rear walls of benches were generally assumed to have been masonry walls and to have also served as dividing walls for ambiguously defined front and rear rooms inside of houses, as observed, for example, at Structures S-30b, S-4a, Z-152a (perhaps), and S-26b. At more complex buildings, the rear rooms are more clearly indicated. Notably large typical houses are few in number (N = 3), but they occur in simple solares that suggest commoner status. We do not view these as a separate category from commoner houses. Elite dwellings that are part of large palace compounds can exhibit a typical commoner house plan but are distinguished by size and the addition of transverse rooms or greater internal subdivisions. They also form part of a large patio group and are situated on an elevated platform. Examples of commoner houses "writ large" in elite groups include some dwellings of the Q-41 and Q-42 groups of Milpa 1 (figure 4.8). Big commoner houses, by contrast, only have a two room plan and are not otherwise elaborate, imposing, or linked to complex groups.

Typical commoner houses (one or two room) are present in all milpas located within or immediately exterior to the city wall, and they are absent in five milpas located 250 meters or more outside of the city wall; these distant milpas contain remains of mixed time periods, so it is not surprising that Mayapán-style houses are absent in them. Typical commoner houses form 77 percent or more of the houses in fifteen milpas—eleven of which consist of 100 percent commoner houses and four of which have between 77 and 88

Typical Commoner Houses P-151c, M-61, X-43, M-58, Z-42b

Large square Houses P-70, P-76, O-54b, P-73, K-68a

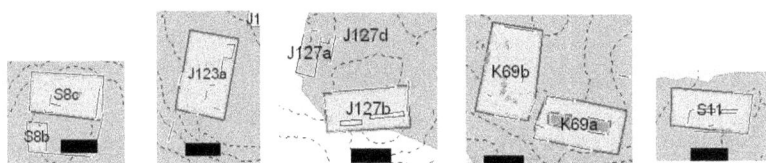

Rectangular alignment Houses S-8c, J-123a, J-127b, K-69b, S-11

FIGURE 5.7. *Commoner house styles at Mayapán. Shown at top are typical houses with benches, the center row illustrates large square house types, including four of five such examples in Milpa 12 and one in Milpa 15 (Str. K-68a). The bottom row illustrates house-sized alignments without benches, including five of seven examples in Milpa 15. Scale (black bar) is 5 meters.*

percent commoner houses (table 5.1). Sample areas around the margins of the city wall have particularly high densities of typical commoner houses (figure 5.8). The term *mid-city* is used for milpas located within at least 500 meters from the epicenter that are not adjacent to the wall. Six areas have between 70 and 75 percent typical commoner houses; these include two milpas adjacent to the monumental zone (1 and 32), one milpa by the north edge of the city wall, and the remaining three are found to the east or southeast of the main group in mid-city locations. Milpas with 57–64 percent typical commoner residences also show no spatial concentration; these include zones near the monumental center—quite distant from it by Itzmal Ch'en—and two mid-city milpas to the east of the epicenter. Two fields with 25 percent typical commoner residences include one located far to the north of the site and another area that is anomalous and likely represents a public access area to two cenotes (Yax-nab

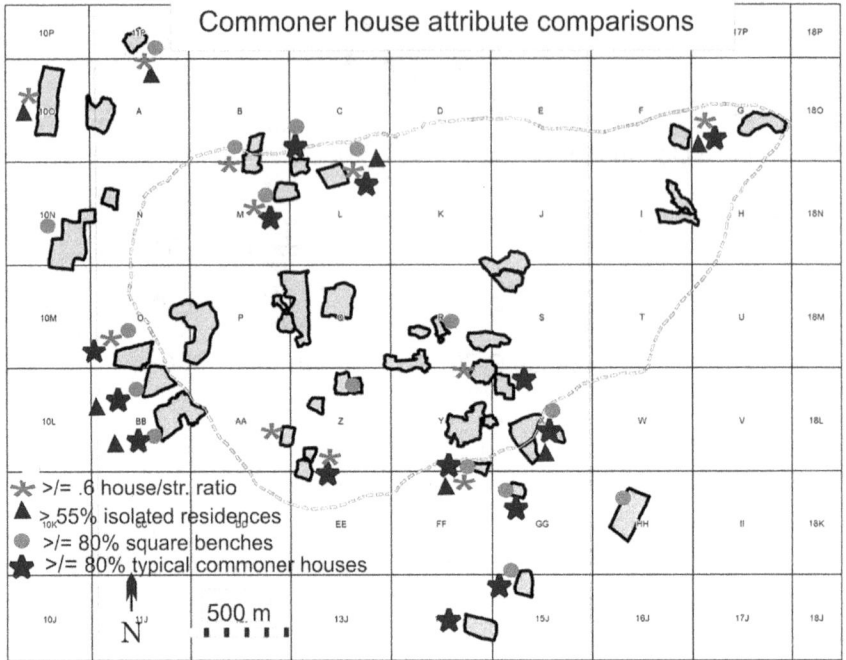

FIGURE 5.8. *Residential zones (milpa samples) near or beyond the city wall tend to have a higher house to ancillary structure ratio, higher frequencies of isolated residences, and more conservative dwelling styles (square benches, typical house forms). These data suggest shorter occupations and less experimentation in style toward the outskirts, which smaller families probably settled later in the city's history.*

and X-te-Toloc). These distributions indicate that occupants of typical commoner houses were widely distributed across the site.

LARGE SQUARE HOUSE-SIZED ALIGNMENTS

Large square alignments or platforms, with or without benches, fall within the size range of large commoner houses, and some exhibit interior room subdivisions (figures 5.7, 5.9). Five versions of these large square houses are spatially concentrated in one milpa (Milpa 12). Of these five, three lack benches but are otherwise of similar size and shape. These structures are located amidst other typical Mayapán houses in this neighborhood, and they are all located within albarrada-defined solares, like those of other residential groups in

Milpa 12 (figure 5.9). Elsewhere, House K-68a (Milpa 15, Square K) also has benches and is embedded within a traditional solare (figure 5.7). One large rectangular structure that lacks benches, Structure G-17 in Milpa 29, may represent housing for a distinct group within a traditional neighborhood (figure 5.10). It forms a wider rectangle than most houses, is twice the size of the largest house in this area, and is located only 60 meters from far northeast Gate G, at the corner of the city wall (figure 5.10). This structure is not surrounded by albarrada walls as are other house groups in the vicinity. Perhaps G-17 was a sleeping facility for guards appointed to the city's defense in this location (i.e., a "warrior house," as described by Freidel and Sabloff [1984:14]). Russell's (2007) discovery of a colonnaded hall outside of this gate also suggests an administrative presence at this location. Other houses in this milpa are humble, isolated residences.

RECTANGULAR HOUSE-SIZED ALIGNMENTS

House-sized rectangular alignments that lack benches may also have been dwellings (figure 5.7). They exhibit the size range of typical Mayapán houses and are positioned within albarrada enclosures. They can be found in isolation, along with typical houses, with other rectangular house-sized alignments, or in a primary position along with smaller outbuildings. These rectangular alignments could represent either unfinished houses that lack benches or simple variants of a Mayapán house style. At Cozumel, single room rectangular dwellings are common. The Mayapán rectangular alignment structures had either one room or two, and the latter were indicated by wall divisions (N = 21) that ran either parallel to or perpendicular to the long axis. A total of forty potential dwellings are represented by rectangular alignments in our sample, including those without visible room divisions. A. Smith (1962:222) classified 1,500 of Mayapán's structures as miscellaneous edifices of unknown function. He suggested their possible use as oratories, men's houses, guesthouses, storage buildings, workshops, toilets, or other unknown purposes. Platforms may have served similar functions, including the support of perishable residences. At Cozumel sites, such rectangular dwellings may predate a period when some Mayapán-style houses were built (Freidel and Sabloff 1984:159–60).

Forty possible house alignments occur in sixteen of our sample areas. Only one or two examples of these structures are present in individual mapped milpas with the exception of three in Milpa 21 and seven in Milpa 15 (Squares J and S, figure 5.7). Milpa 21 is located far to the north of the city wall and was occupied prior to the Postclassic; its rectangular alignments may be earlier. The

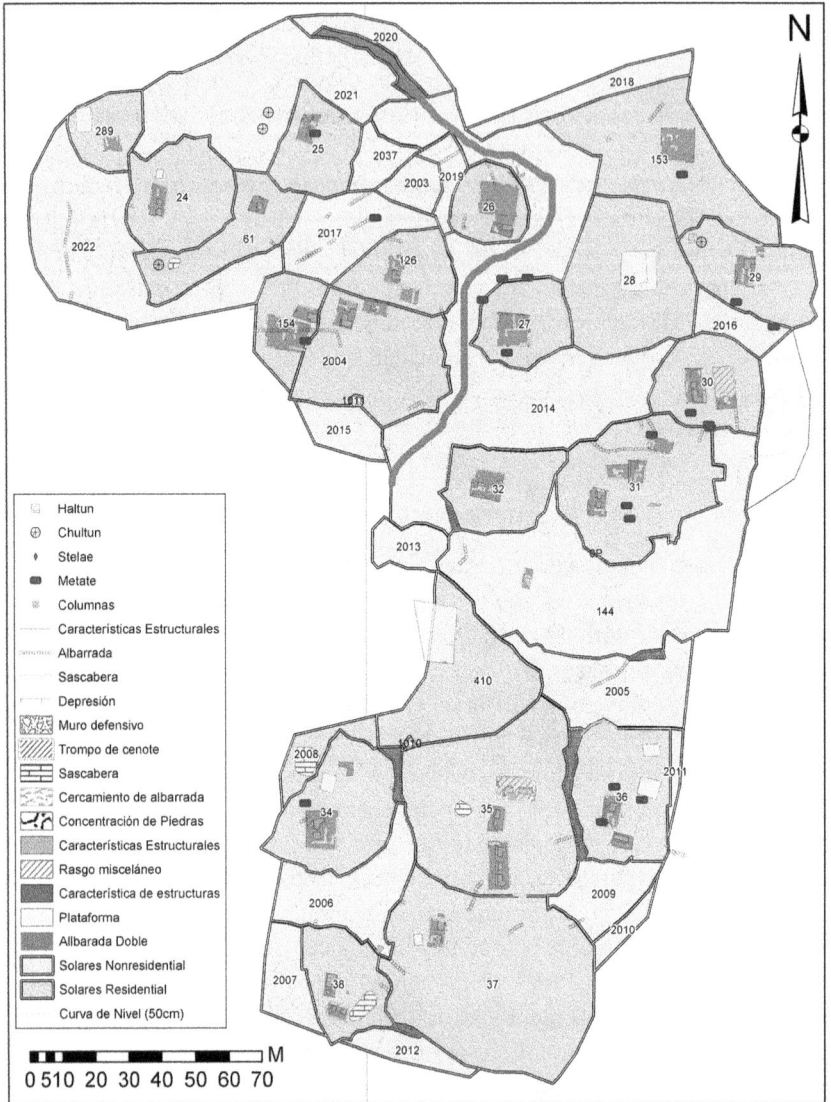

FIGURE 5.9. *Milpa 12 is located in the western part of the city. This zone has typical commoner bench houses and five large square houses (with or without benches) located within walled houselot enclosures. Note also enclosed nonresidential field spaces and the trajectory of a historical trail that follows flat bedrock pavement through the zone. The trail is marked by ancient stone lanes in the upper portion of the map, where it is thicker.*

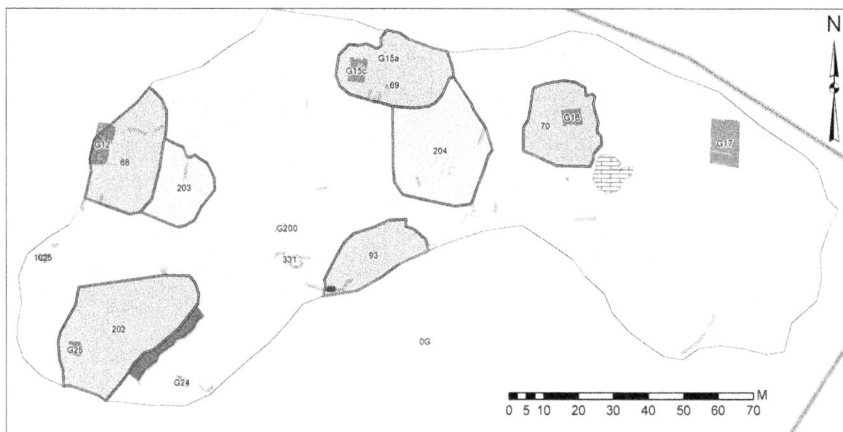

FIGURE 5.10. *G-17 (at far right) is an unusually large rectangular structure compared to other residences in Milpa 29, at the northeast corner of the city wall. G-17 is not enclosed by albarrada. It may represent a guard house, located only 60 meters from Gate G. Note the four enclosed fields in addition to three houselot enclosures in this milpa; two are attached to houselots.*

large number of these structures in Milpa 15, which are within albarrada enclosures, may represent the house style preference of a particular set of families. Only in one case does an alignment house form part of the same patio group as a typical bench house, which further illustrates the distinctiveness of this pattern in Milpa 15. Eight examples of typical commoner houses also exist in Milpa 15. Two other large L- shaped buildings in Milpa 15 are marked by internal wall divisions and could represent additional anomalous dwellings or storage structures (S-4ab, S-5).

MASSIVE PLATFORMS

Massive platforms represent substructures with few alignments that are readily observed on the surface. Massive platforms at Cozumel may represent warehousing facilities (Freidel and Sabloff 1984:145). One such feature is located next to a large open plaza that may have been a market space at Cozumel (Freidel and Sabloff 1984:146), although at other Cozumel sites, houses were sometimes located on these platforms (1984:145). The large, square P-114 platform in Milpa 1A at Mayapán has upper-room block alignments and one possible typical commoner dwelling (figure 5.11). The platform is an

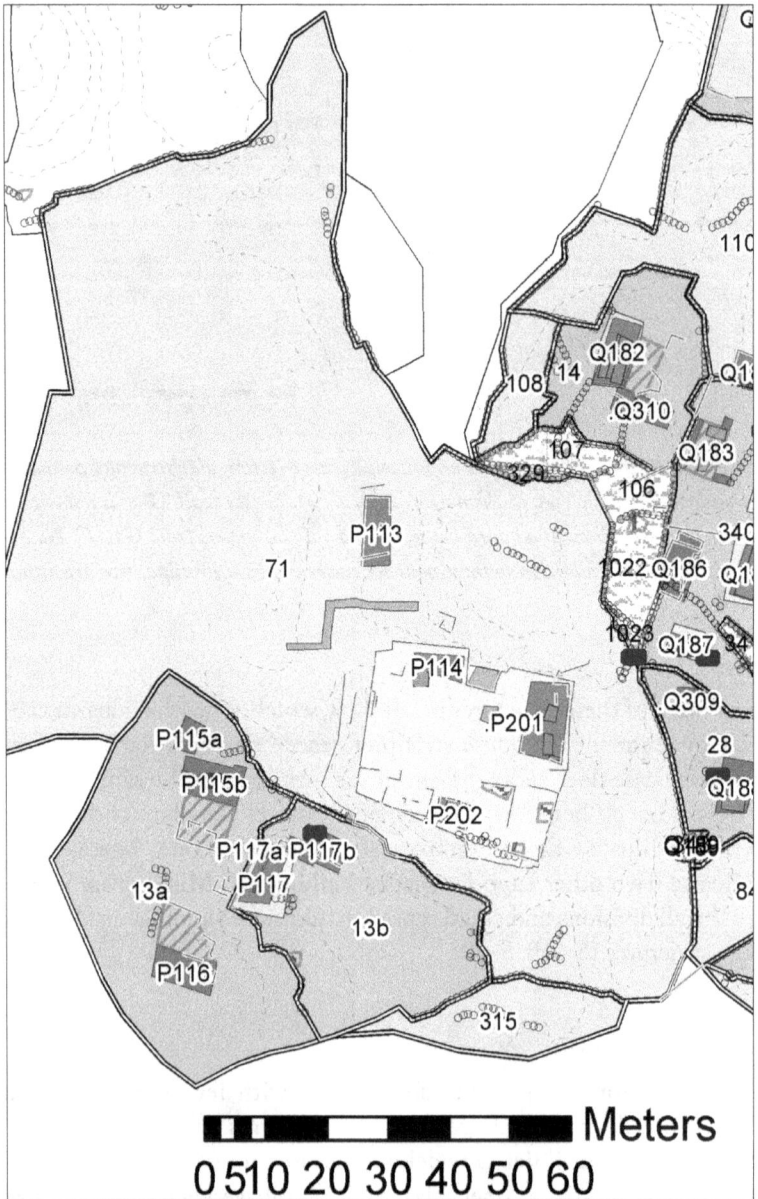

FIGURE 5.11. *Postclassic-era massive platform P-114 (center) is anomalous for Mayapán and may have housed a quadrangle of residential room blocks; midden debris and off-mound burials indicate a domestic function. Note more typical houses and enclosures that border it to the east and west (western edge of Milpa 1).*

atypical residential form for Mayapán. The P-114 platform is embedded in a residential district that includes typical Mayapán houses and excavations and surface collections in soils adjacent to it yielded domestic midden materials and burials. As Freidel and Sabloff suggested for Cozumel, it is possible that the inhabitants were traders who stored merchandise in the room blocks of the platform. Affluent residents of P-114 were indicated by high proportions of obsidian and imported Matillas Fine Orange pottery. They also made surplus chert tools, which attests to diverse sources of residential income (chapter 6). An elongated vacant space in Milpa 1B, just to the north, may have served as a minor market plaza for the city. In chapter 4, we describe a C-shaped massive platform with minimal upper wall alignments in Square K, which may have been a special function (market) feature. Two large U-shaped platforms (Q-240 and Q-243) are observed on Jones's (1962) map of the city. They are unlikely to be residential, but they are located next to dwellings and may have served storage functions. These platforms are positioned on either side of the center of site's principal *sacbe*. Massive platform storage features were tentatively identified near coastal Veracruz, the Bay of Honduras, and at other sites of coastal Quintana Roo, in addition to Zuuk and Cozumel (Freidel and Sabloff 1984:145–46). At Zuuk, they are next to an open plaza, perhaps used as a marketplace, and Freidel and Sabloff (1984:146) suggest that they belonged to merchant families.

Agglutinated substructures were one characteristic of settlement at Cozumel that is not common at Mayapán. Occasionally, conjoined buildings occur, but these are not large or numerous. They may, however, have served similar functions of bulk storage, as proposed for the agglutinated buildings of Cozumel that were probably used in family-level commercial activities at sites like La Expedición (Freidel and Sabloff 1984:137–38, 141, 150, 151). Importantly, agglutinated structures were not associated with elite dwellings at Cozumel (Freidel and Sabloff 1984:142). The P-114 platform is non-elite, in contrast to the Q-240 and Q-243 U-shaped platforms situated in the epicenter, near to major elite dwellings and public buildings.

BI-DIRECTIONAL DWELLINGS

One interesting class of dwelling described by A. Smith (1962) is a building that opens in two directions and has two rooms formed by a medial wall. He identified six of these, and all but one (Z-50a) was located within a predominantly residential group. This type may represent a particular house style, as five of them (J-71a, S-70c, Z-39f, Z-37a, and Z-50a) share an identical plan.

Structure S-133b is a variant, as its medial wall lacks a doorway, and it has an end room (figure 5.12). Based on its size, S-133b is an elite house; Z-50a may also be elite, as it is located within the southern terminus of the principal sacbe. Others are smaller and their occupants were probably of commoner status. In Milpa 10 of our study, Structure R-136b also matches this description. Some spatial clustering is noted in this distribution—S-133b and R-136b are located on adjacent *altillos* (elevated knolls), within Milpa 10, and the structures within the Z square are also near one another.

HOUSE GROUPS

The number of houses within a group may serve as an important indicator of domestic growth cycles or labor organization. Family groups expand their residential architecture through time, and additional houses within a patio group reflect this growth (McAnany 1995; Haviland and Moholy-Nagy 1992). Investment in ancillary structures may also be loosely correlated with duration of occupation. Isolated houses imply smaller domestic pools of labor, and they contrast with agricultural households that require much assistance during key periods of the year (McAnany 2004; King 1994). Residents of isolated houses at some sites produced surplus craft goods, as is sometimes observed at Colha (McAnany 1994; King 1994, 2000). Isolated House X-43, not occupied for long, may have been a temporary dwelling for those performing service to the Mayapán state, or alternatively, the house was newly established by a family that was unable to remain at the city. We favor the interpretation that X-43 was occupied by temporary workers, as the house lacks a full domestic assemblage, including grinding stones, or even average levels of faunal remains in the midden. Most of the houselots in Milpa 7, where X-43 is located, are isolated residences (figure 5.2), as are the majority in Milpa 12 (figure 5.9). Gair Tourtellot (1988:339–41) observed that Mayapán has a high proportion of isolated houses, as does Classic Period Dzibilchaltun, compared to Seibal. He suggested that corvée service may explain this phenomenon at both of the northern sites, perhaps for the salt industry at Dzibilichaltun and military duties at Mayapán.

The albarrada group is an important unit for residential settlement analysis, but spatial clustering must also be considered, especially where albarradas only partially enclose a set of houses and pedestrian traffic would have been easily facilitated between groups. Brown's (1999) analytical unit, the houselot cluster, accounts for spatially concentrated houselots that share albarrada walls. Examples of adjacent houselots that share boundary walls can be seen, for

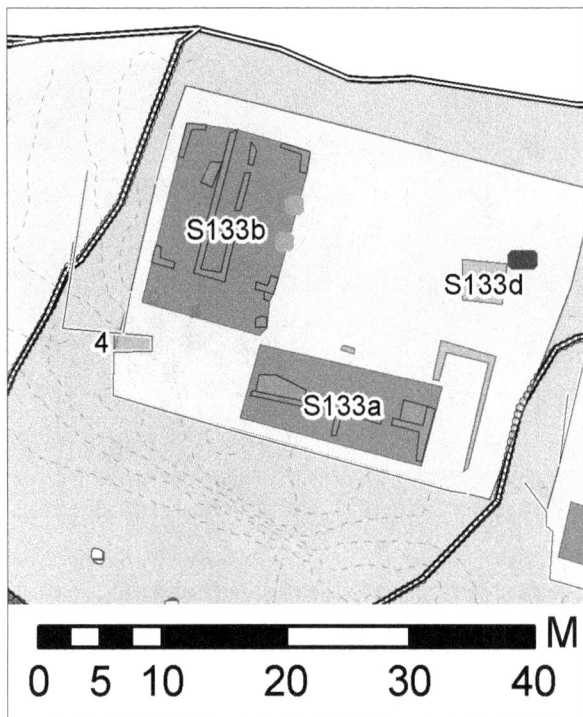

FIGURE 5.12. *Structure S-133b is an example of atypical structures that have a medial wall and open in two directions. This edifice may be an elite house, but other examples are within commoner house size ranges.*

example, in Milpa 12 (figure 5.9). Full cluster analysis requires comprehensive mapping of broader sections of the city and is more difficult with asymmetrically shaped milpa samples (figure 5.1).

Table 5.2 lists the number of residences within albarrada walls that enclose from one to five distinct structure groups. A complicating factor is that some albarrada walls encircle more than one distinct domestic patio (figures 5.1, 5.2). In addition to houselot walls, boundaries are implied by features such as terrace walls or sascabera quarries (Brown 1999:135). For example, in Milpa 4, a commoner neighborhood located in the southern mid-city area, one houselot enclosure contains five houses. This group is really a cluster of four distinct residential groups, one of which has two houses and the remaining three each have a single house (figure 5.13). One could further lump these groups into

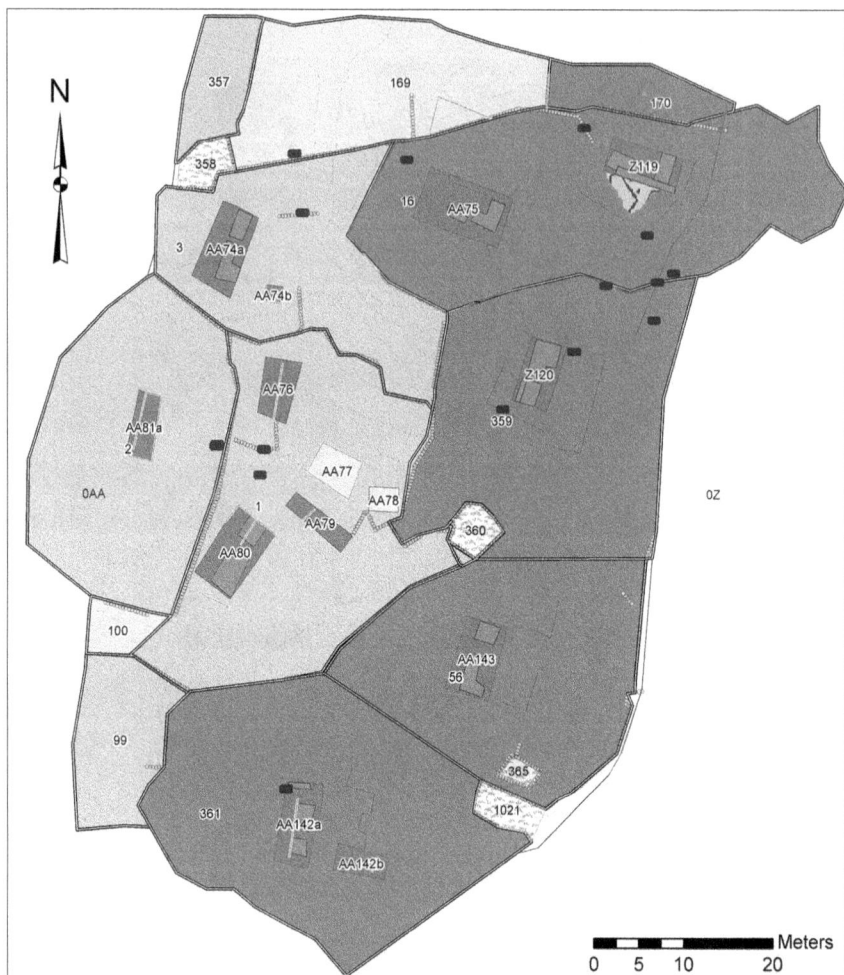

FIGURE 5.13. *Houses along the eastern edge of Milpa 4 are grouped into four residential groups of one or two houses, with open access between their partially enclosing albarrada walls (enclosures shaded dark gray). Houses AA-75, Z-119, and Z-120 were also linked by large quantities of lithic flakes from surplus stone toolmaking. Small dark gray rectangles indicate metate locations.*

all houses found in Milpa 4, as part of a larger houselot cluster defined by shared enclosure walls. Access between the house groups on the eastern edge of the milpa was open despite differences in elevation and spatial distinctiveness. The two house group (AA-75/Z-119) is located atop an altillo, and the isolated house (Z-120) closest to it is located slightly downslope and to the south. These houses specialized in surplus stone toolmaking (chapter 6). The form and size of these five houses in Milpa 4 are otherwise typical for the site. Sets of four (commoner) house groups were also enclosed in Milpas 1 and 32, neighborhoods where additional craft specialists and elites resided. At Mayapán, surplus craft production is not necessarily associated with isolated residences. Other examples of multiple house groups within albarrada enclosures are listed in table 5.2. Nine instances are documented where three houses within an albarrada form two or three spatially separated groups. Three cases are noted where two relatively isolated houses are found within a single albarrada enclosure.

A. Smith reports over 4,000 structures within or near the city wall, including 2,100 dwellings (A. Smith 1962:204–5). Around 2,800 (70 percent) of these structures are located in domestic groups, and those that are not dwellings were probably kitchens or other ancillary buildings and platforms (A. Smith 1962:205). A. Smith (1962:206) observed that over 600 (64 percent) of Mayapán's houses were in single house groups, and over 300 (32 percent) were in two house groups. Fewer houses were located within groups containing three (N = 35) or four (N = 3) dwellings.

Structure groups of the mapped milpa fields in our sample were classified according to how many houses were present in each albarrada group. A total of 146 house groups were located on our maps (table 5.2). These data are improved over those used by A. Smith, who identified groups according to spatial proximity and not houselot boundary walls. But our results generally confirm his findings, with 63.7 percent isolated residences (N = 93), 26.7 percent two house groups (N = 39), 7.5 percent three house groups (N = 11), 1.4 percent in four house groups (N = 2), and 0.7 percent in five house groups (N = 1). The majority of residences in our sample were in single house groups consisting of a single residence, whether or not outbuildings were present.

Spatial Distribution of House Group Types

Three house groups occur more commonly in the central parts of the city, but their distribution is not limited to this zone (table 5.2). They are found twice near the monumental center (Milpa 1), twice in the mid-city zones to the west (Milpa 12), and singly in milpas to the east or southeast (Milpas 6, 9, 15, and 33) of the center. One occurrence is noted near the north (Milpa 24) and east (Milpa 7) edges of the city wall.

TABLE 5.2 Dwelling group types in mapped milpas

Dwelling group type	Milpas (location of occurrences)*	Total
2 house group—commoner	1, 1, 1, 5, 5, 6, 6, 6, 6, 9, 10, 11, 12, 12, 15, 15, 17, 21, 24, 28, 31, 32, 33, 33, 34, 36, 36, 36	28
2 house group—elite	1, 1, 6, 10, 32, 33	6
2 house paired isolated residences in 2 group cluster	1, 4, 15	3
2 house, isolated residence in 4 group cluster	32	1
2 house group, outbuilding, shrine	10	1
3 house in 2 group cluster—elite	2	1
3 house in 2 group cluster	6, 7, 9, 12, 15, 24	6
3 house in 3 group cluster	1, 1	2
3 house, single group	12, 33	2
4 house in 3 group cluster	32	1
4 house in 4 group cluster	1	1
5 house in 4 group cluster	4	1
Isolated residence	1, 1, 3, 3, 6, 6, 6, 7, 7, 11, 12, 12, 12, 12, 13, 15, 15, 15, 15, 17, 18, 18, 18, 18, 19, 21, 21, 24, 26, 29, 29, 33, 33, 33, 35, 36, 36	37
Isolated residence and oratory	1, 32	2
Isolated residence and outbuilding	1, 1, 1, 1, 1, 1, 2, 4, 5, 7, 7, 7, 7, 7, 8, 8, 9, 10, 11, 11, 11, 11, 12, 12, 12, 12, 12, 12, 12, 12, 12, 14, 15, 15, 15, 15, 16, 17, 19, 19, 20, 22, 28, 29, 30, 32, 33, 33, 34, 34, 36,	51
Isolated residence and bench	12, 13	2
Isolated residence, hall, outbuildings	10	1
Grand total (number of dwelling groups)		146

• Figure 1.7 illustrates the location of these milpas.

Two house groups are common and are distributed in eighteen milpas. Milpas 1 and 6 had the greatest numbers of these (N = 5, N = 6, respectively). Like three house groups, they are more common in the central part of the city but are also found in a variety of locations (table 5.2). For example, mapped milpas with the greatest proportions of two house groups (25–67 percent of the total groups per milpa) are located adjacent to the center, in the mid-city areas, and toward the north part of the city wall. Ninety-three single residential groups that lack other structures are distributed in thirty-seven milpas in our sample (table 5.2). All zones of the city have milpas where 43–56 percent of the groups per milpa consist of a single dwelling (figure 5.14). While most areas of the site have at least some milpas with over 64 percent single house groups, this pattern is most prevalent in areas at the southeastern or eastern inner (walled) margins of the city, where half of the milpas have from 64 to 78 percent single house groups.

Ninety-three isolated residences are documented; thirty-seven of these are solitary structures and fifty-six are associated with outbuildings (table 5.2). Solitary residences and single dwellings with outbuildings are found in milpas in all parts of the city. Higher proportions of solitary dwellings without outbuildings are present overall in milpas that are exterior to (but near to) the city wall and near the north edge of the wall. The fewest solitary buildings are in the group of milpas adjacent to the monumental center and far outside the city wall. These data may imply shorter term settlement for certain areas.

RATIOS OF DWELLINGS TO OTHER STRUCTURES WITHIN GROUPS

A. Smith (1962:206) compared the quantities of residences and nonresidences within domestic groups. Within our mapped milpa sample, the ratio of houses to total structures within groups (including houses) varies considerably. Some milpas have average ratios of 0.1 that reflect very few houses while others have only houses within domestic groups, with a ratio of 1.0 (figure 5.15, table 5.3). The spatial distribution of these ratios is revealing. Sample areas located far outside of the city wall have the lowest or highest ratios and thus tend to have groups consisting of primarily outbuildings or isolated houses (three and two milpas, respectively). But two distant milpas have ratios similar to areas within the city (table 5.3). Just outside of the wall, two localities exhibit houses without ancillary structures, while four others had ratios ranging from 0.4 to 0.8. The exceptions indicate that there is not a simple correspondence of isolated residences and location beyond the wall. Milpas within the wall tend to have ratios that range from 0.4 to 0.8. Greater numbers of nonresidential structures nearer to the site center are indicated by more milpas with ratios of 0.2 or 0.3 (table 5.3). This characteristic of downtown Mayapán may reflect more specialized activities, greater settlement longevity, or both.

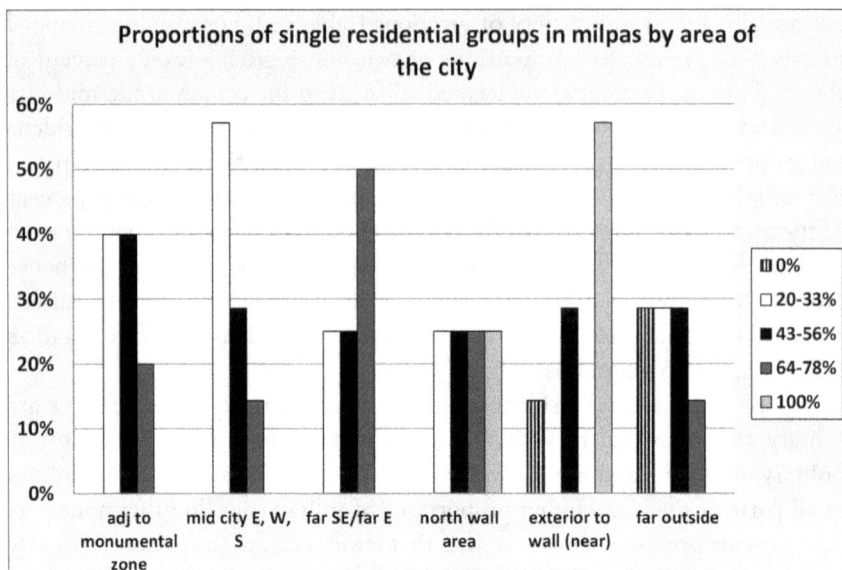

FIGURE 5.14. *Proportions of single residence groups (per interval) distributed in milpas in different portions of the site. Note that areas on the city's periphery (four areas on the right) have more gray bars, indicating greater proportions of single residences.*

HOUSE BENCH PATTERNS

It is generally assumed that benches were used for sleeping, sitting, and a range of other tasks. Bench shapes vary from L-shaped to more square or rectangular forms within Mayapán houses, without any apparent functional differences. Illustrations in figure 5.7 provide examples of houses with square/rectangular benches (M-58, M-61, X-43, and Z-42b) and examples with square and L-shaped forms (O-54b and P-151c). Shapes seem to represent a stylistic choice at the city, and more innovative variation in bench form is observed in the densely inhabited center compared to the more conservative outskirts. As there is no tight clustering of bench forms within specific neighborhoods, these shapes were probably not ethnic markers (table 5.4, figure 5.16). Dwellings with exclusively square/rectangular benches are most numerous in our sample (N = 116), and this convention formed a key part of the typical Mayapán house. Forty-three houses exhibited square/rectangular as well as L-shaped benches, and twenty-one dwellings had the latter exclusively (table 5.4).

Examples with only L-shaped benches tend to be located in residential areas near the site center or toward the south, southeast, or east of the center

Ratio: total dwellings/total structures per milpa

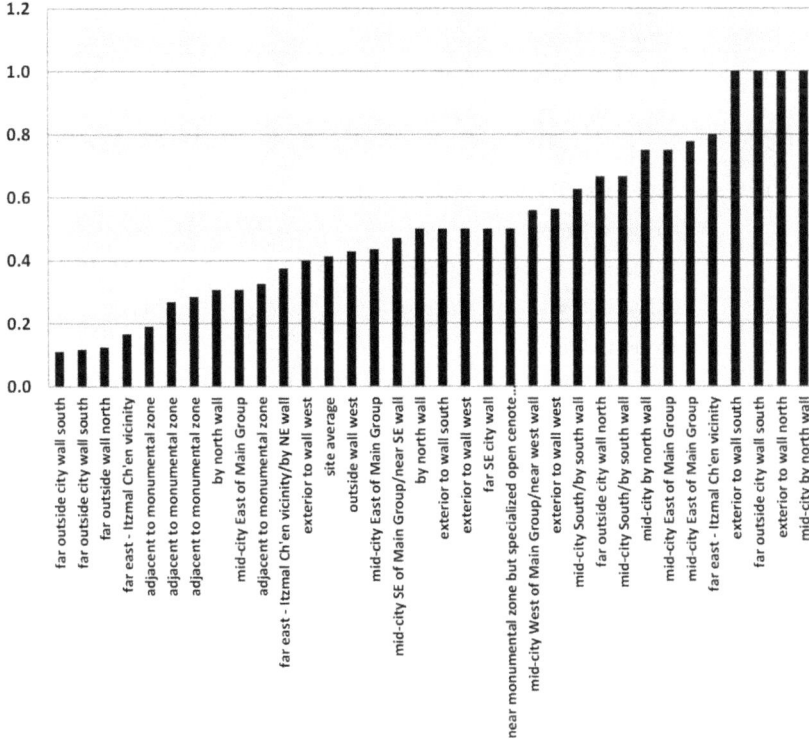

FIGURE 5.15. *The ratio of dwellings to the total number of structures (including ancillary buildings) is charted above by milpas in different parts of the city. Locations far beyond the city wall had more groups of purely outbuildings or only isolated houses. But results are mixed.*

(Milpas 1, 4, 5, 6, 10, 11, 15, 32, and 33), with one exception: Milpa 12. This shape is absent in areas to the north, far southeast, and exterior to the wall (table 5.4, figures 5.8, 5.16). Mixed bench styles within a dwelling are more widespread, as observed in two western and one extreme northeastern mapped milpa (table 5.4, figure 5.8). Although the absence of L-shaped benches in the northern part of the site may be important, this form was widely used at the city. Locations on the margins of the walled city or beyond it containing greater numbers of houses with only square or rectangular benches include Milpas 8, 13, 14, 18, 19, 20, 26, 28, 30, 34, and 35 (table 5.4, figures 5.8, 5.16). These are zones of

TABLE 5.3 Ratios of number of dwellings to all structures, including dwellings and non-dwellings, for all residential groups within each mapped milpa*.

Milpa	Location in city	Ratio
30	Far outside city wall south	0.1
8	Far outside city wall south	0.1
22	Far outside wall north	0.1
16	East—Itzmal Ch'en vicinity	0.2
2	Adjacent to monumental zone	0.2
11	Adjacent to monumental zone	0.3
32	Adjacent to monumental zone	0.3
34	By north wall	0.3
10	Mid-city east of main group	0.3
1	Adjacent to monumental zone	0.3
29	East—Itzmal Ch'en vicinity	0.4
13	Exterior to wall west	0.4
Mean value		*0.4*
28	Outside wall west	0.4
15	Mid-city east of main group	0.4
6	Mid-city southeast of main group/near wall	0.5
19	By north wall	0.5
35	Exterior to wall south	0.5
14	Exterior to wall west	0.5
7	Far southeast city wall	0.5
3	Near monumental zone	0.5
12	Mid-city west of main group/near west wall	0.6
36	Exterior to wall west	0.6
5	Mid-city south/by south wall	0.6
21	Far outside city wall north	0.7
4	Mid-city south/by south wall	0.7
24	Mid-city by north wall	0.8
9	Mid-city east of main group	0.8

continued on next page

TABLE 5.3—*continued*

Milpa	Location in city	Ratio
33	Mid-city east of main group	0.8
17	East—Itzmal Ch'en vicinity	0.8
26	Exterior to wall south	1.0
31	Far outside city wall south	1.0
20	Far outside wall west	1.0
18	Mid-city by north wall	1.0

• Milpa locations are shown in figure 1.7

low-status houses that are not near to focal monumental architecture. Figure 5.8 marks those mapped milpas where at least 80 percent of the houses have exclusively square benches. This illustration also indicates that higher proportions of isolated residences, typical Mayapán houses, and fewer outbuildings overlap with preferences for square benches. These characteristics are markers for the use of more conservative house attribute styles in residential zones that were generally occupied by fewer people of lesser means for shorter time periods. None of these localities housed craft specialists of any significant degree, nor were levels of affluence high. Closer to the center of the city or to focal groups such as Itzmal Ch'en, it is possible that residents were influenced by greater residential density and diversity that might have prompted experimentation, specialization, and elaboration in dwelling features. As chapter 6 indicates, wealthier commoners and crafting houses are usually found near the site center or outlying architectural nodes within the walled settlement. It is worth noting, however, that houses with exclusively L-shaped benches do not form the majority of any mapped milpa, as they almost always occur in areas with equal or greater proportions of houses with square/rectangular benches or combined square/rectangular and L-shaped bench styles (table 5.4, figure 5.16). The prevalence of square/rectangular benches suggests a high degree of conformity to the normative Mayapán style, although it is also true that this form would have been the most practical and simplest to construct.

STRUCTURE GROUP ORIENTATIONS

Most houses of the Colonial era faced east (Tozzer 1941:n357), the direction from which wind and weather arrives in northern Yucatán. The cardinality

TABLE 5.4 Percentages of dwellings with specific bench shapes within mapped milpas*.

Milpa	Houses with L-shaped bench only	Houses with square/rectangular and L-shaped benches	Houses with square/rectangular benches only	Total
1	15	30	55	20
2	0	17	83	6
3	0	100	0	1
4	14	43	43	7
5	25	50	25	4
6	8	38	54	13
7	0	20	80	10
8	0	0	100	1
9	0	33	67	6
10	25	38	38	8
11	20	0	80	5
12	17	33	50	18
13	0	0	100	3
14	0	0	100	1
15	30	10	60	10
17	0	25	75	4
18	0	0	100	4
19	0	0	100	4
20	0	0	100	2
24	0	17	83	6
26	0	0	100	1
28	0	0	100	4
29	0	33	67	3
30	0	0	100	1
31	0	50	50	4
32	30	30	40	10
33	25	8	67	12
34	0	0	100	3
35	0	0	100	1
36	0	25	75	8
Total	21	43	116	180

*Milpa locations are shown in figure 1.7.

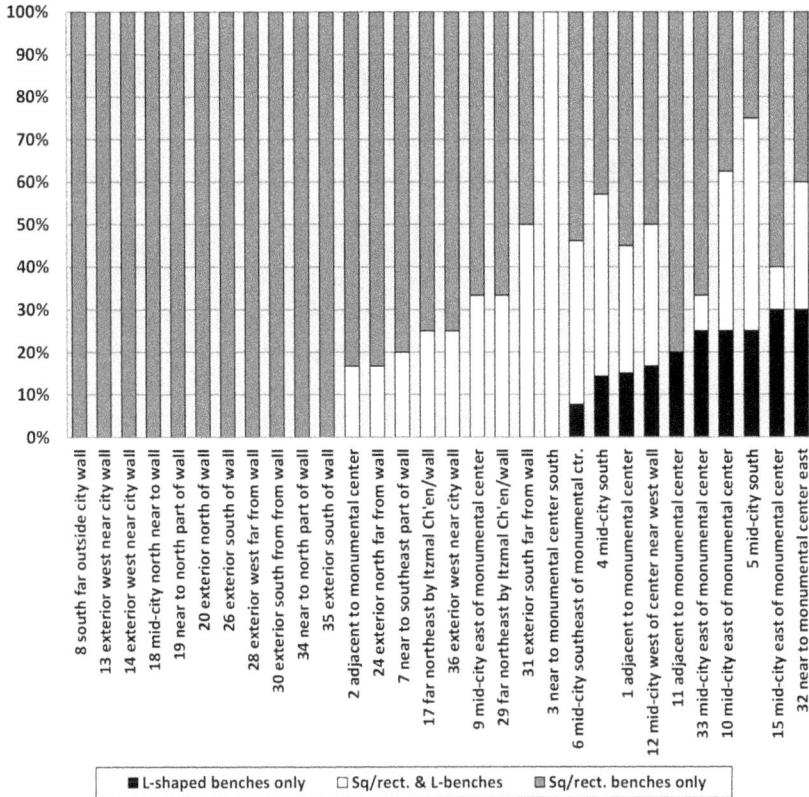

FIGURE 5.16. *Percentage of houses with exclusively L-shaped or square/rectangular benches and houses with combinations of these shapes per mapped milpa at Mayapán. Milpa zones with the highest proportion of square/rectangular benches tend to be near or beyond the city wall.*

of Mayapán houses tends to be skewed east of north and more southeast of east by 10–14 degrees, perhaps due to the position of the sun most of the year (Carlson 1982). A. Smith (1962:208) also observed a strong preference for eastward orientation among Mayapán dwellings, followed by north, then south-facing dwellings, with very few houses facing west. These observations are significant and contribute to our understanding of normative behavior for dwelling construction at the city. But as for earlier Maya cities, multi-dwelling groups at Mayapán exhibit a preference for orientation around an inner patio that allows for only one house to face generally eastward. As most Mayapán residential patios are not closed and instead consist of two (sometimes more) structures that define patio space, we observe that patios themselves are open toward patterned directions. Residents chose where to place their additional houses, and this choice opened up lines of sight for these dwellings toward parts of the cityscape. Here we consider these patio group orientations, which are defined as the direction toward which a patio opened when patios were framed by two or more structures.

A total of 129 groups with more than one house are available for tracking this characteristic in our sample of mapped milpas (table 5.5). As is observed for individual houses across the city, dwelling group orientations show a preference for an eastern direction. Most structure groups formed by two edifices are open toward the northeast (N = 45) or toward the southeast (N = 20). There are fewer cases where two structure groups open toward the northwest (N = 11) or southwest (N = 3). Among groups framed by three structures, eastern patio openings are the most common (N = 9), followed by northern (N = 4), with fewer examples of southern (N = 2) or western (N = 1) orientations. Groups with two mutually facing structures were more variable, with three aligned on an east-west axis and five north-south. Group orientations could not be discerned for eight fully enclosed groups or six dispersed groups, defined as those containing multiple residences that do not form a communal patio space. Eleven other groups without clear patios had back-to-back (N = 3) or side-to-side (N = 9) structures. Overall, residential group patio orientations reiterate the preference for house orientations discussed by A. Smith, as 82.3 percent of a sample of seventy-nine two structure (L-shaped patio) groups open to the northeast or southeast, and nine of sixteen three-sided groups face east. Only 13.9 percent of the two structure groups face northwest.

Choices to have patios open toward the northeast versus southeast, or more aberrantly, toward other directions, were probably influenced by residential zone attractions such as pedestrian pathways or lines of sight to nearby focal architecture (table 5.5, figure 5.17). For example, milpas to the north of the site center do not exhibit groups with northeast orientations that would have resulted in a view of the city wall by individuals looking out of the entranceways of the buildings. Instead, groups in northern Milpas 19, 20, 24, and 34 exhibit preferences for southeastern arrangements that would have faced toward the city center. This desire to face inward toward the site center is commonly observed. For example, in Milpa 6 there are high proportions of groups that face west, northwest, or southwest (67 percent) toward downtown Mayapán. Although nearby Milpa 7 exhibits more variation, more of its groups face northwest than any other direction (table 5.5).

Exceptions to this pattern are instructive. Groups near to Itzmal Ch'en faced this locality rather than the site center. In Milpa 17, by Itzmal Ch'en, patios opened toward the southeast or east and in Milpa 16 they are oriented toward the northeast—each of these respective orientations afforded a vista of the outlying ceremonial group (figure 5.17). Similarly, in Milpa 15 most groups face toward the civic group J-109/111 and the route that led to Itzmal Ch'en (figure 5.17). Milpas 9 and 33, in the same general part of the city, also follow this pattern, with a majority of eastern orientations toward J-109/111 and the Itzmal Ch'en axis and away from the site center (table 5.5). Residents regularly decided to orient their domestic patio viewsheds toward prominent outlying monuments, which served as focal points that defined and divided the city's neighborhoods. Perhaps the popularity of the northeast orientation for central-east dwellings reflects the prior existence of significant pedestrian thoroughfares from the northern and eastern city gates, with the added benefit of early sunlight and better ventilation from eastern winds. Well beyond the city wall, a northeast or southeast group orientation accounts for 50–100 percent of the patios per milpa (Milpas 8, 13, 20, 28, 30, and 34). These choices resulted in the house groups facing toward the city wall (figure 5.17).

SPECIAL FUNCTION BENCHES

Additional bench type features within edifices share morphological similarities with residential benches. Like house benches, some may have been used as beds, seating, tables, or altars. Context provides the key for proposing functional variation using surface settlement data, and we classify nonresidential bench forms according to the following categories: (1) patio shrines, (2) external benches, and (3) enclosed bench structures (figure 5.18). It is important to note that despite their spatial distinctiveness, these features are generally located within the greater context of residential patio groups.

Patio shrines are small, square or rectangular external platforms of equivalent size and construction technology to dwelling benches. They are usually located centrally within the courtyard of a residential or ritual group, and this placement is the primary criterion for identifying them as shrines. This function is also derived from numerous excavations of such features that revealed burials or offerings (A. Smith 1962).

External benches resemble patio shrines in terms of size and form, but they are located within or outside houselots in places other than the residential courtyard (figure 5.18). Some of these benches may have been part of perishable houses or kitchens, as suggested by their occasional association with ephemeral

TABLE 5.5 Percentages of patio group orientations per mapped milpa.

Milpa	L patio NE	L patio SE	L patio NW	L patio SW	En-closed	Dis-persed	3 side E	3 side N	3 side S	3 side W	Facing EW	Facing NS	Back to back	Side by side	Total
1	39	4	–	–	17	4	4	4	–	–	4	13	4	4	23
2	100	–	–	–	–	–	–	–	–	–	–	–	–	–	2
4	50	25	25	–	–	–	–	–	–	–	–	–	–	–	4
5	100	–	–	–	–	–	–	–	–	–	–	–	–	–	3
6	17	–	33	17	17	–	–	–	–	17	–	–	–	–	6
7	–	14	43	–	–	14	14	–	–	–	14	–	–	–	7
8	50	–	–	–	–	–	–	–	50	–	–	–	–	–	2
9	67	–	–	–	–	–	–	–	–	–	33	–	–	–	3
10	17	17	33	–	17	–	–	–	–	–	–	17	–	–	6
11	17	–	–	17	33	–	–	–	–	–	17	–	–	17	6
12	31	31	13	–	–	–	6	–	6	–	–	–	–	13	16
13	100	–	–	–	–	–	–	–	–	–	–	–	–	–	1
14	–	–	–	–	–	–	–	–	–	–	–	–	–	100	1
15	55	9	–	–	–	–	36	–	–	–	–	–	–	–	11
16	100	–	–	–	–	–	–	–	–	–	–	–	–	–	1
17	–	50	–	–	–	–	50	–	–	–	–	–	–	–	2
19	–	50	–	–	–	50	–	–	–	–	–	–	–	–	2
20	–	100	–	–	–	–	–	–	–	–	–	–	–	–	1
21	–	–	–	–	–	100	–	–	–	–	–	–	–	–	1

Milpa	L patio NE	L patio SE	L patio NW	L patio SW	En-closed	Dis-persed	3 side E	3 side N	3 side S	3 side W	Facing EW	Facing NS	Back to back	Side by side	Total
22	–	–	–	–	–	–	–	–	–	–	–	–	–	100	1
24	–	100	–	–	–	–	–	–	–	–	–	–	–	–	2
28	50	–	–	–	–	–	–	–	–	–	–	–	–	50	2
29	–	–	–	–	–	100	–	–	–	–	–	–	–	–	1
30	100	–	–	–	–	–	–	–	–	–	–	–	–	–	1
31	–	–	–	–	–	–	–	–	–	–	–	100	–	–	1
32	33	11	–	–	–	11	11	33	–	–	–	–	–	–	9
33	80	–	20	–	–	–	–	–	–	–	–	–	–	–	5
34	–	100	–	–	–	–	–	–	–	–	–	–	–	–	3
36	17	17	–	17	–	–	–	–	–	–	–	–	33	17	6
Total	45	20	11	3	8	6	9	4	2	1	4	5	3	8	129

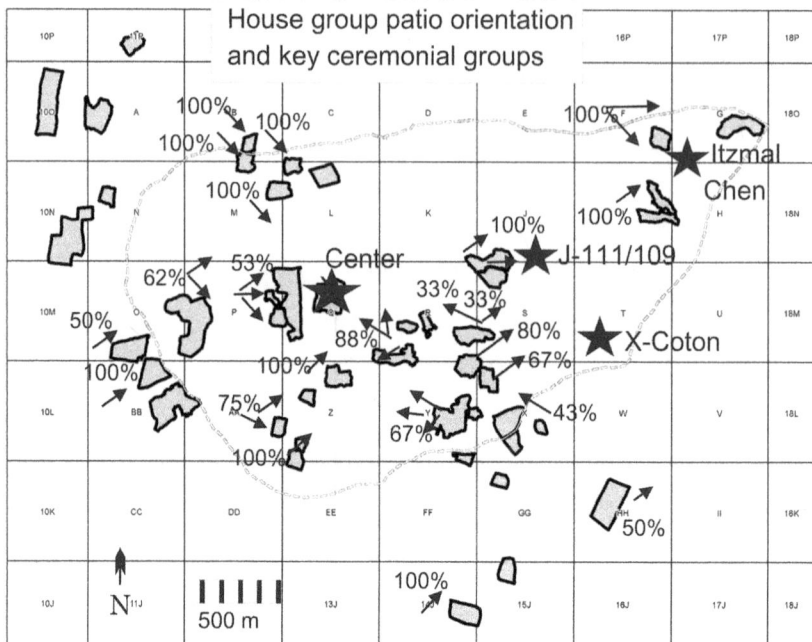

FIGURE 5.17. *House group patio orientations with respect to monumental foci within the city walls. Percentages indicate the proportion of residential groups (> one house) that formed patios within milpas oriented as the arrows indicate.*

wall alignments. Others appear to have been self-standing, but it is difficult to know whether perishable shelters once enclosed them. Pole and thatch structures would have been common at Mayapán, as they are used widely across the peninsula today for sleeping, food preparation, storage, or other domestic tasks. Remains of such features are reported from Cozumel sites (Freidel and Sabloff 1984:21). A. Smith (1962:220) thought that kitchens were likely represented by exterior platforms or benches that were attached to the ends of houses. Alternatively, he suggests that small separate platforms may have also been used for cooking. Smith observed that more than 260 houses at Mayapán had exterior platforms or benches that could have been part of kitchens.

Enclosed bench structures are small wall foundation edifices in which the majority of interior space is filled by a bench (figure 5.18). These small structures may fully encompass a single bench or allow a limited amount of standing room relative to bench-filled space. Most of these are too small to

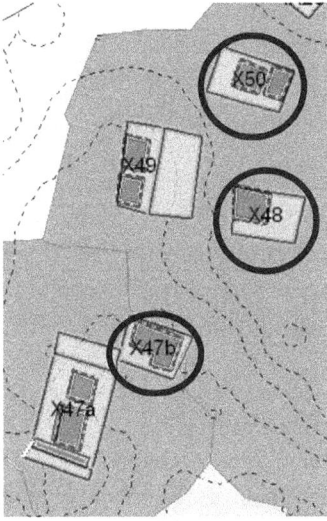

Milpa 7 (Strs. X-47b, X-48, X-52

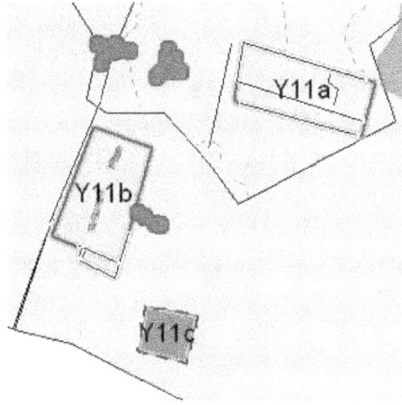

Milpa 32
Str. Y-11c

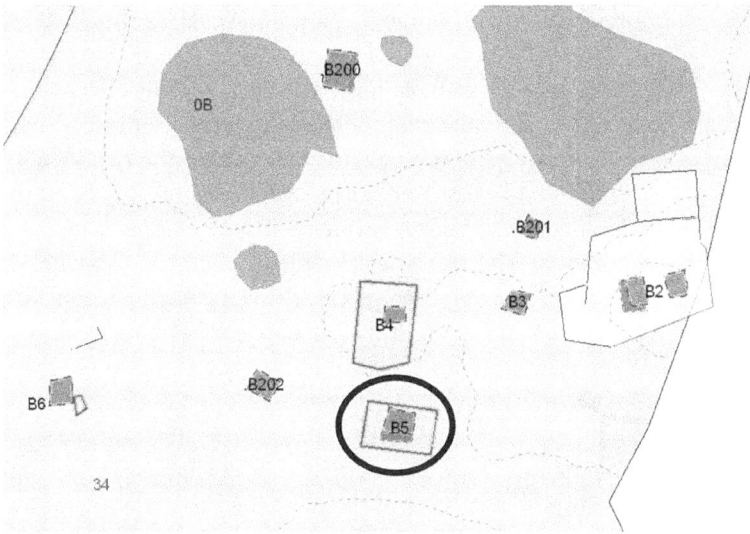

Milpa 34

FIGURE 5.18. *Illustrations of external benches that are within or near residential groups. External bench structures include freestanding quadrangular edifices not contained within other alignments and bench houses in which the majority of an enclosed space is filled by a bench.*

have been houses. Some may have been shrines or sanctuaries. While they are not centrally placed in patios, they usually frame one side of a domestic patio. Occasionally they are isolated at a short distance from dwellings. These structures closely match descriptions of group shrines identified by A. Smith (1962:222, figure 12a–f, n–t), which are essentially altars enclosed by buildings. One possible function for larger bench houses is that men used them as isolation huts during rites of passage (Freidel and Sabloff 1984). Many kinds of outbuildings are described in documentary accounts, including storage huts, granaries, kitchens, sleeping structures, peccary pens, and apiaries (Freidel and Sabloff 1984:11), and all of these edifices, except for peccary pens and apiaries, may be represented by enclosed bench structures. There are many kinds of small buildings without benches indicated by whole or partial wall alignments in the domestic groups and enclosed fields of Mayapán. Outbuildings that lack benches are described separately later in this chapter. Excavation is needed to determine the functional variation of outbuildings, including enclosed benches.

The locations of patio shrines (N = 13), external benches (N = 24), and enclosed benches (N = 16) are listed in table 5.6. Eleven shrines or oratories and two houses with rear shrine rooms are also listed, as these represent additional feature types with benches. Of 506 structures recorded in thirty-six milpa samples, these sixty-six features form only 12.8 percent of the sample. If all of the enclosed benches and external benches were shrines—which we doubt—this is a very small proportion of ritual features at the site. When the forty external benches and bench houses are excluded from this calculation, patio shrines, shrine/oratories, and rear shrine rooms represent only 5.1 percent of our sample. Altars were also rare in perishable dwellings at Cozumel sites, and for that study, the presence of two or more shrines was considered to be an indication of a specialized group rather than a normal house compound (Freidel and Sabloff 1984:16, 57). Such a ritual courtyard (group R-142) was identified in Milpa 10, and Milpa 34 has numerous nonresidential bench features that also suggest an anomalous level of specialized activity (figure 5.18).

Two ritual compounds and one elite residential group in our sample housed oratories while other oratories were with unassuming domestic groups (table 5.7). Fifty oratories were identified by A. Smith (1962:220–21:figure 7) at Mayapán; twenty of these had masonry columns, and all but four were single room structures. They often contain mortuary features. Twenty-two of them are described in detail by Tatiana Proskouriakoff (1962a) and A. Smith (1962), most of which were in the monumental zone or in neighborhoods adjacent to it. Mapped milpa residential zones with oratories tend to have at least

TABLE 5.6 A list of structure numbers, contexts with which they are associated, and location (Milpa) of external benches, enclosed bench, and patio shrine structures.

Exterior bench (self standing)			Enclosed bench structures		
Structure	Context	Milpa	Structure	Context	Milpa
R-178c	Residence	32	Q-184	Residence	1
Y-11c	Residence	32	Z-41a	Outbuilding	2
Q-321 (with Q-46b)	Elite residence	1	Z-200	Outbuilding	2
Q-315	Residence	1	Y-59	Residence	6
P-200	Residence	1	Y-47	Outbuilding	6
Z-47a	Outbuilding	2	X-41b	Isolated residence	7
X-200	Isolated residence	7	X-50	Residence	7
unnumbered	Isolated residence	11	X-54	Outbuilding	7
R-111a	Residence	11	X-47b	Residence	7
R-100a	Elite complex	11	C-200	Isolated residence	19
R-102a	Elite complex	11	R-171c	Isolated residence	32
R-104a	Elite complex	11	R-177a	Residence	32
R-105a	Elite complex	11	B-5	Residence	34
O-29a	Isolated residence	12	M-12a	Residence	34
P-69a	Isolated residence	12	B-7a	Residence	34
BB-206	Isolated residence	13			
J-127d	Isolated residence	15			
14-J-8	Outbuilding	30	Patio shrine		
14-J-9	Outbuilding	30	P-23e	Residence	1
B-200	Bench field/near residence	34	Q-42f	Elite residence	1
B-202	Bench field/near residence	34	Z-191a	Residence	5
B-6	Bench field/near residence	34	HH-1b	Isolated residence	8
B-201	Bench field/near residence	34	X-23d	Isolated residence	9
B-3	Bench field/near residence	34	S-133d	Elite residence	10
			S-130c	Residence	10

continued on next page

TABLE 5.6—*continued*

Exterior bench (self standing)			Enclosed bench structures		
Structure	*Context*	*Milpa*	*Structure*	*Context*	*Milpa*
			R-142e, R-142g	Ritual quadrangle	10
			BB-9b	Isolated residence	13
			Q-244e	Elite residence	32
			Y-41c	Residence	33
			Q-41f	Elite residence	1

one major upper-status house or administrative feature (Milpas 1, 6, 10, 11, 15, and 32). The presence of resident elites within a neighborhood seems to have resulted in the construction of more permanent or formal ritual features. Patio shrines are located at a few commoner houses, although they are uncommon (Milpas 5, 8, 9, 10, 13, and 33).

A. Smith (1962:228, 221–22) observed that one hundred dwellings at Mayapán had altars built within them, and another forty had separate shrines or shrine rooms. He notes that eighty more had group altars. Dividing these 220 features by Smith's 2,100 total surveyed dwellings reveals that 10.5 percent of the site's domestic structures had formal ritual features. Commoners at Mayapán likely shared general belief systems and would have participated in household and public religious acts, as in earlier periods (Gossen and Leventhal 1993). But identifying household religious practice does not imply a decentralization of religious power compared to earlier times, as Donald E. Thompson and J. Eric S. Thompson (1955:238–42) suggested. Household shrines are as frequent (or more so) at Tikal (Becker 1999) as they are at Mayapán, and the rulers of both cities invested heavily in public religious buildings and ceremonies.

DWELLING SIZE

A discussion of elite houses as focal nodes in the city's settlement zone is provided in chapter 4. These edifices are defined by their size and number of rooms; ten Tier 1 residences are identified and eleven Tier 2 smaller elite residences have been located (table 4.1). The three most elaborate palaces are located in Square R (groups R-85–91, R-96–98, and R-100–106), just to the east of the monumental center and its portal gate (chapter 3). Two of these palaces have vaulted tunnels that run beneath their supporting platforms, and

TABLE 5.7 List of oratories or related edifices with shrine rooms identified at Mayapán in our mapped milpa sample. More will probably be found in future mapping, and Carnegie investigators reported at least twenty-two other examples (Proskouriakoff 1962a; A. Smith 1962).

PEMY oratories identified
R-142c (ritual group)
P-28b (residence, also identified by the Carnegie project)
P-21b (possible oratory)
P-23c (possible oratory, also identified by the Carnegie project)
S-10a (residence)
S-10b (residence)
R-172b (residence)
R-168b (residence)
P-21b (or house with rear shrine room)
R-202 (ritual group)
S-2b (residence)
Y-45c (elite residence)
R-100 (elite residence, house with rear shrine)

one of these groups forms the northern terminus of the city's principal sacbe (Proskouriakoff and Temple 1955).

SMALLER ELITE OR WEALTHY HOUSES

Some of the elaborate dwellings identified by A. Smith (1962:218) do not exhibit surface evidence of amplified size or elaboration, although they had rich graves. Similarly, House Q-39, next to elite palace group Q-41 in Milpa 1 (west of the monumental center), appeared relatively simple on the surface, although its size is toward the larger end of the continuum of commoner house sizes (figure 4.8). House Q-39 was encircled by its own albarrada and was considered a logical candidate for the home of domestic servants prior to its excavation in 2009 (M. Delgado Kú 2012a). Full horizontal investigation revealed a stone-lined cist with multiple interments and rich grave goods, including greenstone beads, thirty-six copper bells, a monkey effigy copper bell, copper tweezers, a scrollwork copper ring, a shell ring, shell beads, a ceramic effigy urn, miniature pottery vessels, and figurine fragments. This grave rivals the wealthiest found at Mayapán. Such houses may have been occupied by expanding members of elite families who also occupied adjacent palatial platforms. This example illustrates the problem of identifying secondary elite houses at Mayapán without excavations, especially in cases where surface architecture is of a size that could also represent commoners. While most of the commoner houses at Mayapán lend themselves to more straightforward evaluation using survey data, such efforts must be considered preliminary.

House Size Comparisons

Dwelling size at Cozumel varies considerably and reflects a range of activities performed by occupants of differing size and membership composition (Freidel and Sabloff 1984:181). Cozumel house sizes (40–60 square meters) are at the larger end of the range of ethnographically recorded Maya dwellings (20–60 square meters), which have a mean size of 28 square meters (Freidel and Sabloff 1984:11, table 2). The largest elite dwellings at Mayapán fall within a size range of 81–572 square meters (table 3.1). Palaces are larger than all of the other dwellings (309–572 square meters), except for non-palatial group R-20–23 (413 square meters). Other than the palaces, Tier 1 elite residences are defined as those that range from 152 to 413 square meters and Tier 2 elite residences range from 81.6 to 282 square meters, overlapping with the Tier 1 classification at the upper end. The Tier 1 category is based on architectural elaboration as well as size.

We calculated the size of all probable dwellings from a digitized version of the Carnegie (Jones 1962) map for comparative purposes (figure 5.19). The probable dwelling identification was given to structures exhibiting the rectangular shape, surface characteristics, and association (patio groups) of known domestic architecture for the site. The interval distribution of probable dwellings for the entire site is shown in table 5.8 (figure 5.19); 73.2 percent of these structures fall within 20–70 square meters and 8.5 percent fall within 71–80 square meters. Although the range shown for elite houses on table 4.1 is broad, only 15.9 percent of probable dwelling structures on the comprehensive site map are greater than 80 square meters and only 7.3 percent are larger than 100 square meters. All but two of our elite dwellings on table 4.1 (those 102 square meters or higher) fall within this upper 7.3 percent (figure 5.19). The top eleven values (177 square meters and higher) fall within the upper 1.6 percent of probable dwelling sizes for the entire city. Size appears to be one useful indicator of elite status, and smaller structures such as R-9 and R-100 may merit closer examination for nuancing the concepts of status and wealth at the city.

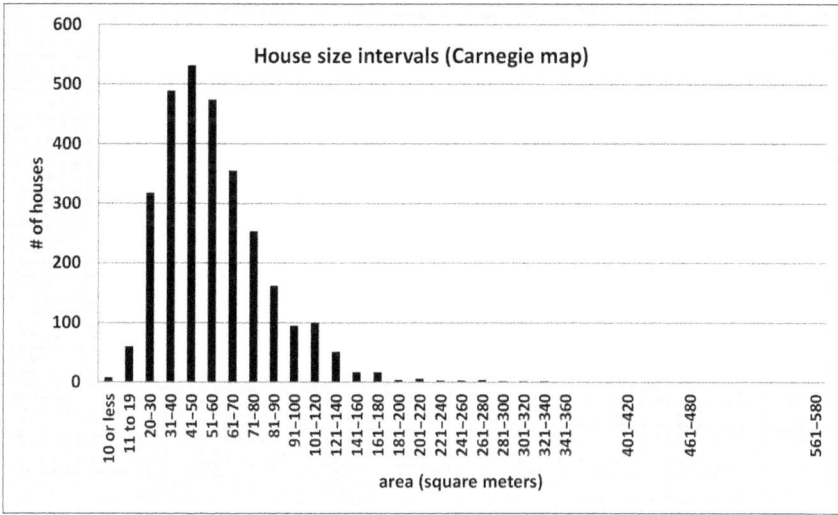

FIGURE 5.19. *House size intervals at Mayapán, as calculated from digitized data from the map by Jones (1962).*

Our probable dwelling calculations described above come from 2,961 structures on the Carnegie map (table 5.8; figure 5.19), although not all have been positively identified as dwellings. The mean for this sample was 58.8 (standard deviation 35.2), with a range of 4.4–572.4 square meters. Only six structures were smaller than 10 square meters (and are unlikely dwellings), and only seventeen edifices in this sample were smaller than 15 square meters. The fact that the sizes of fifty-one houses fall between 15 and 19 square meters suggests that this may have been an important class of small structures—perhaps dwellings—at Mayapán. These small structures were included in the calculations because they share shapes and context types with more average houses. Brown (1999:128) defined a residence as a structure of at least 20 square meters with one or more benches—a reasonable measure given the 28-square-meter average of traditional houses today. Sixty-eight of the structures that we measured from the Carnegie map are less than 20 square meters. If we eliminate those structures, the new mean (60.0) and standard deviation (34.9) are nearly identical to that of the entire sample that originally included them. As discussed previously in this chapter, some houses at Mayapán do not have benches. Most of the probable dwellings (86.9 percent) on the Carnegie map fell within one standard deviation from the mean (ranging from 23.6 to 94 square meters). This range is generally similar to Brown's (1999:122, table 2) calculations for a set of forty Mayapán residences, although more large houses appeared in our sample. Values within one standard deviation of Brown's mean (46.65) ranged from 22.5 to 70.7 square meters. House sizes from our mapped milpas (196 houses, figure 5.20) also yield a smaller mean (52.01 square meters) and standard deviation (29.5) compared to results from the comprehensive Carnegie map. The majority of the samples fall within one standard deviation above or below the mean (figures 5.19, 5.20).

Location and Household Size

We have previously discussed the fact that while larger houses are more commonly found near the site center, secondary elite houses are also clustered near the Square K plaza and are also dispersed as relative isolates in other neighborhoods (figure 5.6, chapter 3). As also noted, house size is not well correlated with albarrada enclosure size. Two other factors exhibit complex relationships with house size: elevation and the number of houses within a group. As we described in chapter 3, construction activities sometimes substantially modified and amplified altillos at Mayapán. All houses larger than 120 square meters were on altillos, which afford natural elevation and the benefits of better air circulation and views. But altillos were plentiful at the city, and commoners regularly built houses on them (figure 5.21). Some larger houses (80–120 square meters) are present in off-altillo locations, and this suggests that other locational factors were sometimes more important than elevation.

The number of houses within a patio group is sometimes a correlate of extended family size and wealth in Maya archaeology (Tourtellot 1988:339; Hendon 1991). Although this attribute has been previously discussed, it is interesting to consider the relative sizes of houses within groups with various numbers of dwellings (figure 5.22). Groups with more houses than the norm (four or five house groups) at Mayapán seem to have been occupied by commoners, according to house size ranges that fall between 30 and 70 square meters for these groups (figure 5.22). Two house groups may well represent a Mayapán ideal, in part due to their ubiquity, and also because this configuration is found for a wide range of elite and commoner house sizes. Isolated residences, as might be expected, exhibit a greater proportion of smaller houses—76 percent of these houses are smaller than 60 square meters.

TABLE 5.8 Intervals of probable house mound sizes, calculated from a digitized version of Jones's (1962) Carnegie project map

Square meters	Number	Percent
10 or less	8	0.30
11–19	60	2.00
20–30	318	10.70
31–40	489	16.50
41–50	532	18.00
51–60	474	16.00
61–70	355	12.00
71–80	253	8.50
81–90	162	5.50
91–100	95	3.20
101–120	100	3.40
121–140	51	1.70
141–160	17	0.60
161–180	17	0.60
181–200	4	0.10
201–220	6	0.20
221–240	3	0.10
241–260	3	0.10
261–280	4	0.10
281–300	2	0.10
301–320	2	0.10
321–340	2	0.10
341–360	1	0.03
401–420	1	0.03
461–480	1	0.03
561–580	1	0.03
Total	2,961	

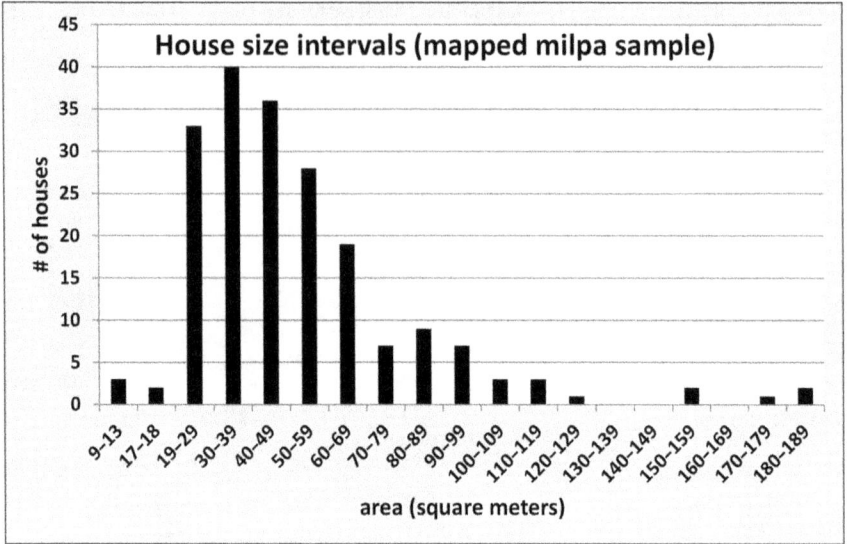

FIGURE 5.20. *House size intervals at Mayapán, as calculated from mapped milpa samples (PEMY project).*

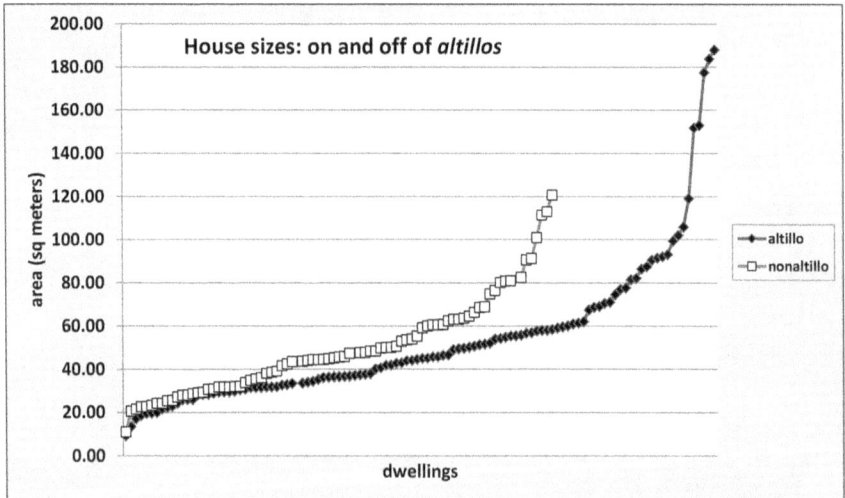

FIGURE 5.21. *House sizes located on and off altillos (natural knolls). Both large and small houses are regularly found on altillos at Mayapán, though some large houses are not on them.*

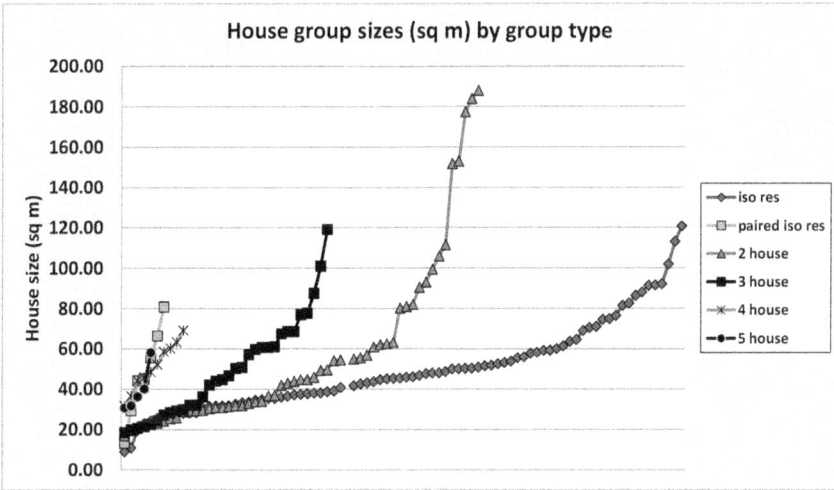

FIGURE 5.22. *House groups classed according to the number of houses within each albarrada enclosure, graphically displayed by frequency and size (area). The largest houses are arranged in two house groups.*

ALBARRADA ENCLOSURES

Albarrada enclosures reflect residential and nonresidential uses of space across the city. As described in chapter 4, some stone walls delineate lanes between residential and open areas for pedestrian traffic. Stone enclosures also define houselot space, much like the solar enclosures of traditional Yucatecan towns today, which contain dwellings, outbuildings, gardens, and animals. Nonresidential enclosures, as defined here, mark spaces without dwellings, including small pens, garden or orchard spaces, or empty lots where diverse agrarian, animal husbandry, or informal activities may have occurred. Although some houses at Mayapán were not enclosed by albarrada walls (see figure 4.5), in this chapter we confine our analysis to enclosed houselots.

HOUSELOT SIZE AND DWELLING SIZE

Property walls at Mayapán and other Maya sites have long captured the interests of archaeologists in terms of their implications for land ownership and wealth. Although wealth differences are evident at the site based on other measures, the area enclosed by houselot walls is not a helpful metric for affluence. A. Smith (1962:209) also observed that larger or more important

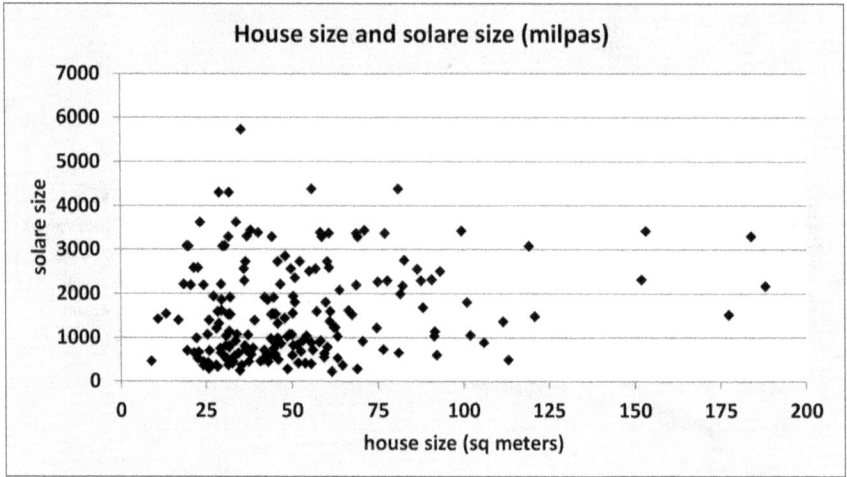

House size and solare size (milpas)

FIGURE 5.23. *The scatterplot illustrates no clear relationship between house size and solare (enclosure) size (as defined by albarrada wall houselot enclosures) at Mayapán. Larger houses were not situated within larger yards.*

house groups were not necessarily situated within greater domestic enclosures. Oddly, greater occupational density in central Mayapán does not result in more divided, smaller houselot enclosures. While some individual houselots show evidence of such fissioning, there is a considerable range of variation in areas within the heart of the city.

The lack of a good correlation between house size (a proxy for wealth and status) and houselot enclosure size indicates that the relationship of property ownership and domestic social groups was complex. The association of nonresidential walled (or open) field spaces with specific dwelling groups is in some cases difficult to ascertain, and in other instances, like Milpa 29 (figure 5.10), linkages are quite clear. There is currently no way to determine the amount of unoccupied land controlled per dwelling, as some fields were not enclosed. Family ownership of orchards, gardens, and other resources would have been important (McAnany 1995). Open fields may have been used for cultivation or as commons areas for a range of pursuits (Dahlin et al. 2010). It is probable that houselots and enclosed fields were used for fruit trees and other crops as they are today.

Notably, domestic enclosure sizes are not statistically linked according to four key variables: (1) the size of structures contained within the albarrada, (2) the number of structures contained within the albarrada, (3) proximity to the site center, or (4) proximity to the city wall. Ordinary least squares and spatial regression were used to assess these relationships with albarrada enclosure size as the dependent variable (Drennan 1996; Anselin 2003; Fotheringham, Brunsdon, and Charlton 2000). For example, the number and area of residential structures produce weak results of low significance, with adjusted R-squared values of 0.28 and 0.29, respectively. Tests for spatial dependence indicate no apparent spatial patterning to the relationships among the variables tested. Our findings are different from those of Brown (1999:136), who documented better statistical correlation between domestic enclosure area and the number and size of structures (r values of .68 or higher). But most of the examples used in his study came from Squares H and I, along the eastern periphery of the city wall. Significantly, Brown (1999:138–40, 142) suggested that cultural norms were influential in setting limited ranges for solar sizes, as space was available in this part of the city for larger enclosures, but residents did not expand accordingly. Comparisons between Mayapán, Cobá, and Cozumel reveal a suprising degree of consistency in houselot enclosure sizes (Brown 1999:142).

Some quantitative comparisons help to demonstrate solar size patterns (table 5.9). House sizes in enclosures larger than 3,000 square meters primarily fall within one standard deviation of the mean house size (20–80 square meters), and all houses in solares larger than 4,000 square meters are also within this range (figure 5.23). But extremely large houses are not found in solares of less than 1,000 square meters—five of the seven largest houses (near 120 square meters or larger) are in enclosures of 2,000–3,500 square meters; the other two are in houselots of 1,000 square meters. Houses smaller than 120 square meters are found in solares of all sizes (figure 5.23).

Houselot Size and Location

In Milpa 1, next to the city's epicenter, houselot enclosures range from 215 to 3,421.1 square meters and the mean is 1,006 square meters. Enclosures in other milpas within 500 meters from the site center range from 140 to 5,238 square meters and have a mean of 1,448.3 square meters (table 5.9). Beyond 500 meters from the center (within the wall), enclosures range from 77.2 to 3,623.6 square meters and have a mean of 1,101.1 square meters (table 5.9). Houselot areas outside of the city wall range from 166.4 to 2,365.6 square meters and have a mean of 603.1 square meters (table 5.9). The degree to which these ranges overlap illustrates the fact that location does not easily predict houselot enclosure size. The mean residential solar area for the total sample of mapped milpas and William R. Bullard, Jr.'s mapped squares (figure 4.3) is 1,084.9 square meters (standard deviation 783.4), with a range of 73.5–6,060.4 square meters. Table 5.9 reveals that the majority of the 587 residential enclosures (87.4 percent) fall within three intervals ranging from 121 to 1,775 square meters in area, with the greatest proportion in the interval of 602–1,189 square meters.

The ranges and means may be less informative than examining aberrant cases in certain parts of the city. For example, solar sizes graphically illustrated in figure 5.24 reveal the existence of a few clusters of larger houselots in the eastern part of the city as well as some clusters of smaller houselots to the south of the site center. The map reveals many solares that are close to the mean value in both areas. The existence of concentrated sets of larger or smaller enclosures may signify special social or economic characteristics for these anomalies.

Comparative information from Laraine A. Fletcher's (1983:table 8.1) study of enclosures at Cobá is provided in table 5.9. The majority of reported Cobá houselot areas fall within the same interval ranges as those of Mayapán, although the greatest proportion of solares from Cobá (30.4 percent) is found in the interval of 120–600 square meters, which is smaller than the most common solar area range for Mayapán. Similarities are revealed by the fact that 60.9 percent of Cobá's solar areas fall within the same three intervals as 87.4 percent of Mayapán's solares, and this suggests that certain size ranges were probably viewed as the most practical by the inhabitants of these sites. Fletcher reported that modern solares around Cobá range from 375 to 2,500 square meters, with a mean of 1,392 square meters, and this value falls within the most common interval ranges for both archaeological sites. Unlike Mayapán, houselot enclosure size is better correlated with residential size and status at Cobá (L. Fletcher 1983:128), although larger solares do not concentrate around the spacious outskirts of either city (Fletcher and Kintz 1983:112).

Hilltop Ring Albarradas

Some houselots are defined by albarrada walls that closely encircle residential and ancillary buildings with little extra space. These ring albarradas reflect a concern with containing architecture rather than the full topographic features on which buildings are placed. Many ring albarradas are on top of altillos, and these are common near to or outside of the city wall (figure 5.25). Hilltop ring albarradas would have afforded good privacy and perhaps a greater sense of defense for those living beyond the wall. Houselots

Table 5.9 Bullard and PEMY (mapped milpa) residential albarrada enclosure area, compared to Cobá (Cobá data from L. Fletcher 1983:table 8.1).

Interval: Enclosure area (square meters)	Bullard/PEMY residential enclosures (number within interval)	Bullard/PEMY residential enclosures (percent within interval)	Cobá residential enclosures (number within interval)	Cobá residential enclosures (percent within interval)
73 or less	2	0.3	2	8.7
92–104	–	–	2	8.7
120–600	147	25.0	7	30.4
602–1189	257	43.8	4	17.4
1205–1775	109	18.6	3	13.0
1803–2379	33	5.6	2	8.7
2437–2861	18	3.1	2	8.7
3297–3577	12	2.0	–	–
3623–4379	6	1.0	–	–
4912–5238	2	0.3	–	–
5884–6060	1	0.2	1	4.3
Total	587	100	23	

E-50 and AA-103 include Mayapán's city wall as part of their enclosures. Of twenty-six ring albarradas identified in the mapped milpa and Bullard survey sample, twenty-three are within 150 meters of the city wall, including nineteen outside of the wall and four at the eastern edge of the site. Three additional examples are near the Square K market plaza. Some tightly ringed enclosures also exist in low-lying areas (e.g., groups AA-107, AA-7, Z-68, Z-162, K-33, and H-9). A concern for privacy or defense in the city's periphery best explains these patterns.

NONRESIDENTIAL ENCLOSURES

The walled field system of Cozumel suggests that Contact Period European claims of communally owned land were inaccurate, or, minimally, oversimplified. While villages or towns may have technically owned land in common, families likely maintained longstanding rights to the fruits of their own labors, including walled areas, orchards, and crops. Developed land was more clearly linked to those who transformed it (McAnany 1995). Freidel and Sabloff

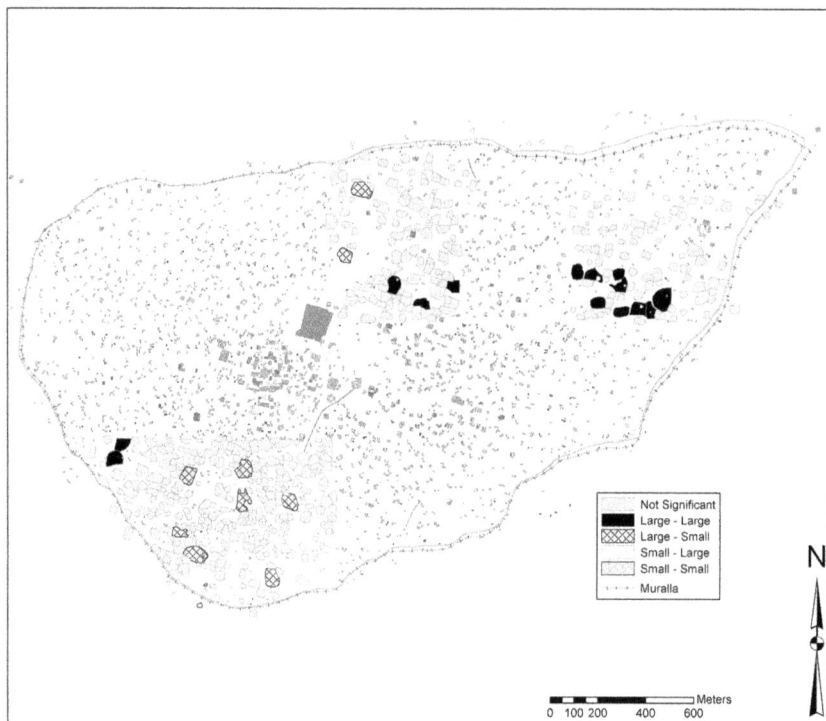

FIGURE 5.24. *The map graphically displays the degree of spatial proximity of larger and smaller albarrada enclosure sizes. The black shaded solares are statistically larger and more clustered together. The crosshatched solares are statistically more dispersed (i.e., larger solares are farther from other, larger, solares and are surrounded by smaller solares). Map by Timothy Hare.*

(1984:183) suggest that nobles probably claimed rights to land and would have wielded political power over rights or obligations to cultivate. As agrarian properties flourished, it is likely that some farmers wielded considerable negotiation power with respect to retaining their holdings. Poorer farmers, newcomers, or enslaved persons would have had less access to resources. Spanish chroniclers had little stake in recognizing property ownership in order to advance their own claims (Kepecs 2003).

Two types of nonresidential walled enclosures at Mayapán include pens and fields. These are working terms that await better evidence with respect to their use. Pens are found in two forms: self-contained units and those that incorporate a portion of a houselot boundary wall for at least one side (figure

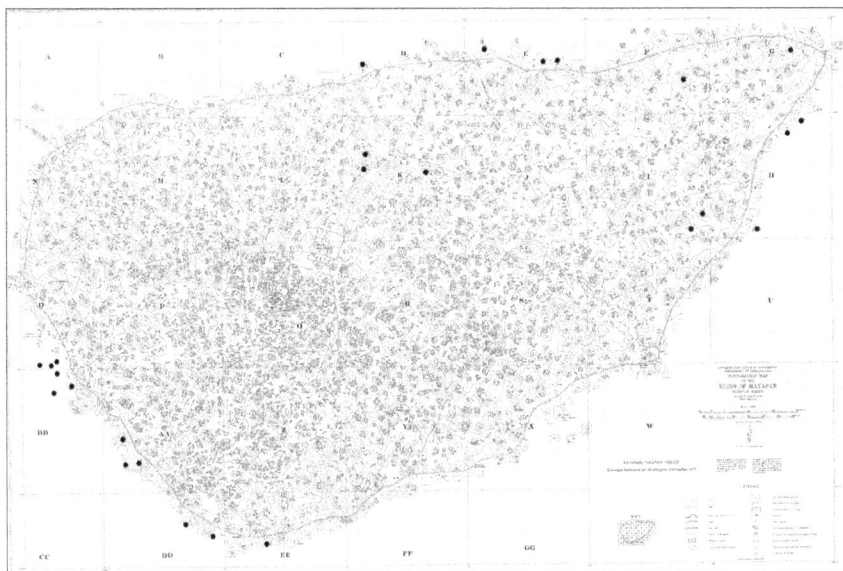

FIGURE 5.25. *Location of hilltop ring albarrada houselot enclosures mapped by the PEMY project.*

5.26, other examples in figures 5.2, 5.11). A total of 105 pens have been identified in our mapped milpa samples, and they are widely distributed within and beyond the city wall (figure 5.27). Pens may have been used for storing agricultural products or to contain animals such as deer, turkeys, dogs, or peccary, as illustrated by a modern example in figure 5.28 (Thompson and Thompson 1955:231; A. Smith 1962:224). Faunal analysis suggests that at least one-third of the city's supply of white-tailed deer derived from husbandry activities in Mayapán's houselots (Masson and Peraza Lope 2008). Many of these deer were consumed upon reaching late adolescence or early adulthood, and their age-at-death profiles do not conform to expectations for a hunting pattern, in contrast to peccary and brocket deer. Some older white-tailed deer may have been obtained in the wild, but the high number of full-size subadult white-tailed deer is far beyond levels normally reported for Maya sites (Masson and Peraza Lope 2008). Turkeys were also a vital component of the city's sustenance. While turkey and dog could have ranged free within houselot boundary walls, pens may have been useful for peccary or deer, which could also have been tethered, as Madrid Codex images reveal (Villacorta C. and Villacorta 1976:42c).

Fields are defined in this study as inter-residential spaces that do not contain domestic structures that are defined on at least three sides by walls (figures 5.9–5.11, 5.29). They could have been used for infield agriculture, as suggested for other northern Maya sites (Killion 1992a, 1992b; Hutson et al. 2007), although other uses are possible. Such spaces are under milpa cultivation today (as are ancient houselots), and their productive potential is adequate. Fields, like pedestrian lanes, are often defined by configurations of houselot boundary walls of the domestic clusters that border them, and some fields may not have been consciously planned.

Field area is highly variable, ranging from 77.2 to 3,275.3 square meters, with a mean of 811.3 square meters. Like pens, fields are widely distributed, and this indicates that no part of the walled city was dedicated exclusively to cultivation (figure 5.30). Generally, fields have low artifact densities. Out of 127 mapped fields, only eleven exhibited surface artifact concentrations identified in systematic survey. No evidence for fertilization of enclosed fields has been found, as many of these areas have red (*kancab*) clays that naturally occur in the area. Some parts of Mayapán exhibit an anthropogenic dark earth soil with a high organic content, but this soil is deeper within residential enclosures compared to areas (such as fields) outside of them.

Other fields at Mayapán may not have been enclosed. Open spaces are discernible in patches across the city (figures 4.5, 4.6). Such open lots could have been cultivated, used as open thoroughfares for pedestrian traffic or commons areas, or for local markets. Given that some houselots were not enclosed by albarrada walls, it possible that some open field spaces were used for similar purposes as enclosed fields. It is significant that denser portions of central Mayapán persisted in maintaining field spaces for agriculture or other recreational, social, and economic uses, and this characteristic has long been noted for dispersed or low-density Maya cities (L. Fletcher 1983:131; R. Fletcher 2012). Families who lived in the city's interior probably maintained their own orchards and gardens, although they could not have provisioned their families solely from these small plots. Agrarian cultivation beyond the city wall would have been an important component of the city's food supply (Russell 2008a, 2008b), and Mayapán also probably traded for some of its food (chapters 6, 8; Masson and Freidel 2012).

BURIALS AT MAYAPÁN

Mayapán mortuary contexts and human remains have been well described and analyzed in prior works (A. Smith 1962; Serafin 2009, 2010; Serafin and

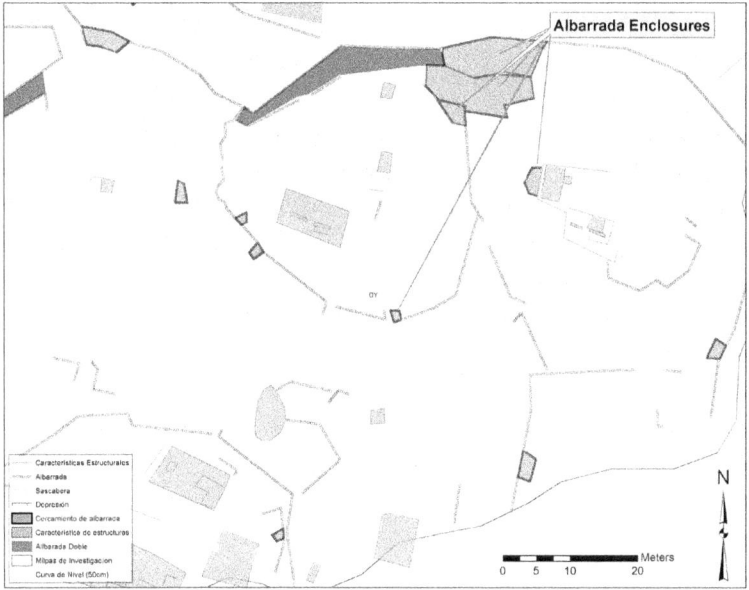

Caracteristicas Estructurales
Albarrada
Sascabera
Decoración
Cercamiento de albarrada
Característica de estructuras
Albarrada Doble
Milpas de Investigacion
Curva de Nivel (50cm)

Albarrada Enclosures

N

Meters
0   5   10   20

FIGURE 5.26. *Examples of pen enclosures adjoining houselot albarrada groups.*

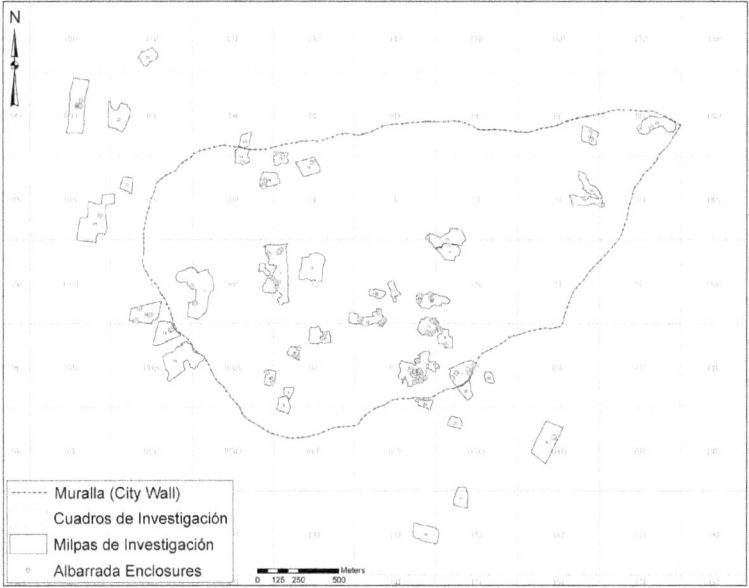

N

Muralla (City Wall)
Cuadros de Investigación
Milpas de Investigación
Albarrada Enclosures

Meters
0 125 250   500

FIGURE 5.27. *Locations of pen enclosures mapped by the PEMY project.*

FIGURE 5.28. *Modern animal pen from a houselot in Telchaquillo, Yucatán (2009). Foundation walls resemble those of ancient examples at Mayapán.*

Peraza Lope 2007; Hutchinson 2010). Our excavations in the settlement zone have recovered thirteen burials of Postclassic age in which the remains of at least forty-two individuals were present (table 5.10). Twenty of these individuals were part of a mass grave at the Itzmal Ch'en ceremonial group (chapter 2; Serafin 2010). The remainder of the sample comes from ten residential contexts, including two multi-interment cists within dwellings as well as a variety of off-structure locations. Brown (1999:124) also found three off-structure burials at Mayapán.

As A. Smith (1962:252) aptly stated, mortuary customs at the site followed "no fixed rule." A wide range of patterns reveals individual and group burials, off-structure burials beneath midden soils in bedrock cavities; cist and tomb burials in structures; and primary, secondary, and cremation interments (figures 5.31, 5.32). The frequent use of bedrock depressions for off-structure burials suggests advanced knowledge or exploration of caprock configuration. Graves were probably marked by perishable materials, as burial intrusions have not been observed despite close spacing. Whistles as well as jointed figurines may have been toys, as they occur in high numbers with child burials (Masson and Peraza Lope 2012). Some grave goods may pertain to a person's profession, as Landa (1941:181) claimed. For example, an individual interred at Q-40a had a stucco-covered, plaster-mixing tool, a red pigment stone, a bird figurine whistle, and a copper bell (figure 5.32). This probable artisan lived at a residence where copper bells and effigy censer faces were made; figurines were likely

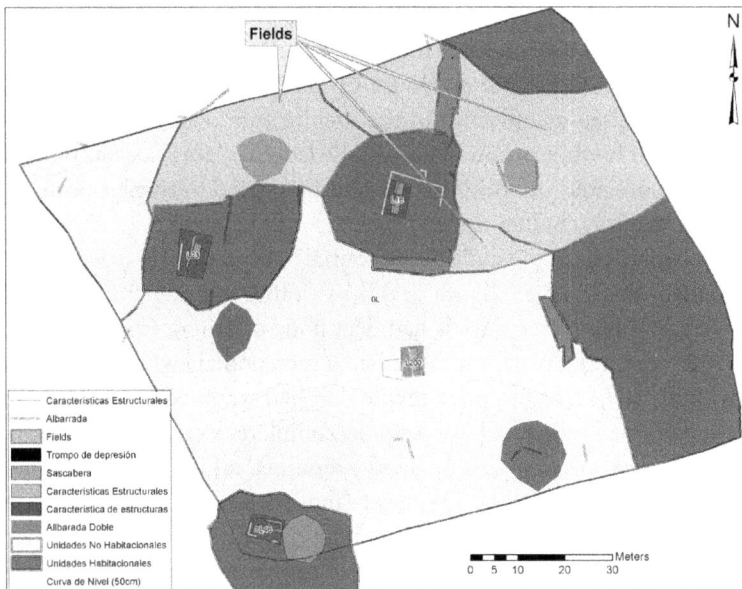

FIGURE 5.29. *Examples of enclosed fields outside of houselot space.*

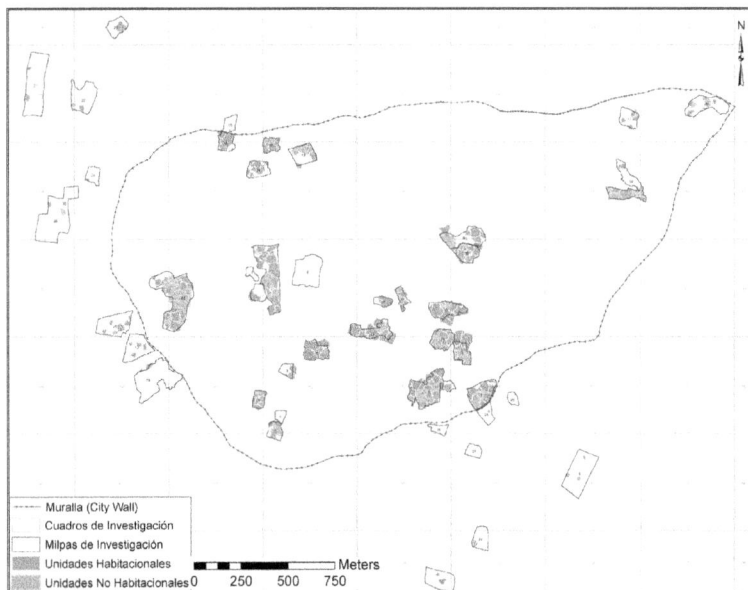

FIGURE 5.30. *Locations of enclosed fields (nonresidential) mapped by the PEMY project.*

manufactured at this locale also. Effigy censer production is indicated at this house by a large number of face molds (Cruz Alvarado et al. 2012). Similarly, an off-structure child burial at House Q-176 included stacked pottery bases that were also used as offerings in the architecture of this dwelling. Russell, Robert H. H. Hutchinson, and Pedro C. Delado Kú (2012) argue compellingly that these anomalous offerings for the site are related to surplus pottery making at this locality (chapter 6).

The rich offerings of the multiple cist burial in Structure Q-39 were described previously in this chapter (figure 5.33). Most other offerings in the settlement zone were humble. Three burials had deer bone offerings. One of two infants buried near domestic platform P-114 had a metapodial awl behind the crania; the awl may have served to pin a textile that had wrapped the infant. Directly beneath this small individual was a single, complete deer cervical vertebra (figure 5.31a). Two whole deer vertebra and a modified antler were also found near a child interment within the Q-39 cist (figure 5.31b). Faunal analysis reveals that deer vertebrae are almost always at least partially fragmented in Mayapán deposits, and the perfect condition of these mortuary examples contrasts with the norm and underscores their use as offerings. Almost no other faunal bone was present in the soils of the burials where the deer vertebrae were found, suggesting that it was unlikely that the bone originated from midden fill. One other Mayapán burial, an adult female next to House R-110a, was buried with a complete left deer radius that was aligned with female's right radius and ulna bones (figure 5.31c). The deer bone was covered with concretion and may have been retrieved from a cenote. Such concretion has not been observed on other Mayapán faunal bone. One other potential female grave good is noteworthy. At House L-28, a 12–16-year-old subadult was found with a *Spondylus* pendant in the pelvic region. Peraza Lope et al. (2008:579) suggest that the teenager was a young woman who was wearing an ornament of purity as described by Landa (1941:106). A similar bivalve pendant was found near a child in the Q-39 cist (figure 5.33). Maxine Oland (2009) also recovered a deer vertebra with a protohistoric Maya burial at Progresso Lagoon, Belize, and deer skulls were included in a Postclassic grave at Caye Coco on this same lagoon. Traci Ardren (2002) argues that the inclusion of deer bone with burials at the Classic-era site of Yaxuna was symbolic of practices of deer raising by women. Our results provide some support for this association in the case of the R-110a female, but the use of deer bone in child burials suggests a broader and more complex meaning that is currently unclear. Possibly, the children were female.

Social identity or occupation is not always expressed explicitly in Mayapán graves. Combinations of interment types and diverse offerings can be found

TABLE 5.10 Burials in Mayapán's settlement zone (PEMY investigations 2002–2009). All were of commoner status except perhaps Q-39.

Burial number	Structure	Age	Offerings, description
03–01	P-114 massive platform	Infant (18–24 months)	Flexed, off-structure Next to Burial 03–02, sherd concentration
03–2	P-114 massive platform	Infant (9–12 months)	Flexed, off-structure Next to Burial 03–01, deer metapodial awl, deer vertebra
03–3	L-28	Child (12–16 years)	Flexed, off-structure Spondylus shell ornament
03–4	F-13a	Adult	Terminal Classic age Off-structure, partly excavated
03–5	L-28	Adult	Secondary (incomplete) burial In sascabera depression
03–6	Milpa 7, Square X, open field	Adult and infant (6 months)	Open field, not near structure Probable mother and child
03–7	R-110a	Adult (50+)	Off structure, side-flexed Female, concretion-encrusted deer radius next to burial's arm, additional half mandible of a 6–7-year-old juvenile human included in grave
03–8	Itzmal Ch'en group	Mass grave 20 individuals	On platform edge near surface by Hall H-15 Mass grave of burned and chopped individuals, mostly adults, effigy censers broken and abundant
none	I-56	Adult	Cavernous pocket of cenote in altillo of I-56 (not excavated) Mama Red jar
03–9	P-115b	Adult	Disarticulated remains Incomplete
08–01	H-11	Adult (50+)	Probable female, Terminal Classic age (pottery sherd offerings) Flexed, next to front structure wall (in patio)

continued on next page

TABLE 5.10—*continued*

Burial number	Structure	Age	Offerings, description
08–02	H-11	Adults (2)	Terminal Classic age (pottery sherd offerings) Side-flexed and tightly flexed, behind structure
09–01	I-55a	Adult	Female, off structure Flexed, time period unknown (possibly Terminal Classic)
09–02	I-55a	Adult	Male, off structure Flexed, time period unknown (possibly Terminal Classic)
09–03	Q-39	Adult (middle-aged)	Female, south end of cist, flexed, shark tooth Same cist as Burials 09–04, 09–05
09–04	Q-39	Mixed adult (at least 3) and infant (2 years)	North end of cist, elaborate, rich offerings of shell, copper, pottery, deer vertebrae, antler tine Same cist as Burials 09–03, 09–05
09–05	Q-39	Child (primarily) (4.5 years)	North end of cist, elaborate, rich offerings of shell, copper, pottery, deer vertebrae, antler tine Same cist as Burials 09–03, 09–04
09–06	Q-176a	Infant (2 years)	Off structure, stacked ceramic plates and small bone awl
09–07	Q-40a	Adult (35 years)	Male, flexed in cist, large sherds, plaster-covered mano Same cist as Burials 09–08, 09–09
09–08	Q-40a	Child (6–9 years)	Large sherds, zoomorphic pottery figurine, copper bell In same cist as Burials 09–07, 09–09
09–09	Q-40a	Adult (35–50 years)	In same cist as Burials 09–07, 09–08

among individuals that are part of a single cist or are among separate burials of the same house group. Mortuary features are not generally a strong indicator of ethnicity or neighborhood affiliation (Masson and Peraza Lope 2010). Three of the Postclassic off-structure graves found by our project did not contain offerings.

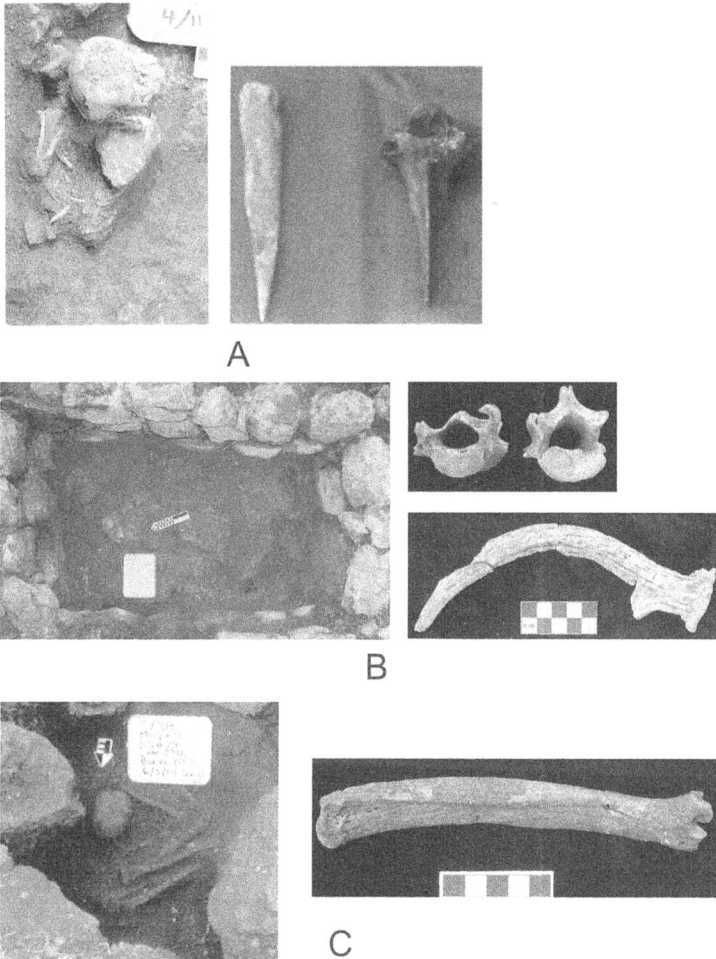

FIGURE 5.31. *Deer bone mortuary offerings in the PEMY settlement zone study area: (A) infant burial near dwelling P-114, with a metapodial awl and a complete vertebra beneath the infant; (B) a child interment in cist burial of dwelling Q-39, with two deer vertebrae and a modified deer antler; (C) an off-structure adult female near House R-110, with a left deer radius (covered in concretion) placed over her right forearm.*

POTTERY

Pottery from recent Mayapán investigations has been fully classified according to time period, type, form, and modes and yields valuable information regarding chronology and distribution that is presented elsewhere (Cruz

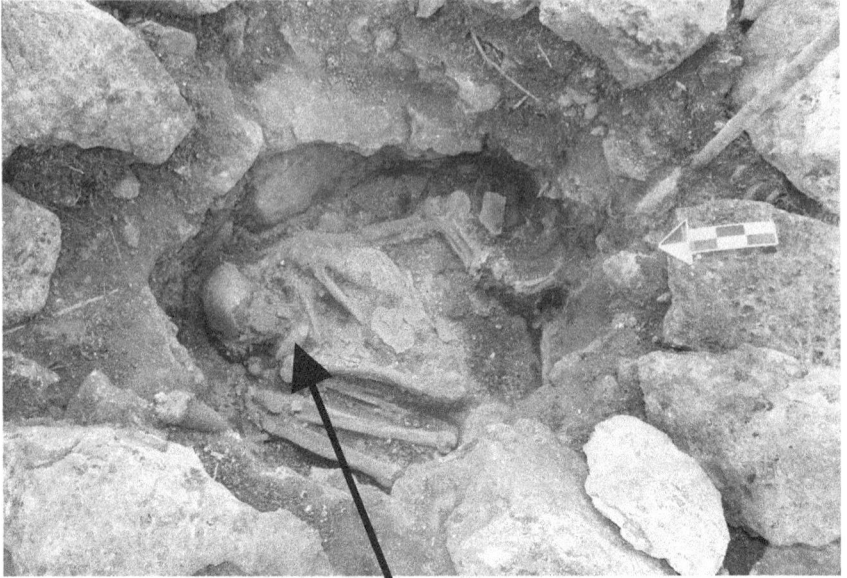

FIGURE 5.32. *An adult burial in a cist within dwelling Q-40a with tools of artisanry, including a stucco plaster-making tool and a chunk of red pigment. Three other plastering tools, a vase filled with plaster, and numerous effigy censer face molds and effigy censer manufacturing failures were recovered at this crafting house.*

Alvarado 2010, 2012a, 2012b; Cruz Alvarado et al. 2009, 2012; Masson and Peraza Lope 2010; Hare and Masson 2010). Here we summarize the basic findings of these detailed studies. A sample of around 250,000 sherds has been analyzed from the PEMY project alone. Most types of Postclassic pottery are widely distributed across various contexts, including commoner and elite residences or public buildings, among surplus crafting houselots and non-crafting houselots, and across various milpa sample units from city neighborhoods (Masson and Peraza Lope 2010; Hare and Masson 2010). These types include the most common jars and dishes of the Mama Red and Navula Unslipped groups, as well as types that are regularly found but in low frequencies, as Robert E. Smith (1971) initially determined. Lower frequency pottery generally represents fancier serving wares, including Matillas Fine Orange imported from the Gulf Coast region and locally made types such as Tecoh Red-on-Buff, Pelé Polychrome, Sulche Black, and Xcanchankan Black-on-Cream. These less abundant types are present throughout the Postclassic Period occupation of the city (Peraza Lope et al. 2006) and are less diagnostic to phase than originally proposed (R. Smith 1971). Modes and subtle form variations are more sensitive indicators of change through time than are the general types of the type-variety classification system (Cruz Alvarado 2010, 2012a). Based on our study of frequency distributions of sherds, we have determined that fancy or imported serving wares are not concentrated in high-status contexts or in contiguous domestic units that might indicate ethnic enclaves. We have argued that Mayapán's finer serving pottery was widely available in the city's marketplace and that many commoners obtained it in equivalent or greater quantities as elites (Masson and Peraza Lope 2010; Hare and Masson 2010; Masson and Freidel 2013:figure 8.11). These findings and interpretations match those reported by Ann Cyphers and Kenneth G. Hirth (2000) for Xochicalco. In a small number of elite contexts, elaborately painted and/or modeled dishes and jars are sometimes concentrated and may be more specific indicators of social groups (chapter 3). As Hirth (1998) argues, wealthy elites in all types of economic systems may be expected to have greater options to obtain high-value goods, and this is certainly the case for Mayapán. At Tikal, even though most polychrome pottery was widely available and may have been obtained through market exchange, specific, high-quality and low-frequency Imix polychrome pottery was limited in its distribution and may have been acquired through nonmarket means (Culbert 2003).

It is noteworthy that households engaged in surplus crafting at Mayapán often have among the highest quantities of imported Matillas Fine Orange (Hare and Masson 2010; Masson and Freidel 2013:figure 8.11). These contexts

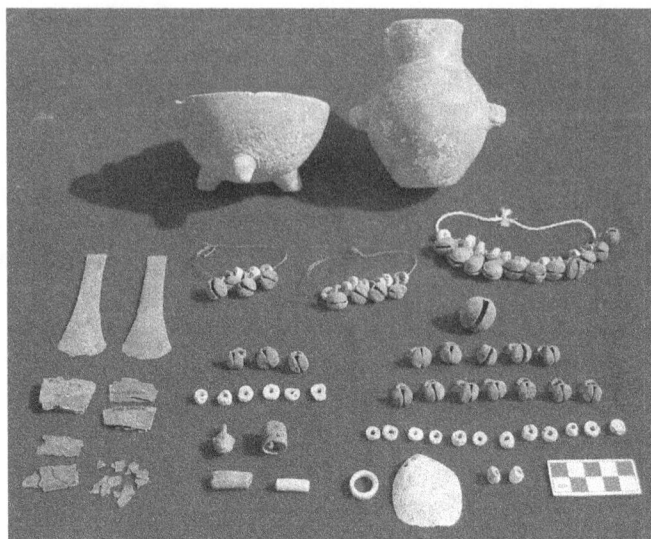

FIGURE 5.33. *Grave goods from a multiple interment in the cist grave of dwelling Q-39. The copper, shell, jade, effigy urn, and miniature vessels were concentrated near a child burial at the north end of the cist.*

also have higher ratios of other imported valuables, which attests to a pattern of greater relative affluence for crafting commoners compared to other commoner occupants of the city. Widespread but low quantities of valuable pottery indicate more about wealth than social identity at Mayapán. But the limited contexts represented by midden test pit samples may not provide the samples needed to identify anomalies such as the special assemblage found at elite House Y-45a (chapter 3). While midden test pits at Y-45a did reveal higher quantities of Buff Polbox group pottery, full excavation discovered ubiquitous quantities of polychrome and painted pottery that contributed to a robust assessment of the possible ethnic ties of its residents (chapter 3).

Only two surplus pottery-making houselots have been identified thus far at Mayapán—at Structures Q-176 and Q-40a (Russell, Hutchinson, and Delgado Kú 2012; M. Delgado Kú 2012b). A significant level of pottery production was initially suspected at Q-176 during our first season in 2001, as sherd density in its vicinity exceeds that for any other context tested at the city (Masson, Delu, et al. 2008; Masson, Delu, and Peraza Lope 2008). For example, three surface collections (84.78 square meters) from Q-176 in 2001 yielded 9,980 sherds, or 23 percent of the entire surface collection from the city's settlement zone. Of seventy-four other collections, all but one had fewer than 1,651 sherds, and all but seven had fewer than 1,151 sherds. Russell et al.'s (2012) investigations in 2009 fully exposed this house and recovered offerings of stacked jar bases that had been used to store clay pigments. The sherd debris from Q-176 consists of a high proportion of slipped Mama Red vessels (33 percent) and Yacman Striated vessels (51 percent), some of which were probably made at this locality (Cruz Alvarado et al. 2012:table 15.5). In contrast, residents of House Q-40a specialized in making molded and modeled elements of Ch'en Mul effigy censers, as mentioned previously (Cruz Alvarado et al. 2012). Both Q-176 and Q-40a are located within a crafts neighborhood, Milpa 1, where there is a concentration of surplus craft-making houses (shell, pottery, chert and chalcedony, and obsidian industries) just to the west of the monumental center (chapter 6). While House Q-176 is not adjacent to any elite or public buildings, House Q-40a is next to the platform of elite Residence Q-41, and it is within the albarrada enclosure of this group. Residents of Q-176 may have been more independent while occupants of Q-40a probably worked under the auspices of the elite compound to which this house was attached. Wilberth A. Cruz Alvarado (personal communication, 2010) observes that the Q-40a artisans were focused on production and decoration of molded and modeled faces rather than entire censers, as fragments of the attached vase portions were scarce at Q-40a. Clearly, specialization at this locality was focused on the stage of production that required the greatest skill. It is the only example of a censer workshop found thus far at the city. This context for effigy censer manufacture supports other evidence that the use of this type of ritual paraphernalia was concentrated in the hands of political and religious elites at the city (chapter 3). More censer workshops surely exist at Mayapán. We offer a full analysis of the crafting industries of the Milpa 1 vicinity and other localities in chapter 6.

Unslipped jar and bowl distributions do not indicate discernible social patterns. Undecorated Navula Unslipped vessels are the most common at the city, and Yacman Striated vessels also form major proportions of context assemblages. Together these two types form 37–70 percent of non-ritual pottery in the settlement zone sample (Peraza Lope et al. 2008). Navula Unslipped sherds consist of 59 percent jars and 30 percent bowls, whereas Yacman Striated sherds are made of 90 percent jars in our test pit and surface collection samples. Based on similarities in form, we infer functional overlap among undecorated Navula and Yacman jars, although the former vary more in size than the latter. The striations are on the exterior of Yacman vessels and do not suggest a specific function. Many contexts have abundant quantities of both Navula and Yacman jars (figure 5.34). Although frequencies for these types are affected by the greater size of Navula jars compared to Yacman examples, the sizes of these jars do not vary at different locations. Comparisons of their relative quantities are thus valid. It is interesting, however, that some contexts used more of one type than the other. The six contexts with the most Navula Unslipped sherds (75 percent or more of the houselot sample) come from six different dwellings in six different milpas (Milpas 6, 8, 12, 17, 26, 34). The five contexts with the most Yacman Striated sherds (50 percent or more of the houselot sample) come from three different milpas, including two houses in Milpa 17, two in Milpa 10, and one in Milpa 26. One of the high contexts for Navula is also in Milpa 17. There is little evidence for spatial clustering that might suggest that the use of these vessels was linked to social identity. While some surface collection samples yield similar Navula and Yacman percentages as the test pit samples, other results were quite different for the same context, which suggests that frequencies sometimes vary according to discard location. For example, test pits in the houselot of the P-115 group yielded sherd samples with 13 percent Navula and 47 percent Yacman, whereas surface collections from this group had 42 percent Navula and 19 percent Yacman. For the fully excavated houses from which samples are more complete, six dwellings had higher proportions of Yacman compared to Navula, including Structures H-11, I-55a, Q-176, Q-39, Q-40a, and L-28 (with percentages of Yacman ranging from 25 to 55 percent). Higher frequencies of Navula compared to Yacman are observed at Structures

I-57, Y-45, and X-43 (with percentages of Navula ranging from 30 to 44 percent). Ceramic frequencies for all contexts are reported by Carlos Peraza Lope et al. (2008) and Cruz Alvarado et al. (2012). Higher relative frequencies for both types are found at houses located near the Itzmal Ch'en group and in downtown Mayapán and thus are not tied to a specific residential zones.

A COMPLEX SOCIAL LANDSCAPE AT MAYAPÁN

Our analysis of Mayapán's domestic features adds new layers of complexity to earlier assessments by A. Smith and Karl Ruppert (1953; Ruppert and Smith 1954; A. Smith 1962) and Brown (1999). The influence of normative styles is indicated by choices made in house and bench style construction, the orientation of houses and house groups, the prevalence of houselot boundary walls, and overlapping pottery assemblages. Mortuary patterns are the most idiosyncratic features at the city. A majority of Mayapán's residents dwelled in single house compounds, reflecting a preference for the establishment of nuclear household units upon marriage. But clusters of houselot enclosures reveal that single dwellings were often nested within a matrix of other similar units. Kin members would have lived near to one another in these clusters, and single dwelling enclosures do not necessarily imply socioeconomic isolation and its disadvantages (Brown 1999). Houselots that are not enclosed by walls tend to closely mimic the composition of those with albarradas.

As might be expected for any socially diverse urban setting, variation is tracked in the details. Individual domestic features may have been constructed in response to multiple and even conflicting influences and purposes. Atypical houses are sometimes clustered in small groups in zones like Milpas 12 and 15, and in other instances they are dispersed among more ordinary dwellings. The influence of a state- or citywide emblematic style may have resulted in normative practices, but experimentation was clearly tolerated. The orientation of patio groups implies the symbolic pull of focal architecture or key avenues within the city, as patios frequently open toward and face the site's monumental center or other nodes such as the Itzmal Ch'en group. Most residents preferred some variant of an easterly patio orientation—a direction from which the wind, rain, and sun arrived—but some oriented their houses to the west, toward the site center. Greater diversity is observed in dwelling features in downtown Mayapán, where more elaborate L-shaped benches are present. This zone seems to have attracted socially diverse crafting families and traders (chapter 6). In contrast, toward the city wall, the tendency to construct more square or rectangular benches reflects conservative preferences.

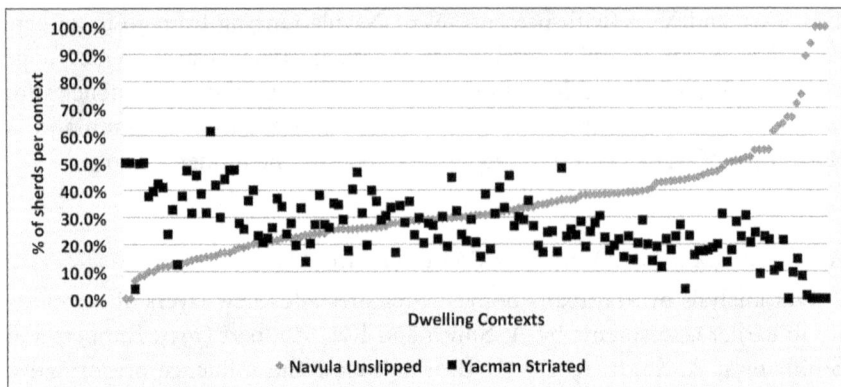

FIGURE 5.34. *Relative percentages of Navula Unslipped and Yacman Striated sherds per surface collections and test pit samples from the settlement zone. The majority of the samples have ample quantities of both of these types of pottery, mainly jars.*

The form and size of pens was largely left to the improvisational whim of individual families, although the significance of these features is clear from their ubiquity. It is probable that these small enclosures served many purposes, as did the larger nonresidential enclosed fields and open spaces between houses. Nonresidential structures in domestic contexts also vary greatly. The identification of enclosed bench edifices may point to key activities of food preparation, storage, or perhaps ritual.

Status differences are reflected in the distribution of Mayapán house sizes, with considerable variation observed for commoner dwellings. Houselot enclosure size does not correlate neatly with status, wealth, or location within the city despite the fact that residential zones near the city wall were less crowded. The construction of Mayapán's wall for defensive purposes (Russell 2008a, 2013), and the fact that peripheral houses were often situated within nucleated, small hilltop albarradas, suggests that privacy and protection were important considerations within and beyond the city wall.

Burials reveal especially diverse social practices. Individual families employed a range of funerary conventions, some more popular than others. Interments were placed in locations that included off-mound, shallow bedrock depressions beneath midden soils; oratories; rectangular or square cists within houses; sascabera depressions; cavernous chambers of cenotes; and in what appear to be open fields. Cremations were rare. Some individuals were buried with deer bones, some with pottery, some with riches, some with the tools of their trade, others with nothing at all. The importance of status and wealth is strongly expressed in mortuary offerings, but this class of data is so variable that it is a poor indicator of specific ethnic groups at Mayapán (Hutchinson 2010).

Pottery distributions attest to a well-stocked city market and the desire of the majority of commoners to own imported or fancy serving vessels. Ceramic types and forms were widely shared among Mayapán's residents, and common types are identical across the northern and eastern parts of the peninsula (Masson 2001b). Regional overlap in common slipped and unslipped pottery has been explained in terms of far-ranging exchange networks that tied the city to its allied polities, especially along the Caribbean side of the peninsula (Connor 1984; Sabloff and Rathje 1975; Masson 2001b; Masson and Rosenswig 2005). Even if ordinary pottery vessels were not exchanged over great distances, trade disseminated normative pottery styles that local potters and consumers chose to adopt. This relative homogeneity means that most domestic sherd assemblages are not useful for identifying social differences. Specialized types and forms that are not commonly distributed represent an exception— as we have demonstrated in chapter 3—including effigy incense burners and Pelé Polychrome pottery. Large samples from extensive excavations are more likely to track anomalous assemblages than small test pit or surface collection samples. Political and religious elites administered the production and use of ritual pottery, as indicated by the top-down distribution of Ch'en Mul effigy censers (chapter 3) and the attached context of their production next to elite House Q-41. Only three contexts in all of the work performed at Mayapán— each representing elite residential or public buildings—have revealed concentrations of Pelé Polychrome vessels (Peraza Lope et al. 2006; chapter 3).

It is interesting that despite Mayapán's status as one of the most densely occupied Maya cities, it can in many ways be characterized as a garden city because of the presence of ample space for cultivation in the vicinity of dwellings. The garden city model has been adapted to the Maya area by colleagues working at Classic Period sites (e.g., Killion et al. 1989; Tourtellot 1993:222; Chase and Chase 1998). This model of mixed and varied agrarian activities, including inner city spaces, is helpful for explaining the general condition of low-density urbanism that characterizes Maya sites. This pattern is largely explained by a commitment to combine urban life with some degree of agrarian production (Chase and Chase 1998; R. Fletcher 2012). Urban cities and capitals of this sort are distinguished from dispersed villages by the sheer numbers of their populations that are distributed over an extensive landscape and the political or military power that they exert. M. Smith (2011b) illustrates these points with case studies taken from Colonial history, including the cities of Addis Ababa and Ouagadougou, which he compares to larger Classic Maya settlements.

Despite Mayapán's cultivation space, its residential density better approximates the character of more traditional expectations of urban places. Like many ancient cities, density varied across the landscape at Mayapán. Even late medieval towns of northern Europe (north of the Alps), which tend to be the archetype for crowded urban living, were not uniform in terms of residential density. Some devoted "considerable areas" to gardening, and marketplaces and church properties could be substantial within walled cities (Pounds 1973:344). Nonetheless, as Norman J. G. Pounds observed, density was much lower outside of city walls in fourteenth-century Europe, as was the case for Mayapán (Russell 2008a). While the characteristics of a site as a whole can be informative, it is clear that housing density varied according to where one resided within a city (figure 4.6). The walled occupational density of Mayapán is 33 people per hectare (pph), which is much higher than southern lowland Maya cities of the Petén (5–10 pph, Rice and Culbert 1990). Mean ranges of 20–23 pph are calculated for the northern Classic-era sites of Sayil and Chunchucmil, as well as for the site of Palenque, and these are closer to the overall density at Mayapán. These pph estimates are loosely based on a calculation of 5 persons per structure from published works (Barnhart 2001:76, derived from Rice and Culbert 1990). Mayapán's average was smaller than that of provincial Aztec centers (50 pph, M. Smith 2011b:58) and significantly lower than northern European towns of the 1300s (110 pph, Hansen 2006:62), But six (500 × 500 meter) squares at Mayapán exhibit pph densities that approximate those of late medieval Europe, with densities of 77–126 pph, although some squares have much lower densities (figure 5.35). It is noteworthy that Mayapán was more populous than most of the European cities and Aztec provincial centers. Only 1 percent of northern late medieval towns reached Mayapán's size of 15,000–17,000, and few medieval cities enclosed more than 100 hectares (Pounds 1973:table 6.5), a small area compared to Mayapán's enclosure of 450 hectares. Provincial Aztec city-state capitals also tended to be about one-half to one-third the size of Mayapán's population (M. Smith 2005:table 4).

The settlement patterns outlined in this chapter indicate a dynamic, growing urban environment throughout Mayapán's Postclassic occupation. The 15,000 or so occupants probably arrived at various intervals as diverse constituents of hometowns of the confederacy, and perhaps from allied localities further afield. The influence of citywide norms on residential architecture is apparent. Although Colonial-era documents are largely silent on the matter of Mayapán's effort to symbolically impose or encourage state style or identity on

A 1   B 5.8   C 9.4   D 24   E 23.4   F 23.2   G 20   O.6

N 24.8   M 74.6   L 68.6   K 75.4   J 76   I 55   H 21.2

O 25   P 69.8   Q 126.4   R 98.4   S 81.6   T 35   U 2.8

BB 4.8   AA 77.2   Z 108.4   Y 71.8   X 25.4

DD 5   EE 15.8   FF 2.6

People per Hectare

	77 - 126
	36 - 76
	24 - 35
	6 - 23
	1 - 5

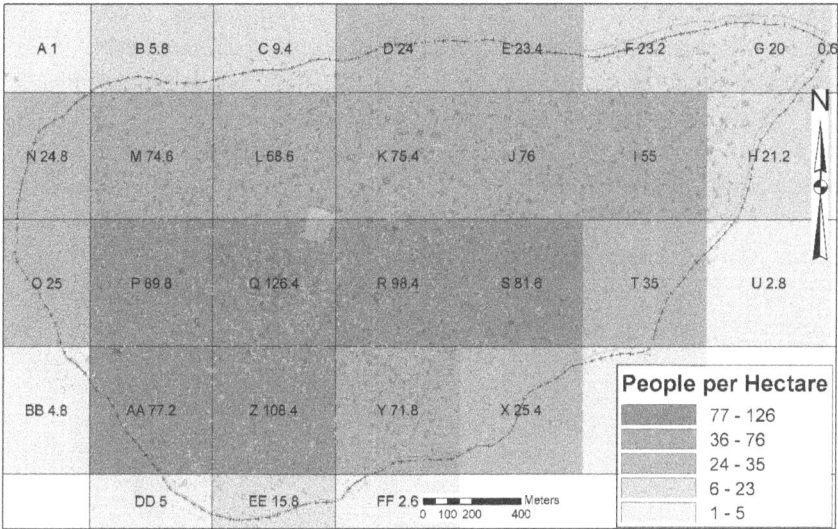

FIGURE 5.35. *Comparisons of variable densities of people per hectare for 500 × 500 meter grid squares within Mayapán's walled enclosure, based on an estimate of five persons per dwelling.*

its subjects in the realm of domestic architecture style and organization, such policies would be in line with Mayapán's other integrative strategies of religious proselytization (chapter 2; Landa 1941:27; Masson 2000), forced resettlement (Landa 1941:23–26), replication of public buildings in the epicenter and nodal locations (chapters 3, 4), state terror (chapter 2), and unitary, propagandistic declarations (Landa 1941:26). The institutionalization of a transformative strategy to promote cohesion, or urban ethnogenesis (e.g., Oudijk 2002; Pohl 2003b; Attarian 2003; Janusek 2004), seems to have influenced norms of the built environment and assemblages of household goods at Mayapán. The promotion of state unity may have been incomplete, which would explain abberant house types that crop up in Mayapán's residential zones. Bottom-up influences are sometimes important factors that affect neighborhood architecture, and these are occasionally evident in our sample (M. Smith 2010a:151). Hostility as well as friendship can characterize neighborhood relationships (M. Smith 2010a:140), and the construction of albarrada walls may have sometimes represented a useful way to separate one's nuclear family from neighbors or relatives. From a bottom-up perspective, the amplified urban opportunities for interaction may have also contributed to the spread of normative conventions for domestic life (Attarian 2003), although this process may have been coeval with top-down efforts. In adjusting to urban life, families may have weakened their ties to their original familial roots in confederated towns as the relative importance of an urban social identity took hold. Exceptions are known at some ancient states where familes maintained diverse ties to city and countryside (Janusek and Blom 2006:248). This chapter builds new layers of evidence pointing to the complexity of urban life and landscape at Mayapán, although many lingering questions remain. The next chapter outlines the evidence for a high degree of economic heterogeneity among the houselots of the city.

6

MARILYN A. MASSON AND
CARLOS PERAZA LOPE

The Economic Foundations

Our research into the economic foundations of Mayapán has focused on the relationships of both commoner and elite producers and consumers across the urban landscape. Evidence for occupational specialization and interhousehold economic dependencies reflects economic interaction at the houselot, regional, and interregional scales. Determining the degree to which Mayapán households were provisioned by others residing within the city or far beyond its borders is crucial for reconstructing the complexities and impacts of market exchange. The importance of labor and labor's rewards in terms of affluence is closely tied to a continuum of craft production and value that incorporates the mundane at one end and the exquisite at the other. Many households produced items at Mayapán, and part of our task is to distinguish those houselots engaged in significant levels of goods manufacture that exceeded their own needs. Variation in systems of circulation such as gifting, tribute, and trade have long been assigned to differentially valued material goods in the Maya past, but we observe considerable overlap in the modes of exchange for the array of desirables at Mayapán. In this chapter we compare the material assemblages of domestic and public contexts and provide the basis for inferring a complex economy at the city that was founded upon regional dependencies for raw materials and finished products and occupational specialization at the household level.

It is well known that the Mayapán state existed in the context of a well-developed system of commercial exchange. Ethnohistorical documents attest to the existence of marketplaces in Contact-era northern Yucatán of varied function, scale, and periodicity. A

DOI: 10.5876/9781607323204.c006

hierarchy of merchants and traders operated at various town, regional, and long-distance scales (Landa 1941; Tozzer 1941; Sabloff and Rathje 1975; Piña Chan 1978; Freidel and Sabloff 1984:185–90; Berdan et al. 2003). A full treatment of the systems of interaction in the Postclassic Mesoamerican world can be found in Michael E. Smith and Frances F. Berdan's (2003a) compilation, which details the variation among polities and regions in terms of the significance of international commerce. Many local and political networks were inextricably embedded in a network of exchange of information and goods that elevated the status and wealth of local elites in their quest for cosmopolitanism and legitimation (Smith and Berdan 2003b; Pohl 2003b). These networks stimulated producers, both noble and commoner, to provide basic goods and luxuries desired for exchanges. For example, royal women created fine woven cloth that was integral to political cohesion (Pohl 2003b). At the other end of the spectrum, commoners paid tribute in goods not made locally, which forced them to trade in marketplaces (table 6.1, Berdan 1988). Although the importance of Postclassic Period marketplace exchange has been generally accepted, the strongest evidence is documentary, and markets and their effects were not monolithic across a region within any time period (Blanton 1996; Smith and Berdan 2003a; Masson and Freidel 2012). More archaeological research is needed to refine knowledge for specific localities. Jeremy A. Sabloff and William L. Rathje (1975) attributed some key characteristics of Postclassic Maya society to the amplification of commercial exchange along maritime routes that shortened transport distances around the Yucatán Peninsula. This emphasis on commerce has been used to explain the weakened foundations of royal authority from the Classic to Postclassic Periods (e.g., Webb 1964; Sabloff and Rathje 1975; Rathje 1975).

This trade "amplification" is now dated to at least the Terminal Classic era (AD 800–1000) of Chichén Itzá (Kepecs, Feinman, and Boucher 1994; Kepecs 2003, 2007; West 2002; Braswell 2010). Zones of small polities that lacked major political centers such as Chichén Itzá or Mayapán also represented thriving commercial zones during the Postclassic Period (M. Smith 2003b). As for Chichén Itzá, Mayapán's trade network was facilitated by social, political, and ideological ties maintained by elites extending from at least coastal Honduras to coastal Tabasco (Ringle, Negrón, and Bey 1998; Ringle 2004). The importance and reach of Maya markets prior to the Terminal Classic Period merits more detailed study than it has received, and Mayapán's economic differences with the deeper Maya past were probably less pronounced than has been generally assumed (Masson and Freidel 2012). This point is an important one, as it bears on Mayapán's relevance for

TABLE 6.1 Economic specialization in Maya territories at the time of Spanish contact, according to Román Piña Chan's (1978:38–39) summary of the Lista de Tributos y Encomiendas 1549 (Paso y Troncoso 1939–1942).

Jurisdiction	Economic attributes
Ah Canul	Coastal strip, little agriculture, rich in saltworks and fish.
Calkiní	Tribute to Montejo in the form of corn, turkeys, honey, cotton.
Other towns	Tribute also included salt, fish, cotton.
Chakan	Tribute of salt and fish obtained directly from the coast or through intermediaries.
Cehpech	Tribute of salt and fish. The capital, Motul, also gave cotton mantles as tribute.
Hocabá	Constantly at war with neighbors, taking them as prisoners, perhaps selling them as slaves.
Maní	Agricultural zone, corn carried from Xul to Oxkutzcab (32.6 km). Annual feasts at Mani in honor of Kukulcan, a religious center.
Ah Kin Chel	High rainfall, cedar forests, northern coastal salt, rich in fishing. Cansahcab town sold salt to other towns. Town of Buctzotz captured people for slavery and produced cedar lumber. At Dzidzantun greenstones arrived through commerce.
Chikinchel or Chauaca	Rich in saltworks, produced fish and great quantities of copal for export. Other important towns, including Sinsimato, had copal monopoly.
Tases	Smallest, a group of towns. Capital of Chancenote had a road to Conil, important commercial centers.
Cupul	Agricultural lands and numerous cenotes, possibility of cacao plantations there. Town of Sodzil paid tribute of red beads, greenstones, corn, and wild turkeys to Lord Naobon Cupul, who lived at Chichén Itzá.
Cochuah	Controlled Bahía de Ascención. Temples in town of Ichmul, where lords of Chichén Itzá made offerings on trips to and from Honduras. Ichmul had cacao orchards. Halach uinic lived in Tihosuco, and he was of the Cochuah lineage, which had commercial agents in the Ulúa River towns.

continued on next page

TABLE 6.1—*continued*

Jurisdiction	Economic attributes
Ecab	Halach uinic lived in the town of Ecab. This town and Cachí were commercially important. Ports of Conil and Pole were in this jurisdiction. Encomenderos received salt, fish, corn, and ornaments from elsewhere in tribute. Isla Mujeres produced corn and salt. Cozumal center of pilgrimage and made honey and wax, paid tribute in salt and fish.
Uaymil	Forests of mahogany, cedar, Palo de Campeche, and copal. Roads from Bacalar to Cochuah and Ichmul. Bacalar was a port of embarkation for merchandise destined for interior, especially cacao. Mani went to Bacalar in search of cacao.
Chetumal	Exported corn, honey, cacao, maintained direct ties to Bacalar. Lord Nachan Kan had commercial agent on Ulúa River.
Campech	Good agricultural lands for corn and fruit trees, produced much cotton, maize, honey, and wax. Salt and fish given to Spanish for tribute.
Champotón	Produced large amounts of fish, ruled by halach uinic of Couah lineage. Commerce with interior via Río Champotón. Tixchel produced turtle shell objects and feather fans.
Acalan	Río Candelaria dominated by Acalan merchants. Commercial ties to Xicalanco, Tabasco, Petén Itzá, and Cimatán. Merchants barrio in Nito.
Cehache or Mazatlán	Forests, lakes, swampy land, riverine ties to Uaymil, Chetumal, and perhaps Belize, reached Petén Itzá via this jurisdiction.
Cimatán	Extended to Gulf Coast, ties with Tabasco along Río Grijalva and tributaries. Carried amber from town of Tatalapa to Tabasco.

diachronic comparisons in the Maya area. Postclassic Maya society's breaks with the past tend to be more greatly emphasized than its similarities, and this impedes the recognition of long-term patterns in the realm of political economy (Ringle and Bey 2001). But much variation in market-oriented impacts on daily life through time should be expected among different towns and cities across the lowlands in the Maya area, as prior studies have shown (A. Chase 1998; Chase and Chase 2001, 2004a; Fry 2003; Culbert 2003;

Dahlin et al. 2010). Greater concentrations of regional populations in earlier periods may help to explain the existence of multiple constricted ceramic style zones and spheres of exchange, whereas broader geographic networks of smaller towns promoted more outward-looking networks through time (Stark 1997; Masson 2001b).

The lack of hieroglyphic references to markets has little to do with whether or not they existed (Masson and Freidel 2012), and elite luxury good enterprises oriented toward accruing or maintaining social capital only represent a partial view of Maya economic systems (e.g., Houston and Stuart 2001; McAnany 2010). Merchants and their activities would have posed a potential threat to members of royal courts, and the exclusion of the mercantile realm in royally commissioned works of art may have been no accident (McAnany 2010). As for the Classic Period, the lords of Mayapán also circulated luxury items such as copper bells, polychrome vessels, exotic faunas or pelts, and similar goods.

In this chapter, we examine archaeological indicators of the importance of market exchange to daily life. The simplest approach to this problem is to determine where households were situated along a continuum defined by complete autonomy at one end and full-time occupational specialization and full dependency on others at the other end. Both of these extremes are unrealistic expectations for ancient agrarian states such as Mayapán (e.g., Wolf 1982:19). Dependency on the outside world is measured by two indices: To what degree were households making surplus products for exchange and to what degree do households' consumed goods reflect acquisitions from others? At the most basic level, residents of Mayapán produced some items with resources of local origin, such as clay for certain pottery types or white-tailed deer. Another correlate of trade's importance is the fact that a significant majority of households obtained an admixture of rarer finished items from distant lands—in Mayapán's case, serpentine axes from the Maya highlands or Gulf Coast Fine Orange pottery. The quantity of the most valuable goods and their distribution across social status lines is one important consideration for identifying the significance of market exchange (Hirth 1998). Reconstructing exchange at Mayapán is quickly complicated by the fact that crafting households relied on imported raw materials (shell, obsidian, cotton thread) for their surplus industries. Dependencies on the outside were layered, beginning with the raw material supply chain into the city and ending with the circulation of more valuable finished craft goods out of the city to smaller towns in the northern peninsula. All of these patterns observed for Mayapán are also reported for Tikal and other earlier prominent centers (Haviland 1963; Rathje 1971; Becker 1973; Fedick 1991; Masson and Freidel 2012). Identifying occupational heterogeneity at Mayapán, as outlined in the details of this chapter, represents fundamental evidence in our case for for a complex economy.

The study of currencies is an additional approach to reconstructing past economic systems. Although historical documents establish with clarity that monetary systems were in use at Postclassic Mesoamerican markets (including those of Yucatán), the archaeological study of potential monetary units has not been well developed for the Maya area, with the exception of studies of art or hieroglyphs (Stuart 2006; Freidel and Reilly 2010; Dahlin et al. 2010). The use of currencies is tied closely to the question of governing institutions. Who made and controlled Postclassic Maya currencies such as cotton mantles, copper bells, jade and shell beads, and cacao beans, and how were their values set in various regions according to their scarcity? David A. Freidel and his colleagues have argued for the importance of elite roles in the creation and valuation of currencies and their commercial worth from the Late Preclassic through Contact Periods (Freidel 1978:258; Freidel, Reese-Taylor, and Mora-Marin 2002; Freidel and Reilly 2010). Freidel and Justine Shaw (2000) propose that the use of durable currencies helped to resolve local crop shortages by providing the option to purchase grain. Corn could not be stored for long in the tropical Maya area, and as crop shortages are often locally experienced, trade across different rainfall zones was feasible. We know that ancient Maya polities, including Mayapán, regularly experienced such shortages (chapter 8).

Janet L. Abu-Lughod (1989:57–58) attributes the rise of prosperous market towns in late medieval times (e.g., Champagne and Bris) to the strategic successes of town authorities in attracting and securing passage for merchants and controlling luxury good supply networks. According to her, before institutions such as money lending were well developed, merchants would commission the production of fine textiles from producers to be picked up on their next journey. This study is illuminating in that it provides a historical example of complicated transactions during the premodern era (the twelfth and thirteenth centuries AD) prior to the adoption of more formal banking institutions in northern Europe.

Our analysis of shell objects in this chapter considers the distribution of different types of shell ornament manufacture in an effort to differentiate shell monetary units from other types of objects. Marine shell has been largely treated as a uniform material class in the Maya region, with the exception of *Spondylus* (Freidel et al. 2002, Graham 2002). We suggest that olive shells and beads and pendants of large, white marine gastropods (such as *Strombus*) also served as currency units; like *Spondylus*, they more commonly entered Mayapán in finished form and, in contrast to more ordinary marine bivalve objects, were not broadly manufactured at the city's shell workshops. This examination of shell debris and finished objects will hopefully provide a useful study for continued work on the manufacture of standardized shell ornaments of potential currency status at Maya sites.

This chapter's treatment of the multiple dimensions and scales of production and exchange contributes an important component of our overall argument for the complexity of Mayapán's urban life. The distribution patterns of various nonperishable items made and obtained by the city are considered individually, as each artifact class was positioned differently on the continuum of value in the city's economy. Archaeological recognition of the complexity of ancient Maya economies has not been fully realized despite the detailed testimonies found in ethnohistorical accounts (Masson and Freidel 2012).

RECOGNIZING ANCIENT ECONOMIC COMPLEXITY: ISSUES OF SIMPLIFICATION AND ELITE CONTROL

A tendency to oversimplify models of past market exchange, in addition to a preoccupation with the issue of elite control of production, has impeded archaeological reconstruction of regional economic complexity (C. Smith 1976; Pyburn 1997; Masson and Freidel 2012). The first issue is well articulated by Stephen A. Kowalewski (1990:54), who states, "What concerns me is that in current social science theories, millennia of change and variation are often subsumed under one typological concept." He argues that the search for variation, change, and reorganization should be of major concern to archaeologists and cautions against rendering "unto the tributary mode" as a default explanation for the economic underpinnings of ancient states (Kowalewski, 1990:55). "When we find scraps of information about the state or tribute," he asks, do we also consider the importance of other networks of exchange? (Kowalewski, 1990:54). As Kenneth G. Hirth (1998) points out, the development of complex economies is cumulative, and in complex systems, gifting, tribute, and marketplace exchange can coexist. It is a simple matter to acknowledge the existence of simple, informal, or barter markets, which are present even among nonstate societies, but priority should be given to determining when and where market exchange was a primary condition of life.

A second question that shadows the study of ancient economic systems is the question of elite control (Kowalewski 1990:54). The degree to which government is underwritten by the contributions of labor and tribute by supporting populations has been central to investigations of Mesoamerican political economies; some have focused primarily on whether control was centralized or decentralized, but this approach leaves plenty of unanswered questions (e.g., Blanton et al. 1996; Chase and Chase 1998; Aoyama 1999; King 2000; Scarborough, Valdez, and Dunning 2003; Braswell 2010). Market philosophy of the industrial era has led Mesoamerican scholars to view ancient market development primarily in juxtaposition to state control (Garraty 2010; Feinman and Garraty 2010). Some influential books within (Weiner 1992) and outside (Davis 2001) of anthropology address this flawed ideological standpoint in the context of traditional societies in greater detail than is possible here.

Marketplaces facilitate direct exchanges between producers, consumers, and a range of middlemen who are beyond the scope of direct elite supervision (C. Smith 1976; Berdan 1988; Hirth 1998). Some argue that markets counteract elite control in ancient settings by countermanding efforts to restrict luxury goods and allowing opportunities for entrepreneurism and affluence in ranks below the noble class (Eisenstadt 1980, 1981; Gailey and Patterson 1987). In extensive, relatively unbound geopolitical landscapes like the Maya area, top-down constraints on exchange would have been difficult to impose (M. Smith 2003b), but central market events hosted at core cities would have been the richest and most diverse and would have presented elites with opportunities for profitable exchanges or taxation (Berdan 1988; Blanton 1996; Masson and Freidel 2012). The study of ancient market exchange in Mesoamerica is now moving beyond simple dichotomous schemes of decentralized "free markets" versus centralized tributary systems (Feinman and Garraty 2010). The Mexica of central Mexico stand as the clearest example of a Mesoamerican civilization deeply invested in a market system, yet, as Kowalewski (1990:53) notes, studies of their economy concentrated for many years on the importance of tribute (with notable exceptions [e.g., M. Smith 1999, 2003b, 2010a; Blanton 1996]).

What material gains might elites have garnered from organizing and fostering major market events at central cities? Contact Period Maya literature on partially administered markets reveals that judges presided over weights and measures and resolved disputes. Trading was officially permitted only in the marketplace (Feldman 1978:12; Piña Chan 1978:40; Tozzer 1941:96). Markets themselves were differentiated by scale, periodicity, and content (Tozzer 1941:9; Piña Chan 1978:42; Freidel 1981:381). Merchants had sufficient incentives to undertake high-risk, long-distance voyages with assurances of state protection. Archaeological and documentary accounts also indicate that elite households produced as well as consumed wealth. Market exchange provided greater opportunities for converting one type of good into another (Berdan 1988). To what degree were elite production activities geared toward the generation of bride wealth and other inter-elite exchanges (e.g., Pohl 2003a) versus commercial profit?

The need to provision elite households with basic goods could also be augmented by regular local and diverse marketplaces. Pilgrimage market fairs and regularly scheduled more secular events are known from Contact Period historical accounts; archaeological features at Cozumel sites affirm these testimonies (Feldman 1978; Freidel 1981; Freidel and Sabloff 1984:186–87, 189). The concern of Classic Period monuments with periodicity and calendrical celebration certainly suggests that complementary opportunities for commercial exchanges at multifunctional gatherings would have been hard to ignore (P. Rice 2009g).

POSTCLASSIC MAYA ECONOMY—
ETHNOHISTORY AND ARCHAEOLOGY

Documentary accounts provide snippets of testimonies concerning marketplaces, merchant/trader hierarchies, currencies, tribute demands, agriculture, property ownership, and occupational specialization for the Postclassic Maya realm. But these sources require comparison with empirical archaeological data. Here we summarize key pieces of information that provide a broader framework for understanding the meaning of the economic activities of Mayapán's households and the regional exchange system in which they were embedded.

Production Diversity in the Contact Period

Products made in the lowland Maya area may have been widely exchanged between neighboring territories and beyond. The resource heterogeneity of this region promoted community-scale specialization in surplus production for exchange well before the Postclassic era (Potter and King 1995; Masson 2003b). Román Piña Chan (1978:38–39) pored through the Lista de Tributos y Encomiendas de 1549 to identify goods associated with specific polities across the Yucatán just after the Spanish conquest of the northern Maya area (table 6.1). Figure 6.1 displays this product diversity for selected provinces and indicates how Maya settlements exploited different environmental zones in a manner that would have promoted exchange (from Piña Chan 1978:figure 12). The 1549 tribute list attests to community- and polity-scale economic specialization prior to Spanish arrival, although it is probable that more complexity existed during Mayapán's heyday. Salt and fish were provided from the following polities that were near the coast or within close coastal trading distances: Ah Canul, Chakan, Cehpech, Ah Kin Chel, Chikinchel/Chauaca, Ecab, Campech, and Chanputun (Champotón). Lumber came from Uaymil and Ah Kin Chel. The polities of Maní, Campech, Chetumal, Isla Mujeres, and Cupul were said to have had good agricultural lands for corn and fruit trees. Copal was made in quantity in Chikinchel/Chauaca, especially in the town of Sinsimato. Cacao production was significant for Chetumal, Ichmul (Cochuah polity), and possibly Cupul. Slaves, sometimes captured during warfare, were sold from Buctzotz (Ah Kin Chel polity) and Hocabá (table 6.1). Some towns paid tribute in trade objects obtained elsewhere, or they produced special luxuries. For example, greenstones were made in Dzidzantun (Ah Kin Chel polity), whereas Sodzil (Cupul polity) paid tribute in red beads, greenstones, corn, and turkeys to an overlord who resided at Chichén Itzá (table 6.1). Ecab provided Spanish *encomenderos* (estate holders) with ornaments of nonlocal origin, and turtle shell objects and feather fans were made in Tixchel (Chanputun). Cimatan carried amber from Tatalapa as far as Tabasco. Several places paid tribute in combinations of these goods along with fish, salt, honey, wax, copal, and cedar. Bacalar was a point of embarkation for goods destined for the interior and was known for its cacao merchants (Piña Chan 1978). Commercial agents resided at Ulúa River towns and at Acalan, Chanputun, and Chetumal. Piña Chan's (1978:41) discussion alludes to the conversion of raw materials into more valuable products for exchange—for example, at towns where carpenters converted wood into wooden effigies. It is important to note, however, that enmities among Yucatecan provinces sometimes impeded trade (Roys 1972:53), which may explain some of the overlap among territories that might have belonged to fluctuating alliance networks.

With the exception of coastal towns, all localities had significant agricultural production (Roys 1972:53; Piña Chan 1978:41), as is expected. Much salt was carried from the Yucatecan coast to Tabasco and beyond to central Mexico and Honduras (Kepecs 2003). Roasted fish was imported inland to a distance of 20–30 leagues and salted, dried fish could be traded farther into the interior. Principal exports from Yucatán were salt, cacao, wax, honey, cochineal, achiote, indigo, and cotton products, but as Piña Chan's (1978:42) analysis indicates, these originated from different peninsular towns. From the Gulf Coast locality of Xicalanco, Aztec traders obtained lowland Mesoamerican products of jaguar skins, turtle shells, jade, and salt and exotic items from highland Chiapas (Scholes and Roys 1938:318). Piña Chan emphasizes that northern Maya long-distance merchants served as middlemen by brokering a wide array of products, including those that did not originate in northern towns. Salt, made on

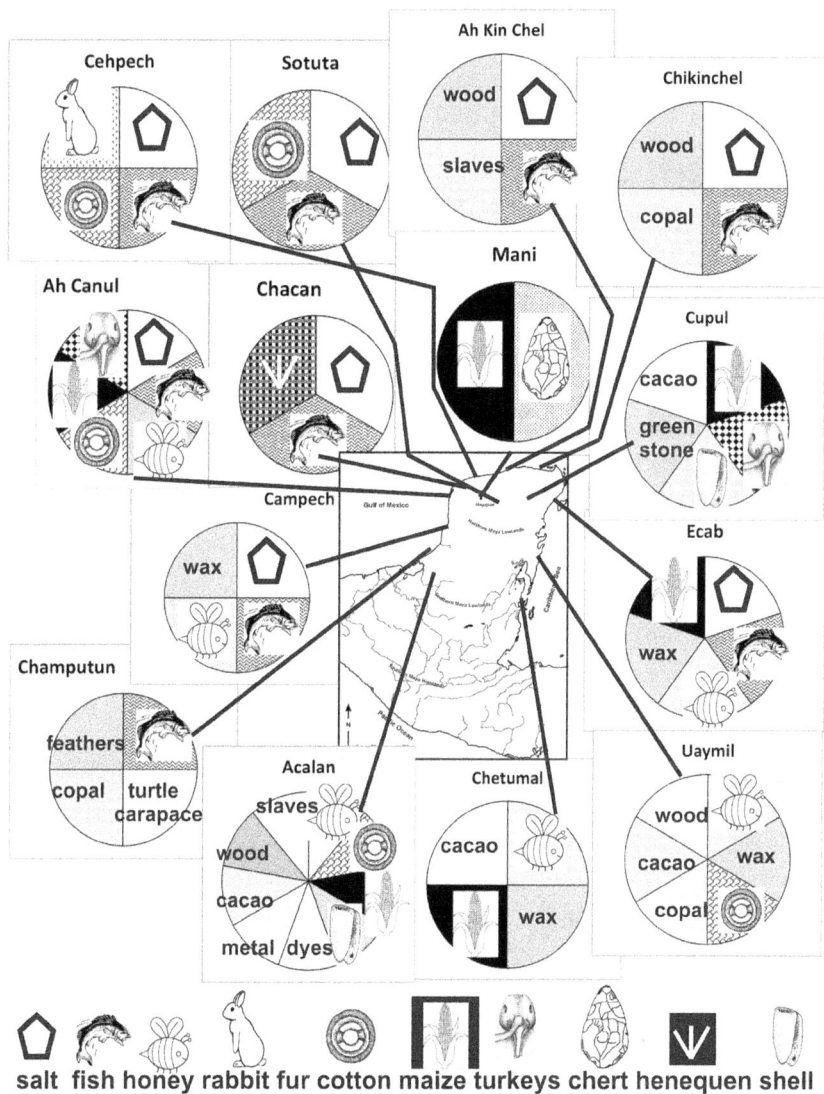

FIGURE 6.1. *Different provinces of the Contact Period paid tribute in different sets of products, as indicated graphically for selected territories in this figure; adapted from Piña Chan (1978:figure 12). This pattern illustrates regional scale productive heterogeneity that provided ideal conditions for market exchange and trading dependencies.*

the coast, would have been especially important for Mayapán's distant trading merchants, even though the city itself was in an area that offered access to few unique resources. Although cacao was grown in cenotes and other depression features, the currency needs of the city's markets would have required more than could be grown locally. Great quantities of cacao were imported to the northern peninsula from Honduras (and probably Belize) and Tabasco (Tozzer 1941:37). Frans Blom (1932:548) also notes that canoes departed from Yucatán for Ulúa, laden with clothing and other goods, and returned "loaded with cacao" (from Fernández de Oviedo y Valdés 1853:253).

Other items obtained from beyond the Maya area include *tuchumitl*, a woolen thread made of dyed rabbit fur, and wooden swords with "flint" (perhaps obsidian) edges. Products available at Xicalanco (Piña Chan 1978:42) include woven cloth, ornaments, slaves, and large greenstones, perhaps serpentine, used to make small axes common in the Maya area. Most of Mayapán's obsidian is from the Guatemalan highlands (especially Ixtepeque) and would have been traded northward along coastal routes. Slave trade apparently occurred into and out of the area, as Maya traders brought slaves along with salt and cloth to Tabasco in exchange for currency items, cacao, and stone beads (Landa 1941:94; Piña Chan 1978:43). It is possible that slaves from distant lands were more desirable in order to dislocate them from hometown connections that might have invited flight (e.g., Inomata 2001). The return voyage would have been relatively light in bulk, consisting of primarily currencies. Diego de Landa (1941:96) further notes these stone beads and cacao were reinvested—that is, these profits were used to buy slaves (presumably for further trade). Red shell beads were an especially valuable currency item (Blom 1932:546). As for many agrarian complex societies, functional overlap existed for shells valued as monetary units and personal jewelry (Blom 1932:546). Caravans of porters carrying merchandise also traveled overland via established trails between towns, and Mayapán represents one such inland location that relied on roads. One cacao transport route extended from the lower Río Hondo to Xiu territory in Yucatán, an aerial distance of 235 kilometers (Roys 1972:52). Francisco de Montejo went to Chichén Itzá and Ake via established roads and routes for merchandise transport connected Valladolid to Bacalar (Piña Chan 1978:40). Stopping places were often marked by roadside shrines honoring the North Star; such shrines have been found archaeologically (Blom 1932:546; Freidel and Sabloff 1984).

These accounts imply a complex commercial system in which different kinds of cloth were exchanged into and out of the Maya area along with other functionally overlapping goods such as pottery, greenstone, and slaves. Although the Maya highlands are a source for serpentine and other types of greenstone, diverse bead colors and stone types are observed archaeologically that suggest a variety of sources. Many houselots at Mayapán possessed at least one Matillas Fine Orange pottery dish of the type made by Maya groups of the Gulf Coast (Forsyth 2004).

NONPERISHABLE PRODUCTS IN THE ARCHAEOLOGICAL RECORD

Archaeological information on production industries at Mayapán is limited primarily to nonperishable materials. Items made at Mayapán's houselots are known from production debris that includes debitage, tools discarded in manufacture, and cores of raw material. Our best data reveals industries that made chert or chalcedony stone tools (bifaces and projectile points), obsidian blades and projectile points, animal bone objects, a variety of pottery vessels and effigies, shell implements and ornaments, stucco sculptures, and copper artifacts. Some tools that reflect the production of perishable industries are also found. Spindle whorls, bone tools, flake tools, and informal bifaces reflect production of cotton thread, weaving, embroidery, or hide working. Bifacial axes and grinding stones indicate agricultural cultivation and food processing. Imported small greenstone axes were likely used to carve wooden objects. Plaster used to surface architecture, sculpture, and friezes was in high demand, and its production was a major undertaking requiring much fuelwood (Russell and Dahlin 2007). Carlos Peraza Lope's team found a cache of plaster-working tools beneath a floor of one hall (Q-72) in Mayapán's monumental center (Peraza Lope, Delgado Kú, and Escamilla Ojeda 2002:101). Evidence for fine plaster work was also found at an effigy censer workshop at House Q-40a, where a vase filled with plaster and a smoothing tool were found (M. Delgado Kú 2012b). Animal use represents an additional production industry at Mayapán; white-tailed deer, turkeys, and dogs were raised in the city's houselots, and a range of other animals were hunted, fished, or obtained through trade (Masson and Peraza Lope 2008). Game was an important export of Sotuta during the Contact Period (Landa 1941:40), and artifacts of bone and antler are ubiquitous at the site.

Clearly, Landa's (1941:23–26) account is accurate in stating that Mayapán's lords brought people to the site to "perform services." Local production activities met many basic needs, but the city was not self-sufficient. Chert/chalcedony, weaving, obsidian, and marine shell industries relied on raw materials that were not local to the site. Mayapán's tribute list suggests that the city also needed to import cotton mantles, fish, salt, and other basic goods (Landa

1941:26). Although one cave has been found that may reflect clay quarrying (Clifford Brown, personal communication, 2003), we do not know to what degree local sources supplied Mayapán's pottery industry, as some slip and paint colors show considerable diversity (Brown 1999; Cruz Alvarado 2012a). Local resources included plaster, some proportion of wood and agricultural products, animal meat and hides, and orchard fruits. We argue that cotton thread production at Mayapán was low based on the scarcity of spindle whorls compared to other Postclassic sites, but mantles were probably woven and embellished (Masson, Hare, and Peraza Lope 2006). Spatially segregated phases of textile production may have occurred at different towns, with significant quantities of spun thread traded to Mayapán for later stages of manufacture. Colonial-era dictionaries are specific about textile-making tasks that individuals performed, including cotton carding, thread spinning, weaving, and further embellishment. Twenty-one different terms are found in the Motul dictionary for grades and thickness of thread along with twelve terms for cloth (Clark and Houston 1998:37–38). Spindle whorl holes can sometimes indicate whether maguey or cotton was spun in central Mexico (Feinman and Nicholas 2007), and this should be true for the Maya area as well. Different fibers were specified for making brooms, mats, or baskets (Roys 1972:46; Clark and Houston 1998:36). Residents at the city had a robust appetite for trade goods, as the distribution of obsidian, greenstone axes, copper bells, and Matillas Fine Orange pottery indicate. Perishable products that are described by Piña Chan, including fine dyes, pigments, beautiful wood, salt, honey, and cacao, would have entered the city's market along with more conspicuous durable objects. Mayapán was a place where raw materials or basic goods were often converted to more valuable finished products.

Market Institutions at Spanish Contact

Montejo observed abundantly supplied markets in the towns of Ecab, Cachi, Chauaca, and Sinsimato during his 1528 entrada (Piña Chan 1978:41). Staples and other goods were obtainable at Cachi, which had a "great market or plaza with many traders and much merchandise" (Piña Chan attributes this quote to Oviedo y Valdés 1853). The beach town of Ecab had fairs in conjunction with commerce (Piña Chan 1978:43, referring to Martyr de Anglería 1892). Although Piña Chan claims that Mayapán had a "house of commerce and trade to which the merchants repair with their merchandise" so that items could be purchased by stewards of governing elites, we were unable to find the original passage describing such an interesting facility in the 1938 Spanish publication of Landa's *Relacion de las Cosas de Yucatán* (Rosado Escalante and Ontiveros 1938, cited by Piña Chan 1978:43). Piña Chan (1978:43, referencing Fernández de Oviedo y Valdés 1851:55), describes the existence of inspectors of weights and measures at the Cachi market who served as judges to litigate disputes in a building at the end of the plaza. Aztec markets also had presiding judges (Blom 1932:545). Perhaps the most vivid description is that found by Blom (1932:545) in *Historia de la Provincia de San Vincente de Chiapa y Guatemala de la orden de predicadores* (Ximenez [1929] 1999, I:94); Blom's translation is as follows:

> The rulers took great pains that there should be held great and celebrated and very rich fairs and markets, because at these come together many things; those who are in need of something will find it there and can be exchanged with those other necessary things: they held their fairs and exhibited what they had for sale close to the temples. The selling and buying is to exchange which is the most natural form of trade; they gave maize for black beans and black beans for cacao, exchanged salt for spices which were *aji* or chile . . . also they exchanged meat and game for other things to eat; they swapped cotton cloth for gold and for some hatchets of copper, and gold for emeralds, turquoises and feathers. A judge presided over the market, to see that nobody was exploited. He appraised the prices and he knew of everything, which was presented at the market.

Blom (1932:545) emphasized the importance of religious festivals, pilgrimage, and commerce and suggests the antiquity of these institutions at sites like Chichén Itzá and Cozumel. He anticipated the pilgrimage/market fair model elaborated on by Freidel and Sabloff (Freidel 1981; Freidel and Sabloff 1984), in which large market events were regularly scheduled within the festival cycle to augment the backdrop of smaller, routine markets.

Archaeological signatures of marketplaces can be difficult to discern, but cases made for some Classic Period cities are compelling. At these sites, central plaza features with nonresidential basal alignments or soil signatures suggest their use as market plazas (recently reviewed by Dahlin et al. 2010; Masson and Freidel 2012; Shaw 2012). Evidence for a potential market plaza in Square K at Mayapán is outlined in chapter 4. In this space, floor level alignments are found and a massive platform is present; these do not resemble domestic architecture. The Square K platform is unique for the site, with the potential to represent a house of weights and measures or some other oversight facility. Also anomalous is Structure P-114 (chapter 5), located in a residential zone to the west of the site center, where residential and warehousing activities may have occurred. Until these structures are investigated, we can only speculate about their function. Other large nonresidential platforms are also suggestive of warehousing and storage linked to market exchange. Freidel and Sabloff (1984:190–92) review the location of possible warehouse platforms in the Maya area, including those from Ulúa, Naco, coastal Veracruz, and Monte Bravo and Vista Alegre (eastern coastal Yucatán); some are up to 70 meters in length and 20 meters wide. Storehouses are sometimes mentioned in documentary accounts; Tiquibalon, Yucatán, had them for wax and honey (Piña Chan 1978, citing Landa in Rosado Escalante and Ontiveros 1938).

MERCHANTS AND TRADERS

Hierarchies of traders existed across Mesoamerica during the Postclassic Period (Berdan et al. 2003). Professional merchants were known as *ppolom*, and traveling merchants were known as *ah ppolom-yoc* (Piña Chan 1978:43); the latter stayed at inns along their routes. Some merchants who traveled were armed. There is reason to believe that merchants were skilled hunters and warriors (Bill 1997:144). In the Madrid Codex (page 95b) they hold pointed knives identical to those found archaeologically at Mayapán (Bill 1997:115, figure 4.5), and they are sometimes linked to captive sacrifice (Bill 1997:144). God "M" is thought to represent the merchant deity Ek Chuah. He is portrayed with a black-painted face, projecting nose, hollowed eyes, whiskers, or a scorpion tail (J. Thompson 1957; Taube 1992; Bill 1997:144). Merchant figures have been identified on mural segments of Chichén Itzá's Temple of the Warriors; they travel along a coastal road and have striped bodies, tumplines, or walking sticks (Kristan-Graham 2001:356). Mayapán sculptures also portray this entity (chapter 7).

Merchant houselots have not been particularly easy to identify at Mayapán, but the distribution of imported pottery hints of their existence. Distinctive ethnic or foreign merchant enclaves of the type identified at Teotihuacan (Millon 1981) and Matacapan (Santley et al. 1987) are not evident in the residential zones explored by our project, at least as indicated by small test pit samples. Assemblages from contexts with higher proportions of imported pottery or effigy sculptures with international iconography also have a majority of local pottery and images (chapter 5; Masson and Peraza Lope 2010). There is also little co-association of atypical dwellings with distinguishing attributes such as high quantities of Matillas Fine Orange pottery, rare cremation burials, or effigies of Aztec gods (Masson and Peraza Lope 2010). While some typical houses with greater quantities of imported pottery or rare, local pottery (Buff Polbox) may have been those of merchants who retained some of the exotic vessels that they vended, this is difficult to verify. Such cases are not limited to elite contexts. Craft production houselots in general were also affluent and tended to have slightly higher proportions of Matillas Fine Orange (Masson and Freidel 2013:figure 8.11).

CURRENCIES AND EXCHANGES

Currencies in use at Spanish contact (figure 6.2) included cacao beans, cotton, cotton thread, cotton cloth, red stone or red shell beads (known as *kan*), white shell beads, greenstone beads (*tun*), copper bells, and axes (Landa 1941:96; Scholes and Roys 1938:612). Blom (1932:542) notes that quetzal feathers were used for money in Verapaz. These items had different values according to geographic location, which was probably determined by their availability and other factors of local economies (e.g., Blom 1932:538). No copper axes, for example, have been recovered at Mayapán.

Currency exchange values vary in the scarce Contact-era sources (table 6.2). According to Piña Chan (1978:43), 200 cacao beans equaled one Spanish *real*, a *contle* was a unit of 400 cacao beans, *xiquipile* units equaled 1,800 beans, and a *carga* was 24,000 beans. These Yucatecan equivalencies differ from figures cited by Blom (1932:538) from central Mexico, where a real was worth 80–100 cacao beans (one-eighth of a peso) and a carga (about fifty pounds) was worth 28–30 pesos (or 3.5–3.75 reales). Other equivalencies are listed in the Relación de Valladolid (Rosado Escalante and Ontiveros 1938:237–38). Jars (of unknown size) of cacao or beads were used for trade, as payment for hired labor, and to purchase slaves. Such jars were worth strands of beads of one or two fathoms (about 6 feet) in length. Coral-colored (*Spondylus*) beads of a length of one handspan (*jeme*, or *cuarta*) were valued at one *tostón* (four reales) according to the Relación de Valladolid, and this is consistent with values reported by Ralph L. Roys ([1943]1972:52). The Relación states that some shell beads were cheaper or more expensive, and this was probably based on color, with *Spondylus* worth more than other shell beads.

Copper bells may have had different values according to size (Piña Chan 1978:43; Tozzer 1941:231n418), and woven cloth of certain sizes and grades also corresponded to monetary standards (Blom 1932:541; Reents-Budet 2006). The existence of weights and measures inspectors at some marketplaces suggests that weight, volume (jars), and lengths may have been important in calculating value, in addition to counts. Factors such as shape, form, raw material, and craftsmanship may have further distinguished currency value, as qualitative variation is evident among shell, greenstone, and copper bells.

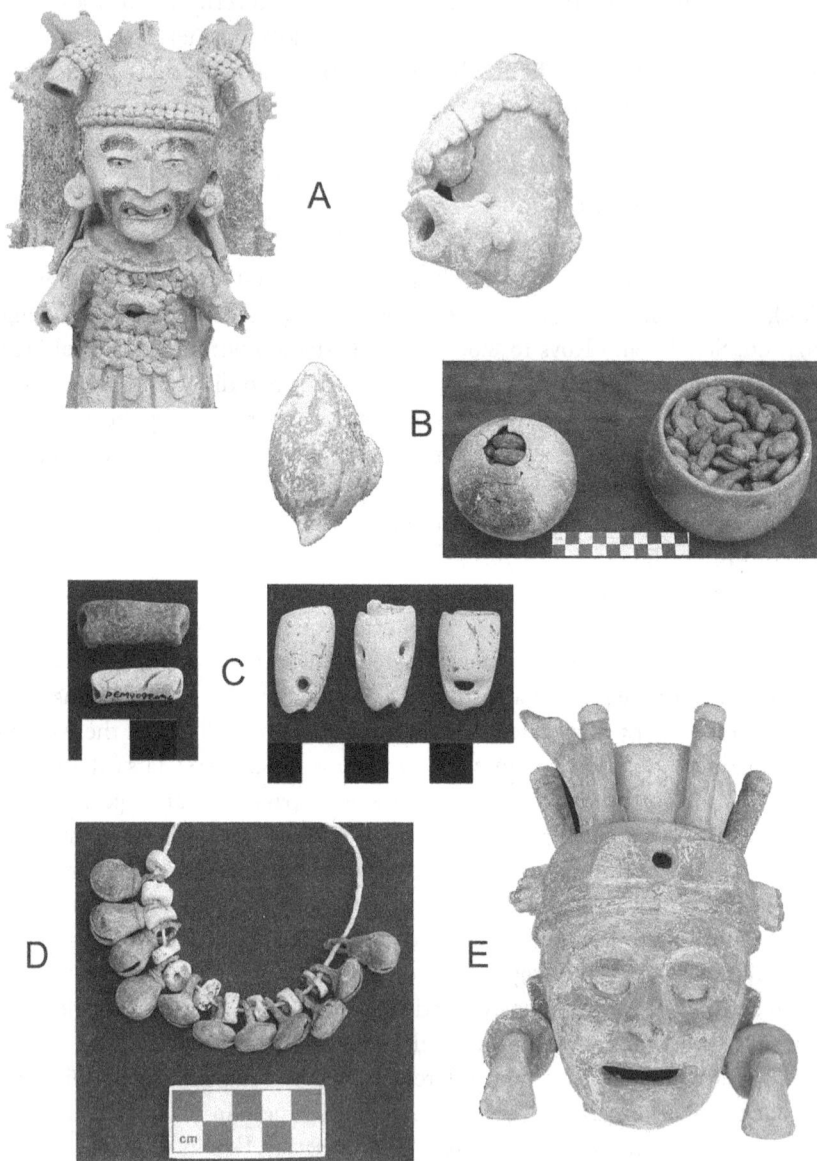

FIGURE 6.2. *Currencies in use at the Contact Period: A) cotton mantles, B) cacao, C) greenstone and shell beads/ornaments, D) copper bells and white shell beads (as found in a burial at dwelling Q-39), E) red and white shell beads and greenstone beads (stacked in headdress of Itzamna effigy).*

TABLE 6.2 Examples of equivalencies among currency units of the Contact Period in the greater Maya area.

Spanish Real	Peso	Cacao beans	Contle	Xiquipile	Carga ~50 lbs	Shell beads (white?)	Shell beads (red)	Toston	Source
4	1/2	–	–	–	–	–	Handspan, ~18 cm	–	Roys (1972:52)
4	–	–	–	–	–	–	–	–	–
1	–	200	–	–	–	–	–	–	Piña Chan (1978:43)
–	–	400	1	–	–	–	–	–	
–	–	1,800	–	1	–	–	–	–	
–	–	–	–	–	–	–	–	–	
–	–	24,000	–	–	1	–	–	–	
1	1/8	80–100	–	–	–	–	–	–	Blom (1932:538)
3.5–3.7	–	–	–	–	1	–	–	–	
–	–	Jar	–	–	–	1–2 fathoms (~182 cm)	–	–	Rosado Escalante and Ontiveros (1938:237–38)
4 (or 1 silver real de a cuatro)	–	–	–	–	–	–	Handspan, (jeme, cuarta, ~13.9–20 cm)	1	

The best information on cacao bean value is from Nicaragua, although these beans were widely used across the Aztec, Mayan, and Nicaraguan regions and as far as Panama. Blom reports from Gonzalo Fernández de Oviedo y Valdés's (1851:316–17) account that a rabbit was worth 10 beans, a chicotlzapotl fruit was worth 4 beans, a slave cost up to 100 beans, and a prostitute could be hired for about the price of a rabbit (8–10 beans). Blom (1932) points out that the greater scarcity of cacao in Nicaragua gave it more worth than in Mesoamerica. In the Maya area, sacrificial victims were purchased at a price of 5 to 10 red shell beads per person (Scholes and Roys 1938:612). Cotton mantles were used as units of exchange across the Maya lowlands (Tozzer 1941:94), the Maya highlands (Feldman 1985:21–23), and other parts of Postclassic Mesoamerica (M. Smith 2003c:124). According to Landa (1941:96), merchants "gave credit, lended, and paid courteously and without usury." Blom (1932:549) reports from the Tulan Tabi documents that one money lender (Francisco Quen) advanced cacao beans on credit to two others (Diego Huchim and Francisco Chim). Units of exchange may have been relatively stable, if Gaspar Antonio Chi's testimony is to be believed: "With provisions there was no bargaining, because the prices (were always) . . . in the same way, except for maize which sometimes (rose in price when the crop failed, and) it never went above the price of one *real* or a little more (per load)" (Tozzer 1941:231).

LABOR

Corvée military service was requested by the Mayapán state of its subjects (Roys 1962:50), and authorities also demanded corvée service for agricultural or other labors in the Contact era (Roys 1972:62). Slaves were essential for major fishing industries, agriculture, and canoe travel, and as porters for overland goods (Tozzer 1941:190n995; Roys 1972:35; Kepecs 2003:267). Large numbers of laborers were required seasonally for factory-scale industries such as salt production (Kepecs 2003:265), but it is not known whether such services were obligatory or compensated. In the early Contact Period, Blom (1932) reports that native carriers were paid wages of 100 beans per day in "Mexico." Montejo paid his troops in cacao beans in Yucatán (Blom 1932:538). Women spinners or weavers were also sometimes hired and paid in cacao beans, corn, or raw cotton, as John E. Clark and Stephen D. Houston (1998:37–38) infer from terms in Colonial dictionaries. Men sold their labor to clear, till, plant, weed, and harvest agricultural fields (Clark and Houston 1998:38). Although there is little direct evidence that wage labor had pre-contact origins, the possibility exists due to the fact that such arrangements were prevalent early in the Contact Period (mid-sixteenth century). The payment of a prostitute, as mentioned previously, provides one example of currency given for services. Midwives, curers, porters, and other service providers may have been similarly paid, as claimed in the Relación de Valladolid (Rosado Escalante and Ontiveros 1938:237–38).

TRIBUTE IN THE DOCUMENTARY SOURCES

Tribute sent to Mayapán included birds, maize, honey, salt, fish, game, cotton mantles, exotic stones, and "everything produced in the country" (Landa 1941:26; Tozzer 1941:30n159). Mayapán's nobility who lived at the city were exempt from tribute, if Chi's testimony is accurate (Tozzer 1941:230; Roys

1962:64). Northern coastal zones provided salt to towns of the interior, and this included Mayapán prior to its demise, according to Chi (Tozzer 1941:230). Trade would have also occurred. Landa (1941:40) describes game and fruit as commodities exchanged by the Cocom with coastal Ah Kin Chel after the fall of Mayapán from their home near Sotuta. Archaeological data reveal a significant deer husbandry industry at Mayapán that calls to mind the "game" traded by the Cocom as mentioned by Landa (Masson and Peraza Lope 2008).

The nature of Mayapán's oversight of cacao production in distant lands of Honduras (including Belize) is not described in detail, but this practice implies hierarchical rights that may have been part of the tribute system (Roys 1962:50, 55–60; Tozzer 1941:37n179, 94n417). A mural segment at the Temple of the Warriors at Chichén Itzá displays cotton mantles, a feather headdress, bowls, and copal or jade beads; the scene resembles aspects of the Aztec Codex Mendoza and likely portrays goods received in tribute (Kristan-Graham 2001:356, figure 12.14) that overlap with those demanded later by the Mayapán state. Another Temple of the Warriors mural emphasizes links between pilgrimage to the great cenote and tribute payment (Kristan-Graham 2001:356), and these activities may also have been complementary at Mayapán.

The term *tribute* was commonly used by Spanish Colonial chroniclers for payments that more closely meet the definition of taxation (M. Smith 2010c). Michael Smith (2010c) argues that payments to the Aztec empire were delivered consistently at regularly timed intervals and more appropriately represent taxes. The Codex Mendoza reveals such explicit expectations of subject polities. In contrast, Smith points out that tribute payments tend to be variable and delivered in the context of specific occasions. Regular requests for disbursement of goods to Mayapán (and other Postclassic Maya political centers) by the same criteria may also have constituted taxes. The line is blurred, however, if payments were timed with pilgrimage occasions (more like tribute). This distinction in terminology is important, as European classifications may be biased (M. Smith 2010c). Unfortunately, there are few other records available that permit a more objective evaluation of this form of state support for Mayapán.

PROPERTY OWNERSHIP

The issue of Postclassic Maya land ownership is considered by Freidel and Sabloff (1984:181–83) in the context of field wall systems at Cozumel sites that suggest a high degree of control and use by specific groups. Nobles frequently administered land rights and oversaw the use of lands across Contact Period Mesoamerica, but land ownership can be described as both communal and held by villages or towns (Freidel and Sabloff 1984:183). The products of labor or other improvements to land, such as cacao or fruit orchards, may have been privately owned (Roys 1972:37; Piña Chan 1978:37, 41; McAnany 1995). Cases of family property ownership can be found upon close examination of the documents. For example, Susan M. Kepecs (2003:259) observes that members of the Euan family owned certain salt beds in Chakan. Roys (1972:37) also reports family ownership of domestic properties and lands. He suggests that in pre-Spanish times, houselots and their gardens were considered to be private property, and this was probably true for the walled houselots and fields of Mayapán (chapter 5).

Matthew Restall's (2001) characterization of the *cah*, a town and its network of affiliated villages and territory, reveals that boundaries were fluid at the time of Spanish contact. But authorities were quite concerned with affirming the boundaries of polity territories, as suggested by rites of circumambulation that were regularly timed with calendrical celebrations (P. Rice 2004:79, 147). The maintenance of boundary shrines and a suite of other landmarks also reinforced concepts of place and belonging (P. Rice 2004:79, 147). It is probable that legal affiliations of social groups to land were complex and variable during the time of Mayapán's regime.

Economic Goods at Rituals and Feasts

Lavish feasts occurred at Mayapán. Priests and high-ranking political elites hosted them at public buildings on a variety of occasions. The presence of rich middens next to certain colonnaded halls and other ceremonial buildings (Q-97, Q-127, Q-151, Q-213) at Mayapán's center attest to these consumption activities (Strömsvik 1953:140; Shook 1954b; Shook and Irving 1955:322–23). Animal foods and maize breads were consumed and gifts of cotton mantles, food, and ceramic vessels were given to guests with the expectation of eventual reciprocity (Landa 1941:92). Landa outlines multiple occasions for gifting, including rites of passage for boys and girls (Landa 1941:106), calendrical festivals (Landa 1941:141), or deity festivals such as the *Chic Kaban* rite for Kukulcan (Landa 1941:158). Food offerings for rituals were often divided among the guests during ensuing feasts. At some temple events, gifts brought by guests were exclusively distributed among high-ranking participants, including lords, priests, and dancers (Landa 1941:158).

At Mayapán, it is not always useful to characterize goods or their production contexts in the dichotomous categories of luxury and utilitarian items, although differences are evident at the extremes of the continuum. Many types of items given at feasts and festivals overlap with goods also transferred as tribute or exchanged in markets. Patronage of certain fine craft production is documented at Mayapán for copper bells and effigy censers (Cruz Alvarado et al. 2012; Paris 2008; Paris and Cruz Alvarado 2012). The distribution of speleothems in household contexts is limited and may be related to commissioned sculpture industries. Speleothems helped form the skeletal framework around which anthropomorphic plaster sculptures were molded; these are found in halls, temples, oratories, and shrines (e.g., Adams 1953:153; Shook and Irving 1955:131). Other limited crafting materials include pigment-mixing shell cups and ceramic palettes.

Elite sponsorship of luxury item manufacture at Mayapán is a pattern with great time depth in Mesoamerica (Feldman 1985:23; Ball 1993; Reents-Budet 1994; Inomata and Stiver 1998; Freidel, Reese-Taylor, and Mora-Marin 2002; Foias 2002:229, 239). At Mayapán, although elites had more objects of the highest value, many classes of valuables are widely distributed across contexts of varying social status. Small, portable valuables, including shell ornaments, greenstone beads, serpentine axes, or (to a lesser extent) copper bells are found in most commoner contexts in low quantities (figure 6.3).

SCALES OF PRODUCTION AND CONSUMPTION AT MAYAPÁN

The importance of marketplace exchange is evident at Mayapán in the degree to which residents were heavily dependent on others for goods deemed essential to daily life. Patterns at individual houses exhibit much variation in part-time work activities and in the amount of surplus created at crafting houselots. Production of crafts at Mayapán clearly occurred on a part-time basis, but differences exist in the quantity of debris at domestic workshop localities where surplus production was clearly intended. We infer part-time production at Mayapán due to the fact that the amount of debris is lower than at other Mesoamerican crafting sites where estimations of the number of objects made per year also suggest part-time production. For example, at Colha, lithic debitage from certain workshops is estimated to have densities of 603,000 pieces of debris per cubic meter or higher, yet it is possible that each flintknapper made around 150 or so of each of four tool types per year over occupations as long as 250 years (Shafer and Hester 1991:83). As the most dense lithic workshops at Mayapán fall considerably short of this quantity (e.g., 16,993 and 9,850 flakes per cubic meter at I-57 and Z-120), presumably these craftsmen made fewer tools than at Colha in a quantity that would not have entailed a full-time commitment. But multi-crafting was common at

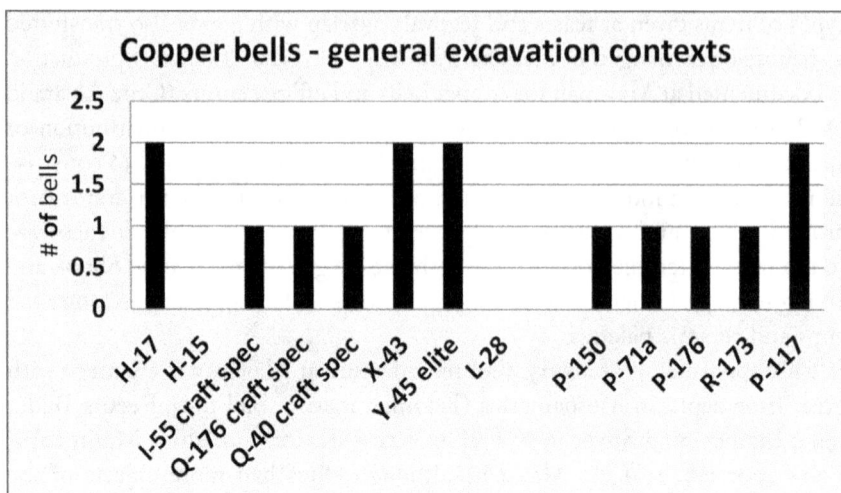

FIGURE 6.3. *Copper bells were recovered in similar amounts in general excavation or surface collection contexts across social status categories and domestic or nondomestic localities, suggesting that these valuables were widely accessible.*

Mayapán's houselots, as at domestic contexts such as Ejutla, Oaxaca (Feinman and Nicholas 2000), which means that the total output of all kinds of surplus goods would sometimes double or triple that of a single product. Occupants of House Q-176 made pottery vessels, figurines, shell objects, and obsidian blades, as we discuss later in this chapter.

The household has long been recognized as an activity group and a locus of production, consumption, and reproduction (Wilk and Netting 1984), although it is important to remember that members of a household can be spatially dispersed and do not necessarily reside within a spatial cluster of dwellings. Nonetheless, residential groups represent a logical starting point for studying the work activities of individuals related by blood or other ties. Domestic refuse represents the cumulative debris of a "household series" (M. Smith 1992:30) and is thus the result of sequential occupation in the same location that may surpass a single generation.

Quantifying and explaining surplus craft production has long concerned scholars of the Mesoamerican past. Although Prudence M. Rice (2009h:125–26) objects to archaeological uses of the terms *craft specialization* and *craft workshops*, in favor of more neutral terms such as *craft production*, the concept of craft specialization remains useful if employed with a quantitative approach and a set of well-defined expectations (e.g., Clark 2003). Identifying specialization or surplus production is a matter of degree (Costin 1991:4). For Mayapán, the key distinction is between craft producers making low numbers of objects and those engaged in making significant surplus quantities beyond those necessary for their own use. Surplus production of selected goods represents choices made by residents to specialize in crafting over other work options, at least for some of their time.

Cathy Lynne Costin's (1991) influential multidimensional crafting typology underestimates the importance of both scale and intensity at the household level, which is ranked below other levels of nonresidential workshop or attached production contexts. But as some attached artisans produced low quantities of exquisite goods (e.g., Inomata and Stiver 1998), scale in some attached contexts is small compared to that of a flinknapper who made hundreds of tools annually from his home. Gary M. Feinman and Linda M. Nicholas (2000:136, 138, 2004:170, 187, 2007:209, 2010) have effectively illustrated the importance of intensive production activities at household contexts and the adequacy of this scale for provisioning some thriving regional market systems in ancient Mesoamerica. Context types and scale do not always fit neatly into the scheme proposed by Costin. Patterns that Feinman and Nicholas report for Ejutla for the production of shell objects and figurines closely resemble those of the domestic workshops that we have documented at Mayapán in terms of intensity and scale. At Mayapán, one nonresidential workshop has been documented, but activities at this segregated context (residences are located nearby) differ little from workshop deposits that are within houselot enclosures (Kohut et al. 2012). General overlap in scale and intensity is also observed at isolated (nonresidential) workshop deposits and residential workshops at Colha (Shafer and Hester 1983; Hester and Shafer 1984; Masson 2001c). These findings negate the importance that has been assigned to nondomestic workshops in typological schemes (e.g., Santley and Kneebone 1993:table 1). The expectation that nonresidential production is accompanied by a scalar increase is not necessarily true.

Michael Deal's (1998:23) ethnoarchaeological study in modern Tzeltal communities defines three scales of production. At the domestic scale, activities merely replace a household's inventory; the elementary scale involves production beyond a household's needs; and the artisan scale involves year-round work (Deal 1998:23–25). Of these three, Mayapán workshops most closely match the elementary scale. Similarly, Mayapán's patterns match descriptions of a "household industry," where part-time production is undertaken for surplus exchange, as described by Robert S. Santley and Ronald R. Kneebone (1993:table 1). Deal emphasizes that greater investment in crafting (in his case, at the artisan scale) represents a necessary strategy to supplement household income for those with poor access to agricultural land. These artisans tended to be poorer than agriculturalists. This scenario contrasts with our data from Mayapán, which indicates that surplus crafting households tend to exhibit greater affluence than houselots engaged in more generalized activities that presumably included cultivation. The same pattern is reported from the Classic Period sites of Chunchucmil (Dahlin 2009:353) and Colha (Potter and King 1995:28; Shafer and Hester 1986:163).

In general, primary debris is rare at Colha (Shafer and Hester 1983; Hester and Shafer 1984) and the large urban center of Tikal (Fedick 1991). A focus on late-stage production seems to have characterized some larger towns and cities of the Maya area. At Mayapán, this pattern is also the norm. The majority of chert and chalcedony workshop debris reflects late-stage biface production. Cores are rare at the site and preforms were probably brought to the city. Segregation of stages of production may have been relatively common between sites and regions of Mesoamerica. This process correlated with an increase in commodity value (such as cloth) with each transfer and embellishment (Berdan 1988). Mayapán imported much of the raw materials it needed for its household craft industries; similarly, houses at Ejutla, in the landlocked portion of the Valley of Oaxaca, produced surplus objects made of imported Pacific coast marine shell (Feinman and Nicholas 2000).

Commoner household contexts at Mayapán vary in terms of productive activities but can generally be grouped into two categories: crafting houses that made significant surplus quantities of shell, stone, or pottery goods and non-crafting houses where such surpluses were absent. The locations of crafting houses thus far identified are illustrated in figure 6.4; five crafting houses (figure 6.5) and three non-crafting houses (figure 6.6) were fully excavated. While many houses at the city engaged in low levels of production, as suggested by low quantities of flakes or shell debris, crafting houses were identified arbitrarily as those with debris in outlier quantities beyond one standard deviation above the mean—and in many cases at levels far beyond this measure (table 6.3). Material assemblages of non-crafting houses reflect a range of general activities (H-11 and L-28) or specialized activities other than crafting, such as domestic (Z-42b) or military or corvée service (X-43).

ENGENDERED CRAFTING

Julia A. Hendon (1996:48) calls for a consideration of craft production and other work activities within dwellings that may identify gender-specific

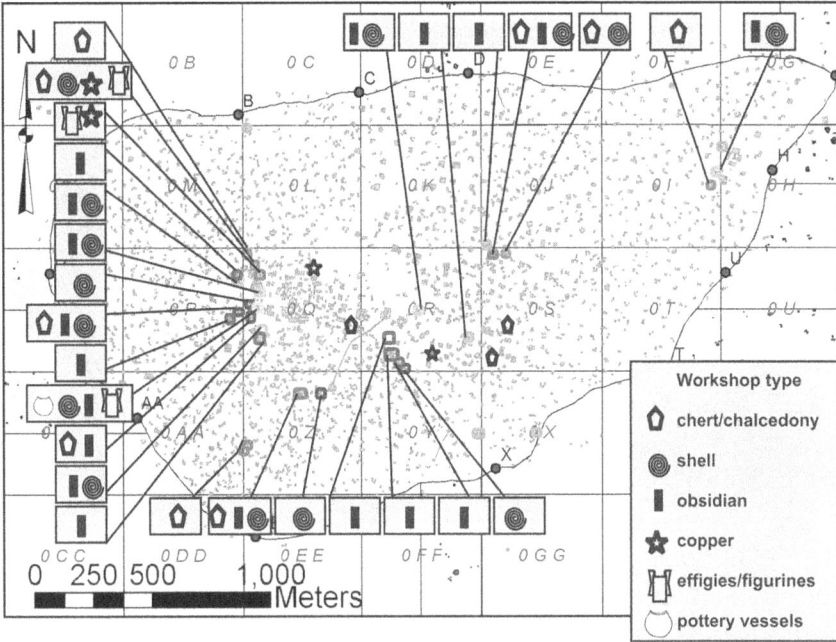

FIGURE 6.4. *The location of surplus crafting household workshops identified in PEMY research in the Mayapán settlement zone is indicated by gray boxes and arrows. These localities had workshop debris in quantities at least one standard deviation above the mean. Three additional localities are identified by icons plotted on the map (two copper and three chert); these were not investigated by the PEMY project (table 6.3).*

undertakings. Ethnohistorical sources provide limited information. To what extent did the burdens of food acquisition, processing, cooking, and child rearing permit female involvement in crafting (Clark and Houston 1998:34)? Such factors probably depended on family size and whether groups of women in a household shared routine tasks. Making thread, weaving, and embroidery represented a female domain across Mesoamerica, as implied by figurines (Hendon 1996:56), women's activities in the Maya codices (Vail and Stone 2002), and historical documents (Clark and Houston 1998:34; McAnany 2010). Raising domestic game and fowl was also primarily the responsibility of females (Landa 1941:127; Ardren 2002; Masson and Peraza Lope 2008).

Landa's description of the Contact-era rite of *Yolob u dzab kam yax* (thought by Alfred M. Tozzer [1941:n814] to mean "ceremony of the blue color") involves smearing the tools linked to specific occupations with blue pigment.

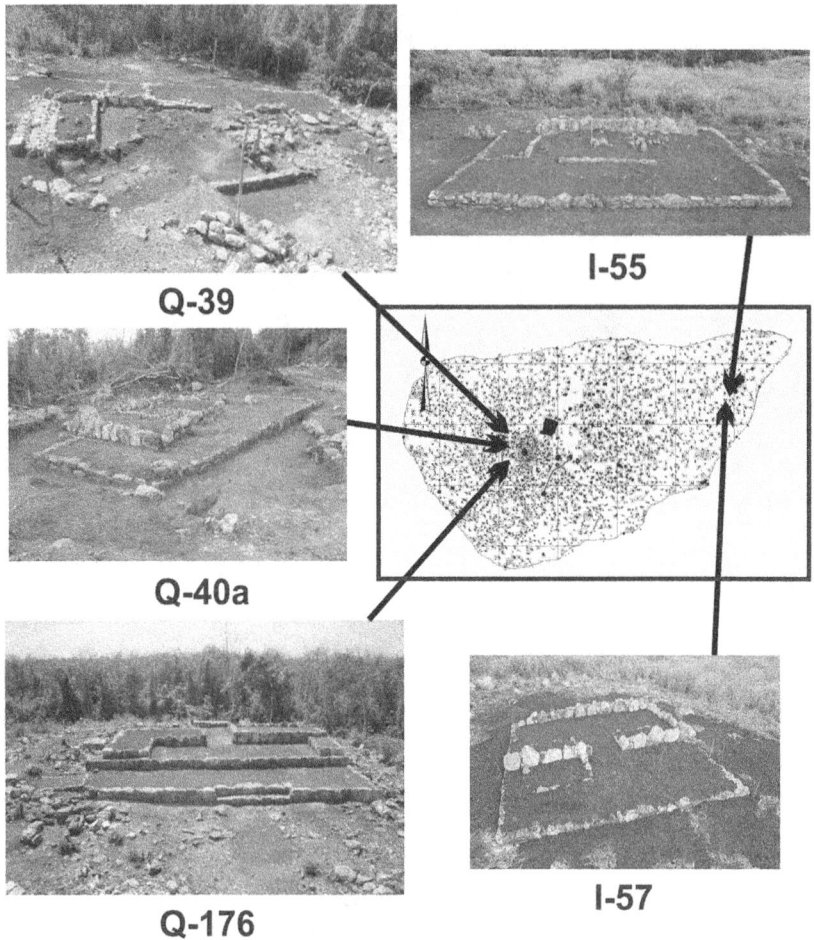

FIGURE 6.5. *Localities engaged in surplus craft production fully excavated by the PEMY project. All were dwellings except for I-57, a special-purpose shelter (in its own enclosure next to House I-56) associated with chert and chalcedony flaking debris. House I-55 made obsidian blades and shell products; House Q-39 made chert/chalcedony and shell products; House Q-40a made effigy censers, copper, and shell items; and House Q-176 made pottery vessels, obsidian blades, and shell items.*

Such tools ranged from articles used by priests to spindles used by women in weaving. Boys and girls were struck lightly nine times on the backs of their hands, a ritual linked to their future involvement in the hereditary occupa-

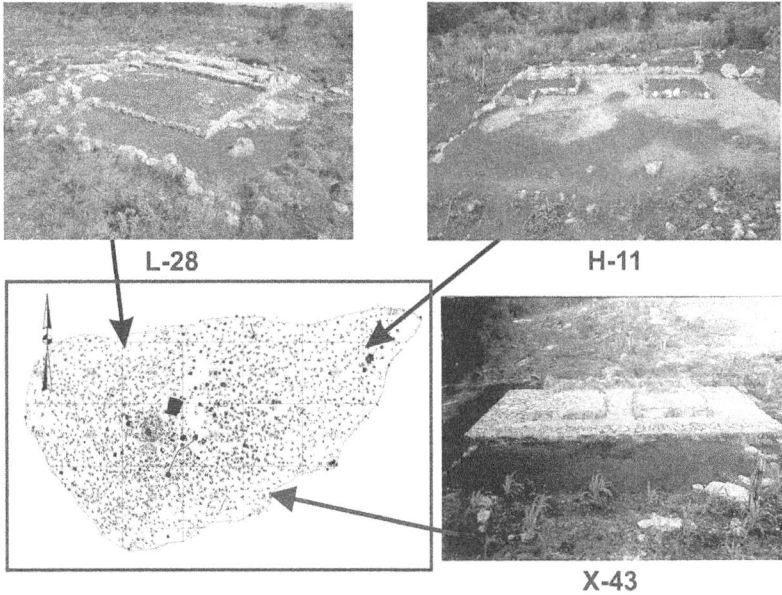

FIGURE 6.6. *Dwellings fully excavated by the PEMY project not associated with surplus craft production. Houses L-28 and H-11 were associated with a range of general activities and low levels of shell crafting while House X-43 was briefly occupied, lacked a full domestic assemblage, and contained a higher proportion of projectile points that may suggest it was occupied by males who were performing military service for the city.*

tions of their parents (Landa 1941:159). This rite was geared toward artisans (Tozzer 1941:n813) and recalls similar role-bestowal rites for children that are featured in the Codex Mendoza (Berdan and Anawalt 1992). Crafting and other occupations were described as "oficios" by some chroniclers, which may signify a role, a calling, or a duty (Clark and Houston 1998:34–35). As these authors note, men's responsibilities included farming, fishing, hunting, bee-keeping, and forest resource extraction; women raised children and animals, prepared food, and made thread, cloth, and clothing (Clark and Houston 1998:35). Genders sometimes overlapped in certain forms of curing or sorcery and a few crafts (perhaps pottery making), but complementary participation in productive activities was common. It is possible that increased demands on women to create cloth tribute in the Colonial era led to a greater focus on textiles than before (Clark and Houston 1998:38). The section that follows

TABLE 6.3 Craft production workshops identified in PEMY sample areas in Mayapán's settlement zone through systematic surface collection, test pits, or full excavation. Fully excavated contexts are indicated with an asterisk.

Neighborhood/Structure/Product		Neighborhood/Structure/Product	
Barrio Itzmal Ch'en (Milpa 16)		Crafts Barrio Downtown (Milpa 1)	
I-57*	Chert	Q-39*	Chert, shell, copper, figurines
I-55*	Obsidian, shell	Q-37	Chert
–	–	P-115	Obsidian
Mid-city east (Milpa 15)		P-24	Obsidian
S-12	Chert, shell	Q-196	Obsidian
S-10	Obsidian, chert, shell	P-114	Obsidian, chert, shell
J-130	Obsidian	Q-188	Obsidian, chert
–	–	P-28b	Obsidian, shell
Downtown (Milpa 2)		Q-303	Obsidian, shell
Z-39	Obsidian, chert, shell	Q-46a	Obsidian, shell
Z-47	Shell	Q-176*	Obsidian, shell, pottery vessels, figurines
Z-43	Shell	Q-40a*	Pottery effigy censers, copper
Downtown (Milpa 32)		Q-183	Shell
R-177	Shell	–	–
R-173	Obsidian	–	–
R-174	Obsidian	–	–
Mid-city east (Milpa 10)		–	–
R-137	Obsidian	–	–
Downtown (Milpa 11)		South between center and wall (Milpa 4)	
R-155	Obsidian	Z-119	Chert, shell
R-110b	Obsidian, shell	Z-120	Obsidian, chert, shell
Workshops known at Mayapán (not investigated by PEMY)			
S-139 (mid-city east, near Milpa 10)	Chert	Brown (1999:459)	
S-82/S-129 (mid-city east, near Milpa 10)	Chert	Masson, personal observation, 2002	
Q-242 (downtown next site center)	Chert	Masson, personal observation, 2002	
R-183 (downtown near Milpa 32)	Copper	Paris and Cruz Alvarado (2012)	
Q-92 (in site center)	Copper	Paris and Cruz Alvarado (2012)	

Note: Z-119/Z-120 are adjacent houselots and are not fully divided by walls. They form part of the same residential group presents the archaeological data from Mayapán that reveals a complex record of production and consumption activities at the city.

MAYAPÁN'S PRODUCTION INDUSTRIES

Mayapán's location is not physiographically unique for the northwestern Yucatán plains. The city was not situated in a place that offered special agricultural, aquatic, or other natural resource advantages. Its location is most likely due to specific political and historical contingencies that have yet to be identified. The city was centrally located and could have taken advantage of inland routes across the confederacy and it was not prohibitively distant from the northern coast of the peninsula. The ability to attract an artisan work force would have been essential for establishing and maintaining its position of political importance. Residents of the urban center were busy and productive: crops were cultivated; game, fish, and fowl were hunted and raised; and raw materials were converted into more useful and valuable craft items at the city's houselots. The acquisition of money, in the form of cacao beans, shell beads, and other items (figure 6.2) was an essential component of trade that fostered houselot dependencies (e.g., Freidel, Reese-Taylor, and Mora-Marin 2002; Freidel and Shaw 2000).

Textiles

Spindle whorls are scarce at Mayapán compared to other Postclassic Maya sites near the Caribbean coast (figure 6.7). Ratios of ceramic spindle whorls to ceramic sherds are less than .00003 for Mayapán in contrast to those from the small Belize sites of Laguna de On and Caye Coco, with .002 and .0001, respectively (Masson, Hare, and Peraza Lope 2006). A high number of 76 whorls is reported from Cozumel samples (Phillips 1979). This low ratio for Mayapán was consistent in data examined from the Carnegie, INAH, and PEMY projects. From our test pit excavations, three spindle whorls were found in a sample of over 100,000 sherds, and similarly, the Carnegie project publications (Masson 2009) report thirteen spindle whorls despite the recovery of a sample of 390,144 sherds analyzed by Robert E. Smith (1971:table 1a). Of the nineteen total spindle whorls recovered from INAH and PEMY project investigations through 2009, two are of Terminal Classic slate pottery and predate the city (Shiratori 2008:table 16.1). Molded forms recovered include flat, biconvex, hemispherical, and "cupcake" cross-sections (Shiratori 2008:table 16.1). Sampling issues are not responsible for the paucity of whorls

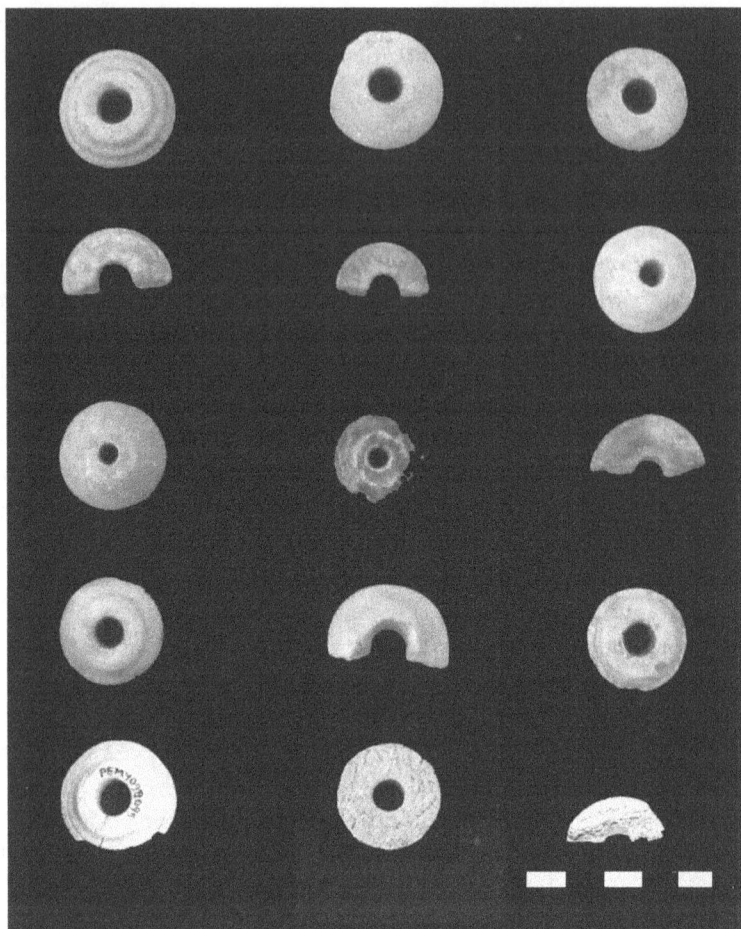

FIGURE 6.7. *Spindle whorls from Mayapán. At the bottom right are two human bone spindle whorls recovered from House Q-40a and Hall Q-54.*

at Mayapán, as the sample includes eight fully excavated houses in four neighborhoods. One clay spindle whorl was present among these houses, from a family grave at House Q-39. An unusual example includes a spindle whorl–sized, perforated, flat human bone disk recovered from dwelling Q-40a (figure 6.7). A fragment of a similar human bone whorl was found by Peraza Lope's INAH project at a nearby hall, Q-54 (figure 6.7). The Q-40a example measures 2.6 centimeters in external diameter, and its hole diameter is .78 centimeters, similar to dimensions reported by Yuko Shiratori (2008) for pottery whorls.

Notably, House Q-40a is an artisan locality that is attached to elite group Q-41; it is not difficult to imagine the symbolic importance of thread woven with a human bone whorl.

Cotton is grown in small quantities in Yucatán today in the kitchen gardens of Telchaquillo. Ideal growing conditions for cotton are not uniform in the northwest part of the peninsula compared to everywhere else in the Maya lowlands. Soil depth and moisture requirements (Reents-Budet 2006:115) are particularly substandard around Mayapán. But production of cotton thread may have been less important at the ancient city than weaving and embroidery. Significant quantities of thread may have been exchanged into the site. Similarly, while some cacao can be grown in moisture sinks in the Yucatecan landscape (Kepecs and Boucher 1996), Mayapán was deeply vested in obtaining these beans in quantity from distant locales. As the city's elites received cotton mantles as tribute, we know that at least some cotton products arrived at the city from other towns. The earlier Classic-era site of Dzibilchaltun also may have emphasized other industries and opted to import thread, as perforated sherds and molded pottery whorls are uncommon at that settlement (Taschek 1994:214, 219). The labor-intensive nature of cotton production makes it a logical industry for the spatial segregation of labor for a state with the power to make this happen (Berdan 1988). Dorie Reents-Budet (2006:116) describes the arduous tasks of tilling, hoeing, weeding, culling, eliminating pests, and watering cotton plants. She points out that once bolls are harvested, they must be hand processed and cleaned, their seeds removed, and the fibers combed and fluffed before being spun into thread. Given that tribute in mantas numbered in the tens of thousands in the Contact Period (Reents-Budet 2006:116), we can surmise that the needs were great during Mayapán's era. We suspect that Mayapán textile makers concentrated on later production stages that accorded cloth with greater value.

The environs of Mayapán are among the driest of the Maya region (Folan 1983:figure 3), and plants like maguey and henequen thrive locally. It is probable that fiber industries from these plants were also important for the site. Abundant bone tools are present in many contexts that resemble those associated with rope, mat, and basket production at other Mesoamerican sites, as we discuss in detail in the next section. Whorl weight may be more important than whorl diameter for distinguishing maguey from cotton whorls, but this distinction is complicated by the fact that some maguey fibers could be fine and of high quality (Carpenter, Feinman, and Nicholas 2012). The Mayapán whorls measured by Shiratori (2008:table 16.1) exhibit a close range of measurements, with an average whorl diameter of 2.8 centimeters (range 2.4–3.2

centimeters, standard deviation .2 centimeter) and an average hole diameter of .9 centimeter (range .7–1.0 centimeter, standard deviation .1 centimeter). These fall within the ranges of almost all of the whorls reported for El Palmillo, Oaxaca, where cotton and maguey thread was spun, but they are in the upper range of sizes for that site (Carpenter, Feinman, and Nicholas 2012:figure 3).

Bone Tools

The ubiquity of bone tools found at Mayapán suggests that their production was an important industry and a logical outgrowth of the abundance of game and fish. Deer bone tools are especially important (Pollock and Ray 1957:653). Animal bones were sometimes fashioned into tools needed for the manufacture of other crafts such as weaving and sewing. Animal products were also made into fine craft items such as animal crania headdresses, musical instruments, or ornaments. The bone tool industry at Mayapán may reflect, among other activities, later stages of cloth production. Thread may have been woven into mantles or plain mantles converted and embellished through embroidery and the use of dyes. Sharpened, polished bone implements and deer metapodial bone awl-like tools are particularly common in the site's assemblage (figure 6.8). A total of 372 bone tools have been analyzed from the PEMY (N = 116) and INAH (N = 256) projects in the site center. Ongoing faunal analysis from the 2008–2009 seasons will likely reveal more examples. Initial studies by Juliana Novic (2008) and Jonathan White et al. (2012) have been augmented by additional lab analysis by Marilyn A. Masson and Elizabeth H. Paris, and this work provides a general morphological and functional classification. The combined results of these studies are presented in tables 6.4 and 6.5.

Worked bone was used for a variety of functions. Table 6.4 lists 233 objects that were probably tools used to make other products. A total of 139 ornaments, instruments, and other decorative items are listed in table 6.5. Split deer metapodials (commonly referred to as awls) represent just over one-third of the entire collection of 372 objects (N = 127, 34 percent). The awls exhibit variation in the symmetry and workmanship of the pointed end and broken fragments were sometimes resharpened (figure 6.8). Eighteen other pointed bone artifacts (including eleven antler tines) and twenty thin perforator-like objects (including seven fish spines) were present in the sample. Perforators and needles (figure 6.8) are identified by their small circumference, and sea bass dorsal spines were sometimes perforated for threading (17 of 28 needles were fish spines). Sharpened fish spines may have been used for bloodletting or tattooing, if Tozzer's analogy to practices in Panama is correct (Pollock

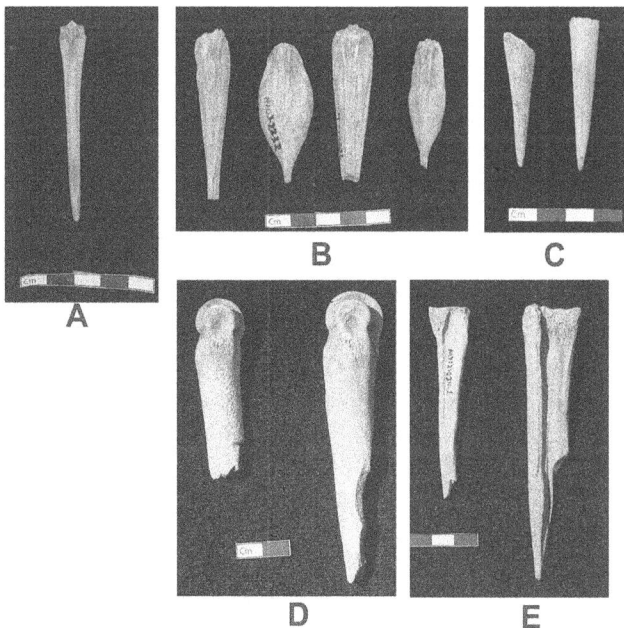

FIGURE 6.8. *Bone tools are common at Mayapán and reflect the importance of late-stage textile-working activities such as weaving, embroidering, and embellishing. Such tools include modified fish spines (A, B) and metapodial awls (C, D, E).*

and Ray 1957:652; Tozzer 1941:notes 396, 525). The working end of some awls was flattened with a spatulate appearance that appears designed for a specific task (twelve of 127), and eight other spatula-like (non-metapodial) tools were found along with flattened mammalian long bones that closely resemble weaving picks (table 6.4). Other items included one bone scoop, one scraper, and twenty unfinished, worked bone splinters (table 6.4). We have previously described drilled bone disks that resemble spindle whorls (figure 6.7).

The probable use of needles and bone spindle whorls is relatively clear, in contrast to deer metapodial (and other tapered long bone) tools that had a range of potential applications. For example, pointed bone objects were used for nose perforation in the context of nose plug insertion. Deities in the Borgia Codex are also equipped with pointed femurs used as ritual weaponry, sometimes linked to eye-gouging or other violent or sacrificial acts, and they are also

TABLE 6.4 Animal bone tool contexts and classifications, N = 233 (INAH-PEMY 1996–2009). Asterisks mark fully excavated contexts for which analysis is ongoing.

Deer metapodial bone tools (tapered, pointed)					
Q-151 (hall)	Tapered	1	Q-96 (platform)	Tapered	1
Q-152 (temple)	Tapered	1	Q-97 (hall)	Tapered	6
Q-152c (hall)	Spatulate	1	Q-99 (hall)	Spatulate	1
Q-162 (temple)	Tapered	1	F-13 (house)	Blunted	1
Q-162 (temple)	Blunted	1	H-11* (house)	Tapered	4
Q-162 (temple)	Spatulate	1	H-15z/e* (grave)	Tapered	2
Q-163 (hall)	Tapered	1	I-55a* (house)	Tapered	6
Q-163 (hall)	Spatulate	1	J-130 (house)	Tapered	1
Q-176a* (house)	Tapered	4	INAH Lote 1254	Tapered	1
Q-303 (workshop)	Tapered	1	INAH Lote 4000	Spatulate	1
Q-39* (house)	Tapered	2	INAH Lote 6392	Tapered	1
Q-54 (hall)	Tapered	18	INAH n/a	Tapered	2
Q-54 (hall)	Blunted	1	Milpa 11 surface	Spatulate	1
Q-54 (hall)	Spatulate	1	P-114 (house)	Tapered	2
Q-56 (house	Tapered	3	P-117 (house)	Tapered	1
Q-57 (unknown)	Tapered	4	P-117 (house)	Spatulate	1
Q-58 (temple)	Tapered	5	P-150 (house)	Tapered	1
Q-61/Q-58	Tapered	1	R-106 (palace)	Tapered	1
Q-64 (hall)	Tapered	3	R-108 (palace)	Spatulate	1
Q-66 (oratory)	Tapered	1	R-137 (house)	Tapered	1
Q-67 (house)	Tapered	1	R-151b (house)	Tapered	1
Q-69 (shrine)	Tapered	1	R-155 (house)	Tapered	1
Q-70 (hall)	Blunted	1	Y-43 (house)	Tapered	1
Q-72 (hall)	Tapered	1	Y-43 (house)	Spatulate	1
Q-74a (shrine)	Tapered	2	Y-44 (house)	Tapered	1
Q-79a (shrine)	Tapered	5	Y-45* (house)	Tapered	1
Q-82 (temple)	Spatulate	1	Z-120 (house)	Tapered	1
Q-87 (hall)	Tapered	1	Z-43 (outbuilding)	Tapered	1
Q-88a (hall)	Tapered	1	Z-47 (house)	Blunted	1
Q-92 (house)	Tapered	11	–	–	
Q-94 (shrine)	Tapered	1	–	–	
Q-95 (temple)	Tapered	3	–	–	
Q-95 (temple)	Curved splinter	1	–	–	
Subtotal metapodial tools					127

TABLE 6.4—continued

Flattened mammal long bone weaving pick-like implement			Bone spindle whorl		
I-55a* (house)	–	1	Q-54 (hall)	Human	1
Q-152c (hall)	–	1	Q-40a* (house)	Human	1
Q-54 (hall)	–	3	Q-56 (house)	Large mammal	1
Q-80 (temple)	–	1	Subtotal bone whorl		3
S-132a (house)	–	1			
Subtotal weaving pick	7				

Bone perforator			Needle		
Q-162 (temple)	–	3	I-55a (house)	Bone splinter	1
Q-54 (hall)	–	2	K-69b (house)	Bone splinter	1
Q-67 (house)	–	1	P-71a (house)	Bone splinter	1
Q-64 (hall)	Fish	1	P-28b (house)	Bone splinter	1
Q-81 (hall)	Fish	1	INAH n/a	Bone splinter	3
Q-92 (house)	Fish	1	H-20 (house)	Fish bone	1
Q-79 (shrine)	Fish	1	Q-152 (temple)	Fish bone	3
Q-97 (hall	Fish	1	Q-72 (hall)	Fish bone	2
Q-53 (house)	Fish	1	Q-95 (temple)	Fish bone	1
Q-74a (shrine)	Fish	1	Q-54 (hall)	Fish bone	4
Q-64 (hall)	–	1	Q-303 (workshop)	Fish bone	1
Q-72 (hall)	–	1	P-117 (house)	Fish bone	1
Q-92 (house)	–	2	K-69b (house)	Fish bone	1
Q-95 (temple)	–	1	I-55a (house)	Fish bone	1
R-183b (house)	–	1	Q-64 (hall)	Fish bone	2
R-137 (house)	–	1	Q-79 (shrine)	–	1
Subtotal perforator	20		Q-92 (house)		1
Other pointed bone tools			Q-97 (hall)		1
H-11* (house)	–	1	R-151b (house)	–	1
P-114 (house)	–	1	Subtotal needles		28
Q-152 (temple)	Triangular	1	*Mammal bone splinters—partly worked*		
Q-162 (temple)	Triangular	1	L-28* (house)	–	1
Y-44 (house)	Triangular	1	INAH Lote 163	–	1
Q-163 (hall)	–	1	M-60a (house)	–	1

continued on next page   *continued on next page*

TABLE 6.4—*continued*

Other pointed bone tools (continued)			Mammal bone splinters (continued)		
Q-67 (house)	–	1	Q-54 (hall)	–	1
Q-64 (hall)	Antler tine	1	P-114 (house)	–	1
Q-92 (house)	Antler tine	5	P-28b (house)	–	1
Q-54 (hall)	Antler tine	1	P-71a (house)	–	2
Q-55 (oratory)	Antler tine	1	INAH n/a	–	1
Q-95 (temple)	Antler tine	1	Q-152 (temple)	–	2
Q-97 (hall)	Antler tine	2	Q-176* (house)	–	1
Subtotal other pointed tools		18	Q-41 (palace)		1
Scoop, scraper, spatula			Q-41 (palace)		1
Q-83 (oratory)	Scoop	1	Q-56	–	1
Y-45* (house)	Scraper	1	Q-92 (house)	–	1
Q-152 (temple)	Spatulate	1	R-137 (house)	–	1
Q-162 (temple)	Spatulate	1	R-155 (house)	–	1
Q-54 (hall)	Spatulate	1	R-204 (house)	–	1
R-155 (house)	Spatulate	2	S-132a (house)	–	1
Y-43 (house)	Spatulate	1	Subtotal unfinished splinters		20
Q-64 (hall)	Spatulate	2			
Subtotal scoops, etc.		10			

part of sacred bundles (e.g., Díaz, Rodgers, and Byland 1993:6, 26, 62, plate 16). The Borgia bones appear as femurs (of human or deer size), with red-painted proximal epiphyses intact. Similarly, in the Madrid Codex (pages 40c–41c), pointed bones were used as perforators and bloodletters (Von Nagy 1997:53). Use wear and residue analysis are needed to positively ascertain the functions of awls and other pointed bones, but it is reasonable to suggest that a significant proportion were dedicated to textile industries. High quantities of quite similar bone tools are reported from the site of El Palmillo, Oaxaca, where they are associated with a cotton and maguey fiber industry (Feinman and Nicholas 2011:42, figure 12; Carpenter, Feinman, and Nicholas 2012:table 6, figure 8). The function of some modified bones is unclear, such as 13 modified pneumatic marine fish spines. These bulbous fish spines (N = 32) were regularly shaped into pointed objects that may have had a utilitarian purpose; a few of these were long and tapering, but most were ovoid in shape (table 6.5, figure 6.8b).

TABLE 6.5 Animal bone ornaments, flutes, rasps, and other crafted objects (N = 139).

Bone tube, possibly a flute			Bone tube, partly worked		
Q-58 (temple)	–	1	Y-45* (house)	Large animal	1
Q-72 (hall)	–	1	Y-111 (house)	Large animal	1
Q-80 (temple)	–	1	P-28b (house)	Turkey	1
Y-111 (house)	–	1	Q-54 (hall)	–	1
Lot 5129	–	1	Q-92 (house)	–	2
R-155 (house)	–	1	Subtotal unfinished tube		6
Subtotal bone flute		6	Rasp		
Drilled tooth pendant			Q-54 (hall)	Deer	1
Q-66 (oratory)	Human	1	Q-72 (hall)	Large mammal	1
H-11* (house)	Dog	1	Q-54 (hall)	Human	2
Q-54 (hall)	Dog	1	Q-55 (oratory)	Human	1
Q-54 (hall)	Peccary	1	Q-68 (house)	Human	1
Q-83 (oratory)	Dog	1	Q-92 (house)	Human	1
Q-79A (shrine)	Mammal	1	H-11* (house)	Human	1
INAH 3475	Mammal	1	Q-55 (oratory)	Large mammal	1
Q-69 (shrine)	Peccary	1	Q-58 (temple)	Large mammal	1
Q-70 (hall)	Peccary	1	Q-92 (house)	Turkey	1
Q-82 (temple)	Peccary	1	Subtotal rasp		11
P-28b (house)	Peccary	1	Bone bead		
Q-39* (house)	Shark	1	Q-303 (workshop)	Fish	1
Q-95 (temple)	Crocodile	1	Q-79 (shrine)	Fish	1
Subtotal drilled tooth		13	INAH 5130	Fish	1
Animal tooth filed and polished			INAH 165(10)	Fish	1
H-11* (house)	Dog	1	Q-64 (hall)	–	1
INAH 4000	Mammal	1	Q-92 (house)	–	1
Q-92 (house)	Dog	1	Q-95 (temple)	–	1
Subtotal worked tooth		3	Q-74a (shrine) (house)		1
Misc. shaped bone object—human			P-115b (house)	Shark/ray	2
Q-81 (hall)	–	1	P-71a (house)	Shark/ray	2
Q-64 (hall)	Spatulate	1	Q-54 (hall)	–	1
Q-92 (house)	Notched	1	Q-58 (temple)	Shark/ray	1

continued on next page   continued on next page

TABLE 6.5—*continued*

Misc. shaped bone object—human			*Bone bead*		
Q-95 (temple)	Perforated	1	P-114 (house)	Shark/ray	2
Q-58 (temple)	Pointed, shaped	2	Q-41 (house)	Shark/ray	2
Q-74a	Pointed	1	R-155 (house)	Shark/ray	1
Subtotal misc. shaped bone object—human		7	Q-97 (hall)	Shark	1
			Q-39* (house)	Shark	1
			Q-69 (shrine)	Turtle	1
			Q-162 (temple)	Turkey (tube bead)	1
			Q-58 (temple)	Turkey (tube bead)	1
			P-28b (house)	Turkey (tube bead)	1
			Q-303 (workshop)	Turkey (tube bead)	1
			F-13 (house)	Turkey (tube bead)	1
			Subtotal bead		27

Misc. shaped bone object—animal			*Spines*		
Q-162 (temple)	Fragment	1	Q-152 (temple)	Pneumatic	3
Q-54 (hall)	Fragment	1	Q-54 (hall)	Pneumatic	7
Q-58 (temple)	Fragment	1	Q-80 (temple)	Pneumatic	1
R-106 (palace)	Fragment	1	R-171c (house)	Pneumatic	2
R-142c (oratory)	Fragment	2	Y-43 (house)	Pneumatic	1
Q-58 (temple)	Fragment	1	INAH 5175	Pneumatic	1
F-13 (house)	Rectangular	1	INAH 6352	Pneumatic	1
Y-45 (house)	Rectangular	1	INAH 163	Pneumatic	1
R-155 (house)	Rectangular	1	P-117 (house)	Pneumatic	1
P-28b (house)	Rectangular	1	INAH	Pneumatic	1
Itzmal Ch'en	Rectangular	1	Q-57 (unidentified alignment)	Pneumatic	2
Q-54 (hall)	Rectangular	1	Q-64 (hall)	Pneumatic	2
Subtotal shaped animal		13	Q-92 (house)	Pneumatic	4
Highly burned and polished bone			Q-95 (temple)	Pneumatic	2
L-28 (house)		1	Q-97 (hall)	Pneumatic	2
I-55a* (house)		1	R-183b (house)	Pneumatic	1

continued on next page   *continued on next page*

TABLE 6.5—*continued*

Highly burned and polished bone		Spines		
H-15* (mass grave/hall)	1	Q-152 (temple)	Stingray	1
Q-95 (temple)	2	Q-162 (temple)	Singray	1
Q-74a (shrine) (house)	1	Q-82 (temple)	Stingray	1
Subtotal burned/polished	6	Q-54 (hall)	Stingray	1
Perforated, notched, grooved		P-117b (house)	Stingray	1
Q-54 (hall) –	3	INAH	Stingray	1
Q-95 (temple) –	1	Subtotal spine		38
Q-81 (hall) –	1	*Earspool*		
INAH –	1	Q-95 (temple)	Human	1
Q-92 (house)	1	Q-80 (temple)	Shark	1
Subtotal engraved	7	Subtotal earspool		2

Figure 6.9 illustrates some of the more exceptional craft items made from animal bone. A total of 139 bone craft objects or fragments are represented in the sample (table 6.5). Thirteen drilled teeth were identified, including those of dog, peccary, shark, crocodile, and one human (table 6.5, figure 6.9a). Six bone tubes with perforated holes were probably flutes, and six additional tubes may represent unfinished flutes (table 6.5, figure 6.9b). A puma or jaguar femur was nicely cut and may have been intended to be part of a staff (figure 6.9c). The sample included twenty-seven bone beads of fish, shark, ray, turtle, or turkey (table 6.5, figure 6.9d). Two bone earspools were present, one of human bone and the other made from a shark vertebra (figure 6.9d). Eleven notched shafts made of human, large mammal, and turkey long bone represented rasps (figure 6.9e). Six stingray spines were identified. Other worked fragments of ornamental bone that were polished, shaped, perforated, or engraved are listed in table 6.5.

The spatial distribution of bone objects indicates the widespread nature of activities involving their use. In general, bone artifacts are recovered across much of the site in low frequencies, with some exceptions that might link structures to specialized activities (tables 6.4, 6.5). Ornamental or musical objects were more common at the site center, as indicated by the number of structures from grid Square Q listed in table 6.5. Only seven of thirty-five test pit or surface collection contexts in the settlement zone had four or more bone tools; five were located in downtown Mayapán next to the site center (P-114, P-28b, R-155, Q-41, Q-303) and two were in other locations (Y-43, P-71a).

All but group Q-41 were commoner dwellings. Faunal analysis (still in progress) from fully excavated dwellings has identified four bone tools from Y-45a and Q-39, five from Q-176; and Houses H-11 and I-55a are distinguished by slightly higher quantities. Ten pointed bone objects were found from House I-55a. Two needles were among the I-55a assemblage, along with two tapered metapodials and one flattened long bone weaving pick-like item; these suggest that textile production was important at this locality. One piece of burned and polished bone was also at I-55a. Metapodial or other tapered bone tools were also particularly abundant in full excavation samples of House H-11 (N = 5) and House Q-176 (N = 4). In contrast, no awls were recovered in the assemblage from fully excavated House L-28, which contained only one bone splinter and one piece of polished bone. House X-43 (fully excavated) had no bone artifacts. The quantity and type of metapodial tools at I-55a and, to a lesser extent, H-11 and Q-176 implies greater involvement in textile production than at houses like L-28 and X-43; these items were not a regular part of every household toolkit. Although Q-176 is slightly larger and more elaborate, the other houses are comparable in terms of size and degree of elaboration. Additional houses identified from test pit samples that may have been involved in textile working, as suggested by two or more metapodial or other weaving tools, include Y-43 (N = 2), P-114 (N = 3), and R-155 (N = 3).

A different type of concentration is present in the patio of house group P-28, in the downtown crafts district west of the site center (as indicated by a 1 × 2 meter test pit sample). At P-28, six bone objects included two beads or pendants, one needle, one inlay fragment, one turkey bone tube, and one polished bone splinter (tables 6.4, 6.5). This assemblage is more likely to reflect a combination of activities that involved making musicial instruments, sewing (and/or bloodletting), and making or acquiring bone ornaments. Other contexts also had a mixture of items that represent ornaments, instruments, or crafting tools. For example, a midden associated with House R-155, next to a cluster of palaces east of the site center, revealed seven bone objects (1 × 2 meter test pit sample), including one bead, one possible flute, two spatulate tools, one metapodial tool, one unfinished splinter and one rectangular inlay piece. Like that of P-28, this assemblage suggests involvement in a variety of crafting activities.

Monumental zone samples were hand sorted and not routinely screened, but this method was generally consistent due to continuity in a local, highly skilled labor force. While some sampling errors may plague the data, differential frequencies at structures in the site center imply specific activities involving bone objects at several locations. A total of 256 bone artifacts in

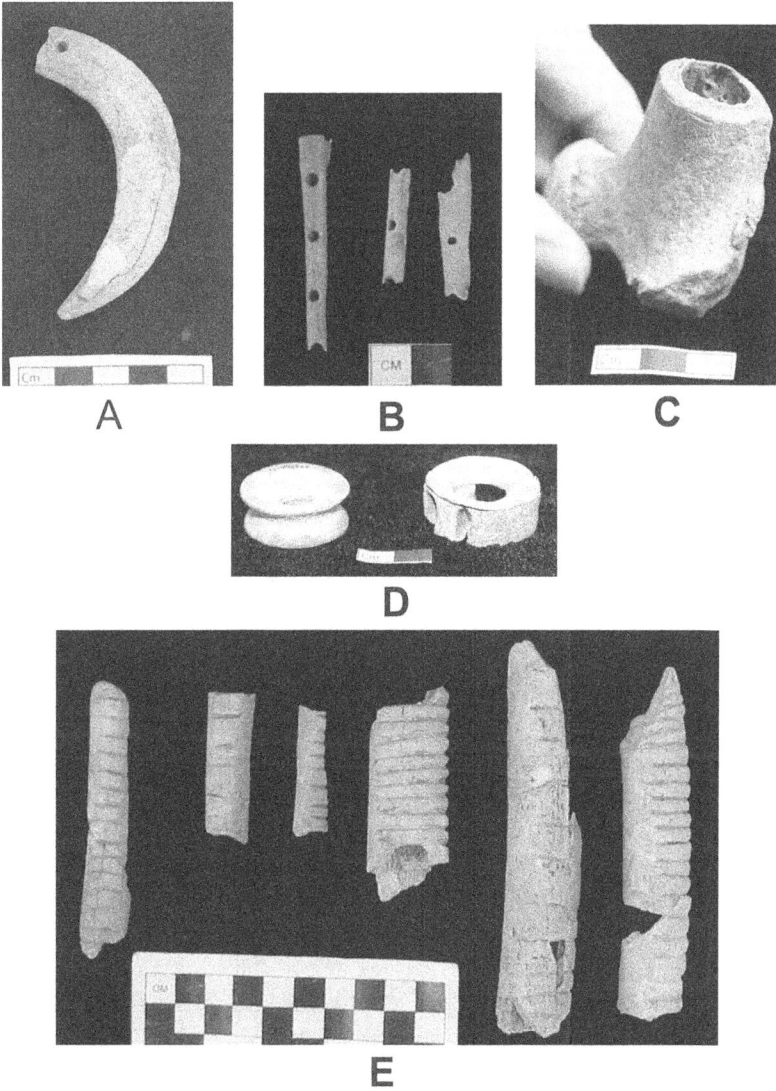

FIGURE 6.9. *Bone ornaments and instruments from Mayapán, including a perforated peccary tooth (A), bird bone flutes (B), a carved puma or jaguar femur (C), a shark vertebra earspool and a shark vertebra bead (D), and human long bone rasps (E).*

the sample came from the monumental center—of these, 236 are from thirty-three secure contexts (tables 6.4, 6.5). Nineteen of these contexts had one to three objects, five had four to six items, and nine contexts had eleven or more artifacts. Generally, the distribution of bone objects by monumental building type is close to the proportion each building type represents in the sample, but three types of buildings had more bone artifacts than might be expected. Halls, monumental zone houses, and temples formed 36 percent, 18 percent, and 21 percent of the sample of structures yet had 42 percent, 21 percent, and 25 percent, respectively, of the monumental center assemblage of bone objects. Oratories and shrines represented 9 percent and 12 percent of the structure samples, and these building types had 3 percent and 8 percent, respectively, of the bone artifacts. A tendency for greater use of bone items at halls, monumental zone houses, and temples is thus inferred, and this variation is accounted for by examining the frequencies at individual structures. Seventy percent of the 236 bones from known monumental contexts are from nine structures with eleven to fifty-three artifacts. Hall Q-54 had the largest sample, with fifty-two modified bones (tables 6.3, 6.4). The next largest assemblage is found at House Q-92, with thirty-three bones, followed by Temple Q-95 (N = 16), Halls Q-64 (N = 14) and Q-97 (N = 13), and Temples Q-58 (N = 13), Q-152 (N = 12), and Q-162 (N = 11).

The Hall Q-54 assemblage includes twenty deer metapodial tools, three rasps, three probable weaving picks, two animal tooth pendants, one shark vertebra bead, four other pointed objects, four fish bone needles, seven altered pneumatic spines, one bone tube, and seven other artifacts. The metapodial tools, weaving picks, and needles suggest some production activities at this locality, although ceremonial use is a possible alternative. Analogous assemblages of artifacts are present at two other halls. Hall Q-64 had three metapodial tools, two spatulates, two needles, two perforators, one antler tine, two pneumatic spines, and a bead, a spatula, and a shaped bone fragment. Hall Q-97 had six metapodial tools, one needle, one perforator, two antler tines, two pneumatic spines, and a shark vertebra bead. Material from monumental zone House Q-92 had 11 metapodial tools, four pneumatic spines, three bone perforators, one splinter, one needle, five antler tines, a polished dog tooth, one fish vertebra bead, two bone tubes, two rasps, and two pieces of shaped bone. Copper bell production also occurred at this house, which is identified as a luxury crafting locality (Paris 2008).

Bone items at temples overlapped with those found at halls. Temples Q-58, Q-95, Q-152, and Q-162 had the greatest number of bone artifacts. All had metapodial tools, although sacrificial Temples Q-58 and Q-95 had greater quantities (N = 5, N = 4). While only one metapodial tool was found at the other two temples, each also had a spatulate tool and another pointed bone object. Q-162 had three perforators, and both Q-152 and Q-162 had a stingray spine. Q-58 was distinguished from the other two by the presence of a flute and a rasp. Temple Q-158, unlike the other two, had three bone needles, three pneumatic fish spines, and two bone splinters. Beads were present at Q-58 and Q-162, and a crocodile tooth pendant and human bone earspool were found at Q-95. Temple Q-95 had the greatest diversity, with nine different categories of objects, including (beyond those already mentioned) a needle, perforator, other pointed bone, shaped pieces (N = 4), and pneumatic spines (N = 2) while the other temples had from five to seven types of artifacts (tables 6.4, 6.5). The large drilled crocodile tooth pendant from Q-95 is the only example found at Mayapán. The sacrificial rites at this burial shaft temple may explain the presence of trophy objects, including the human bone earspool and perforator. A crocodile is featured in the fisherman mural atop this building, and the pendant may have reflected a reference to the Tlatecuhtli deity (chapter 2).

Small Shrines Q-79, Q-79a, Q-74a, and Q-69 had eight metapodial tools among them as well as two fish spine perforators and one needle, three bone beads, two animal tooth pendants, and two pieces of shaped bone. As these vicinities were associated with public buildings of the site center, overlap in the objects recovered from their general facilities is not surprising But Shrine 74a, more isolated and within the site's Main Plaza, had two metapodial tools.

Like the other monumental buildings with higher quantities of bone objects, the temples and shrines have a mixture of items that represent personal possessions, musical instruments, and ritual use. Ceremonious usage of these items is easily envisioned. Metapodial tools could also have been used for ritual mutilation; awls or weaving picks may have been worn in headdresses of deity impersonators (e.g., Vail and Stone 2002); fish spines may have been useful in bloodletting; and finished objects such as beads or rasps could have been discarded in the context of many possible behaviors. Rasps made of human bone were probably deeply symbolic, representing relics of revered ancestors or, perhaps, sacrificed war captives. But the overlap of hall and domestic assemblages within the monumental center may suggest some use of the public buildings for production. Production of certain items may have itself been of great symbolic importance and geared toward special occasions (e.g., McAnany 2010:115–21). Some ritual occasions may have also called for offerings that included goods essential to daily life (chapter 2, figure 2.13).

Who used the public plazas and the buildings that framed them, especially the relatively open colonnaded halls? It is difficult to say whether tools were discarded casually or formally at these locations or whether they belonged to the noble patrons of the edifices or visitors who frequented the Main Plaza. At Xochicalco, artifact distributions also suggested overlap in the use of public precinct buildings and domestic contexts, leading the investigators to suggest that retainers living in the precinct sometimes undertook ordinary activities in support of patrons or events sponsored at the site center (Cyphers and Hirth 2000:130–31). At Mayapán, similar behavior seems likely. Parallels are observed for many artifact categories beyond bone tools. Small houses such as Q-92 were next to public buildings and probably housed retainers. Other houses excavated in Mayapán's monumental precinct, such as Q-56, had fewer bone tools (three metapodial tools, one bone spindle whorl, and one splinter) that indicate lesser engagement in textile production. Some halls—for example, Q-72—had fewer bone tools (N = 6), and while activities may have overlapped with other central edifices, they were not as important.

MARINE SHELL

Shell ornament production at Mayapán is widespread and diverse, and the city was fully reliant on trade networks with coastal sites to obtain raw marine shell materials for this industry. A total of 2,632 shell items have been identified from the INAH and PEMY projects, including 2,601 marine shells, of which 2,304 were identified and 296 consisted of unidentified fragments (table 6.6). An additional 32 specimens include fossil shells, coral, or inland aquatic *Pomacea* snail fragments. The marine shell sample is closely split between gastropods (55.3 percent) and bivalves (44.7 percent). A variety of products were made, including ornaments, cups, and occasional tools (chisels or celts). One of the more remarkable shell objects found previously at Mayapán is a shell "collar" type of object carved with hieroglyphs and numerical coefficients that Tatiana Proskouriakoff (1953:283) identified as part of the Tzolkin day count.

Ornaments are of particular interest due to the use of beads (particularly red ones) as currency (Tozzer 1941:95, 231n418). Two main bead forms are present in our sample: discoidal and cylindrical. Other than red and white shell beads, what other ornaments may have been used as units of exchange? We argue that suspended olive/*Prunum* and *Spondylus* ornaments also fit reasonable criteria for currency items (figure 6.10), as Colonial Spanish references to "beads" may have included a variety of suspended, drilled shells beyond the

TABLE 6.6 List of identified shell from INAH (1996–2004) and PEMY (2001–2009) projects. Percent given is that of 2,304 identified shells. Total sample included 2,632 shells, with 296 unidentified shell fragments and 32 fossils, coral, or non-marine shells.

Taxonomic name	Number	Percent of 2,304	Common name, attributes of interest
Strombus sp. and conch	873	37.90	Conch
Dinocardium	338	14.70	Giant cockle
Dosinia sp.	154	6.70	Small bivalve
Oliva sp.	149	6.50	Olive
Bivalve	90	3.90	Bivalve
Mercenaria campechiensis	69	3.00	Quahog
Phacoides sp.	68	3.00	Small bivalve
Prunum sp.	56	2.40	Common Marginella, small gastropod, olive size
Natica sp.	52	2.30	Moon shell, small gastropod
Spondylus sp.	39	1.70	Thorny oyster
Chione sp.	38	1.60	Small bivalve
Gastropod (marine)	25	1.10	Gastropod
Anadara	24	1.00	A genus of ark clam
Arca zebra	23	1.00	Turkey wing clam
Busycon	20	0.90	Lightning whelk
Cardiidae	20	0.90	Cockles
Trachycardium sp.	20	0.90	Yellow cockle
Mytilidae	20	0.90	Mussels
Pleuroploca gigantea	17	0.70	Horse conch
Ostreidae	16	0.70	Oyster
Pectinidae	16	0.70	Scallop
Pinna carnea	16	0.70	Amber pen shell, reddish and textured like *Spondylus* but thin, fan shaped, translucent
Ficus communis	15	0.70	Paper fig shell, similar to pear whelk
Polinices lacteus	15	0.70	Also a moon shell and similar to *Natica*

continued on next page

TABLE 6.6—*continued*

Taxonomic name	Number	Percent of 2,304	Common name, attributes of interest
Anomia	10	0.40	Jingle shell/saddle oyster, very thin, uneven margins, bumpy, can be translucent when flaked
Barbatia tenera	10	0.40	Delicate ark shell
Conus sp.	10	0.40	Cone snail, gastropod, variants used in traditional African currency and kula ring exchange, brown and white coloring
Anomalocardia	7	0.30	Caribbean pointed Venus family Veneridae
Cassis	6	0.30	Helmet shell
Gouldia cerina	6	0.30	Waxy gould clam Veneridae, brown and white markings
Diodora cayenensis	5	0.20	Keyhole limpet, conical, ribbed purplish/white markings, rings
Nerita sp.	5	0.20	Checkered nerite, ribbed, black/white checkered pattern, ribbed
Haliotis sp.	4	0.20	Abalone, pearly ear shells, Venus's ear iridescent interior, pearly
Fasciolaria tulipa	4	0.20	Tulip shell
Isognomon alatus	4	0.20	Flat tree oyster
Terebra	4	0.20	Auger shell, long tapering spire
Crassostrea virginica	4	0.20	Atlantic oyster
Chama sp.	3	0.10	Leafy jewelbox oyster, looks like *Spondylus*, preserves redness
Asaphis deflorata	3	0.10	Gaudy asaphis, clam
Cyphoma sp.	3	0.10	Flamingo tongue shell, small, olive-sized but with ring-like lateral ridge
Cypraea sp. (cowry)	3	0.10	Cowry
Littorina sp.	3	0.10	Periwinkle
Melongena corona	3	0.10	Crown conch
Carditamera floridana	2	0.10	Cardita
Euvola ziczac	2	0.10	Scallop

continued on next page

TABLE 6.6—*continued*

Taxonomic name	Number	Percent of 2,304	Common name, attributes of interest
Ischadium recurvum	2	0.10	Mussels
Lucinidae	2	0.10	Clam
Marginella sp.	2	0.10	Olive-like
Plicatula gibbosa	2	0.10	Kitten paw, related to oyster, pronounced ridges and reddish color, triangular in shape, like *Spondylus* but no spines
Pteria sp.	2	0.10	Pearly oyster, produces pearls and pearly interior
Tellina radiata	2	0.10	Sunrise tellin, smooth shell, nice color when fresh
Turbinella angulata	2	0.10	West Indian chank, large conch
Veneridae	2	0.10	Venus clams
Aequipecten muscosus	1	0.04	Scallop
Architectonica nobilis	1	0.04	Atlantic sundial, pronounced spiral, pattern of square markings around spiral
Brachydontes	1	0.04	Scorched mussell
Busycotypus canaliculatus	1	0.04	Channeled whelk
Callista	1	0.04	Clam
Crepidula fornicate	1	0.04	Common Atlantic slipper snail
Cypraea or *Cymatium*	1	0.04	Cowrie or hairy trumpet, very different unless worked, both have brown markings, hard, smooth
Oliva or *Strombus*	1	0.04	Either olive or conch
Pholas	1	0.04	Campeche angel wing
Phyllonotus pomum	1	0.04	Apple murex
Pseudochama radians	1	0.04	Atlantic jewelbox, like *Chama*
Pterioida	1	0.04	Clam
Trivia candidula	1	0.04	small ribbed gastropods, olive sized, ribbed, called "cowries" in Britain, not closely related, superficial resemblance, little white trivia
Urosalpinx cinerea	1	0.04	Atlantic oyster drill, predatory, knobby rugged

discoidal and cylindrical forms. Like these latter beads, olive shell ornaments were often perforated in systematic ways and suspended as belts, tunic elements, or collars in Maya art (figure 6.10). An example that is contemporary with Mayapán is the olive shell collar worn by Kukulcan/Quetzalcoatl illustrated in the Dresden Codex (Taube 1992:figure 93). Individually suspended pendants may also have represented currency units—most notably, drilled bivalve shell forms that have longstanding use histories at Maya archaeological sites (e.g., Buttles 1992:93). The Atlantic thorny oyster (*Spondylus americanus*) shell is often shown in Classic Period art, and it was also a valuable offering in sites dating as early as the Formative Period, along with a related Pacific species (e.g., Freidel, Reese-Taylor, and Mora-Marin 2002; Moholy-Nagy 2003, 2008). *Spondylus* and other bivalves were made into pendants (figure 6.10) that were probably used as pectorals or shell chastity objects (Tozzer 1941:106). One subadult burial of about twelve years of age was identified at Mayapán commoner House L-28. This individual was probably female, as a *Spondylus* pendant was placed in the pelvic region (Peraza Lope et al. 2008:576).

Red beads made of *Spondylus* shell found archaeologically represent the red bead monies in use at the time of Spanish contact (Freidel, Reese-Taylor, and Mora-Marin 2002). But most shell beads at Mayapán are white. Similarities in the form and size of white shell beads and red *Spondylus* beads suggest to us the parallel use of white shell beads as monetary units. As discussed previously, the Relacion of Valladolid explicitly distinguishes different lengths and probable values of coral-colored beads from other beads (presumably white ones). The contextual association of white shell beads with other known currency units also implies that they functioned similarly. For example, white and red shell discoidal beads are stacked with green jade cylindrical beads in the painted, bejeweled headdress of a Chen Mul effigy censer portraying the god Itzamna (figure 6.2e). This association of these beads of three different colors supports the case that they functioned similarly as ornaments in the city's exchange system. Another example is evident in the bracelets or anklets found with a child burial at House Q-39 (figure 5.33). These adornments consisted of strings of alternating white discoidal beads and copper bells (bells were also monies). Other suspended shell objects in the grave included a white marine bivalve shell pendant (not *Spondylus*) and numerous *Spondylus* discoidal and cylindrical beads (figure 5.33). The overlap in the use of certain beads and pendants as decorative ornaments and monetary units at Mayapán matches cross-cultural expectations for premodern currencies. Freidel, Kathryn Reese-Taylor, and David Mora-Marin (2002) argue effectively that adornment is a

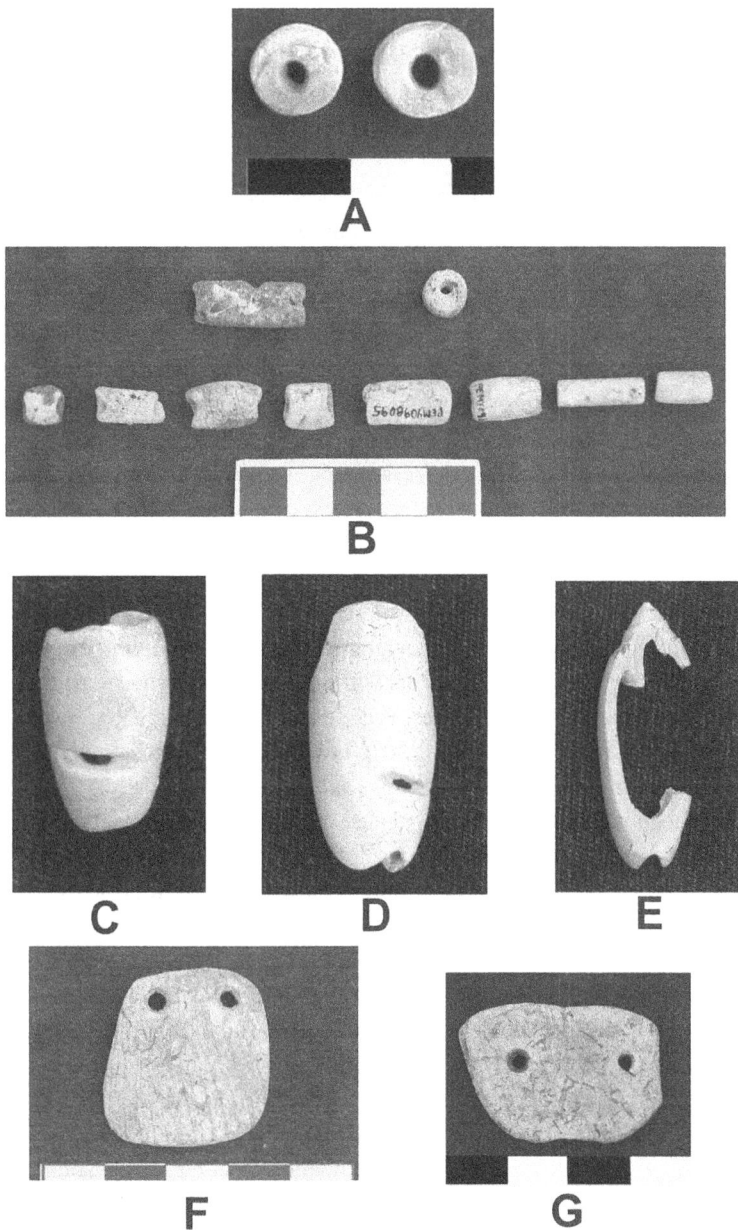

FIGURE 6.10. *Suspended shell objects likely to be currencies at Mayapán, including discoidal red (Spondylus) and white beads (A), cylindrical beads (B), modified Oliva and Prunum shells (C, D, E), and bivalve pendants (usually Spondylus), as shown here (F, G).*

critical component of assigning value to shell monies in the commercial realm. These authors point out that the display of these items by high-status persons establishes their value, desirability, and sanctification. Evidence abounds among ethnographic case studies for the practice of wearing monies as part of personal attire (Quiggin 1949:258).

Pieces of shell are regularly found in test pits across Mayapán. As for other craft industries, surplus shell-working contexts must be distinguished from other locations with minor quantities of debris. Shell workshops are indicated by statistical outliers with quantities equal to or beyond one standard deviation above the mean. A second important distinction is the type of shell remains that are present. Preforms and shell-working debris indicate production contexts while contexts with primarily finished ornaments are more likely to represent consumer assemblages. Examining the distribution of finished objects also contributes toward wealth assessments of elite and commoner houselots at the city. In the following paragraphs, we also suggest that distinguishing between currency and non-currency shell-object production represents a third important consideration.

There are two specific objectives to our analysis of shell. The first compares scales and types of production according to context. The second examines the products made at the city and compares them to potential shell-currency items and ornaments at other Maya sites. We identify varying scales of involvement of houselots in ornament making at Mayapán, from occasional pursuits to manufacture for exchange. Workshops that focused specifically on shell beads have not been identified, perhaps because a low rate of manufacturing failures is associated with this industry. Houselots that were engaged in surplus production used a broad range of marine shell taxa that are represented by shell flakes, cores (marine shells from which sections have been removed), ornament fragments, and partially worked pieces.

Most marine shells were brought whole to the site for the purpose of craft production. Shell species were not uniformly available along the west and north coasts of the Yucatán Peninsula (E. Andrews 1969:41–45), and this fact attests further to Mayapán's reliance on a matrix of exchange relationships to supply its craft industries and sources of currency. Mayapán was closest to the north coast, about 55 kilometers as the crow flies. While *Prunum* shell (worked similarly to olive shell) was available at some north coast beaches, *Oliva* shells are only available on the east and west coasts (E. Andrews 1969:41, table 1; Andrews et al. 1974:table 2). Due to preservation problems, shellfish would not have been a viable component of the Mayapán diet.

Frequencies of Marine Shells and Finished Shell Objects

A total of 2,632 shells were analyzed from the INAH and PEMY projects (tables 6.6, 6.7), which included 2,304 pieces of identified marine shell, 296 unidentified fragments, and 32 miscellaneous items (coral, fossil coral, fossil shell, a crab claw, and inland aquatic or terrestrial snails). These materials were identified in the field lab by Elizabeth L. France (2008), Gina Lasalla (2009), and White (White et al. 2012). *Strombus* species (conch) dominated the assemblage, forming 37.9 percent of the sample, followed by *Dinocardium* (giant cockle, 14.7 percent), *Dosinia* clams (6.7 percent), and various *Oliva* species (6.5 percent). Some identified bivalves were also relatively abundant, including *Mercenaria* (quahog, 3.0 percent) and *Phacoides* (3.0 percent) as were bivalve fragments not identified to species (3.9 percent). Other taxa forming 1 percent or more of the sample include *Prunum* (Common Marginella, 2.4 percent), *Natica* (moon shell, 2.3 percent), *Spondylus* (thorny oyster, 1.7 percent), *Chione* (a small bivalve, 1.6 percent), gastropods not identified to species (1.1 percent), *Anadara* (ark clam, 1.0 percent), and *Arca zebra* (turkey wing clam, 1.0 percent). A total of sixty-seven taxonomic identifications are listed on table 6.6, most of which formed less than 1 percent of the sample. The large amount of *Strombus* shells may reflect their large size, which would have created more debris. But their importance is also evident in the city's shell-working industries. Thirty-eight classifications of bivalves account for 44.5 percent of the total shell sample. Twenty-nine categories of gastropods form 55.5 percent of the shells, which includes *Strombus* (37.9 percent) and all other gastropods (17.6 percent).

Shells were clearly used for different purposes, and the abundance of worked or finished gastropod artifacts provides a clearer picture of their crafting trajectory. With some important exceptions, bivalve trajectories are more difficult to ascertain, as many examples merely reflect flaked debris. Table 6.6 lists some important characteristics of identified shells, many of which had specific coloring that may have contributed to their value. Table 6.7 groups identified shells based on form, size, and coloring. A group of larger, more robust gastropods, dominated by *Strombus*, also includes whelks and similar species and forms 42.6 percent of the sample. These shells were used to make the greatest range of objects, permitted in part by their large size. As noted elsewhere in the Americas, conch and whelk tools can be utilitarian, including cups, picks, chisels, and adzes (Eaton 1974; Luer et al. 1986; Masson 1988), although such objects are uncommon at Mayapán (figure 6.11). Conch shells were often used to make small discoidal or cylindrical beads, plaques, or pendants. In this respect they were used for some of the same products as bivalves. Pendants

TABLE 6.7 Identified shell taxa INAH-PEMY projects, organized into general taxonomic/morphological categories. (Percent shown is that of identified marine shell specimens, N = 2,304.)

Robust gastropod group	Percent of 2,304	Bivalve group (except for Spondylus-like)	Percent of 2,304
Strombus sp. and conch	37.90	*Dinocardium*	14.70
Gastropod (marine)	1.10	*Dosinia* sp.	6.70
Busycon	0.90	Bivalve	3.90
Pleuroploca gigantea	0.70	*Mercenaria campechiensis*	3.00
Ficus communis	0.70	*Phacoides* sp.	3.00
Conus sp.	0.40	*Chione* sp.	1.60
Cassis	0.30	*Anadara*	1.00
Fasciolaria tulipa	0.20	*Arca zebra*	1.00
Terebra	0.20	*Trachycardium* sp.	0.90
Melongena corona	0.10	*Cardiidae*	0.90
Turbinella angulata	0.10	Pectinidae	0.70
Busycotypus canaliculatus	0.04	*Barbatia tenera*	0.40
Phyllonotus pomum	0.04	*Anomalocardia*	0.30
Urosalpinx cinerea	0.04	*Gouldia cerina**	0.30
Total	42.60	*Diodora cayenensis**	0.20
Olive and similar types		*Isognomon alatus*	0.20
Oliva sp.	6.50	*Asaphis deflorata*	0.10
Prunum sp.	2.40	*Crassostrea virginica*	0.20
Cyphoma sp.	0.10	*Carditamera floridana*	0.10
Cypraea sp. (cowry)	0.10	*Euvola ziczac*	0.10
Marginella sp.	0.10	Lucinidae	0.10
Cypraea or *Cymatium*	0.04	*Tellina radiata**	0.10
Trivia candidula	0.04	Veneridae	0.10
Total	9.30	*Architectonica nobilis*	0.04
Other small, delicate gastropods		*Brachydontes*	0.04
Natica sp.	2.30	*Callista*	0.04
Polinices lacteus	0.70	*Crassostrea*	0.04
Nerita sp.	0.20	*Pholas*	0.04
Littorina sp.	0.10	*Pterioida*	0.04

continued on next page

TABLE 6.7—*continued*

Other small, delicate gastropods	Percent of 2,304	Bivalve group (except for Spondylus-like)	Percent of 2,304
Architectonica nobilis	0.04	Mytilidae**	0.90
Total	3.30	Ostreidae**	0.70
Spondylus group		*Anomia***	0.40
Spondylus sp.	1.70	*Haliotis* sp.**	0.20
Pinna carnea	0.70	*Ischadium recurvum***	0.10
Chama sp.	0.10	*Pterioida***	0.04
Plicatula gibbosa	0.10	Total bivalve	42.00
Pseudochama radians	0.04	*Other*	
Total	2.60	*Crepidula fornicate*	0.04
		Oliva or *Strombus*	0.04

* special coloring when fresh
** pearly interior characteristics

and beads were made from bivalves such as *Plicatula gibbosa* and *Spondylus*, as well as species similar to *Spondylus*, including *Pinna carnea*, *Chama*, and *Pseudochama radians*. Some of the shells in this *Spondylus* group share the red color of the thorny oyster, including *Chama* and *Pinna carnea*. The *Spondylus* group forms 2.6 percent of the sample (table 6.7). As the spines of *Spondylus* were usually removed in pendants found at the city, the resemblances between these species increased with processing. The Olive group forms 9.3 percent of the sample and includes small elongate gastropods used for suspended ornaments (table 6.6). They exhibit an overlapping range of modifications: spires are often removed and horizontal notches or round perforation holes are present. These shells include *Oliva*, *Prunum*, *Cyphoma*, *Cypraea* (cowry), *Cymatium*, *Marginella*, and *Trivia candidula* (known as "cowries" in Britain but not closely related). An additional group of small, more delicate gastropods (table 6.7) tend to be about the same size as Olive group shells, but they have a more rounded and less elongate shape. These gastropods include *Natica*, *Polinices lacteus*, *Nerita*, *Littorina*, and *Architectonica nobilis*, and they form 3.3 percent of the sample. Bivalves other than the *Spondylus* group represent 42 percent of the identified shells (table 6.7); within this group, 2.3 percent are oyster or mussel shells with pearly qualities that may have been important for crafting. Some bivalves are also notable for their markings or color—for example, *Tellina radiata* (Sunrise Tellin), *Chama* (retains red coloring), *Nerita*

A

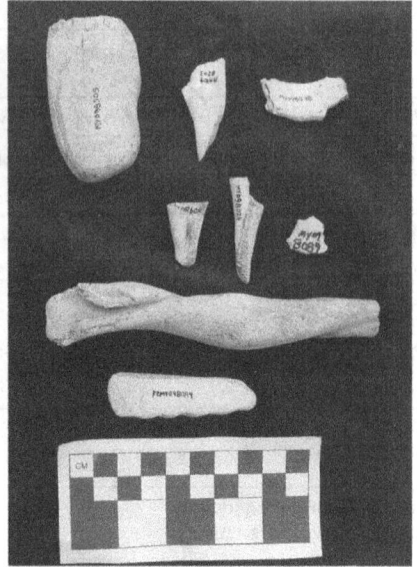

B

C

FIGURE 6.11. *Bivalve (Dinocardium) debris (A) and Strombus (B, C) debris from Mayapán shell workshops. These types of shells were used to make a range of ornaments and objects that are infrequent and non-systematic and were not likely to have served as currencies, unlike Spondylus and olive/Prunum suspended ornaments shown in figure 6.10 (although white discoidal beads of Strombus were probably also currencies).*

TABLE 6.8 Finished shell objects—INAH/PEMY contexts, N = 326.

General category	Taxa/artifact type	Number	Percent of 326
Bivalve pearly	Abalone worked	2	0.6
Bivalve pearly	*Anomia* ornament	2	0.6
Bivalve	*Barbatia* pendant	1	0.3
Bivalve	Bivalve pendant	3	0.9
Gastropod	*Busycon* ornament fragment	2	0.6
Bivalve	*Chione* pendant	5	1.5
Gastropod	*Conus* ornament	3	0.9
Olive group	*Cypraea* pendant	1	0.3
Bivalve	*Dinocardium* pendant/rectangular	2	0.6
Bivalve	*Dinocardium* worked	1	0.3
Bivalve	*Dosinia* worked	1	0.3
Bivalve	*Mercenaria* pendant	1	0.3
Bivalve pearly	Mytilidae bead	1	0.3
Bivalve pearly	Mytilidae pendant	1	0.3
Olive group	*Oliva* various	96	29.4
Bivalve	Pectinidae disc bead	1	0.3
Bivalve	Pectinidae pendant	1	0.3
Bivalve	*Phacoides* pendant	1	0.3
Other small gastropod	*Polinices* pendant	2	0.6
Olive group	*Prunum* various	22	6.7
Spondylus group	*Spondylus* bead	3	0.9
Spondylus group	*Spondylus* pendant	23	7.1
Spondylus group	*Spondylus* worked	1	0.3
Gastropod	*Strombus* bead	28	8.6
Gastropod	*Strombus* columnella	6	1.8
Gastropod	*Strombus* dentiform	1	0.3
Gastropod	*Strombus* pendant, not all drilled	43	13.2
Gastropod	*Strombus* bracelet	5	1.5
Gastropod	*Strombus* spoon/spatulate	4	1.2
Gastropod	*Strombus* lip tool	2	0.6

continued on next page

TABLE 6.8—*continued*

General category	Taxa/artifact type	Number	Percent of 326
Gastropod	*Strombus* cup	1	0.3
Gastropod	*Strombus* worked fragment	36	11.0
Unidentified	Unidentified bead	12	3.7
Unidentified	Unidentified pendant, not all drilled	4	1.2
Unidentified	Unidentified worked	3	0.9
Fossil	Fossil shell, 2 worked bivalve, 2 longitudinally cut Marginella, 1 flattened and filed olive	5	1.5
			100.0
Pendant total			30.1
Bead total			14.7
Olive and *Prunum* ornament total			36.2

(black and white checkered pattern), *Diodara* (purplish white markings), and *Gouldia cerina* (brown and white markings).

It is interesting that some of the rarer shells found at Mayapán were important in other ancient societies for ornament making or as currencies. Close to home, *Chama* was used to make red shell beads in the Caribbean (Keegan and Carlson 2008/2009), and at the site of Ejutla, Oaxaca (Feinman and Nicholas 1993:108). The spiral of the *Conus* shell was important for currency in Africa and Oceania (Quiggin 1949:figures 7, 73) and was also used for the famed kula ring bracelets. Cowries were widely used across the Old World as a unit of exchange (Einzig 1949:147–51; Quiggin 1949:25–39).

A total of 326 finished artifacts were present in our sample of 2,632 shell objects (table 6.8). This tally is provisional, as it was sometimes difficult to determine from small fragments of worked debris (smoothed, polished, incomplete specimens) whether or not they were from completed ornaments or broken manufacturing failures. Numerous *Oliva* or *Prunum* shells exhibit a removal of the spire, lip, and/or columnella (figure 6.10) and represent a finished ornament type that dates back to the Late Preclassic in the Maya area (e.g., Garber 1989:figure 23; Aizpurúa and McAnany 1999:122–23). Figure 6.12 illustrates examples of polished or partially worked *Oliva* and *Prunum* shells and a whole *Cypraea*. Such specimens were often completely smoothed and polished, and this may have been an early step in ornament making. Although

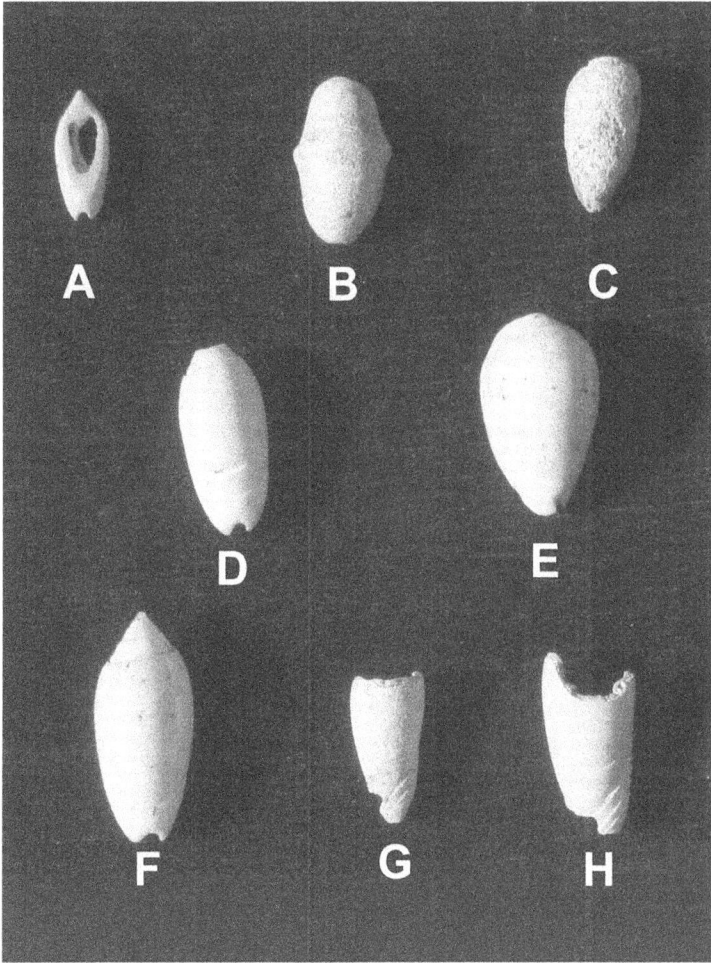

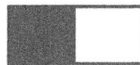

FIGURE 6.12. *Partly worked olive/Prunum small marine gastropod group shells from Workshop I-55, including a split example (A), an unworked Cyphoma (B), a fossil shell perhaps unrelated to the shell-working industry (C), an incompletely notched shell (D), polished Cypraea and Prunum (E, F), and unsmoothed spire-lopped shells (G, H).*

polished shells are included in the finished-object inventory, they may represent preforms. Finished shells consist of 77.3 percent marine gastropods, 15.4 percent marine bivalves, 1.5 percent fossil shells, and 5.8 percent unidentified shells (table 6.8).

The most numerous completed ornament types were *Oliva* shell ornaments (29.4 percent). It is worth noting that *Prunum* shell ornaments—closely related to *Oliva* shells in shape, modification, and use—formed an additional 6.7 percent; the total of *Oliva* and *Prunum* combined forms over one-third of the finished-object sample (36.2 percent). The remainder of the sample is largely comprised of pendants or related, shaped geometric pieces (30.1 percent)— some not drilled—and beads (14.7 percent) (figure 6.13). Pendants, beads, and olive/*Prunum* objects together form 81 percent of the finished objects. The remaining 19 percent includes small quantities of fossil tools, *Strombus* objects, and unidentified fragments. Fossil shells (figure 6.12c) were probably used as abraders or for other crafting tasks; two were merely smoothed, two were longitudinally split, and one was flattened.

Most of the pendants are made of conch shell (23.2 percent), including worked fragments and undrilled pieces (table 6.8). *Strombus* was also popular for bead making, as beads of conch formed 8.6 percent of the finished-object sample, and beads unidentified to species (3.7 percent) are also likely to be of conch shell. *Spondylus* pendants (and worked fragments) formed 7.4 percent of the completed-object sample. All other artifact types except for *Oliva/Prunum* shells form less than 1.9 percent of the sample. Additional patterns are apparent when considering the five general type groups listed in table 6.7. Pendants and non-drilled geometric ornaments made of bivalves (other than *Spondylus*) formed 6.4 percent of the sample (Abalone, *Anomia*, Barbatia, miscellaneous bivalves, *Chione, Dinocardium, Dosinia, Mercenaria*, Mytilidae, Pectinidae, and *Phacoides*). Beads of this group of bivalves form 5.2 percent of the sample. More utilitarian *Strombus* columnella and lip objects, including spatulas, spoons, and a cup, form 4 percent of the finished tools (table 6.8). *Oliva* and *Oliva*-like ornaments and pendants make up 36 percent of the finished-object sample, and beads made of all types of shell represent nearly 15 percent of the sample (table 6.8). Given the importance of shell "beads" as units of monetary exchange, the ubiquity of *Oliva* group ornaments and pendants (made from various shells) suggests to us that these items had a place in the currency system. They are more abundant than cylindrical or discoidal beads.

The production side of shell industries at Mayapán can be assessed by the characteristics of the sample of shell-working debris. The INAH and PEMY project samples included fragments with modification (cut marks, smoothing,

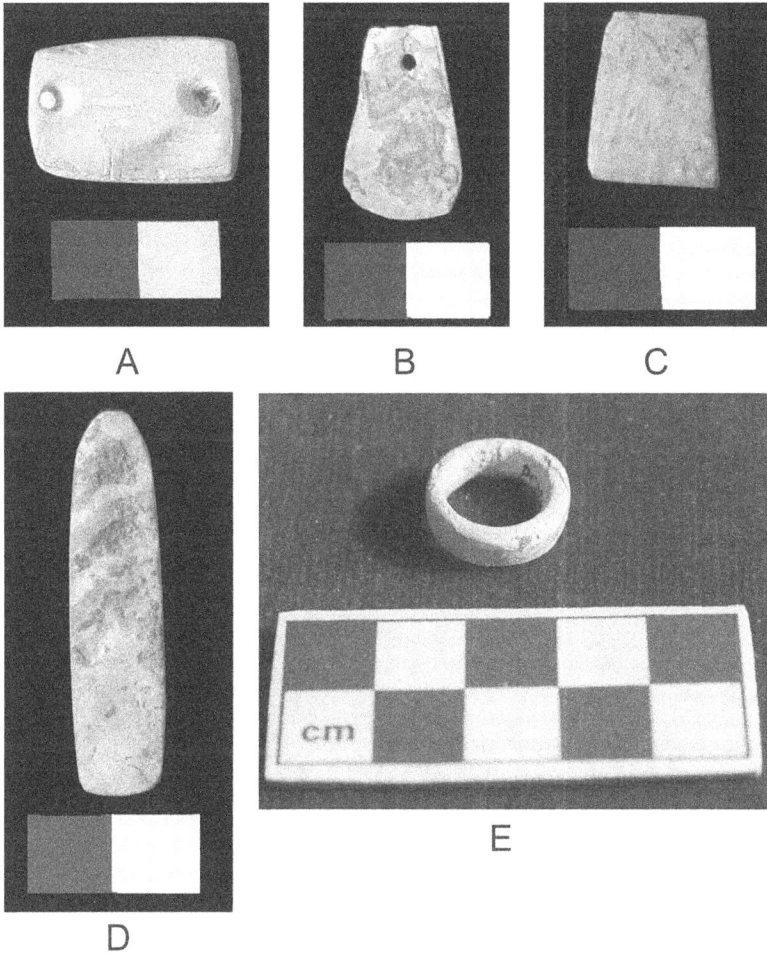

FIGURE 6.13. *Marine shell ornaments from Mayapán that are not thought to have been currency items, including an incompletely drilled Strombus rectangular pendant (A), an ax-shaped pendant (B), a wedge-shaped plaque (C), an elongate plaque (D), and a shell ring (E). All are from the I-55 workshop except for the ring (from a burial in Q-39).*

polish, partly drilled pendants or beads and other preforms), and debris that lacked signs of modification other than natural or cultural percussion breakage. A total of 99 debris pieces were visibly altered (table 6.9), and 2,207 pieces of debris lacked evidence for impacts beyond breakage.

TABLE 6.9 INAH/PEMY preform shell debris exhibiting significant modification (all contexts, N = 99).

Taxa/Modification	Number	Percent of 99
Anadara ornament preform	1	1.0
Anomia discoidal bead preform, not drilled	1	1.0
Anomia ornament preform	2	2.0
Bivalve cut fragment	1	1.0
Bivalve pendant preform half drill hole	1	1.0
Busycon ornament nearly finished	1	1.0
Busycon pendant preform drilled	1	1.0
Busycon worked fragment unfinished	1	1.0
Dinocardium cut	1	1.0
Dinocardium ornament preform	2	2.0
Dinocardium smoothed	2	2.0
Dinocardium smoothed drilled	1	1.0
Dosinia polished preform	1	1.0
Dosinia smoothed	1	1.0
Mercenaria campechiensis cut	1	1.0
Mercenaria cut smoothed	1	1.0
Mercenaria unfinished ornament, not drilled	1	1.0
Oliva fragment	22	22.2
Oliva preform partial groove	2	2.0
Oliva preform smoothed	1	1.0
Oliva tinkler preform partial groove	2	2.0
Ostreidae, cut, rectangular, unfinished	1	1.0
Ostreidae ornament preform	2	2.0
Pectinidae ornament preform	4	4.0
Prunum no spire preform partly drilled	1	1.0
Prunum preform	3	3.0
Spondylus rectangular, not drilled, colored orange	1	1.0
Strombus, shell cup fragment, unfinished	1	1.0
Strombus claw shape fragment	1	1.0
Strombus cut fragment	2	2.0

continued on next page

TABLE 6.9—*continued*

Taxa/Modification	Number	Percent of 99
Strombus disc fragment not drilled	1	1.0
Strombus bead preform, discoidal, not drilled, colored blue	1	1.0
Strombus ornament fragment	2	2.0
Strombus ornament preform	1	1.0
Strombus pendant preform partly drilled	6	6.1
Strombus rectangular, notched	1	1.0
Strombus rectangular not drilled	1	1.0
Strombus rectangular preform	3	3.0
Strombus rectangular preform partly drilled	1	1.0
Strombus rough cut paint pot	1	1.0
Strombus smoothed	5	5.1
Strombus spatulate ornament fragment	1	1.0
Strombus square rough	1	1.0
Strombus columnella ornament preform	1	1.0
Strombus columnella object polished unfinished	1	1.0
Strombus columnella pointed object unfinished	1	1.0
Strombus worked fragment unfinished	1	1.0
Trachycardium smoothed	1	1.0
Unidentified grooved fragment	1	1.0
Unidentified triangular pendant preform	1	1.0
Unidentified rough square partly drilled	1	1.0
Unidentified rounded edge	1	1.0
Unidentified smoothed	2	2.0
Total	99	100

Modified debris was limited to fourteen different identified taxonomic categories, inlcuding Anadara, *Anomia*, bivalves not identified to genus, *Busycon*, *Dinocardium*, *Dosinia*, *Mercenaria*, *Oliva*, Ostreidae, Pectinidae, *Prunum*, *Spondylus*, *Strombus*, and *Trachycardium*. Nearly two-thirds of the modified shell debris is represented by *Strombus* (33.3 percent) and *Oliva* or *Prunum* shells (31.3 percent); less abundant taxa of note include *Dinocardium* (6.1 percent), Ostreidae (5.1 percent), *Anomia* (3 percent), and *Mercenaria* (3.0 percent). All other identified taxa formed 2 percent or less of the sample (table 6.9). Beyond

TABLE 6.10 Summary of ornament types by taxa in sample of modified shell debris (itemized in detail in table 6.9). (INAH/PEMY projects)

Olive and related Olive group shells	31.3%
Bivalve pendant preform	19.2%
Strombus/Busycon pendant unfinished	13.1%
Spondylus rectangular object unfinished	1.0%
Strombus rectangular object unfinished	7.1%
Unidentified taxa pendant/ornamament	3.0%
Bivalve ornament fragment	5.1%
Gastropod ornament fragment	9.1%
Bead unfinished	2.0%
Strombus miscellaneous fragment	6.1%
Unidentified taxa worked fragment	3.0%

the *Oliva/Prunum* ornaments, the majority of the sample was comprised of unfinished pendants or ornaments (57.6 percent). Bead preforms comprised only 2 percent of the modified debris and 6.1 percent is represented by miscellaneous *Strombus* objects (an unfinished cup, a spatulate, columnella objects, and various worked fragments). Clearly, *Oliva/Prunum* ornaments and pendants made of various other shells dominate this assemblage of altered debris, as together they form 88.9 percent of the sample (table 6.9). This pattern does not necessarily mean that these objects were produced in abundance at the city, as the overall number of modified (rather than finished) items is small, with only 99 specimens listed in table 6.9. It is difficult to know whether modified fragments represent manufacturing failures or pieces of broken finished objects.

Bivalves were popular for pendant manufacture, although a variety of shells were used for this purpose (tables 6.9, 6.10). Unfinished pendants made of bivalves formed 19.2 percent of the modified debris and one *Spondylus* example is present. Thirteen percent of the partially worked pendants were made of *Strombus* or *Busycon* (figure 6.13a, d); others were not identified species (3 percent). Rectangular or square ornaments are listed separately in table 6.10 (figure 6.13a), and these were relatively common in the sample of unfinished *Strombus* objects (7.1 percent); one *Spondylus* example was also present.

Shell Debris

Unmodified shell debris represents percussion flakes (figure 6.11), unworked fragments, or slightly (incompletely) worked fragments; taxa frequencies are

TABLE 6.11 Debris (percussion flakes, unworked fragments, or slightly worked fragments), all seasons, N = 2,207 (PEMY project).

Taxa	Number	Percent of 2,207	Taxa	Number	Percent of 2,207
Strombus	721	32.70	*Crassostrea virginica*	4	0.20
Dinocardium	329	14.90	*Fasciolaria tulipa*	4	0.20
Unidentified	218	9.90	*Isognomon alatus*	4	0.20
Dosinia sp.	156	7.10	*Terebra*	4	0.20
Bivalve	73	3.30	*Asaphis deflorata*	3	0.10
Phacoides sp.	67	3.00	*Chama* sp.	3	0.10
Mercenaria campechiensis	65	2.90	*Cyphoma gibbosum*	3	0.10
Natica sp.	58	2.60	*Littorina* sp.	3	0.10
Fossil shell	41	1.90	*Melongena corona*	3	0.10
Chione sp.	32	1.40	Abalone	2	0.10
Prunum sp.	25	1.10	*Carditamera floridana*	2	0.10
Anadara	23	1.00	*Cypraea zebra* (cowry)	2	0.10
Arca zebra	23	1.00	*Euvola ziczac*	2	0.10
Oliva sp.	23	1.00	*Ischadium recurvum*	2	0.10
Cardiidae	21	1.00	Lucinidae	2	0.10
Mytilidae	19	0.90	*Lucinoma filosus*	2	0.10
Trachycardium sp.	18	0.80	*Marginella*	2	0.10
Gastropod (marine)	17	0.80	Ostreidae or Mytilidae	2	0.10
Pleuroploca gigantea	17	0.80	*Plicatula gibbosa*	2	0.10
Busycon	15	0.70	*Pteria colymbus*	2	0.10
Ficus communis	15	0.70	*Turbinella angulata*	2	0.10
Ostreidae	15	0.70	Veneridae	2	0.10
Pinna carnea	15	0.70	*Aequipecten muscosus*	1	0.05
Arcoidea	14	0.60	*Architectonica nobilis*	1	0.05
Polinices lacteus	13	0.60	*Brachydontes*	1	0.05
Spondylus	12	0.50	*Busycotypus canaliculatus*	1	0.05
Coral	11	0.50	*Calista*	1	0.05
Pomacea	11	0.50	Crab claw	1	0.05
Barbatia tenera	9	0.40	*Crepidala fornicata*	1	0.05

continued on next page

TABLE 6.11—*continued*

Taxa	Number	Percent of 2,207	Taxa	Number	Percent of 2,207
Pectinidae	9	0.40	*Cypraea* or *Cymatium*	1	0.05
Spondylus or Ostreidae	8	0.40	Fossil coral	1	0.05
Anomalocardia	7	0.30	Pteroidea	1	0.05
Cassis sp.	7	0.30	*Pholas*	1	0.05
Conus sp.	6	0.30	*Phyllonotus ponum*	1	0.05
Gouldia sp.	6	0.30	*Pseudochama radians*	1	0.05
Anomia	5	0.20	*Tellina radiata*	1	0.05
Diodora cayenensis	5	0.20	*Trivia candidula*	1	0.05
Nerita sp.	5	0.20	*Urosalpinx cinerea*	1	0.05

listed in table 6.11. *Strombus* fragments were most common (32.7 percent), followed by several kinds of bivalves: *Dinocardium* (14.9 percent), *Dosinia* (7.1 percent), *Phacoides* (3 percent), *Mercenaria* (2.9 percent), and bivalves unidentified to species (3.3 percent). *Natica* formed 2.6 percent of the unmodified debris sample, and all other taxa formed 1.4 percent or less. The majority of shell debris from the site appears to reflect industries using many taxonomic categories of shell for which finished tools are not present. This discrepancy may be due to the fact that finished products were modified to an extent that prohibited taxa identification or, alternatively, tools or ornaments of these taxa were not made according to ubiquitous, standardized trajectories.

Ratios of Debris to Finished Objects

Evaluating the site's shell industry is aided by comparing the proportions of debris to finished tool frequencies per taxa. Table 6.12 provides the ratios of all shell-working debris (modified or unmodified) to finished products for nineteen taxa for which finished products were identified. Very low ratios for some taxa suggest that some key finished products were exchanged into Mayapán and not solely supplied from local production. Large ratios indicate an inverse pattern for other taxa where local industries generated abundant debris relative to the quantity of finished products. We suggest that taxa with lower ratios are the best candidates for imported shell currency items, as these objects would have been obtained in the city's regional commercial activities. Only six taxa fit this expectation, with low ratios between .1 and .3 pieces of

TABLE 6.12 Ratio of all debris (with or without modification) to finished ornaments—only species listed are those with finished tools present in sample (PEMY project).

Taxa	Percent of taxa	Percent of all debris combined	Percent of finished ornament	Debris/finished tool ratio
Oliva sp.	6.5	2.2	29.4	0.1
Spondylus sp.	1.7	0.9	8.3	0.1
Haliotis sp.	0.2	0.1	0.6	0.1
Prunum sp.	2.4	1.3	6.7	0.2
Conus sp.	0.4	0.3	0.9	0.3
Cypraea sp. (cowry)	0.1	0.1	0.3	0.3
Anomia	0.4	0.3	0.6	0.6
Strombus sp. and conch	37.9	32.7	38.7	0.8
Chione sp.	1.6	1.4	1.5	0.9
Polinices lacteus	0.7	0.6	0.6	0.9
Pectinidae	0.7	0.6	0.6	0.9
Barbatia tenera	0.4	0.4	0.3	1.3
Busycon	0.9	0.8	0.6	1.3
Mytilidae	0.9	0.8	0.6	1.3
Bivalve	3.9	3.3	0.9	3.6
Phacoides sp.	3.0	2.9	0.3	9.5
Mercenaria campechiensis	3.0	2.9	0.3	9.6
Dosinia sp.	6.7	6.9	0.3	22.3
Dinocardium	14.7	14.5	0.6	23.7

debris per finished item. These include *Oliva* and *Prunum* (ratios of .1 and .2, respectively), *Spondylus* (.1), Abalone (.1), *Conus* (.3), and *Cypraea* (.3). Of these taxa, *Oliva/Prunum* and *Spondylus* are numerically far more significant in the sample than the others, which implies their currency status.

In contrast, seven shell taxa exhibit nearly a 1:1 ratio of debris to finished products, which indicates the importance of specific local manufacturing trajectories. These taxa include *Strombus*, *Chione*, *Polinices*, *Barbatia*, Pectinidae, *Busycon*, and Mytilidae. Of this list, only *Strombus* is present in major proportions in the debris and finished-item samples. Large, versatile *Strombus* shells were made into a variety of useful objects and currency beads or pendants. For this reason, *Strombus* ratios are not specifically indicative of bead manufacture.

Two taxa had ratios of debris to finished items of nearly 10:1, including *Phacoides* and *Mercenaria* (9.5 and 9.6, respectively). Two other taxa had higher ratios of over 20:1, including *Dosinia* and *Dinocardium* (22.3 and 23.7, respectively). These comparisons imply a hierarchy of shell values and different trajectories of production and consumption for shell working at Mayapán (table 6.12).

There is not an even correspondence in the proportions of species represented and the types of finished or worked shell items in the assemblage. For example, olive shells comprise 6.5 percent of the taxa identified but 29.4 percent of the completed objects (or object fragments) in the sample (and 27.3 percent of the modified production debris). As mentioned earlier, modified olive and *Prunum* fragments are the primary category for which finished products and incomplete fragments may be difficult to discern; but their importance in both categories is indicated by their ubiquity. Similarly, *Spondylus* forms 1.7 percent of the species list yet 7.1 percent of the completed-shell artifact list. In contrast, there are far more other (non-*Spondylus*) bivalves in the sample of debris than in the ornament or tool categories.

Oliva/Prunum and *Spondylus* shells in particular have long-term significance in the Maya area, as they were important valuables as early as the Formative Period (Buttles 1992; Masson and Freidel 2013). Their status at Mayapán as potential currency items is thus not surprising. Despite a widespread shell-working industry within the city, finished, valuable ornaments of these shell groups were also probably obtained through exchange on a regular basis.

Shell Production Workshops

The best information on surplus shell production contexts at Mayapán are from the set of horizontally excavated structures (PEMY project), which provide the largest samples. Table 6.3 lists seventeen surplus shell production contexts detected by various collection methods; in four contexts, shell was the only surplus craft industry, and the others represent multi-crafting localities. These contexts were identified arbitrarily as those with shell quantities occurring at or above one standard deviation from the mean (table 6.13). Quantification per square meter was straightforward for systematic (28.26 square meters) surface collections. The number of shells per area of excavation is our best metric for test pits and horizontal excavations. Table 6.13 also quantifies shell according to excavation unit volume. Comparisons of shells per square meter and per cubic meter at fully excavated houses highlight the same three workshop contexts—I-55a, Q-39, and Q-176 (table 6.13). Shells per cubic meter were less useful for excavation samples due to the diluting effect of sterile levels near bedrock or in fill. Most debris at houselot workshops was

TABLE 6.13 Quantities of shell at shell workshops identified by the PEMY project. Values indicate the number of shells per square meter of surface collections, and number/square meter and number/cubic meter for test pits and fully excavated structures*.

Structure	Surface collections number/ square meter	Test pits number/ square meter	Test pits number/cubic meter	Horizontal excavations number/ square meter	Horizontal excavations number/cubic meter
P-114 house	1.00	14.6	34.4	–	–
Q-183 house	0.50	–	–	–	–
Z-120/ and Z-119/ AA-75 adjacent houses	0.80	–	(17.7)	–	–
Z-43 house	0.50	10.0	25.1	–	–
R-110b*	0.40	7.0	(8.0)	–	–
R-177*	0.40	–	–	–	–
Q-46a*	0.40	–	–	–	–
Z-39 elite house	–	15.5	52.0	–	–
Q-303 workshop	–	15.0	(18.1)	–	–
S-10bc house	–	11.0	37.9	–	–
S-12b house	–	11.0	(21.6)	–	–
P-28 house	–	10.5	(16.0)	–	–
Z-47b house	–	8.0	(14.2)	–	–
I-55a house	–	(6.0)	(11.5)	1.30	5.4
Q-39 house	–	–	–	1.20	4.1
Q-176 house	1.00	19.3	45.6	0.90	3.6
H-11 house	–	–	–	0.50	1.9
H-15 hall	–	–	–	0.10	0.3
H-15 grave	–	–	–	0.90	1.3

continued on next page

TABLE 6.13—*continued*

Structure	Surface collections number/ square meter	Test pits number/ square meter	Test pits number/cubic meter	Horizontal excavations number/ square meter	Horizontal excavations number/cubic meter
H-17 temple	–	–	–	0.10	0.2
I-57 workshop	–	2.0	8.8	0.30	1.1
L-28 house	–	–	–	0.30	1.8
Q-40a house	–	–	–	0.30	1.3
X-43 house	–	–	–	0.03	0.4
Y-45 elite house	–	–	–	0.10	0.3
Mean	0.17	3.9	12.8	0.50	1.8
Standard deviation	0.28	3.5	12.0	0.50	1.7
Mean + standard deviation	0.46	7.4	24.8	1.00	3.5

• All horizontally excavated structures are shown, but only I-55a, Q-39, Q-176 are workshops. The list includes those with quantities equal to or greater than the mean value plus 1 standard deviation, with close exceptions, other probable workshops are marked by an asterisk, equal to twice the mean value and almost > / = 1 standard deviation above the mean). Values in parenthesis do not meet outlier criteria for the column in which they occur, for reasons explored in the text.

within around 40 centimeters of midden above bedrock. Similarly, artifacts concentrated within the top 40 centimeters of horizontally excavated structures; these investigations for the most part terminated at floors and wall bases or on bedrock patios that were close to the surface. Some structures are identified as outliers according to only one set of data, while others are identified as workshops by surface collections, excavation area, and/or volume (table 6.13). Reasons for these different results vary by structure. For example, the shell-working area at House I-55a was in front of the building, in the patio area, and the test pit data come from a midden behind the house where shell had not been discarded. The test pit data identified debris from surplus obsidian blade making while the full excavations revealed shell working in front of the house. Although test pits in middens may not fully represent activities at houses, these data represent a good starting point for examining production patterns

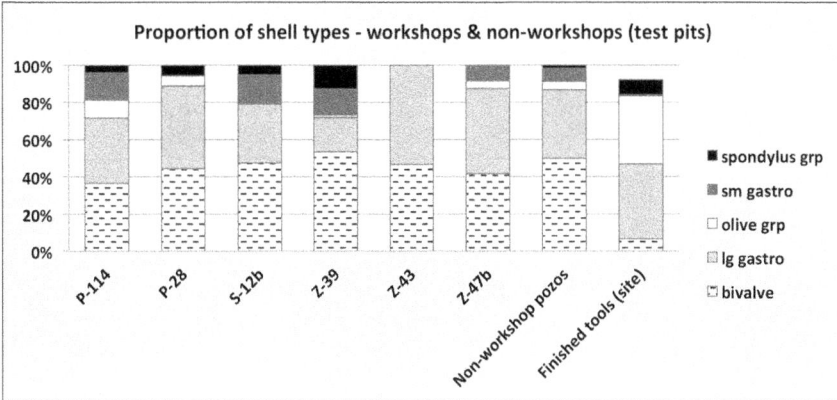

FIGURE 6.14. *Types of selected shell material in workshops compared to non-workshops and the finished tool assemblage for the entire site (test pit data).*

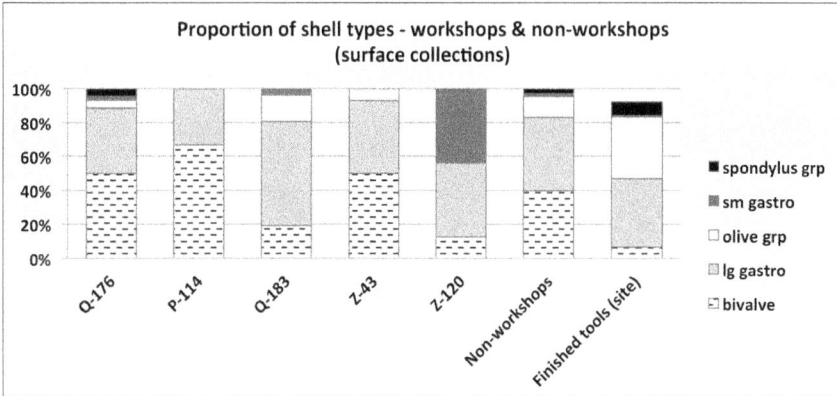

FIGURE 6.15. *Types of selected shell material in workshops compared to non-workshops and the finished tool assemblage for the entire site (surface collection data).*

across many contexts at the city, as indicated by cases in table 6.13 where more than one type of sampling unit pointed to a surplus crafting industry. The seventeen domestic contexts where surplus shell ornament production was identified include Houses Q-176, P-114, Q-183, Q-46a, Q-303, Q-39, P-28, Z-120, Z-119/AA-75, Z-43, R-110b, R-177, S-10, S-12, Z-47, Z-39, and I-55a. Five of these localities were identified by surface collection densities, six additional houselots were identified from test pit densities, and two were determined from horizontal excavations (table 6.13).

TABLE 6.14 Proportions of finished tools of major shell groups at workshops, non-workshops, and the composite site assemblage. Non-workshops are marked with an asterisk. Percentage given is that of total taxonomically identified shells. Note that P-114, Z-43, and Q-176 were sampled by multiple sample units (PEMY project).

Sample type	Context	Bivalve misc. (percent)	Large gastropod (percent)	Olive group (percent)	Small gastropod (percent)	Spondylus group (percent)	Total identified shell tool
Test pit	P-114	36.0	35.0	9.0	15.0	4.0	74
Test pit	P-28	44.0	44.0	6.0	–	6.0	18
Test pit	S-12b	47.0	32.0	–	16.0	5.0	19
Test pit	Z-39	54.0	18.0	1.0	14.0	13.0	71
Test pit	Z-43	47.0	53.0	–	–	–	15
Test pit	Z-47b	42.0	46.0	4.0	8.0	–	24
Test pit	Q-303	–	100.0	–	–	–	8
Test pit	S-10bc	25.0	63.0	–	13.0	–	8
Test pit	All workshops	43.0	36.0	4.0	11.0	6.0	237
Test pit	Non-workshops	49.9	36.9	4.4	7.1	1.8	339
Surface collection	Q-176	50	39.0	5.0	2.0	5.0	44
Surface collection	P-114	67	33.0	–	–	–	15
Surface collection	Q-183	19	62.0	15.0	4.0	–	26
Surface collection	Z-43	50	43.0	7.0	–	–	14
Surface collection	Z-120	13	44.0	–	44.0	–	16
	All workshops	40	44.0	6.0	8.0	2.0	114

Surface collection	Non-workshops	40	43.0	12.0	2.0	3.0	168
Horizontal excavation	I-55a	51.0	36.0	12.0	–	1.0	251
Horizontal Excavation	Q-39	60.0	31.0	9.0	–	1.0	134
Horizontal excavation	Q-176	47.0	39.0	12.0	1.0	1.0	114
Horizontal excavation	H-11*	44.0	44.0	9.0	–	3.0	66
Horizontal excavation	Y-45*	33.0	56.0	6.0	4.0	–	48
Horizontal excavation	H-17*	26.0	46.0	26.0	–	2.0	54
Horizontal excavation	L-28*	33.0	63.0	2.0	–	2.0	49
Horizontal excavation	H-15*	29.0	62.0	6.0	3.0	–	34
Horizontal excavation	H-15 grave*	42.0	53.0	6.0	–	–	36
Horizontal excavation	Q-40a*	55.0	38.0	7.0	–	–	29
Horizontal excavation	I-57*	53.0	41.0	6.0	–	–	17
Horizontal excavation	X-43*	33.0	67.0	–	–	–	6
Horizontal excavation	All workshops	53.0	35.0	11.0	0.0	1.0	499
Horizontal excavation	Non-workshops	37.0	51.0	9.0	1.0	1.0	339
Grand total	Finished tools (entire site)	6.7	40.2	36.5	0.6	8.3	326

Contexts R-110b, R-177, and Q-46a are not included, as their shell quantities were not quite 1 standard deviation above the mean value.

TABLE 6.15 Results of chi-square tests between workshop and non-workshop contexts for the proportions of five major shell taxa groups; chi-square test value for 4 degrees of freedom is 9.487, p = .05 (PEMY).

Sample type	Comparisons	Chi-square result	Significance
Test pit	Workshops and non-workshops	11.39000	Reject the null hypothesis of no difference
Surface collection	Workshops and non-workshops	8.73000	Fail to reject the null hypothesis of no difference
Horizontal excavation	Workshops and non-workshops	49.52000	Reject the null hypothesis of no difference
Horizontal excavation	Non-workshops (excluding H-17) and H-17	19.69910	Reject the null hypothesis of no difference
Horizontal excavation	Workshops and H-17	18.47457	Reject the null hypothesis of no difference
Horizontal excavation	Workshops and non-workshops (excluding H-17)	27.39013	Reject the null hypothesis of no difference

Comparisons of the distribution of the five major taxa groups of shell (as defined in table 6.7) show few striking differences in the proportions and ranges of shell taxa present at workshop versus non-workshop locales (table 6.14, figures 6.14, 6.15). The importance of bivalve shell working is indicated by percentages ranging from 40 to 53 for all workshops and by 37–40 percent bivalves in non-workshops sampled by various collection units (table 6.14). Large gastropod shell fragments similarly formed 35–44 percent of all workshop samples and 37–51 percent of all non-workshops. Chi-square statistical tests were employed to determine whether differences existed between surplus workshop contexts and the other (non-workshop) sampling units (table 6.15). These results failed to indicate that workshop and non-workshop samples were significantly different from one another, with the exception of surface collection data (table 6.15). Sample sizes may have affected surface collection results. These data suggest a close relationship between shells made in surplus production contexts and consumer contexts.

Fully excavated contexts provide the most robust data on differences between samples. Olive group shells are more abundant in the Temple H-17

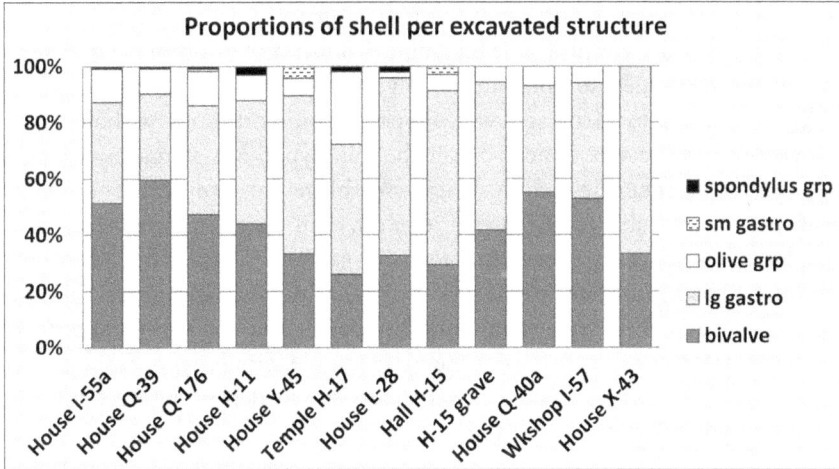

FIGURE 6.16. *Comparisons of shell proportions in five taxa groups among horizontally excavated structures—Workshop houses I-55a, Q-39, and Q-176 are shown at the left of the graph. Other contexts did not engage in significant surplus production. Much overlap exists between workshop shells and other contexts; the temple stands out for higher proportions of olive shell.*

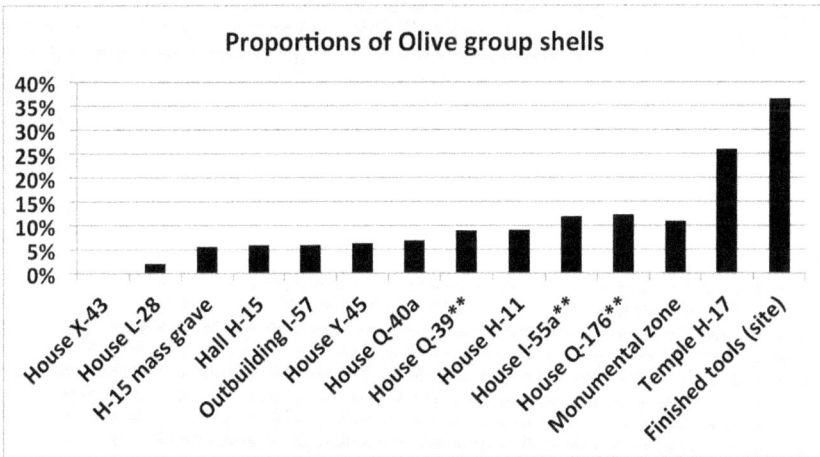

FIGURE 6.17. *Proportions of Olive group shells (within five major shell taxa groups) of each fully excavated structure compared to those of the monumental center and the finished shell assemblage for the entire site. Shell workshops are indicated by asterisks. Temple H-17 and the finished-tool sample have much higher proportions than other contexts, including the monumental zone.*

assemblage (26 percent) compared to other contexts in which these taxa form 0–12 percent of the sample (table 6.14, figures 6.16, 6.17). Additional chi-square tests were performed to compare non-workshop contexts without H-17 to H-17, workshops to H-17, and workshops to non-workshops without H-17, respectively—all results indicated that the null hypothesis should be rejected and that the frequencies of the H-17 assemblage are significantly different from the others (table 6.15, figures 6.16, 6.17), even though the same range of taxa groups is generally observed among the samples. Despite the chi-square results, table 6.14 indicates slightly greater quantities of Olive group shells or *Spondylus* group shells at certain workshops, such as I-55a, Q-176, and Z-39, but not in quantities as great as at the H-17 temple. Similarly, workshop I-55a is associated with unfinished *Oliva/Prunum* group debris (figure 6.12) and more idiosyncratic ornaments (Figure 6.13).

Although the INAH monumental zone sample was not collected with the use of screens, it provides valuable supplemental information regarding the proportions of the five major taxa groups under consideration (table 6.16). For samples with twenty identified shells or more, the proportions of Olive group shells (ranging from 2 percent to 14 percent) are more similar to Workshops I-55a and Q-176 than to the high quantities at Temple H-17. The numerically robust sample from Temple Q-58, the most analogous context to H-17, had only 7 percent olive shells. The high proportions of Olive group shells from Temple H-17 are thus anomalous, even when compared to monumental center buildings. As observed for the PEMY settlement zone samples, bivalve and large gastropod shells form the majority of material from the site center.

Further differences are noted between surplus production workshops and most other contexts tested in terms of the proportion of finished tools for the site (figure 6.17). Specifically, Olive group shells occur in much lower proportions (12 percent or less) in our workshop and non-workshop contexts than they do in the finished composite tool sample (36.5 percent, table 6.14). The Temple H-17 assemblage (with 26 percent Olive group shells) is more like the overall finished-tool sample than the domestic contexts (figure 6.17). This observation lends support to the idea that more Olive group shells were entering Mayapán as currency items than were produced at the city's house-lots. Overall, the distribution of Olive group shells across contexts of different social status or function at Mayapán is relatively equitable. This pattern is clearly illustrated in figure 6.17 (also table 6.16), where most proportions range from 6 to 12 percent, including ordinary commoner houses not engaged in shell surplus production, such as Q-40a and H-11 (7 percent and 9 percent, respectively) and outlying elite House Y-45 (6 percent). Except for Temple

TABLE 6.16 Monumental zone structures—frequencies of five major taxa groups (INAH project).

Structure	Bivalve (percent)	Large gastropod (percent)	Olive group (percent)	Small gastropod (percent)	Spondylus group (percent)	Other shell (percent)	Total identified shell taxa
Monumental zone House Q-56	36	55	–	9	–	–	11
House Q-57	34	45	2	–	18	–	44
Monumental zone House Q-63	–	50	50	–	–	–	2
Monumental zone House Q-67	33	52	11	–	4	–	27
Monumental zone House Q-68	25	50	19	–	6	–	16
Monumental zone House Q-92	41	38	13	3	4	1.0	130
Monumental zone House Q-93	48	38	9	2	4	–	82
Hall Q-54	27	54	14	4	1	–	78
Hall Q-97	37	41	12	–	10	–	41
Oratory Q-55	38	62	–	–	–	–	21
Oratory Q-66	20	60	10	–	10	–	10
Shrine Q-61	25	25	50	–	–	–	16
Shrine Q-98	–	67	33	–	–	–	3
Temple Q-58	29	56	7	1	6	–	109
All monumental zone structures	35	47	11	5	2	0.2	590

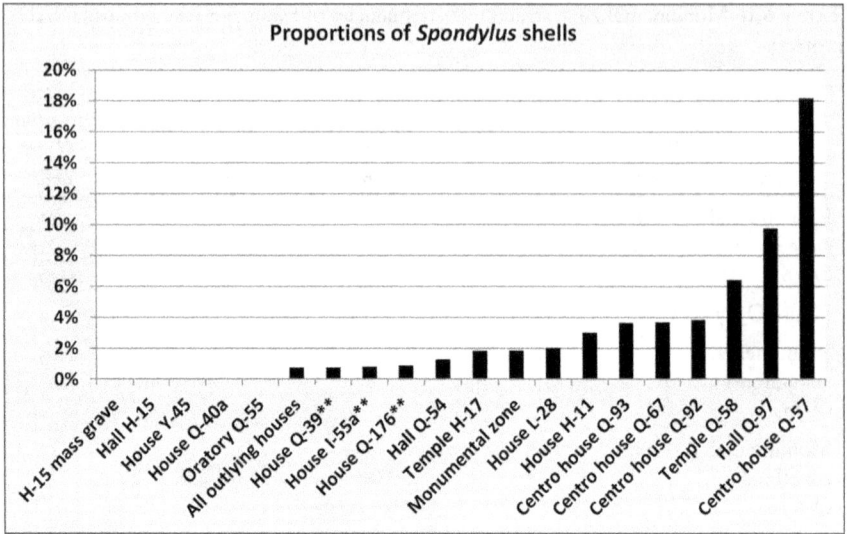

Proportions of Spondylus shells

FIGURE 6.18. *Proportion of Spondylus group shells in horizontally excavated contexts from the monumental zone and settlement zones (contexts with shell samples of 20 or more specimens).*

H-17, the distribution of Olive group shells is not hierarchical and does not accord with expectations of a prestige-goods model.

Similarly, the *Spondylus* group represents 8.3 percent of the entire site finished-tool sample, yet forms only 1 percent of all of the outlying horizontally excavated structures and 2 percent of the monumental zone contexts (figure 6.18). Only two of twenty horizontally excavated contexts within and outside of the site center have proportions of *Spondylus* group shells above 6 percent: Hall Q-97 and commoner custodial House Q-57 (site center). Four other contexts have proportions of 3–4 percent that are above the 2 percent monumental zone average—these include Itzmal Ch'en's custodial House H-11 and other custodial houses in the site center (Q-93, Q-67, and Q-92). In contrast, Hall H-15 had no *Spondylus* group shells and Hall Q-54 and Temple H-17 had average *Spondylus* proportions of 1–2 percent that are like those of the humble outlying dwelling of L-28 (2 percent). As with Olive group shells, individual structure anomalies exist, but proportions are relatively equitable across contexts representing different social statuses and functions. There is no consistent evidence for top-down distribution of *Spondylus* group shells. As argued for Olive group shells, *Spondylus* group shells were probably valued as monetary units of exchange at Mayapán.

Smaller test pit samples are of more limited use in comparing shell frequencies, as two household shell workshops (Q-39, I-55a) were not detected until full excavation. Nonetheless, it is noteworthy that of the sixty-two non-workshop test pits in which shell was recovered, Olive or *Spondylus* shells were present at 29 percent of the contexts, 24.2 percent had at least one Olive shell, and 6.5 percent had at least one *Spondylus* shell. These contexts represent ten different vicinities (milpa fields) of the settlement zone and eighteen different houselot contexts, only two of which are elite. Minimally, these test pit results reflect widespread access to potential shell currencies—nearly one in three contexts yielded specimens despite the small sample per houselot.

Troubling in our study of shell items at Mayapán is the relative scarcity of beads—as conventionally defined—in houselot or production contexts. Although Olive and *Spondylus* group ornaments are good candidates for shell media of exchange, surely discoidal or cylindrical beads were also used, as these best fit Landa's description. A total of thirty-six beads are present in our sample of all excavated units; most of those identified to genus were made of conch shells (N-24), two were made of *Spondylus*, and one was made of oyster shell. The beads are not concentrated in elite or public buildings; only two came from elite House Y-45, three came from monumental zone custodial House Q-92, outlying commoner Houses H-11, P-150, and Q-40a each had one, commoner Houses P-117 and Q-176 each had three, and Hall H-15 had four. Six were recovered from workshop House I-55a, one from workshop House Z-43, and eleven from workshop House Q-39, but the latter were concentrated as grave goods in a single burial feature. This distribution does not indicate a tendency for bead manufacture within workshop contexts, with the possible exception of I-55a. Beads were highly curated and not frequently lost. All of the beads were completed, and partly manufactured examples were not found. Ten were of a cylindrical shape, eleven were discoidal, two were rectangular, and one was trapezoidal.

Although Carnegie excavators rarely cleared entire structures horizontally, they tested a number of architectural features, particularly graves and caches that provide supplementary information. Lot lists compiled from the Carnegie Institution of Washington's *Current Report* series (Masson 2009) reveal that this work recovered at least 151 finished shell ornaments, of which 63 were from nineteen commoner domestic contexts and 88 were from six elite residences and fourteen monumental building groups. Abundant shell beads (N = 22) were recovered from a burial in an epicentral custodial house (Q-62), which resembles our findings at the family tomb of House Q-39 (figure 5.33). The interchangeability of shell beads with other kinds of suspended shell ornaments as grave offerings implies their mutual status as shell currency units.

Although beads were present at House Q-62, two other commoner burials (Q-37a and K-57) had shell pendants and/or Olive shell ornaments. In only six cases investigated by the Carnegie were shell beads solely recovered without being accompanied by other kinds of shell ornaments (three commoner and three monumental contexts). This observation emphasizes the close symbolic and functional association of beads with bivalve pendants and tinklers. Rarer objects such as shell rings clearly served only as adornments (figure 5.33). Jade beads were also placed into caches with shell beads or ornaments in domestic settings investigated by the Carnegie (J-71b, A-1, and Q-244d) and at the site center. In general, shell ornaments and beads were regularly recovered by this earlier project at commoner dwellings.

Why might shell beads be relatively scarce in non-mortuary domestic contexts at Mayapán? Their relative scarcity may reflect their value, as might be expected for a monetary unit, along with the necessary characteristics of durability and portability. Commoners regularly possessed beads in low numbers. The lack of evidence for significant quantities of shell bead production at Mayapán may also reflect the fact that beads were obtained in significant numbers from external sources through commercial exchanges and that city artisans did not primarily supply them. In this respect, patterns for shell beads, a known currency, match those that we have previously described for Olive and *Spondylus* group suspended ornaments, or their close imitations. Toward the end of this chapter, we discuss consumption patterns of potential shell currencies in greater detail.

Metallurgy

One other currency item, copper bells, was made at Mayapán. Two contexts for bell production have been well documented in Peraza Lope's INAH-sponsored investigations (Paris 2008), and two additional multi-crafting houses (Q-40a and Q-39) have recently been added to the list by the recovery of bell-casting ceramics (Paris and Cruz Alvarado 2012; Cruz Alvarado et al. 2012:figure 15.13). The INAH project investigated an outlying secondary elite house (R-183b) and a custodial caretaker house (Q-92) behind Temple Q-95 in the monumental center and recovered small crucible vessels that were filled with copper alloy material and bell clusters (Paris 2008:figures 5–7). Paris (2008:54) argues that production at these houses was for local consumption and that activities focused on reworking imported metal objects into numerous small bells. Most of Mayapán's 381 studied metal artifacts are bells (85 percent), according to Paris (2008:table 2). The production debris found at

R-183 and Q-92 was of a limited scale and metal production was not common at the city. No crucibles were present at Q-40a or Q-39; both were adjacent to elite group Q-41.

Six bell shapes have been defined for Mayapán, with variable suspension styles (Paris 2008:table 5). Bells found across the site at non-production locales exhibit a wide size range with a relatively even distribution (Paris 2008:figure 17). It has not been possible to discern standardized intervals of size and potential value despite Tozzer's suggestion regarding bell monies (1941:n418). Their scarcity, and the probability that the majority of Mayapán's bells were opportunistically exchanged from beyond the Maya region, would have made it difficult to impose production standards. Nonetheless, they were clearly one of the most valuable objects in circulation. Bells were uncommon at Mayapán, and like shell beads, they are concentrated in a few wealthy mortuary contexts and also distributed relatively evenly in general excavation contexts of elite and commoner dwellings. We discuss consumption patterns in more detail later in this chapter. We infer that if bells were used as currency items, this occurred infrequently compared to shell, cacao beans, and cotton mantles.

Obsidian Production and Consumption

Obsidian was a common household tool at Mayapán. Its availability reflects the importance of distant trade for inventories used in daily life. Most residents of the city would have obtained their obsidian from workshops within Mayapán or market stalls maintained by craftspersons who removed blades from imported blade cores. Two sets of questions guide the examination of obsidian frequencies with respect to production and consumption patterns in this chapter. First, where were obsidian blades made, who made them, and what can be said about the scale of production? Second, to what degree were blades widely accessible? Former studies of obsidian distributions in Postclassic northern Belize (Masson 2000) and elsewhere (P. Rice 1987) suggest that by this period, obsidian was a valued item, although it was not prohibitively expensive and could be obtained without restriction in the marketplace.

Obsidian Workshops

We calculated the mean and standard deviation of the number of obsidian blades per square meter of surface collection or the area and volume of test pits and horizontal excavations (table 6.3). Contexts with frequencies at least one standard deviation above the mean are identified as potential surplus production contexts. Cores are sometimes present in these high-density contexts that

TABLE 6.17 Surface collection obsidian interval frequencies. Asterisks mark intervals that are density outliers (mean plus 1 standard deviation) and represent probable workshops (PEMY project).

Number of obsidian pieces within 28.26 square meter-collection unit	Number of structures per interval	Percent of structures per interval	Percent of commoner contexts per interval
	36	35.3	97
0.5–4	29	29.3	97
5–13	23	23.2	83
15–21*	5	5.1	100
23–26*	3	3.0	66
30–48*	3	3.0	100
Total	99		

* Mean pieces per 3 meter dog leash collection unit (28.26 square meter): 5.38, standard deviation is 8.64, values above 14.02 per collection represent the mean value plus 1 standard deviation. Workshops/densities: Q-196 (48 pieces), Q-176 (40 pieces), Q-46a (30 pieces), R-174 (26 pieces), Z-39 (25 pieces), Q-188 (23 pieces), P-114 (21 pieces), Q-303 (20 pieces), P-115b (19 pieces), R-173b (18 pieces), P-24 (15 pieces).

support their status as probable houselot workshop deposits. As with all types of manufacturing traditions at Mayapán, a continuum may have existed in the scale of obsidian production, and it is important to recognize that test pits or surface collections may not have sampled the areas of densest debris. For example, at fully excavated House I-55a, two 1 × 2 meter test pits probed a rich midden behind the house from which obsidian densities were almost (but not quite) one standard deviation beyond the mean. Full excavation of the house sampled areas to the front and side of the building and revealed exceptionally high obsidian frequencies.

A total of nineteen individual houselots were associated with surplus obsidian workshop activity, as indicated by the surface collection, test pit, and/or horizontal excavation densities (table 6.3, figure 6.4). These contexts have frequencies at or beyond one standard deviation above the mean, with the exception of R-137, which was the only other case in the test pit sample that qualified as an outlier/workshop when two anomalously high contexts were removed and the mean and standard deviation recalculated. Some of the same contexts were flagged by higher densities through multiple sampling methods (tables 6.17, 6.18, 6.19). Future research at Mayapán will surely encounter additional blade-making workshops.

TABLE 6.18 Test pit obsidian interval frequencies. Intervals with one asterisk represent outliers for the entire test pit sample (mean value plus 1 standard deviation). Two asterisks indicate an interval that is close to this arbitrary cutoff.

Interval:Number of obsidian pieces per square meter of excavation unit	Number of contexts per interval	Percent of contexts per interval	Percent of commoner houses per interval
0	7	11.7	100
1–3.5	16	25.0	100
4–8	11	20.0	100
9–15	12	20.0	83
17–23	3	5.0	66
27–30**	4	6.7	75
31–37*	3	5.0	100
42–47*	2	3.3	100
91–95*	2	3.3	100
Total	60		

Mean: 13.1, standard deviation: 31.9, mean + standard deviation = 31.9 (includes all cases).Mean: 10.4, standard deviation: 11.6, mean + standard deviation = 21.9 (excludes two cases in highest interval).

Workshops (densities): Q-303 (95), Q-176 (91), P-28 (47), P-114 (42), Z-120 (37), R-155 (31), S-10 (31). Other high density contexts (not above standard deviation) include R-110 (30), J-130 (28), Z-39 (27), R-137 (27).

Interval: Number of obsidian pieces per cubic meter	Number of contexts per interval	Percent of contexts per interval	Percent of commoner houses per interval
0	7	11.7	100
1–3	4	6.7	100
4–6	6	10.0	100
10–20	13	21.7	100
23–34	14	23.3	78.5
40–54	4	6.7	100
61–68**	4	6.7	100
69–72*	2	3.3	100
90–109*	4	6.7	75
157–172*	2	3.3	100

Mean: 32.2, standard deviation: 37.6, mean + standard deviation = 69.7 (includes all cases)
Mean: 27.6, standard deviation: 28.7, mean + standard deviation = 56.3 (excludes two highest cases)
Workshops (densities): Q-303 (172), J-130 (157), P-114 (109), Q-176 (107), S-10 (105), Z-39 (91), P-28 (72), R-110 (69)

TABLE 6.19 Obsidian densities for horizontally excavated contexts in the settlement zone (calculated from Masson, Escamilla Ojeda, and Peraza Lope 2008; Escamilla Ojeda 2009, 2012). Surplus production locations are listed at the bottom (I-55a and Q-176).

Structure	Number of cores	Number of obsidian pieces	Area (square meter)	Obsidian pieces per square meter	Area (cubic meter)	Obsidian pieces per cubic meter
House X-43	0	14	252.00	0.1	18.59	0.8
Temple H-17	4	408	601.60	0.7	328.20	1.2
Elite house Y-45	1	277	376.00	0.7	176.10	1.6
House L-28	0	55	212.00	0.3	30.40	1.8
Hall H-15	0	351	475.34	0.7	126.40	2.8
Workshop I-57	0	125	74.25	1.7	18.91	6.6
H-15 grave	0	316	40.25	7.9	28.66	11.0
House H-11	7	542	133.30	4.1	35.88	15.1
House Q-39	7	656	120.00	5.5	34.23	19.2
House Q-40a	11	682	88.50	7.7	21.74	31.4
House Q-176*	11	1,141	140.00	8.2	33.07	34.5
House I-55a*	8	2,351	196.00	12.0	47.35	49.7

Mean density per square meter was 4.12, standard deviation 4.03. Mean density per cubic meter was 14.6, standard deviation 16.0. Significant obsidian working activity was also present at Q-40a and Q-39, as illustrated by cores and higher densities, although they are not 1 standard deviation above the mean value.

Surface collection densities are calculated from the total number of blades within standardized 28.26-square-meter (3 meter dog leash) collection units. Of ninety-nine surface collections, 35.3 percent of the samples had no obsidian and 29.3 percent had less than one blade within each collection unit (table 6.17). Values of less than one blade were calculated when more than one collection was taken from a single context, as the total number of blades from all collections per context was divided by the total collection area. Higher quantities are present in the remaining contexts, as 23.2 percent of the collections had 5 to 13 blades within a single dog leash sample, 8.1 percent had 15 to 26 blades within a surface collection, and three cases had 30 to 48 pieces (table 6.17). The mean number of obsidian pieces per sample unit was 5.38 (standard deviation 8.64), thus, there are eleven contexts with over 15 pieces per unit that represent outliers in quantities of one standard deviation beyond the mean. These include collections taken at Structures Q-196, Q-176, Q-46a, R-174, Z-39 (the only elite house), Q-188, P-114, Q-303, P-115, R-173, and P-24; these contexts are listed in order of descending density. From this list, Houses Q-303, Q-176, P-114, and Z-39 were also identified as surplus obsidian-working localities by other sampling methods. Excavation data provide a more robust look at obsidian densities.

Test pit densities are calculated by excavation area and volume (table 6.18). These calculations almost always identified the same contexts as significant outliers in terms of obsidian frequencies. For cases where a context represented an outlier according to only one of these measures, and if it was close to one standard deviation beyond the mean in the other measure, it was included in the workshop list. Eleven percent of the test pits had no obsidian. Low densities ranging from 1 to 15 pieces per square meter or from 1 to 34 pieces per cubic meter were found in most of the test pit samples, according to the number of contexts within intervals of square meter (65 percent) or cubic meter (61 percent) densities (table 6.18). Seven workshops were identified by quantities of obsidian in excess of 31 pieces per square meter, and eight workshops were flagged by densities in excess of 69 pieces per cubic meter (table 6.18). These contexts include those that are equal to or greater than one standard deviation above the mean of the entire test pit sample. Densities per square meter identify the following houses as workshops: Q-303, Q-176, P-28, P-114, Z-120, R-155, and S-10. According to densities per cubic meter, outliers include the following contexts: Q-303, J-130, P-114, Q-176, S-10, Z-39, P-28, and R-110. Four contexts were outliers by both measures (Q-303, Q-176, P-114 and S-10). As this sample includes two cases with far more obsidian than the remainder (91 and 95 pieces at Q-303 and Q-176, respectively), means and standard deviations without these two cases are also presented in table 6.18. The interval of 27–30 pieces that is indicated by two asterisks on table 6.18 adds four cases to the workshop list. Of these four, three qualify as workshops according to densities per cubic meter on the same table; House R-137 is the only case that does not, but it is included in our workshop tally. It is interesting that House I-55a, an outlier in the fully excavated sample, falls below the qualifying intervals in table 6.18, with only 25 pieces per square meter and 45.5 pieces per cubic meter in the test pit samples.

Support for the correlation between obsidian densities and production activities is found in the co-occurrence of obsidian blade cores in five of the nine test pits thought to represent workshops. Three contexts, Z-120, Z-39 and R-155, had one obsidian core, and Q-303 had two. House J-130 also had two obsidian cores and had very high densities (157 pieces per cubic meter).

Obsidian assemblages were analyzed for twelve fully excavated localities in the settlement zone (table 6.19; Escamilla Ojeda 2009, 2012). Obsidian densities for these contexts are lower than for test pits, as full excavations include clean-swept interior architectural spaces. Two contexts, I-55a and Q-176, are identified as surplus obsidian-working localities, according to the number of pieces per square meter and per cubic meter (table 6.19). With densities per cubic meter of 49 and 34 pieces, respectively, they exceed the mean (14.6) plus one standard deviation (16.0). House Q-40a has values that are close to this measure and obsidian working may have been among its varied other crafting pursuits (table 6.3), but we have not technically counted it as a workshop for this study. Similarly, obsidian is abundant at Q-39, which ranks fourth in density per cubic meter. The recovery of 8 to 11 blade core fragments at I-55a, Q-176, and Q-40a provides additional evidence of blade making, although two other houses had 7 core fragments each, including Q-39 (table 6.19). The surplus production of obsidian at Q-176 was initially indicated by surface collection and test pit sampling (tables 6.17, 6.18). It is noteworthy that Houses Q-40a and Q-39 are both multi-crafting houses that are adjacent to elite group Q-41, and their partial engagement in some obsidian working below the levels of Q-176 and I-55a is not surprising. House Q-176 is also a multi-crafting house in Milpa 1, next to the site center. House I-55a is close to the Itzmal Ch'en group, which it faces.

The type and location of these contexts reveals important information about the social context of craft production. All but one of the nineteen high-frequency surface collections, nine test pits, and two horizontally exposed obsidian workshop locales represent commoner residences, with the exception of Z-39, a secondary elite house next to the southern edge of the monumental center and the southern terminus (Z-50) of the site's principal sacbe. This context was identified as an obsidian production locality from both surface collection and test pit samples. The most striking observation about the location of these residential workshops is their tendency to be located near the monumental center (table 6.3, figure 6.4). Nine of the nineteen obsidian workshop localities are within Milpa 1, to the immediate west of the site center. Milpa 1 has the highest density of surplus crafting houselots, and we suggest that it represents a crafts barrio (figures 6.4, 6.19). Including nine houselots that made surplus obsidian, there are thirteen total crafting houselots in Milpa 1, and as only four of these thirteen made a single surplus item, multi-crafting was common in this neighborhood. Of the nine obsidian workshops in Milpa 1, three exclusively made obsidian blades, and the remainder made other crafts as well (table 6.3). Some of the highest obsidian densities come from Milpa 1 crafting houselots such as Q-303, Q-176, P-28, and P-114 (table 6.18). The proximity of the Milpa 1 houselots to the site center is likely to be

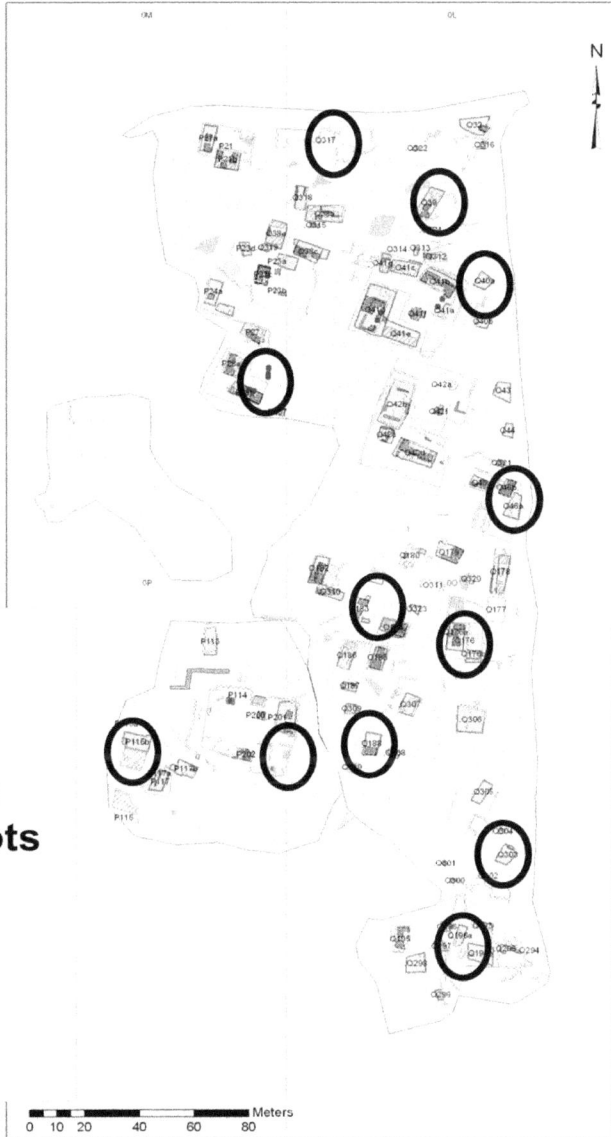

Milpa 1

crafting houselots

FIGURE 6.19. *Milpa 1, located immediately to the west of Mayapán's monumental center, has a concentration of surplus craft production houses and represents the only crafts barrio identified at the city.*

significant, and although all of these obsidian workshops are within independent houselot walls, manufacture for elite clients may partially explain the concentration of activity in this part of the city. But Milpa 1 is also located in downtown Mayapán, at the nexus of a number of roads leading to the site center from the city gates (chapter 4). This location may also have offered ample opportunities for vending or participation in central or neighborhood marketplaces at Mayapán.

Surplus obsidian-working contexts outside of Milpa 1 also tend to be located near nodal architecture in the settlement zone (figure 6.4). Two such contexts are in Milpa 32 (R-173b and R-174) and two are in Milpa 11 (R-155 and R-110). These locations, like Milpa 1, represent downtown settlement zones. Milpa 32 also has a large elite residential group in its midst (Q-244) and Milpa 11 (R-155 and R-110) is near a row of the three largest palaces at Mayapán (R-86, R-96, and R-103). House I-55a, in Milpa 16, faces the Itzmal Ch'en group, the largest focal node outside of the site center. A less clear spatial association is noted for Workshops S-10 and J-130, which are within 250 meters of a colonnaded hall (J-111). One workshop context is not located near any elite residences or public architecture, House Z-120 in Milpa 4 (figure 6.4), in the southeastern residential zone of the city.

Our data suggest that the highest levels of obsidian production are associated with craftsmen living near elites and who possibly worked in their service. Exceptions may be represented by I-55a; although it is 50 meters to the southeast of Itzmal Ch'en, elites did not reside in this area. House Z-120 also represents an exception, which illustrates that commoners may have sometimes produced obsidian at home without close supervision. House Z-120 is also a chert and shell workshop. Nineteen surplus obsidian production localities have been identified using basic statistical criteria.

Obsidian Consumption

Obsidian frequencies for surface collections and test pits described above reveal that 35 percent of the ninety-nine surface collection contexts had no obsidian, but the majority of these contexts had no lithic tools at all (tables 6.17, 6.18, 6.20). Surface collections were taken in all parts of the city, even where dense midden concentrations were not visible at the surface in sparsely inhabited areas. For this reason, some collections have low densities of all materials. The majority of both surface collections and test pit samples suggest that obsidian was used regularly for daily activities of commoners. The right-hand column of tables 6.17 and 6.18 indicates the proportion of commoner contexts represented by the obsidian frequency intervals. Affluent craft specialists tended to possess more obsidian,

TABLE 6.20 PEMY surface collection obsidian-chert/chalcedony tool ratio intervals.

Interval: Ratio of obsidian pieces to other lithic tools	Number of contexts	Percent of total contexts per interval of 96	Percent of commoner contexts (non-workshops)	Percent of elite contexts per interval	Number of contexts (workshops) per interval	Percent of contexts (workshops) per interval	Percent of commoner contexts (non-workshops and workshops)
No lithic tools	21	21.9	100	0	0	0	100
No obsidian	12	12.5	92	8	0	0	92
Only obsidian (1–30 pieces)	24	25.0	79	8	3	12.5	92
.3–.7	4	4.2	100	0	0	0	100
1	6	6.3	100	0	0	0	100
1.5–2.9	7	7.3	71	14	1	14.3	86
3.0–6.5	11	11.5	73	9	2	18.2	91
8–11	7	7.3	43	14	3	42.9	86
12–15	4	4.2	50	0	2	50.0	100
Total	96		79	6	11		96

Below: Ratios of obsidian to all other chipped stone tools, recalculated to include used chert and chalcedony flakes.

No lithic tools	33	34.4	97	3	0	0.0	97
Only obsidian	12	12.5	92	8	0	0.0	92
.1–.8	19	19.8	84	11	1	5.3	89
1–2.6	17	17.7	59	12	5	29.4	88
3.0–6.5	8	8.3	63	0	3	37.5	100
7–11	6	6.3	67	0	1	33.3	100
30	1	1.0	0	0	1	100.0	100
Total	96		79	6	11		96

even when they did not manufacture obsidian blades, compared to non-crafting houselots. As table 6.18 reveals, the interval of 9–15 pieces per square meter includes seven ordinary (non-crafting) houselots, three surplus craft-producing (commoner, non-obsidian) houselots, and two elite houses. Houselot samples in the higher interval of 17–25 pieces per square meter include one ordinary, two craft-production (non-obsidian) commoner houselots, and one elite context. These data suggest that commoners were able to obtain obsidian with ease. It was not prohibitively expensive and elites did not control its distribution.

The relative importance of obsidian in consumer contexts is also reflected by the ratio of obsidian to other kinds of lithic artifacts. Obsidian blades at Mayapán were used for a range of light to heavy cutting tasks (Masson, Escamilla Ojeda, et al. 2008; Escamilla Ojeda 2009), and some functions probably overlapped with sharp chert or chalcedony tools. Here we assess three different ratios that attest to the relative importance of obsidian. The ratio of obsidian to chert/chalcedony tools (formal and retouched tools) represents our first measure. Chert and chalcedony unifacial and bifacial tools are not as ubiquitous as blades or other types of artifacts, so additional ratios are also employed. We also calculate the obsidian to all chert/chalcedony artifact ratios (formal and retouched tools and all used flakes, cores, and flaking debris). We are especially partial to a third ratio, which considers the quantity of obsidian to all modified chert/chalcedony artifacts, including unifaces, bifaces, and used flakes but excluding unused production debris. This is the most valuable ratio, as it considers all lithics used for work activities at Mayapán's houselots. But few comparable case studies exist, as the number of used flakes has been rarely assessed in the Maya area. At Mayapán, these tools were identified by examining every chert/chalcedony flake with an 8x magnification geological loupe for evidence of retouch or edge damage attributable to utilization. Artifact-sherd ratios are employed in other studies (e.g., M. Smith 2003d), as sherds potentially represent a type of constant for occupational duration or intensity. But the quantity of sherds can also be related to other functional factors. As pottery production areas such as Q-176 have greater sherd densities that dwarf the quantities of stone tools, we do not employ sherd ratios.

Both obsidian and chert tools were recovered in thirty-nine of ninety-six surface collections that were clearly associated with a structure (table 6.20). Of the total sample, 36.5 percent had ratios of one or more obsidian blades per chert/chalcedony stone tool. When used chert flakes are included in the ratio, at least 32 percent of the surface collections had one or more obsidian blades per stone tool (table 6.20). Commoner contexts represented the majority of the sample, and they form 50–73 percent of the cases with 3 to 15 obsidian blades per stone tool (higher ratio intervals, table 6.20). Elites and obsidian workshop localities also used blades in equal or greater numbers to chert or chalcedony tools, as might be expected.

TABLE 6.21 PEMY test pit sample obsidian to chert/chalcedony tool ratio intervals.

Interval: Ratio of obsidian to other lithic tools	Number of contexts	Percent of total contexts per interval of 96	Percent of commoner contexts (non-workshops) per interval	Percent of elite contexts per interval	Number of contexts (workshops) per interval	Percent of contexts (workshops) per interval	Percent of commoner contexts (non-workshops and workshops)
No tools	4	6.8	100	0	0	0.0	100
No obsidian	3	5.1	100	0	0	0.0	100
Only obsidian	22	37.3	91	5	1	4.5	95
0.8	1	1.7	100	0	0	0.0	100
1.3–3.7	6	10.2	83	0	1	16.7	100
5.5–11.7	9	15.3	89	0	1	11.1	100
14–31	7	11.9	71	14	1	14.3	86
36–77	5	8.5	20	20	3	60.0	80
110, 285	2	3.4	0	0	2	100.0	100
Total	59		47	3	9 (plus 1 elite workshop)		59

Note: only one elite house workshop is represented, within a ratio of 54 pieces of obsidian per other stone tools.
Below: ratios of obsidian to all other chipped stone tools, recalculated to include used flakes.

No obsidian	7	11.9	100	0	0	0.0	100
Only obsidian	2	3.4	100	0	0	0.0	100
.02	1	1.7	100	0	0	0.0	100
.1–.9	31	52.5	84	6	3	9.7	94
1–3.8	16	27.1	56	6	6	37.5	94
4.8–8	2	3.4	100	0	0	0.0	100
Total	59		47	12	9		59

TABLE 6.22 PEMY obsidian to chert/chalcedony uniface and biface ratios, horizontally excavated structures.

Structure	Context type	Obsidian/lithic tool ratio	Obsidian/lithic tool ratio, including used flakes
X-43	Commoner house by city wall, short and incomplete domestic history	0.7	0.1
I-57	Chert/chalcedony workshop out-building, near commoner houses	1.2	0.2
Q-39	House, multi-craft workshop, next to elite Palace Q-41 and down-town monumental center	1.9	1.4
Y-45	Elite house in southeast settlement zone	2.5	.4
H-17	Temple, Itzmal Ch'en group	4.4	3.6
L-28	Commoner house by city wall	5.0	0.4
Q-176	Commoner house, obsidian and multi-craft workshop, downtown near monumental center	6.9	6.0
H-11	Commoner house, custodial to Itzmal Ch'en group	7.2	2.5
H-15 hall	Colonnaded hall, Itzmal Ch'en group	7.5	2.4
H-15 grave	Mass grave by Hall H-15	7.9	2.3
Q-40a	Commoner house, multi-craft workshop, next to elite Palace Q-41 and downtown monumental center	8.4	8.3
I-55a	Commoner house, obsidian and multi-craft workshop, near Itzmal Ch'en	20.8	10.2

Test pit data affirm these findings that obsidian tools were equally or more important than chert tools at Mayapán houselots, including those of ordinary residents who were not surplus crafters. These data indicate that 37.3 percent of the test pit contexts had from 1 to 31 obsidian blades per chert/chalcedony tool. These ratios were reflected in a sample consisting of 71–89 percent non-crafting commoner houselots (table 6.21). Obsidian blades were, as expected, more ubiquitous relative to stone tools at workshop localities, with ratios of 36 to 285 blades per chert tool. When used chert flakes are added to the calculations, results are similar: 30.5 percent of the contexts had 1 to 8 blades per chert tool, and these intervals are made up of 56–100 percent ordinary (non-crafting) commoner houselots (table 6.21).

Ratios of obsidian to chert/chalcedony tools for horizontally excavated structure intervals are provided in table 6.22, and these generally confirm the findings of surface collection and test pit samples. Only one of twelve contexts has a ratio below 1.2 obsidian fragments per other stone tool, indicating common access to obsidian across social and functional contexts. Ratios of non-workshop houses vary from 0.7 to 7.2. Except for the high ratio at obsidian workshop I-55a (20.8 pieces of obsidian per chert tool), ratios of obsidian to chert tools do not distinguish obsidian workshops well from other localities (table 6.22). This fact is not surprising, as it simply reflects that multi-crafting localities like Q-176 used a high number of chert tools for diverse activities. It is interesting, however, to note that obsidian to chert tool ratios tend to be higher at obsidian workshops when used flakes are included in the chert tool ratio (table 6.22).

Setting obsidian workshops aside, comparisons of non-workshop commoner houses, elite residences, and public buildings are informative. Commoner Houses L-28 and H-11 have more obsidian (ratios of 5.0 and 7.2, respectively) than elite House Y-45 (2.5) or Temple H-17 (4.4). The ratio of House H-11 is essentially the same as that of contexts from Hall H-15. While House H-11 is located next to the Itzmal Ch'en group (H-15 and H-17), this is not the case for L-28, a house located in an unassuming neighborhood near the north part of the city wall. A low ratio at I-57 (1.2) indicates the singular focus of chert/chalcedony toolmaking at this workshop and a lack of other domestic activities at this locality. The very low ratio at commoner House X-43 concurs with other assessments that this house was occupied only briefly, and a full range of domestic activities did not occur there.

Obsidian to chert tool ratios that include used chert flakes reveal that elite House Y-45a and commoner House L-28 have a very low ratio (0.4), and this ratio is exceeded significantly by all other contexts (2.3–10.2) except for chert Workshop I-57 and commoner House X-43 (table 6.22). By this measure, obsidian-working contexts have the three highest ratios (10.2, 8.3, 6.0), and public buildings Temple H-17 and Hall H-15 have more relative obsidian than five other houses tested, probably because utlitized flakes are less ubiquitous at ceremonial structures.

TABLE 6.23 Composite comparisons for PEMY project chipped tool assemblage.

	Obsidian (number)	Lithic tools (number)	Used flakes (number)	Flakes (not used) (number)
Fully excavated contexts	6,918	1,200	1,974	38,187
Test pits	2,110	104	4,354	34,474
Surface collections	811	164	558	8,320
Total	9,839	1,468	6,886	80,981
	Obsidian (percent)	Lithic tools (percent)	Used flakes (percent)	Total chipped stone tools (excluding non-used flakes)
Fully excavated contexts	68	12	20	10,092
Test pits	32	2	66	6,568
Surface collections	53	11	36	1,533
Total	obsidian	lithic tools	utilized flakes	

Composite site ratios:
Ratio obsidian/lithic tools: 6.7
Ratio obsidian/lithic tools + used flakes: 1.2
Ratio obsidian/lithic tools + used flakes + unused flakes: 0.1

The total obsidian to lithic tool ratio for Mayapán is 6.8 pieces of obsidian per uniface or biface, and when used flakes are added to the other non-obsidian chipped stone tools, there are 1.2 obsidian pieces for all lithic tools, including the most expedient categories (table 6.23). When these ratios are expressed as percentages (table 6.23, figure 6.20), obsidian forms 68 percent of the entire chipped stone tool assemblage of excavated contexts (retouched unifaces and bifaces form 12 percent, used flakes form 20 percent). Obsidian also forms 32 percent of the chipped stone tools from test pits and 53 percent of the surface collection tools (figures 6.21, 6.22). Overall, these composite values attest to the importance of this material in daily life at the city, especially considering the fact that 95 percent our test pit and 93 percent of our surface collection are commoner dwellings.

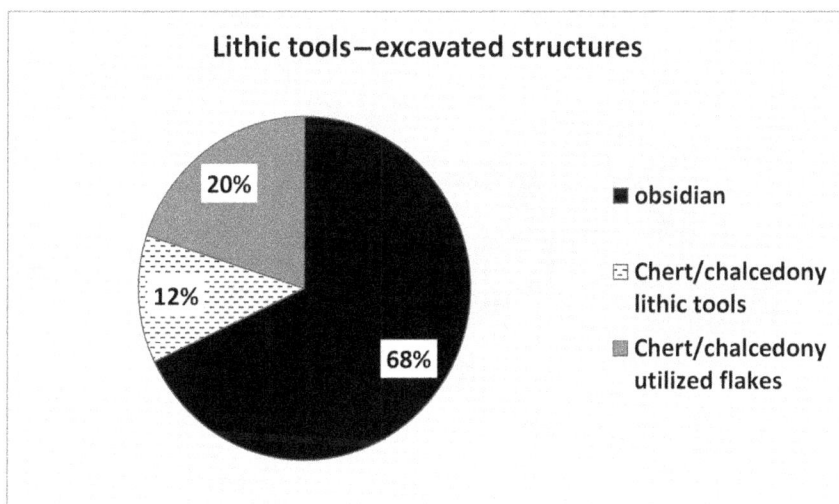

Lithic tools—excavated structures

- ■ obsidian
- ⊡ Chert/chalcedony lithic tools
- ▨ Chert/chalcedony utilized flakes

20%

12%

68%

FIGURE 6.20. *Proportion of obsidian to chert/chalcedony chipped stone tools and used flakes (fully excavated contexts).*

Obsidian Artifacts

Almost all obsidian artifacts from Mayapán are blade fragments. Except for the low numbers of prismatic blade cores mentioned previously, the sample includes occasional flakes, chips, small side-notched projectile points, and, rarely, thumbnail-sized scrapers (Proskouriakoff 1953:283). As outlined in detailed studies by Bárbara Escamilla Ojeda (2009, 2012), core fragments were highly expended, ranging from 1.2 to 3.5 centimeters in length and from 1.6 to 2.1 centimeters in width. Average obsidian blade length was 4.1 centimeters (ranging from 1.6 to 7.6 centimeters), and average width was 1 centimeter (ranging from .2 to 3.31 centimeters). These blade widths are not much smaller than those of Laguna de On, Belize, for which the mean width was 1.2 (Masson 2000). Laguna de On is around 400 kilometers from the highland Guatemala volcanic sources; Mayapán was nearly twice as far. Their relatively comparable mean blade sizes suggest general parity in the small size of blade cores that were traded up the coast of Yucatán and into inland sites. Perhaps blades of this size were most greatly desired. Light, medium, and heavy wear on the edges of blades was commonly observed. Visual sourcing by Escamilla Ojeda (2009, 2012) suggests that most (80.8 percent) of the obsidian traded to Mayapán was from Ixtepeque, and other sources present include El Chayal (15.6 percent) and San Martín Jilotepeque (3.4 percent). The dominance of

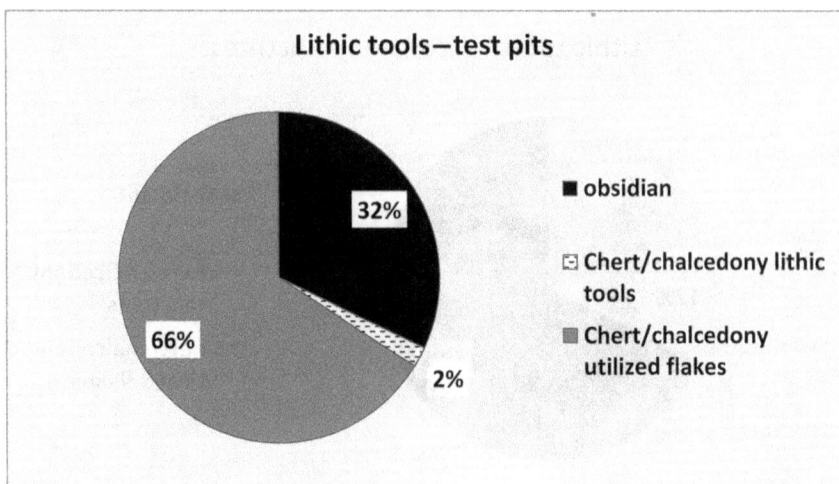

Lithic tools—test pits

- obsidian
- Chert/chalcedony lithic tools
- Chert/chalcedony utilized flakes

32%

66%

2%

FIGURE 6.21. *Proportion of obsidian to chert/chalcedony chipped stone tools and utilized flakes (test pits).*

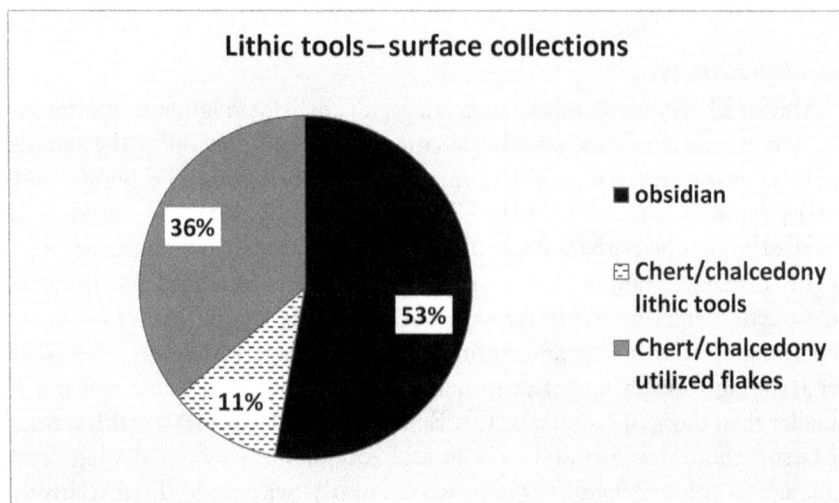

Lithic tools—surface collections

- obsidian
- Chert/chalcedony lithic tools
- Chert/chalcedony utilized flakes

36%

53%

11%

FIGURE 6.22. *Proportion of obsidian to chert/chalcedony chipped stone tools and utilized flakes (surface collection contexts).*

the Ixtepeque source in the Late Postclassic Period has been established for sites contemporary to Mayapán in the Maya area (Masson and Chaya 2000; Braswell 2010).

A   B

C

FIGURE 6.23. *Greenstone axes from Mayapán houselots. The majority are from commoner dwellings, and the chisel (A) is from an offering on top of Hall H-15.*

WOODWORKING INDUSTRIES: GREENSTONE CELTS

Although wooden objects do not preserve at Mayapán, this industry was probably important. Small greenstone celts and chisels were likely used for woodworking (figure 6.23). Carved wooden effigies of important deities are referred to regularly in documentary sources. For example, twenty wooden masks were present at one Colonial Period ceremony in Yaxcaba (Scholes and Roys 1938:614); buckets were also made of wood during the Contact Period (Tozzer 1941:198). In Cenote Dzab-Na of Tecoh, not far from Mayapán, a wooden statue was also found (Strömsvik 1956).

Greenstone celts and chisels at Mayapán exhibit variation in color from shades of nearly black to dark green. These stones probably originated from the Maya highlands of Chiapas or Guatemala, where small river cobbles of similar composition and coloring are abundant. Test pit and surface collection data reveal that greenstone celts were commonly found at commoner and elite houselots near the epicenter but were also regularly recovered in mid-city and more peripheral locations within the city wall (table 6.24). Fully excavated contexts revealed that similar quantities of axes were found in smaller surface collection or test pit samples (i.e., no context had more than two greenstone axes). They are found at houses engaged in surplus craft work and at houses where such activities were not undertaken. Although an ax was not recovered at fully excavated House L-28, one was found on the surface of a nearby similar house (L-23). Split axes, which perhaps entered this state as a result of use-related breakage, were commonly reused as chisels. Of the eighteen axes and chisels that could be measured, the mean length was 4.0 (standard deviation of 0.9) when an unusual example that is 11.5 centimeters long is eliminated from the calculation.

Four greenstone ax fragments or pieces of raw material were also found in the interior floors of Hall H-15 and Temple H-17, and two of these were concentrated in offerings of smashed incense burners (figures 3.11, 3.12, 6.23a). The use of greenstone fragments as offerings attests to this material's symbolic value. Commoners regularly possessed greenstone objects, but they are not distributed as regularly as obsidian. One of the finest greenstone axes, represented by a small polished medial fragment, was found at Hall H-15. Offering pieces at Itzmal Ch'en consisted of one piece of raw material and one fragmented tool (chapter 3); these may have symbolized original whole objects of symbolic or historical value (Weiner 1992; Lesure 1999). Some of the finest examples are from the monumental center, including the large ax of 11.5 centimeters in length. Variation in ax size, workmanship, quality and the color of the greenstone material attests to a gradation of value among these objects (figure 6.23). The greenstone ax is an artifact class with a long-standing history in the Maya area (Freidel and Reilly 2010). Other greenstone objects were scarce at Mayapán, including the PEMY settlement zone samples. Beads were found in similar quantities at commoner crafting houselot Q-176 (N = 3) compared to Hall H-15 (N = 3) and Temple H-17 (N = 2) but are largely absent from other houselot contexts.

TABLE 6.24 Greenstone objects recovered by PEMY project horizontal excavations, surface collections, and test pits.

Unit type	Structure	Greenstone ax	Greenstone polisher	Greenstone raw material	Greenstone jade, onyx, or micaceous ornament/bead
Horizontal	H-11 house	1	–	–	–
Horizontal	H-15 hall	2	1	–	3
Horizontal	H-17 temple	1	–	1	2
Horizontal	I-55a craft specialist	1	–	–	–
Horizontal	Q-39 craft specialist	2	–	–	1
Surface	Q-176 craft specialist	2	–	–	3
Surface	Q-40 craft specialist	2	–	–	–
Surface	Y-45 elite house	1	–	–	–
Surface	L-28 house	–	–	–	–
Surface	X-43 house	–	–	–	–
Surface	L-23 house	1	–	–	–
Surface	M-59a house	1	–	–	–
Surface	Q-179 house	1	–	–	–
Surface	Q-181 house	1	–	–	–
Surface	Q-185 house	1	–	–	–
Surface	Q-195 house	1	–	–	–
Surface (2)	Q-42 elite house	2	–	–	–
Surface	R-175b house	1	–	–	–
Surface	Y-106 house	1	–	–	–
Test pit	Z-120 craft specialist	1	–	–	–
Test pit	S-8c craft specialist	1	–	–	–
Test pit (2)	P-114 craft specialist	2	–	–	–

TABLE 6.25 Mayapán tool typology.

Type	Characteristics	Use
Pointed bifaces	Elongated, thin bifaces with one pointed end, clear shoulders, and rounded or tapered proximal sides	Knives, lanceolates
Diamond-shaped bifaces	Small bifaces with diamond shape, shoulders tend to be at center of artifact	Perforators or projectiles
Wedge-shaped bifaces	Also known as triangular bifaces	Axes
Oval bifaces (small)		Axes
Hammerstones	Spherical or sub-spherical, sometimes made from cores	Battering
Small hammerstones or polishing stones	Wedge-shaped and planoconvex in cross section	Crafts
Thick bifaces—celtiform	Resemble northern Belize general utility biface type, blunt, battered end	Heavy pounding and smoothing tasks
Stage 1 and 2 bifaces	Larger, thicker bifaces that appear unfinished, perhaps preforms of types listed above	Cores, expedient heavy tasks, preforms
Narrow bifaces type 1	Parallel sided (or nearly so), thick, proximal and distal ends are similarly shaped	Perforators, drills, or fragments of bifacial projectile points
Narrow bifaces type 2	Narrow bifaces like type 1 but with thick oval base	Perforators or drills
Narrow bifaces type 3	Narrow bifaces that are thinner in cross-section than types 1 or 2	Probable bifacial projectile points
Side-notched points	Most are primarily unifacial with bifacial edge trimming, some are fully bifacial; rounded, squared, and concave bases	Projectile points
Eccentrics	Zoomorphic, crescent, S-shaped—rare	Symbolic
Rare tool forms (from monumental center)		
Long bifacial knives	Proximal fragments of 12 cm and 15 cm in length, appear to be made of Colha chert; resemble Proskouriakoff's (1962:356, figure 27) "large, leaf shaped blades"	Ceremonial knives

continued on next page

TABLE 6.25—*continued*

Type	Characteristics	Use
Large thick biface	Well made and appears to be made of Colha chert	Miscellaneous
Thin stemmed biface		Knife
Thick stemmed biface	Resembles Proskouriakoff's (1962:357, figure 7) "stemmed points"	Lanceolate
Thin oval biface	Fully oval and symmetrical	Celtiform
Expedient unifaces and bifaces		
Retouched flakes	Much variation in form and modification	A variety of cutting tasks
Gravers, spurs, denticulates	Some variation in form and modification	Crafting
Scrapers	Some variation in form and modification	Crafting

CHERT AND CHALCEDONY TOOLS

Frequencies of Mayapán Stone Tool Types

A total of 1,497 chert and chalcedony unifaces and bifaces were recovered from the PEMY investigations; 1,493 of these are inferred to be of Postclassic date. In 2008 we outlined a descriptive typology for the formal tools from the site that is summarized in table 6.25 (Masson, Escamilla Ojeda, and Peraza Lope 2008). Proskouriakoff (1962b:330) was not particularly impressed by the workmanship of chipped stone tools at the city in terms of style, standardization, or raw material; she went so far as to state that the variable tool morphology was "symptomatic" of deep social disorder and cultural poverty. But Mayapán, like earlier centers, has examples of finely crafted stone tools alongside a wide array of more simply made examples that have been modified through extended lives of recycling or resharpening.

As noted by Proskouriakoff (1962b:355), Mayapán's stone tools are smaller in size than earlier, southern lowland precedents. The size and scarcity of chert or chalcedony axes at Mayapán perplexed Carnegie project investigators, so much so that Joseph A. Hester, Jr. (1953) undertook experiments to see if land could be cleared using unmodified limestone hand axes. We attribute the use of small agricultural oval and wedge-shaped axes to differences in local land use and forest. Drier Yucatán areas may have been more easily cleared with burning and the use of smaller bifaces. Chert or chalcedony cobbles also appear to be small in this region, and this would have provided its own constraints on tool size.

Triangular hatchets (wedge-shaped bifaces) are common at Mayapán (Proskouriakoff 1953:282) and represent one of the formal bifacial tool categories (figure 6.24e). Similar hafted examples appear in the Dresden, Madrid, and Borgia codices (e.g., Dresden Codex:11 [Bill, Hernández, and Bricker 2000]; Madrid Codex:55b, 54b [Villacorta C. and Villacorta 1976]; Borgia Codex:52, plate 26 [Díaz, Rodgers, and Byland 1993]), where they are used as weapons, although they were also likely useful for a variety of agricultural and wood-working activities (e.g., Borgia Codex:59, plate 19; Díaz, Rodgers, and Byland 1993). These objects closely resemble the "triangular bifaces" made by Colha flintknappers in the Postclassic Period (Shafer and Hester 1983; Michaels 1987:153, figure 30). Pointed bifacial knives resemble those of contemporary central Mexico in form and also constitute a formal lithic tool type for the city. These knives are typically pointed on either end and have straight or slightly convex sides, with some variations in the definition of a shoulder in the basal half of the artifact. They are distinguished from lance or spear points (in the Borgia Codex), which have a clear, elongate triangular shape (e.g., Díaz, Rodgers, and Byland 1993:53, plate 25). Mayapán pointed bifaces are similar to the Postclassic lenticular bifaces at Colha in northern Belize (Shafer and Hester 1988; Michaels 1987:146, figure 27), although the Belize artifacts tend to be narrower, thinner, and have more standardized shoulders and straight, tapering edges, whereas the Mayapán versions are more variable in terms of edge convexity.

Table 6.25 lists recurring chipped stone tool types at Mayapán, and their overall frequencies are charted in figure 6.25. Those that exhibit significant standardization in morphology, size, and, presumably, function (figure 6.24) can be classified as formal tools, including the following: side-notched projectile points (most often unifacial with bifacial edge retouch), pointed bifaces (useful as knives and lanceolates), wedge-shaped (triangular) axes, small oval biface celts, and narrow bifaces (Types 1 and 2) that, when complete, may have been used as perforators or drills. Fragments of certain, thinner narrow bifaces, sometimes with stems (Type 3), can be difficult to distinguish in width, thickness, and length from elongated bifacial projectile points, which are relatively rare at the site (figure 6.24i, j, k). Spherical (or sub-spherical) chert or chalcedony hammerstones also occur with regularity. Informal, more expediently manufactured tools exhibit greater variation (figure 6.26) and include gravers made on the points or projections of retouched flakes, a variety of retouched flakes, composite flake tools, used cores, and thick or other nonstandardized

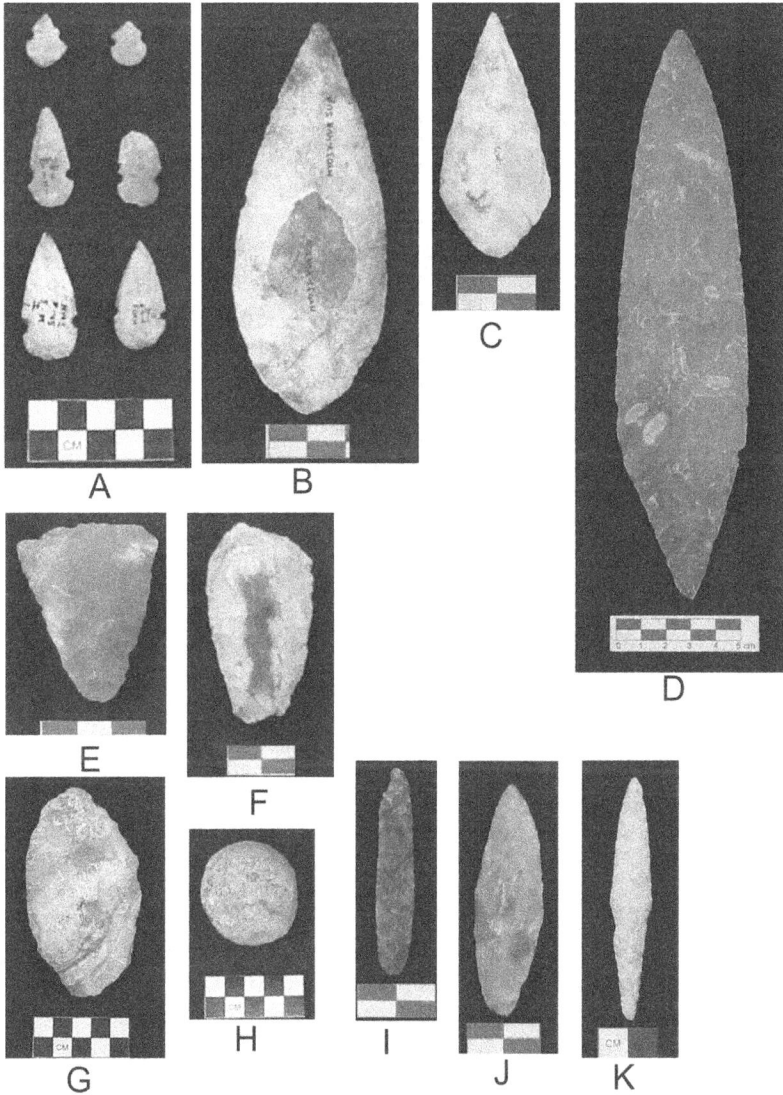

FIGURE 6.24. *Formal tool types at Mayapán, including side-notched projectile points, rounded base variety with varied degrees of resharpening shown (A), pointed bifacial knives with rounded or converging bases (B, C, D), wedge-shaped (triangular) axes (E), oval biface celts (F), thick (Stage 1 or 2) bifaces (G), spherical hammerstones (H), narrow bifaces with parallel sides (I), convex sides (J), or with metric/morphological characteristics of either projectile points or perforators/drills (K). The large, elongated pointed biface (D) is rare for its size at Mayapán, and examples B and C exhibit more typical size ranges.*

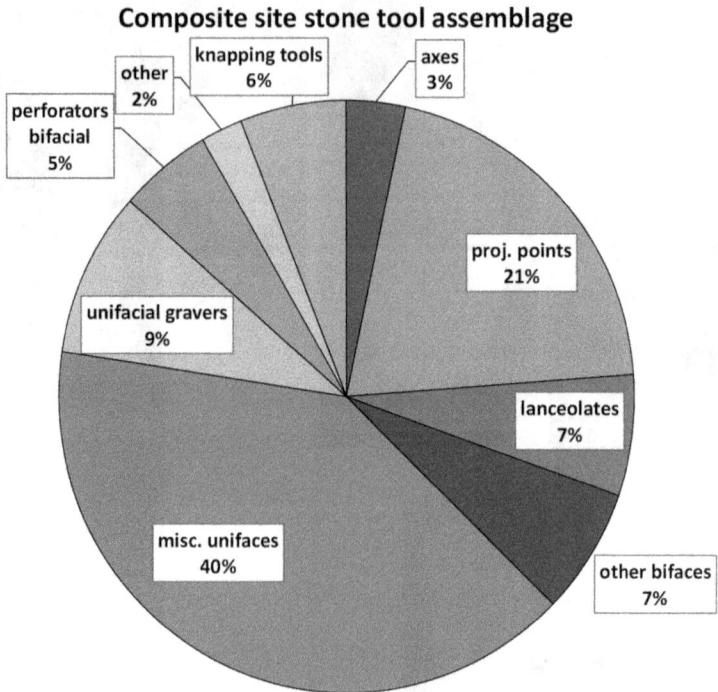

Composite site stone tool assemblage

FIGURE 6.25. *Proportion of major stone tool types from all contexts at Mayapán (details in table 6.23).*

bifaces. The relative quantities of these general tool categories from the PEMY project are summarized in table 6.26, which indicates that the most frequent tool categories are various expedient unifacial tools (40.1 percent). Next most common were side-notched projectile points (20.4 percent), followed by unifacial gravers (9.0 percent), miscellaneous bifaces (6.9 percent), pointed bifacial knives (6.6 percent,), artifacts related to chipped stone production (6.0 percent), bifacial perforators (5.2 percent), axes (3.3 percent), and other items amounting to 2.3 percent of the sample, including eccentrics, greenstone axes, and polishing stones (table 6.26).

These frequencies provide the basis of four primary observations about lithic tool use and activities at the city. First, expedient technology was highly significant for crafting and ordinary tasks. Second, crafting activities represented

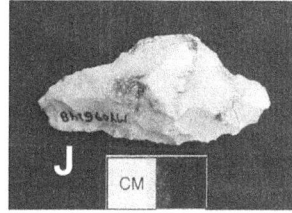

FIGURE 6.26. *Flake tools at Mayapán, including gravers (Row A, example D), miscellaneous retouched flakes (Rows B, C, examples G, H, I), a burin spall graver (F), retouched flakes with notches (E, left, H), a mini-scraper (E, right), and a composite flake tool (J). Examples A–I are from shell Workshop Q-39 and example J is from shell Workshop I-55.*

TABLE 6.26 Stone tool types from Mayapán (PEMY project, surface collection, test pit, and fully excavated contexts). Materials are chert/chalcedony unless otherwise indicated.

Projectile point	Total	Percent	Subtotal (%)
Projectile point (66 are obsidian)	304	20.4	
Subtotal points			20.4

Knife and lanceolate	Total	Percent	Subtotal (%)
Pointed biface	85	5.7	
Other knives/lanceolates	14	0.9	
Subtotal knife/lanceolate			6.6

Ax	Total	Percent	Subtotal (%)
Wedge-shaped biface	24	1.6	
Oval biface celt (25) and informal celtiform (1)	26	1.7	
Subtotal ax			3.3

Other biface	Total	Percent	Subtotal (%)
Biface formal fragment (pointed knife or ax)	12	0.8	
Biface informal	11	0.7	
Biface informal discoidal	3	0.2	
Biface informal planoconvex	19	1.3	
Biface informal thick	22	1.5	
Biface, informal GUB	3	0.2	
Biface fragment	33	2.2	
Subtotal other biface			6.9

Perforator/drill	Total	Percent	Subtotal (%)
Perforator/drill (narrow biface types 1 and 2)	36	2.4	
Narrow biface (informal)	1	0.1	

Perforator/drill/bifacial point	Total	Percent	Subtotal (%)
Perforator/drill/bifacial point (narrow biface type 3)	41	2.7	
Subtotal perforator/drill/graver			5.2

Unifacial tools	Total	Percent	Subtotal (%)
Graver (mainly unifacial tools)	135	9.0	
Subtotal unifacial graver			9.0
Uniface scrapers (26)/scraper and composite tools (2)	28	1.9	

continued on next page

TABLE 6.26—*continued*

Unifacial tools	Total	Percent	Subtotal (%)
Unifaces/retouched flake	567	38.0	
Trimmed blade (formal)	4	0.3	
Subtotal misc. uniface			40.1

Misc. crafting/industry tools	Total	Percent	Subtotal (%)
Greenstone ax	26	1.7	
Limestone disk	2	0.1	
Polished pebble	7	0.5	
Subtotal misc. greenstone/limestone/pebble tools			2.3

Chipped stone production tools or by-products	Total	Percent	Subtotal (%)
Hammerstone (various shapes)	14	0.9	
Oval biface (Stage 2 preform or core)	2	0.1	
Pointed biface (preform)	3	0.2	
Projectile point preform (9 are obsidian)	28	1.9	
Core/core fragment, used	9	0.6	
Core, not used (not including obsidian)	28	1.9	
Burin core	5	0.3	
Subtotal misc. chipped stone production tools			6.0

Eccentric	Total	Percent	Subtotal (%)
Eccentric, mini	1	0.1	
Subtotal eccentric			0.1
Total Postclassic tools	1,493	100.0	100.0

Pre-Mayapán artifact	Total
Pre-Mayapán projectile point (stemmed biface)	2
Pre-Mayapán projectile point (stemmed triangular point)	1
Constricted adze	1
Total tools	1,497

by gravers, perforators, and some proportion of the unifacial tools were a key component of urban life. Third, agricultural activities (forest clearing, hoeing) are poorly represented due to low frequencies of axes of any kind (wedge-shaped or oval, 3.3 percent, figure 6.25). Fourth, military activities were a dominant concern, as implied by the high proportion of projectile points (figure 6.25). Projectile points and pointed knives/lanceolates combined comprise over one-fourth of the assemblage (27.1 percent) of all formal and expedient flake tools. That these projectiles and knives were used in warfare is clear from the mass graves unearthed at Mayapán. A pointed knife was embedded in the rib cavity of a victim near Q-79 (Adams 1953:figure 1). An enlarged, personified pointed knife is aimed at a death god on the inner Kukulcan Temple (Q-162a) frieze (chapter 2, figure 2.12). A mass grave at group Itzmal Ch'en (H-15) is also littered with projectile point fragments.

Was Mayapán populated to a large extent by craftspeople and warriors or citizen militia? The stone tool frequencies imply that farming was minimal and reiterate the concerns of Carnegie investigators regarding how the city sustained itself (J. Hester 1953:289; Proskouriakoff 1956:340; A. Smith 1962:214). Four considerations may explain these findings, and they are not mutually exclusive. First, agrarian activities may have been directed at a largely cultivated landscape that required little tree felling. Burning is an effective clearing technique in the area today (J. Hester 1953). Second, agricultural activities involving stone tools may have been practiced in outfield locations, resulting in low household recovery. We doubt that this is the case, as Bradley W. Russell's (2008a) surveys outside the city wall also revealed few bifacial axes. Third, Mayapán may have traded for significant portions of its food. Fourth, corvée service or tribute obligations may have provided Mayapán with some of its agricultural staples. The agrarian landscape of the city would have been complex and varied, involving houselot gardens, cultivation of enclosed or open spaces in the city's neighborhoods, fruit orchards, and outfield plots for corn and other staples. It is probable that residents of all houselots engaged in some subset of these activities. At the minimum, part-time craftspersons would surely have had gardens in their houselots. But from the perspective of the stone tool assemblage, agrarian activities required far less use of heavy chopping tools than in the Classic Period. It is interesting that oval bifaces were also relatively scarce at Postclassic Laguna de On, Belize (14 percent of the assemblage) despite the fact that raw materials were readily available and oval biface celts were a primary product made for exchange in the earlier Classic Period at nearby Colha (Shafer and Hester 1983; Hester and Shafer 1984).

Mayapán farmers would have used the small oval biface celts or wedge-shaped axes that are found at the city's ancient houselots. It is notable that bifacial celts were also diminished in size at the Postclassic settlements of northern Belize, home to the larger Classic Period technology (Shafer and Hester 1983; Michaels 1987; Masson 1993; Galup 2007). There is great similarity in the length and thicknesses of oval biface celts and wedge-shaped axes at Mayapán, as revealed by our own measurements of these artifacts, and both shapes would have likely sufficed to do the job. The forest today at Mayapán differs from that of northern Belize (and much of Quintana Roo), even when conditions of secondary growth prevail in both environments. Vegetation around Mayapán is lower, drier, and scrubbier; the tool of choice for Belizean workers is the machete while farmers in the towns around Mayapán employ a *coa*, a short, hooked, sickle-like hafted tool.

Spatial Comparisons of Stone Tool Assemblages

The distribution of chipped stone tools per context helps to identify variation in the different kinds of activities at Mayapán dwellings. Among fully excavated structures, comparisons are made of the relative quantities of aggregated stone tool categories, including projectile points, axes, miscellaneous bifaces, perforators, gravers, artifacts related to flintknapping activities, and other tool groups listed in table 6.27. Relative percentages of tool types with each structure's assemblage are considered, along with the number of tool types per square meter and per cubic meter of excavation (tables 6.27, 6.28). The latter values are instructive, as they are independent of the presence or absence of other types of tools. With this measure we can compare the number of axes between localities irrespective of whether or not a context also used a large number of gravers or other tools for specific activities. But densities are also affected by the degree of activity specialization or length of occupation.

Overall, the numbers of specific tool types per square meter or per cubic meter are low, due to the fact that full excavations include a significant amount of relatively clean interior space (tables 6.27, 6.28, figures 6.27–6.32). Axes at fully excavated dwellings were present in densities of 0.04 to 0.1 per cubic meter (table 6.28). Some differences of potential importance are observed in the other metrics provided. Axes, never common, are in greatest abundance at Houses H-11 and X-43. House H-11 also has among the three highest percentages of axes of its total tool assemblage (11.4 percent) along with two other outlying houses, X-43 (12.5 percent) and L-28 (9.1 percent), as indicated in table 6.27 and figure 6.27. Axes are present in lower proportions at Houses Y-45 (4.1 percent), I-55, Q-176, and Q-40 and Temple H-17 (the latter four range from 1.1 to 1.8 percent). Notably, they are absent at Hall H-15 and its associated mass grave and at two chert/chalcedony workshop contexts (I-57 and Q-39).

House Q-39 has the highest relative quantities of miscellaneous bifaces (excluding axes) per square meter and per cubic meter, but the differences

TABLE 6.27 Percentage of tool types for horizontally excavated structures (PEMY).

Type	Temple H-17 (percent)	House I-55 (percent)	Workshop I-57 (percent)	House Q-176 (percent)	House Q-39 (percent)	House Q-40a (percent)
Projectile point	6.3	7.1	12.5	6.3	3.4	3.3
Projectile point obsidian	1.1	0.9	–	4.6	2.3	6.7
Subtotal projectile point	7.4	8.0	12.5	10.9	5.7	10.0
Pointed biface	4.2	3.5	3.8	3.4	1.4	4.4
Biface stemmed lanceolate	–	1.8	–	–	–	–
Biface informal knife	–	0.9	1.0	–	–	1.1
Biface informal pointed	–	0.9	–	0.6	0.3	–
Subtotal knife/lanceolate	4.2	7.1	4.8	4.0	1.7	5.6
Wedge-shaped biface	1.1	0.9	–	1.1	–	1.1
Oval biface celt	–	0.9	–	0.6	–	–
Biface informal celtiform	–	–	–	–	–	–
Subtotal ax	1.1	1.8	0.0	1.7	0.0	1.1
Biface formal fragment	2.1	–	1.9	2.9	0.6	–
Biface informal	2.1	1.8	–	1.1	1.1	–
Biface informal discoidal	–	–	–	–	–	–
Biface informal planoconvex	1.1	1.8	–	0.6	0.9	–
Biface informal thick	–	–	1.0	–	–	1.1
Biface informal "gub"	–	0.9	–	0.6	–	1.1
Biface fragment	2.1	0.9	–	1.7	3.2	–
Subtotal misc. biface	7.4	5.3	2.9	6.9	5.7	2.2
Perforator/drill	1.1	1.8	1.9	0.6	1.4	1.1
Narrow biface informal	–	–	–	1.1	–	–
Perforator/drill/bifacial point	–	–	1.0	–	0.3	–
Subtotal perforator	1.1	1.8	2.9	1.7	1.7	1.1
Subtotal graver	16.8	10.6	4.8	16.6	16.9	3.3
Scrapers (includes only 1 bifacial, and 2 graver/ scrapers)	4.2	1.8	1.0	0.6	4.0	1.1

continued on next page

TABLE 6.27—*continued*

Type	Temple H-17 (percent)	House I-55 (percent)	Workshop I-57 (percent)	House Q-176 (percent)	House Q-39 (percent)	House Q-40a (percent)
Unifaces/retouched flakes	49.5	52.2	63.5	48.0	58.7	70.0
Blade/flake blade	2.1	–	1.9	1.1	1.1	–
Subtotal misc. uniface	55.8	54.0	66.3	49.7	63.9	71.1
Greenstone ax	1.1	0.9	–	0.6	0.6	1.1
Limestone disk	1.1	–	–	–	–	–
Polished pebble/cobble smoother	1.1	0.9	–	1.1	0.3	1.1
Subtotal misc. crafting tools	3.2	1.8	0.0	1.7	0.9	2.2
Hammerstone	–	–	–	–	–	1.1
Pointed biface preform	–	–	1.9	–	–	–
Projectile point preform	–	–	–	0.6	0.9	–
Projectile point preform obsidian	–	2.7	1.0	1.7	0.3	1.1
Core/core fragment	2.1	3.5	1.0	2.9	1.4	1.1
Core used	1.1	2.7	1.9	–	0.3	–
Core burin	–	0.9	–	1.7	0.3	–
Subtotal production tools	3.2	9.7	5.8	6.9	3.2	3.3
Total postclassic tools	95	113	104	175	349	90

Type	House H-11 (percent)	Hall H-15 (percent)	Hall H-15 grave (percent)	House L-28 (percent)	House X-43 (percent)	House Y-45 (percent)	Grand total (number)
Projectile point	14.3	43.5	80.0	22.7	18.8	47.1	149
Projectile point obsidian	–	–	–	50.0	0.0	8.3	45
Subtotal projectile point	14.3	43.5	80.0	72.7	18.8	55.4	16.7
Pointed biface	11.4	8.7	10.0	–	12.5	11.6	51
Biface stemmed lanceolate	–	–	–	–	–	–	2

continued on next page

TABLE 6.27—*continued*

Type	House H-11 (percent)	Hall H-15 (percent)	Hall H-15 grave (percent)	House L-28 (percent)	House X-43 (percent)	House Y-45 (percent)	Grand total (number)
Biface informal knife	2.9	–	–	–	–	–	4
Biface informal pointed	8.6	–	–	–	–	–	6
Stemmed biface asymmetrical	2.9	–	–	–	–	–	1
Subtotal knife/ lanceolate	25.7	8.7	10.0	0.0	12.5	11.6	5.5
Wedge-shaped biface	5.7	–	–	4.5	–	1.7	10
Oval biface celt	2.9	–	–	4.5	12.5	2.5	9
Biface informal celtiform	2.9	–	–	–	–	–	1
Subtotal ax	11.4	0.0	0.0	9.1	12.5	4.1	1.7
Biface formal fragment	–	–	–	–	–	–	11
Biface informal	2.9	–	–	–	–	–	11
Biface informal discoidal	2.9	–	–	–	–	0.8	2
Biface informal planoconvex	5.7	–	–	–	–	0.8	10
Biface informal thick	–	–	–	–	25.0	1.7	8
Biface informal "gub"	–	–	–	–	–	–	3
Biface fragment	–	–	–	–	6.3	–	18
Subtotal misc. biface	11.4	0.0	0.0	0.0	31.3	3.3	5.4
Perforator/drill	2.9	4.3	–	–	6.3	1.7	17
Narrow biface informal	–	4.3	–	–	–	–	3
Perforator/drill/ bifacial point	2.9	–	5.0	–	6.3	5.8	12

continued on next page

TABLE 6.27—*continued*

Type	House H-11 (percent)	Hall H-15 (percent)	Hall H-15 grave (percent)	House L-28 (percent)	House X-43 (percent)	House Y-45 (percent)	Grand total (number)
Subtotal perforator	5.7	8.7	5.0	0.0	12.5	7.4	2.8
Subtotal graver	8.6	4.3	–	–	–	4.1	133
	–	–	–	–	–	–	
Scrapers	5.7	4.3	–	4.5	–	1.7	29
Unifaces/ retouched flakes	8.6	21.7	5.0	9.1	6.3	4.1	541
Blade/flake blade	–	–	–	–	–	3.3	14
Subtotal misc. uniface	14.3	26.1	5.0	13.6	6.3	9.1	50.2
Greenstone ax	2.9	8.7	–	–	–	0.8	10
Limestone disk	–	–	–	–	–	0.8	2
Polished pebble/ cobble smoother	–	–	–	–	–		6
Subtotal misc. craft tools	2.9	8.7	0.0	0.0	0.0	1.7	1.5
Hammerstone	2.9	–	–	–	6.3	0.8	4
Pointed biface preform	2.9	–	–	–	–	–	3
Projectile point preform	–	–	–	4.5	–	0.8	6
Projectile point preform obsidian	–	–	–	–	–	–	9
Core/core fragment	–	–	–	–	–	1.7	20
Core used	–	–	–	–	–	–	7
Core burin	–	–	–	–	–	–	5
Subtotal production tools	5.7	0.0	0.0	4.5	6.3	3.3	4.6
Subtotal eccentric							1
Total Postclassic tools	35	23	20	22	16	121	1,163

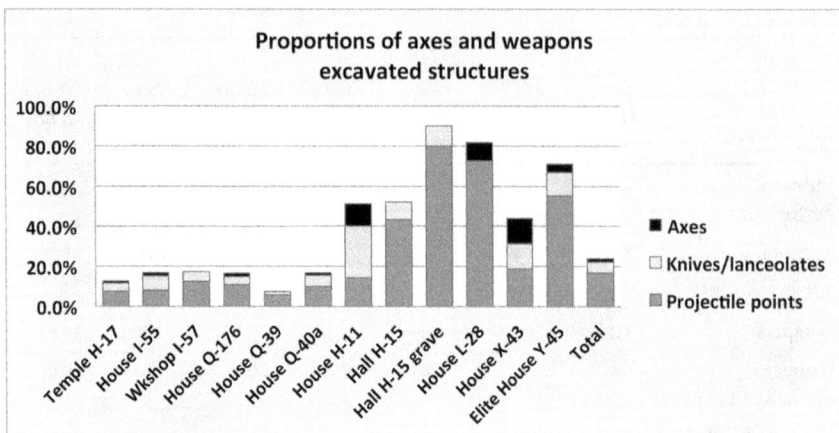

Proportions of axes and weapons excavated structures

FIGURE 6.27. *Comparison of proportions of weaponry to axes per structure at horizontally excavated PEMY structures. Note that non-crafting Houses H-11, L-28, and X-43 have slightly more axes.*

among contexts are not great (table 6.28). The percentages of tools per context reveal that House X-43 has the most relative miscellaneous bifaces (31.3 percent), followed by House H-11 (11.4 percent). Lower proportions ranging from 2.2 to 7.4 percent are present at Temple H-17, Houses Q-176, Q-39, I-55, Y-45, and Q-40, and Workshop I-57 (table 6.27). They are absent at Hall H-15 contexts and House L-28. High proportions of miscellaneous bifaces are not associated with biface Workshops Q-39 and I-57 (5.7 percent and 2.9 percent, respectively), perhaps due to a low error rate. Miscellaneous bifaces with varied morphologies performed a range of functions and have less potential to differentiate activities as an aggregate group. There are no other distinguishing attributes of House X-43 that help to explain its high proportions of these tools, except that it also had among the highest proportions of axes.

Projectile points are slightly more ubiquitous at the Hall H-15 mass grave per square meter compared to other contexts, but per cubic meter, the quantity (0.6) is not significantly different from Houses Q-176, Q-39, L-28, and others. But projectile points make up 80 percent of the stone tools in the mass grave. While Houses Y-45a and L-28 also have high proportions of projectiles (55 percent and 73 percent, respectively), as does Hall H-15 (44 percent), all other contexts have less than 20 percent (table 6.27). The predominance of projectiles at the massacre locality is not surprising. Points are a standard component of

TABLE 6.28 Aggregated tool quantities per square meter and per cubic meter at fully excavated contexts.

	Structure					
	Temple H-17	House I-55	Workshop I-57	House Q-176	House Q-39	House Q-40a
Square meter	601.650	196.00	72.25	136.00	120.00	88.50
Cubic meter	328.200	47.35	18.91	33.07	34.23	21.74
Projectile points/square meter	0.010	0.05	0.18	0.14	0.17	0.10
Projectile points/cubic meter	0.020	0.20	0.70	0.60	0.60	0.40
Knives/lances/square meter	0.010	0.04	0.07	0.05	0.05	0.06
Knives/lances/cubic meter	0.010	0.20	0.30	0.20	0.20	0.20
Axes/square meter	0.002	0.01	0.00	0.02	0.00	0.01
Axes/cubic meter	0.003	0.04	0.00	0.09	0.00	0.05
Misc. bifaces/square meter	0.010	0.03	0.04	0.09	0.17	0.02
Misc. bifaces/cubic meter	0.020	0.10	0.20	0.40	0.60	0.10

	Structure						
	House H-11	Hall H-15	Grave H-15	House L-28	House X-43	Elite House Y-45	Grand total
Square meter	133.30	475.340	40.25	212.00	252.00	376.00	2703.290
Cubic meter	35.88	126.420	28.66	30.44	18.59	176.13	899.616
Projectile points/square meter	0.04	0.020	0.40	0.08	0.01	0.18	0.070
Projectile points/cubic meter	0.10	0.080	0.60	0.50	0.20	0.40	0.200

continued on next page

TABLE 6.28—*continued*

	Structure							
	House H-11	Hall H-15	Grave H-15	House L-28	House Q-176	House X-43	Elite House Y-45	Grand total
Knives/lances/square meter	0.07	0.004	0.05	0.00	0.00	0.01	0.04	0.020
Knives/lances/cubic meter	0.25	0.020	0.07	0.00	0.00	0.10	0.08	0.070
Axes/square meter	0.03	0.000	0.00	0.01	0.01	0.01	0.01	0.010
Axes/cubic meter	0.10	0.000	0.00	0.07	0.07	0.10	0.03	0.020
Misc. bifaces/square meter	0.03	0.000	0.00	0.00	0.00	0.02	0.01	0.020
Misc. bifaces/cubic meter	0.10	0.000	0.00	0.00	0.00	0.30	0.02	0.070

	Temple H-17	House I-55	Workshop I-57	House Q-176	House Q-39	House Q-40a
Square meter	601.650	196.00	72.25	136.00	120.00	88.50
Cubic meter	328.200	47.35	18.91	33.07	34.23	21.74
Perforators/square meter	0.002	0.05	0.08	0.14	0.31	0.05
Perforators/cubic meter	0.003	0.20	0.30	0.60	1.10	0.20
Gravers/square meter	0.030	0.06	0.07	0.21	0.49	0.03
Gravers/cubic meter	0.050	0.30	0.30	0.90	1.70	0.10
Misc. unifaces/square meter	0.090	0.31	0.96	0.64	1.86	0.72
Misc. unifaces/cubic meter	0.200	1.30	3.60	2.60	6.50	2.90
Misc. crafting tools/square meter	0.005	0.01	0.00	0.02	0.03	0.02

continued on next page

TABLE 6.28—continued

	Temple H-17	House I-55	Workshop I-57	House Q-176	House Q-39	House Q-40a
Misc. crafting tools/cubic meter	0.010	0.04	0.00	0.09	0.09	0.09
Flintknapping tools/square meter	0.005	0.06	0.08	0.09	0.09	0.03
Flintknapping tools/cubic meter	0.010	0.20	0.30	0.40	0.30	0.10

	House H-11	Hall H-15	Grave H-15	House L-28	House X-43	Elite House Y-45	Grand total
Square meter	133.30	475.340	40.25	212.000	252.000	376.00	2703.290
Cubic meter	35.88	126.420	28.66	30.440	18.590	176.13	899.616
Perforators/square meter	0.05	0.004	0.02	0.000	0.030	0.03	0.040
Perforators/cubic meter	0.20	0.020	0.03	0.000	0.400	0.07	0.100
Gravers/square meter	0.02	0.002	0.00	0.000	0.000	0.01	0.050
Gravers/cubic meter	0.08	0.010	0.00	0.000	0.000	0.03	0.100
Misc. unifaces/square meter	0.04	0.010	0.02	0.010	0.004	0.03	0.220
Misc. unifaces/cubic meter	0.10	0.050	0.03	0.100	0.100	0.10	0.600
Misc. crafting tools/square meter	0.01	0.004	0.00	0.000	0.000	0.01	0.010
Misc. crafting tools/cubic meter	0.03	0.020	0.00	0.000	0.000	0.01	0.020
Flintknapping tools/square meter	0.02	0.000	0.00	0.005	0.004	0.01	0.020
Flintknapping tools/cubic meter	0.06	0.000	0.00	0.030	0.050	0.02	0.060

the assemblages of any structure at Mayapán, and none of our horizontally excavated structures lacked them. Major differences are not obvious in the continuum of values of projectile points per square meter or per cubic meter. Surplus crafting houses (Q-176, Q-39, and Q-40a) had lower percentages of points (5.7 percent to 10.9 percent), presumably due to the abundance of other types of informal tools used at these contexts (table 6.27).

According to the percentage of tools, H-11 exhibits the most knife/lanceolate tools (25.7 percent) while other contexts have frequencies ranging from 1.7 to 12.5 percent. House X-43 (12.5 percent), Y-45 (11.6 percent), and the H-15 mass grave (10 percent) are at the upper end of this range (table 6.27, figure 6.27). The quantity of knives per square meter or per cubic meter fails to distinguish fully excavated contexts from one another, with the exception of House H-11 (0.25 per cubic meter, table 6.28), which may signal the importance of activities calling for pointed bifaces at H-11.

House Y-45, the H-15 mass grave, and X-43 had among the highest percentages of projectile points and lanceolate/knives compared to other localities (figure 6.27). This correspondence was not observed for House H-11, which had points in proportions below these other edifices (but more than five other domestic contexts) yet had the greatest relative quantity of lanceolates/knives. Mayapán's pointed knives were used as weaponry, as indicated by their iconographic contexts in codices and art at the site. Their general co-occurrence with points at some contexts may help to identify the importance of martial activities. But these implements would have also been useful as knives in a domestic setting, as their wide distribution suggests. The recovery of pointed biface preforms in low numbers at I-57 suggests that these tools were among those manufactured at this workshop (Masson and Escamilla Ojeda 2012:figure 18.20).

Percentages of perforators are highest at House X-43 (12.5 percent), followed by Hall H-15 (8.7 percent) and House Y-45a (7.4 percent); all others have 5.7 percent or fewer (table 6.27, figure 6.28). Quantities per square meter and per cubic meter distinguish crafting House Q-39 (1.1 per cubic meter, 0.3 per square meter) above all others (table 6.28). Beyond this observation, other commoner houses have similar densities to one another (0.2 to 0.6 per cubic meter), and these are more abundant than observed for elite House Y-45 or public buildings (0.02 to .003 per cubic meter). There is little agreement among the relative percentage and density data for these objects. But the density data reveal the importance of low numbers of perforators at all types of commoner houses, and perhaps an emphasis on textile working at Q-39. It is perhaps noteworthy that a spindle whorl was placed as an offering in

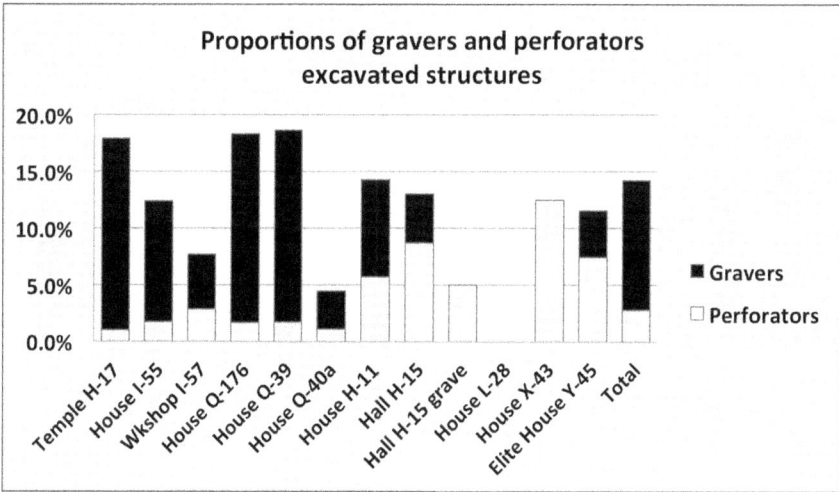

FIGURE 6.28. *Proportions of gravers and perforators at horizontally excavated PEMY structures.*

the family grave at this house. Perforators are low-frequency objects that are made on carefully crafted narrow bifacial tools (figure 6.24i), unlike gravers, which are more ubiquitous, as they are made expediently on various pointed flakes (figure 6.26).

Gravers form the greatest proportion of the assemblages at Houses Q-39 and Q-176 and at the H-17 temple; these contexts have percentages ranging from 16.6 to 16.8 percent (table 6.27, figure 6.28). Shell working at the two houses would seem to explain these high frequencies. The abundance of gravers at these two shell workshops is confirmed by the quantity per square meter and per cubic meter, which far exceed other contexts (table 6.28); their density is low for Temple H-17. Although gravers formed 10.6 percent of House I-55's assemblage, density was low for this additional shell workshop and indicates that the use of gravers was less important relative to other activities at this locality (table 6.28). All others have gravers in the amount of 3.3–8.6 percent. House Q-39 seems to be particularly distinguished from the others by the quantity of gravers and perforators. Such subtle patterns hint at variability in emphasis at houselot workshops and suggest that perishable industries such as textiles probably existed alongside those dedicated to chert, obsidian, pottery, and shell. Gravers are often associated with shell working, but they are simply pointed protuberances on flakes that exhibit a great deal of variation at the individual artifact level and could have been used for a range of purposes. Work

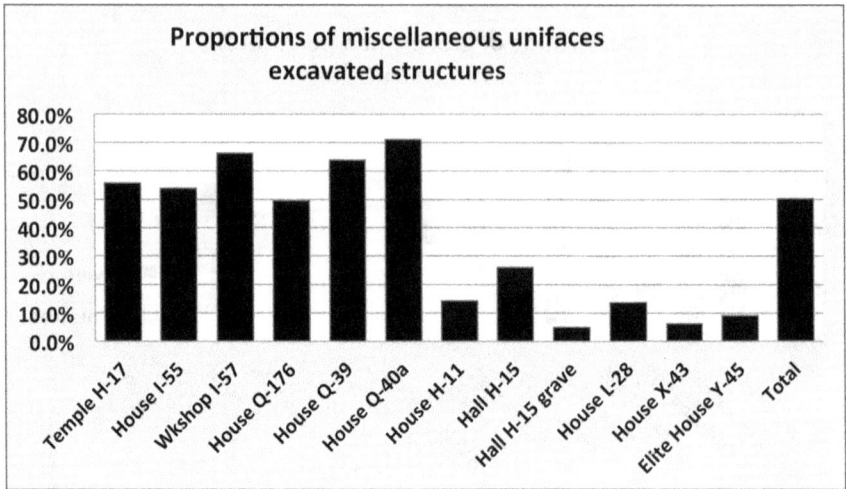

FIGURE 6.29. *Proportions of unifaces at horizontally excavated PEMY contexts. In general these were more significant at crafting houses versus non-crafting houses.*

on Mayapán's gravers is ongoing, and evidence is emerging for patterned variants of pointed flakes that are systematically modified in one or more places on the dorsal and ventral flake surfaces.

Unifaces (other than gravers) were often the most common tool at the contexts that we compared, representing 50.2 percent of the fully excavated structure tool sample (figure 6.29). This term encompasses a wide variety of informal tools. As a group, these tools were most frequent at crafting localities Q-40a, I-57, Q-39, I-55a, Q-176, and at Temple H-17, with percentages ranging from 54 percent to 71 percent (table 6.27). All other contexts had half or less of this percentage range. Density values reveal nearly identical results for crafting houses and indicate that unifaces were not abundant overall at the temple. Unifaces were most ubiquitous at Q-39 (6.5 per cubic meter), I-57 (3.6 per cubic meter), Q-176 (2.6 per cubic meter), Q-40a (2.9 per cubic meter), and I-55a (1.3 per cubic meter); all other contexts had densities well below 1 per cubic meter (table 6.28). Multi-crafting activities seem to have required a greater number of flake tools than at other houses.

Stone artifacts related to flintknapping (hammerstones, preforms, cores) are not present in greater abundance at lithic workshops that are identified from flaking debris (I-57 and Q-39). Such artifacts form 3.2–9.7 percent of fully excavated contexts, with the greatest frequency at House I-55a (table 6.27, figure 6.30). They form from 0.02 to 0.1 per cubic meter of residential structures

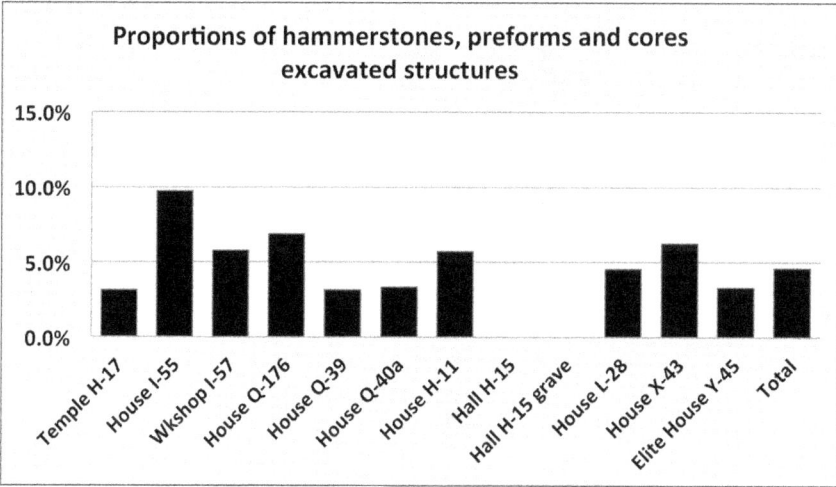

Figure 6.30. *Proportions of stone tools used in lithic production (hammerstones, preforms, cores) at horizontally excavated PEMY contexts. Lithic working is not distinguished by high amounts of these materials.*

and are scarcer at public buildings (table 6.28). We conclude that the presence of such objects is not a strong indicator of a stone tool workshop and that household tool kits included such items for expedient use. The lack of high numbers of preforms suggests a low failure and discard rate at flintknapping houselots. Pointed biface preforms were recovered at only two localities: House H-11 and Workshop I-57.

Projectile point preforms were present at Q-176, Q-39, L-28, and Y-45. We surmise that projectile point making was a regular household activity and that men were not dependent on workshops for obtaining this type of weapon. Mayapán's typical side-notched points are not technologically complex and involve edge retouch and side notching of otherwise non-elaborate elongate flake blades. Most points are not fully bifacially flaked. These elementary lithic modification skills were probably widely shared, enabling hunters or warriors to replenish this low-investment tool type without constraint. Points could be made easily on flakes from small polyhedral flake cores. Pointed knives, however, involve greater skill in thinning and shaping and require access to cobbles of a greater size than is evident in Mayapán's collection of flake cores. The average maximum dimension of cores in the sample was 4.4 centimeters (standard deviation 1.7, range 2.1–7.2, N = 13), whereas the mean length for whole pointed bifaces is 6.6 centimeters (standard deviation 1.6, range 4.3–9.9,

N = 19), including smaller, resharpened examples. To illustrate this discrepancy more fully, only one core in the sample had a maximum dimension of 7.2 centimeters, while eight of nineteen pointed bifaces were 7.2–9.9 centimeters long. A sample (N = 35) of whole pointed bifaces from the INAH project had a mean length of 8.8 centimeters (standard deviation 3.8) and twenty-three of the thirty-five were at least 7 centimeters long. Large cores were needed for new pointed bifaces, and such cores were not widely available to the city's residents. Biface manufacturing workshops may have had special access to them. Intensive reduction and use of cores is reflected by the absence of large examples at the city.

Miscellaneous crafting tools, including greenstone axes, limestone disks, and polished pebbles or cobbles, represent different types of activities. Miniature greenstone axes, usually made of dark green serpentine-like or other river cobble material, were present at Houses I-55, Q-176, Q-39, Q-40, H-11, and Y-45 and were absent at two houses (L-28 and X-43) and the I-57 workshop. Our data suggest that commoners regularly possessed greenstone axes; similarly, Payson Sheets (2000) points out that houses preserved by a volcanic eruption at the site of Cerén usually possessed one ax. Limestone disks were rare in our sample, found only at Temple H-17 and elite House Y-45. Freidel and Sabloff (1984:33) were among the first to discuss the use of limestone disks as beehive covers. Polished pebbles were present at H-11, I-55, Q-176, Q-39, and Q-40 and absent elsewhere. Such objects are expected from crafting houselots, perhaps for polishing artisanal objects.

The differences and similarities of stone tool types in household assemblages reveal, on the one hand, a tendency toward task specialization and on the other hand, well-equipped household tool kits that were suitable for an array of daily tasks. Chi-square tests were performed to evaluate the variation that we have described. These tests compared tool assemblage frequencies of each conceivable pair of dwellings from our fully excavated sample (table 6.29). Four of twenty-eight tests failed to reject the null hypothesis of no difference, suggesting that it is highly probable that twenty-four pairs of houses were drawn from a different population (df = 5, p = 0.05). Chi-square tests did not suggest significant differences between Houses I-55 and Q-176 or I-55 and Q-40a, all of which are multi-crafting houselots. Significant differences were also not detected for H-11 and X-43 or for L-28 and Y-45; none of these are surplus crafting localities, however, more differences might be expected for Y-45, an elite house, and L-28, a peripheral commoner dwelling. The latter structure has a low sample size that may have skewed the results, but high percentages of projectile points at L-28 and Y-45a also set them apart from other dwellings

TABLE 6.29 Results (chi-square comparisons of frequencies of axes, bifaces, projectile points, lanceolates, perforator/gravers, and unifaces between fully excavated houses), p = .05, df = 5, values > / = 11.07 reject the null of no difference

	House I-55	House Q-176	House Q-39	House Q-40a	House H-11	House L-28	House X-43	House Y-45
House I-55	/							
House Q-176	No difference (4.01)	/						
House Q-39	Different (18.69)	Different (16.78)	/					
House Q-40a	No difference (8.90)	Different (18.87)	Different (24.91)	/				
House H-11	Different (25.64)	Different (35.25)	Different (106.66)	Different (40.82)	/			
House L-28	Different (58.42)	Different (62.74)	Different (155.67)	Different (49.25)	Different (26.83)	/		
House X-43	Different (23.13)	Different (21.41)	Different (65.98)	Different (41.54)	No difference (4.86)	Different (24.89)	/	
Elite House Y-45	Different (82.36)	Different (98.87)	Different (222.01)	Different (91.56)	Different (21.57)	No difference (9.008)	Different (24.49)	/
Total tools	108	176	365	88	36	21	21	119

(table 6.27). Perhaps the most revealing outcome of the chi-square tests is the implication that the stone tools of crafting houselots are more similar to one another than to non-crafting houselots, and vice versa.

In summary, the frequencies and densities of certain stone tools help to pinpoint activity differentiation at Mayapán houselots. Unifaces and greenstone axes tended to distinguish crafting houselots from other commoners. Conversely, axes were more common at some non-crafting houses (H-11 and X-43) where residents may have engaged in agricultural activities. The quantity of pointed knives does not set apart any structure, although these tend to be more ubiquitous at crafting localities and at House H-11. These knives were made at Workshops I-57 and Q-39. Perforators and gravers are absent at L-28 and there are no gravers at X-43. Thus, these objects were not always part of ordinary household toolkits. Perforator and graver quantities at House Q-39 are well beyond those of other contexts, and this ubiquity hints at a perishable textile industry at this houselot. Shell working occurred at Q-39 but graver densities are lower at shell Workshops Q-176 and I-55 (table 6.28). Hammerstones, preforms, and cores did not concentrate at stone tool workshops and were instead stocked routinely at dwellings, presumably for expedient flake tool industries or other broad uses. Projectile points are uniformly ubiquitous and do not tend to differentiate dwellings well from one another. Although higher frequencies of certain tools highlight inter-context differences in our sample, the data also reveal that most dwellings had low quantities of the majority of tools reviewed in this analysis. Most tools served both specialized industries and equipped houses with implements useful for daily tasks. A view emerges of a flexible stone technology in which a suite of formal tools had multiple applications; these implements were supplemented by a wide array of expedient flake tools that were made at home.

Surface Collection and Test Pit Sample Stone Tools

The surface collection and test pit data supplement the observations just presented for larger samples. Twenty-one surface collection contexts had only one stone tool, fourteen had two tools, eight had three, seven had four, and only a few had five (N = 2), six (N = 2), seven (N = 3), eight (N = 1), nine (N = 1) or twelve (N = 1) tools. These data have been fully described elsewhere (Masson, Delu, and Peraza Lope 2008), and here we provide some summary observations. Contexts with three or more tools (tables 6.30, 6.31) hint at interesting patterns. Only five surface collection contexts had two axes (oval biface or wedge-shaped)—four of these were commoner houses not engaged in surplus shell production and one was a shell workshop. Stone tool workshops

TABLE 6.30 Stone tools from PEMY surface collections where three or more tools were recovered (excluding utilized flakes).

Structure	Context type	Number of tools	Tools within 3 meter dog leash collection unit
Q-176	Obsidian/shell workshop, house	12	3 biface fragments, 1 thick biface, 2 perforators, 1 graver, 1 pointed biface, 1 projectile point, 2 projectile point preforms, 1 retouched flake
R-174	Obsidian workshop, house	9	2 planoconvex bifaces, 1 constricted adze, 1 hammerstone, 1 oval biface, 1 perforator, 2 projectile points, 1 retouched flake
P-146b	House	8	1 thick biface, 2 hammerstones, 1 pointed biface, 2 wedge-shaped axes
BB-12	House	7	1 core, 1 hammerstone polisher, 2 oval bifaces, 1 perforator drill, 1 pointed biface, 1 projectile point
Z-119/ AA-75	Stone tool/obsidian/ shell workshop, houses	7	1 hammerstone, 2 perforators, 2 pointed bifaces, 1 planoconvex biface, 1 projectile point
Z-43	Stone tool workshop, house	7	2 hammerstones, 1 oval biface preform, 1 wedge-shaped ax, 1 planoconvex biface, 1 pointed biface, 1 projectile point
Y-111	House	6	1 biface, 1 discoidal biface, 1 planoconvex biface, 1 pointed biface, 2 projectile points
Z-190a	House	6	1 thick biface, 1 biface, 1 hammerstone, 1 perforator 1 pointed biface, 1 projectile point
Q-39	Obsidian/stone tool/shell workshop, house	5	1 biface, 1 planoconvex biface, 1 projectile point preform, 2 retouched flakes
Z-120	Obsidian/stone tool/shell workshop, house	5	2 bifaces, 1 thick biface, 2 projectile points
L-18	House	4	2 perforators, 1 projectile point, 1 wedge-shaped ax
L-23	House	4	2 bifaces, 1 pointed biface, 1 retouched flake
P-114	Obsidian/stone tool/ shell workshop	4	1 thick biface, 1 perforator, 2 projectile points

continued on next page

TABLE 6.30—*continued*

Structure	Context type	Number of tools	Tools within 3 meter dog leash collection unit
Q-244b	Elite house	4	1 oval biface, 2 perforators, 1 retouched flake
Q-188	Obsidian/stone tool workshop	4	1 biface, 1 core, 1 projectile point, 1 retouched flake
Q-196	Obsidian workshop	4	1 pointed biface, 3 projectile points
10-O-3	House	3	1 core, 1 perforator, 1 pointed biface
I-57	Stone tool workshop	3	1 thick biface, 1 projectile point, wedge-shaped ax
P-115b	House	3	1 perforator, 1 pointed biface, 1 wedge-shaped ax
R-184	House	3	2 oval bifaces, 1 pointed biface
R-168b	House	3	2 oval bifaces, 1 pointed biface
R-170a	House	3	1 perforator, 1 pointed biface, 1 projectile point
R-172a	House	3	1 thick biface, 2 projectile points
Z-47	Shell workshop, house	3	2 oval bifaces, 1 hammerstone

tended to have a range of bifaces, including fragments, thick (unfinished or expedient) bifaces, and formal bifaces (axes, pointed bifaces) that may have been made at these locations. Hammerstones, as noted previously, occur in all sorts of dwellings. In the surface collections, three were present at workshops and two were at ordinary houses (table 6.30).

Test pit stone tool frequencies provide little definitive information regarding houselot specialization. Of fifteen contexts with three or more tools from test pits, only four axes (oval or wedge) were found; three of these were from houselots with stone tool workshops associated with them (table 6.31). Test pits at non-crafting houses revealed no axes that might indicate a focus on agrarian production. As with the surface collection data, stone tool workshop houselots had a diverse array of tools that point to bifacial reduction, household activities and other craft-working. Most of the workshops were involved in multi-crafting.

Despite the limitations of sample size, some interesting comparisons emerge in charts of the distribution of agricultural bifaces (wedge-shaped and oval) versus potential weaponry (projectile points and pointed bifaces). These items

TABLE 6.31 Stone tools from test pit contexts where three or more stone tools were recovered (excludes utilized flakes).

Structure	Context type	Number of tools	Type of tools in test pit sample
S-10b/c	Obsidian/stone tool/ shell workshop, house	17	1 oval biface, 6 perforators, 2 pointed bifaces, 7 projectile points, 1 projectile point preform
S-12ab	Stone tool/shell workshop, house	10	8 projectile points, 2 projectile point preforms
Z-120	Obsidian/stone tool/ shell workshop, house	10	1 biface fragment, 3 perforators, 5 projectile points, 1 wedge-shaped ax
Z-43	Stone tool workshop, house	6	2 perforators, 1 pointed biface, 1 projectile point, 2 flake blades
BB-12	House	5	1 oval biface, 1 projectile point, 2 flake blades, 1 scraper
Q-176	Obsidian/shell workshop, house	5	1 oval biface, 4 projectile points
X-43	House	5	1 biface, 4 projectile points
F-13	House	5	1 perforator, 4 projectile points
P-151	House	4	1 core fragment, 1 perforator, 2 projectile points
S-132	House	4	1 biface, 1 core fragment, 2 projectile points
P-114	Obsidian/stone tool/ shell workshop, house	3	1 perforator, 1 projectile point, 1 projectile point preform
P-115b	House	3	1 core fragment, 1 perforator, 1 projectile point preform
P-150	House	3	1 pointed biface, 1 projectile point, 1 projectile point preform
Z-39	Obsidian/stone tool/ shell workshop, elite house	3	3 projectile points
Z-47b	Shell workshop, house	3	1 biface, 1 hammerstone, 1 perforator

only rarely overlapped in systematic surface collections (figure 6.31). Of forty-seven cases with any of these tool types, ax forms were recovered together with pointed bifaces or projectiles in only eight cases. Remaining contexts either had only pointed knives (N = 15), only projectiles (N = 7), only knives and

projectiles (N = 6), or only axes (N = 11). We have shown from the fully excavated assemblages that projectile points tend to be constantly ubiquitous at
Mayapán houselots and that axes tend to be scarce. The surface collection data
suggest that more full-scale investigations of Mayapán's houselots are merited
to determine the degree to which non-crafting residents devoted their time to
agricultural or military pursuits.

The tendency for axes and weaponry to be recovered in different sample
units is not strongly indicated for test pit samples (figure 6.32), due in part to
the mixed assemblages from three lithic workshop contexts where a variety
of tools were made (Z-120, Q-176, and S-10). Figure 6.32 shows that a single
projectile point was recovered from sixteen test pits, and pointed knives were
present in only five contexts. Contexts with three to eight projectile points
included four stone tool workshops—Z-39, S-12, Z-120, and S-10—and
House Q-176, where surplus chert tools were not manufactured. House X-43
is the only non-crafting locality with more than three projectiles. Despite the
likelihood that Mayapán's residents made their own technologically simple
projectile points, the ubiquity of points at these stone tool workshops implies
that point making may have also been undertaken by specialists. It is conceivable that access to preferred raw material and well-executed elongate flakes at
the city's workshops would have encouraged point making, even if residents
were otherwise capable of doing the job.

MILITARISTIC INDUSTRIES AT MAYAPÁN

The quantities of projectile points and knives at Mayapán attest to the
importance of warfare at the city. Kenneth G. Hirth (1993a:136) determined
that elites had more projectile points at Xochicalco, which may indicate their
association with militaristic activities. Elite contexts in our sample (Hall H-15,
Y-45) had among the highest relative percentages, but overall, densities were
low (tables 6.27, 6.28). Warfare was one activity that elites shared with commoners at Mayapán, and war captains and conscripted warriors assuredly
resided within the city.

David Webster (2000:79) argues that Maya militia armies were quickly
mobilized to fight the Spaniards at the time of contact. In the Maya highlands,
military operations were organized under a pair of war chiefs, including one
hereditary and one rotating position. Four war gods were recognized. Women
carried supplies for armies and battles were loud, with shouting, drums, sticks,
whistles, and conch shells adding to the din (Follett 1932:376–78). Warfare was
employed to acquire slaves, for revenge, or to control strategic resources such

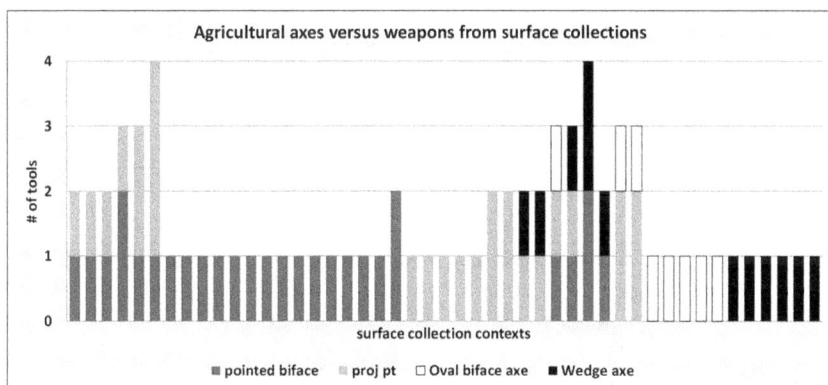

FIGURE 6.31. *Comparisons of ax to weaponry frequencies from surface collection contexts.*

as land or salt sources (Webster 2000:81). Weapons included spear-throwers, slings, bows, thrusting spears, blade-edged swords, war clubs, knives, hatchets, and "bee bombs" (Follett 1932:380; Webster 2000:79). Slings have not been documented archaeologically but were definitely used (Tozzer 1941:note 1150). It is possible that spherical hammerstones doubled as sling stones. Stanley Serafin (personal communication, 2010) has identified a healed cranial blow made with a dull, sling stone-like weapon on one of the burials near House I-55. As mentioned previously, hatchets were weapons for decapitation in some scenes of the Postclassic Maya codices. Tools of agriculture and flintknapping probably doubled as weapons of warfare.

The size ranges of Mayapán's projectiles suggest that both atlatl darts and bows and arrows were used, although these points are technologically similar and are distinguished mainly by the length of the projectile. The most common point type is made from an elongate, triangular side-notched flake (figure 6.24a). These points are usually not fully bifacially flaked, but bifacial edge trimming is common; retouched bases can exhibit a square, round, or concave shape. A sample of 55 whole points reveals an average length of 2.8 centimeters (standard deviation .9, range 1.2–6.1). Some side-notched points at Mayapán are fully bifacially flaked; these exhibit a similar size range to that of predominantly unifacial points. The mean length for a sample of five complete bifacial examples is 2.8 centimeters, with a standard deviation of 0.7 and a range of 2.1–3.5. Fully bifacial points are not common, nor do they concentrate in specific spatial contexts that would link them with different ethnic groups. Compared to unifacial points, bifacial points are often narrower,

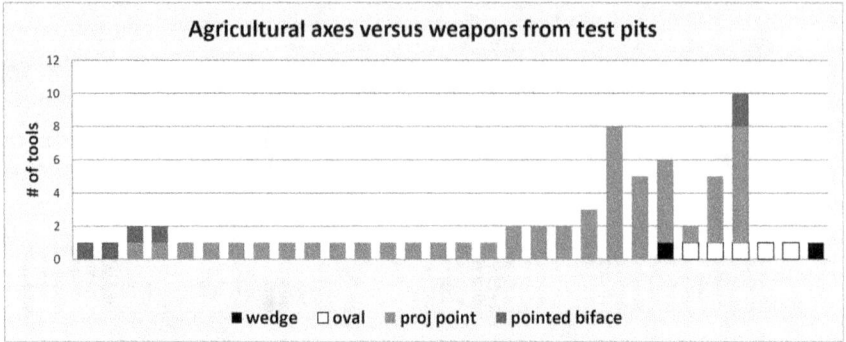

FIGURE 6.32. *Comparisons of ax to weaponry frequencies from test pit contexts.*

longer, and exhibit greater workmanship (figure 6.24). Smaller, shorter, unifacial points have a more pronounced, wider or more elongated triangular shape above the base; base sizes tend to be the same size irrespective of point length. Large bases with short point lengths often represent resharpened points; in other cases, short points have more proportionate bases and were probably small arrow points to begin with. Obsidian points include both elongate and shorter side-notched forms observed in chert/chalcedony examples. The differences in point lengths, triangular proportions, and base sizes likely reflect that fact that side-notched flake points were commonly made and refurbished by a variety of hunters and warriors at Mayapán. While general similarities were important, the details of length, proportion, and base shape were not tightly standardized. Projectile point assemblages from individual fully excavated structures show considerable variety, and we infer that shape and size do not closely reflect systematic stylistic choices made by family groups. For example, we found concave, round, and square base points at a single residence, Y-45.

Despite prior efforts to seriate some of these variations in Postclassic Maya projectile forms (Shafer and Hester 1988:112; Simmons 1995), the co-occurrence and overlap in technology, context, and raw material of tiny triangular projectile points and more elongated examples at Mayapán and the hinterland site of Laguna de On suggest they were contemporary (Masson 2000; Masson and Peraza Lope 2010:90). As Mayapán was abandoned during the mid-fifteenth century AD, these points cannot be assigned to an exclusively Terminal Postclassic or Colonial Period date.

Projectile points were used in hunting and warfare, and they provide a good indication of the importance of the latter when combined with other archaeological and iconographic evidence for conflict and the importance of war and sacrifice. The evidence for white-tailed deer husbandry practices at Mayapán suggests that fewer projectiles were needed for deer hunting (Masson and Peraza Lope 2008). Other staples include turkey (also home-raised) and iguana, neither of which needed to be hunted with projectiles. We do not deny, however, that Mayapán's residents hunted; some portion of the white-tailed deer population is of a more advanced age and was likely hunted; snares were also key hunting devices.

Warfare would have been essential to the commercial interests of the Mayapán state, as for other Postclassic Maya centers (Carmack 1981a; Blake 1985:24). War captives became slaves, and some slaves were sold commercially (Scholes and Roys 1938; Roys 1972:34–45; Sabloff 2007:24). Although we have yet to identify slave dwellings archaeologically, or distinguish them from other low-status residences, the slave industry provided a motive for martial activities, and this research question looms significantly in the background of any consideration of warfare at Mayapán.

ANIMAL INDUSTRIES: MAYAPÁN FAUNA

Hunters, or *ah ceh* (he of the deer), during the Contact Period employed pit capture, snares (spring pole), and projectiles to obtain deer, armadillo, peccary, and other animals (Carr 1996). Another name for hunters was *tok bate*, or "flint warrior" (Von Nagy 1997:58). The use of dog, deer, and peccary goes back to the Formative Period at early sites such as Cerros or Colha (Carr 1996:254; Shaw 1999), but their signifance varies greatly at Maya sites in different locations and time periods (Masson 1999a, 2004). For example, deer were rare at Cozumel Island, where fish and turtles were more important (Hamblin 1984). Deer products, including antler and bone (and presumably perishable hides), were traded to coastal sites like Cozumel and Isla Cerritos (Carr 1996:255, table 15.1).

Animals were used in ritual as well as for food (Pohl 1981, 1985a, 1985b, 1990; Moholy-Nagy 2008; Masson and Peraza Lope 2013). As scenes in the Madrid Codex (pages 40, 41) show, deer were ritually hunted and sacrificed in a variety of ways that were also employed for humans. Spear-throwers, spears, heart extraction, disembowelment, beheading (perhaps after death) were used, and deer head offerings were sometimes displayed on platforms (Von Nagy 1997:50). The use of deer heads for offerings continued into the Contact Period along with bread and cacao at the town of Hocabá (Scholes 1938:139; Von Nagy 1997:52).

Harry E. D. Pollock and Clayton E. Ray (1957) were the first to study animal use at Mayapán, concentrating mainly on monumental center contexts and lots with large samples. Their findings were similar to our own, in that the major mammals included white-tailed and brocket deer, dog, and two types of peccary (1957:638). According to these authors, turkey, iguana, rabbit, catfish, and other kinds of marine fish are also common. White-tailed deer were the most important animal resource and dog were used primarily in ceremonies of the site center (1957:653). Exotic animal bones were found in the site center in low numbers (puma and jaguar foot bones, a spider monkey bone, a manatee rib, tapir teeth) that suggest they were imported as isolated elements (1957:653). Pollock and Ray observe that most of the fish were marine, lending support to Landa's (1941:40) claim that fish trade was important for inland sites. Tozzer (1941:notes 993–1147) provides lengthy notes regarding a wide range of plant and animal species used in Yucatán.

Birds identified by Pollock and Ray (1957) include wild turkey (*Meleagris ocellata*), heron, hawk, parakeet, motmot, chachalaca, great curassow, and pigeon or dove (Columbidae). Identified turtles include primarily aquatic terrapin (*Pseudemys scripta*), box turtle, *Geomyda areolata*, mud turtle (Kinosternidae), and *Dermatemys mawii* (Pollock and Ray 1957:648). They found a skeleton of a toad with hallucinogenic properties that was regularly exploited by Mesoamerican peoples, *Bufo marinus*. Most fish were marine except for a Cichlid (mojarra) that could have survived in freshwater cenotes. Catfish included the saltwater variety, and *Rhamdia guatemalensis* (a common cenote catfish) is absent (Pollock and Ray 1957:650). Other identified marine fish include sergeant fish, snook, grouper, mullet, sheepshead, and spadefish, as well as sharks (tiger and great white) and rays.

Faunal analysis from the INAH and PEMY projects has been comprehensive (Masson and Peraza Lope 2008, 2013); we are currently finishing the analysis of the 2008 and 2009 seasons that include fully excavated contexts. Animals were commodified and manipulated for different social and functional occasions, much like other material goods. Some animal products represented exotic, valuable trade items. Other more common animals were imported or obtained from nearby forests or *aguadas* (ponds), and supplemented daily staples. Animals, including staple faunas, were also valued for ritual sacrifice and consumption.

The highlights of our faunal research can be summarized as follows. An analysis of 97,416 bones has been published for the monumental center and outlying settlement zone (Masson and Peraza Lope 2008:tables 1–3). White-tailed deer comprised 23 percent of the sample (an additional 26 percent is represented by deer-sized large mammal long bone fragments that are likely to be deer), and this taxon was clearly the dominant meat source for the city. Wild turkey, probably raised in captivity, forms 12.9 percent of the sample. An additional 6.6 percent of the faunal remains consist of large bird long bone fragments that are likely to be turkey. Iguana forms 10.2 percent of the sample and dog represents 4.4 percent. Less frequent, but regularly recovered taxa include brocket deer (2.6 percent) and peccary (1 percent). The proportions described above are for the monumental center, but deer retained its status as the major meat source in the residential zone, followed in importance by iguana, turkey, and dog. Fish, primarily marine, formed 1.2 percent of the samples in the monumental center and 3.6 percent of the settlement zone samples (Masson and Peraza Lope 2008:table 3).

White-tailed deer remains are ubiquitous across Mayapán, and we have argued that at least one-third of the deer consumed at the city were raised through animal husbandry in houselots, based on the fact that as many as 42 percent of the long bones of these animals are adult-sized but exhibit unfused (late-fusing) epiphyses. This high proportion of young animals in their prime is an expectation of the processes of domestication—or alternatively, careful wildlife management or animal husbandry. This demographic profile for Mayapán's white-tailed deer matches that of dog, a known domesticate, and contrasts with patterns for peccary and brocket deer (Masson and Peraza Lope 2008:177). Dog remains are most often those of full-sized subadults while it is rare to find unfused long bones of peccary or brocket deer. Measurements of white-tailed deer long bone ends by Karime F. Gazdik (2009) confirm that the size of large subadult deer (with unfused epiphyses) matches that of adult animals at Mayapán, and this age profile indicates that these animals were generally butchered upon reaching full size but before bone fusion was complete. Such animals were in the prime of life and should not represent nearly half of a sample hunted in the wild (Masson and Peraza Lope 2008). Game was an important resource for the city, and Contact-era accounts suggest that game exports from the Mayapán region were essential for obtaining fish and salt from coastal sites (Landa 1941:40). The fact that white-tailed deer, turkey, and dog formed as much as 73 percent of the site's protein sources (counting long bone fragments only provisionally identified to species)—49 percent of which may have been white-tailed deer and 20 percent of which may have been turkey—points to a commitment at the city to ensuring dietary stability through engaging in husbandry of white-tailed deer and oscellated turkeys. Opportunistic hunting and the capture of iguana and turtles supplemented the diet, as did the trade for marine fish—but these contributions were minor by comparison. Enclosed pens are frequently found in the city's houselots, and these probably sheltered animals (chapter 5). The city's *albarrada* houselots themselves represent enclosures that would have contained turkeys, dogs, and tethered deer (e.g., Madrid Codex:42c; Villacorta C. and Villacorta 1976).

AGRICULTURE AND PROPERTY

Mayapán is one of several northern Maya sites that are distinguished by residential boundary walls and a large circumferential wall around the densest portion of the settlement zone (chapter 5). Residential property was not strictly delineated by walled houselot enclosures (A. Smith 1962). As we observe in chapter 5, boundary walls seem to reflect a concern for privacy and containment as a consequence of urban life. Lot sizes do not correlate well with factors of wealth, status, or location. Cycles of family growth best account for the division of residential space within the city. In outer Mayapán, where vacant land was ample, many houselots tightly circumscribed their dwellings with boundary walls, presumably for the safekeeping of domestic resources.

Access to agricultural lands was institutionalized, yet it was also subject to negotiation (Freidel and Sabloff 1984). Residents would have cultivated gardens within or near their houses. Other orchards or infields may have existed at Mayapán, as indicated by tracts of enclosed nonresidential fields or nonenclosed vacant spaces. Outfield cultivation would have also been important. The system would have been more complex than a simple infield-outfield model due to options for small-plot agriculture closer to home (Killion 1992a:figure 6.3, Alexander 1999a:83–84). Household gardens and outlying milpas are the primary cultivated spaces for residents of modern Telchaquillo (1 kilometer north of Mayapán). This mixed strategy has great time depth in the region (Alexander 1999a:87).

How much land could have been cultivated within the city wall? Figures 6.33 and 6.34 illustrate the amount of cultivable space in mapped milpas of the PEMY project. All nonresidential space was calculated by including the area of enclosed fields (that lacked houses), open spaces, and other nonresidential areas per milpa. Milpas with more than 50 percent nonresidential space were predominantly located near or outside the city wall. Only two mid-city milpas exhibited this pattern. Of twenty-one milpas consisting of a majority of nonresidential space, all but one had more than 60 percent nonresidential space, and fourteen of these had more than 80 percent nonresidential space. For those located specifically within the city wall, twelve milpas located toward the outer edges of the settlement and one mid-city milpa had more than 60 percent nonresidential space. Seven other milpas outside the wall were at least 60 percent vacant. Only four milpas near the city wall had less than 50 percent nonresidential space. Eight milpas had less than 30 percent nonresidential space. Downtown residents of Mayapán did not live next to ample infield or orchard space. Land available for gardening varied according to settlement density, which was denser near the site center. Motivations for living in downtown Mayapán seem to have trumped the advantages of living next to generous tracts of open land, at least for a significant portion of the urban population. During the Contact Period, Maya communities of Yucatán, including farmers, also generally preferred town life (Restall 2001). Walking to moderately distant agrarian plots is a tradition that continues today.

To what degree were local lands farmed to supply the city? We suppose that the periphery of Mayapán was a hub of agrarian activity, although more research is needed beyond the city wall. Land was ample within at least 1 kilometer of the wall, according to surveys performed thus far. Russell's (2008a, 2008b) survey reveals an extensive landscape that was partly inhabited and partly cultivated. Within 500 meters of the wall, Russell has documented fields, pens, possible granaries or apiaries, and low densities of modest dwellings, many of which were contemporary with Mayapán. Artifact densities are low in this area and it is difficult to know whether agriculturalists living and working outside of the wall were permanent or temporary occupants. Sayil's dispersed rural houses may have been occupied seasonally, according to Kelli N. Carmean, Nicholas P. Dunning, and Jeff Karl Kowalski (2004:440), as they had no water supply features. At Mayapán, however, cenotes exist both within and outside the city wall and were shared by families who would have had to walk daily to fill vessels to supply their homes. Most houses are within 250 meters of a water source (Russell 2008a). Unlike the Puuc area, chultuns are rare at Mayapán. More water sources exist at the city than are currently documented (chapter 5).

Joseph Hester (1952) thought that agricultural soil was poor around Telchaquillo and explored aguadas within 15 kilometers of that vicinity. His assumption about the low productivity of land within and adjacent to Mayapán was overstated. Many modern milpas successfully feed families from this terrain, and we have observed corn growing from pockets of soil even where bedrock outcrops on the surface. Hester (1952:270) found no evidence that aguadas were used for dry-season agriculture, and this is not surprising, as population pressure seems to have been low outside of Mayapán's urban zone. More extensive slash and burn methods were probably viable closer to the city throughout its occupational history. Soils outside of downtown Mayapán are poor in the sense that they tend to be shallow, hold little water, and have some

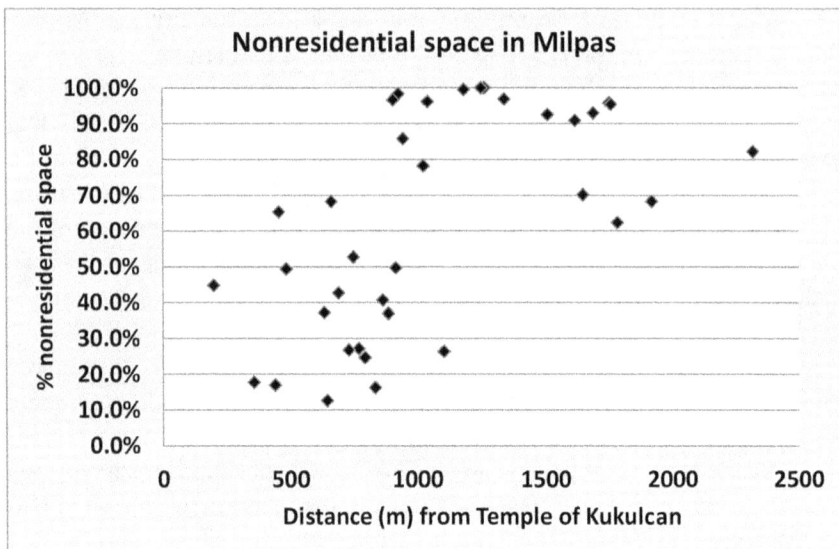

FIGURE 6.33. *Amount of nonresidential space in milpas plotted against distance from the Temple of Kukulcan.*

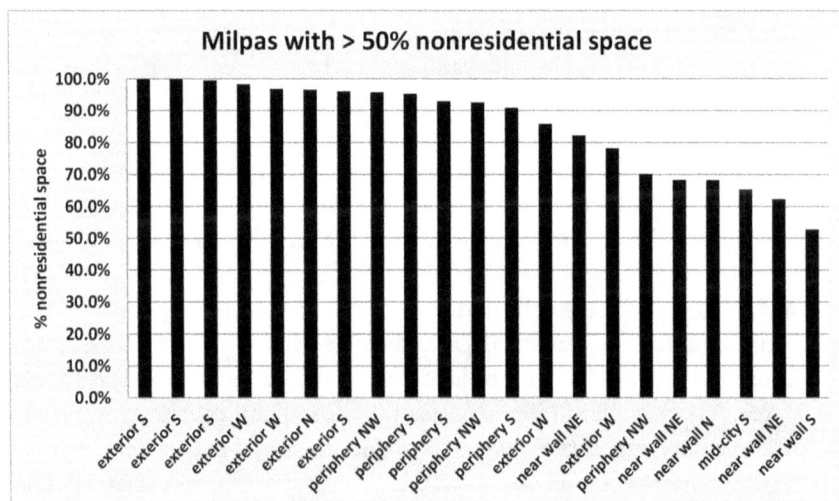

FIGURE 6.34. *Milpas with greater than 50 percent nonresidential space tend to be located near the wall (inside it and within 200 meters), exterior to the wall (within 200 meters), or in the peripheral areas farther from the wall. Only one mid-city location in our sample is in this group (Milpa 3, a relatively open space with two cenotes).*

mineral deficiencies (Beach 1998), whereas soil in the more densely inhabited areas of the city has been enhanced by high charcoal and other organic contributions by the ancient inhabitants. The Mayapán dark earth midden is an anthropogenic horizon (Brown 1999). Figure 6.35 illustrates Russell, who is 6 feet 4 1/2 inches tall, in a field of tall corn in downtown Mayapán (Milpa 1) in August 2009; the Mayapán dark earth is a meter or more deep in this part of the city. Gardens within the city's houselots would have supplemented more distant milpa plots. The potential existed in parts of Mayapán for rich agricultural harvests. All modern farmers do not have the luxury of cultivating in Mayapán's dark earth middens that concentrate in the central part of the city. Much of the site and its environs have shallow kancab soils that are adequate in normal years for productive milpas.

During droughts, Mayapán's environment would have been especially harsh. Evidence suggests that such perils struck regularly from the time of the city's rise to power by AD 1200 to its fall in the mid-fifteenth century and beyond (chapter 8). Pollen records suggest that vegetation was dominated by a combination of maize and disturbance taxa (Leyden 2002:96). The collapse of the city's government and its subsequent abandonment may be linked to a constellation of severe climatic events that resulted in drought and colder conditions. Richardson B. Gill and Jerome P. Keating (2002:136–37) outline correlating events that include volcanic eruptions, droughts, and the onset of the Little Ice Age that began around AD 1450. They note that droughts and cold are mentioned in the books of the Chilam Balam of Mani and Chumayel— "the fields, having been impoverished shall be searched for food and water which will not be found anywhere . . . the people . . . were chilled"—during K'atun 8 Ahau, possibly corresponding to the K'atun 8 interval when Mayapán fell (AD 1441–1461). A parallel event includes the famine of 1 Rabbit in central Mexico in AD 1454, which prompted starving people to sell themselves into slavery. In 2009 we witnessed the effects of a one-year drought. Corn failed to grow and cattle were dying regularly of starvation. The Chilam Balam of Maní describes the risks vividly: "Three times it has been necessary to make bread with the cup root because of the famine" (Craine and Reindorp 1979:84–85).

TRANSPORTATION OF FOOD

Regional exchange within Mesoamerican states has been traditionally viewed as limited by the constraints of transporting food with human porters, who must be fed. Michael H. Logan and William T. Sanders (1976:46) argue that large cities like Tenochtitlan could not transport food effectively beyond

Figure 6.35. *Bradley Russell (6 feet 4 1/2 inches tall) stands in a farmer's cornfield in Milpa 1, just west of the monumental center (photo taken in August 2009). Mayapán soils are sufficiently productive for corn agriculture today, as in the past.*

a maximum distance of 150 kilometers—smaller urban places would have a range of up to 50 kilometers. Robert D. Drennan, Philip T. Fitzgibbons, and Heinz Dehn (1990:179) and Sanders and Santley (1983:246–49) suggest 150–275 kilometers as the maximum distance for urban food supplies. Both sets of scholars favor the model that prestige goods (and not food) were traded over greater distances.

Theoretical limitations on food exchange are pertinent to the question of drought relief. Although surplus food is often available and within reach of settlements undergoing famine, failures of communication, logistics, or politics can intervene in successful transfers (Pounds 1973:433; Gill 2000:76; Davis 2001). Plainly stated: for the right price, food is for sale even in times of shortages. Droughts do not affect all areas evenly, including the Maya lowlands, which has a mosaic of soils and hydrology (Dunning, Beach, and Luzadder-Beach n.d.). Freidel and Shaw (2000) argue that storage limitations on maize in the Maya area presented a major obstacle, and they propose that Maya states resolved this problem with a currency system. More easily stored cacao bean and shell monies could be exchanged for surplus grain in times of hardship, and arguably, to supply cities like Mayapán on a regular basis. Freidel and Shaw (2000) and Freidel and F. Kent Reilly III (2010) analyze the conspicuous symbolism that links heads of Maya states with the maize deity and cacao. They argue that these associations were an integral component of assigning value to these items in the commercial realm. Gill (2000:79) takes a more pessimistic view for the Classic Period: "the ability to redistribute foodstuffs to famine stricken areas in the Lowlands . . . was most likely non-existent." We would agree that there is little evidence for chiefly accumulation and direct redistribution of foodstuffs and argue instead that food would have at times been a lucrative trade good. Given the ongoing exchange of foodstuffs during times not plagued by droughts in northern Yucatán during the Postclassic (e.g., Landa 1941:40), we think it likely that opportunities for profit during food shortages would have fostered supply networks during all but the most severe episodes. For those who could afford it, the stores were open. A monolithic view of food exchange in the context of shortfalls is not helpful, as the scope of dire impacts fluctuated in space and time. Clearly the mid-fifteenth-century suffering, which coincides with the fall of Mayapán, proposed challenges that could not be met by political will or institutions of exchange. Prior to the city's collapse, it is reasonable to consider that food flowed regularly across the *cahob* of the northern peninsula. Gill (2000:77) points out the need for military enforcement and security in desperate times. The militaristic nature of the Mayapán state may have been geared in part toward such challenges.

The area of northern Quintana Roo is more humid and lush than the arid environs of Mayapán. For example, around Punta Laguna, situated in a rich agrarian zone between Valladolid and Cancun, annual rainfall averages 1,519 millimeters (Curtis, Hodell, and Brenner 1996:37) compared to less than half that amount (about 777 millimeters per year) around Mérida (and Mayapán). This lush area was one potential breadbasket for drier northwest Yucatán, including Mayapán, although it was probably not the only one. Ancient settlements around Valladolid and Tizimin lie near the Quintana Roo/Yucatán state borders and are 150 kilometers from Mayapán, within the arbitrary distance constraint imposed by Logan and Sanders (1976) for the transportation of maize in supply of major urban places.

It is also important to remember the advantages of coastal transportation networks that thrived during the Postclassic Period (Sabloff and Rathje 1975). The significant differences in moisture and vegetation between Mayapán's heartland in northwest Yucatán and the eastern Caribbean area (now the state of Quintana Roo) merit more concerted scholarly attention. Crops from the eastern breadbasket could have been traded through coastal sites such as Tulum, Cozumel, and other localities and could have been brought by canoe to ports closer to the northwest coast. The historical port town of Progreso, Yucatán, is located within 70 kilometers of Mayapán, well within the most conservative transport ranges proposed for human porters. This part of the north coast is dotted with dozens of other settlements within 100–150 kilometers of Mayapán that could have serviced the city in the way that Isla Cerritos may have functioned for Chichén Itzá (Andrews et al. 1988). Modern towns have obliterated Pre-Columbian port remains along the north coast, some of which were occupied during the Postclassic Period (A. Andrews 2008:figure 1).

Overland transport networks in the Yucatán would have been important for transporting all manner of goods, including food, when environmental hazards were confined to specific locations. Hurricanes provide an example of localized effects. The devastation of Cancun (Hurricane Wilma in 2008) or small towns near Mérida (Hurricane Isidore in 2002) has been recently witnessed; when one of these areas was hit, the other scarcely noticed the effects.

AGRICULTURAL FOOD PROCESSING

Agricultural processing tools such as manos and metates are regularly found in low numbers at Mayapán houselots. Metates are made from very large limestone boulders and were often reused in architecture. House Q-40a had five manos that may have been used for grinding corn or for stucco production. We favor the latter function, as one mano was found in a grave at this house that was covered with fine plaster. Manos were found at other houses too: four were recovered at H-11, one at L-28, and fifteen at elite House Y-45. Hall H-15 had seven manos. All structures except X-43 had groundstone; occupants of this house may not have processed their own food. The abundance of manos from elite House Y-45, which had an associated kitchen structure, may be related to the hosting of large feasts in the frontal gallery; high numbers of polychrome serving vessels at this house also imply such activities.

HEALTH OF MAYAPÁN'S POPULATION

Mayapán's population seems to have had ample access to game and fowl. Animal bones are ubiquitous at domestic and public contexts, and we have argued that deer and turkey were raised in abundance at the city's houselots. Although raising deer may have been uncommon at other contemporary Postclassic sites, the availability of rich animal proteins seems to link lowland Maya towns across the peninsula, with variations in emphasis on fishing and hunting strategies (Hamblin 1984; Coyston, White, and Schwarcz 1999; Masson 2004). In comparison to southern sites of the Terminal Classic, Mayapán and its contemporaries enjoyed an abundance of meat, fowl, and fish. The paucity of animal bone at Terminal Classic sites in northern Belize suggests severe levels of game depletion in some portions of the Maya lowlands (Masson 2004).

The proportion of maize and other crops in the diet are more difficult to assess, although grinding stones are common. Analysis of stable carbon and nitrogen isotopes by Lori Wright (2007:5) suggests that, like other Maya sites, maize was a staple in the Mayapán diet. The carbon isotope results indicate slightly lower levels than are observed at most southern Classic Period sites, perhaps because marginally lower levels of maize were consumed at Mayapán. The importance of terrestrial proteins is affirmed by nitrogen isotope data that is similar to some earlier cities (Wright 2007:5). Disease may have plagued the city, as infant and child graves are regularly found, although it is hard to know whether this is due to the excellent preservation of human bone at the site. Child mortality is generally high in ancient societies. Mass graves that might be attributed to epidemics have not been found, but those related to warfare and violence have been revealed in the site center and at the Itzmal Ch'en group (Adams 1953; Peraza Lope et al. 2006; chapter 3). The greatest threat to Mayapán's population was likely warfare, as we have previously discussed.

According to Serafin (personal communication, 2010), a human osteologist, childhood stress was a considerable problem for Mayapán's residents, as indicated by linear enamel hypoplasia and porotic hyperostosis. Caries were relatively low. Serafin (2009) suggests that crowded urban living conditions and proximity to animals (deer, turkeys, dogs) resulted in significant infectious disease—one case of treponemal disease has been identified along with other evidence for systemic infections. Rampant disease cycles are described in the Chilam Balam chronicles in the years prior to and following Spanish contact, as are drought cycles that can lead to famine and epidemic diseases. A pestilence in K'atun 4 Ahau (AD 1480–1485) may have been experienced by lingering occupants of Mayapán, according to Tozzer (1941:note 205). We do not currently have accurate demographic data from Mayapán. Many skeletons recovered from the site center are disarticulated and probably represent the remains of sacrificed war captives (Serafin and Peraza Lope 2007; Serafin 2010). A small sample of domestic burials from the settlement zone has been recovered that includes infants and adults. Very few individuals of elderly (more than fifty years old) status have been found, although this is normal for a premodern agrarian population.

WEALTH AND STATUS AT MAYAPÁN

Two types of data are particularly amenable to tracking wealth and status variation archaeologically: architectural size and elaboration and the quantification of valuable local and nonlocal items. Hirth's (1998) distributional approach compares fancy and imported artifact frequencies across social status contexts to evaluate the importance of marketplace exchange for making valuables available in relatively equitable quantities to elites and commoners. This approach has proven valid in at least one ethnohistorically documented market society in the Aztec towns of Morelos, Mexico (M. Smith 1999), and much equitability is reported for the central Mexico Epiclassic center of Xochicalco (Hirth 1993b, 1998; Cyphers and Hirth 2000). At Mayapán, four types of contexts have been tested by our project that are relevant for these comparisons: surplus craft production houselots, other houselots not engaged in significant craft production, elite houses, and public buildings (the Itzmal Ch'en colonnaded hall and temple). The majority of our contexts are commoner dwellings, and prior analysis has determined that surplus craft production households were wealthier than other commoners. Here we compare the distribution of imported goods, including obsidian, marine shell, greenstone axes, and other greenstone ornaments. As previously discussed, the distribution of imported and fancy locally made goods is widespread among commoner houselot contexts (Hare and Masson 2010).

Obsidian consumption has already been addressed in this chapter and will only be summarized here. To reiterate our findings, 37 percent of the test pit contexts had 1–31 obsidian blades per chert tool, and these intervals were made up of 71–89 percent non-crafting commoner houselots. Including used flakes in the calculation reveals that 30 percent of the test pits had 1–8 obsidian blades per chert tool, and these contexts included 56–100 percent non-crafting commoner houselots (table 6.21). The fact that craft producers tended to have more obsidian than non-crafting houselots is indicated by the fact that seven of twelve contexts, with 9–15 pieces of obsidian per square meter, were non-crafting houselots (two were crafting houselots), whereas the 17–25 piece-per-square-meter interval includes only one non-crafting houselot, two crafting houselots, and one elite context. Elite House Y-45a had obsidian/chert tool ratios that were on par with commoner House L-28 (table 6.22). Other specific details add to this argument of equitability in access to obsidian. Three non-crafting houses (H-20, F-13, and P-117) had 12–15 pieces per square meter of obsidian (or 40–67 pieces per cubic meter)—more than elite House R-103/104 (12 pieces per square meter, 33 pieces per cubic meter) and equivalent to or more than elite House Q-41b (16 pieces per square meter, 29 pieces per cubic meter). Commoner House Z-43 had 22 pieces per square meter (54 pieces per cubic meter), more than elite House S-131/132 (17 pieces per square meter, 21 pieces per cubic meter). Non-obsidian crafting Houses P-115 and Z-47 also had much obsidian (11.7 and 12.8 pieces per square meter and 15 and 22 pieces per cubic meter, respectively). These results are also confirmed by fully excavated contexts (table 6.19). Non-crafting House H-11 had 4.1 pieces per square meter (15 per cubic meter), more than elite House Y-45a (0.7 pieces per square meter, 1.6 pieces per cubic meter). Two other non-crafting houses (X-43 and L-28) had less obsidian than other dwellings (0.1 and 0.3 per square meter and 0.8 and 1.8 per cubic meter, respectively), which reveals the important fact that commoners differed in terms of their wealth. Overall, our patterns reveal that some commoners had access to obsidian in levels equivalent to those of elites and meet expectations of the distributional model for obsidian marketplace accessibility.

Copper Bell Distribution

Bells in consumer contexts are found in both elite and non-elite residences and meet expectations of a marketplace distribution (Paris 2008:60, table 7). One commoner context with three bells is House X-43, an isolated and otherwise relatively impoverished residence near the southeast portion of the city wall. Other humble houses excavated by the Carnegie project similarly yielded bells or other metal objects (Paris 2008:table 7). One burial in House Q-39 (in downtown Mayapán, just west of the monumental center) had a large quantity of bells (N = 36), including one of the city's few bell effigies in the form of monkey head (figure 5.33). This house is located next to one of the site's largest elite residences (group Q-41), and its residents may have had special benefits or a social affiliation with this group. Bells are concentrated in at least one other mortuary context from the Carnegie investigations (J. Thompson 1954:figure 2h).

The frequency of copper bell recovery from general (non-mortuary) excavations reveals few differences in wealth or accessibility across social status lines, as illustrated in figure 6.3. Table 6.32 indicates the context types where bells were recovered from either test pits or fully excavated structures. Regardless of sampling methods, only one or two bells were found from all of these structure or midden contexts. Elite House Y-45a had two bells, as did commoner Houses X-43 and P-117 and Temple H-17. Four other ordinary (non-crafting) houses (P-150, P-71a, P-176, and R-173) each had one bell, as did commoner craft producers at I-55, Q-176, and Q-40.

Greenstone Distribution

Greenstone celts also represent valuable imported items (figure 6.23), and we have already discussed the probability that these objects were part of many ordinary household toolkits. A total of 49 greenstone items have been recovered from surface collections (not systematic, N = 13), test pits (N = 4), horizontal excavations (N = 20), and INAH project work in the site's monumental center (N = 12). The PEMY project greenstone objects are listed by context in table 6.24. These durable artifacts occur in low frequencies and were highly curated. Thus, chances are low of recovering them from one or two test pits at a single locality. Ad hoc surface collections indicate the regular presence of these artifacts at commoner houses (L-23, Y-106, Q-179, R-175b, M-59a, Q-176, Q-185, Q-195, and Q-181) and three elite houses in our survey area (two at Q-42, one at Y-45a). Despite the extensive amount of work done at the monumental center, frequencies at that vicinity are not greater than in domestic contexts outside of this zone. This distribution suggests that greenstone axes were available to commoners in the city's marketplace. They are found in craft-production houselots and at more generalized commoner domestic localities. Only one to two of these objects was found at any single context, irrespective of the amount of area excavated.

TABLE 6.32 Copper objects recovered in PEMY contexts.

Unit type	Structure, context type	Copper bell	Copper fragment, folded copper	Ring, tweezers
Horizontal excavation	H-17 temple	2	–	–
Horizontal excavation	H-15 hall	–	1	–
Horizontal excavation	I-55 surplus craft production house	1	–	–
Horizontal excavation	Q-176 surplus craft production house	1	–	–
Horizontal excavation	Q-40 surplus craft production house, next to elite palace	1	–	–
Horizontal excavation	Q-39 surplus craft production house, next to elite palace	26	8	2
Horizontal excavation	X-43 commoner house	2	–	–
Horizontal excavation	Y-45 elite house	2	–	–
Horizontal excavation	L-28 commoner house	–	–	–
Test pit	P-150 commoner house	1	–	–
Test pit	P-71a commoner house	1	–	–
Test pit	P-176 commoner house	1	–	–
Surface collection	R-173 commoner house	1	–	–
Test pit	P-117 commoner house	2	–	–

Marine Shell Ornament Distribution

Shell distributions are considered at length in a previous section of this chapter. Here we consider specifically the relative quantity of marine shell ornaments that were most likely to have been used as currencies: Olive group ornaments, *Strombus* and *Spondylus* pendants or beads, and other bivalve-shaped pendants. Tables 6.33, 6.34, and 6.35 indicate the low frequencies of these items for surface collections, test pits, and fully excavated structures. All but one of twenty-three surface collections with one to three of these items are commoner dwellings. Shell workshops similarly had from one to three such objects (table 6.33), indicating a low incidence of errors or a focus on making non-currency products. In sixteen test pits with these ornaments (all but one are commoner houses), most contexts had from one to three such objects, including shell workshops. Two exceptions in the test pit sample have from four to six items (table 6.34). Higher quantities of shell ornaments per square

TABLE 6.33 Selected finished shell objects from PEMY surface collection units.

Structure	Olive/ Prunum tinkler	Strombus bead	Strombus pendant/ ornament	Spondylus pendant	Other bivalve pendant	Total
EE-26b house	1	–	–	–	–	1
Y-51 house	1	–	–	–	–	1
Y-111 house	2	–	–	–	–	2
Q-189 house	–	1	–	–	–	1
Y-107 house	–	1	–	–	–	1
Z-101 house	–	1	–	–	–	1
M-60a house	–	–	2	–	–	2
R-170a house	–	–	1	–	–	1
R-171 house	–	–	–	1	–	1
R-111 house	–	–	–	1	–	1
R-168b house	1	–	2	–	–	3
Q-42 elite house	1	–	–	–	–	1
R-177 craft specialist (shell)	1	–	–	–	–	1
P-24 craft specialist	2	–	–	–	–	2
Q-196 craft specialist	2	–	–	–	–	2
Q-183 craft specialist (shell)	3	–	–	–	–	3
R-110 craft specialist (shell)	1	1	–	–	–	2
S-10 craft specialist (shell)	2	1	–	–	–	3
Z-120 craft specialist (shell)	–	–	1	–	–	1
Q-46 craft specialist (shell)	–	–	1	–	–	1
Z-119 craft specialist (shell)	1	–	2	–	–	3
Q-37 craft specialist	–	–	–	1	–	1
Q-176 craft specialist (shell)	3	2	2	2	1	10

meter and per cubic meter were recovered in fully excavated shell workshop contexts Q-176, Q-39, and I-55a and at Q-40a, where some shell working may also have occurred (table 6.35). It is noteworthy that two of three ordinary commoner houses (L-28 and H-11) had these shell objects in similar quantities to elite House Y-45a, Temple H-17, and Hall H-15. Marine shell ornaments and currencies in particular were nonlocal items of value. They were widely available to commoners at the site, although they are not highly ubiquitous. These two characteristics meet the expectations for monetary units.

THE ECONOMIC FOUNDATIONS OF MAYAPÁN

The economy of the political capital of Mayapán was founded on a complex set of of strategies that fostered interdependence among households within the city and region and with distant trading partners. Evidence that surplus craft production was an important part-time occupation for city households supports a model of an urban place in which residents were bound together in a fabric of local production and consumption.

The most marked finding in our comparisons is the distinction between surplus crafting houselots and those that engaged in other activities. Crafting localities differed among themselves in the types and quantity of debris, and nearly half of these contexts produced more than one type of commodity. Altogether, twenty-nine surplus production localities were found in our settlement zone study areas; four others have been documented by other investigations (table 6.3). All but one was within a houselot, and the exception (I-57) was a self-standing building contained within its own albarrada wall, between two nearby houselots. Crafting houses were of commoner status, with the exception of elite House Z-39, and perhaps House Q-39, a wealthy house next to elite group Q-41. House Q-40a was the only house engaged in spatially attached production, as suggested by its location within the albarrada wall of elite group Q-41 and the fact that its burials had modest, craft-related grave goods (figure 5.32). Fourteen of the twenty-nine workshops that we identified produced a single item: four focused on shell (Q-183, R-177, Z-43, and Z-47), eight on obsidian (R-137, R-173, R-174, R-155, J-130, P-115, P-24, and Q-196), and two on chalcedony/chert tools (I-57 and Q-37). The remaining fifteen produced multiple materials (table 6.3). Two localities made chert and shell objects (S-12 and Z-119), four worked obsidian, chert, and shell (P-114, Z-39, Z-119, and S-10), five worked obsidian and shell (R-110, Q-303, P-28b, Q-46, and I-55), and one worked obsidian and chert (Q-188). More varied crafting industries were observed in Milpa 1 at Q-40a (pottery effigy censers,

TABLE 6.34 Selected finished shell objects from PEMY test pit samples.

Structure	Olive/ Prunum tinkler	Strombus bead	Strombus pendant/ ornament	Spondylus pendant	Total
Q-303 craft specialist (shell)	1	–	–	–	1
R-110b craft specialist (shell)	–	–	1	–	1
I-55a craft specialist (shell)	1	1	–	–	2
P-28 craft specialist (shell)	1	–	1	–	2
Q-176 craft specialist (shell)	1	2	1	–	4
F-13a house	1	–	–	–	1
S-80 house	1	–	–	–	1
P-117 house	3	3	–	–	6
P-150 house	–	1	–	–	1
Z-39 elite house	–	2	1	–	3
Z-43 house	–	1	–	–	1
P-71/O-28 house	–	–	1	–	1
R-155 craft specialist	–	–	–	1	1
P-115b craft specialist	–	–	–	1	1
S-10bc craft specialist	–	–	1	–	1
P-114 craft specialist	6	–	3	–	9

copper bells, and probably shell objects), Q-39 (chert, shell, copper bells, and possibly clay figurines), and Q-176 (obsidian, shell, pottery vessels, and clay figurines). These localities together represent ten locations where chert tools were made, seventeen shell-working contexts, nineteen obsidian workshops, and two ceramic workshops. These workshops were identified using measures of outlier frequency status for the quantity of debris present by surface collection, test pit, and horizontal excavation results.

Most of the identified workshops were located not far from elite residential or public buildings, but evidence for attached patronage is minimal (figure 6.4). Thirteen are present in Milpa 1, just west of the monumental center, in an area that includes two of the seven largest elite residences of the city (figure 6.19). We identify this area as a crafts barrio (Masson, Peraza Lope, and Hare 2008; Hare and Masson 2012). Two other workshops are within 150 meters of the Itzmal Ch'en outlying ceremonial group. As elites did not live in this area, patronage, if it existed, would have been at a distance. Six workshops

TABLE 6.35 Selected finished shell objects from PEMY fully excavated structures. None were recovered from X-43.

Ornament	House L-28	House H-11	Elite House Y-45	House Q-176	House Q-40	House Q-39	House I-55a	Temple H-17	H-15 hall, grave
Bivalve pendant, ornament	–	3	–	1	2	3	4	–	–
Oliva, Prunum, Cypraea tinkler	1	2	3	11	5	5	11	6	3
Strombus bead	–	–	2	–	3	9	3	–	5
Spondylus bead	–	1	–	1	–	–	–	–	–
Bivalve bead	–	–	–	–	–	1	1	–	–
Spondylus pendant	1	–	–	–	2	1	–	–	–
Strombus, Busycon pendant, ornament	4	1	7	1	3	3	10	4	1
Strombus spatulate, spoon	–	–	1	–	–	–	1	–	–
Total shell objects	6	7	13	14	15	22	30	10	9
Total square meters	212.00	133.30	376.00	136.00	88.50	120.00	196.00	601.65	515.00
Objects per square meter	0.03	0.05	0.03	0.10	0.17	0.18	0.15	0.02	0.02
Total cubic meters	30.44	35.88	176.10	33.07	21.74	34.23	47.35	328.20	155.10
Objects per cubic meter	0.20	0.20	0.07	0.42	0.69	0.64	0.63	0.03	0.06

are found in Milpas 11 and 32, near the eastern and southeastern edges of the monumental center. Four of the seven largest elite dwellings at the city are in these milpas. Two workshops are located in Milpa 2, just south of the site center, where a large public group is present that formed the terminus of the site's central sacbe; elite House Z-39 is one of these two workshops. Exceptions to this pattern exist. Two workshops in Milpa 4 are not near any elite architecture, and three workshops in Milpa 15 do not appear spatially associated with the nearest public building, J-111, 250 meters away. Clifford T. Brown (1999:457–62) found an additional chert/chalcedony biface workshop at S-139, located 120 meters to the south of an elite dwelling (S-133), with which it exhibits no clear association.

In general, craft producers were concentrated in downtown Mayapán, as were the largest elite residences and most of the public architecture. This area of the city would have offered enhanced opportunities for commerce and affluence near the nucleus of political and religious activities. Other clustered craft activity may exist at Mayapán outside of our sample areas, perhaps near the concentration of elite houses in Square K, next to the probable market-place—but this is unconfirmed. Away from focal architecture, a pattern of outlying, isolated houses or sets of two houses engaged in surplus crafting is observed in the cityscape, as reflected by workshops identified in Milpas 4, 15, and perhaps 16 (Itzmal Ch'en area). These craftspersons may have provisioned the neighborhoods in which they were situated in addition to making goods destined for market exchange. It is unclear at this point whether proximity to elite houses and the monumental center in the downtown areas of Milpas 1, 2, 11, and 32 was fostered by some form of patronage or supervision, or more indirectly, by the concentration of affluent consumers in these zones. Hirth (1993b:141) argues that dispersed producers at Xochicalco produced for market exchange rather than neighborhood vending. Chert, obsidian, and shell products made at Mayapán's workshops are distributed widely and were also probably obtained in the city's marketplace. Simpler tools may have been made at home or were acquired from local markets in the residential zone or neighborhood vendors; more sophisticated items may have been obtained at the larger central market (e.g., Fry 2003; Masson and Rosenswig 2005). Many households probably made or modified some of their own projectile points and expedient lithic tools. Bifaces and flakes or flake cores for expedient use may have been obtained from workshops.

Overlap in shell, obsidian, and chert production occurs among the down-town and outlying workshops, although more obsidian working is concentrated downtown. Qualitative differences are observed among chalcedonies used at the outlying I-57 workshop compared to epicentral House Q-39, where flakes were of much finer material (Kohut et al. 2012). The location of a censer workshop within the albarrada of elite group Q-41 most clearly suggests attached specialization; this is the most specialized and artisanal type of production documented for Mayapán. These data suggest that crafting occurred for a variety of purposes, much of it to provision the city with its basic needs.

Crafting households were affluent compared to other commoner residents at the city, and this pattern contrasts with ethnographic models that propose that crafting was undertaken by the poorest households to buttress meager agricultural options (D. Arnold 1985:192–93). Jeanne Arnold (1995:91–95) identifies affluence among Chumash craft-workers, and this pattern is also observed at the Early Classic Maya city of Chunchucmil, Yucatán (Dahlin 2009:353; Hutson, Dahlin, and Mazeau 2012). Kin-based learning and residential patterns may also account for the growth and concentration of the downtown craft district at Mayapán, as has been proposed for other societies (D. Arnold 1989:181).

The practice of part-time specialization is attested to in a review of ethnohistorical sources (Clark and Houston 1998:38), and this is confirmed by our assessment of the scale of production at Mayapán houselots. The ubiquitous references in the Colonial Period to female roles in textile manufacture suggest to Clark and Houston (1998:38) that cloth production was as essential to daily subsistence as corn. Was this a consequence of amplified Colonial-era demands, as these authors wonder? The low frequency of spindle whorls at Mayapán suggests that women at this city were not as heavily burdened with spinning thread as were their contemporaries at other towns in the peninsula or central Mexico. Other textile industries, such as weaving or embroidery, were probably more important. The regular distribution of pointed bone tools may reflect these later stages of textile producton. Some earlier Maya cities of the southern lowlands engaged in significant thread spinning, as indicated by an abundance of spindle whorls (A. Chase and D. Chase 2004:119), and an emphasis on late-stage textile working may be a pattern specific to northwest Yucatán at sites like Mayapán and Dzibilichaltun.

Documenting occupational specialization in its varied combinations and scales at Mayapán's houselots is a cornerstone category of evidence supporting a model of an integrated and complex economy at this political capital. Craft production also reflects dependence on a regional exchange network of towns and polities connected to the city. The array of crafting activities provides a clear case of diversification in the economic activities of houselots. This dimension of heterogeneity in productive work contrasts with relative homogeneity in the consumption of valuables across social class lines. The scale of production and indicators of wealth vary in degree along a continuum among commoner houselots, as might be expected in any market economy and urban place (Hirth 1998). Production heterogeneity and relative consumption homogeneity meet two essential expectations of a well-developed market economy and match patterns documented for some earlier Mesoamerican political centers discussed at the beginning of this chapter (Masson and Freidel 2012). Despite a diverse set of thriving production industries, Mayapán was not an economic isolate. Producers depended heavily on outside sources—within Yucatán and beyond—for raw materials that were transformed into useful and valuable goods within the city walls. As consumers, residents of the city also fulfilled appetites for regular quantities of finished imported goods such as greenstone celts or Matillas Fine Orange pottery that originated in the distant corners of the Maya area. Mayapán's economy conforms well to general comparative patterns documented across the Postclassic Mesoamerican world system in the degree to which households depended on others, both locally and distantly, to provision themselves with the inventories that they needed or desired (Kepecs, Feinman, and Boucher 1994; Kepecs 2003; Smith and Berdan 2003a). Large quantities of cacao (along with cotton thread or mantles) and basic raw materials (lithic cores, shells) and other perishables (such as hardwoods, copal, and salt) were exchanged into the city from distant lands to supplement local supplies. The city's production economy does not fit simple models that have been proposed for ancient Maya states. Instead, the data exhibit diverse configurations that might be expected from an urban place that was occupied for over two hundred years. The city was neither autonomous nor a "consumer city" that depended largely on its hinterland (e.g., P. Rice 1987; Ball 1993).

The analysis of shell industries in this chapter proposes that certain suspended shell objects served as currencies along with beads, including *Spondylus* (and other bivalve) pendants and Olive group tinkler-type ornaments. Significant quantities of these potential monetary units were exchanged into the city, and they are not well represented compared to more idiosyncratic objects in the city's workshops. Future analyses of market economies at ancient Maya states will benefit from a deeper consideration of valuable items that served not only as adornments but also as currencies (Freidel, Reese-Taylor, and Mora-Marin 2002). Like other material classes at Mayapán, shell objects varied in quality along a continuum of value. Dichotomous classifications of prestige versus utilitarian goods are of limited utility for understanding complex systems of value and exchange (Lesure 1999; Masson and Freidel 2012, 2013).

The most pressing and unresolved question is the scale of food production

at Mayapán. Craft-producing houselots may not have been able to fully supply their own food. Martin Biskowski (2000:293, 302) considers the heavy
time investment required for maize preparation in Postclassic central Mexico.
Full-time tortilla vendors helped to solve this problem by eliminating the need
for redundant tasks at every household (Biskowski 2000:296); occupational
specialization also alleviates this burden. He suggests that urban residents
were supplied with food by agrarian houselots at the city margins through the
marketplace, petty vendors, or other mechanisms (Biskowski 2000:293, 302).
In general, this model for urban provisioning is a good fit for Mayapán, with
two qualifications: not all houselots in the peripheral zone (near or beyond
the city wall) were agrarian and a significant number of downtown houses
prepared food for themselves and probably for others. One house, Z-43, next
to a large public group (Z-50, southern sacbe terminus), had five metates clustered at the surface, surely more than a nuclear family required. Residents
of this house likely prepared food for feasts at nearby elite House Z-39 and
Hall Z-50, but the possibility that surplus tamales were also produced for sale
merits consideration. Houses such as L-28 and H-11 may have been engaged
primarily in agriculture or food production; H-11's occupants may have also
fulfilled custodial duties for Itzmal Ch'en. In contrast, commoner houses like
X-43, whose occupants may have resided temporarily at the city for the duration of their corvée service obligation, had no grinding stones and may have
been dependent on others for food.

The agrarian foundations of Mayapán are not well understood. Our sample
of fully investigated houses is weighted toward surplus craft producers, and
smaller test pit samples of dozens of other locations yield little direct evidence
for households devoted to farming or food processing. By default, houses of
agrarian specialists may be those that exhibit a more generalized domestic
assemblage without an emphasis on crafting or other occupations. Agricultural
tools may be infrequent at Mayapán houselots due to the possibility that male
farmers discarded broken implements in outfield locations (McAnany 1989;
Brown 1999:457), although we doubt that this explanation fully accounts for
the problem. Nonresidential walled fields within the city wall, along with scattered residences beyond the city wall that were near to extensive cultivable
tracts (Russell 2008a), suggest that agricultural production contributed in an
important way to Mayapán's diversified economy. Future work will hopefully
provide more detailed information on farming strategies and capacities.

Addressing the question of elite oversight of the city's economy is complex,
as the data reviewed in this chapter reveal an array of economic relationships
across class lines. In general, elite encouragement of production industries is

inferred. In some cases specialized goods were directly commissioned. In other cases, dispersed workshops seemed to operate more independently—a circumstance that was tolerated, perhaps strategically so, by governing authorities. Promoting, organizing, or administering local or central markets that allow residents to self-provision solves basic supply problems for city life and contributes to overall economic and political stability (Garraty 2010:19; Masson and Freidel 2012). Markets also attract the most skilled artisans and merchants, and they provide elites with greater opportunities for wealth (Blanton 1996:83). Instead of viewing the varied manifestations of craft production at Mayapán as a laissez-faire, chaotic system, we interpret these patterns as a complex and layered adaptation to the diverse needs and opportunities of the urban setting. Downtown Mayapán was a hub of activity that would have drawn diverse craft artisans, yet at the same time, residents in the settlement zone would have also benefited from neighborhood workshops. Occupants of outlying houselots had the option to diversify their income through craft production. Other forms of service were probably directly recruited to serve elite needs, such as preparing food, supplying ritual paraphernalia, stucco working, stone carving, or masonry.

The economic foundations of Mayapán thus reflect an intricate, complicated system that supported urban life. Governing elites encouraged diverse local production that provisioned the city with many of its essentials—a wise strategy for polity stability. Opportunities for wealth and exchange stimulated production and would have also contributed to the quantity and diversity of potential tribute payments. The landlocked city was not autonomous, and it depended significantly on the outside world within and beyond northwest Yucatán. Political officials would have been integral in maintaining—peaceably or otherwise—solid relationships with trading partners who were in possession of key resources. It is noteworthy that the city itself sits on no unique mother lode of spatially constrained resources. Most of its workshops did not produce goods that could not have been acquired elsewhere, although it is probable that the urban zone lured artisans who produced objects of top quality for the region. In this respect, Mayapán differs little from earlier Maya cities. Regional traders may have moved Mayapán's game, fruit, and finished products to coastal towns in exchange for fish, salt, marine shell, and other items. Long-distance merchants, including members of the city's noble class, would have traveled these paths as well and brokered valuables farther south along Gulf and Caribbean routes. They would have returned with currencies (cacao, marine shell, copper bells), nonlocal raw materials (obsidian cores, cotton thread, *Spondylus*), or finished products (greenstone axes, jade beads,

Matillas Fine Orange vessels). Mayapán's formidable military clout would have guarded these interests across the peninsula. Alliances would have also been maintained through diplomatic channels, including elite marriages, gifts, investiture, and general participation in shared elite culture that included religious beliefs, ritual knowledge, and symbolic paraphernalia (e.g., Pohl 2003a, 2003b; Masson 2003a; Boone and Smith 2003). The study of Mayapán's religious influence on allied hinterland polities and their leaders has been well documented (e.g., Sidrys 1983; Masson 2000; Rice and Rice 2009). In chapter 7 we examine the diversity and distribution of the city's pantheon of gods and other supernaturals portrayed in pottery, stucco, and stone sculptures.

7

Religious Practice

CARLOS PERAZA LOPE AND
MARILYN A. MASSON

The distribution of sculptural art at Mayapán provides new perspectives on religious practice at the city. Marilyn A. Masson (2000:197–216) originally analyzed some patterns of sculpture distribution at Mayapán using Tatiana Proskouriakoff's (1962a, 1962b) published illustrations of examples from temples, halls, oratories, shrines, and elite residences. This chapter focuses specifically on religious art and builds on the earlier study by incorporating all published examples of Mayapán effigy ceramic sculptures from Robert E. Smith (1971), chapters in the Carnegie *Current Report* series, and stone sculptures and censers recovered by Carlos Peraza Lope's INAH-Mayapán project from the 1996 through 2004 seasons. As the personages portrayed in ceramic, stone, and stucco sculptures overlap considerably across these media, we analyze these objects together as part of composite assemblages per architectural group. Iconographic themes are also manifested in a variety of media at other sites that are contemporary with Mayapán. For example, gods, decorative attributes, costume elements, and ritual paraphernalia are replicated among effigy censers, figures illustrated in Maya codices, and entities on the mural paintings of Tulum (Masson 2000:225) and Santa Rita (Chase and Chase 1988:82). Most stone sculptures are relatively small, and like ceramic objects, they could have been portable. Exceptions are represented by stucco sculptures that decorated freestanding or interior altars or columns of major buildings and serpent heads that originated at the base of columns or balustrades.

Effigy censers were necessary accoutrements for all kinds of ceremonies, and reconstructing the specific ritual occasions associated with archaeologically

DOI: 10.5876/9781607323204.c007

recovered censers is an inexact process. Effigy and non-effigy censers have great time depth in the Maya area, although the full-bodied Ch'en Mul censers of the Postclassic Period are distinctive in style (P. Rice 1999). Although Mayapán's censers have been analyzed for many years for their iconographic meaning (J. Thompson 1957; Taube 1992; Milbrath and Peraza Lope 2003a; Milbrath et al. 2008; Milbrath and Peraza Lope 2013), the arrays of effigies at particular buildings has not yet been examined. In this chapter, we review the inventories per structure of each identifiable entity. Our findings indicate that rare effigies tend to concentrate at a few specific buildings or architectural groups while more common Maya gods tend to be widely distributed, with some exceptions. For example, the death god is common but also concentrates at the group of the Q-95 burial shaft (sacrificial) temple. We identified effigies using classifications of Postclassic Maya gods published by J. Eric S. Thompson (1957) and Karl A. Taube (1992). In addition to gods, the Mayapán censer and stone sculptures may also reflect historical individuals or ancestors important to the city's cadre of nobles, lords, priests, and military captains. A full argument for portrayal of apotheosized ancestors among some effigy censers in the Postclassic Maya area is offered elsewhere (Masson 2000:221–24). Similarly, difficulties with assigning Aztec figurines to particular deities leads Michael E. Smith (2002:105–6) to infer that some of them represented people rather than gods.

We leave out non-effigy censers from this analysis, although such vessels were important components of ceremonious ceramic use at other Postclassic sites (P. Rice 2009f). Non-effigy ritual ceramics that potentially represent composite censers include Cehac-Hunacti Composite vessels and Acansip Painted cups (R. Smith 1971; P. Rice 2009f). In the Maya area, non-effigy composite vessels can have mat signs, step frets, rosettes, and other geometric designs that are also observed on sacred buildings, such as Tulum Structure 16 (Masson 2000:figure 7.11). But with the exception of applique rosettes and banding, these designs are rare at Mayapán, where composite vessels are defined as those with filleted bands, as well as applique motifs, and are sometimes painted. Unfortunately, ordinary jars may also exhibit one of these decorative elements (Thul Applique, Chenkeken Incised, Huhi Impressed), and it is difficult to know from the perspective of a sherd sample whether these elements represent a ritual vessel or simply a decorated storage or water jar, especially as most of them exhibit minimal decoration with no interior evidence of burning. Such vessels were not commonly recovered from our test pit and horizontal excavations; of a total excavation sample of 242,996 Postclassic sherds, only 1,728 sherds (0.7 percent) represented the combined total of Cehac-Hunacti (N = 155), Thul (N = 992), Chenkeken (N = 475), or Huhi (N = 144) unslipped vessels. A small quantity of 81 Acansip Painted sherds were found. Cehac-Hunacti Composite formed only 0.03 percent of Temple H-17's assemblage (Cruz Alvarado et al. 2012). The study of non-effigy decorated pottery at Mayapán merits further careful investigation, but the use of composite censers was minimal at this site in comparison to effigy censers.

TEMPORAL AND SPATIAL CONTEXTS OF EFFIGY USE

Mayapán was arguably the nucleus of the effigy censer tradition, if the ubiquity, diversity, size, and quality of effigies at this site are any indication. By these measures, the effigies of Mayapán far exceed the caliber of censers at any other contemporary site. Harry E. D. Pollock (1962) argues for a late introduction of effigy censers at Mayapán, and in general terms, effigy censers concentrate in the upper, later stratigraphic deposits at all Postclassic sites (Masson 2000). Good evidence supports a date in the mid-thirteenth century rather than late fourteenth century for the onset of effigy censer use (Milbrath et al. 2008:105; Milbrath and Peraza Lope 2013). Mayapán was likely in decline by at least the end of the fourteenth century AD (chapter 8). While duress is certainly a provocation for revitalization and cultic activities (Masson 2000), the widespread adoption and ubiquity of effigy censer use across the Maya area seems unlikely to have arisen from a political center with ever-diminishing power and influence during its final decades. A second consideration that supports the thirteenth-century origins of effigy censer use is the sheer ubiquity of these objects at Mayapán and its contemporaries. The abundance of these objects (in certain contexts) is more easily explained by the probability of two centuries of production, use, and discard rather than a few decades, as Pollock (1962:8) originally proposed. It is possible that some jars with modeled appliques or other elements are precursors to effigy censers, as has been suggested for Zacpetén (P. Rice 2009f:283).

From historical accounts one gets the impression that most calendrical occasions called for the use of an effigy, whether a ceramic burner, a wooden statue, or an idol made of another material (Russell 2000). Alfred M. Tozzer (1941) suggested that effigy censers were used in Ch'en or Yax monthly ceremonies that Diego de Landa described while J. Thompson (1957:602) felt that they were used on the day 1 Imix in the 260-day almanac, which happened to occur on 18 Yax when Landa recorded his observations. This interpretation is confirmed in Donald H. Graff's (1997:163–64) study of almanacs in the Madrid Codex. Many other "idols" were required for monthly rituals (Russell

2000), the commemoration of the four divisions of the 260-year cycle (Bricker 1997), deer hunting and agricultural ceremonies (P. Rice 2004:246), Uayeb rites and their cardinal shrines, the completion of the 52-year cycle, and the passage of K'atuns or half-K'atuns (D. Chase 1985b, 1988; P. Rice 2009f:300–301).

Mayapán's public buildings were probably used for many different ritual events over the nearly three centuries of the city's occupation, and this resulted in a cumulative overlay of ceremonial debris. Despite this potential for mixing, most of the sculpture assemblages from the site center in this study were recovered from the latest phase of use of each building, as the monumental center has been subjected to little penetrating excavation by the Carnegie or INAH projects. Penetrating excavations rarely recovered sculptures or ceramic effigies. Most examples from building assemblages probably served as decorative or ritual accessories of the latest use of the edifices, making their comparisons a valid exercise. A comparison of faunal use at the monumental center revealed results similar to this effigy study, with common animals widely distributed at public buildings, and at the same time, concentrations indicated the special importance of some taxa at specific localities. In particular, dog use was far above the norm at the Templo Redondo buildings (Masson and Peraza Lope 2013).

The manufacture and use of elaborate ritual paraphernalia at Mayapán was centralized at elite residences and public buildings (chapters 3, 6). Older models of decentralized ritual practice in Postclassic Maya society, based on the impression that portable effigy censers were widely distributed (A. Smith 1962:267), are not supported in our analysis. The spatial constraint of religious practice is also described in historical accounts of patronage and supervision of religious effigy manufacture (Clark and Houston 1998:35–36, 41). Males made them in seclusion under strict ritual guidelines, and the "carving of idols had to be approved by priests" (Landa 1941:159–60; Clark and Houston 1998:41). The specialized molding, modeling, plastering, and painting of effigies at House Q-40a, under the watchful eye of elite group Q-41, certainly fits well with Landa's observation. At hinterland sites, including Santa Rita, Laguna de On, and Caye Coco, caches and censers concentrate at elite residences, special ritual buildings, or ritual dumps located away from the settlement (D. Chase 1986; Masson 1999a, 1999b, 2000; Russell 2000).

In general, the contexts for effigy recovery are similar to those reported at other sites. Paired effigies are sometimes found at Mayapán that match those attributed by Diane Z. Chase (1986) to Uayeb ceremonies—for example, pairs have been reported from Hall Q-151 and Round Temple (Templo Redondo) Q-152 (Peraza Lope et al. 2003; Milbrath and Peraza Lope 2013).

Paired effigies may also be related to K'atun intervals of the *may* cycle, during which "guest" idols were sometimes introduced halfway through the K'atun to accompany the interval's patron deity; the guest effigy would then preside as the new patron over the first half of a subsequent K'atun before being joined by a new guest (P. Rice 2009f:301). As at Santa Rita, pairs of effigies have also been reported from Zacpetén (P. Rice 2009f:304). Some incomplete effigies were located in situ on the floors of monumental buildings at Mayapán that had been broken elsewhere prior to their final deposition (chapter 3; Milbrath et al. 2008:106; Milbrath and Peraza Lope 2013). The recovery of incomplete effigies is common; these have been reported for Zacpetén (Pugh and Rice 2009b:147–50) and Laguna de On (Masson 2000; Russell 2000). At least some effigies were broken when the city was abandoned, perhaps as part of a revolt by those who may have sided with the Xiu (Milbrath and Peraza Lope 2013); other fragments remained within small shrine buildings such as Q-79 and Q-79a. Most anthropomorphic sculptures were defaced or decapitated and were found fallen on or around the structures that they had decorated. One act of reverential abandonment was observed at palace group R-86, where censers were cached within a family tomb for probable conservation (Proskouriakoff and Temple 1955). A few were funerary offerings, as for Xipe Totec censer fragments in the grave at elite House Q-208 (J. Thompson 1954:79). At the Itzmal Ch'en ceremonial group, portions of several censers were broken, mixed together, and deposited on the final floors of Hall H-15 and Temple H-17 in an act of ritual termination (chapter 3, figures 3.11, 3.12). On the other hand, many effigy censers were smashed and thrown in a mass grave of chopped human remains at Itzmal Ch'en. Given these depositional contexts, it appears that most censers were recovered in or near contexts of their use. The censers amid the mass graves of Hall H-15 or in the plaza by Shrines Q-79/79a of the Templo Redondo group may have been ritually dumped (Adams 1953; Paris and Russell 2012). There is no published information on the effigy censers from the burial shaft of Temple Q-95 that Edwin M. Shook (1954a:271) excavated. From the interior room of the other burial shaft temple (Q-58), the INAH project recovered censer fragments that were probably strewn around at the time that the shaft was looted, long before Shook (1954a:257) investigated this temple. Thus, the Q-58 censers may come from the shaft.

Compared to Mayapán, effigy faces in the hinterlands exhibit fewer variations and are generally smaller along the east coast of Quintana Roo and Belize as well as in the Petén. At least sixteen distinct entities are identified in this chapter among the Mayapán censers, whereas most effigies found in northern Belize are one of five entitites, including old and young male faces, the death god, a female deity, and Itzamna (Sidrys 1983:245; Masson 2000:239; Russell 2000). Raymond V. Sidrys (1983:245) also observed single instances of Chac and a merchant deity in Belize. This short inventory is similar at Zacpetén, with Chac/Tlaloc, Itzamna, a merchant deity, and a female deity thus far identified (P. Rice 2009f:304). The distribution of these censers is extensive, as they occur across the Yucatán Peninsula and into the Petén and highland Guatemala regions (e.g., Pendergast 1986; Schele and Mathews 1998:figure 8.12; Masson 2000; Milbrath et al. 2008; Rice and Rice 2009). Some Mayapán censer faces are made from the same facial mold. Modeling and painting were used to dress and embellish molded faces and form the bodies. Precedents for these effigy vessels are known in Mesoamerica from the Classic Period Oaxaca urn tradition and, closer to home, figurine traditions from Veracruz and Jaina, but direct historical relationships are poorly understood. The Maya area has a longstanding tradition of the use of both censers and effigy vessels (Ringle et al. 1998; P. Rice 1999). Susan Milbrath et al. (2008) argue that central Mexican contact contributed importantly to the iconographic content of Mayapán's effigy censers, although the vessels themselves are all but absent at Aztec sites. The international influences of this era must be acknowledged (Pollock 1962:14; Taube 1992; Smith and Berdan 2003a), but it is also true that the majority of deities represented in the effigies of Mayapán are traditional Maya gods (Masson and Peraza Lope 2010).

TALLYING EFFIGY ART

The data examined in this chapter were compiled from illustrations or photographs. We compiled a separate page of images for each structure; we then classified the images and entered this information into a Microsoft Excel database that generated the tables of this chapter. We used our own photographs of recently recovered stone and ceramic sculptures from the INAH investigations (1996–2004); other illustrations were published in the Carnegie Institution of Washington's *Current Reports* (table 7.22), or by J. Thompson (1957), R. Smith (1971), or Proskouriakoff (1962a, 1962b). The work of establishing deity identifications and taking photographs of the INAH project collection was accomplished in 2004 with the invaluable assistance of Bradley W. Russell and Elizabeth H. Paris. Josalyn Ferguson and Morgan Houston helped to organize the published Carnegie images. Table 7.22 lists the structures that are referred to in this chapter along with the published sources for each structure from which these images were tallied. Figure 2.10 illustrates the location and arrangement of Mayapán's monumental center structures.

Although our effort was comprehensive, it is in part dependent on the material originally chosen for publication. Investigators of the Carnegie project generally published photographs of whole vessels or faces of incense burners in the *Current Reports* series, and examples of some of these vessels were later published in a ceramic monograph by Robert Smith (1971). Our work represents a systematic attempt to reconstruct the assemblages per structure and is comprehensive with regard to the choices made by prior investigators to publish illustrations or photographs. The INAH sample is more complete, as effigies from this project were studied directly.

Sculptures discovered in 2009 from the Itzmal Ch'en group are described in detail in chapter 3. As ceramic analysis from that season is still in progress, we have not included the tallies of Itzmal Ch'en sculptures and effigy censer faces in the 2009 inventory analyzed in this chapter, which is primarily concerned with large samples from the site's central monumental plazas and surrounding buildings. We do include some of the materials from the Carnegie-era investigations of the Itzmal Ch'en group. Our own work to date on the Itzmal Ch'en sculpture and censer assemblage reveals that there are no conspicuous concentrations of any particular deity other than the recovery of a high number of serpent sculptures (chapter 3).

HUMAN PORTRAITS

Human portrait sculptures are defined in this study as those that lack deity markers and may indicate historical individuals (table 7.1). Six stone torsos were recovered from the Q-69 shrine, and they exhibit idiosyncratic, personalized adornments (figure 7.1). None exhibit armor that might suggest that they were warriors. A string of beads or beaded cloth is draped from the neck of one figure and another has a circular pendant, perhaps a mirror. The other four figures have pectoral collars. The lower arms are missing from all but one, which holds a spiked incense cone held in a shallow bowl (figure 7.1). Three turbaned human faces were found in the same context, and two of these headdresses support the base of a priestly miter. The torsos and heads appear to be male, except for the individual who holds the incense cone, who wears a long dress. The sculptures are from the general area of the shrine and were not in situ within it. This dispersal of sculpture fragments around buildings is commonly observed at the site center and may be attributed to desecration events at the time of the city's demise. The figures could be portraits of the lords, priests, or important ancestors of families linked to the Q-70 hall group.

TABLE 7.1 Stone/stucco human faces and bodies.

Context	Portion	Description of faces and torsos
Cenote X-Coton	1 face	Male with animal pelt headdress
Temple H-17	1 face	1 eroded face (see also chapter 3)
House J-71b	1 face	Male in reptile headdress
Temple Q-127a	1 face, 1 limb	Helmeted male with closed eyes
Temple Q-149	1 limb	
Hall Q-151	3 limbs	
Hall/Temple Q-151/152	1 face	Fragment
Round Temple Q-152	1 limb	
Hall Q-152c	1 face	Shallowly carved head with long hair
Hall Q-156	1 face, 1 torso, 1 limb	1 human with shield, 1 sculpted column with feet preserved
Shrine Q-157a	1 torso	Nude female torso
Temple Q-159	1 torso	Seated banner holder
Hall Q-161	3 faces, 2 with bodies	1 human head, 2 full-figured turbaned male and female pair
Hall Q-163	1 face	Miniature pot-bellied figure
House Q-168	1 face	Anthropomorphic figure
Round Temple Q-214	1 face	Female with shawl
Temple Q-218	2 limbs	
House Q-244	1 face	Turbaned fanged male
Shrine Q-69	1 face, 6 torsos, 1 limb	2 turbaned males, 6 priest/lord tunic torsos (1 could be female)
Hall Q-70	3 faces, 1 limb	1 male with bird headdress, 1 male with plumed feather head-dress, 1 other horizontal-bodied turbaned figure
Hall Q-72	1 torso	
Shrine Q-84	1 torso	Anthropomorphic figure
Platform Q-84	1 face, 1 torso	1 male face, 1 torso with mirror or shell pendant
Shrine Q-90	3 torsos	1 reclining Chacmool-like miniature

continued on next page

TABLE 7.1—*continued*

Context	Portion	Description of faces and torsos
Temple Q-95	1 limb	
Platform Q-96	1 limb	
Shrine Q-98	2 faces	1 goggled seated figure with turban, 1 old person with side flap headdress
House R-86	1 face, 2 limbs	1 male with large headdress
House R-87	1 limb	
House R-89	2 face	1 male with headdress, 1 human emerging from snake mouth
Temple Q-149	1 face	Cone headdress with triple knots, possibly closed eyes, mouth open
Hall Q-145	1 face	Cone headdress with triple knots, eyes and mouth open

Quite similar in style to the Q-69 figures are two examples from Hall Q-161 (figure 7.1), adjacent to the Temple of Kukulcan's eastern side. These turbaned figures wore miters and represent a male and female pair. They may have been important dynastic founders. The female's abdominal region has a circular cavity into which offerings or a mirror may have been set. An additional turbaned head fragment was recovered at the hall. Tenoned snake and skull sculptures were also present at Q-161, which may have fallen from the Temple of Kukulcan.

Another set of large carved human stone heads was recovered at Hall Q-70, adjacent to the Q-69 shrine (figure 7.1). These were probably the heads of full-bodied human figures. One human face emerges from a bird or serpent mouth, and another face is bedecked in elaborate feathered headgear. This latter figure has prominent cheekbones and may depict an elderly personage, perhaps Itzamna or God N. The noses of both sculptures are broken and may have been defaced. They may represent individuals of two distinct offices, deities, or ancestors. A third turbaned head sculpture from Q-70 may have been set into a shrine or wall program, as it was not part of a full figure. From the Q-98 shrine, two human effigy sculptures were found. These examples represent an older male with a side flap headdress and a seated anthropomorphic figure with traces of goggle eyes and a turban headdress.

Mayapán Stela 14 is similar in many ways to the self-standing human sculptures. This stela was set next to round Temple Q-126 (figure 7.1), and

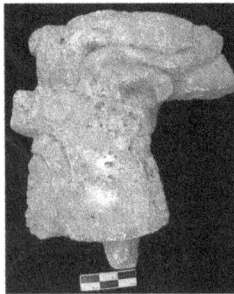

FIGURE 7.1. *Examples of human sculptures that probably portray historical individuals. Illustrations of examples from Q-149, Q-161, Q-126, and Q-69 are by Kendra Farstad from Proskouriakoff (1962a:figures 8c, 9a, 9b, 11L, 9c, 9k). Photos from Q-70 courtesy of Carlos Peraza Lope, photos by Bradley Russell.*

the turbaned figure is carved in deep relief, except for the rear side, which is part of a flat rectangular slab (Proskouriakoff 1962a:135). A robust, well-rounded human figure carved into Stela 7 from Round Temple Q-152 also resembles self-standing sculptures to a certain degree, but the relief is not as pronounced.

Human head sculptures with cone-shaped headdresses come from two structures located adjacent to one another, the Q-145 hall and the Q-149 temple. Each head has a series of three knots above the forehead out of which a tall vertical cone emerges (figure 7.1). The faces clearly depict two different personages, but their shared group provenience suggests that this headdress was a marker for the individuals that used this architecture. A third cone headdress figure was recovered at a more humble residence, P-33b, but it lacks the triple knots; unlike the others, it is in the form of a tenoned head. A cone headdress is one attribute that is linked to central Mexican depictions of Quetzalcoatl, which sometimes also have two horizontal ribbons at the base (e.g., Miller and Taube 1993:141). Perhaps the Mayapán examples portray a headdress worn by Kukulcan priests, whose activities concentrated at group Q-149. This group is part of a courtyard just to the east of the Temple of Kukulcan, in front of Hall Q-151 and Temple Q-153; the latter is situated on the edge of the Ch'en Mul cenote. Such priests have been described for other late Mesoamerican cities, including Cholula and Chichén Itzá (Ringle 2004).

Other human sculptures include the head of a male from Q-127a (portal vault temple) whose eyes are closed and who wears a side flap helmet. At the residential altar (Q-244d) of elite House Q-244 a male is portrayed with a turban/miter and fangs. At the R-86 palace compound a male portrait sculpture wears a large headdress and the R-89 sanctuary has two eroded heads and one tenoned head. Other human faces, many of which are eroded, are listed in table 7.1 along with fragments of arms, legs, and hands.

Overall, human figure sculptures (heads, torsos, or limbs) come from eight halls, eight temples, six houses, five shrines, two platforms, and one cenote (table 7.1). Many of them wear headdress miters that Taube (1992) links to the priesthood. Other examples have flap, cone, feather, or animal headdresses. Eyes appear to be open in most cases, although many faces are too eroded to make a determination. Male heads are the most numerous item (N = 10), and an additional four humans (probably male) have animal headdresses or emerge from an animal's mouth. These sculptures likely portray important governing elites, priests, and warriors from Mayapán's major families. Other categories of human sculptures with more specific attributes are discussed in the remainder of this chapter, including females.

Tenoned sculptures also take the form of deities or humans (table 7.2), and except for the tenon spikes, the personages resemble non-tenoned pieces. One tenoned Itzamna head came from the Ch'en Mul cenote. Two other examples portray human faces that emerge from serpent mouths (Temple Q-126, Hall Q-97), a theme that is observed in other forms of sculpture. Three additional human tenoned faces come from round Temple Q-214, Hall Z-50, and a cone-headed figure from House P-33b (previously mentioned). As table 7.2 shows, three human tenoned pieces have closed eyes, and the eyes are open on two others. All mouths are open on the human examples, where this can be determined, as if to enable speech. The human tenoned sculptures may depict important ancestors and were recovered from a variety of structure types.

Skull tenoned sculptures are concentrated at Shrine Q-89, which has nine of these examples (figure 7.2) and is located in the plaza space in front of burial shaft Temple Q-95. This shrine may have functioned as a skull platform at Mayapán (P. Delgado Kú 2004), analogous to an earlier example at Chichén Itzá. The architecture of this shrine looks like many others at Mayapán in that it has a single, small upper chamber that opens to a staircase ascending from one side (east in this case). Two additional tenoned skulls are found at Hall Q-54, and one each is present at Hall Q-64, Shrine Q-69, Platform Q-94/94a, Hall Q-161, Sanctuary (of the Temple of Kukulcan) Q-162b, and round Temple Q-214 (table 7.2).

At the Q-163a sanctuary, a bird-beaked human face is present; this image represents the wind god (Ehecatl) aspect of Kukulcan. Notably, Q-163a abuts the west side of the Temple of Kukulcan, as it is part of Hall Q-163 that extends to the west of the temple. The association of this deity with the temple is not surprising.

DEITY STONE AND CERAMIC EFFIGIES

Stone or stucco sculptures and ceramic effigies that seem to represent deities are listed in table 7.3. The censer sample consists largely of faces, most of which were not part of restored vessels. An occasional diagnostic torso or headdress is included in this analysis. A total of 265 fragmented or whole censers or effigy cups were examined, of which 237 were classified and are included in table 7.4. The remaining 28 were miscellaneous unidentified fragments. Five deities are far more common than the others when the percentages of identified (237) censers are compared. These five major entities include Itzamna (N = 31, 13.1 percent), the merchant god/whiskered god group (11.8 percent; 15 whiskered, 13 merchants), Chac (N = 39, 16.5 percent), the young face male group that may

TABLE 7.2 Human or deity tenoned stone sculptures

Type	Structure	Number	Description
Skulls	Hall Q-54	2	
	Hall Q-64	1	
	Shrine Q-69	1	
	Shrine Q-89	9	
	House Q-94/94a	1	
	Hall Q-97	1	
	Hall Q-161	1	
	Sanctuary Q-162b	1	
	Round Temple Q-214	1	
	Total	17	
Humans	Temple Q-126	1	Emerges from bird/serpent mouth, closed eyes, mouth open
	Round Temple Q-214	1	Eyes closed, mouth broken
	House P-33b	1	Cone headdress, eyes closed, mouth open
	Hall Z-50	1	Eyes open, mouth open
	Hall Q-97	1	Emerges from serpent mouth, open eyes
Total		5	
Deity	Sanctuary Q-163	1	bird-beaked human/ wind god, eyes open
Cenote Ch'en Mul	1	Itzamna or an old god	

represent warriors and/or maize gods (N = 59, 25.5 percent), and skeletal death god images (N = 18, 7.4 percent). Other censers that occur regularly in the assemblage include the old god (N = 7, 3.0 percent) that shares characteristics with Itzamna, old (N = 2) and young (N = 5) female deities (combined equaling 4.6 percent), and Xipe Totec (N = 7, 3.0 percent). Four examples are present for each of the following: males with scrolls painted on their faces, diving figures, a possible Venus god, and a Monkey Scribe. Occurring in only one or two examples are the maize god, a censer representing Kukulcan (Winters 1955b),

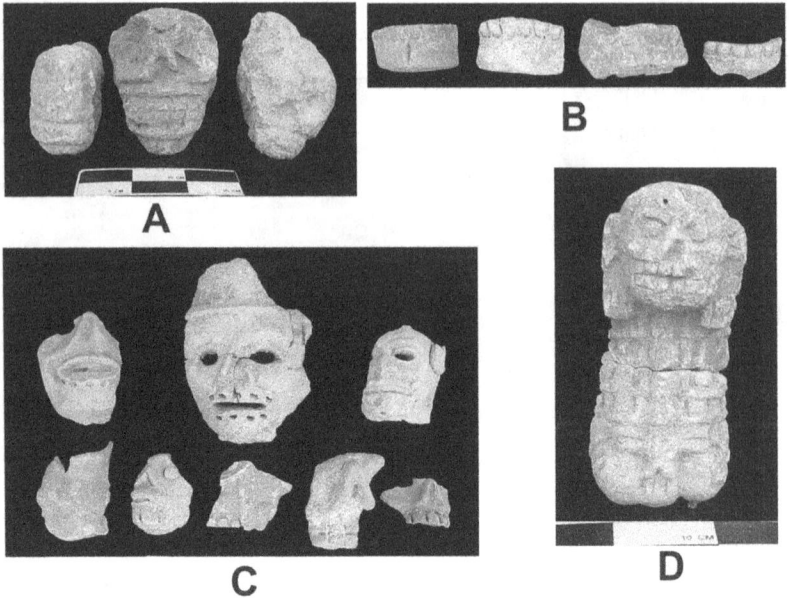

FIGURE 7.2. *Death god images, including three of nine tenoned skulls from Shrine Q-89, effigy skull cup mandibles and faces from various monumental center contexts (B, C), and a small death god sculpture from Temple Q-95. Courtesy of Carlos Peraza Lope, photos by Bradley Russell.*

bird-beaked human faces that may represent the Ehecatl form of Kukulcan/ Quetzalcoatl, a fire god (identified by Taube 1992, with a face identical to Itzamna), two males with nose plugs, a male with hair inset perforations, and a torso displaying intestinal sacrifice. Felines are represented in the form of headdresses that exhibit feline faces or pelts, feline paws, or feline effigies. A recurring symbol is the quincunx (five-point turquoise symbol) medallion worn by two male effigies; an additional example was found in isolation from its original censer.

OLD GODS / ITZAMNA

Stone sculpture examples of Itzamna heads were recovered from the Q-87a hall and the Q-146b statue platform. A tenoned head Itzamna was recovered from the Cenote Ch'en Mul (previously mentioned); it was probably moved from its original location and discarded at this locality. Another Itzamna sculp-

TABLE 7.3 Structures with stone and stucco human or deity figures.

Structure	Entity
Shrine Q-77	Xipe Totec
Hall Q-163	Xipe Totec
Hall Q-163	Tlaloc
Oratory Q-87a	Itzamna
Statue Platform Q-146	Itzamna
Altar H-17a	Itzamna
Round Shrine H-18	Earth lord
Palace R-88	Earth lord
Oratory Q-83	Earth lord
Temple Q-159	Earth lord
Hall Q-163	Young female goddess
Hall Q-161	Female/ancestral figure
Sanctuary Q-157a	Old female goddess
Round Temple Q-214	Old female goddess
Temple Q-162	Ehecatl
Temple Q-162	Puffy cheek human
Hall H-15	Puffy cheek human
Hall Q-163	Merchant/whiskered entity and other unidentified males (sculpted columns)

ture was present at a plaza altar, H-17a (Itzmal Ch'en). This entity is abundantly represented in the censer collection of Mayapán, forming 14 percent of the identified censers. Itzamna is a primary deity of the Maya codices, and he was associated with the priesthood and sorcery (J. Thompson 1970; Taube 1992).

Itzamna's diagnostic characteristics include a gaping, largely toothless mouth (sometimes with short fangs); an old, drawn face with high cheekbones and a large hooked nose; portions of the mouth area and eyelids that are sometimes painted yellow; and the presence of a spherical ornament on the nose bridge (figure 7.3a; J. Thompson 1957). Some idiosyncratic attributes of Itzamna faces include a bird headdress (Q-80), a bejeweled headdress consisting of upright ornaments of tubular jade beads topped by white and red shell discoidal beads (Q-70, figure 6.2e), and a nose plug (Q-162). A single Itzamna has a cleft chin (Q-161), suggesting a relationship with old god images. Two

Table 7.4 Percentage of identified Chen Mul Modeled effigy censers and effigy cups.

Identification	Number	Percent of 237
Whiskered	15	6.3
Merchant	13	5.5
Old god	7	3.0
Itzamna	31	13.1
Chac (including cups)	39	16.5
Possibly Chac (fanged entity)	2	0.8
Maize god or Kukulcan	2	0.8
Death head	17	7.2
Death torso	1	0.4
Young males	28	11.8
Filed-tooth males	9	3.8
Male with bird headdress	9	3.8
Bird headdress fragment	6	2.5
Male with reptile headdress	2	0.8
Reptile headdress fragment	2	0.8
Helmeted male	1	0.4
Male with shield	2	0.8
Young female goddess	5	2.1
Old female goddess	4	1.7
Female body fragments	2	0.8
Monkey Scribe	4	1.7
Bird-beaked human (Ehecatl)	2	0.8
Venus	4	1.7
Fire god	1	0.4
Tzalolteotl	2	0.8
Xipe Totec	7	3.0
Diving figure	4	1.7
Other (perforated hair, scroll face, quetzal feather headdress, feline, intestinal sacrifice torso, nose plug figures, red face/blue cheek figure)	16	
Total identified	237	
Other/unidentified fragments	28	

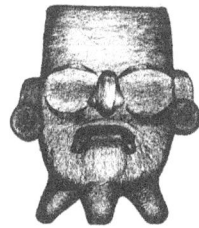
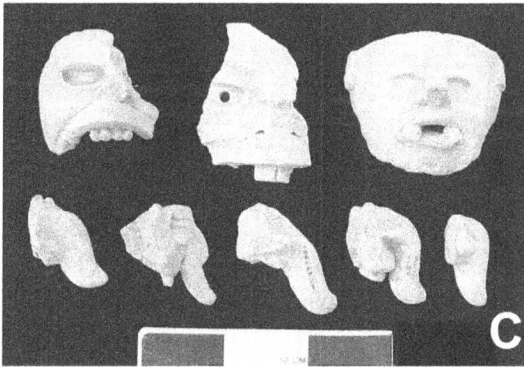
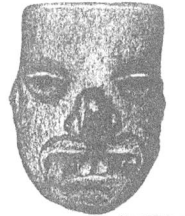

FIGURE 7.3. *Effigy incense burners and cups identified as Itzamna (A), an old god (B), and Chac (C, D, E). Courtesy of Carlos Peraza Lope, photos by Bradley Russell.*

Itzamna censers and three other examples share a horizontal strap and knot headdress element at palace group R-86.

One Itzamna effigy head has a face that is identical to other Itzamna examples, but Taube (1992:125) classifies this censer as Huehueteotl, an aged fire god of central Mexico and the Gulf Coast, based on its quincunx headdress element. This example is unique in combining this face and headband at the site. Without the headdress it would likely be classified as Itzamna. Notably, the fire god effigy comes from the R-86 palace group, where two additional Itzamna censers were found. We do not dispute Taube's identification, although it raises questions about the importance of face versus headdress elements for the classification of effigies. Many of the examples in this study lacked headdresses; thus, Itzamna identifications should be considered with this qualification in mind. Quincunx symbols were represented on other costume elements in our sample that were not in association with older male faces.

Other examples of old male effigy faces share a subset of these characteristics. Overlapping with Itzamna are the gaping mouths and drawn old faces, but differences include the presence of a cleft chin or closed eyes and the absence of a nose bridge ornament (figure 7.3b). Some old god censers may represent God N, although identifying attributes of this deity are not present among our fragments, such as associations with turtle or conch shells, quadripartite symbols, sky markers, or other indicators of Pauahtuns (Taube 1992:93–94). An exception may be an example reported by Milbrath and Peraza Lope (2013) in which an old god effigy has an oval pectoral that is centrally placed within a mat symbol, which they compare to the central Mexican *oyohualli* symbol. J. Thompson (1957) similarly suggests that the old cleft chin could be linked to Mam or Itzamna. It is thus possible that some of our old god examples may represent Itzamna or other more specific entities, but they lack the diagnostic attributes that are needed for verification. Another deity that has an old face and an Itzamna-like Roman nose in the codices is God G, or the Sun God (Taube 1992:50). This entity sometimes has a beard and is shown with serpent eye markings (Taube 1992:50, figure 22b, c). Our old god faces do not have serpent eye markings, beards, or kin sign markings, and thus probably do not portray God G.

One example of an old male face has closed eyes (Q-88). This characteristic is not normally associated with either God N or Itzamna. Closed eyes are a formal attribute of Xipe Totec, who is not portrayed as an aged entity. Five other non-aged censer faces in our sample also had closed eyes but were otherwise relatively generic and not distinguishable as Xipe Totec. One of these faces comes from the same context as the aged closed-eye example (Q-88); three others come from Hall Q-151 and one is from Palace R-86. It is difficult to interpret closed-eye effigies that may not be Xipe Totec. It is tempting to infer that they represent revered ancestors, who are often shown with closed eyes that refer to their deceased status in other Mesoamerican traditions, although other explanations are possible. Except for the eyes, these effigies closely resemble other censers. They are likely gods shown in death. The maize god is sometimes shown with closed eyes, which links this entity to death and the agricultural cycle (Taube 1992), as we discuss in greater detail in the maize god section of this chapter. The majority of Mayapán's censers and sculptures do represent recognizable deities (J. Thompson 1957; Peraza Lope 1999; Milbrath and Peraza Lope 2003a, 2013), supporting the idea that the closed-eye censers are also versions of gods in stages of sleep or death.

Thirty-one Itzamna faces are present in our sample, and the fire god example discussed by Taube would bring this count to thirty-two (tables 7.4, 7.5). Itzamna censer faces are broadly distributed at individual structures at the site center and are present in only one outlying elite residence, the R-86 palace group. Multiple clusters of structures account for the majority of the sample, including a temple group forming the borders of the North Plaza (Q-58/66/62/64), the Q-80 cluster (Q-80/81/79/79a), structures of the Templo Redondo platform (Q-151/152/152b/152c/88a), the Castillo group (Q-162/161), and the R-86 palace. The greatest concentrations are in Temple Q-80 and Temple Q-152 clusters, with 21.9 percent each, followed by the North Plaza Q-58 group and the R-86 palace (12.5 percent each); 9.5 percent of the faces were from the Temple of Kukulcan group. An additional 21.9 percent of the Itzamna faces are thinly distributed among six other contexts. In comparison to other censer types described in this chapter, Itzamna faces are concentrated in a greater number of groups, suggesting that the use of this entity was more widely distributed, as might be expected given the weighty importance of this deity in the Postclassic pantheon (J. Thompson 1957; Taube 1992). Prudence M. Rice (2009f:304) observes that Itzamna was also important for the K'owoj Maya of Zacpetén, who had historical roots at Mayapán. An Itzamna effigy vase was placed as an offering in Hall H-15 of the Itzmal Ch'en group (figure 3.13). Portraits of this god on cups or vases are rare at Mayapán; such vessels normally are linked to Chac or Tlaloc.

Although the identication of an old god in the censer collection is tentative, some observations are noteworthy. At least five examples had cleft chins. The seven occurrences come from five structures that belong to four architectural groups. Three of these groups are the same as those that had Itzamna faces, including the Q-80 cluster (Q-81), the Templo Redondo group (Q-151), and the Q-208 residential group. Considering the old god and Itzamna effigies together, the Q-80 cluster accounts for 20.5 percent of the faces and the Templo Redondo group has 25.6 percent. One of the three stone heads representing Itzamna was also from the Templo Redondo group (Q-87a). If the old god with closed eyes from Q-88 is more closely affiliated with the young face

TABLE 7.5 Structures with Itzamna/old god Ch'en Mul Modeled effigy censers. Three additional stone examples are listed in table 7.3.

	Itzamna censers		Old god censers	
Structure	No.	%	No.	%
Temple Q-58	1	3.1	–	–
House Q-62	1	3.1	–	–
Hall Q-64	1	3.1	–	–
Shrine Q-66	1	3.1	–	–
Hall Q-70	2	6.3	–	–
Hall Q-72	–	–	1	14.3
Shrine Q-79/79a	2	6.3	–	–
Temple Q-80	2	6.3	–	–
Hall Q-81	3	9.4	1	14.3
Hall Q-88a	1	3.1	–	–
Oratory Q-88	–	–	1	14.3
Shrine Q-89	1	3.1	–	–
Shrine Q-98	1	3.1	–	–
Portal Vault Q-127	1	3.1	–	–
Hall Q-151	1	3.1	2	28.6
Round Temple Q-152	2	6.3	–	–
Sanctuary Q-152b	1	3.1	–	–
Hall Q-152c	2	6.3	–	–
Temple Q-153	1	3.1	–	–
Hall Q-161	1	3.1	–	–
Temple Q-162	2	6.3	–	–
Elite House Q-208	1	3.1	2	28.6
Elite House R-86	4	12.5	–	–
	32	100	7	

Note: Old gods have cleft chins. The old god example from Structure Q-88 has closed eyes, and the Itzamna from Q-151 also has a cleft chin.

closed-eye personages, it may be important that three out of four examples of the latter are concentrated in the Templo Redondo compound; the old personage is from Q-88, which is part of that architectural group.

Old god images are distributed at three halls, one oratory, and one residence (Q-208). This residence is an upper-status house at the south end of the monumental center. Itzamna effigies are present at many types of structures, including five shrines, five temples, seven halls, one portal vault, one palace (R-86), and two residences (Q-208, Q-62), as tables 7.4 and 7.5 indicate. This entity has not been found at commoner residences in the settlement zone.

Chac and Tlaloc

Mayapán Chac censers depict this deity with traditional attributes that resemble Maya codex figures; some hinterland peninsular sites display this god with attributes of Tlaloc, the central Mexican rain deity (Milbrath et al. 2008:107–8). It is interesting that, unlike the censers, Chac cups or vases at Mayapán often blend Chac and Tlaloc features (figure 7.3d). Representations of Chac (tables 7.6, 7.7) are divided almost evenly among effigy cups (N = 19) and effigy censers (N = 20), as J. Thompson (1957:622) originally noted. Effigy cups almost always portray Chac rather than any other god. The presence of Tlaloc goggles on Chac figures reveals some fusion in the traits of these deities (Taube 1992:133). A more typical Tlaloc stone sculpture is known from Hall Q-163. Another goggle-eyed personage was present at Q-98, although it lacks fangs. Chac is not among the deities that are well represented in stone and ceramic form, in contrast to Itzamna, Ehecatl, the death god, or female entities. When both effigy cups and censers are tallied, Chac is the most abundantly portrayed entity at Mayapán. Two additional fanged male faces may also be Chac, but it is not certain whether fangs represent Chac in the absence of other identifying features.

Chac cups are usually found as caches in rear interior building altars, singly or paired with plain cups (e.g., Adams 1953:figure 5; Winters 1955b:384, figure 40). Other variations of these caches include single or paired plain cups without Chac representations. Offerings within the cups typically include jade and/or shell beads (e.g., Smith and Ruppert 1956:figure 8i, j; Pollock 1956:535; Shook 1954a:figure 2j). Of interest is a possible parallel practice in offerings to Tlaloc at the Templo Mayor, where "cloud jars" contained greenstone beads (López Luján 1998:180). Nineteen Chac effigy cups are present in the structures available for study (table 7.6). These come from sixteen different contexts, as six of the cups came in three pairs. Where supports could be determined, there are six tripod cups, ten pedestaled cups, and two pedestaled vases. Given their contexts, cups are inferred to represent cache vessels, but non-effigy examples are sometimes recovered from dwellings. The possibility

TABLE 7.6 Structures with Chac cups and pedestal vessels, including those with Tlaloc attributes. Chac effigy censers are listed separately in table 7.7.

Structure	Number	Form/ID	Identifying attributes
Hall Q-64	1	Chac tripod	Nose, side fangs not visible
Shrine Q-71	1	Chac pedestal	Long nose and fangs
Hall Q-87a	1	Chac/Tlaloc pedestal vase	Goggles and elaborate nose, no fangs
Temple Q-127a	1	Chac fragment	Only fanged mouth visible
Hall Q-151	1	Chac/Tlaloc tripod	Has goggles, fangs, long nose
Temple Q-153	1	Chac pedestal	Long nose and fangs
Hall Q-161	1	Chac cylinder vase	Long nose, upcurling and drooping variety
Hall Q-164	1	Chac pedestal	Long nose and fangs
House Q-208	2	Chac pedestal, Chac tripod	Both have long nose, fangs, pedestal is painted
Round Temple Q-214	1	Chac tripod	Long nose
Serpent Temple Q-218	1	Chac tripod	Long nose and fangs, eye bridge bobble
Shrine A-1	2	Chac/Tlaloc pedestals	Both examples have goggle eyes, one has fangs
Temple H-17	1	Chac pedestal	Only fanged mouth visible
House R-86/87	1	Chac tripod	Long and cruller nose, fangs
Oratory R-91	2	Chac/Tlaloc pedestal, Chac tripod	Pedestal vessel has goggle eyes and fangs, long nose, tripod has cruller nose
Structure Y-30	1	Chac pedestal	Fangs

that they also represented drinking vessels cannot be ruled out, as this was the case for the Aztec realm (Smith, Wharton, and Olson 2003). The fact that they are infrequent suggests that drinking involved other types of vessels in addition to cups.

Two primary variants are observed in the Chac representations (figure 7.3c, d, e). One has a more naturalistic face, with a long nose and fangs; these are

TABLE 7.7 Contexts with Chac Ch'en Mul Modeled effigy censers.

Structure	Chac censers (number)	Chac censers (percent)
Shrine Q-79/79a	1	4.8
Temple Q-80	2	9.5
Hall Q-81	1	4.8
Oratory Q-88	1	4.8
Hall Q-88a	4	19.0
Platform Q-88b	1	4.8
Altar Q-88e	1	4.8
Temple Q-95	1	4.8
Hall Q-151	1	4.8
Temple Q-152	1	4.8
Hall Q-152C	2	9.5
House R-86	4	19.0
Total	20	

present on both pedestal and tripod cups. In two cases a braided nose ornament is present. One cup has an upcurling/drooping nose that closely resembles codex representations of Chac, and one pedestal vase reveals this nose form. The other variation shares many attributes with the first, but Tlaloc-like goggles are present on the eyes. Only five cases have goggles—these are pedestal cups, with a single exception. One example is paired at R-91 with a braided nose cup. A combination of Chac and Tlaloc attributes is also reported from some Zacpetén censers (Pugh and Rice 2009b:162; P. Rice 2009f:304). The mingling of the Mexican and Mayan rain god characteristics probably attests to high levels of interregional interaction and their functional parallels in the religious systems of both regions.

Almost half of the contexts (N = 7) with Chac cups do not have censers, and this reflects the fact that the use of Chac vessels was widespread. The sample of nineteen Chac cups originated from temples (26 percent); halls (26 percent); shrines, sanctuaries, and altars (21 percent); oratories (11 percent); and houses (16 percent). They were most commonly found in or around the interior altars of these buildings (table 7.6). The majority of these vessels were originally altar offerings; when found near the altars, the altars had been looted in antiquity and the vessels had been discarded in close proximity. Only two contexts, shrines at A-1 and Y-30, are associated with small commoner domestic groups, and all others are from elite residential or public buildings in or near the monumental zone. J. Thompson (1957) observed that Itzamna's importance in the Postclassic Period did not continue into Colonial times. He contrasts this pattern with that of Chac. Thompson suggested that Itzamna may have been a god who was more important to the nobility, whereas Chac was more broadly important to commoners and continued traditions of village agriculture. Although his idea resonates compellingly, elites at Mayapán seem to have appropriated Chac effectively for rites involving altar offerings at monumental buildings or palaces.

Non-effigy tripod cups, sometimes associated with Chac cups, functioned in similar ways and may pertain to rituals involving Chac. There are thirty-one plain cups in our sample that originate from twenty-three contexts, only three of which are outside of Square Q on the Mayapán map (the epicenter). Two of these plain cups are from non-elite contexts. Eight structures have multiple tripod or pedestal cup offerings of two or three vessels, and only three combine non-effigy cups with Chac effigy cups. Non-effigy cups come from eight altar, shrine, or sanctuary structures, five halls, four temples, three oratories; and three houses, and are distributed across all major groups of the Main Plaza.

Chac effigy censers (table 7.7) are among the five most common censer groups in the sample (9 percent). Over half of them (57.4 percent) come from the Templo Redondo compound that includes Q-88, 88a, 88b, 88e, Q-151, Q-152, and Q-152c. Although these structures face different directions and might have been part of courtyard groups shared with nearby buildings, they are back to back or side by side with each other or the Templo Redondo, and they represent an elevated, intimate group that shares refuse zones, passageways, alleys, or staircases. The concentration of Chac censers at the Templo Redondo group is probably significant. This group forms the east border of the Main Plaza of the city. An additional 19 percent of the Chac censers were recovered from the adjacent cluster of buildings that forms the north border of the Main Plaza (Q-80, Q-81, and Q-79/79a). Milbrath and Peraza Lope (2009:598) suggest that Xiu nobles, known as "rain-bringers," were the patrons of Hall Q-151 (Hall of the Chac Masks), which is located at the southern end of the Templo Redondo cluster and faces its own courtyard. These authors' assessment represents one plausible explanation for the prevalence of Chac effigies at this group.

Like the Templo Redondo cluster, the Q-80 cluster includes structures that face opposite courts, but they share a narrow alley. The rear room of the Q-80 temple, where the serpent mural is located, opens toward the alley and the back of the Q-81 hall. Although 19 percent of the Chac effigies are concentrated at the Q-80 group, this quantity is less than half of the amount (57.4 percent) found at the Templo Redondo group. The Q-80 group has a diverse assemblage, with examples of almost every kind of censer present. An additional five Chac effigies were present at palace group R-86, just east of the monumental zone. Including these groups, Chac censers were present at four halls, three temples, one palace, a platform, a shrine, and an oratory. The greatest concentration at individual structures is observed at the Q-88a hall and the R-86 palace group, which had four and five Chac effigies, respectively. All other contexts had one example, except for Q-80 (N = 2) and Q-152c (N = 2).

MERCHANT GOD / WHISKERED GOD

The merchant god is primarily observed in censer form (table 7.8, figure 7.4), although one stucco portrait was present on a sculpted column at Hall Q-163 (figure 2.10). Ten faces and three noses were present among the censers. J. Thompson's (1957) unidentified "whiskered god" was also common, with fifteen examples (figure 7.4). The whiskered god censers probably portray merchants, although they are separately tabulated and evaluated in this discussion. Together whiskered entities and merchant effigies represent the most ubiquitous category of censers (26.7 percent, N = 28). Only Chac is more numerous when cups and censers are considered.

Merchant effigies exhibit interesting variation. The most diagnostic attributes include an elongated nose and hollow eyes. Hollow eyes were present on all of the faces (N = 10) discussed here and three additional noses belonged to this deity (from Q-74, Q-98, and Q-162). Less uniform attributes of merchants include the presence of a bird headdress (N = 1, Q-81), the presence of whiskers on merchants (N = 3, Q-81, Q-163a, and R-86), the presence of a side flap headdress (N = 2, Q-79/79a and Q-163a), and the presence of a protruding lip plug and flat cap (N = 4, two at Q-81, also at Q-172 and Y-8b). Two major variants can be discerned that include the whiskered, side flap, or bird headdress variety and the protruding lip, flat cap variety that resembles God M (J. Thompson 1957), as illustrated in figure 7.4.

Fifteen effigy censers are classified as deities with whiskers (table 7.8). As some clearly identified merchants have whiskers, and most other known Postclassic Maya deities do not, it is likely that whiskered entities are also merchants, perhaps shown without hollow eyes. Taube (1992:figures 44b, 45) illustrates multiple examples of whiskered merchants from the Maya codices and other art. Two whiskered entities have bird headdresses, and at Q-81 this

TABLE 7.8 Structures with whiskered and merchant Chen Mul Modeled effigy censers.

	Whiskered gods		Merchant gods		Combined whiskered and merchant gods
	No.	%	No.	%	%
House Q-62	1	6.7	–	–	3.6
Platform Q-74	–	–	1	7.7	3.6
Shrine Q-79/79a	2	13.3	1	7.7	10.7
Temple Q-80	3	20.0	–	–	10.7
Hall Q-81	1	6.7	3	23.1	14.3
Oratory Q-82	1	6.7	–	–	3.6
Temple Q-95	1	6.7	–	–	3.6
Shrine Q-98	1	6.7	1	7.7	7.1
Hall Q-152c	1	6.7	–	–	3.6
Hall Q-161	–	–	1	7.7	3.6
Temple Q-162	2	13.3	1	7.7	10.7
Sanctuary Q-162b	1	6.7	–	–	3.6
Sanctuary Q-163a	–	–	1	7.7	3.6
House Q-172	–	–	1	7.7	3.6
House K-67	1	6.7	–	–	3.6
House R-86	–	–	1	7.7	3.6
Oratory Y-8b	–	–	2	15.4	7.1
Total	15	100.0	13	100.0	100.0

headdress is also worn by a whiskered merchant. A whiskered, hollow-eyed merchant figure of stucco is observed at Q-163, and he wears a bird headdress (figure 2.10). The whiskered entity on the Santa Rita mural (Tun 6 Ahau figure) also has a bird headdress (J. Thompson 1957). Males with young faces are the only other censer category with multiple examples of bird headdresses (one Itzamna example is present), and as we discuss in chapter 6, this may be linked to military roles that are one aspect of merchant activities. One unique whiskered figure from K-67 wears a helmet with a spike on top. Outside of the Maya area, some other Mesoamerican gods had whiskers, including Quetzalcoatl/Ehecatl in the Borgia Codex. The single trait of whiskers is not

FIGURE 7.4. *Effigy censer burners identified as merchant gods (A) and gods with whiskers (possibly also merchant gods) (B). Courtesy of Carlos Peraza Lope, photos by Bradley Russell.*

sufficient to propose a Quetzalcoatl/Kukulcan identity for Mayapán, especially when some clear examples of merchants also have whiskers. Whiskers may also connote a jaguar association (J. Thompson 1957:611).

The distribution of merchant and whiskered god effigy censers is shown in table 7.8. These are concentrated in two localities of the Main Plaza—the

Q-80 group and the Q-162 group. The Temple Q-80 group accounts for 46.7 percent of the whiskered effigies and 30.8 percent of merchants (including Q-81, Q-79, Q-79a, and Q-82). The Temple of Kukulcan group accounts for 20 percent of the whiskered entities and 23.1 percent of merchants (Q-162, Q-161, Q-162b, and Q-163a). All other occurrences are single censers from different groups—except for Oratory Y-8b, where two merchant effigies were found. Whiskered and merchant censers are not linked to a particular building type, as whiskered effigies are found at three temples and two houses, and merchants are found at one platform, one temple, and two residences. Both are found at one oratory, three shrines, and two halls.

Together, the Q-80 and Q-162 clusters account for 66.7 percent of the whiskered god censers and 53.8 percent of the merchant god censers (table 7.8, Structures Q-81, 81, 82, 161, 162, 162b, 163). The fact that these two categories cluster at the same architectural groups lends support to our suggestion that they both represent merchants. These concentrations occur at two of the most important sets of architecture in the monumental center of Mayapán and reveal the central place given to merchant deities in rites of the Main Plaza.

Maize God and Kukulcan

Maize gods and Kukulcan were difficult to identify in a sample of fragmented censers and censer faces (table 7.9, figure 7.5). Both entities might be expected to have young male faces, of which we found many. Loose costume elements cannot be securely linked to these faces. In the Maya codices, the maize god has a vertical jagged line that crosses his face (Schellhas 1904:167; Taube 1992:41) that was not present in any of the examples in our sample. Since our analysis, however, a new censer was recovered from Hall Q-54 that has a stepped cut-out face, maize foliation, youthful features, and a blue paint that probably represents the maize god (Milbrath and Peraza Lope 2013:220; Milbrath, Peraza Lope, and Delgado Kú 2010). Other ceramic art may portray the maize god, who Taube (1992:41) connects to diving figures at Tulum and a small stone sculpture at Mayapán. Many such descending figures are represented in stone sculptures (N = 13) and effigy ceramics (N = 4). Flowers and maize foliage adorn possible maize god images at Tulum (Taube 1992:41); botanical elements are abundant in our sample, including ten buds, fourteen flowers, sixteen maize plants, and twelve maize tamales (or copal balls). We suspect that these botanical embellishments were part of censers belonging to some of the young male faces, although this association was not constant.

Eight of the structures where young male faces were found had either flowers or maize elements while seven did not.

The maize god is occasionally linked to sacrifice, particularly disembowelment, as in two cases in the Dresden and Paris codices (Taube 1992:44). Disembowelment is closely associated with harvesting maize (especially green corn) elsewhere in Mesoamerica (Taube 1992:44). In these instances and others, Taube notes that the maize god is shown with closed eyes, indicating death. We have one censer body that is disemboweled from Oratory Q-82 (figure 7.5b). A slit was modeled into the censer torso in its lower right abdomen, from which applique entrails protrude. At the top of the sternum area, a wound is also painted on this torso from which blood flows. Perhaps this effigy represents a sacrificed maize deity. As mentioned previously, four young-faced male censers have closed eyes but lack any other attributes that would link them to closed-eye Xipe Totec figures. These examples from Oratory Q-88, Hall Q-151 (N = 2), and Palace R-86 may represent the maize deity.

Other young-faced male effigies may represent the maize god. One vessel has a youthful face that is modeled on the side of a simple vase. Corncob elements may be present in the headdress. Sixteen other young faces are also possible contenders (table 7.9, first column on left), although they may also represent warriors. These young faces are generally attractive, and some resemble a maize god effigy identified by Howard D. Winters (1955b). A complicating factor is that the maize god is not the only male deity who is youthful or beautiful in the Postclassic Period; the Venus deity and Kukulcan could also be put into this category (J. Thompson 1957; Winters 1955b). In fact, the faces of one Kukulcan example and one maize god example from Hall Q-81 were made from the same censer face mold (Winters 1955b). Masson has argued that it difficult to know whether the Tulum descending figures portray Kukulcan or the maize god, as the former was said to descend from the heavens to receive offerings on certain ritual occasions (Landa 1941:158; Masson 2000:221, 231–37). The painted design on the face of the Venus entity aids in identification, but paint has eroded from some of our youthful male examples. Warriors may also have been young and attractive, as suggested by two males with bird headdresses from H-17a and K-67.

Carnegie investigators were conservative with identifications of the maize god or Kukulcan, and they often resorted to describing censers as having youthful faces. A single example of each god was reported by Winters (1955b) from Hall Q-81, made possible by the recovery of fully restorable effigies. Each of these reconstructed censers carries ball adornos, and maize foliage sprouts from the ball held by the maize god. The Kukulcan censer wears a conch shell pendant that represents the primary identifier and has a puma

TABLE 7.9 Chen Mul effigy vessels with male faces that represent unknown entities.

	Young male faces	Other adult male faces	Filed-tooth male	Male w/bird beaddress	Bird beaddress	Male w/ reptile beaddress	Reptile beaddress	Male w/5-point shield	Male w/ belmet	Total
Temple Q-58	–	1	–	–	1	–	–	–	–	2
House Q-62	1	–	–	1	–	1	–	–	–	3
Hall Q-64	–	1	–	–	–	–	–	–	1	2
Hall Q-70	1	–	2	–	1	–	–	–	–	4
Hall Q-72	1	–	–	–	–	–	–	–	–	0
Shrine Q-79/79a	2	–	–	1	–	1	1	–	–	5
Temple Q-80	2	1	6	–	–	–	–	–	–	9
Hall Q-81	–	2	–	–	–	–	–	–	–	2
Oratory Q-82	–	–	–	–	1	–	–	–	–	1
Oratory Q-88	1	1	–	–	–	–	–	–	–	2
Hall Q-88a	1	–	–	–	–	–	1	–	–	2
Platform Q-88b	1	–	–	–	–	–	–	–	–	1
Shrine Q-89	1	–	–	–	–	–	–	–	–	1
Hall Q-151	2	1	–	–	–	–	–	–	–	3
Temple Q-95	1	–	–	–	1	–	–	–	–	2
Temple Q-126	–	–	–	–	–	1	–	–	–	1
Portal Vault Q-127	–	1	–	–	–	–	–	–	–	1

	Young male faces	Other adult male faces	Filed-tooth male	Male w/bird headdress	Bird headdress	Male w/ reptile headdress	Reptile headdress	Male w/5-point shield	Male w/ helmet	Total
Cenote Chèn Mul	1	–	–	–	–	–	–	–	–	1
Temple Q-162	1	–	–	–	2	–	–	–	–	3
Sanctuary Q-162c	–	–	–	–	–	–	–	1	–	1
Altar Q-162h	–	–	–	1	–	–	–	–	–	1
House Q-208	–	1	–	–	–	–	–	–	–	1
Temple H-17	–	1	–	–	–	–	–	–	–	1
Altar H-17a	–	–	–	1	–	–	–	–	–	1
House K-67	–	1	–	1	–	–	–	–	–	2
Palace R-86	2	–	–	1	–	–	–	–	–	3
House J-71a	–	–	–	1	–	–	–	–	–	1
Other	–	–	1	–	–	–	–	1	–	2
Totals (number)	17	11	9	7	6	3	2	2	1	58
Total (percent)	29	19	16	12	10	5	3	3	2	

Note: The North Plaza has 9 percent (Q-58/62.64, N = 5), the West group (Q-70, N = 4) has 7 percent, the North group (Q-79/79a/80/81/82, N = 17) has 29 percent, the East group (Q-151/88/88a/88b, N = 9) has 16 percent, the Castillo group (Q-162, 162c/162h, Cenote Chèn Mul, N = 6) has 10 percent, and the Itzmal Chèn group (H-17/17a, N = 2) has 3 percent. The Q-72 example is from a Lacandon-style head vessel and could be the maize god. It is not included in the percentages calculated.

headdress (Winters 1955b; J. Thompson 1957). This figure does not have the flanking knots or turquoise disk that the Dresden Kukulcan possesses (Taube 1992:60, figure 27a). The Dresden figure has a collar of olive shells, as do comparative examples shown by Taube from Aztec codices. No olive shells were present in our study collection of censer adornos, but one conch shell adorno was found, from the Temple of Kukulcan. This shell may have been part of a Kukulcan censer.

The fisherman mural figure on the bench of Q-95 wears an oversize olive shell in his midsection and may represent Kukulcan (figure 2.24; Masson and Peraza Lope 2007). Unfortunately, the face of this mural was obliterated in antiquity. The presence of a water serpent in this scene is additional evidence for the identification of this figure as God H, who is linked separately to water serpents and Quetzalcoatl in the Dresden Codex (Taube 1992:56, 60). The Classic Period Water Lily Serpent is also linked to the wind glyph (Taube 1992:59). It is curious that this deity, so important to Mayapán, is not clearly represented in human form, in contrast to numerous zoomorphic and architectural referents. Kukulcan is well represented by serpent columns and balustrades, round temples (Milbrath and Peraza Lope 2003a:23; Pollock 1936; Ringle, Négron, and Bey 1998), and bird-beaked Ehecatl sculptures that depict this entity as the wind god.

OTHER MALE CENSERS

Some censers published in the Carnegie *Current Reports* were not identified to specific deities, particularly those with adult male faces that did not look particularly old or young (table 7.9). In our analysis of the INAH assemblage, we had a similar problem. Some adult male censer faces in our sample have distinctive markings that may be linked to specific deities that have yet to be identified, particularly those with scroll designs on their faces or filed teeth. Both of these unusual types concentrate at the Q-80 group (figure 7.5c).

The bodies of restored effigies with adult male faces that were recovered by Peraza Lope's INAH project, along with examples from Chichén Itzá, reveal costume elements that are suggestive of warriors. Animal headdresses, helmets, thick cotton breastplates, and pectoral quincunx shields or medallions may attest to this role (figure 7.5d–f). Fragments of censer bodies from the INAH sample reveal more examples of possible braided cotton armor. Rather than armor, such textile elements may have been part of aged deities (Milbrath and Peraza Lope 2013:218). Proskouriakoff and Charles R. Temple (1955) identified one censer from the R-86 palace as an "Eagle Knight." Bird

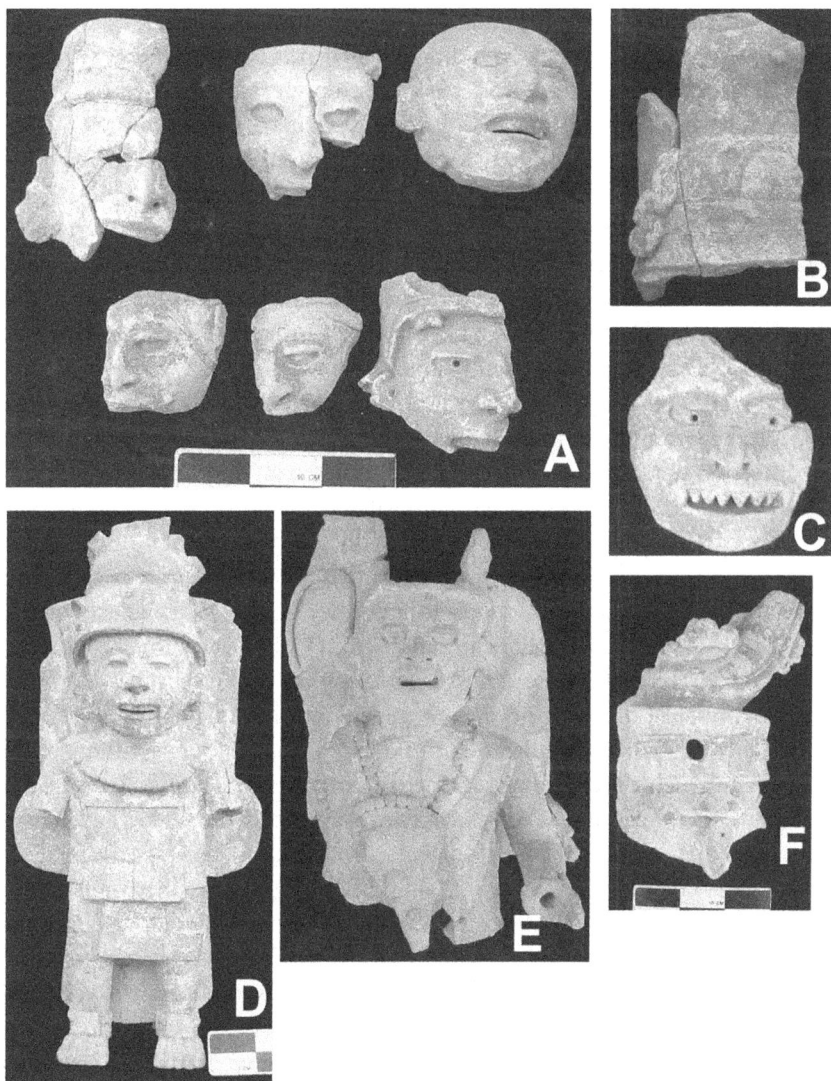

FIGURE 7.5. *Effigy censers with young male faces, including some that may represent the maize god (A), a sacrificial torso with intestines emerging (B), and an example of filed-tooth males (C). Some males have a helmet (D), with a medallion (probably the five-point turquoise symbol (E), or commonly wear bird or reptile (F) headdresses. Courtesy of Carlos Peraza Lope, photos by Bradley Russell.*

or reptile headdresses are common among the adult male effigies; other animal elements are also found, including a jaguar pelt (Q-162) and bat imagery (Q-79). Human tenoned and freestanding sculptures, as discussed previously, have similar headdresses. Some adult male faces may represent warriors, perhaps those who were associated with military orders, as proposed for other Mesoamerican cities (Hirth 1989:69, 73, 77; Sugiyama 2004:118).

Types of headgear may be particularly diagnostic at Mayapán. Recognizable deities such as Itzamna, Chac, Venus, the Monkey Scribe, and various females have turban or miter-style headdresses while males with adult faces that lack diagnostic facial markings tend to have bird or reptile headdresses. Only rarely do other identified gods have animal headdresses, with the exception of merchants, who were known to be armed and martially skilled. Of thirty-one examples of Itzamna ceramic or stone sculptures at the site, only one has a bird headdress (Q-80), and two examples of the merchant god have animal headgear (Q-81 and Q-62). Whiskered gods (also possibly merchants) sometimes have bird headdresses (Q-81 and Q-62), as does a sculpted column whiskered head from Q-163. J. Thompson (1957) states that Chac censers are occasionally associated with reptile headdresses, although we do not see evidence for this in our sample. The single Kukulcan censer from Q-81 has a puma headdress.

If the bird and reptile headdresses (and perhaps other animals) do indicate the presence of warrior orders at the site, we have new insight into the importance of such an organization in the city's rituals. There are hints of the existence of such orders from documents, notably the Chumayel chronicle's metaphorical description of conflict at Mayapán, where the snakes and jaguars are said to bite each other, and also where the "kinkajou claws the back of the jaguar" (Roys 1962:44, Roys 1933:197). Ralph L. Roys long ago interpreted these passages to refer to the existence of warrior orders at Mayapán analogous to those of central Mexico and Chichén Itzá (Roys 1962:44, Roys 1933:197). But the animals referred to in these passages do not correspond neatly to the prevalent bird and reptile headdresses worn by the effigies.

Although jaguars or pumas are present in the iconography of Mayapán, they are not as common as birds or reptiles in the headdresses. Jaguars are not dominant in any particular building program, as they are at Chichén Itzá, and there are very few representations of felines in censer or stone art. At the Temple of Kukulcan one censer (face missing) has a jaguar pelt headdress; separately, four feline effigy censer paws were found by Peraza Lope's team. A Kukulcan censer has a puma headdress from Q-81 (Winters 1955b). One full figure effigy censer seems to have the body of a feline (Q-151). Stone or stucco representations of jaguars are also found at an altar and dance platform aligned with the Temple of Kukulcan (Q-162d and Q-77), one other serpent temple (Q-159), the shrine of an additional hall (Q-72b), and the Itzmal Ch'en temple (H-17). It is odd that feline imagery is so rare at Mayapán, given the references in the chronicles and important precedents at Chichén Itzá. Felines are also rare in the site's faunal record. The dominance of bird imagery in the head-dresses of male adult censers differs from the dominance of serpent imagery in stone sculpture and architecture.

Quincunx emblems include five dots that mark the four corners of a square and a center point (Freidel, Schele, and Parker 1993). Shields with this design may represent jeweled banners such as those carried to or placed in front of temples in the Nuttall Codex (e.g., Nuttall 1975:1, 18). This symbol also decorates certain temples (Nuttall 1975:15, 18), which Bruce E. Byland and John M. D. Pohl (1994:77). identify as a jewel in its roof. Taube (1992:125) states that this symbol is characteristic of a Mexican fire god at Mayapán. Two examples of quincunx banners are present in our collection. Two additional censers display a shield-sized pectoral with this design that is draped over the midsection of adult males, possibly warriors. One of the males is helmeted and the other is missing its headgear; these pieces originate from Sanctuary Q-162c and the Q-64 hall. Two cases of helmet-like headgear are documented, including one each from the Carnegie and INAH projects (figure 7.5d). One wears the quincunx pectoral just discussed (Q-162c, figure 7.5e). The helmet fits close around the face and tapers to a point at the top, and it is unique in the collection. The other helmet is worn by a whiskered entity from house group K-67.

A total of fifty-eight male faces are present in our sample (figure 7.5a, d, e). Of these, seventeen have beautiful faces and might represent the maize god. Assuming that other entities might also have had beautiful faces, these hand-some examples cannot be definitively identified. Some young or mature (not aged) males have distinguishing characteristics such as bird or reptile head-dresses, helmets, quincunx shields, or filed teeth (figure 7.5). Eleven faces could not be identified to any specific deity and could not be classified as especially attractive. Nine filed-tooth males were present in the sample, and these were concentrated in two contexts—seven from the Q-80 temple and two from the Q-70 hall.

Ten examples had bird or reptile headdresses, and six additional isolated bird and two isolated reptile headdresses were present in the collection that had been detached from the faces. The spatial distribution of bird and reptile headdresses is broad (table 7.9). Censer headdresses of both types are found at the Q-79/79a shrine and at a house (Q-62) next to Hall Q-64. All other contexts have exclusively bird (N = 8) or exclusively reptile (N = 2) censer headdress figures. The thirteen different contexts with either headdress type include two halls, three shrine/altars, four temples, and four houses. At least one house and one shrine are linked directly to an adjacent hall. Bird headdress elements (N = 13) are much more common than reptiles (N = 5). Stone sculpture examples of reptile headdress figures are known from two residential groups—J-71b and R-89—and a stone bird headdress figure was found at Hall Q-70. All stone examples are from architectural groups where censer examples were also found.

Bird headgear is exclusively present on censers at Temples Q-58 and Q-95, Altar H-17a (of Temple H-17), Q-162 (along with one of its altars, Q-162h), Hall Q-70, Oratory Q-82, and one upper-status house (K-67). Reptile headdress censers (figure 7.5f) are exclusively present at two contexts: the Q-88a hall and the Q-126 round temple. Some of the most important major groups at the site center are represented by these contexts, including the North Plaza (Q-58/62), a group along the Main Plaza's western edge (Q-70), the Q-80 group that connects the North and Main Plazas (Q-79/79a/82), the Templo Redondo group (Q-88a), the Temple of Kukulcan group (Q-162/162h), and other major features, including the Q-95 Fisherman Temple, the round portal vault Temple Q-126, and three major domestic compounds (R-86/87, K-67, and J-71a). The outlying ceremonial group of Itzmal Ch'en (H-17a), in this respect, replicates art from the site center. From Chichén Itzá, fully restored examples of male effigy censers with bird and reptile headdresses and cotton braided breast plates are currently on display at El Gran Museo del Mundo Maya de Mérida.

Generic adult male faces from which headdresses have been detached are sometimes found in the same contexts as those with bird or reptile headdresses (N = 3). Sometimes they are present in locations without other censers with such headdresses (N = 6). The same pattern is observed for beautiful face males without headdresses; in six cases, they are found with those wearing animal headdresses, and in eight cases, they are not. But twenty-two of twenty-eight adult male faces (beautiful or not) overlap with the same six architectural groups listed above for the bird/reptile headdress distributions. Closed-eye faces are also present at Q-151 (N = 2), R-86 (N = 1), Q-88, and Q-151; they also have the potential to represent ancestral or patron gods rather than specific entities from the Maya codices. Two examples of male faces with nose plug ornaments were also found in the INAH collection, although such ornaments were not unique to warriors. The nose plug censers were also from the Q-80 temple.

A group of censer faces found by the INAH project exhibits distinctive teeth that are filed to a point (table 7.9). This tooth modification provides a fierce appearance, and although Landa (1941:125) describes this practice as one of beautification for women, the censer examples from Mayapán have cropped hairstyles that clearly identify them as male (figure 7.5c). It is interesting that they are concentrated at only two contexts. Most of them are from the Q-80 temple group (seven of nine examples), and two others are present at the Q-70 hall. An effigy censer with filed teeth was recovered at Zacpetén from an oratory or temple, Structure 605; this variant is unusual for that site (Pugh and Rice 2009b:150–53). Another example at that site is reported from group 719 (Pugh, Rice, and Cecil 2009:194). Few examples of such censers have been reported; we are not aware of any in the Maya area other than Zacpetén and these two edifices at Mayapán. It is tempting to interpret these findings as evidence for affinity between the two sites (e.g., chapter 3; Rice and Rice 2009).

Warriors are infrequently portrayed in solid figurines in the Postclassic Maya realm. Known cases include Mayapán House Q-214 and at Santa Rita Corozal in Belize (Chase and Chase 1988:figure 3). Effigy censer portraits of warriors are also reported from Champotón (Milbrath et al. 2008:108). Perhaps the veneration of patron gods of warrior orders was important, or alternatively, revered ancestral lords were portrayed in military gear, as was common in earlier Maya art (Schele and Freidel 1990). War captains would have been influential in Mayapán society as the chief enforcers of state policy (Restall 2001:table 11.3, Roys 1962:50). When they failed, the city recruited mercenaries (Roys 1962:59). Like some of its predecessor capitals in Mesoamerica, Mayapán could have instituted ideological events and objects celebrating the importance of service to the state through the military (e.g., Sugiyama 2004; Headrick 2007).

One problem with the warrior identification is the lack of weapons in the censer assemblage. The Q-214 solid figurine carries a spear. We are left with the conclusion that entities who wore animal headdresses probably carried objects of copal, rubber, maize, or cacao, as did other censer effigies at the site. Perhaps these effigies were patron gods of warrior orders and thus held offerings presented for success in battle.

Warriors are well glorified elsewhere in Mesoamerican art, as exemplified in the eagle/jaguar battle scenes of the Cacaxtla murals (Nagao 1989). Closer in time to Mayapán are the Mixtec codices, where many actors (including some females) in the Nuttall Codex wear bird or reptile headdresses (along with feline headdresses). In many scenes, these figures are not engaged in acts of war (e.g., Nuttall 1975:91). Many actors are ultimately involved in dynastic combative struggles, although it is not clear that their primary occupation was the role of warrior. The Mixtec codices suggest that animal headdresses are more closely related to mythology rather than military institutions in that region. Most striking is a scene from the War of Heaven involving 9 Wind, the Mixtec equivalent of Quetzalcoatl. Patriarchal/priestly figures, the Yaha Yahui, descend from the sky in this scene on page 48 of the Codex Vindobonensis, wearing bird and serpent headdresses (Byland and Pohl 1994:figure 38). They are identified as avatars of 9 Wind by Byland and Pohl (1994:88). A mythological underpinning for these elements of Mayapán's censers and sculptures cannot be ruled out. Kukulcan would have been as important at Mayapán as 9 Wind would have been to Mixteca dynasties, and perhaps the bird/serpent headdresses of the censers signal entities that were devoted to this founding deity. Eagle headdresses are most commonly depicted in the Nuttall and other codices, but the Mayapán birds lack the hooked beak and appear to represent different species. When Mixtec priests are shown (Byland and Pohl 1994:figures 60, 61), they do not have animal headdresses, although their headgear changes with the occasion. Their gear includes miters similar to those of the gods of the Maya codices and many Mayapán censers. Guilhem Olivier (2003:plate 1) notes examples where the Aztec deity Tezcatlipoca appears in the guise of both a turkey and a vulture in highland codices. This example illustrates the point that certain actors could adorn themselves in animal gear for specific occasions.

At Chichén Itzá, evidence is stronger that bird headdresses were associated with military officials—for example, as observed on the Mercado (3D11) balustrades and sculptured dais (Ruppert 1943:236, figure 23). The combatants on the Temple of the Wall Panels (north panel) have hovering snakes and jaguars that face off with their human counterparts (Ruppert 1931:plate 11). Warriors, identified by their weapons, also wear serpent/reptile headdresses at Chichén Itzá, as on two (south and north) sculpted pilasters of the Mercado (Ruppert 1943:figure 20a, f). Many more examples of warriors with animal headdresses exist at Chichén Itzá, although this is not the only type of headgear that warriors have at that site. Two complete bird and reptile headdress censers from El Gran Museo del Mundo Maya in Mérida are from Chichén Itzá, and they link this iconography to the censers.

Headdresses on other effigies come in several basic forms that could be lumped under the general classifications of turbans, flaps, feathers, and cones. Turbans often have large discs across a wide band over the forehead, with a cylinder or funnel-shaped priestly miter element extending above the band (Taube 1992); these are present on censers and the stucco sculptures of the Q-163 hall (Peraza Lope 1999). Another common turban variant is a band that is covered in rows of beaded or knotted cloth, above which rise similar elements to the disc band turbans. Side flap headdresses are rare (figure 7.4a), and only two examples are known from censer sample. Feathers are common back rack elements for many censers, but a few stone sculptures have feathered headdresses as observed at Q-70 (figure 7.1). Torsos on censers and stone sculptures have various layered tunics, pectoral cloth collars, finely made loincloths, and occasional pendants.

FEMALES

Females are rare in Mayapán art compared to males. One female sculpture was paired with a male at Hall Q-161 (figure 7.1), and she is likely an ancestor or other key historical person. Other examples probably represent goddesses. A female torso was found at Sanctuary Q-157a (figure 7.6e). This figure has bare breasts and is broad and crudely made. Another female was reported (Shook 1954a) from round Temple Q-214 and is thought to represent a deity. She wears a V-shaped shawl to the back, although her breasts are bare, and her braided hair is crossed in the rear. She is seated with her knees drawn up, perhaps in a childbearing position. Shook (1954c:19) suggested that she represents Goddess O/Ixchel, as this portrait evinces broad, mature, and authoritative qualities. Both of the females from Q-157a and Q-214 may represent Ixchel, as they share the attributes of broad bodies and bare breasts (figure 7.6d). There are no other specific deity attributes on these sculptures of older women.

Another female sculpture was found at the base of the Castillo's (Q-162) east stair (figure 2.13). Her age is not discernible, as her head has been removed. She is shown grinding at a metate, and this piece perhaps celebrated female roles in the food production process (figure 2.13). Alternatively, the sculpture may refer to a creation myth. A female with a mano and metate is present in the upper celestial realm of the Tulum Structure 16 mural; the scene seems to celebrate dynastic history and mythology (Miller 1982:plate 37; Masson 2000).

At Hall Q-163, a young female was portrayed in plaster around a sculpted column (figure 7.6c). This beautiful, pregnant young woman is identified by Milbrath and Peraza Lope (2003a:26, figure 21) as Tlazolteotl, the Aztec goddess of childbirth. But the column figure does not bear any diagnostic facial markings, including those of the Aztec goddess. Her beauty and youth also recall the younger aspect of Postclassic Maya Goddess I, as shown in the codices (Taube 1992:figure 29), although it is the older Ixchel who is more closely linked to childbirth (Taube 1992, Tozzer 1941:129). Merideth Paxton (2001:148) makes a compelling case that these old and young female portrayals depict the same goddess (Ixchel) at different ages, as they share numerous attributes and

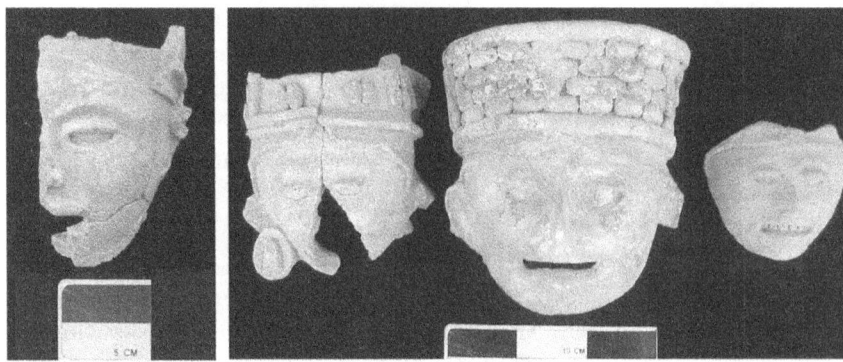

A   B

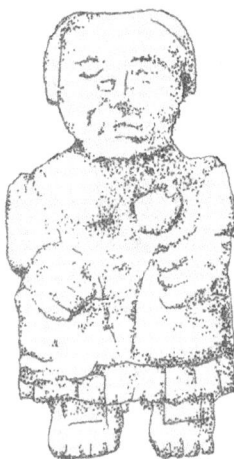
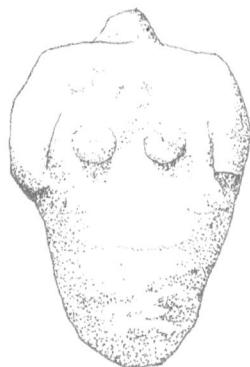

C   D   E

FIGURE 7.6. *Young (A) and older (B) female effigy censers from Mayapán's monumental center (courtesy of Carlos Peraza Lope, photos by Bradley Russell), and monumental center female sculptures, including a young female (stucco column, Hall Q-163, courtesy of Carlos Peraza Lope), a seated older female sculpture from round Temple Q-214 (D), and another sculpture from Shrine Q-157a (E). Objects in D and E drawn by Kendra Farstad from Proskouriakoff (1962a:figure 10f and 10b).*

an identification glyph in the codices. Thompson (1950:83) at one point made a similar argument, as Taube (1992:64) acknowledges. Old and young goddesses in the Maya codices reflected ideal roles for women in Postclassic Maya society (Vail and Stone (2002).

Tlazolteotl's face was identified by J. Thompson (1957) in two examples in the Carnegie censer assemblage, based on distinctive markings, including a U-shaped nose ornament and a yellow and white face with black lip and cheek markings (table 7.10). He states that she is closely associated with weaving, Xipe Totec rituals, and merchants in the central Mexican documentary records. Thompson found examples from Palace R-86 and the Q-208 elite residence. Notably, rare Xipe Totec effigy censers were also found at these two structures.

Eleven other fragments of female censers were recovered by the INAH project, representing a minimum number of seven women in six faces and one fully restored censer (table 7.10). Four other torso fragments with breasts were found. Female effigies are concentrated at the Temple Q-80 group, including six with young faces and two with old faces. Two female torso fragments originate from the Q-80 temple itself, and the other examples are from adjacent Hall Q-81 and Oratory Q-55. Three of the females have blue-painted faces (figure 7.6a). One female effigy was fully restored (Peraza Lope et al. 1997); it had been smashed and thrown into a mass grave just below the plaza surface at the corner of Hall Q-81 and Shrines Q-79 and 79a (Pedro Delgado Kú, personal communication 2013). A portion of the mass grave was originally investigated by Robert M. Adams, Jr. (1953), and additional work by Peraza Lope et al. (1997) reveals that this deposit is spatially extensive. Milbrath suggests (personal communication, 2013) that this restored female may represent a version of an Aztec female maize goddess (Chicomecoatl), as she wears a central Mexican–style V-shaped shawl (*quechquemitl*). This effigy, and five other examples with young faces, may represent Goddess I, and the two older ones with gaping mouths could either be an older aspect of her or Goddess O/ Ixchel, according to Taube's (1992) classification. This explanation is the simplest. Females wore V-shaped shawls in other instances of Postclassic Maya public art. For example, the rear side of the female figure in figure 7.6d has such a shawl (as shown in Proskouriakoff 1962a:figure 10f), as do the female ancestral figures shown on the Tulum murals (Masson 2000, 2003a). Mayapán figurines, however, most commonly wear simple dresses that cover the chest, as do some portraits of probable historical personages (Masson and Peraza Lope 2012). It is probable that many of Mayapán's figurines represented people rather than gods (e.g., M. Smith 2002:105–6).

TABLE 7.10 Structures with female Ch'en Mul Modeled effigy censers.

Structure	Young face (number)	Old face (number)	Female body fragment (number)	Tlazolteotl goddess* (number)
Oratory Q-55	–	–	1	–
Temple Q-80	4	2	2	–
Hall Q-81	–	–	1	–
Residence Q-208	–	–	–	1
Palace R-86	–	–	–	1
Shrine/Hall Q-79/Q-81	1	–	–	–

* Identified by J. Thompson (1957)

The seven female faces are clearly identified as female by centrally parted long hair that drapes partially over the forehead, with one exception (figure 7.6b). Male censer figures have short cropped hairstyles and the female faces are noticeably more gracile than the males. One female face fragment lacks the hair portion of the censer but exhibits delicate facial features. The concentration of these censers at Temple Q-80 and adjacent Hall Q-81 is striking and suggests that specific ritual practices at this temple were connected to Goddesses I and O. Two Tlazolteotl effigies identified by J. Thompson (1957) come from two residences. Stone or stucco women are present at additional contexts, including public buildings Q-157a, Q-214, Q-162, and Q-163. Women in the city's art are thus represented by four general entity types: young goddess, old goddess, Tlazolteotl, and ancestral figures. The only effigy censers in residential contexts are those of Tlazolteotl, perhaps incorporated by nobility to emphasize their foreign connections (J. Thompson 1957; Masson and Peraza Lope 2010), although some residences had numerous female solid or hollow figurines. These figurines lack distinctive deity characteristics (Masson and Peraza Lope 2012). Female figurines are also reported from Zacpetén, although they are not common (P. Rice 2009f:292–95). A very small proportion of the Mayapán female figurines appear pregnant, as is sometimes the case for the Zacpetén assemblage. Figurines are not found from the coeval sites of Laguna de On or Caye Coco, Belize, with the exception of one articulated puppet-like example from the latter site. Prudence Rice (2009f:292–95) reports that female figurines are found in public and residential contexts, and this distribution is also observed at Mayapán (Masson and Peraza Lope 2010:figures 2–7, 9, 10; Masson and Peraza Lope 2012). The lack of distinctive deity attributes on female figurines in the Postclassic Maya area contrasts with examples reported from Otumba (C. Charlton 1994). As Prudence Rice (2009f) suggests for Zacpetén, the Mayapán examples were probably important for curing and practices that included household rituals. It is interesting that reverence regarding these figurines also resulted in their deposition in and around monumental buildings; they are also common in child burials at Mayapán (Masson and Peraza Lope 2012).

Venus

Venus deities had a youthful appearance like that of the maize god (Milbrath and Peraza Lope 2013). J. Thompson (1957) tentatively identified a central Mexican Venus god in the Carnegie project assemblage, based on a painted checkerboard facial pattern (figure 7.7a). Four examples are known, and they are concentrated at Shrine Q-79/79a (N = 3) and Hall Q-81 (N = 1), with which these shrines share a platform. This tally includes Thompson's identification of one face at each building; two more were found associated with Q-79/79a by the INAH project. Thompson's examples had lower skeletal jawbones, which he linked to the central Mexican deity Tlauizcalpantecutli and other Venus figures in the Mexican codices (J. Thompson 1957:616). The newly found examples have checkerboard patterns delineated by yellow paint on a white background. Kukulcan was sometimes associated with Venus (Milbrath and Peraza Lope 2003a). It is possible that he is indirectly referenced by these Venus effigies.

Xipe Totec

Two Xipe Totec sculptures are reported—one of stucco from Hall Q-163 (Peraza Lope 1999; Milbrath and Peraza Lope 2003a) and one of stone from a plaza trench dug between the Temple of Kukulcan and the Q-77 platform (Adams 1953). A couple of other examples of human stone sculptures have closed eyes, as do three additional human tenoned heads, four ceramic masks (figure 7.7d), and the old and young face male censer effigies described previously. It is not certain that all figures with closed eyes represent Xipe Totec, in the absence of other identifying attributes. But at least seven censer effigies definitively portray this entity (figure 7.7c). Two faces each originate from Hall Q-88a and elite Residence Q-208, and one each was found from Altar Q-72b, Temple Q-80, and palace compound R-86 (table 7.11). Two additional censer limbs that exhibit flayed skins come from Q-208, and these fragments probably belong to the same vessels as the faces (J. Thompson 1957). Xipe Totec is the

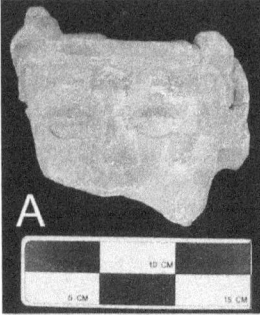

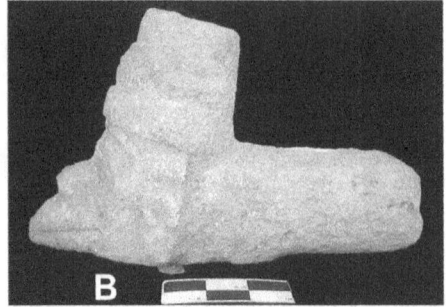

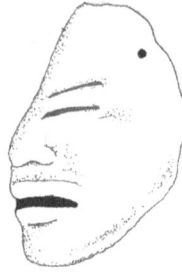

FIGURE 7.7. *Examples of a checkered-face Venus ceramic effigy (A), a stone Ehecatl sculpture from the Temple of Kukulcan (B), a Xipe Totec effigy (C), a ceramic mask resembling Xipe (D), and two Monkey Scribe effigy censers (E, F). Examples A–C and E–F are from the monumental center, courtesy of Carlos Peraza Lope. Photos A, B, C, and E by Bradley Russell; photo F by Phil Hostetler; example D is from Structure Q-119, drawn by Kendra Farstad from R. Smith (1971:figure 32d).*

most clearly identified central Mexican deity at Mayapán, and he is present at three major compounds of the Main Plaza and two upper-status residential groups located near the monumental zone. In all contexts where Xipe Totec is found, the assemblage of effigies also includes a majority of more traditional Maya gods. The presence of this deity does not necessarily indicate foreign residences at Mayapán, as this entity was incorporated in a cosmopolitan fashion into rituals involving local supernatural beings (Masson and Peraza Lope 2010). House Q-208 has the greatest number of Xipe representations due to the presence of body fragments and faces, and it is noteworthy that a representation of Tlazolteotl was also found there. This concentration may attest to especially strong international ties of the Q-208 residents. The Xipe Totec censer fragments come from a multiple child burial at this house. There is nothing else that is unusual about the grave, and the presence of this god may be related to the deity's association with renewal in the cycle of death and rebirth.

Descending Figures

Effigies of diving or descending figures are found in ceramic (N = 4) and stone (N = 12). They are distributed at both domestic and public buildings in quantities of one or two per edifice (table 7.12). Diving figures are likely to represent different individual deities, or perhaps ancestors, rather than a specific entity known as the diving god (Masson 2000). Other possibilities are discussed in the section treating the maize god and Kukulcan. The lack of diagnostic attributes prohibits the identification of descending entities with specific deities.

Ceramic Masks

Four ceramic masks were recovered by Carnegie investigators from Structures Q-244b (N = 2), Q-119 (N = 1), and Q-59b (N = 1). Three were from residential contexts and one was from Q-59b, a burial altar in front of Temple Q-58 (table 7.13). These masks may depict deceased humans or gods (figure 7.7d), as suggested previously in the discussion of the maize god, young-faced males, and Xipe Totec. Their slit eyes are closed or partially open and their mouths are open as if to permit speech. Three mouths are oval shaped, and one is an open slit. The masks are all perforated for suspension but are too small to have been worn over a human face, around 7 centimeters in height (Taube 1992:122). A. Ledyard Smith and Karl Ruppert (1956:figure 10f) suggest that the example from Q-244b was used as a pectoral. It is not possible to determine whether the masks were intended for covering skeletal bundles

TABLE 7.11 Structures with Xipe Totec Chen Mul Modeled effigy censers.

Structure	Number
Altar Q-72b	1
Temple Q-80	1
Hall Q-88a	2
Residence Q-208	2
Palace R-86	1

of the deceased, as has been argued for other mask traditions of Mesoamerica (Headrick 2007:55–56). Only one of these contexts is a burial (Q-59b). No burials are reported from Q-119a and the mask from Q-244b was not in one of the burials. Thus, their use as funerary masks cannot be inferred from the present data, although they all come from residences and may have been part of mortuary bundles removed at some point from funerary contexts. These items are rare at the site, and while each is unique, all share basic similarities. They originate from contexts that are not spatially clustered. One derives from a temple group at the site center (Q-59b), two from a large elite residential group to the southeast of the center (Q-244b), and one is from a large residential group to the center's northeast (Q-119). Masks are rare at Zacpetén, although one example was recovered that represents the face of a rain deity that is unlike the human face masks of Mayapán (P. Rice 2009f:297).

Taube (1992:122, figure 74) identifies these masks as representations of Xipe Totec. They might represent pectorals linked to the veneration of this deity rather than representations of deceased residents of the city. They do not originate from any contexts where Xipe Totec censers were found. If these masks do represent Xipe Totec, then the total number of contexts with this god at the city would be increased to thirteen. The only attributes that these masks share with Xipe Totec are the closed eyes and open, prominent mouths and lips. Human sculptures at Mayapán can also have closed eyes and open mouths yet may not represent this god, as observed on the figures from Q-127a and Q-149 and tenoned heads from Q-126 and P-33b (Proskouriakoff 1962a:figure 8). The ceramic masks closely resemble some of the faces of figurines that also have closed eyes and open mouths and are not Xipe Totec (e.g., two figurines from Q-244b and a figurine from the R-86 palace group). A personified, ground stone celt from the R-86 group exhibits the same face. It is hard to know whether deceased entities were Xipe Totec without additional identifying attributes such as flayed skin (Proskouriakoff and Temple 1955). The faces from Q-244b are missing their

TABLE 7.12 Structures with ceramic and stone diving figures.

Structure	Ceramic	Stone
Temple H-17	–	1
Altar H-17a	–	1
Residence R-86	1	1
Residence S-133b	–	1
Hall Z-50	–	2
Hall Q-54	–	1
Shrine Q-89	–	1
Portal vault Q-127	–	1
House Q-208	2	1
House Q-244	–	2
Hall Q-81	1	–
Total	4	12

bodies. The theme of a dead or sleeping posture with an open mouth is probably not unique to Xipe Totec and may in some cases represent ancestral personages.

MONKEY SCRIBE

Four Monkey Scribe ceramic effigies have been found at three different groups, including one from Temple Q-58, two from the Templo Redondo group (Q-152, figure 7.7e), and one from the R-86 noble residence. The most elaborate example is from Temple Q-58 (figure 7.7f), the subject of a recent article by Milbrath and Peraza Lope (2003b), who document this entity's links to Maya creation myths. The presence of two Monkey Scribe effigies in the Templo Redondo group provides further indications of an emphasis on traditional Maya gods at this locality, including Itzamna and Chac. The Q-58 example was found buried facedown in the soil behind this large burial shaft temple, the second biggest structure in the monumental zone. The effigy was probably removed from the pyramid's temple, perhaps at the time of the city's destruction. This scribe holds a shell ink cup and brush, and numerical banners are painted on his tongue, headdress, and arms. Human sacrifice at Q-58 would have been linked to creation mythology, of which the Monkey Scribe was an integral component (Milbrath and Peraza Lope 2003b).

TABLE 7.13 Structures with human face ceramic masks.

Structure	Description of structure	Description of mask
Q-59b	Burial shrine in front of temple Q-58	Mask has half open, narrow eyes with elongated, open oval mouth.
Q-119a	Residence to northeast of monumental center	Mask has closed-eye slits and a wide, straight open mouth.
Q-244 group	Elite house	Mask has barely open eyes with an elongated, open oval mouth. A second mask has closed eye slits with an elongated, open oval mouth.

CHACMOOL-LIKE RECLINING FIGURE

A miniature reclining ceramic sculpture with its head missing was found from the Q-90 shrine (figure 7.8). The body posture mimics that of larger Chacmool stone sculptures known from Chichén Itzá, but it is hard to know whether this figure portrayed the same entity; it lacks an offering dish on its midsection.

DEATH GODS

A small skeletal sculpture from the Q-95 temple resembles the central Mexican deity of Cihuateteo (Milbrath and Peraza Lope 2003a:figure 21b), and it shares characteristics with a variety of Mesoamerican death gods (figure 7.2d). A skeletal effigy stone ring was found at a dance platform (Q-96) in front of Temple Q-95. Nine tenoned skeletal faces decorated Shrine Q-89, which is located in the courtyard formed in part by Temple Q-95 (figure 7.2a). Twenty-one of thirty-nine death images—including censers, skull effigy cups, tenoned skulls and other sculptures—are concentrated in the Q-95 temple group. Skull art is similar across all of these different media, and the inverted V-shaped nose element is also common in central Mexico death god representations. Ceramic effigies of the death god take three major forms (table 7.14, figure 7.2b, c), including a skeletal head that was formerly part of a full-bodied censer, mandibles that were part of skeletal cups, or modeled skull elements that were part of censer headdresses that featured multiple skulls (R. Smith 1971:figure 71a). Headdress skulls (death bonnets) are not included in our tally, as they were not fully published in the *Current Reports*. Two molds for effigy censer–sized death heads were found by the Carnegie project, from Residence S-133b and Oratory Y-8b. One variant of the full-bodied censer death figures

FIGURE 7.8. *A miniature Chacmool sculpture from Structure Q-90 (top) and an example of several earth lord sculptures at Mayapán, this one from Q-83 (bottom).*

TABLE 7.14 Death effigy ceramic vessels. All are Ch'en Mul effigy censers unless otherwise described.

Structure	Number	Description
Hall Q-70	1	1 death torso (Chapab Modeled vessel with applique decoration)
Temple Q-80	2	1 death face, 1 skeletal mandible
Oratory Q-82	2	1 death cup, 1 death censer face
Hall Q-88a	1	Death face fragment, skeletal mandible
Shrine Q-90	1	Death face has perforated mouth, no nose
Temple Q-95	8	2 skeletal mandibles from probable skull cups, 1 skull cup, 2 maxilla, 2 perforated mouths without noses, 1 skull face
Temple Q-162	1	Perforated mouth with nose
Elite Residence Q-170	1	Death face censer
Elite Residence R-86	1	Death face cup
Residence R-126a	1	Death head mold

has a perforated mouth (figure 7.2c). Bradley Russell (personal communication, 2004) suggests that these holes represent teeth. Three examples of these perforated mouth censers have no nose—just like the skeletal faces—and this trait equates them with death god images (figure 7.2c).

PUFFY FACE FIGURES

Two puffy-faced figures with enlarged cheeks are found in Mayapán's sculpture assemblage, one is from the Temple of Kukulcan (Q-162), and the other is from Itzmal Ch'en Hall H-15. The Q-162 example has a beaded turban headdress. This curious personage has yet to be linked to a known deity.

WIND GOD / EHECATL

Two stone tenoned heads and one ceramic representation of a bird-beaked human are found at Mayapán. All are from the Temple of Kukulcan group; the censer and one stone sculpture are from the temple itself (figure 7.7b). The other example is from an adjacent structure at the temple's southwest corner (Sanctuary Q-163a). This exclusive distribution reveals an association of the site's main temple with Quetzalcoatl/Kukulcan, including his aspect in the form of the wind god (see Milbrath and Peraza Lope 2003a:26, figure 22). The ubiquity of serpent sculptures in the site center and at the Itzmal Ch'en group is discussed in chapters 2 and 3. Sometimes these sculptures indicate serpent column temples (Proskouriakoff 1962a; Pugh 2001), and in other cases they demonstrate the importance of the feathered or other serpent deity sculptures at public buildings of the city.

EARTH LORD

Earth lord effigies are found at Mayapán in multiple media (figure 7.8). A modeled stucco altar on the plaza floor of the Itzmal Ch'en group—Shrine H-18a—depicts this deity, specifically, the central Mexican god Tlaltecuhtli (Proskouriakoff 1962a:137; Taube 1992:128–30; Milbrath and Peraza Lope 2003a:26). Taube (1992:128–30) suggests that this god may have had a Late Classic Maya precedent in Itzamna Cain, Itzamna's earth monster manifestation. A miniature stone sculpture of a scaly earth monster was found at R-88, part of the R-86 palace group. Another clawed, long-limbed earth lord figure rides a diving figure from the Q-83 oratory. A pair of earth lord riders are mounted like jockeys atop the heads of serpent columns from Temple Q-159 (Proskouriakoff 1962a:figure 7).

SCROLL FACE EFFIGIES

Four examples of a scroll-faced censer entity come from Temple Q-80. Each has a yellow square scroll that extends from the nose across the cheekbones and cheek. The identification of this entity is unknown.

PERFORATED HAIR ENTITY

One censer has rows of perforations that extend along the hairline. Perhaps hair was embedded into these indentations when the censer was used. This attribute is rare, but a similar characteristic is observed on a death god image from the Templo Mayor of Tenochtitlan (Solís 2004).

ANIMALS

Animal heads, full-bodied images, tenoned sculptures, or ring sculptures occur regularly at Mayapán's buildings. Except for the felines and serpents discussed previously, these sculptures tend to represent animals that are not fierce predators (table 7.15). Most examples have been found at the site center, the Itzmal Ch'en group, or high-status residences. A monkey and a coati ring were present at Sanctuary Q-162b along with a dog or coati head. Dog head sculptures were also found in a niche in Cenote X-Coton and at Halls Q-81 and H-15 (figure 3.10). Monkey stone sculptures are found at Itzmal Ch'en Temple H-17 (figure 3.8) and on two panels from the Z-8b house (Proskouriakoff 1962a:figure 11b, c). Bird effigies are found at elite contexts including Palace R-86, Altar H-17a, and at Halls Q-151 and Q-152c; some of these have perforated eyeholes and could have been ring sculptures or cord holders. A single crocodile sculpture was found at House J-71b and an iguana column was present at House Q-113a. Felines are confined to the Main Plaza and Itzmal Ch'en. They were recovered from the Q-159 temple, dance Platform Q-77, Altars Q-72b and Q-162d, Hall Q-88a, and Hall H-15; the latter is probably a sacrificial stone (Proskouriakoff 1962a:figure 10x). The miniature jaguar from Q-88a, inscribed with calendrical hieroglyphs, may represent the maize god in feline form (Peraza Lope et al. 1997:41–49). A variety of structure types have animal sculptures, including four houses; two platforms; five halls, five altars, shrines, or sanctuaries; one cenote; and three temples (table 7.15). All of the houses except for Z-8b are elaborate.

Animal vessels, most of which are not censers, are few at Mayapán. Rodent, pisote, or turkey head applique pots were found at P-114 and Y-45a. Four large ceramic feline paws and a feline censer headdress came from Q-162b; one feline effigy vessel was found in the Q-151/152 passage; one pelt from a censer headdress came from Q-152c; and two effigy vessels were found at elite Residence Q-169. The paws from the Castillo sanctuary (Q-162b) and the feline effigy vessels resemble those from Classic Period Monte Alban, although the vessel slips and form are local. While we do not propose a direct historical relationship, earlier Oaxacan precedents are worth noting, as these are not limited to jaguars but also to the representation of a variety of animals, deities, and warriors in ceramic vessels (Caso and Bernal 1952). Other animals are fewer in number at Mayapán. One monkey sculpture was found at H-18a and at the Q-151/152 passage, and the feet of an odd zoomorphic entitity, with toes made of three cacao pods, came from Q-58.

MISCELLANEOUS STONE SCULPTURES

Effigy Banners, Bundles, and Stone Houses

A few stone banners or banner holders are preserved at Mayapán. They were located at round Temple Q-214, monument Platform Q-84, Temple Q-159,

TABLE 7.15 Contexts with zoomorphic stone and stucco sculptures.

Structure	Identification
Temple H-17	Monkeys (N = 3)
House Z-8b	Monkeys (N = 2)
Elite House R-86	Parrot
Hall Q-151	Bird
Altar H-17a	Bird
Hall Q-152c	Bird
House J-71b	Crocodile
Hall Q-81	Dog
Cenote X-Coton	Dog
Sanctuary Q-162b	Dog/coati
Platform Q-77	2 feline
Temple Q-159	Feline
Altar Q-72b	Feline
Altar Q-162d	Feline
Hall H-15	Feline (N = 2), sacrificial stone shown in Proskouriakoff 1962a:figure 10x, and a miniature sculpture
Hall Q-88a	Feline, miniature with glyphs
House Q-113a	Iguana column
Platform Q-96	Unidentified body
Temple Q-95	Unidentified body
Shrine Q-90	Unidentified body
Temple H-17	Turkey
Temple H-17	Serpents (N = 11)
Hall H-15	Serpents (N = 2)
Temple H-17	Turtles (N = 3)
Hall H-15	Turtles (N = 2), 1 with human face
Hall H-15	Dog

Platform Q-172, and House Z-8b. A stone bundle was recovered at Temple Q-80 (table 7.16). Banners and bundles would have been an important part of rituals conducted at Mayapán, and most would have been made of perishable materials. They are rarely represented in stone and their distribution is not particularly revealing. They are not found at the same structures as column ball sculptures. Three small stone effigy temple sculptures are reported for Mayapán at Houses Q-66 and S-133b and Palace R-86. Such temple effigies are reported for the Aztec area (e.g., Marquina 1960:figures 3–6) and Copán, where they may have represented sleeping houses for deities (Stuart 1998:400).

COLUMN BALL SCULPTURES

Thirteen column ball sculptures have been found at Mayapán, from contexts that include four temples (including two round temples); two halls; five altars, sanctuaries, or oratories; one house; and one monument platform (table 7.17). They generally resemble earlier war banners or marker stones documented for sites such as Teotihuacan, Tikal, and El Tajín (Freidel, Schele, and Parker 1993:figures 7:4b, 7.6; Koontz 2002:109–14). Rex Koontz also identifies them in Postclassic central Mexican codices. The art at El Tajín shows banners at a scale that approximates the large size of some Mayapán examples. The earlier banners have circular disks on top rather than rounded balls on top of a straight stone column, as at Mayapán. In our sample, these sculptures were central components of the structures in which they were found, particularly at Itzmal Ch'en Shrine H-18 (Proskouriakoff 1962a:figure 10). There is no direct evidence for their association with war activities at Mayapán, but they may be linked to sacrificial rituals that could have been the end product of war. Shrine H-18 had a burial shaft in which sacrificial victims were placed (Chowning 1956). Alternatively, they may have been installed as part of cosmological or calendrical ceremonies, perhaps involving the world tree as the axis mundi. Symbolic links between sacrifice, warfare, and cosmology are not mutually exclusive at Mesoamerican sites (Freidel, Schele, and Parker 1993:299–303; Koontz 2002; Sugiyama 2004).

Column ball sculptures were not concentrated at specific groups, although important groups seem to possess them. They are found at an oratory at the Main Plaza's northeast entrance (Q-83), a monument platform within the plaza (Q-84), a skull platform/shrine (Q-89), two major halls just to the southeast of the Main Plaza (Q-142 and Q-145), the Templo Redondo (Q-152) and its sanctuary (Q-152a), the Temple of Kukulcan (Q-162), a temple to the south of the Main Plaza (Q-218), a round shrine (H-18) and altar (H-17a) of the Itzmal Ch'en group, and a palace structure (R-87) and its sanctuary (R-90). In three cases, two column ball sculptures are found within a single group, and two of these groups include a round temple. The presence of column ball sculptures marks the Itzmal Ch'en, Templo Redondo, and Temple of Kukulcan groups;

TABLE 7.16 Structures with stone banner holders or bundles.

Structure	Description
Temple Q-80	1 bundle
Round Temple Q-214	1 zoomorphic banner holder
Monument Platform Q-84	1 banner holder
Temple Q-149	1 stone bowl
Temple Q-159	1 banner holder or spool element
House Q-172	1 socketed banner holder
House Z-8b	1 banner holder

TABLE 7.17 Structures with column ball altars.

Structure	Number
Oratory Q-83	1
Monument Platform Q-84	1
Shrine Q-89	1
Hall Q-142	1
Hall Q-145	1
Round Temple Q-152	1
Shrine Q-157a	1
Temple Q-162	1
Temple Q-218	1
Altar H-17a	1
Round Temple H-18	1
House R-87	1
Sanctuary R-90	1

the example at Itzmal Ch'en is the largest at the city. Some interesting spatial overlap is observed in the distribution of these columns with that of sacrificial stones, as described in the next section.

SACRIFICIAL STONES

Seven sacrificial stones are reported from the site (table 7.18). They are identified by a tapered shape at one end. Examples are found at four temples, one altar linked to a temple, one hall, and one monument platform. The Temple of Kukulcan (Q-162), the Q-218 temple, the H-17a altar, and the Q-84 monument platform have these stones and column ball sculptures. The Q-141 temple, which has a sacrificial stone, is situated across a courtyard from Hall Q-142, where a column ball altar was found. The contexts of five of seven sacrificial stones thus overlap with structures or groups that have column ball sculptures, suggesting a functional relationship between these two types. The two other contexts include burial shaft Temple Q-95, where the presence of a sacrificial stone is not surprising, and the Z-50 hall that is located at the southern end of Mayapán's principle sacbe.

SPATIAL DISTRIBUTION OF EFFIGIES AT MAYAPÁN: A SUMMARY

The distribution of stone, stucco, and ceramic effigies at individual structures has been explored in detail in the foregoing sections of this chapter, where the tallies of effigy ceramics have been presented in separate tables from those of stone or stucco. Here we summarize the composite characteristics of these structure group assemblages and examine combined proportions of deities represented in multiple media. There is a tendency for the majority of entities to be represented primarily in stone/stucco or ceramic forms. The percentage of effigy types of all media within these groups is presented in tables 7.19 and 7.20. Table 7.19 provides row totals that examine the proportion of all specific effigies within each structure and within each structure group. Table 7.20 presents column totals that reveal the proportion of each effigy in the sample that is found at individual structures and groups. These tables provide percentages that differ from those offered previously in this chapter, as they combine all examples of stone, stucco, and ceramic effigies. Common effigy types are widely distributed (figure 7.9), and the Q-80 group has twice as many effigies as all other groups (figure 7.10) other than the Templo Redondo group (Q-152).

Within specific architectural groups, some effigies are present in large proportions. Chac (N = 39) and Itzamna (N = 35) censers or cups are common in the assemblages from the Templo Redondo (Q-152) compound (28.9 percent, 21.1 percent) and elite residential group R-86 (33 percent, 19.0 percent), as indicated in table 7.19. Itzamna is also common at the Temple Q-58 group (25 percent) and the Q-127 and Itzmal Ch'en groups (20 percent each). These patterns suggest the importance of local gods at these groups, although the Templo Redondo and R-86 assemblages also include the central Mexican entity Xipe Totec and a wide range of other traditional Maya deity effigies

TABLE 7.18. Structures with tapered sacrificial stones.

Structures	Number
Monument Platform Q-84	1
Burial shaft Temple Q-95	1
Temple Q-141	1
Temple Q-162	1
Temple Q-218	1
Altar H-17a	1
Hall Z-50	1

(figures 7.11–7.14). In the K'ich'ean area, Mexican-style architecture such as twin temple complexes and Mexican deity effigies such as Xipe Totec are also reported, but as is observed at Mayapán, these features are not numerically dominant in the assemblages (Carmack 1971:16–17).

When the distributions of all examples among the groups are calculated (table 7.20, figure 7.11), the Templo Redondo group has 28.2 percent of the sample's Chac effigies and 22.9 percent of the Itzamna effigies. The R-86 compound has 17.9 percent of the sample's Chacs but only 11.4 percent of the Itzamnas. Temple Q-58 has 11.4 percent of the site's Itzamna figures. At the Q-80 temple cluster, which has the most censers of any group, 20 percent of all Itzamna and 10.3 percent of all Chac effigies in the sample were found. But these were not the most important censers at the Q-80 group, as merchants, other males, and females are present in higher proportions (figure 7.11). Although important at several particular groups, Chac and Itzamna effigies were popular and widely distributed in lower proportions at many other localities.

Merchant/whiskered gods are present in high proportions in two groups: the Temple Q-80 cluster and the Temple of Kukulcan (Q-162) group, which have 16.7 percent and 25.9 percent of these effigies, respectively (table 7.19). Other male figures are also relatively abundant at these groups, representing 19.4 percent of the Q-80 group assemblage and 14.8 percent of the Q-162 group sample. Other male effigies are particularly ubiquitous at Q-58 (37.5 percent) and Itzmal Ch'en (40 percent), where they are more abundant than other types. Hall Q-70 (18.8 percent) and Portal Gate Q-127 (20 percent) also have high proportions, although other males are not the most common type at these groups. It may be significant that the Q-80 and Q-162 groups are the only localities where other male effigies are ubiquitous along with high proportion of merchant and whiskered entities (figures 7.11, 7.12).

TABLE 7.19 Distribution percentage of effigy types within structures and groups (row totals).

Structure	Itzamna	Old god	Merchant/ whiskered	Chac	Maize	Other male	Closed-eye human	Xipe Totec	Death head	Female
Q-80 GROUP										
Q-80 temple	2	–	3	2	2	7	–	1	2	8
Q-81 hall	3	1	4	1	–	2	–	–	–	2
Q-79/79a shrine	2	–	3	1	2	3	–	–	–	–
Q-83 oratory	–	–	–	–	–	–	–	–	–	–
Q-82 oratory	–	–	1	–	–	1	–	–	2	–
Subtotal	7	1	11	4	4	13	0	1	4	10
Q-80 group (percent)	10.6	1.5	16.7	6.0	6.0	19.4	0.0	1.5	6.0	14.9
R-86 GROUP										
R-86 residence	4	–	1	5	2	1	1	1	1	1
R-91 oratory	–	–	–	2	–	–	–	–	–	–
Subtotal	4	0	1	7	2	1	1	1	1	1
R-86 group (percent)	19.0	0.0	4.8	33.3	9.5	4.8		4.8	4.8	4.8
Q-162 GROUP										
Q-162 temple	2	–	3	–	1	2	–	–	1	–
Q-161 hall	1	–	1	1	–	–	–	1	1	1
Q-163 hall	–	–	1	–	–	–	–	–	–	1
Q-162b	–	–	1	–	–	–	–	–	1	–

continued on next page

TABLE 7.19—*continued*

Structure	Itzamna	Old god	Merchant/ whiskered	Chac	Maize	Other male	Closed-eye human	Xipe Totec	Death head	Female
Cenote Chèn Mul										
Q-162c	—	—	—	—	—	I	—	—	—	—
Q-162h	—	—	—	—	—	I	—	—	—	—
Q-163a sanctuary	—	—	I	—	—	—	—	—	—	—
Subtotal	3	0	7	I	2	4	0	I	3	2
Q-162 group (percent)	11.1	0.0	25.9	3.7	7.4	14.8	0.0	3.7	11.1	7.4
Q-95 GROUP										
Q-95 temple	—	—	I	I	—	I	—	—	9	—
Q-89 shrine	I	—	—	—	I	—	—	—	9	—
Q-90 shrine	—	—	—	—	—	—	—	—	I	—
Q-94 house	—	—	—	—	—	—	—	—	I	—
Q-97 hall	—	—	—	—	—	I	—	—	I	—
Subtotal	I	0	I	I	I	2	0	0	21	0
Q-95 group (percent)	3.7	0.0	3.7	3.7	3.7	7.4	0.0	0.0	77.8	0.0
Q-152 GROUP										
Q-88a hall	I	—	—	4	—	—	—	2	2	—
Q-151 hall	I	2	—	2	2	I	2	—	—	—
Q-88 oratory	—	I	—	I	I	I	2	—	—	—

continued on next page

TABLE 7.19—continued

Structure	Itzamna	Old god	Merchant/ whiskered	Chac	Maize	Other male	Closed-eye human	Xipe Totec	Death head	Female
Q-152c hall	2	–	1	2	–	–	–	–	–	–
Q-87a oratory	1	–	–	–	–	–	–	–	–	–
Q-152 temple	2	–	–	1	–	–	–	–	–	–
Q-87a hall	–	–	–	1	–	–	–	–	–	–
Q-152b sanctuary	1	–	–	–	–	–	–	–	–	–
Subtotal	8	3	1	11	3	2	4	2	2	0
Q-152 group (percent)	21.1	7.9	2.6	28.9	7.9	5.3	10.5	5.3	5.3	0.0
Q-70 GROUP										
Q-70 hall	2	–	–	–	1	3	–	–	1	–
Q-54 hall	–	–	–	–	–	–	–	–	2	–
Q-72b altar	–	–	–	–	–	–	–	1	–	–
Q-69 shrine	–	–	–	–	–	–	–	–	1	–
Q-72 hall	–	1	–	–	1	–	–	–	–	–
Q-74 platform	–	–	1	–	–	–	–	–	–	–
Q-71 shrine	–	–	–	1	–	–	–	–	–	–
Q-55 oratory	–	–	–	–	–	–	–	–	–	1
Subtotal	2	1	1	1	2	3	0	1	4	1
Q-70 group (percent)	12.5	6.3	6.3	6.3	12.5	18.8	0.0	6.3	25.0	6.3

continued on next page

TABLE 7.19—*continued*

Structure	Itzamna	Old god	Merchant/ whiskered	Chac	Maize	Other male	Closed-eye human	Xipe Totec	Death head	Female
Q-58 GROUP										
Q-58 temple	1	—	—	—	—	2	—	—	—	—
Q-62 residence	1	—	1	—	1	2	—	—	—	—
Q-64 hall	1	—	—	1	—	2	—	—	1	—
Q-59b shrine	—	—	—	—	—	—	1	—	—	—
Q-66 shrine	1	—	—	—	—	—	—	—	—	—
Subtotal	4	0	1	1	1	6	1	0	1	0
Q-58 group (percent)	25.0	0.0	6.3	6.3	6.3	37.5	6.3	0.0	6.3	0.0
Q-214 GROUP										
Q-214 temple	—	—	—	1	—	—	1	—	1	1
Q-218 temple	—	—	—	1	—	—	—	—	—	—
Subtotal	0	0	0	2	0	0	1	0	1	1
Q-214 group (percent)	0.0	0.0	0.0	40.0	0.0	0.0	20.0	0.0	20.0	20.0
ITZMAL CH'EN										
H-17a altar	1	—	—	—	—	1	—	—	—	—
H-17 temple	—	—	—	1	—	1	—	—	—	—
H-18 shrine	—	—	—	—	—	—	—	—	—	—
Subtotal	1	0	0	1	0	2	0	0	0	0
Itzmal Ch'en (percent)	20.0	0.0	0.0	20.0	0.0	40.0	0.0	0.0	0.0	0.0

continued on next page

TABLE 7.19—continued

Structure	Itzamna	Old god	Merchant/whiskered	Chac	Maize	Other male	Closed-eye human	Xipe Totec	Death head	Female
Q-127 GROUP										
Q-126 TEMPLE	–	–	–	–	–	1	1	–	–	–
Q-127 portal	1	–	–	–	–	–	–	–	–	–
Q-127a temple	–	–	–	1	–	–	1	–	–	–
Subtotal	1	0	0	1	0	1	2	0	0	0
Q-127 group (percent)	20.0	0.0	0.0	20.0	0.0	20.0	40.0	0.0	0.0	0.0
MISC. STRUCTURES										
Q-88b platform	–	–	–	1	1	–	–	–	–	–
Q-153 temple	1	–	–	1	–	–	–	–	–	–
Q-159 temple	–	–	–	–	–	–	–	–	–	–
Q-164 hall	–	–	–	1	–	–	–	–	–	–
Q-157 sanctuary	–	–	–	–	–	–	–	–	–	1
Q-244 house	–	–	–	–	–	–	2	–	–	–
Q-149 temple	–	–	–	–	–	–	1	–	–	–
Q-146 platform	1	–	–	–	–	–	–	–	–	–
Q-208 house	1	2	–	2	–	1	–	2	–	1
Q-98 shrine	1	–	2	–	–	–	–	–	–	–
Q-77 shrine	–	–	–	1	–	–	–	1	–	–
Q-88e	–	–	–	–	–	–	–	–	–	–

continued on next page

TABLE 7.19—continued

Structure	Itzamna	Old god	Merchant/ whiskered	Chac	Maize	Other male	Closed-eye human	Xipe Totec	Death head	Female
Q-119a house	—	—	—	—	—	—	1	—	—	—
A-1 shrine	—	—	—	—	—	—	—	—	—	—
P-33b	—	—	—	2	—	—	1	—	—	—
R-126a	—	—	—	—	—	—	—	—	1	—
J-71a	—	—	—	—	—	1	—	—	—	—
Q-172 house	—	—	1	—	—	—	—	—	—	—
Y-30	—	—	—	1	—	—	—	—	—	—
Y-8b oratory	—	—	2	—	—	—	—	—	—	—
Q-170 house	—	—	—	—	—	—	—	—	1	—
K-67 house	—	—	1	—	—	2	—	—	—	—
Subtotal misc. structures	4	2	6	9	1	4	5	3	2	2
Misc. structures (percent)	9.5	4.8	14.3	21.4	2.4	9.5	11.9	7.1	4.8	7.1
Grand total per column	35	7	28	39	16	38	14	9	39	17

Structures continued	Monkey Scribe	Ehecatl	Diving figures	Tlaloc	Nose plug	Scroll face	Earth lord	Venus	Total
Q-80 GROUP									
Q-80 temple	—	—	—	—	2	4	—	—	33
Q-81 hall	—	—	1	—	—	—	—	1	13
Q-79/79a	—	—	—	—	—	—	—	3	11

continued on next page

TABLE 7.19—continued

Structures continued	Monkey Scribe	Ebecatl	Diving figures	Tlaloc	Nose plug	Scroll face	Earth lord	Venus	Total
Q-83 oratory	–	–	–	–	–	–	1	–	1
Q-82 oratory	–	–	1	–	2	4	–	4	4
Subtotal	0	0	1	0	2	4	1	4	66
Q-80 group (percent)	0.0	0.0	1.5	0.0	3.0	6.0	1.5	6.0	100.0
R-86 GROUP									
R-86 house	1		1				1		19
R-91 oratory	–	–	–	–	–	–	–	–	2
Subtotal	1	0	1	0	0	0	1	0	21
R-86 group (percent)	4.8	0.0	4.8	0.0	0.0	0.0	4.8	0.0	100.0
Q-162 GROUP									
Q-162 temple	–	3	–	–	–	–	–	–	12
Q-161 hall	–	–	–	–	–	–	–	–	5
Q-163 hall	–	–	–	–	–	–	–	–	3
Q-162b sanctuary	–	–	–	–	–	–	–	–	2
Cenote Chén Mul	–	–	–	–	–	–	–	–	1
Q-162c	–	–	–	–	–	–	–	–	1
Q-162h	–	–	–	–	–	–	–	–	1
Q-163a sanctuary	–	–	–	–	–	–	–	–	1
Subtotal	0	3	0	1	0	0	0	0	26
Q-162 group (percent)	0.0	11.1	0.0	3.7	0.0	0.0	0.0	0.0	100.0

continued on next page

TABLE 7.19—*continued*

Structures continued	Monkey Scribe	Ehecatl	Diving figures	Tlaloc	Nose plug	Scroll face	Earth lord	Venus	Total
Q-95 GROUP									
Q-95 temple	—	—	—	—	—	—	—	—	12
Q-89 shrine	—	—	—	—	—	—	—	—	11
Q-90 shrine	—	—	—	—	—	—	—	—	1
Q-94 house	—	—	—	—	—	—	—	—	1
Q-97 hall	—	—	—	—	—	—	—	—	2
Subtotal	0	0	0	0	0	0	0	0	27
Q-95 group (percent)	0.0	0.0	0.0	0.0	0.0	0.0	0.0	0.0	100.0
Q-152 GROUP									
Q-88a hall	1	—	—	—	—	—	—	—	10
Q-151 hall	—	—	—	—	—	—	—	—	8
Q-88 oratory	1	—	—	—	—	—	—	—	5
Q-152c hall	—	—	—	—	—	—	—	—	5
Q-87a oratory	—	—	—	—	—	—	—	—	1
Q-152 temple	—	—	—	—	—	—	—	—	3
Q-87a hall	—	—	—	—	—	—	—	—	1
Q-152b sanctuary	—	—	—	—	—	—	—	—	1
Subtotal	2	0	0	0	0	0	0	0	34
Q-152 group (percent)	5.9	0.0	0.0	0.0	0.0	0.0	0.0	0.0	100.0

continued on next page

TABLE 7.19—*continued*

Structures continued	Monkey Scribe	Ebecatl	Diving figures	Tlaloc	Nose plug	Scroll face	Earth lord	Venus	Total
Q-70 group									
Q-70 hall	—	—	—	—	—	—	—	—	7
Q-54 hall	—	—	—	—	—	—	—	—	2
Q-72b altar	—	—	—	—	—	—	—	—	1
Q-69 shrine	—	—	—	—	—	—	—	—	1
Q-72 hall	—	—	—	—	—	—	—	—	2
Q-74 platform	—	—	—	—	—	—	—	—	1
Q-71 shrine	—	—	—	—	—	—	—	—	1
Q-55 oratory	—	—	—	—	—	—	—	—	1
Subtotal	0	0	0	0	0	0	0	0	16
Q-70 group (percent)	0.0	0.0	0.0	0.0	0.0	0.0	0.0	0.0	100.0
Q-58 GROUP									
Q-58 temple	—	—	—	—	—	—	—	—	4
Q-62 house	—	—	—	—	—	—	—	—	5
Q-64 hall	—	—	—	—	—	—	—	—	5
Q-59b shrine	—	—	—	—	—	—	—	—	1
Q-66 shrine	—	—	—	—	—	—	—	—	1
Subtotal	1	0	0	0	0	0	0	0	16
Q-58 group (percent)	6.3	0.0	0.0	0.0	0.0	0.0	0.0	0.0	100.0

continued on next page

TABLE 7-19—continued

Structures continued	Monkey Scribe	Ebecatl	Diving figures	Tlaloc	Nose plug	Scroll face	Earth lord	Venus	Total
Q-214 GROUP									
Q-214 temple	—	—	—	—	—	—	—	—	4
Q-218 temple	—	—	—	—	—	—	—	—	1
Subtotal	0	0	0	0	0	0	0	0	5
Q-214 group (percent)	0.0	0.0	0.0	0.0	0.0	0.0	0.0	0.0	100.0
ITZMAL CH'EN									
H-17a altar	—	—	—	—	—	—	—	—	2
H-17 temple	—	—	—	—	—	—	—	—	2
H-18 shrine	—	—	—	—	—	—	1	—	1
Subtotal	0	0	0	0	0	0	1	0	5
Itzmal Ch'en (percent)	0.0	0.0	0.0	0.0	0.0	0.0	20	0.0	100.0
Q-127 GROUP									
Q-126 temple	—	—	—	—	—	—	—	—	2
Q-127 vault	—	—	—	—	—	—	—	—	1
Q-127a temple	—	—	—	—	—	—	—	—	2
Subtotal	0	0	0	0	0	0	0	0	5
Q-127 group (percent)	0.0	0.0	0.0	0.0	0.0	0.0	0.0	0.0	100.0

continued on next page

TABLE 7.19—continued

Structures continued	Monkey Scribe	Ehecatl	Diving figures	Tlaloc	Nose plug	Scroll face	Earth lord	Venus	Total
MISC. STRUCTURES									
Q-88b platform	—	—	—	—	—	—	—	—	2
Q-153 temple	—	—	—	—	—	—	—	—	2
Q-159 temple	—	—	—	—	—	—	1	—	1
Q-164 hall	—	—	—	—	—	—	—	—	1
Q-157 sanctuary	—	—	—	—	—	—	—	—	1
Q-244 house	—	—	—	—	—	—	—	—	2
Q-149 temple	—	—	—	—	—	—	—	—	1
Q-146 platform	—	—	—	—	—	—	—	—	1
Q-208 house	—	—	2	—	—	—	—	—	11
Q-98 shrine	—	—	—	—	—	—	—	—	3
Q-77 shrine	—	—	—	—	—	—	—	—	1
Q-88e	—	—	—	—	—	—	—	—	1
Q-119a house	—	—	—	—	—	—	—	—	1
A-1 shrine	—	—	—	—	—	—	—	—	2
P-33b	—	—	—	—	—	—	—	—	1
R-126a	—	—	—	—	—	—	—	—	1
J-71a	—	—	—	—	—	—	—	—	1

continued on next page

TABLE 7.19—*continued*

Structures continued	Monkey Scribe	Ehecatl	Diving figures	Tlaloc	Nose plug	Scroll face	Earth lord	Venus	Total
Q-172 house	—	—	—	—	—	—	—	—	1
Y-30	—	—	—	—	—	—	—	—	1
Y-8b oratory	—	—	—	—	—	—	—	—	2
Q-170 house	—	—	—	—	—	—	—	—	1
K-67 house	—	—	—	—	—	—	—	—	3
Subtotal misc. structures	0	0	2	0	0	0	1	0	41
Misc. structures (percent)	0.0	0.0	4.8	0.0	0.0	0.0	2.4	0.0	100.0
Grand total per column	4	3	4	1	2	4	4	4	263

Note: Closed-eyed column includes four possible maize god, other male, or old god figures with closed eyes. Where there is overlap, these examples are not included in percentage calculations. The remaining closed-eye examples include ceramic masks.

TABLE 7.20 Distribution percentage of effigy types between structures and groups (column totals).

Structure	Itzamna	Old god	Merchant/ whiskered	Chac	Maize	Other male	Closed-eye human	Xipe Totec	Death head	Female
Q-80 GROUP										
Q-80 temple	2	–	3	2	2	7	–	1	2	8
Q-81 hall	3	1	4	1	–	2	–	–	–	2
Q-79 shrine	2	–	3	1	2	3	–	–	–	–
Q-83 oratory	–	–	–	–	–	–	–	–	–	–
Q-82 oratory	–	–	1	–	–	1	–	–	2	–
Subtotal	7	1	11	4	4	13	0	1	4	9
Q-80 group (percent)	20.0	14.3	37.9	10.3	25.0	34.2		11.1	10.3	58.8
R-86 GROUP										
R-86 residence	4	–	1	5	2	1	1	1	1	1
R-91 oratory	–	–	–	2	–	–	–	–	–	–
Subtotal	4	0	1	7	2	1	1	1	1	1
R-86 group (percent)	11.4	0.0	3.4	17.9	12.5	2.6		11.1	2.6	5.9
Q-162 GROUP										
Q-162 temple	2	–	3	–	1	2	–	–	1	–
Q-161 hall	1	–	1	1	–	–	–	–	1	1
Q-163 hall	–	–	1	–	–	–	–	1	–	1

continued on next page

TABLE 7.20—*continued*

Structure	Itzamna	Old god	Merchant/ whiskered	Chac	Maize	Other male	Closed-eye human	Xipe Totec	Death head	Female
Q-162b sanctuary	—	—	1	—	—	—	—	—	1	—
Cenote Chen Mul	—	—	—	—	—	—	—	—	—	—
Q-162c	—	—	—	—	—	1	—	—	—	—
Q-162h	—	—	—	—	—	1	—	—	—	—
Q-163a sanctuary	—	—	1	—	—	—	—	—	—	—
Subtotal	3	0	6	1	2	4	0	1	3	2
Q-162 group (percent)	8.6	0.0	24.1	2.6	12.5	10.5	0.0	11.1	7.7	11.8
Q-95 GROUP										
Q-95 temple	—	—	1	1	—	1	—	—	9	—
Q-89 shrine	1	—	—	—	1	—	—	—	9	—
Q-90 shrine	—	—	—	—	—	—	—	—	1	—
Q-94 house	—	—	—	—	—	—	—	—	1	—
Q-97 hall	—	—	—	—	—	1	—	—	1	—
Subtotal	1	0	1	1	1	2	0	0	21	0
Q-95 group (percent)	2.9	0.0	3.4	2.6	6.3	5.3	0.0	0.0	53.8	0.0
Q-152 GROUP										
Q-88a hall	1	—	—	4	—	—	—	2	2	—

continued on next page

TABLE 7-20—continued

Structure	Itzamna	Old god	Merchant/whiskered	Chac	Maize	Other male	Closed-eye human	Xipe Totec	Death head	Female
Q-151 hall	1	2	—	2	2	1	2	—	—	—
Q-88 oratory	—	1	—	1	1	1	2	—	—	—
Q-152c hall	2	—	1	2	—	—	—	—	—	—
Q-87a oratory	1	—	—	—	—	—	—	—	—	—
Q-152 temple	2	—	—	1	—	—	—	—	—	—
Q-87a hall	—	—	—	1	—	—	—	—	—	—
Q-152b sanctuary	1	—	—	—	—	—	—	—	—	—
Subtotal	8	3	1	11	3	2	4	2	2	0
Q-152 group (percent)	22.9	42.9	3.4	28.2	18.8	5.3	30.8	22.2	5.1	0.0
Q-70 GROUP										
Q-70 hall	2	—	—	—	1	3	—	—	1	—
Q-54 hall	—	—	—	—	—	—	—	—	2	—
Q-72b altar	—	—	—	—	—	—	—	1	—	—
Q-69 shrine	—	—	—	—	—	—	—	—	1	—
Q-72 hall	—	1	—	—	1	—	—	—	—	—
Q-74 platform	—	—	1	—	—	—	—	—	—	—

continued on next page

TABLE 7.20—*continued*

Structure	Itzamna	Old god	Merchant/ whiskered	Chac	Maize	Other male	Closed-eye human	Xipe Totec	Death head	Female
Q-71 shrine	—	—	—	1	—	—	—	—	—	—
Q-55 oratory	—	—	—	—	—	—	—	—	—	1
Subtotal	2	1	1	1	2	3	0	1	4	1
Q-70 group (percent)	5.7	14.3	3.4	2.6	12.5	7.9	0.0	11.1	10.3	5.9
Q-58 GROUP										
Q-58 temple	1	—	—	—	—	2	—	—	—	—
Q-62 house	1	—	1	—	1	2	—	—	—	—
Q-64 hall	1	—	—	1	—	2	—	—	1	—
Q-59b shrine	—	—	—	—	—	—	1	—	—	—
Q-66 shrine	1	—	—	—	—	—	—	—	—	—
Subtotal	4	0	1	1	1	6	1	0	1	0
Q-58 group (percent)	11.4	0.0	3.4	2.6	6.3	15.8	7.1	0.0	2.6	0.0
Q-214 GROUP										
Q-214 temple	—	—	—	1	—	—	1	—	1	1
Q-218 temple	—	—	—	1	—	—	—	—	—	—
Subtotal	0	0	0	2	0	0	1	0	1	1
Q-214 group (percent)	0.0	0.0	0.0	5.1	0.0	0.0	7.1	0.0	2.6	5.9

continued on next page

TABLE 7-20—continued

Structure	Itzamna	Old god	Merchant/ whiskered	Chac	Maize	Other male	Closed-eye human	Xipe Totec	Death bead	Female
ITZMAL CH'EN										
H-17a altar	1	–	–	–	–	1	–	–	–	–
H-17 temple	–	–	–	1	–	1	–	–	–	–
H-18 shrine	–	–	–	–	–	–	–	–	–	–
Subtotal	1	0	0	1	0	2	0	0	0	0
Itzmal Ch'en (percent)	2.9	0.0	0.0	2.6	0.0	5.3	0.0	0.0	0.0	0.0
MISC. STRUCTURES										
Q-88b platform	–	–	–	1	1	–	–	–	–	–
Q-153 temple	1	–	–	1	–	–	–	–	–	–
Q-159 temple	–	–	–	–	–	–	–	–	–	–
Q-164 hall	–	–	–	1	–	–	–	–	–	–
Q-157 sanctuary	–	–	–	–	–	–	–	–	–	1
Q-244 house	–	–	–	–	–	–	2	–	–	–
Q-149 temple	–	–	–	–	–	–	1	–	–	–
Q-146 platform	1	–	–	–	–	–	–	–	–	–
Q-208 house	1	2	–	2	–	1	–	2	–	1
Q-98 shrine	1	–	2	–	–	–	–	–	–	–
Q-77 shrine	–	–	–	–	–	–	–	1	–	1

continued on next page

TABLE 7.20—*continued*

Structure	Itzamna	Old god	Merchant/ whiskered	Chac	Maize	Other male	Closed- eye human	Xipe Totec	Death head	Female
Q-88e				1						
Q-119a house							1			
A-1 shrine				2						
P-33b							1			
R-126a									1	
J-71a						1				
Q-172 house	—	—	1	—	—	—	—	—	—	—
Y-30 shrine	—	—	—	1	—	—	—	—	—	—
Y-8b oratory	—	—	2	—	—	—	—	—	—	—
Q-170 house	—	—	—	—	—	—	—	—	1	—
K-67 house	—	—	1	—	—	2	—	—	—	—
Subtotal misc. structures	4	2	6	9	1	4	5	3	2	2
Misc. structures (percent)	11.4	20.7	20.7	23.1	6.3	10.5	38.5	33.3	5.1	11.8
Grand total per column	35	7	29	39	16	38	14	9	39	17

TABLE 7-20—*continued*

Structures continued	Monkey Scribe	Ebecatl	Diving figures	Tlaloc	Nose plug	Scroll face	Earth lord	Venus	Total
Q-80 GROUP									
Q-80 temple	–	–	–	–	2	4	–	–	33
Q-81 hall	–	–	1	–	–	–	–	1	13
Q-79 shrine	–	–	–	–	–	–	–	3	11
Q-83 oratory	–	–	–	–	–	–	1	–	1
Q-82 oratory	–	–	–	–	–	–	–	–	4
Subtotal	0	0	1	0	2	4	1	4	62
Q-80 group (percent)	0.0	0.0	25.0	0.0	100.0	100.0	25.0	100.0	24.0
R-86 GROUP									
R-86 residence	1	–	1	–	–	–	1	–	19
R-91 oratory	–	–	–	–	–	–	–	–	2
Subtotal	1	0	1	0	0	0	1	0	21
R-86 group (percent)	25.0	0.0	25.0	0.0	0.0	0.0	25.0	0.0	8.0
Q-162 GROUP									
Q-162 temple	–	3	–	–	–	–	–	–	12
Q-161 hall	–	–	–	–	–	–	–	–	5
Q-163 hall	–	–	–	1	–	–	–	–	3
Q-162b sanctuary	–	–	–	–	–	–	–	–	2

continued on next page

TABLE 7.20—*continued*

Structures continued	Monkey Scribe	Ebecatl	Diving figures	Tlaloc	Nose plug	Scroll face	Earth lord	Venus	Total
Cenote Chèn Mul									
Q-162c	—	—	—	—	—	—	—	—	1
Q-162h	—	—	—	—	—	—	—	—	1
Q-163a sanctuary	—	—	—	—	—	—	—	—	1
Subtotal	0	3	0	1	0	0	0	0	26
Q-162 group (percent)	0.0	100.0	0.0	100.0	0.0	0.0	0.0	0.0	10.3
Q-95 GROUP									
Q-95 temple	—	—	—	—	—	—	—	—	12
Q-89 shrine	—	—	—	—	—	—	—	—	11
Q-90 shrine	—	—	—	—	—	—	—	—	1
Q-94 house	—	—	—	—	—	—	—	—	1
Q-97 hall	—	—	—	—	—	—	—	—	2
Subtotal	0	0	0	0	0	0	0	0	27
Q-95 group (percent)	0.0	0.0	0.0	0.0	0.0	0.0	0.0	0.0	10.3
Q-152 GROUP									
Q-88a hall	1	—	—	—	—	—	—	—	10
Q-151 hall	—	—	—	—	—	—	—	—	8
Q-88 oratory	1	—	—	—	—	—	—	—	5

continued on next page

TABLE 7-20—continued

Structures continued	Monkey Scribe	Ebecatl	Diving figures	Tlaloc	Nose plug	Scroll face	Earth lord	Venus	Total
Q-152c hall	–	–	–	–	–	–	–	–	5
Q-87a oratory	–	–	–	–	–	–	–	–	1
Q-152 temple	–	–	–	–	–	–	–	–	3
Q-87a hall	–	–	–	–	–	–	–	–	1
Q-152b sanctuary	–	–	–	–	–	–	–	–	1
Subtotal	2	0	0	0	0	0	0	0	38
Q-152 group (percent)	50.0	0.0	0.0	0.0	0.0	0.0	0.0	0.0	14.4
Q-70 GROUP									
Q-70 hall	–	–	–	–	–	–	–	–	7
Q-54 hall	–	–	–	–	–	–	–	–	2
Q-72b altar	–	–	–	–	–	–	–	–	1
Q-69 shrine	–	–	–	–	–	–	–	–	1
Q-72 hall	–	–	–	–	–	–	–	–	2
Q-74 platform	–	–	–	–	–	–	–	–	1
Q-71 shrine	–	–	–	–	–	–	–	–	1
Q-55 oratory	–	–	–	–	–	–	–	–	1
Subtotal	0	0	0	0	0	0	0	0	16
Q-70 group (percent)	0.0	0.0	0.0	0.0	0.0	0.0	0.0	0.0	6.1

continued on next page

TABLE 7-20—*continued*

Structures continued	Monkey Scribe	Ebecatl	Diving figures	Tlaloc	Nose plug	Scroll face	Earth lord	Venus	Total
Q-58 GROUP									
Q-58 temple	—	—	—	—	—	—	—	—	4
Q-62 residence	—	—	—	—	—	—	—	—	5
Q-64 hall	—	—	—	—	—	—	—	—	5
Q-59b shrine	—	—	—	—	—	—	—	—	1
Q-66 shrine	—	—	—	—	—	—	—	—	1
Subtotal	1	0	0	0	0	0	0	0	16
Q-58 group (percent)	25.0	0.0	0.0	0.0	0.0	0.0	0.0	0.0	6.1
Q-214 GROUP									
Q-214 temple	—	—	—	—	—	—	—	—	4
Q-218 temple	—	—	—	—	—	—	—	—	1
Subtotal	0	0	0	0	0	0	0	0	5
Q-214 group (percent)	0.0	0.0	0.0	0.0	0.0	0.0	0.0	0.0	1.9
ITZMAL CH'EN									
H-17a altar	—	—	—	—	—	—	—	—	2
H-17 temple	—	—	—	—	—	—	—	—	2

continued on next page

TABLE 7.20—continued

Structures continued	Monkey Scribe	Ebecatl	Diving figures	Tlaloc	Nose plug	Scroll face	Earth lord	Venus	Total
H-18 temple	–	–	–	0	–	–	1	–	1
Subtotal	0	0	0	0	0	0	1	0	5
Itzmal Ch'en (percent)	0.0	0.0	0.0	0.0	0.0	0.0	25	0.0	1.9
Q-127 GROUP									
Q-126 temple	–	–	–	–	–	–	–	–	2
Q-127 vault	–	–	–	–	–	–	–	–	1
Q-127a temple	–	–	–	–	–	–	–	–	2
Subtotal	0	0	0	0	0	0	1	0	5
Itzmal Ch'en (percent)	0.0	0.0	0.0	0.0	0.0	0.0	25	0.0	1.9
MISC. STRUCTURES									
Q-88b platform	–	–	–	–	–	–	–	–	2
Q-153 temple	–	–	–	–	–	–	–	–	2
Q-159 temple	–	–	–	–	–	–	1	–	1
Q-164 hall	–	–	–	–	–	–	–	–	1
Q-157 sanctuary	–	–	–	–	–	–	–	–	1
Q-244 house	–	–	–	–	–	–	–	–	2
Q-149 temple	–	–	–	–	–	–	–	–	1
Q-146 platform	–	–	–	–	–	–	–	–	1

continued on next page

TABLE 7.20—continued

Structures continued	Monkey Scribe	Ebecatl	Diving figures	Tlaloc	Nose plug	Scroll face	Earth lord	Venus	Total
Q-208 house	—	—	2	—	—	—	—	—	11
Q-98 shrine	—	—	—	—	—	—	—	—	3
Q-77 shrine	—	—	—	—	—	—	—	—	1
Q-88e	—	—	—	—	—	—	—	—	1
Q-119a house	—	—	—	—	—	—	—	—	1
A-1 shrine	—	—	—	—	—	—	—	—	2
P-33b	—	—	—	—	—	—	—	—	1
R-126a	—	—	—	—	—	—	—	—	1
J-71a	—	—	—	—	—	—	—	—	1
Q-172 house	—	—	—	—	—	—	—	—	1
Y-30	—	—	—	—	—	—	—	—	1
Y-8b oratory	—	—	—	—	—	—	—	—	2
Q-170 house	—	—	—	—	—	—	—	—	1
K-67 house	—	—	—	—	—	—	—	—	3
Subtotal misc. structures	0	0	2	0	0	0	1	0	41
Misc. structures (percent)	0.0	0.0	50.0	0.0	0.0	0.0	25.0	0.0	15.9
Grand total per column	4	3	4	1	2	4	4	4	263

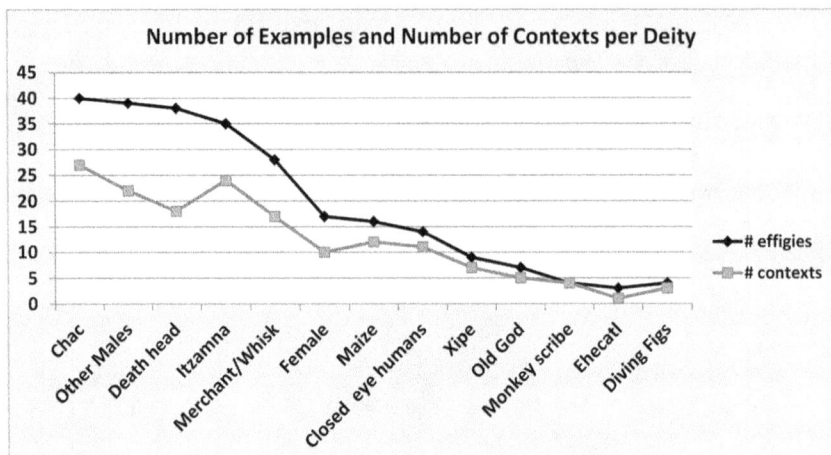

FIGURE 7.9. *Common stone and ceramic effigies are widely distributed among different contexts—in particular, Chac, various males, death gods, Itzamna, and merchant gods. As might be expected, rarer representations are limited to fewer contexts.*

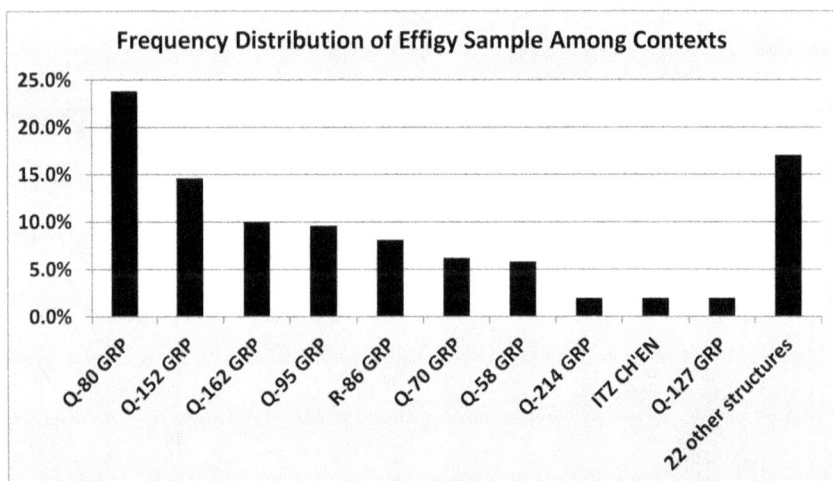

FIGURE 7.10. *Graph indicating the distribution of all ceramic and stone effigies in our sample by group. Percentage calculated is that of all effigies in the sample analyzed.*

The Q-80 and Q-162 groups have the highest proportions of female effigies at the site, especially Q-80, where they form 14.9 percent of this group assemblage (table 7.19, N = 10). Eight censer examples come from Temple

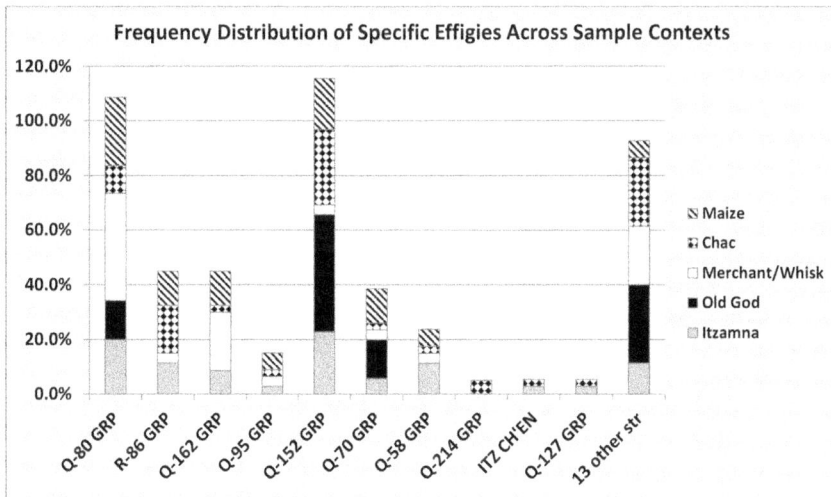

FIGURE 7.11. *Percentages reflect the proportion of the total number of specific effigy censers in the sample that are present at different groups.*

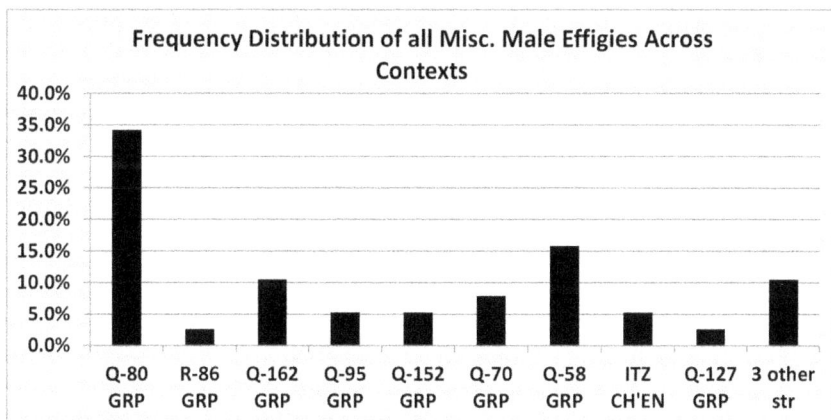

FIGURE 7.12. *Graph indicating the distribution of all "other male" effigies across the groups compared; some may represent warrior figures. The ubiquity at the Q-80 group may be related to the large sample size at this locality.*

Q-80; females were especially important at this locality. Fifty-nine percent of all of the female images recovered are from Q-80 (table 7.20, figure 7.15). The Kukulcan temple group stands out for having three sculptures, which make up 7.7 percent of the Q-162 group assemblage (table 7.19) and 11.8 percent of the total sample of females (table 7.20).

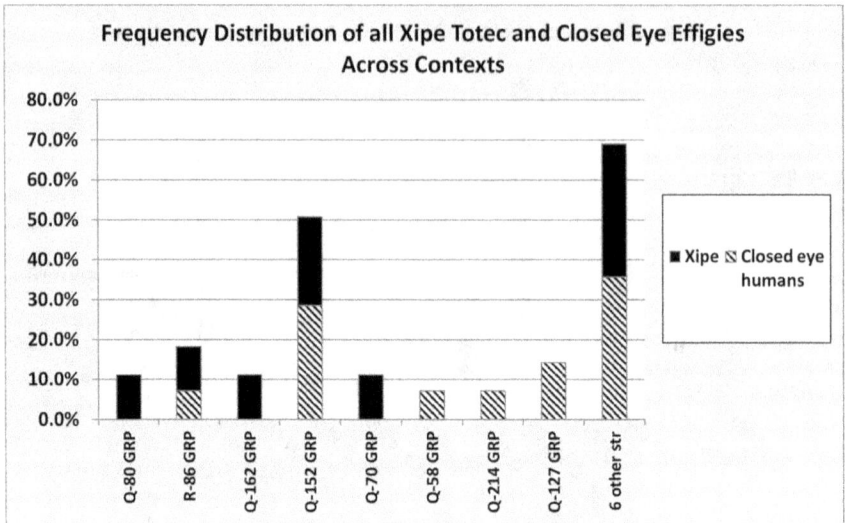

FIGURE 7.13. *Distribution of the total number of Xipe Totec and closed-eye (stone and ceramic) effigies across the groups in the sample. Note: closed eye censers from R-86 and Q-152 groups overlap with censers also classified as maize gods, other males, and old gods.*

Venus god faces were concentrated (three out of four) at the Q-79/79a shrine (part of the Q-80 cluster), and the fourth example is within the same group, from Hall Q-81 (tables 6.19, 6.20, figure 7.16). The Kukulcan temple group has the only Ehecatl effigies at Mayapán (figure 7.16), and they form 11.1 percent of this group's assemblage (table 7.19). This concentration fits nicely with the fact that this temple was dedicated to Kukulcan, of whom Ehecatl was a wind god manifestation.

Other males represent a composite category that may include warrior effigies. Potentially, Q-80 and Q-162 centralize images linked to female gods, merchants, and warriors or ancestral figures. Merchants often had a bellicose dimension. Most filed-tooth males derive from the Q-80 group, where seven of nine were recovered; two others come from nearby Hall Q-70. Other males are also present in higher proportions at colonnaded hall group Q-70 (18.8 percent), burial shaft Temple Q-58 (37.5 percent), and the outlying Itzmal Ch'en group (40 percent, table 6.19). Death effigies were also significant at Q-70 (25 percent). But the structures with the most death imagery—Q-95 and Q-89—do not have high proportions of other males (table 6.19).

What might the high proportions of merchant, miscellaneous male, and female effigies mean? The Q-80 and Q-162 compounds are among the three

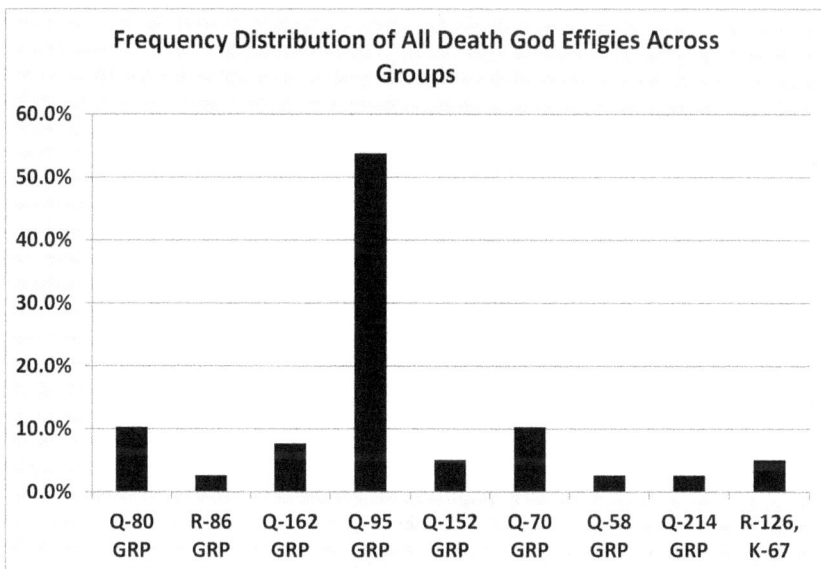

Frequency Distribution of All Death God Effigies Across Groups

FIGURE 7.14. *Distribution of the total number of death god effigies across the groups in the sample. Group Q-95 (Fisherman Temple group) has the highest concentration.*

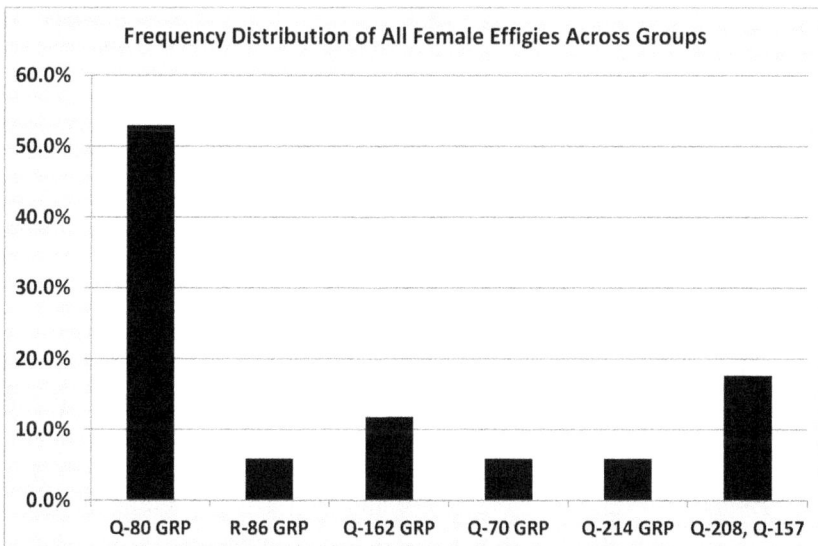

Frequency Distribution of All Female Effigies Across Groups

FIGURE 7.15. *Distribution of the total number of female stone and ceramic effigies across the groups in the sample. From the monumental center, all but one ceramic effigy censer was found at the Q-80 group (eight from Temple Q-80 and one from Hall Q-81), suggesting that the invocation of female deities was significant at this locality.*

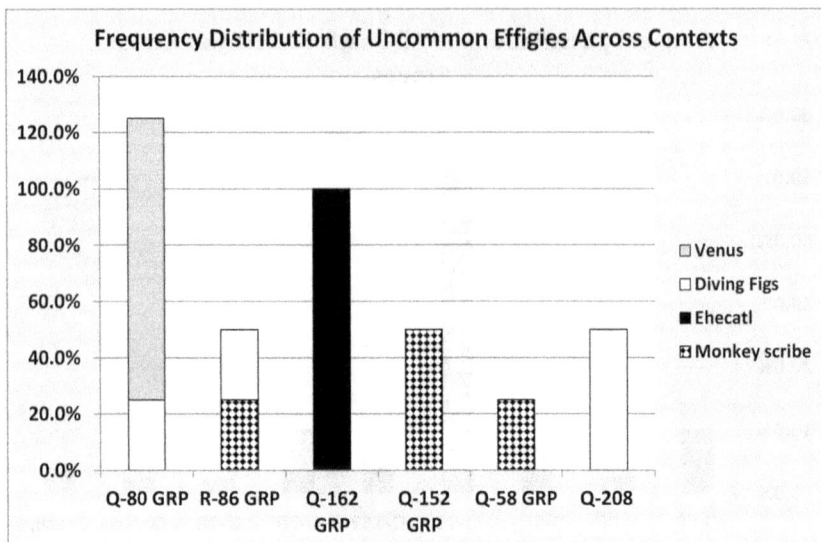

FIGURE 7.16. *Distribution of the total number of Venus god, diving figure, Ehecatl, and Monkey Scribe stone or ceramic effigies across the groups in the sample. Ehecatl, the wind god aspect of Kukulcan/Quetzalcoatl, concentrates at the Temple of Kukulcan (Q-162). Venus effigies concentrate at Q-80. The other rare types do not concentrate at a single group.*

most conspicuous architectural groups in the site center along with the Templo Redondo. These deities have symbolic implications for the commercial and productive industries of the city. Merchant effigies show a range of stylistic variation, and to facilitate synthesis we lump whiskered gods with them here. The Temple Q-80 group has 37.9 percent of the merchant/whiskered effigies in the entire sample and the Temple of Kukulcan (Q-162) group has 24.1 percent (table 7.20). Temples Q-80 and Q-162 probably served as major pilgrimage nodes or locations for ceremonies that emphasized trade, war, and female contributions to society and the supernatural realm. One of the goddess sculptures from the Q-162 group is pregnant, and one large sculpture portrays a woman grinding at a metate (figures 2.13, 7.6). Both young and old female faces are found among the Q-80 group censers, which may represent at least two different deities—Goddesses I and O—or a central Mexican maize goddess, as Milbrath has suggested (personal communication, 2013). Other female sculptures are found at round Temple Q-214, and Q-157a may also be linked to Ixchel (Shook 1954a).

Although the Q-80 and Q-162 groups have notable concentrations of certain effigies, these samples are diverse and among the top three most ubiquitous group assemblages from the site. A broad array of effigies was used for different ritual occasions within the buildings of these central compounds of the city. J. Thompson (1957) discusses six central Mexican deities that were important to travelers, and these included the merchant god (Yacapitzauac, with a pointed nose), a female goddess (Chalmecaciautl), and a version of Quetzalcoatl (Nacxitle). Perhaps the Q-80 and Q-162 array of entities reflects gods that were important for travelers to Mayapán. Ixchel was similarly the focus of pilgrimage on the island of Cozumel, a hub for merchants (Tozzer 1941:109; Freidel and Sabloff 1984; Paxton 2001:51, 143).

Old god faces are not common in the sample (N = 7), as they are only present at four groups (figure 7.11). At these localities, they are found in similar or lesser proportions to other censers (table 7.19), including the Q-80 group (1.5 percent), the Templo Redondo group (7.9 percent), the Q-70 hall group (6.3 percent), and the Q-208 residence (18.2 percent). The Templo Redondo (Q-152) compound has nearly half (42.9 percent, N = 3) of the old god faces in the sample (table 7.20); two examples are at the Q-208 residence and two other occurrences are single. The faces lack insignia linking them to Pawatuns, with which old God N is often identified (Taube 1992), although diagnostic attributes may have been present on the bodies or headgear that they now lack (Milbrath and Peraza Lope 2013:218). One example has closed eyes. The multiple presence of old god entities at the Templo Redondo, where the well-known gods of Itzamna and Chac are abundant, suggests further links to the more conservative ritual emphasis of this compound, especially considering the likelihood that they represent Pawatuns.

Potential maize god images (N = 16) do not dominate the assemblage of any group (table 7.19, figure 7.11). They may be common at the site (Milbrath and Peraza Lope 2013), even if specific diagnostic attributes are not present on fragmentary censers. Carnegie scholars were able to identify only one definitive maize god from a fully restored example decorated with maize foliage (Winters 1955b; J. Thompson 1957). Taube (1992) notes that the maize god is linked to death and disembowelment and is sometimes depicted with closed eyes. Four young, attractive "other male" censer faces have closed eyes and may thus represent the maize god, as might a disemboweled torso fragment. Fourteen ceramic effigies and sculptures have closed eyes in the sample, but some of these are old or mature individuals that could represent deceased humans, Xipe Totec, or the maize god.

Xipe Totec (N = 9) is found in seven contexts at Mayapán (table 7.19, figure 7.13). In two groups, two faces of this god are present, the Templo Redondo (Q-152) group and the Q-208 residence. Other cases occur singly. Xipe Totec represents only 5.3 percent of the Templo Redondo group but is 18.2 percent of the Q-208 assemblage, counting the limbs and faces that may be part of only one or two examples (table 7.19). Xipe Totec is not an exclusive deity for any group, and all groups with this effigy have at least six types of entities present, including local traditional Maya gods (figures 7.11, 7.13). The use of these images may reflect the foreign connections of some of Mayapán's local groups or, alternatively, newcomers undergoing assimilation (Masson and Peraza Lope 2010). Some closed-eye old face censers, ceramic masks, and sculptures may also represent Xipe Totec, but as they overlap with other categories, percentages of closed-eye personages are not calculated in tables 7.19 and 7.20. We hesitate to identify this deity based on the single attribute of closed eyes.

Four diving figures are reported in the sample (table 7.19, figure 7.16) These form low proportions of the samples at three contexts, Residences R-86 (N = 1) and Q-208 (N = 2) and the Q-80 compound (N = 1). Their identities are difficult to ascertain from published photos, but one example may represent the maize god and another might be Chac. At Tulum and Mayapán, diving figures have previously been identified as the maize god (Taube 1992). The two elite houses where Xipe Totec was found (R-86 and Q-208) also had diving effigies. The presence of this east coast icon at these structures may further reflect their occupants' cosmopolitan trading ties. Most diving figures at Mayapán are in the form of thirteen miniature stone sculptures described by Proskouriakoff (1962a). Two other upper-status residences also had diving figures (S-133 and Q-244), which were also present at two halls (Q-54 and Z-50), a shrine (Q-89), and a portal vault (Q-127) as well as the Itzmal Ch'en temple and altar (H-17 and H-17a). The stone divers are broadly distributed among a range of elite houses and public buildings.

Death head images include skeletal faces in cup or censer form and stone sculptures, including tenoned heads, totaling thirty-nine examples (figure 7.14). Although widespread among eighteen contexts, death imagery is heavily concentrated at one group, that of the Q-95 Fisherman Temple, which has 53.8 percent of the death images at the site (table 7.20). This group's assemblage is comprised of 77.8 percent death images (table 7.19). Four death god heads were found at each of two other groups, Q-80 and Q-70. They formed a mere 6 percent of the Q-80 assemblage but were more significant at Q-70 (25 percent).

Eighteen of twenty-one death images at the Q-95 group come from two structures: eight ceramic effigies and one death god sculpture from the Q-95 temple itself and nine tenoned skull heads from the Q-89 shrine. The tenoned head concentration at Shrine Q-89 suggests it may have served as a skull platform similar to those reported at Chichén Itzá and Postclassic central Mexico. At Temple Q-95, the death god sculpture has been identified as a central Mexican deity (Milbrath and Peraza Lope 2003a). Death head ceramics are more abundant here than anywhere else at Mayapán. These effigies underscore the importance of sacrifice at Q-95, as indicated by the central burial shaft in which the remains of over forty men, women, and children were thrown. A sacrificial stone was found on top of the temple (Shook 1954c). The structure's fisherman mural also relates a story of sacrifice and rebirth (chapter 2).

CACAO PODS

The Carnegie project occasionally recovered cacao pod censer adornos. Thirty-seven examples were recovered from eighteen different contexts tested by the INAH and PEMY projects. Most contexts only had one or two ceramic pods, but three were found at Hall Q-88/88a, five were found at elite House Y-45a, and eleven were from Temple Q-80. Effigy censers at these latter two structures probably held cacao pod offerings, or they formed part of the foliage that emanates from the elaborate costumes of some censer figures (table 7.21). As we have discussed, Q-80 was a pivotal temple at Mayapán, and the structures in its vicinity had abundant and diverse effigies, including many merchant deity censers. The association of cacao pods with this group is probably linked to its importance to commercial agents and activities.

Cacao beans were the most common form of money (Tozzer 1941:37). Unfortunately, most cacao pod adornos are not part of restored vessels, and we do not know which deities held them. Milbrath et al. (2008:108) report cacao pods in the headdress of merchant deity censers at Mayapán, and they also describe an example from Champotón. The association of merchant effigies with cacao pods is a clear indication of the symbolic importance of commerce. House Y-45a was a large residence located in a neighborhood near the southeast portion of the city wall, with a rear shrine room, receiving room, and two storage rooms. Its residents may have been merchants, provisioners, or tribute collectors. Other objects held by censer figures at the city include cones and balls of copal or rubber, flowers, tamales, and maize foliage.

LAYERS OF RELIGIOUS PRACTICE

Our results reflect complex patterns of censer and sculpture effigy use at Mayapán. While concentrations imply different emphases at the city's buildings in rituals that invoked various entities, the prevailing pattern is the use

TABLE 7.21 Contexts with ceramic cacao pods. These adornos probably derive from headdress or handheld elements of Ch'en Mul Modeled effigy censers.

Structure	Project sample	Number
House Q-62	INAH	1
Hall Q-70	INAH	1
Shrine Q-79/79a	INAH	1
Temple Q-80	INAH	11
Hall Q-81	INAH	1
Oratory Q-82	INAH	2
Oratory Q-88	INAH	1
Halls Q-88/88a	INAH	3
House Q-94/94a	INAH	1
Shrine Q-98	INAH	1
Round Temple Q-152	INAH	2
Hall Q-161	INAH	1
House R-142c	PEMY	1
House Z-39	PEMY	1
House R-101	PEMY	1
House Q-303	PEMY	1
House L-28	PEMY	2
House Y-45	PEMY	5

of a broad range of entities at major structures and groups. The larger the sample of effigies from a particular location, the more diverse is the assemblage. The most prominent groups of the Main Plaza at Mayapán have the greatest number of effigies, with outlying structures rarely having more than two. Noble families of Mayapán rotated the burden of calendrical festivals linked to the effigies (Landa 1941:133–57; D. Chase 1985a, 1986; P. Rice 2004:77–83; P. Rice 2009c; Milbrath and Peraza Lope 2013), and our analysis indicates that this practice resulted in the use of many different kinds of gods at specific structures.

Concentrations hint at the importance of certain deities at specific architectural groups. Death imagery concentrates at the Q-95 burial shaft temple and a shrine in its courtyard, Q-89. But burial shaft temples may have focused on different aspects of sacrificial ritual and cosmology, as other temples and shrines lack death god imagery (Q-58, H-18, and T-70). All of these temples have some link to Kukulcan creation myths, as indicated by the presence of serpent sculptures or related imagery (Masson and Peraza Lope 2007).

The Q-80 and Q-162 temple groups had effigies that may have appealed to merchants and creation mythology. Temple Q-80 has an important concentration of female effigy censers. Wind god effigies are only found at the Temple of Kukulcan, and all but one of the Venus gods were found at a shrine within the Q-80 compound. Filed-tooth male entities also concentrated almost exclusively at this group. In contrast, the Templo Redondo group and the R-86 noble residence have high proportions of Chac and Itzamna, two of the most important local gods. These groups, along with Q-80, also had diving figure effigies. Both the Templo Redondo and R-86 groups have diverse assemblages that include Xipe Totec. These shared characteristics may link the R-86 noble family to the Templo Redondo group along with the Pelé Polychrome fish dishes found at both of these groups. Multiple examples of old gods and Xipe Totec are found only at the Templo Redondo group and Q-208, another elite residence.

The most perplexing problem—one that may never be resolved—is to determine the specific occasions for which effigy censers were produced, used, and discarded. Beyond monthly festivals and yearly Uayeb ceremonies, K'atun intervals also had patron gods in effigy form; curiously, the faces of K'atun effigies may have been those of historical figures rather than faces with deity markers (Love 1994:19–25). This possibility may explain the large number of male face effigies that lack specific deity attributes (Masson 2000). Some effigy censers from Utatlán and its neighbors may also have been apotheosized ancestors (Carmack 1971:17).

Chapter 8 considers the evidence for the collapse of the Mayapán polity, including deposits linked to willful acts of destruction at many of the city's public buildings. As discussed at the beginning of this chapter, many of the broken censers and sculptures were deposited in the context of episodes of abandonment.

TABLE 7.22 Citations for investigations of structures mentioned in chapter 7, which report effigies of ceramics, stone, or stucco. Some effigy ceramics were republished by Robert Smith (1971).

Structure/group	Carnegie project	INAH or PEMY project
A-1	Smith and Ruppert 1956	
A-3	Ruppert and Smith 1954	
AA-13	Ruppert and Smith 1954	
AA-31	Ruppert and Smith 1954	
AA-37	Ruppert and Smith 1954	
AA-60	Ruppert and Smith 1954	
AA-94	Ruppert and Smith 1954	
AA-103	Ruppert and Smith 1954	
AA-112	Ruppert and Smith 1954	
H-12	Chowning 1956	
H-13	Chowning 1956	
H-14	Chowning 1956	
H-15	Chowning 1956	Delgado Kú, Escamilla Ojeda, and Peraza Lope 2012a
H-16	Chowning 1956	
H-17	Chowning 1956; D. Thompson 1955; J. Thompson 1957	Delgado Kú, Escamilla Ojeda, and Peraza Lope 2012b
H-18	Chowning 1956	
I-94	Ruppert and Smith 1952	
J-122	Ruppert and Smith 1952	
J-131	Ruppert and Smith 1952	
J-49	Ruppert and Smith 1952	
J-50	Ruppert and Smith 1952	
J-71	Smith and Ruppert 1956	
K-52	Smith and Ruppert 1953	
K-67	Smith and Ruppert 1956	
P-14	Smith and Ruppert 1956	
P-23	Smith and Ruppert 1956	

continued on next page

TABLE 7.22—*continued*

Structure/group	Carnegie project	INAH or PEMY project
P-28	Smith and Ruppert 1956	
Q-37	Smith and Ruppert 1956	
Q-58	Shook 1954a	
Q-59	Shook 1954a	
Q-60	Shook 1954a	
Q-61		Peraza Lope et al. 2003
Q-62	Ruppert and Smith 1954	
Q-64		Peraza Lope et al. 2003
Q-65		Peraza Lope et al. 2003
Q-69	Adams 1953	Peraza Lope, Delgado Kú, and Escamilla Ojeda 2002
Q-70		Peraza Lope, Delgado Kú, and Escamilla Ojeda 2002
Q-71	Adams 1953	Peraza Lope, Delgado Kú, and Escamilla Ojeda 2002
Q-72		Peraza Lope, Delgado Kú, and Escamilla Ojeda 2002
Q-73		Peraza Lope et al. 1997
Q-74		Peraza Lope et al. 1997
Q-75		Peraza Lope, Delgado Kú, and Escamilla Ojeda 2002
Q-76		Peraza Lope et al. 1997
Q-77	Adams 1953	Peraza Lope et al. 1997
Q-78		Peraza Lope, Delgado Kú, and Escamilla Ojeda 2002
Q-79	Adams 1953	Peraza Lope et al. 1997
Q-80	Winters 1955a	Peraza Lope et al. 1997
Q-81	Winters 1955b	Peraza Lope et al. 1997
Q-82	Shook 1954a	Peraza Lope et al. 1997, 1999a
Q-83		Peraza Lope et al. 1999b
Q-84	Adams 1953	Peraza Lope et al. 1999c
Q-85		Peraza Lope et al. 1997

continued on next page

TABLE 7.22—*continued*

Structure/group	Carnegie project	INAH or PEMY project
Q-86		Peraza Lope et al. 1999c
Q-87		Peraza Lope et al. 1997
Q-88	Shook and Irving 1955	Peraza Lope et al. 1997
Q-89		Peraza Lope et al. 2003
Q-90	Adams 1953	Peraza Lope et al. 2003
Q-91		Peraza Lope et al. 2003
Q-92		Peraza Lope et al. 2003
Q-93		Peraza Lope et al. 2003
Q-94		Peraza Lope et al. 2003
Q-95	Shook 1954a	Peraza Lope et al. 2003
Q-96		Peraza Lope et al. 2003
Q-97	Shook and Irving 1955	
Q-98		Peraza Lope et al. 2003
Q-119	Smith and Ruppert 1953	
Q-126	Shook 1955	
Q-127	Strömsvik 1953	
Q-143	Winters 1955c	
Q-146	Winters 1955c	
Q-147	P. Smith 1955	
Q-148	P. Smith 1955	
Q-149	P. Smith 1955	
Q-151	Shook and Irving 1955	Peraza Lope et al. 1997
Q-152	Shook and Irving 1955	Peraza Lope et al. 1999a
Q-153	P. Smith 1955	Peraza Lope, Delgado Kú, and Escamilla Ojeda 2002
Cenote Ch'en Mul	R. Smith 1954	
Q-157	R. Smith 1954	
Q-159	Winters 1955c	
Q-160		
Q-161		Peraza Lope et al. 1997

continued on next page

TABLE 7.22—*continued*

Structure/group	Carnegie project	INAH or PEMY project
Q-162		Peraza Lope et al. 1997, 1999b
Q-163		Peraza Lope et al. 1999b
Q-164	Shook 1954a	
Q-165	Chowning and Thompson 1956	
Q-166/167	Chowning and Thompson 1956	
Q-168	Chowning and Thompson 1956	
Q-169	Thompson and Thompson 1955	
Q-172	Thompson and Thompson 1955	
Q-173	Thompson and Thompson 1955	
Q-208	J. Thompson 1954	
Q-209	J. Thompson 1954	
Q-213	Shook 1954b	
Q-214	Shook 1954b	
Q-217	Winters 1955c	
Q-218	Winters 1955c	
Q-244	Smith and Ruppert 1956	
R-100	Smith and Ruppert 1953	
R-126	Smith and Ruppert 1956	
R-142	Smith and Ruppert 1956	
R-171	Smith and Ruppert 1956	
R-30	Smith and Ruppert 1956	
R-85 to R-90	Proskouriakoff and Temple 1955	
R-91	Smith and Ruppert 1956	
S-133	Smith and Ruppert 1956	
T-70	Shook 1953	
T-72	Shook 1953	
Cenote X-Coton	R. Smith 1953	
Y-2	Smith and Ruppert 1956	
Y-8	Smith and Ruppert 1956	
Z-4	Ruppert and Smith 1954	
Z-50	Pollock 1956	

8

Militarism, Misery, and Collapse

Marilyn A. Masson and Carlos Peraza Lope

"That which came was a drought, according to their words, when the hoofs burned, when the seashore burned, a sea of misery."

(The Book of the Chilam Balam of Chumayel, Roys 1967:76).

Mayapán's collapse is traditionally associated with the short-term events of factional strife and abandonment during K'atun 8 Ahau, AD 1441–1461 (Landa 1941:36–37). A longer view of the last half of the city's history reveals that its fall was the culmination of a struggle lasting at least a century against natural and social forces that would have abutted against the survival capacities of any ancient political capital. Interrelated factors that aggravated the stability of Mayapán were three-fold—environmental catastrophes, factional divides, and warfare. Although these issues challenged the city's regimes throughout its history, they coalesced and were amplified during the fourteenth and fifteenth centuries AD, leading to the mid-fifteenth-century abandonment. This chapter outlines the prolonged obstacles that eroded the centralizing capacities of the confederacy government. In the face of improbable odds, the polity and city of Mayapán persevered through a series of severe disasters that would have fueled discontent by threatening the agrarian base of the city and its supporting towns. The protracted process of collapse involved at least three episodic acts of abandonment and destruction over the final 150 years, as suggested by recent archaeological findings and ethnohistorical accounts. The escalation of regional warfare was one response to political and climatic stress, although this short-term reaction contributed little toward long-term regional recovery.

DOI: 10.5876/9781607323204.c008

When the end finally came, it happened quickly. The political fractures that tore apart the Mayapán state had deep historical roots dating back to the era of Chichén Itzá. Why did the actions of the Xiu against the Cocom in the fateful K'atun 8 Ahau gain traction at this particular time? We suggest that the city was by this point brought to its knees, suffering diminished size, food shortages, and loss of political support among subject populations. The Cocom, who commanded much authority in the confederacy throughout Mayapán's history, bore the brunt of the blame for this ill fortune. It is difficult to sort out accusatory doctrine regarding poor governance from the agendas of competing factions. The Cocom were accused of tyranny, slavery, and bringing Mexican mercenaries (probably from Tabasco) into the city (Roys 1962:47–48). This testimony, however, was provided by a descendant of the Xiu family, Gaspar Antonio Chi, who was one of Diego de Landa's principal informants (Landa 1941:59–62). Some accusations, including the extent of the slave trade, were disputed (Tozzer 1941:note 178). The Xiu and their allies orchestrated the massacre of the Cocom authorities, broke down the city wall in a broad-scale attack, and brought about the collapse and abandonment of Mayapán (Landa 1941:36–37).

THE LONG DECLINE: K'ATUN 9 AHAU (1302–1323) UNTIL SPANISH CONTACT (1511)

What evidence exists for longer term strife affecting the Mayapán state? Events mentioned in Colonial Period sources are outlined below in chronological order, along with relevant archaeological data that contribute new information. Although some Colonial-era Maya documents are of questionable accuracy concerning earlier history (Gunsenheimer 2002), evaluating these accounts with empirical scientific data helps to bring greater resolution to models of the city's fall. Table 8.1 presents a selection of events suggested by interdisciplinary sources for the fourteenth and fifteenth centuries AD.

In K'atun 9 Ahau (1302–1323), there was a period of terror and war (Roys 1962:44). K'atun 9 Ahau, along with subsequent K'atuns 7 Ahau and 5 Ahau, encompassed a period from 1302–1362, characterized in general by political decentralization and factionalism, described by Ralph L. Roys (1962:45) as a "revolution." These difficulties dissipated in K'atun 3 Ahau (1362–1382). The restoration of order during this K'atun included a tumultuous inquisition in which political leaders were questioned and tortured. Their tongues were cut off, their eyes were torn out, and they were trampled and dragged while alive. Some of this purging of the nobility was seen as illegitimate (Roys

TABLE 8.1 Events from various sources in the K'atun history of Mayapán. Arrows indicate full two sigma AMS ranges, dark gray boxes indicate the most probable timing.

K'atun	Ethnohistory (Roys 1962; Landa 1941)	Environmental (Curtis, Hodell, and Brenner 1996)	Archaeological AMS-dated events
1200–1272			
1272–1292			
1292–1302			
K'atun 9 Ahau 1302–1323	Terror and war	Q-79 mass grave	Mass grave Itzmal Ch'en
K'atuns 7, 5 Ahau 1323–1362	Factionalism, revolution		
K'atun 3 Ahau 1362–1382	"[S]torm broke," inquisition, purging of nobility	Drought, "one of the driest periods in the 3,500 year sequence of Punta Laguna" (most probable dating)	House Y-45 ritually abandoned Q-88 Hall burned to ground (3 Ahau effigy jaguar date)
K'atun 1 Ahau 1382–1401	Order restored, some out-migration, Cocom invited Canul allies into city		
K'atun 12 Ahau 1401–1421	Benevolent leaders, peace, prosperity, abundant food		
K'atun 10 Ahau 1421–1441	Severe famine	Little Ice Age effects?	
K'atun 8 Ahau 1441–1461	Cold, famine, drought, Xiu-Cocom war, abandonment	Local droughts	Some building destruction may also date to this K'atun
K'atun 6 Ahau 1461–1481	"[H]urricane of the four winds" (1464) decimated game, leveled and uprooted forests, destroyed tall buildings		
K'atun 4 Ahau 1480–1500	Plague (blood vomit, 1480–1485+/-), "when vultures entered the houses" (at Mayapán), lingering Xius evacuate		
Ensuing years	Warfare ravaged the land, 150,000 men died in battle		
+/- 1511	Peace established, European diseases		

1962:45). Following this interrogation, order was restored during K'atun 1 Ahau (1382–1401), although considerable out-migration may have occurred. Chichén Itzá's Postclassic town may have been largely depopulated during K'atun 1 Ahau, with occupants resettling at Champotón (Roys 1962:45). The Chumayel chronicle states that the "men of Tancah [Mayapán] were dispersed and the batabs of the towns were scattered" during this interval (Roys 1933, 1962:78). Alfred M. Tozzer (1941:note 180) suggests that these abandonments may be confused in historical accounts with the final K'atun 8 Ahau event, but archaeological evidence indicates that earlier acts of destruction and departure occurred prior to 1400 (table 8.1). During K'atun 1 Ahau, the Cocom invited more allies from Tabasco—the Canuls—into the city (Roys 1962:46; Landa 1941:61). The Canuls were not hated or penalized after the city's fall and were allowed to settle peacefully in the western peninsula after the final collapse of the city (Roys 1962:48).

Archaeological and paleoenvironmental evidence may coincide with these K'atun histories. Two mass graves are dated with AMS radiocarbon samples (of burned human bone) to calibrated ranges extending from 1271–1394 (Itzmal Ch'en) and 1200–1390 (Q-79/Q-80, epicenter), respectively (Peraza Lope et al. 2006). These two sigma date ranges coincide well with the 1302–1362 "revolution." There are indications that these mass graves were deposited earlier rather than later within these ranges. Given the bimodal probability curve for Postclassic-era dates (Bronk Ramsey 1995, 2001), there is an 86 percent chance that the mass grave in the plaza near Q-79 dates to within 1200–1320. The massacre represented by this grave best fits the strife described for K'atun 9 Ahau (1302–1323). The probabilities are about even for the early and late bimodal radiocarbon date ranges for the Itzmal Ch'en mass grave. The dates for both mass graves leave open the possibility that human interments represent victims of warfare any time between K'atun 9 and K'atun 5 Ahau (1302–1362)—or alternatively, they are potentially related to the inquisition of the nobility in K'atun 3 Ahau (1362–1382). The noble status of the victims is implied by their proximity to monumental contexts and the deposition of abundant smashed effigy censers amidst the chopped, disarticulated, and/or burned human bones.

The burning and abandonment of epicentral Hall Q-88a is also radiocarbon dated to the interval of 1271–1400 (calibrated two sigma range), and this act of destruction may correspond to the same disjunctive K'atuns as one or both of the mass graves (Peraza Lope et al. 2006). Dates come from burned thatch cinders that covered the floor of this edifice. The belongings of the hall's patrons were found beneath the roof. A K'atun 3 Ahau date inscribed on a glyphic miniature jaguar sculpture from Q-88a's floor likely refers to the

K'atun ending in 1382 (Milbrath and Peraza Lope 2003a:40), around the time when certain nobles were being prosecuted. During this same period, elite House Y-45a was abandoned after its residents smashed their fancy serving vessels, burned offerings, and buried the rooms containing these deposits with fill (chapter 3). Burned carbon from a buried offering of smashed pottery and charcoal revealed a two sigma range of 1270–1400 (Peraza Lope et al. 2006). This abandonment event probably predates 1382, the beginning of a prosperous period.

The strife experienced during the fourteenth century at Mayapán may have been aggravated by a drought detected in the Punta Laguna lake core (Curtis, Hodell, and Brenner 1996:46). Jason H. Curtis, David A. Hodell, and Mark Brenner suggest that the drought probably occurred during the last half of the fourteenth century, although a mid-fifteenth-century date cannot be ruled out (1368–1429 +/–50). This episode is described as one of the driest periods on record in the 3,500-year sequence of this Quintana Roo lake core (Curtis, Hodell, and Brenner 1996:43). Presumably a drought of this magnitude affected much of the peninsula, including the Mayapán area. Recently, more specific information on droughts from the speleothem record has been published. Between 1300 and 1400, severely dry years occurred in the greatest frequency and severity since the fall of Chichén Itzá in the eleventh century (Kennett et al. 2012:figure 2). This record shows a rebound to a period of wetter years in the first part of the fifteenth century followed by droughts of equal or greater magnitude and longer duration from the time Mayapán fell until the Spanish conquest of Yucatán (1450–1550).

The stability that may have been established in K'atun 1 Ahau (1382–1401) lasted around forty years, as the subsequent K'atun 12 Ahau (1401–1421) is described as a peaceful one in which leaders were perceived as benevolent, the populace prospered, and the food supply was abundant (Roys 1962:46). It is possible that a late fluorescence at sites contemporary with Mayapán corresponds to this interval (Masson 2000:249–64).

This reprieve was truncated in K'atun 10 Ahau (1421–1441), when severe famine struck the region (Roys 1962:46). The final K'atun 8 Ahau (1441–1461) overthrow of the Cocom-dominated confederacy involved fighting with stones, an unclear reference that may include slings or projectiles, as well as the seizure of the city wall and the dissolution of the ruling council (Roys 1962:47–48). The wall was broken down, which may explain its deteriorated condition. Destruction of the wall (9.1 kilometers in circumference) would have represented a major attack by a large military force (Roys 1962:47–48). The Xiu aggressors must have summoned their allies in the attack. This war probably occurred in the year 1448 (Roys 1962:78). The Cocom lords were the targets of this war, and all members of this family who were at Mayapán were killed. One individual survived, as he happened to be absent on a trading expedition to Honduras, and he resettled with allies and relatives at the locality of Tibolón, in the vicinity of Sotuta (Tozzer 1941:note 178; Landa 1941:39).

The timing of the drought indicated by the Punta Laguna core and the speleothem record may signal pressures faced by the Mayapán state and its network of allied polities and trading partners in the fourteenth century. These events served as a rehearsal for the final collapse of the city. Severe or widespread shortages would have strained the capacities of regional trade systems through which food and other goods were normally distributed. While the period of 1382–1421 may have offered a reprieve, the region subsequently suffered the impacts of global volcanic activity, and possibly the Little Ice Age, in the form of local droughts (Gill 2000:289; Gill and Keating 2002:136). Approaching 1450 the state's incapacitation was probably inevitable. Traumatic testimonies of suffering in Yucatán in the Chilam Balam books regarding K'atun 8 Ahau (1441–1461) describe cold and starvation (Gill 2000:301). Notably, the central Mexican famine of the Year 1 Rabbit had its most severe effects by 1454, when Moctecuhzoma I gave his subjects in the Valley of Mexico permission to migrate to other regions in an effort to save themselves (Hassig 1981:171). Inland towns of northern Yucatán suffered pronounced shortages of food and water during K'atun 8 Ahau (Craine and Reindorp 1979:83). In too many cross-cultural instances, famine leads to greater susceptibility to disease (Davis 2001). The populations of the peninsula were weak at the time of Spanish arrival and may have suffered from indigenous epidemics only to be hit by European-introduced diseases of even greater severity.

Plagues hit the region at the time of Mayapán's fall and in the immediate decades to follow. If populations lingered in the city after K'atun 8 Ahau, they experienced further suffering. A great "hurricane of the four winds" in 1464 decimated regional game populations, uniformly reduced the height of trees in large tracts of Yucatán, and destroyed tall buildings (Landa 1941:40; Tozzer 1941:note 201). According to one account, trees were uprooted, resulting in regrowth to equal heights (Tozzer 1941:note 204). Forest resources and orchard fruits would have been destroyed. This loss of landesque capital would have resulted in impoverishment and hunger, as orchards and other multi-generational investments in agrarian development had an important role in assuring the stability of the food supply (Erikson 2006).

Approximately eighteen years later, in 1482, a great plague hit. This "blood-vomit or *xe kik*" is recorded in K'atun 4 Ahau (Landa 1941:41; Tozzer 1941:note 205). The disease was also referred to as the "general death" (*cimil*) or when "the vultures entered the houses within the fortress (of Mayapán)." This intriguing reference suggests that some level of occupation continued at Mayapán past 1441–1461; the Xiu may have remained in residence until K'atun 4 Ahau (1480–1500) (Pollock 1962:15; Milbrath and Peraza Lope 2003a:33). The epidemic may have prompted their ultimate evacuation, which probably occurred between 1480 and 1485 (Roys 1933:11, 1962:73). Warfare ravaged the land during some of the years that followed. Landa (1941:41) states that 150,000 men died in battle in this period. When peace was finally established, smallpox broke out in 1517, perhaps introduced by Spanish explorer Francisco Hernández de Córdoba (Tozzer 1941:note 207). These political, environmental, and epidemiological factors gave Postclassic Maya society in northwest Yucatán little opportunity to stabilize in the decades leading up to the Spanish conquest (Tozzer 1941:41n206).

A wider view of these effects considers the economic implications of environmental stress among interacting Postclassic polities. With central Mexico in trouble in the years bracketing the famine of 1 Rabbit that peaked in 1454, trade networks between the Maya area and its neighbors may have been interrupted long enough for Mayapán to fail. On a more regional level, trade provides one viable solution to periodic agricultural shortages (Freidel and Shaw 2000), particularly those arising from short-term, local events. The Aztec Triple Alliance bounced back from the famine of 1 Rabbit; similarly, Yucatán managed short-term recoveries between calamities of the fourteenth and early fifteenth centuries (Landa 1941:41–42), and coastal Maya towns were prospering from trade at Spanish contact (Berdan et al. 2003; Kepecs 2003). Mayapán's political and religious leaders may have sponsored a revitalization movement, probably during the fourteenth century, in response to such hardship. This movement reached and recharged hinterlands polities along the east coast of the peninsula (Masson 2000).

WARFARE AND THE MAYAPÁN STATE

Why was war undertaken by protohistoric Maya states? The goals of seizing property, children, and wives were principal motivating factors (Tozzer 1941:41n206). Taking captives was related to an escalating slave trade, which continued into the Colonial era. For example, sixteenth-century Iuit rulers of Hocabá conducted war in order to capture slaves for sale (Roys 1962:48;

see also Tozzer 1941:note 175; Roys 1940). The episodic hardships encountered across Yucatán during Mayapán's final century and a half, which continued through the Colonial Period, may have also contributed to revitalization rituals involving increased human sacrifice of children and adults that greatly disturbed sixteenth-century Spanish priests. France B. Scholes and Roys (1938) suggest that such acts may have been part of a desperate response to the social disorder caused by conquest and disease.

There are plentiful indications of the importance of warfare to the Mayapán state that began with its foundation and the construction of the first Temple of Kukulcan, which was decorated with stucco death figures and niches for trophy skulls (chapter 2, figure 2.12). Throughout the occupation, the nucleated settlement pattern, great city wall, and abundance of projectile points and knives reveal a society ever conscious of military concerns (chapter 6; Russell 2008a, 2013). Households armed themselves with projectiles, knives, and lances, and these were the most common tools in domestic assemblages, comprising a combined total of 28 percent of all stone tools, including informal unifaces (figure 6.25). Axes, seemingly benign, also sometimes served as tools of decapitation (Bill, Hernández, and Bricker 2000). At burial shaft Temple Q-95, Edwin W. Shook (1954c) observed that the upper half of the shaft deposit of human remains contained Ch'en Mul censers, but the lower half did not. This fact suggests that ritualized sacrifice preceded the onset of Ch'en Mul effigy censer rituals during the latter half of the city's occupation and were perhaps conducted from the late part of the thirteenth century onward (Milbrath et al. 2008:105; Milbrath and Peraza Lope 2013). Analysis of human remains at the epicenter reveals that violent trauma, sacrifice, and trophy taking in the context of warfare and building dedication are commonly reflected. Many of the burials in the site center's alleys, construction fill, and other features were probably sacrificial victims (Serafin and Peraza Lope 2007; Serafin 2010:200). The slave trade meant that raids were waged to forcibly capture individuals. A strong military was needed to defend Mayapán's interests in circum-peninsular and overland trade and to protect merchants (chapter 6). Postclassic codex scenes reiterate these themes of captive taking and sacrifice (Bill 1997). Military service was emphasized in corvée demands placed on subjects of the confederacy. The Report of Tekal informs us that "they did not take tribute from their vassals more than what the latter wished to give, except that they served them with their persons and arms in war, whenever the occasion offered" (Roys 1962:50).

Mass graves and sacrificial burial shaft temples point to warfare as a key activity of the Mayapán state. The extensive deposits around 30 centimeters below the plaza floor near edifices Q-79 and Q-80, and starting at 10 centimeters below the ground surface along the platform of the Itzmal Ch'en ceremonial group, are similarly defined by extensive disarticulated human remains and effigy censer fragments (figure 8.1). The remains probably belonged to residents of Mayapán, whose bones were desecrated and dishonored in shallow graves during one of the violent upheavals of the late thirteenth or fourteenth centuries that have been described previously. Projectile points are common in the Itzmal Ch'en grave, and three knives were found in the rib cages of two individuals and near the pelvis of a third in the vicinity of Q-79/Q-80 (Adams 1953:145). At Itzmal Ch'en, the bones were intentionally chopped apart and burned (Vidal Guzmán 2011). Additional mass graves that include skulls and disarticulated postcranial elements have been found at Mayapán in an alley next to Round Temple (Templo Redondo) Q-152, between the Temple of Kukulcan and one of its sanctuaries, and other locations (Shook and Irving 1955; Serafin and Peraza Lope 2007; Serafin 2010). At least two shaft temples and one shrine (H-18) also received sacrificial victims (Chowning 1956; Masson and Peraza Lope 2007). Monumental plazas at Mayapán doubled as resting places for victims of violence at the hands of warlords of the Mayapán state. Some of these victims may have been casualties of internal strife or external raids on the city. In contrast, skulls or long bones in shrine contexts would have represented ancestral relics (Landa 1941:131). The grim realities of warfare and conflict seem to have permeated life at the city throughout much of its history.

What was the reach of Mayapán's army? Ross Hassig (1988:23) argues that armies mobilized by empires or other extensive political entities could control large territories and meet foes at borders. In contrast, city-states tended to attack a rival's political center and then sack it following victory. Although alliance networks were capable of joining together large forces during the Postclassic Period in central Mexico, warfare was not conducted on a major scale and military expeditions tended to be appropriative rather than destructive (Hassig 1988:24, 259; Pohl and Robinson 2005:28). Mayapán's confederacy was geographically extensive enough to have commanded a conscripted militia of considerable size; such units were efficient and could be rapidly mobilized (Webster 2000:79). The need for a city wall, coupled with evidence for periodic destruction, indicates that the city was not immune to deadly skirmishes at home. Aztec armies acted punitively but stopped short of wholesale slaughter in order to establish obedient tributaries (Hassig 1988:259). Raids and punitive expeditions, like those of the Aztec, seem to have been conducted by the Mayapán state, and the acquisition of captives for sacrifice, sale, or servitude was a key motive (Scholes and Roys 1938).

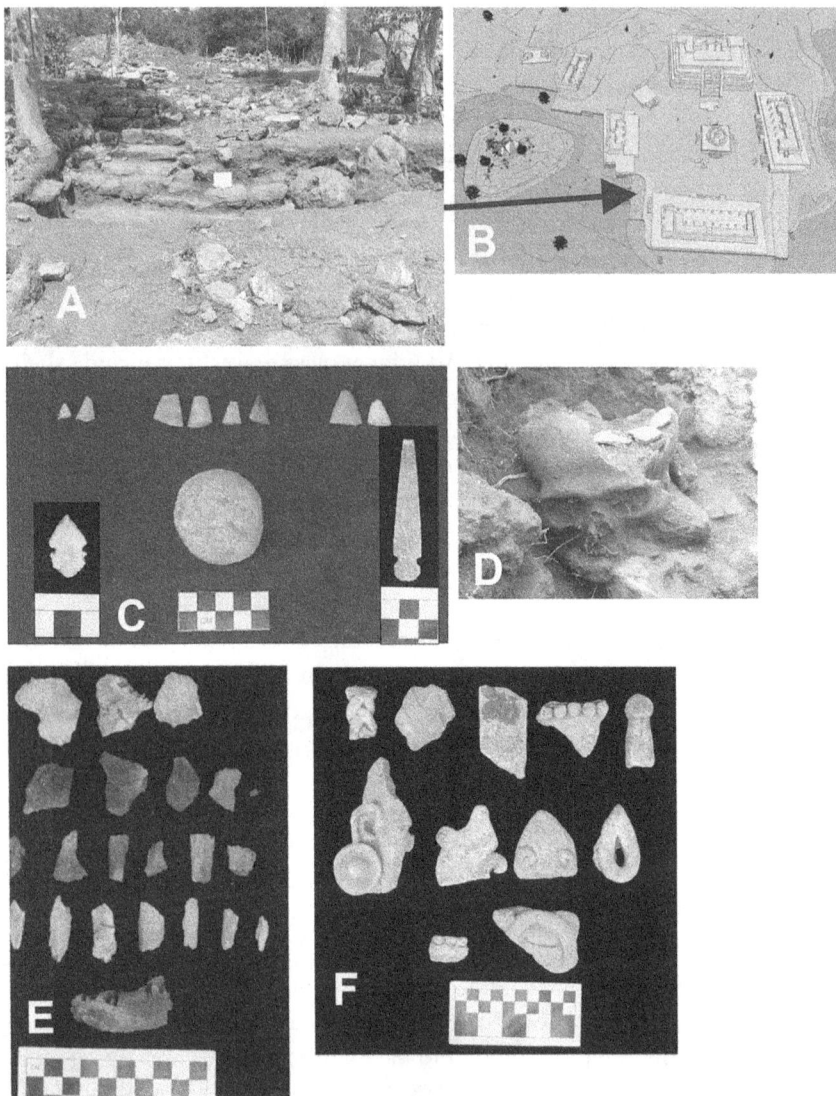

FIGURE 8.1. *The mass grave at the staircase of the Itzmal Ch'en group (A, B) was deposited prior to AD 1400. The feature contained projectile points (C); hammerstones (C); disarticulated, smashed, and burned human bones (D, E); and broken effigy censers (F).*

RAPID ABANDONMENT IN MAYAPÁN'S ARCHAEOLOGICAL RECORD

The archaeology of rapidly abandoned sites has received much recent attention in Mesoamerica. Some mortuary features at the Classic-era Maya city of Yaxuna were ritually desecrated (Ardren 2002; Suhler et al. 2004:475). Evidence for burning, smashing, and scattering of materials and the removal of funerary materials has been reported from this site. In central Mexico, Xochicalco was also rapidly abandoned, and although central public structures were burned and destroyed, residential structures were not widely impacted (Webb and Hirth 2003:41). This political capital ended in violent conflict, perhaps due to an internal rebellion, as is reported for Mayapán (chapter 2). At Xochicalco, artifacts were strewn on temple floors and dismembered corpses were discovered over structures (Webb and Hirth 2003:41). Abandoned Xochicalco buildings retained a large proportion of their inventories (Webb and Hirth 2003: 38–40). Takeshi Inomata (2003:46–47) also reports much burning during the rapid exodus from the Maya city of Aguateca, where metates were probably broken from fire and falling debris. Where possible, it is important to distinguish abandonment versus termination ritual (Mock 1998). At Aguateca, abandonment was inferred when there was a good fit between material assemblages and presumed building functions, suggesting that items remained in the contexts of their use (Inomata 2003:47). Termination is documented at Aguateca in cases where artifacts were burned or interred within fill (Inomata 2003:54–56). Abandonment and termination behaviors are potentially related; when the former is imminent, termination rites can be undertaken (Inomata 2003:57). As for Xochicalco, burning did not occur at structures outside of the epicenter at Aguateca, leading Inomata to deduce that outlying residences were more slowly abandoned and that their occupants had the opportunity to carry away valued possessions (Inomata 2003:57–58). Joel W. Palka (2003:126) argues that elites may be the first to leave in cases such as the city of Dos Pilas, where public buildings were dismantled and later reoccupied or scavenged. Rapid abandonment results in many usable items being left behind (Palka 2003:122). Some low-status houses at Dos Pilas had few usable items while other occupants departed more suddenly and left smashed refuse on floors (Palka 2003:128). Similarly, much burning occurred at Teotihuacan in the central precinct and at outlying temples, but only 45 of 965 apartment compounds exhibit evidence of burning (Manzanilla 2003:94).

Twenty-one contexts at Mayapán with signs of destruction are listed in table 8.2 and are plotted in figures 8.2 and 8.3 for the monumental center and the outlying settlement zone. The abandonment of Mayapán was also associated with much burning and looting prior to the collapse of some dwellings and public buildings with masonry roofs (Pollock 1954:266, 1962:15). A variety of edifices reveal the remains of destruction and burning (Peraza Lope et al. 1997; Peraza Lope, Masson, and Delgado Kú 2008). Effigy censers and other precious goods are smashed over floors (Adams 1953; Winters 1955b; Peraza Lope et al. 1997, 2008; Delgado Kú, Escamilla Ojeda, and Peraza Lope 2012a, 2012b) and sculptures were decapitated and fell or were thrown down from their original locations (Proskouriakoff 1962a; Delgado Kú, Escamilla Ojeda, and Peraza Lope 2012a, 2012b). Care was sometimes taken to cover offerings with fill or place cherished effigies into tombs for safekeeping (Proskouriakoff and Temple 1955; Peraza Lope et al. 1997, 1999a, 2008), and some caches and burials were later looted in antiquity (Pollock 1954:266; Shook 1954c; A. Smith 1962:264). Susan Milbrath and Carlos Peraza Lope (2009:602) attribute the destruction, burning, and broken monuments of Mayapán's public buildings to the Xiu and their allies in the context of the final revolt in K'atun 8 Ahau. As table 8.1 indicates, however, some acts of termination and abandonment predate 1400 (see also figures 8.2, 8.3). Additional radiocarbon dates from terminal assemblages indicate that other destructive events may have occurred in the fourteenth century. As figure 8.2 reveals, nine other similar contexts have yet to be dated. At the minimum, the impacts of violence at the city left a number of public buildings in disrepair before the city's final abandonment, and at least one elite house was ceremoniously terminated.

In addition to the mass graves, three contexts that we have investigated are particularly illustrative of this pattern, including Q-88a, Y-45, and the Itzmal Ch'en group (table 8.1). Colonnaded Hall Q-88a, adjoined to the complex of Mayapán's central Templo Redondo group, was completely burned; cinders from its thatch roof covered the floor. It was left this way, in ruins, from an event that predates 1400 until the final departure of the city's population. Outlying elites at House Y-45a smashed all of their fine pottery in the back rooms of their house, burned some offerings, and then filled these rooms with rubble in a ceremonious late thirteenth- or fourteenth-century departure (Masson and Peraza Lope 2005; Peraza Lope et al. 2008; chapter 3). At Itzmal Ch'en, portions of the floors of an upper temple (H-17) and a colonnaded hall (H-15) were burned in acts of desecration or abandonment (chapter 3; Delgado Kú, Escamilla Ojeda, and Peraza Lope 2012a, 2012b). Termination rituals also occurred at these structures as indicated by twelve concentrations of broken pottery—mostly effigy censers—and two pieces of greenstone over the floors of the hall and temple and in front of the temple (chapter 3, figures 3.11, 3.12). If the termination deposits are contemporary with the mass grave, this event occurred prior to 1400.

TABLE 8.2 Evidence for the intentional destruction or termination of buildings from the Carnegie project investigations.

Structure	Heavy burning final floor	Heavy burning roof, objects on floor	Dense surface deposits of effigy censers	Other abandonment rituals	Looted altar/shrine under roof fall	Contents of altar/shrine cache nearby	Skeleton (violent death)	Thrown down sculpture
Temple T-72 (Shook 1953)	X		X					
Temple Q-58 (Shook 1954a)			X				X	
Temple Q-82 (Shook 1954a)	X		X		X	X		
Hall Q-81 (Winters 1955a)			X		X	X		
Houses J-71a and J-71b (Smith and Ruppert 1956)		X						
House S-133 (Smith and Ruppert 1956)		X (partial)						
Hall Z-50c (Pollock 1956)		X (partial)						
House Q-208 (J. Thompson 1954)		X			X			
Kukulcan Temple Q-162 (Shook 1954b)	X		X		X	X		
Temple H-17 (PEMY)	X (partial)			X				
Hall H-15 (PEMY)	X (partial)		X	X				

continued on next page

TABLE 8.2—continued

Structure	Heavy burning final floor	Heavy burning roof, objects on floor	Dense surface deposits of effigy censers	Other abandonment rituals	Looted altar/shrine under roof fall	Contents of altar/shrine cache nearby	Skeleton (violent death)	Thrown down sculpture
Y-45a (PEMY)				X				
Q-88a (INAH)		X						
Hall Q-97 (Shook and Irving 1955)		X	X		X	X		X
Hall Q-151 (Shook and Irving 1955)			X					
Alley Q-151/Q-152 (Shook and Irving 1955)			X				X	
Q-79 (Adams 1953)			X				X	
H-15/Itzmal Chen platform edge			X				X	
House Q-169 (Thompson and Thompson 1955)					X			
Round Temple Q-126 (Shook 1955)	X		X		X	X		X
Palace R-87/R-86 (Proskouriakoff and Temple 1955)	X	X		X	X	X		
Temple Q-80 (Winters 1955a)			X				X	

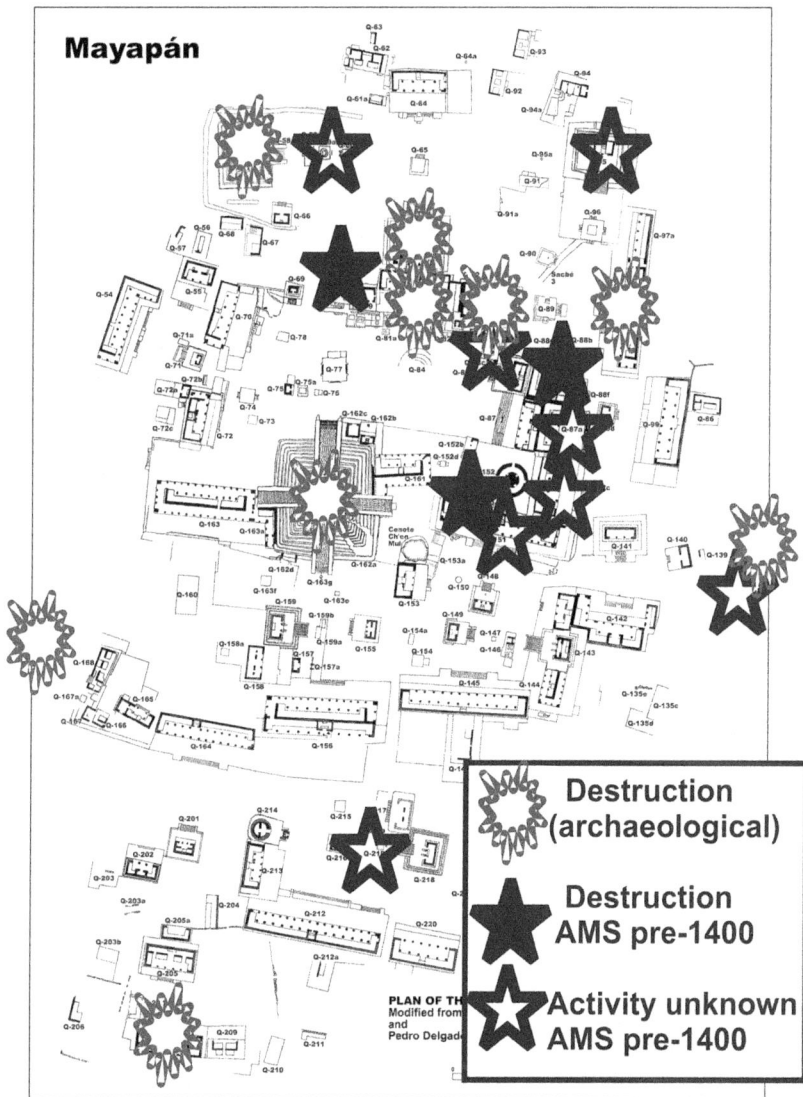

FIGURE 8.2. *Destruction and abandonment events recorded at Mayapán's monumental center.*

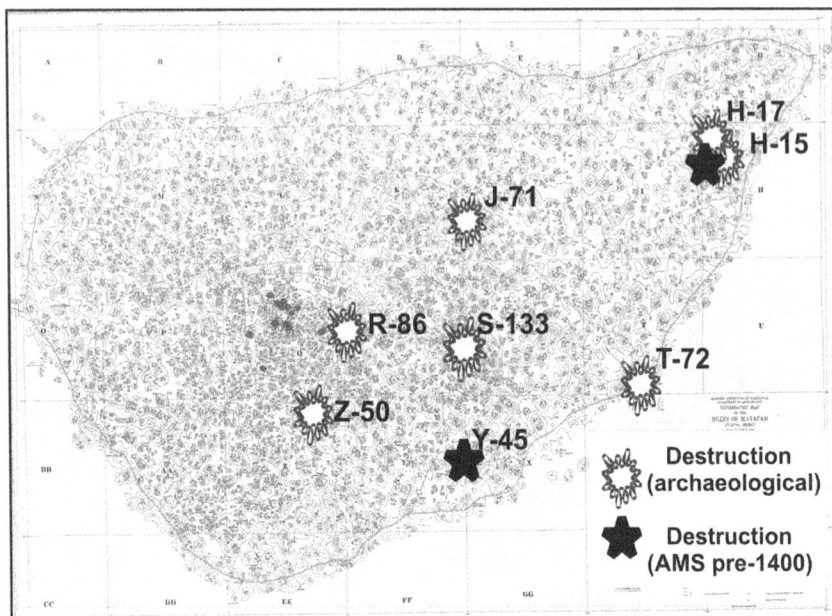

FIGURE 8.3. *Destruction and abandonment events recorded in Mayapán's settlement zone.*

POPULATION AND COLLAPSE

Issues of the Classic-era Maya collapse continue to be a source of scholarly debate (Turner and Sabloff 2012; Masson 2012). The abandonment of many Classic Period sites suggests that there was a dramatic decline in regional populations (Rice and Culbert 1990). Although fertility declines in mobile populations that are under stress, rapid resettlement can result in a quick recovery. Richardson B. Gill (2000:98) doubts that fertility was a factor that contributed to demographic decline in the Terminal Classic Maya lowlands. Until systematic survey is performed in well-watered zones away from Classic Period centers in areas such as northeastern Belize, it is difficult to fully document this process. Terminal Classic settlements are populous in northeastern Belize at a time when central Petén sites are abandoned (Sidrys 1983; Masson 2000; Masson and Mock 2004), but full-coverage survey has never been undertaken. The issue of population recovery during the Postclassic era is also poorly chronicled, especially as new sites are sometimes founded in locations away from conspicuous earlier centers. Coastal Yucatecan sites of the Postclassic era are numerous (A. Andrews 1977; Andrews and Vail 1990). How many small towns dotted the landscape? Settlement data is hard won in the Maya area, and until more studies are done, arguments for the scale of demographic decline or recovery are weakly supported. We do not doubt the severe impacts that have been documented at many Classic-era sites and their immediate hinterlands (Rice and Culbert 1990), but other areas are more poorly understood. Susan Kepecs's (1999, 2003) years of survey in the Chikinchel region revealed a landscape dotted with towns occupied from Chichén Itzá's apogee into the Colonial Period.

Unfortunately, we have little demographic data for the regional settlement system associated with Mayapán. The fact that members of the city's confederacy returned to their hometowns or founded new polities after the city's fall is well known (Landa 1941; Tozzer 1941; Restall 2001). The majority of these towns were occupied when the Spanish arrived and are occupied today. Many of these longstanding localities were also settlements of the Postclassic era. Colonial churches were constructed on or near monumental architecture of Preclassic or Classic Period date that reflect long-term settlement histories for these towns. Archaeological documentation of public and domestic architecture is impaired by Spanish efforts to raze existing temples and use these materials or platforms to construct large Colonial churches at towns like Acanceh, Tecoh, Sotuta, and Mani, among many others. These towns were also reorganized according to a European grid plan, further impacting archaeological remains. Redeposited construction materials of earlier public buildings underlie central plazas in Yucatecan towns today, and in some cases ancient mounds still stand. At Telchaquillo, 1 kilometer north of Mayapán, public and domestic architecture is partially preserved, and the temple in this town's square was substantially modified during the Postclassic Period (R. Smith 1954; Ruppert and Smith 1957; Russell 2008a). Recent archaeological survey in the vicinity of Mayapán has located a number of Postclassic and earlier sites (Brown et al. 2006:7). During Mayapán's heyday, Yucatán may have had a population of 8–13 million (Stannard 1993:37). According to some estimates, 95 percent of this population may have been decimated in epidemics following European contact (Gill 2000:100). More research is necessary to assess pre-European populations, particularly for Postclassic-era Yucatán.

THE COLLAPSE OF THE CONFEDERACY

Droughts are not all alike, and we do not advocate a single cause for the collapse of Mayapán. As Gill (2000:302–4) points out, droughts were periodically experienced in Yucatán throughout the Postclassic Period. Some of the K'atuns in which they occurred did not result in political dissolution or long-term catastrophic demographic effects. The regularity of suffering from shortages during various K'atuns suggests that, at least some of the time, effects were constrained by their short-term duration, limited geographical impact, or the ability to move food through markets (Freidel and Shaw 2000). Effects are difficult to measure from fleeting accounts in the Chilam Balam chronicles. Famines and droughts recorded by Spanish sources from the sixteenth through eighteenth centuries reflect abysmal suffering and death (Gill 2000:304–5). Sources seem to indicate that the fifteenth century was particularly severe in terms of the frequency and scale of environmental and epidemiological calamities (Kennett et al. 2012). Importantly, the fall of Mayapán is not attributable to societal failures and weak political or economic institutions, as was long assumed (chapter 1). Earlier collapses in the Maya sequence reflect oscillations of centralization and decentralization (Marcus 1993). In the forty to sixty years that lapsed between Mayapán's demise and the onset of European diseases, Yucatán towns were struggling with a barrage of natural catastrophes, shortages, and hostile regional relationships. This state of affairs was not uniformly experienced by all towns and polities across the peninsula. Well-watered agricultural zones, salt production towns, and trading centers were thriving on the eve of Spanish arrival (Chase and Chase 1988; Kepecs 2003; Berdan et al. 2003; Masson 2000, 2003b), even though Mayapán did not recover.

Mayapán's decline was prolonged. An increase in late thirteenth- or early fourteenth-century violence suggests an unstable environment and a city besieged by hostility. These circumstances provide a longer term context with which to view the final Xiu-led revolt that annihilated a large contingent of the Cocom nobility. Considering the series of catastrophes that befell the confederacy, it is remarkable that the political capital was able to maintain power to the extent that it did. The monumental buildings of the city were erected by at least 1200, and much of the following century seems to have been an interval of prosperity and growth. There are no historical accounts of disasters, and the radiocarbon sigma ranges for mass graves do not extend before 1270. The troubles of the late thirteenth or early fourteenth centuries seem to have been briefly overcome for the forty years—from 1382–1421—before they resumed. If the historical references correlate accurately with radiocarbon-dated events, then Mayapán thrived unfettered for only seventy years, from around 1200–1270, and regained some traction for forty years around the turn of the fifteenth century. A more interesting question to ponder given these indications is how the city and its polity endured until the mid-fifteenth century. The perseverance of the Mayapán state until K'atun 8 Ahau (1441–1461) attests to the tenacity and power of political institutions and a populace sufficiently tolerant of this mode of governance throughout episodes of economic hardship and the purging of unpopular governors. In a comparative sense, the fits and starts of Mayapán's sequence are not unlike the troubled histories of the *longue durée* that are chronicled for other ancient states in which victorious, popular, leadership becomes legendary amid a backdrop of mediocre or even disastrous regimes. The dynastic legacies of the Classic Maya area are similarly punctuated and defined by exceptional, rare periods of prosperity under long-lived dynasts whose accomplishments far surpass those of their ancestors and descendants (Martin and Grube 2008). Like other ancient political capitals, Mayapán fell, but it is probable that in due course another regional center would have risen once again to unite this part of the peninsula. Some have argued that a new capital may have been developing at the large urban center of Mérida-Tihó, on the eve of Spanish arrival (Restall 1997:33–35).

9

Recognizing Complexity in Urban Life

MARILYN A. MASSON AND
CARLOS PERAZA LOPE

The complexity of urban institutions at the city of Mayapán is reflected in the details of the chapters of this book. This new look at the last major Pre-Columbian Maya political capital reveals multiple layers of political, urban, social, economic, and religious organization. The general history of Mayapán's most influential governors has been known since Diego de Landa's day, and here we have looked beneath the surface to explore evidence for middle-level political cohesion that would have tied the city's lords to its ordinary laborers. Within the cityscape, characteristics of architectural form, size, function, and artifact assemblages attest to subsystems that articulated the teeming daily desires and objectives of at least 15,000 residents. Although this book's chapters consider separate categories of data that reflect neighborhood administration, planning, household settlement, economic production and exchange, and religious images, it is clear that these aspects of life at Mayapán overlapped. Even the city's collapse was not simple or short, and this process testifies as much to Mayapán's resiliency as to its weaknesses. Complexity is reflected at different analytical scales. On a general level, the state successfully unified its citizenry, particularly those who resided at the capital, who adopted a relatively homogenous set of architectural and artifact styles. More specific variation is also tracked at the scale of individual buildings, where assemblages attest to pluralistic constituents who exercised some license in the annual cycle of religious observance, labor investment, marketplace purchases, and houselot characteristics.

Elite-sponsored social gatherings and the materialization of political and religious authority were closely

DOI: 10.5876/9781607323204.c009

founded on the economies of daily life. Activities at all social scales stimulated the production of basic goods in households, as is observed for the Aztec realm (Smith, Wharton, and Olson 2003). Commerce at Mayapán, along with its tribute rosters, would have bound together producers, consumers, traders, elites, commoners, farmers, locals, and visitors. Arguably, such integration has great time depth in the Maya area (Masson and Freidel 2012). The relevance of Mayapán as a comparative case study has yet to be fully recognized by those who study Classic Period Maya economies. While the importance of market exchange may have reached its zenith in Postclassic Mesoamerica (Sabloff and Rathje 1975; Smith and Berdan 2003a), the significance of this institution in earlier periods merits further systematic queries (Feinman and Garraty 2010; Masson and Freidel 2012). A ritual economy perspective focuses on the degree to which production was embedded in a system of beliefs (Wells 2006; McAnany 2010). The production of sacred and mundane goods for major ritual celebrations stimulated the local economy and connected producers to higher authorities in important ways for Mayapán and many other centers. This embeddedness of the city's commercial industries can be viewed as evidence for a highly integrated system. Embeddedness is no longer viewed as a label that points to an inferior level of sociocultural evolution (Feinman and Garraty 2010:173). Undoubtedly, the city's occupants were, for the most part, devout. But we leave open the probability that a secular realm of commercial relationships also existed in which religion was of little or no importance. To what degree were individuals motivated by practical concerns such as craft or agrarian provisioning and market events beyond occasions prompted by religious celebrations? We envision that such practical exchanges were a daily concern of city life.

Occupational diversity and dependency on others is a cornerstone of the definition of ancient urban life, whether one worked in crafts or agriculture or as a merchant, official, priest, or laborer (Childe 1950:11; Haviland 1970). Li Liu (2006:187) eloquently points out that surplus craft production is integral to the development of states and urbanism and that these processes cannot be separated into a linear causal sequence. Cross-culturally, the development of craft specialization at urban places is dependent on access to regional resources needed for the industries (Liu 2006:187). For this reason, the economies of urban places are closely articulated with those of regional towns and villages. At Mayapán, identifying craft production contributes directly toward recognizing that this political capital was a fully functional urban place. The importance of market institutions is revealed as a key mechanism for surplus exchange and household interdependency at this city. Ironically, V. Gordon Childe

(1950) did not consider markets in his treatise on urban life, as he thought that state authorities redistributed surpluses directly. Market institutions have received little attention in the Maya area relative to tribute demands, but this is now changing (A. Chase and D. Chase 2004; Dahlin et al. 2010; Masson and Freidel 2012; Shaw 2012). Even for the Aztec, for whom abundant historical records attest to complex market systems, economic analysis for many years emphasized a tributary mode of exchange (Kowalewski 1990:54). The existence and importance of Postclassic Maya markets has been accepted for many years, particularly due to the emphasis on commerce in the early works of Jeremy A. Sabloff, William L. Rathje, and David A. Freidel (Sabloff and Rathje 1975; Rathje 1975; Freidel and Sabloff 1984; Freidel 1981).

Studying the intersection of hierarchical and heterarchical networks is illustrative, as these configurations can be complementary, potentially conflictive, or both (Crumley 1987:158–59). We discover complexity at the junctures of these arrays of relationships (Crumley 1987:163). In ancient Mesopotamia, investigators have moved away from a top-down view of a hierarchical, temple-centered society in order to acknowledge the flexible, entrepreneurial character of social institutions (Stone 2007b:215). Mayapán, like Mohenjo-Daro and Harappa, exhibits variation in the elite control of production (Wright 1996:126). Elites or those under their close supervision tended to perform highly specialized crafting at Harappan sites as well as at Mayapán and Classic Maya centers (e.g., Ball 1993). Mayapán elites supervised or performed molding, modeling, stuccoing, and painting of deity effigy censers and copper bell production (Paris 2008; Cruz Alvarado et al. 2012). Aside from these cases, the majority of Mayapán's craft industries were organized according to commoner heterarchical networks. Some were concentrated in a downtown neighborhood (Milpa 1) while others were configured into smaller groups in dispersed parts of the city (Grid squares AA, Z, and S and Itzmal Ch'en). We infer that the exchange of these basic goods occurred in the marketplace, and it is also possible that craftspersons sold goods to their neighbors from their homes. Strict rules were enforced that confined trade activities to the marketplace, at least for professional merchants (Tozzer 1941:96n424). It is not known to what degree this was enforced on exchanges of small quantities of low-value goods within a settlement. Lawrence H. Feldman (1978) mentions the existence of petty vendors at the lower end of Contact Period Maya trader hierarchies.

The women and men of Mayapán fabricated the goods that were essential for the matrix of exchange relationships that bound together occupants of the city and other Yucatecan towns. Women wove and embellished fabrics for the textile industry, ever essential to the economies of ancient states (Pirenne

1925:153–55; Reents-Budet 2006). The stamp of female labor is also borne by white-tailed deer husbandry and fruit (garden or orchard) industries; these foodstuffs were traded out to coastal sites and also contributed dietary staples to the city's fare, as did maize tamales, also prepared by women. Although many stone, ceramic, and shell craft items may have been made by men, in the use lives of these objects, they passed through the hands of individuals of varied age and sex in the course of daily work. Aspects of crafting may have also been a family affair, with household members helping with preliminary stages or gathering necessary supplies (e.g., firewood for open pot firing or plaster making). Some households became affluent as a result of crafting or other part-time jobs.

Like the occupants of earlier Maya centers, farmers and craftspersons at Mayapán implemented a range of strategies for organizing their labor and reaping its rewards (e.g., Becker 1973; Scarborough, Valdez, and Dunning 2003; Lohse and Valdez 2004; Masson and Freidel 2012; Dunning, Beach, and Luzzader-Beach n.d. 2003). Commoner households of premodern states were not the faceless proletariat masses of yesteryear's models, as comparative case studies defy views of passive or unchanging social relations of production, particularly between craft and agrarian producers and political elites (Gailey and Patterson 1987; Wailes 1996:4; Tringham 1996:236–37; M. Smith 2002; Robin 2004). Childe's (1950:11) model, which held that disempowered craft specialists made goods for food that was doled to them by a redistributive elite, is no longer tenable.

Heterarchical power networks provide opportunities for their participants and can thwart efforts by a ruling class to control the flow of exchanges. Such dialectical processes have long been recognized and inform the study of specific archaeological cases (Pirenne 1925:168–212; Crumley 1987). For societies with written or artistic records, top-down scorn for the contributions of farmers, craftspeople, traders, and laborers may be reflected in their omission from propagandistic works (Trigger 1980:108–9). Overt suppression of the mercantile sector has long been documented for Postclassic central Mexico (Berdan 1988), and parallel concerns may be reflected in Classic Maya art (McAnany 2010:256–57). Avaricious and decrepit depictions of the merchant deity (God L) are juxtaposed against the beauty, youth, and divinity of the avatar of Classic Maya kings, the maize god. As Patricia A. McAnany (2010) observes, this contrast was initiated by courtly nobles who controlled the artistic and written records and cast themselves as protagonists.

Considerable horizontal differentiation is observed in the work lives of occupants of specific dwellings at Mayapán and at earlier Maya sites (King 1994,

2000; McAnany 1994; Robin 2004; Yaeger and Robin 2004; Lohse and Valdez 2004; Hutson et al. 2012). Similarly, Elizabeth C. Stone (2007b:225–27) reports that neighborhoods in the ancient Near Eastern cities were populated by members of diverse occupations and that crafting was undertaken on a private basis rather than solely under the auspices of elite patronage. As for Mayapán, models of impoverishment of the general population of Mesopotamian city-states are no longer supported (Stone 2007b:218). Residents of both of these ancient societies had a degree of independence in terms of orchard holdings and grain fields, and some citizens combined farming, crafting, or trade with the duties of professional or religious offices (chapters 2, 7; Stone 2007b:219, 228). Chapter 8 reveals, however, that opportunities for affluence would have been truncated when episodes of drought or other pestilences rendered the region's economy particularly fragile.

REGIONAL PERSPECTIVES

A full reconstruction of the complexity of the Mayapán polity and its hinterlands will require a regional approach informed by large-scale survey and testing. In urban history, as well as anthropology, studies have tended to focus on the city as an analytical unit rather than the regional systems in which the cities are embedded (Kowalewski 1990:40). This book is certainly guilty of the same. Data that are needed for understanding regional organization include the size and spacing of cities and the distribution of the population and economic resources (Russell 1972:18; Ashmore 1981; Kowalewski 1990; D. Rice 2006).

We still do not know the urban index—specifically, the proportion of the population in the Mayapán confederacy that lived in cities or large towns (Russell 1972; Kowalewski 1990). Presumably this ratio was high, given the importance assigned to town living at Spanish contact, when very few Maya farmers lived as relative isolates in agricultural zones (Freidel and Sabloff 1984; Restall 2001). Houses located outside of the city wall clustered within 500 meters or closer to this enclosure. Scattered farmsteads are observed in this zone, indicated by dispersed, isolated residential groups in distant tracts of cultivable land (Russell 2008a). Ancient states frequently had at least 50 percent or more of their population residing in cities or towns (Kowalewski 1990:46); Postclassic era Yucatán probably met or exceeded this proportion. The reasons for Mayapán's exact location remain unknown. Unlike cities with longer occupational histories, the Postclassic capital was quickly founded and built, and the commercial activities of the center would have involved some rerouting of overland northern trade traffic that had former destinations in the Puuc, Mérida, and Chichén Itzá areas. Alternatively, preexisting routes to Classic Period Telchaquillo (1 kilometer from Mayapán) assumed greater importance. As for many premodern cities, the ability to attract trade was essential for Mayapán, and political capitals tended to enjoy particular advantages in this regard due to their ability to combine administrative, religious, and economic functions. Placement in a well-integrated and well-settled region also contributed to the stability and growth of ancient cities (Pirenne 1925:145; Russell 1972:234; Blanton 1996). Mayapán was built in a centrally located inland part of the northern peninsula in a well-populated region (Brown et al. 2006), as was its predecessor, Chichén Itzá.

Assessing functional differentiation among settlements is accomplished using qualitative and quantitative variables, with an emphasis on scale, degree, and change through time (Kowalewski 1990:49). Both large and small urban places can serve as seats of political, religious, and economic institutions for the hinterlands that they service (M. Smith 2008). Cities and towns in a regional landscape should be expected to differ significantly. Primate centers are identified by concentrations of goods and features that include civic-ceremonial architecture, state art, exotic objects, craft manufacture, and access to the widest ranges of utilitarian goods; such places linked their regions to the outside world (Kowalewski 1990:49; Smith and Berdan 2003b). Mayapán would have been distinct in the Postclassic Maya realm due to its population, settlement density, status as the political capital and center for religious knowledge, and investment in regional commerce backed by military muscle. This city would have also been home to the greatest concentration of skilled artisans and influential merchants and nobles, representing a cosmopolitan world city (Pollock 1962; Milbrath and Peraza Lope 2003a; Smith and Berdan 2003a). Smaller towns would have performed some of these functions on a lesser scale. For example, craftsmanship declines in quality in the hinterlands compared to Mayapán, as reflected in the attributes of effigy censers (Masson 2000:262; Milbrath et al. 2008).

Investigating horizontal complexity among settlements of equivalent size is a task that is essential for regional scale studies (Kowalewski 1990:50). Although Mayapán lacked equals in the Maya lowlands, the prospect of studying horizontal complexity between secondary centers of the region should be foregrounded in future studies. Horizontal differentiation is expected to correlate with geo-political location and the possibility of specific functions. Sites may be positioned in a core-periphery continuum or they may represent boundary, gateway, or defensive locations (Blanton 1996). Resource access may also result in differentiation, particularly for sites located near particularly rich or marginal cultivable land (Kowalewski 1990:50; Scarborough, Valdez, and Dunning 2003), chert (Shafer and Hester 1983), or salt (Kepecs 2003). In ancient Mesopotamia, a surprising level of rural complexity, wealth, and functional diversity has been documented by aerial surveys (Stone 2007b:229); work in the Maya countryside has revealed the same (Potter and King 1995; Connell 2003; Scarborough, Valdez, and Dunning 2003). Bruce H. Dahlin and his colleagues report striking functional differentiation between Chunchucmil and other Classic-era Yucatecan cities (Dahlin 2009; Dahlin et al. 2010). Spanish chroniclers also describe much productive diversity and specialization at different Maya towns (Roys 1957; Piña Chan 1978; chapter 7, figure 7.1).

Population growth is essential for the establishment of an urban center, but at some point in a city's history, growth can add strain. For example, the division of inherited wealth among siblings reduces prospects for affluence (Stone 2007b:228). Clusters of small *albarrada* groups in downtown Mayapán imply that larger *solares* were divided several times among family members. Unmarried sons at Mayapán may have served in the military or other service sectors, depending on their social status. Declining birth rates and increased mortality are also known problems for ancient cities, which can struggle to maintain their populations without the process of migration (Kowalewski 1990; Paine and Storey 2006). Upon founding the city, Mayapán's nobility resettled subjects in the urban zone so that they could provide necessary services (Landa 1941). The city may have re-implemented this policy with regularity. Mercenaries and slaves were brought to Mayapán at certain points in time along with individuals conscripted for temporary service. Other types of voluntary migrants may have been numerous.

How did cities attract populations other than by coercive means? Incentives such as offering arable land or other opportunities for making a living are sometimes effective (Stone 2007b:228). Cities promise occupations with potentially greater rewards than rural pursuits, although such hopes were not always realized (Pirenne 1925:154). Some workers in premodern urban settings achieved higher standards of living, even if it meant that they toiled harder, and their employment was precarious in the event of injury or illness (Dyer 1989:189–233). The purported individual freedoms associated with medieval European cities have been contrasted to those of the Maya, whose liberties were said to have been constrained by moral authority propagated by leaders at smaller cities like Piedras Negras (Houston et al. 2003). Yet the freedom of medieval laborers at the lower end of the wealth continuum, vulnerably tethered to meager incomes and the whims of their employers, must not be exaggerated; and medieval society was anything but free from the constraints of Christendom. Although Mayapán had no equal peers in the extensive lowlands, the challenge of luring and retaining residents from their hometowns may have been daunting, given the pull of *cahob*, the primary source of social identity (Restall 2001). Beyond material incentives, the magnetism of a cosmopolitan place may have attracted more adventurous newcomers. Migration to late medieval towns primarily occurred from the countryside to the nearest city within one day of travel from the hometown (Russell 1972:231). Intercity migration was rare and limited to very skilled persons during this period in Europe, as more distant cities had fewer kin members who could house migrants, who were perceived as outsiders. Migrants may have traveled further to Mayapán, as urban functions were concentrated at a single settlement rather than across a network of cities.

To what degree did Mayapán promote the concept of political unity across Yucatán, as far as the eastern Caribbean coast, down the Gulf of Mexico, and into the southern interior lowlands? State-making can involve ethnogenesis, or the "creation of an authentic culture" for a group as a whole, that can override ethnic differences (Gailey and Patterson 1987:9; Oudijk 2002). Identities that transcended political boundaries in medieval towns used shared dialects, customs, building patterns, and diet (Russell 1972:18; Pirenne 1925:188, 210; Dyer 1989:189–90), and the same pattern holds for peninsular Postclassic Maya culture (Masson 2000, 2001b; Masson and Rosenswig 2005). Ordinary Mayapán-style pottery was widely emulated across Yucatán, Quintana Roo, and northeast Belize. Ritual effigy censer use is found beyond these zones into the further reaches of the Petén and Guatemalan highlands, with local modifications (Schele and Mathews 1998; Milbrath et al. 2008; Rice and Rice 2009). In terms of overlap in pottery forms and general decorative attributes, the Postclassic Period was one of the most geographically unitary in Maya history (Masson 2001b). Mayapán-style domestic or public architecture was sometimes reproduced at specific structures located at distant sites, including those of Cozumel, Caye Coco, and Zacpetén (Freidel and Sabloff 1984; Rosenswig and Masson 2002; Pugh 2002). Mayapán would have been a place of epic status to hinterland elites. Participation in elite culture was a dynamic force that bound together late Mesoamerican cultures, including those of the Yucatán Peninsula (Ringle, Négron, and Bey 1998; Pohl 2003a, 2003b; Reents-Budet 2006). Elites exchanged marriage partners, with all of the gifting and celebration that these occasions entailed. They also embraced the same or similar belief systems, used parallel religious paraphernalia and artistic symbol sets, and bedecked themselves in luxury goods that were widely circulated across regions (Ringle, Négron, and Bey 1998; Smith and Berdan 2003a). This interaction contributed toward maintaining alliance networks essential for commerce. For distant Caribbean towns such as Caye Coco, a lagoon settlement less than 1/26th the size of Mayapán's walled area, political ties to the Yucatecan center would have been prestigious (Rosenswig and Masson 2002). Commoners at peripheral sites were also linked materially to Mayapán, even though they were unlikely to have visited the city. Ceramic vessels, stone tools, spindle whorls, and many other classes of artifacts are often indistinguishable in most aspects of form, style, or function between the center and east coast sites.

Hinterland interaction with Mayapán intensified during the last half of the Late Postclassic Period, from around AD 1250–1450 (Masson 2000). This pattern is reflected in the adoption of Chen Mul effigy censers, small line-of-stone shrines and altars, the use of other specific ritual paraphernalia (such as calendrical turtle sculptures), the diversification of everyday pottery forms to include more attributes like those at Mayapán, and house or public building styles. This resurgence, as J. Eric S. Thompson (1970:83) called it, is associated with increased public construction and an infusion of nonlocal goods that suggests accelerated development and prosperity in the periphery. Given Mayapán's troubles that occurred during an interval extending from AD 1270/1302 until 1362/1382 (chapter 8), the Caribbean surge seems inversely correlated with Mayapán's woes. Perhaps this is due to the gross chronological measures at our disposal. Mayapán may have bounced back from its slump around AD 1382–1421, and this forty-year interval may align with the acceleration of activity at distant sites (chapter 8). The eastern developmental surge may alternatively coincide with fleeting accounts of a diaspora out of Mayapán in K'atun 1 Ahau (1382–1401), as some of these individuals could have settled at Caribbean or Petén towns (P. Rice 2009a, 2009b). Both scenarios may have coincided: a diaspora could have partially overlapped with a recovery at the political capital. The dark K'atuns of the fourteenth century may have prompted an effective revitalization movement that centered on the use of Ch'en Mul effigy censers and more ancient Maya gods (Masson 2000; Milbrath et al. 2008; Milbrath and Peraza Lope 2009).

The revitalizing efforts of the Mayapán state may have been more effective in the long run for coastal polities than for the northwest peninsula. Once the villages and towns of the Caribbean were kick-started, they became active players in circum-peninsular trade and political interaction. These towns outlived Mayapán and were booming as a consequence of profitable commercial exchanges in the Mesoamerican world system on the eve of Spanish arrival

(Freidel and Sabloff 1984; Chase and Chase 1988; Masson 2003b; Kepecs 2003; Berdan et al. 2003). Political elites at Tulum, San Gervasio, Chikinchel towns, Caye Coco, and Santa Rita seem to have been up to the task of negotiating with the outside world and maintaining the social order that was essential to prosperity.

CITY UNITY

Efforts of the Mayapán state to symbolically promote polity unity within the city are reflected in standardized architecture and material objects used by its populace. This local process was a more intensive version of the types of regional emulation that have been reported in the hinterlands. City life can sometimes foster greater homogeneity in material culture and at other times promote social fragmentation through the effects of occupational specialization or the pull of hometown identities (Attarian 2003). Within Mayapán, the adoption of a normative house style is a particularly strong indicator of polity identity embraced by commoner households, voluntarily or otherwise. Like many ancient states, citizens of Mayapán used similar inventories of pottery and stone tools, and relative unity is observed in ritual practice at altars, shrines, and common deity effigies (see also Chase and Chase 2003:112) The orientation of domestic patio groups toward focal features within the city, especially the site center, suggests that these nodes held great meaning for commoners. A degree of experimentation was tolerated, as atypical house forms are found at the site, sometimes in clusters. Elites who constructed and operated outlying ceremonial groups took a mainstream approach in general attributes of building form, function, decoration, and the types of ritual paraphernalia that they used. The homogenization of outlying buildings makes it difficult to know whether they were built independently by ambitious elite factions or were part of a unified program initiated by governing authorities. We favor the latter interpretation, given the strategic placement of these groups by Major Gates D, H, and T and by large cenotes with long use histories.

The idea that minor ceremonial groups served as an intermediate layer of organization that linked outlying residential zones to governing authorities is not new. Minor centers and other outlying features at Caracol and La Milpa are thought to have performed administrative functions (Chase and Chase 2003:100; Tourtellot et al. 2003a:43, 2003b:106). Although the K'owoj were said to have guarded the east gate, there is little evidence that the eastern ceremonial group of Itzmal Ch'en was used to glorify the identity of any specific ethnic group. Gate H, near to this group, is not the only eastern gate that has nearby monumental buildings. Itzmal Ch'en replicates many characteristics of monumental center public buildings (Proskouriakoff 1962a), but it also has some unique characteristics of unknown inspiration, such as an unusually wide substructure (Delgado Kú, Escamilla Ojeda, and Peraza Lope 2012a, 2012b). Other outlying ceremonial groups have idiosyncratic attributes. Dual shrines grace the top of the temple of the X-Coton group by Gate T, and Temple E-11 has a small *sacbe* by Gate D; these features are unlike edifices of the site center. Identifying similarities and differences of the city's monumental groups is possible using different scales and criteria, and the recognition of replicated features does not mean that the stamp of human agency cannot be detected in the details. One dimension of ritual behavior at Mayapán—mortuary ritual—allowed for a full range of ethnic, family, or individual expression of social identity (A. Smith 1962; Hutchinson 2010). Burial features, positions, and grave offerings are bafflingly diverse, even within individual house groups, and little spatial clustering is observed that might reflect the norms of social subunits.

How effective were state efforts at promoting unity? Conformity was clearly expressed by the majority of citizens in adopting the typical house style, but historical accounts attest to the fact that Mayapán was a place alive with rife competition and critique. Commoner households likely found themselves to be the targets of persuasive rhetoric for and against regimes in power. Some of these households would have had little choice about which side to take in factional strife due to their hometown, kin, or political affiliations. The Mayapán state was not above using "ritual sacrifice to terrorize a restive citizenry" (Dickson 2006:123). The two large burial shaft temples in the monumental center would have hosted bloody spectacles of sacrifice. Mayapán engaged in state-sponsored theater of cruelty and terror, a strategy employed by many ancient states (Sugiyama 2004; Dickson 2006:140). Dissention among the populace is not overtly observed in the material remains of daily existence, but the city's episodic rebellions (chapter 8) would have depended on some degree of public support.

PLANNING

The urban landscape at Mayapán is punctuated and penetrated by nodes, edges, and paths such as those defined by Kevin Lynch (1960), leading us to infer that the city exhibits more evidence for top-down planning than has been previously recognized. Cities are the product of many builders who engage in constant modification for their own reasons (Lynch 1960:2). Late medieval cities grew through time, gradually adding walls to contain newly settled areas (Pirenne 1925:141–42; Russell 1972:22). We do not know whether Mayapán's great wall was built early or late in the settlement history, as its dry-laid stone is nearly impossible to date, but it was the most defining feature of the urban settlement (Russell 2013). Given Landa's (1941:24) description of the construction of walls at the time the city was founded, we favor the idea that the wall was an integral part of the original Postclassic political capital. Parts of this wall were carefully planned to include key features and to exclude others such as Cenote Sac Uayum, rumored even today to host malevolent forces (Brown 1999:157). Currently it is only possible to speculate the degree to which the city wall was perceived as a symbolic boundary between those living on either side of it.

Non-orthogonal layouts do not necessarily imply weak political control or a lack of planning (M. Smith 2007:21). Planning is best evaluated in degrees rather than by the classification of "planned versus unplanned" (M. Smith 2007:7). The latter dichotomy has generally been used to refer to urban places with orthogonal versus non-orthogonal layouts. Although Michael E. Smith (2007:7) observes that epicenters tend to exhibit greater planning principles than residential zones, at Mayapán the strategic placement of nodes defines and differentiates such residential areas and connects them to the larger city settlement system. Many aspects of city planning and organization represent the contributions of elites (Childe 1950:13).

Landmarks at junctions of features are particularly significant at cities (Lynch 1960:81). Focal points, especially public architecture in the settlement zone, as outlined in chapter 4, are distinctive from other features by having greater practical or symbolic meaning to the observer (Lynch 1960:8). Mayapán's focal points tend to cluster in functionally differentiated sets of nodes; for example, three of the city's outlying temple groups are associated with gates, and two of these are next to some of the largest cenotes at the site. Gates can be edges as well as nodes (Lynch 1960:100). Another example of a focal point includes the cluster of the city's three largest palaces, the monumental center portal gate, and the northern terminus of the city's principal sacbe. Focal architecture is spaced at regular distances, and it seems clear that this placement was part of a strategic effort to integrate the settlement zone in the eastern three-fourths of the walled part of the city. For example, distances of 200 meters separate three pairs of temples (E-11/H-17, H-17/T-70, and T-70/R-19) and two others are separated by a distance of 130–150 meters (R-19/E-11 and R-19/Z-50; see figure 4.2). Alignment of these nodes across these distances tends to connect the city gates with the epicenter or other downtown features; a north/northeast-to-south/southwest alignment links Temple E-11 (near Gate D), Hall K-79, Temple R-19, and Hall Z-50 (southern terminus of the principal sacbe) and passes by the city's Square K marketplace, goes through its adjacent elite neighborhood, and intersects with the three-palace cluster and major sacbe (figure 4.2). Pedestrians entering Gate H on the east side of the city could have walked a nearly straight line to the focal points of Temple H-17, Hall J-109, Temple R-19, and the site center. The shared architectural types of halls and temples at these nodes fits an expectation of "coordination among the buildings" for "more planned" urban places (M. Smith 2007:8).

It is difficult to assess the degree of standardization in the planned public features of different Postclassic Maya cities or towns, as so little work has been performed on Mayapán's largest contemporaries. However, Tulum and Santa Rita share mural art styles with the city (Barrera Rubio and Peraza Lope 2004; M. Delgado Kú 2009; Milbrath, Peraza Lope, and Delgado Kú 2010). Tulum, in particular, has a serpent column temple that resembles Mayapán temples. The epicenter of Tulum, like that of Mayapán, was walled, and Tulum's colonnaded halls and large effigy censer assemblages are also closely analogous (Sanders 1960). Ironically, Tulum was built more orthogonally than Mayapán; William T. Sanders (1960) identified linear streets and the city wall is rectangular and symmetrical. Tulum's principal temple overlooks an inner walled compound. The outlying settlement of this coastal town has not been surveyed. Lowland Postclassic Maya towns across the peninsula lack formally built, recognizable ball courts (but see Masson 2000). The reason for this consistent exclusion of a traditional form of public building is not understood, and it contrasts with contemporary Postclassic Maya highland sites where ball courts are ubiquitous (Fox 1987).

Constructed features help to simplify individuals' perceptions of urban places (Lynch 1960:87). In some cases top-down construction of features can be an imposition that divides other logical, preexisting groupings (M. Smith 2010c:151). Cities reach their form from top-down as well as bottom-up processes; creating and using paths are logical aspects attributable to the latter. In preindustrial cities like Mayapán, focal architectural groups may have been particularly significant as landmarks compared to modern cities of several million people, where they tend to be secondary to paths (Lynch 1960). At the ancient city, at least one focal node would have been visible within a short walk from any part of the settlement zone (Shook 1952). In reality, focal nodes, paths, and other features form intersecting clusters that provide access, vistas, and guide the perceptions of mobile pedestrians through urban space (chapter 3; Lynch 1960:8; M. Smith 2007:36–37). "Way-finding" is the original function of an environmental image, including constructed features within cities (Lynch 1960:125). Mayapán's cenotes, like those of other Yucatecan towns, were named features of critical navigational importance (Brown 1999:525–31, 2005, 2006). Today, archaeologists wishing to be escorted to any particular structure group shown on the Carnegie Insitution of Washington's Mayapán map need only to ask residents of Telchaquillo to take them to the nearest named cenote.

To what degree were urban spaces within Mayapán differentiated from one another? Areas designated for formal use provide an additional indication of planning (M. Smith 2007), such as the city's Square K market plaza, civic-ceremonial groups, and public cenotes. Two residential zones are distinctive compared to the rest of the settlement: the cluster of craft specialists in Milpa 1 and the cluster of elite residences in Squares K/R, to the east of the market plaza. More such areas might be found in future work. The three-palace cluster next to the monumental zone's portal gate probably constitutes an additional elite neighborhood, as these palaces are adjacent to one another and far exceed any others at the city in size or elaboration (chapter 4). Unfortunately, knowledge concerning elite residences in Squares K/R and in the three-palace cluster is limited to a single investigation of the R-86 group by Tatiana Proskouriakoff and Charles R. Temple (1955). Currently there are no comparative neighborhood scale data that would permit the evaluation of ethnicity for these clusters of elite dwellings. Commoner residential zones near Gates D, H, and T and their outlying ceremonial groups may have also been defined by these prominent focal points (Hare and Masson 2012). Most of Mayapán's neighborhoods may have grown through time with little formal planning. Migrants who were drawn to the city probably elected to live as near to their relatives as possible (e.g., M. Smith 2010a:151).

COLLAPSE

It is rare for a single ancient political center to maintain a position indefinitely at the top of a regional hierarchy. Dynamic regional shifts in the places of power are inevitable through time (Kowalewski 1990:51). For the Maya area, factors that contribute to the decline of a particular kingdom are well known. Kings were not alike in their leadership skills or longevity (Martin and Grube 2008). Competition for resources and power was manifested in the twin strategies of alliance networking and warfare that provide only tenuous stability. Regional political geography through all periods of Maya statehood may also have been resolved at times through participation in ritual calendrical passages and prescribed rotation of duties of office (Love 1994; P. Rice 2004). Resource shortages wrought by climatic fluctuations would have periodically aggravated and accelerated inter-polity hostilities (Gill 2000; Gill and Keating 2002). Cross-cultural comparisons of ancient states reveal that subjects gauged their leader's divinely sanctioned status with metrics such as battle outcomes, droughts, and pestilence (Houston et al. 2003; Dickson 2006:135). Despite this tendency, across preindustrial Europe subjects tended to have a high tolerance for the failures or weaknesses of divine rulers, perhaps because of the lack of available options (Dickson 2006:135). Leaders of Mayapán can be grouped in this category. The Cocom claimed divine ancestry from Kukulcan (Roys 1962:63).

Internal processes also affected the undulating fates of specific cities. Family growth and wealth division multiply the numbers of nobles in search of new riches or opportunities. Marriage or entrepreneurial activities can reconstitute estates but do not provide a complete solution (Stone 2007b:219). Burgeoning noble sectors can present a major threat to political lords, and efforts to appease this sector are apparent in the late dynastic records of Classic-era Maya sites such as Yaxchilan and Copán (Schele and Freidel 1990). The formation of a council government at Mayapán provided an institutional means for incorporating high-ranking nobles into governance and gave them an official platform for vetting their concerns. Nonetheless, this confederacy was, in practice, a hierarchical system headed by a paramount (Ringle and Bey 2001). Inter-elite competition can result in the abandonment of elite obligations to their subordinates or extended families, and this can spur an exodus out of urban places (Stone 2007b:229). This response occurred at least once at Mayapán before the final fall of the city (chapter 8).

Elite factional competition and agricultural strain led to episodes of turmoil in the history of Mesopotamian states that periodically disrupted prosperous periods (Stone 2007b:229). This characterization is parallel to that of Mayapán. Like its medieval contemporaries (Russell 1972:31), Mayapán reached its maximum urban extent during the thirteenth and fourteenth centuries. Medieval town development was truncated by the bubonic plague, at least temporarily. Ironically, plagues may have been one of the calamities that contributed to the suppression of political cycles in Yucatán after Mayapán's fall, even before the arrival of Europeans and the deadly epidemics that accompanied them.

The growth of militarism through time tends to correlate with an interest in defending accumulated wealth in ancient states, although Bruce G. Trigger (1980:73) points out that Childe, a pacifist, thought that warfare was a futile expenditure of wealth and manpower and did little to resolve city-state conflicts.

It can be difficult to determine whether warfare promoted or impeded the long-term stability of a given polity (Pyburn 1997:147).

Significant achievements of civilizations can survive the collapse of particular states or empires during interim periods of decentralization. Although some loss of elite esoterica will occur, the subsequent reconstitution of core elements of sophisticated knowledge and beliefs may arise from recesses in the countryside such as manors, monasteries, or remote towns (Trigger 1980:113; Blake 1985; Freidel, Schele, and Parker 1993; Stone 2007b:231). The early Colonial era of Yucatán is a case in point. Mayapán fell over six decades before Spanish arrival, yet the towns of the peninsula maintained their knowledge of history, religion, and writing as well as key aspects of political, economic, and social institutions. Informants imparted much of this information to Spanish chroniclers. Naturally the implementation of Colonial policies wrought significant and irreversible organizational changes.

CONCLUDING THOUGHTS

In advocating the recognition of complexity in the Maya lowlands, K. Anne Pyburn (1997:156) observes that it is ethnocentric to draw conclusions about non-Western societal trajectories, ancient or modern, as the outcome of environmental constraints or other unintended accidents and to interpret our own histories as a progressive set of advances that march toward ever-increasing complexity. Charles Mann (2005) also advocates a more nuanced view of ancient New World history, including that of the Maya, in arguing that Native Americans were neither passive victims of environmental catastrophe nor noble poster children for living in harmony with an unaltered wilderness. Mayapán's lords, subjects, and their predecessors should be given credit for a complex array of strategies, agendas, positive accomplishments, and failures that were dynamic and changing, as is appropriate for any other historical polity. Mann (2005:314) makes this argument for Maya kingdoms that collapsed at the end of the Classic Period, but it is also a relevant framework with which to understand Mayapán's trajectory.

This book's goal of documenting complexity in Mayapán's political structure, urban planning, settlement patterns, economy, and religious organization may seem at the surface to be a well-tread response to the tired view of Postclassic Maya civilization as a devolved, decadent, and weak echo of the glory days of Chichén Itzá and its antecedents. While the chapters of this book do address this problematic characterization anew, that has not been our primary goal. We view the argument over Postclassic "decadence" as one that was long ago put to rest (Chase and Rice 1985a, 1985b; Sabloff and Rathje 1975; Sabloff and Andrews 1986; Sabloff 2007; Demarest, Rice, and Rice 2004; Smith and Berdan 2003a). Nonetheless, in some corners the view still lingers that "the practices of the Maya elite were largely extinguished by the 880's [AD]" (R. Fletcher 2012:331). The principal contribution of these chapters has been to recognize that the organizational institutions at Mayapán were more intricate than previously acknowledged. It is time to move past characterizing Mayapán as part of a "progressive deterioration" in the centuries following the Classic-era Maya collapse (R. Fletcher 2012:311). Roland Fletcher's (2012) projection of his doomed-to-fail low-density urbanism model to the Maya area is flawed by monolithic assumptions regarding limited forms of water control and dependency on agrarian worker mobility, about which there is little hard evidence. His ideas about productive homogeneity ignore the prospect of market-based food trade for supplying urban zones. It is also problematic that his criteria for success primarily concern city area and longevity, and he does not consider the fact that catastrophic climatic events have triggered the decline of a great many ancient political capitals. Don S. Rice (2006) offers a far more sophisticated treatment of the diachronic complexity of Maya city sustainability (see also Turner and Sabloff 2012), although Rice also does not discuss the solutions that market exchange can sometimes offer to supplement city food supplies and mitigate shortfalls (Freidel and Shaw 2000).

The recognition of variation, diversity, and institutional complexity within this ancient urban setting, as well its entanglements with external towns, makes research at Mayapán relevant to studies of earlier Maya cities. The definition and characteristics of urban life have not been fully explored for the Classic or Preclassic Periods, nor have the formal mechanisms that linked subjects to governing authorities been investigated in worthy detail. For example, Classic-era scholars disagree over whether, how, or why governing elites may have hosted and administered markets (chapter 6; Masson and Freidel 2012). Settlement data from the massive city of Caracol reveal a strong, centralized government and a planned and administered urban landscape and market exchange system (A. Chase 1998; Chase and Chase 2003; A. Chase and D. Chase 2004; Chase et al. 2011). Variation likely existed in the organizational complexity of different Maya centers, but foundational institutions of economy or government probably differed more in scale than form (Masson and Freidel 2012). In the Aztec realm, differences also existed in city-state affluence and influence, and some towns hosted simple, marginal markets where limited products could be purchased while others presided over large and diverse markets of regional significance (Blanton 1996). Mayapán's internal market exchange, in which traders and craftspersons worked to supply the city's residents, would have had been a significant enterprise in its own right, irrespective of trade with the external world (e.g., Dyer 1989:7–8).

Studies that focus on a single site have emphasized greater local autonomy than may be merited. Such views depend heavily on the constraints of local production and offer little consideration of the role of inter-town exchange dependencies that potentially mitigated local limitations (Pyburn 1997:156,167). Recent work has made positive advances in this direction (e.g., Scarborough, Valdez, and Dunning 2003; Scarborough and Valdez 2003), but an emphasis persists on the relative economic independence of smallholders (Scarborough and Valdez 2009). We agree with Pyburn (1997:156), who criticizes an exoticized view of ancient Maya states that has fostered little recognition of an "economically based political system"—although chapter 6 discusses important exceptions in Maya scholarship. She points out that signs of complexity have long existed in the form of distant trade dependencies, craft production, complex agricultural systems that generated considerable surplus, and warfare. Economic incentives for the latter have rarely been considered in any depth. Major Maya centers were long characterized as nonurban despite indications to the contrary in terms of the occupational density and functional diversity of large settlements (Pyburn 1997:156).

An important question in evaluating the relationships of governors to the governed is the degree to which political elites controlled aspects of the economy. We have considered this issue for Mayapán. Except for a limited set of goods, we argue that elites encouraged but did not directly supervise the majority of basic food and craft production activities. We infer that elites were heavily invested in all types of distribution, particularly in taking tribute and administering large, regular market events (Freidel 1981; Masson and Freidel 2012). These events would have required planning, authorization, promotion, and policing by appointed officials (Piña Chan 1978; A. Chase and D. Chase 2004:117). Products of household labor, as well as market goods, were probably subjected to taxation. Incentives for merchants to frequent the city's market events would have included state protection en route. Multiple modes of exchange coexisted within all ancient Maya economies (Masson 2002). Luxury exchange among elites is also present in all ancient states, and it need not characterize an entire economic system (A. Chase and D. Chase 2004:116; M. Smith 2004:89). A high degree of integration of commoner activities with those of elites, as reflected by replication of artifact assemblages, does not necessarily connote an authoritarian regime (M. Smith 2002).

Little explored in this book is the issue of urban caché. How does a city establish its reputation in a way that attracts desirable and necessary occupants? Hosting one of the largest and most diverse regional markets was an important draw, as these attracted the best artisans and merchants who created more opportunities for luxury exchange for wealthy residents. These factors were important for Aztec centers (e.g., Blanton 1996) and presumably also for Mayapán. In addition to offering major market events and boasting a resident artistic and mercantile community, political and religious spectacle would have also contributed to the cumulative "image of the city" in Lynch's (1960) sense. Mayapán's monumental plazas that defined the heart of the downtown area, as well as key points on thoroughfares leading inward from the city's gates, exceeded in quantity and quality any other constructions at a single site in the Postclassic Maya world. Mayapán's priests and educated nobles were also the gatekeepers of religious and mytho-historical knowledge; the concentration of these literati would have helped to set Mayapán apart from its contemporaries as a wellspring of culture and commerce. A more morbid draw may have been the spectacle of public ritual sacrifice. The "ritual" attraction of a place due to monumental works and events is a centripetal factor (Scarborough, Valdez, and Dunning 2003:xix), and conjunctions of fairs and market events were one of several options for mercantile exchange (Pirenne 1925:143; Pounds 1973:404–6; Freidel 1981). Compulsory migration was probably a key element of Mayapán's strategy to maintain its population, but retention and stability are more effective with the addition of positive tangible and symbolic incentives.

Mayapán's image was not untarnished, and conflict among privileged sectors of society was endemic, if sometimes effectively backgrounded. Merchants and priests are people with connections and wealth who can challenge political regimes (Eisenstadt 1980, 1981; Dyer 1989). A priest, in fact, led the final revolt against the Cocom Mayapán government (chapter 2). But Mayapán survived through some of its dark periods until the very end, and to do so it must have counted on and received the loyalty of a significant number of subjects.

In this reexamination of Mayapán as a civilization, we have loosely followed Childe's (1950) framework for recognizing an urban place. Six of Childe's ten components of urban places have been reviewed in the chapters of this book: (1) urban density, (2) occupational specialization, (3) monumental public buildings, (4) a ruling class consisting of political, religious, and military officials, (5) sophisticated art styles, and (6) significant levels of long-distance trade. Building on this framework, we have documented significant variation in the complex, populous urban landscape of Mayapán in terms of wealth, occupation, and other multiple influences on the social identity of the city's residents. Two other urban characteristics on Childe's list—scientific knowledge and writing—have been recently reviewed in other publications for Mayapán (Aveni, Milbrath, and Peraza Lope 2004; Milbrath and Peraza Lope 2003a; Milbrath, Peraza Lope, and Delgado Kú 2010; M. Delgado Kú 2009). Childe was incorrect in assuming that occupational specialization must have been full time in ancient cities, as it is now known that part-time craft production, in concert with a diverse array of other work, was of a sufficient scale to support the dependencies one expects of a well-developed, preindustrial regional market system (Feinman and Nicholas 2000). Childe's (1950) redistributional model for state economies was also too simple, as all craftspersons were not attached to state authorities. Vestiges of the redistributional model can still be found in the Maya literature, but they are largely discredited (as critiqued in Stark and Garraty 2010:44; Dahlin et al. 2010; Masson and Freidel 2012).

Documenting the complexity of ancient states is an important research problem that has been advocated in recent archaeological theory (M. Smith 2007:17). In order to do so, researchers must first identify all the different parts of a societal system and then determine how they are related (Kowalewski 1990:39). This undertaking may require changing old perceptions. The Mayapán era has in effect been labeled a "dark age," much like regions of western Europe after the fall of Rome (Crumley 1987:158–59). Yet this label is not applicable to certain times and places in the late medieval world (Pounds 1973:25). This framework has stifled Postclassic Period research, with a few hardy exceptions over the years. The complex organization of the city and polity of Mayapán outlined in this book not only sheds "new light on a dark age" (Freidel 1985), it illustrates in many ways that this city was begotten, historically, from a long line of Maya cities that preceded it. The "otherness" of the Postclassic Period Maya may also be an idea that needs reexamination, given the similar principles that probably existed through time for organizing an urban landscape; administering settlement zones; integrating citizenry with religious monuments, art, and celebrations; and helping subjects to self-provision through the sponsorship of central marketplaces. While the tropes of divine kingship were discarded, it is probable that much collective wisdom regarding how to operate a powerful political center was heartily recycled.

Abu-Lughod, Janet L. 1989. *Before European Hegemony: The World System A.D. 1250–1350*. New York: Oxford University Press.

Adams, R. E. W., and Woodruff D. Smith. 1981. "Feudal Models for Classic Maya Civilization." In *Lowland Maya Settlement Patterns*, edited by Wendy Ashmore, 335–49. Albuquerque: University of New Mexico Press.

Adams, Robert M., Jr. 1953. "Some Small Ceremonial Structures at Mayapán." *Current Reports* 9: 144–79. Washington, DC: Carnegie Institution of Washington.

Aizpurúa, Ilean Isel Isaza, and Patricia A. McAnany. 1999. "Adornment and Identity: Shell Ornaments from Formative K'axob." *Ancient Mesoamerica* 10 (1): 117–27. http://dx.doi.org/10.1017/S095653619910107X.

Alcock, Susan E. 2002. *Archaeologies of the Greek Past: Landscape, Monuments, and Memories*. Cambridge: Cambridge UnivCersity Press.

Aldenderfer, Mark, and Charles Stanish. 1993. "Domestic Architecture, Household Archaeology, and the Past in the South-Central Andes." In *Domestic Architecture, Ethnicity, and Complementarity in the South-Central Andes*, edited by Mark Aldenderfer, 1–12. Iowa City: University of Iowa Press.

Alexander, Rani T. 1999. "Mesoamerican House Lots and Archaeological Site Structure: Problems of Inference in Yaxcaba, Yucatán, Mexico, 1750–1847." In *The Archaeology of Household Activities*, edited by Penelope M. Allison, 78–100. London: Routledge.

Alexander, Rani T. 2005. "Isla Civlituk and the Difficulties of Colonization in Southwestern Campeche." In *The Postclassic to Spanish-Era Transition in Mesoamerica: Archaeological Perspectives*, edited by Susan Kepecs and Rani T. Alexander, 161–83. Albuquerque: University of New Mexico Press.

Andrews, Anthony P. 1977. "Reconocimiento arqueológico de la costa norte del Estado de Campeche." *Boletin de la Escuela de Ciencias Antropológicas de la Universidad de Yucatán* 4 (24): 64–77.

Andrews, Anthony P. 1993. "Late Postclassic Lowland Maya Archaeology." *Journal of World Prehistory* 7 (1): 35–69. http://dx.doi.org/10.1007/BF00978220.

Andrews, Anthony P. 2008. "Facilidades Portuarias Mayas." In *El Territorio Maya: Memoria de la Quinta Mesa Redonda de Palenque*, edited by Rodrigo Liendo Stuardo, 15–40. Mexico, D.F.: Instituto Nacional de Antropología e Historia.

Andrews, Anthony P., E. Wyllys Andrews V, and Fernando Robles Castellanos. 2003. "The Northern Maya Collapse and its Aftermath." *Ancient Mesoamerica* 14 (1): 151–56. http://dx.doi.org/10.1017/S095653610314103X.

Andrews, Anthony P., and Fernando Robles Castellanos, eds. 1986. *Excavaciones Arqueologicas en El Meco, Quintana Roo, 1977*, 77–130. Coleccíon Científica 158. Mexico, D.F.: Instituto Nacional de Antropología e Historia.

Andrews, Anthony P., Tomás Gallareta Negrón, Fernando Robles Castellanos, Rafael Cobos Palma, and Pura Cervera River. 1988. "Isla Cerritos: An Itzá Trading Port on the North Coast of Yucatán, Mexico." *National Geographic Research* 4: 196–207.

Andrews, Anthony P., and Gabriela Vail. 1990. "Cronología de sitios Prehispánicos costeros de la Peninsula de Yucatán y Belice." *Boletin de la Escuela de Ciencias Antropologicas de la Universidad de Yucatán* 18 (104–105): 37–66.

Andrews, E. Wyllys, IV. 1942. "Yucatán: Architecture." *Carnegie Institution of Washington Year Book* 41: 257–63.

Andrews, E. Wyllys, IV. 1943. "The Archaeology of Southwestern Campeche." Carnegie Institution of Washington Publication 546. Washington, DC: Carnegie Institution.

Andrews, E. Wyllys, IV. 1969. *The Archaeological Use and Distribution of Mollusca in the Maya Lowlands*. Middle American Research Series Publication 34. New Orleans, LA: Tulane University.

Andrews, E. Wyllys, IV, and Ralph T. Patton. n.d. "A Preliminary Study of the Ruins of Mayapan, Yucatan, Mexico." A copy of the unpublished manuscript is in the Department of Anthropology, University at Albany–SUNY, Albany, NY.

Andrews, E. Wyllys, IV, Michael P. Simmons, Elizabeth S. Wing, and E. Wyllys Andrews V. 1974. *Excavation of an Early Shell Midden on Isla Cancun, Quintana Roo, Mexico*. Middle American Research Series Publication 31. New Orleans, LA: Tulane University.

Andrews, E. Wyllys, V, and Jeremy A. Sabloff. 1986. "Classic to Postclassic: A Summary Discussion." In *Late Lowland Maya Civilization: Classic to Postclassic*, edited by E. Wyllys Andrews V and Jeremy A. Sabloff, 433–56. Albuquerque: University of New Mexico Press.

Anselin, Luc. 2003. *GeoDa 0.9 User's Guide.* Spatial Analysis Laboratory (SAL). Urbana: Department of Agricultural and Consumer Economics. University of Illinois, Urbana-Champaign.

Anselin, Luc, and Anil K. Bera. 1998. "Spatial Dependence in Linear Regression Models with an Introduction to Spatial Econometrics." In *Handbook of Applied Economic Statistics,* edited by Amman Ullah and David E. A. Giles, 237–89. New York: Marcel Dekker.

Anselin, Luc, Ibnu Syabri, and Oleg Smirnov. 2002. "Visualizing Multivariate Spatial Correlation with Dynamically Linked Windows." In *New Tools for Spatial Data Analysis: Proceedings of a Workshop,* edited by Luc Anselin and Serge Rey. Santa Barbara: Center for Spatially Integrated Social Science, University of California, Santa Barbara. (CD-ROM).

Aoyama, Kazuo. 1999. *Ancient Maya State, Urbanism, Exchange, and Craft Specialization: Chipped Stone Evidence from the Copán Valley and the La Entrada Region, Honduras.* Memoirs in Latin American Archaeology 12. Pittsburgh: University of Pittsburgh.

Ardren, Traci. 2002. "Death Becomes Her: Images of Female Power from Yaxuna." In *Ancient Maya Women,* edited by Traci Ardren, 68–88. Walnut Creek, CA: AltaMira.

Arnauld, M. Charlotte, Linda R. Manzanilla, and Michael E. Smith, eds. 2012. *The Neighborhood as a Social and Spatial Unit in Mesoamerican Cities.* Tucson: University of Arizona Press.

Arnold, Dean E. 1985. *Ceramic Theory and Cultural Process.* Cambridge: Cambridge University Press.

Arnold, Dean E. 1989. "Patterns of Learning, Residence and Descent Among Potters in Ticul, Yucatan, Mexico." In *Archaeological Approaches to Cultural Identity,* edited by Stephen J. Shennan, 174–84. London: Unwin-Hyman.

Arnold, Jeanne E. 1995. "Social Inequality, Marginalization, and Economic Process." In *Foundations of Social Inequality,* edited by T. Douglas Price and Gary M. Feinman, 87–104. New York: Plenum. http://dx.doi.org/10.1007/978-1-4899-1289-3_3.

Ashmore, Wendy, ed. 1981. *Lowland Maya Settlement Patterns.* Albuquerque: University of New Mexico Press.

Attarian, Christopher J. 2003. "Cities as a Place of Ethnogenesis: Urban Growth and Centralization in the Chicama Valley, Peru." In *The Social Construction of Ancient Cities,* edited by Monica L. Smith, 184–211. Washington, DC: Smithsonian Institution.

Aveni, Anthony F. 1980. *Skywatchers of Ancient Mexico.* Austin: University of Texas Press.

Aveni, Anthony F., and Horst Hartung. 1978. "Three Maya Astronomical Observatories in the Yucatan Peninsula." *Interciencia* 3 (3): 136–43.

Aveni, Anthony F., Susan Milbrath, and Carlos Peraza Lope. 2004. "Chichén Itzá's Legacy in the Astronomically Oriented Architecture of Mayapán." *RES* 45: 123–43.

Ball, Joseph W. 1993. "Pottery, Potters, Palaces, and Polities: Some Socioeconomic and Political Implications of Late Classic Maya Ceramic Industries." In *Lowland Maya Civilization in the Eighth Century A.D.*, edited by Jeremy A. Sabloff and John S. Henderson, 243–72. Washington, DC: Dumbarton Oaks.

Barnhart, Edwin. 2001. "The Palenque Mapping Project: Settlement and Urbanism at an Ancient Maya City." PhD diss., University of Texas at Austin.

Barrera Rubio, Alfredo, and Carlos Peraza Lope. 2004. "La Pintura Mural de Mayapán." In *La Pintura Mural Prehispánica en México: Área Maya*, edited by Leticia Staines Cicero, project directed by Beatriz de la Fuentes, 419–46. México, D.F.: Instituto de Investigaciones Estéticas, Universidad Nacional Autónoma de México.

Barrera Vasquez, Alfredo, and Sylvanus G. Morley. 1949. *The Maya Chronicles*. Carnegie Institution of Washington Publication 585, Contribution 48. Washington, DC: Carnegie Institution.

Beach, Timothy. 1998. "Soil Constraints on Northwest Yucatán, Mexico: Pedoarchaeology and Maya Subsistence at Chunchucmil." *Geoarchaeology: An International Journal* 13 (8): 759–91. http://dx.doi.org/10.1002/(SICI)1520-6548(199812)13:8<759::AID-GEA1>3.0.CO;2-B.

Becker, Marshall Joseph. 1973. "Archaeological Evidence for Occupational Specialization Among the Classic Period Maya at Tikal, Guatemala." *American Antiquity* 38 (4): 396–406. http://dx.doi.org/10.2307/279144.

Becker, Marshall Joseph. 1999. *Excavations in Residential Areas of Tikal: Groups with Shrines*. Tikal Report no. 21. Philadelphia: University of Pennsylvania Museum of Archaeology and Anthropology.

Becker, Marshall Joseph. 2003. "Plaza Plans at Tikal: A Research Strategy for Inferring Social Organization and Processes of Cultural Change at Lowland Maya Sites." In *Tikal: Dynasties, Foreigners, and Affairs of State*, edited by Jeremy A. Sabloff, 253–80. Santa Fe, NM: School for Advanced Research Press.

Berdan, Frances F. 1988. "Principles of Regional and Long-Distance Trade in the Aztec Empire." In *Smoke and Mist: Mesoamerican Studies in Memory of Thelma D. Sullivan*, edited by J. Kathryn Josserand and Karen Dakin, 639–56. British Archaeological Reports, International Series no. 402. Oxford: BAR.

Berdan, Frances F., and Patricia R. Anawalt, eds. 1992. *The Codex Mendoza*, vol. 2, *Description of the Codex Mendoza*. Berkeley: University of California Press.

Berdan, Frances F., Marilyn A. Masson, Janine Gasco, and Michael E. Smith. 2003. "An International Economy." In *The Postclassic Mesoamerican World*, edited by

Michael E. Smith and Frances F. Berdan, 96–108. Salt Lake City: University of Utah Press.

Bey, George J., III, and William M. Ringle. 2007. "From the Bottom Up: The Timing and Nature of the Tula-Chichen Itza Exchange." In *Twin Tollans: Chichén Itzá, Tula, and the Epiclassic to Early Postclassic Mesoamerican World*, edited by Jeff Karl Kowalski and Cynthia Kristan-Graham, 377–428. Washington, DC: Dumbarton Oaks.

Bill, Cassandra R. 1997. "The Roles and Relationships of God M and Other Black Gods in the Codices, with Specific Reference to Pages 50–56 of the Madrid Codex." In *Papers on the Madrid Codex*, edited by Victoria R. Bricker and Gabrielle Vail, 111–45. New Orleans: Middle American Research Institute, Tulane University.

Bill, Cassandra R., Christine L. Hernández, and Victoria R. Bricker. 2000. "The Relationship Between Early Colonial Maya New Year's Ceremonies and Some Almanacs in the Madrid Codex." *Ancient Mesoamerica* 11 (1): 149–68. http://dx.doi.org/10.1017/S0956536100111034.

Biskowski, Martin. 2000. "Maize Preparation and the Aztec Subsistence Economy." *Ancient Mesoamerica* 11 (2): 293–306. http://dx.doi.org/10.1017/S0956536100112040.

Blake, Michael. 1985. "Canajaste: An Evolving Postclassic Maya State." PhD diss., University of Michigan.

Blanton, Richard E. 1976. "Anthropological Studies of Cities." *Annual Review of Anthropology* 5 (1): 249–64. http://dx.doi.org/10.1146/annurev.an.05.100176.001341.

Blanton, Richard E. 1978. *Monte Alban: Settlement Patterns at the Ancient Zapotec Capitol*. New York: Academic Press.

Blanton, Richard E. 1996. "The Basin of Mexico Market System and the Growth of Empire." In *Aztec Imperial Strategies*, by Frances F. Berdan, Richard E. Blanton, Elizabeth H. Boone, Mary G. Hodge, Michael E. Smith, and Emily Umberger, 47–84. Washington, DC: Dumbarton Oaks.

Blanton, Richard E., Gary M. Feinman, Stephen A. Kowalewski, and Peter N. Peregrine. 1996. "A Dual Processual Theory for the Evolution of Mesoamerican Civilization." *Current Anthropology* 37 (1): 1–14. http://dx.doi.org/10.1086/204471.

Blom, Frans. 1932. "Commerce, Trade and Monetary Units of the Maya." In *Middle American Papers*, 533–56. Middle American Research Series Publication 4. New Orleans, LA: Tulane University.

Boone, Elizabeth H., and Michael E. Smith. 2003. "Postclassic International Styles and Symbol Sets." In *The Postclassic Mesoamerican World*, edited by Michael E. Smith and Frances F. Berdan, 186–93. Salt Lake City: University of Utah Press.

Brainerd, George W. 1958. "The Archaeological Ceramics of Yucatan." University of California Anthropological Records, vol. 19. Berkeley and Los Angeles: University of California Press.

Brasseur de Bourbourg, C. E. 1867. "Rapport sur les ruines de Mayapan et d'Uxmal au Yucatan (Mexique)." *Archives de la Commission Scientifique de Mexique* 2: 234–88.

Braswell, Geoffrey E., ed. 2003. *The Maya and Teotihuacan: Reinterpreting Early Classic Interaction.* Austin: University of Texas Press.

Braswell, Geoffrey E. 2010. "The Rise and Fall of Market Exchange: A Dynamic Approach to Ancient Maya Economy." In *Archaeological Approaches to Market Exchange in Ancient Societies,* edited by Christopher P. Garraty and Barbara L. Stark, 127–39. Boulder: University Press of Colorado.

Braudel, Fernand. 1981. *The Structures of Everyday Life: The Limits of the Possible.* Berkeley: University of California Press.

Braudel, Fernand. 1992. *Civilization and Capitalism, 15th–18th Century,* vol. 2, *The Wheels of Commerce.* Berkeley: University of California Press.

Bricker, Victoria, and Cassandra Bill. 1994. "Mortuary Practices in the Madrid Codex." In *Seventh Palenque Round Table, 1989,* edited by Virginia M. Fields, 195–200. San Francisco: Pre-Columbian Art Research Institute.

Bricker, Victoria R. 1997. "The Structure of Almanacs in the Madrid Codex." In *Papers on the Madrid Codex,* edited by Victoria R. Bricker and Gabriella Vail, 1–25. Middle American Research Series Publication 64. New Orleans, LA: Tulane University,.

Bronk Ramsey, Christopher. 1995. "Radiocarbon Calibration and Analysis of Stratigraphy: The OxCal Program." *Radiocarbon* 37: 425–30.

Bronk Ramsey, Christoper. 2001. "Development of the Radiocarbon Program OxCal." *Radiocarbon* 43: 355–63.

Brown, Clifford T. 1999. *Mayapán Society and Ancient Maya Social Organization.* PhD diss., Tulane University. University Microfilms, Ann Arbor.

Brown, Clifford T. 2005. "Caves, Karst, and Settlement at Mayapán, Yucatán." In *In the Maw of the Earth Monster: Mesoamerican Ritual Cave Use,* edited by James E. Brady and Keith M. Prufer, 373–402. Austin: University of Texas Press.

Brown, Clifford T. 2006. "Water Sources at Mayapán, Yucatán, México." In *Precolumbian Water Management: Ideology, Ritual, and Power,* edited by Lisa J. Lucero and Barbara W. Fash and, 171–85. Tucson: University of Arizona Press.

Brown, Clifford T. 2008. "Un Nuevo cenote hallado en Mayapán." In *Proyecto Los Fundamentos del Poder Económico de Mayapán, Temporadas 2001–2004: Informe final para el Consejo Nacional de Arqueología de México,* edited by Marilyn A. Masson, Carlos Peraza Lope, and Timothy S. Hare, 645–46. Albany, NY: University at Albany–SUNY; Mérida, México: Centro INAH Yucatán.

Brown, Clifford T., Carlos Peraza Lope, Walter R. T. Witschey, and Rhianna Rogers. 2006. "Results of Survey in Central Yucatán, México." Paper presented at the 76th

Annual Meeting of the Society for American Archaeology, San Juan, Puerto Rico, April 29, and posted online at http://mayagis.smv.org/papers.htm.

Brown, Clifford T., and Walter R. T. Witschey. 2003. "The Fractal Geometry of Ancient Maya Settlement." *Journal of Archaeological Science* 30 (12): 1619–32. http://dx.doi.org /10.1016/S0305-4403(03)00063-3.

Brüggemann, Jürgen K. 1992. *Tajin: Guía Oficial*. México, D.F.: Instituto Nacional de Antropología e Historia.

Bullard, William R., Jr. 1952. "Residential Property Walls at Mayapán." *Current Reports* 3: 36–44. Washington, DC: Carnegie Institution of Washington.

Bullard, William R., Jr. 1953. "Property Walls at Mayapán." *Carnegie Institution of Washington Year Book* 54: 276–77.

Bullard, William R., Jr. 1954. "Boundary Walls and House Lots at Mayapán." *Current Reports* 13: 234–53. Washington, DC: Carnegie Institution of Washington.

Buttles, Palma. 1992. "Small Finds in Context: The Preclassic Artifacts of Colha, Belize." Master's thesis, University of Texas at Austin.

Byland, Bruce E., and John M. D. Pohl. 1994. *In the Realm of Eight Deer: The Archaeology of the Mixtec Codices*. Norman: University of Oklahoma Press.

Canuto, Marcello A., and William L. Fash, Jr. 2004. "The Blind Spot: Where the Elite and Non-Elite Meet." In *Continuities and Changes in Maya Archaeology: Perspectives at the Millenium*, edited by Charles W. Golden and Greg Borgstede, 51–75. New York: Routledge.

Carlson, John B. 1982. "'The Structure of Mayapan: A Major Post-Classic Maya Site in Northern Yucatan." In *Proceedings of the Symposium: Space and Time in the Cosmovision of the Mesoamerica*, edited by Franz Tichy, 43–61. Munich: Wilhelm Fink Verlag.

Carmack, Robert M. 1971. "Quichean Art: A Mixteca-Puebla Variant." *Katunob* 12: 12–35.

Carmack, Robert M. 1977. "Ethnohistory of the Central Quiche: The Community of Utatlan." In *Archaeology and Ethnohistory of the Central Quiche*, edited by Dwight T. Wallace and Robert M. Carmack, 1–19. Albany, NY: Institute for Mesoamerican Studies, University at Albany–SUNY.

Carmack, Robert M. 1981a. *The Quiché Mayas of Utatlán*. Norman: University of Oklahoma Press.

Carmack, Robert M. 1981b. "New Quichean Chronicles from Highland Guatemala." In *Estudios de Cultura Maya*, vol. 13, 83–103. México, D.F.: Universidad Nacional Autónoma de México.

Carmack, Robert M., and James L. Mondloch. 1983. *Titulo de Totonicapán: Texto, Traducción, y Comentario. Instituto de Investigaciones Filologicas, Centro de Estudios Mayas*. México, D.F.: Universidad Nacional Autónoma de México.

Carmack, Robert M., and Dwight T. Wallace. 1977. "Overview." In *Archaeology and Ethnohistory of the Central Quiche*, edited by Dwight T. Wallace and Robert M. Carmack, 1–109. Albany, NY: Institute for Mesoamerican Studies, University at Albany–SUNY.

Carmean, Kelli, Nicholas P. Dunning, and Jeff Karl Kowalski. 2004. "High Times in the Hill Country: A Perspective from the Terminal Classic Puuc Region." In *The Terminal Classic in the Maya Lowlands: Collapse, Transition, and Transformation*, edited by Arthur A. Demarest, Prudence M. Rice, and Don S. Rice, 424–49. Boulder: University Press of Colorado.

Carpenter, Lacey B., Gary M. Feinman, and Linda M. Nicholas. 2012. "Spindle Whorls from El Palmillo: Economic Implications." *Latin American Antiquity* 23 (4): 381–400. http://dx.doi.org/10.7183/1045-6635.23.4.381.

Carr, H. Sorayya. 1996. "Precolumbian Maya Exploitation and Management of Deer Populations." In *The Managed Mosaic: Ancient Maya Agriculture and Resource Use*, edited by Scott L. Fedick, 251–61. Salt Lake City: University of Utah Press,.

Carrasco, David. 1982. *Quetzalcoatl and the Irony of Empire: Myths and Prophecies in the Aztec Tradition*. Chicago: University of Chicago Press.

Caso, Alfonso, and Ignacio Bernal. 1952. *Urnas de Oaxaca*. México, D.F.: Instituto Nacional de Antropología e Historia.

Cecil, Leslie G. 2009. "Technological Styles of Slipped Pottery and Kowoj Identity." In *The Kowoj: Identity, Migration, and Geopolitics in Late Postclassic Peten, Guatemala*, edited by Prudence M. Rice and Don S. Rice, 221–37. Boulder: University Press of Colorado.

Cecil, Leslie G. 2012. "Inter-Regional Socioeconomic and Sociopolitical Relations of the Postclassic Maya of North-Central Yucatan, Mexico, Belize, and Guatemala." Final Report to the National Science Foundation. Manuscript on file at the Sociology Department, Stephen F. Austin State University, Nacogdoches, TX.

Charlton, Cynthia Otis. 1994. "Plebeians and Patricians: Contrasting Patterns of Production and Distribution in the Aztec Figurine and Lapidary Industries." In *Economies and Polities in the Aztec Realm*, edited by Mary G. Hodge and Michael E. Smith, 195–219. Albany, NY: Institute for Mesoamerican Studies.

Charlton, Thomas H. 1994. "Economic Heterogeneity and State Expansion." In *Economies and Polities in the Aztec Realm*, edited by Mary G. Hodge and Michael E. Smith, 221–56. Albany, NY: Institute for Mesoamerican Studies.

Charlton, Thomas H., Deborah L. Nichols, and Cynthia Otis Charlton. 2000. "Otumba and Its Neighbors: Ex Oriente Lux." *Ancient Mesoamerica* 11 (2): 247–65. http://dx.doi.org/10.1017/S0956536100112088.

Chase, Arlen F. 1998. "Planeación civica e integración de sitio en Caracol, Belice: Definiendo una economía administrada del periodo Clásico Maya." *Los Investigaciones de la Cultura Maya* 6, vol. 1, 26–44. Campeche, México: Universidad Autónoma de Campeche, Campeche, México

Chase, Arlen F., and Diane Z. Chase. 1998. "Scale and Intensity in Classic Period Maya Agriculture: Terracing and Settlement at the 'Garden City' of Caracol, Belize." *Culture and Agriculture* 20 (2–3): 60–77. http://dx.doi.org/10.1525/cag.1998.20.2-3.60.

Chase, Arlen F., and Diane Z. Chase. 2001. "Ancient Maya Causeways and Site Organization at Caracol, Belize." *Ancient Mesoamerica* 12 (2): 273–81. http://dx.doi.org/10.1017/S0956536101121097.

Chase, Arlen F., and Diane Z. Chase. 2003. "Minor Centers, Complexity, and Scale in Lowland Maya Settlement Archaeology." In *Perspectives on Ancient Maya Rural Complexity*, edited by Gyles Iannone and Samuel V. Connell, 108–18. Los Angeles: Cotsen Institute of Archaeology, University of California, Los Angeles.

Chase, Arlen F., and Diane Z. Chase. 2004. "Exploring Ancient Economic Relationships at Caracol, Belize." *Research Reports in Belizean Archaeology* 1:115–27.

Chase, Arlen F., Diane Z. Chase, John F. Weishampel, Jason B. Drake, Ramesh L. Shrestha, K. Clint Slatton, Jaime J. Awe, and William E. Carter. 2011. "Airborne LiDAR, Archaeology, and the Ancient Maya Landscape at Caracol, Belize." *Journal of Archaeological Science* 38 (2): 387–98. http://dx.doi.org/10.1016/j.jas.2010.09.018.

Chase, Arlen F., and Prudence M. Rice. 1985a. "Introduction." In *The Lowland Maya Postclassic*, edited by Arlen F. Chase and Prudence M. Rice, 1–8. Austin: University of Texas Press.

Chase, Arlen F., and Prudence M. Rice, eds. 1985b. *The Lowland Maya Postclassic*. Austin: University of Texas Press.

Chase, Diane Z. 1985a. "Ganned But Not Forgotten: Late Postclassic Archaeology and Ritual at Santa Rita Corozal, Belize." In *The Lowland Maya Postclassic*, edited by Arlen F. Chase and Prudence M. Rice, 104–25. Austin: University of Texas Press.

Chase, Diane Z. 1985b. "Between Earth and Sky: Idols, Images, and Postclassic Cosmology." In *Fifth Palenque Round Table, 1983*, edited by Virginia M. Fields, 223–34. San Francisco: Pre-Columbian Art Research Institute.

Chase, Diane Z. 1986. "Social and Political Organization in the Land of Milk and Honey: Correlating the Archaeology and Ethnohistory of the Postclassic Lowland Maya." In *Late Lowland Maya Civilization: Classic to Postclassic*, edited by Jeremy A. Sabloff and E. Wyllys Andrews V, 347–78. Albuquerque: University of New Mexico Press.

Chase, Diane Z. 1988. "Caches and Censerwares: Meaning from Maya Pottery." In *A Pot for All Reasons: Ceramic Ecology Revisited*, edited by Charles C. Kolb, Louana M. Lackey, and Muriel Kirkpatrick, 81–104. Philadelphia, PA: Laboratory of Anthropology, Temple University.

Chase, Diane Z. 1992. "Postclassic Maya Elites: Ethnohistory and Archaeology." In *Mesoamerican Elites: An Archaeological Assessment*, edited by Diane Z. Chase and Arlen F. Chase, 118–34. Norman: University of Oklahoma Press.

Chase, Diane Z., and Arlen F. Chase. 1988. *A Postclassic Perspective: Excavations at the Maya Site of Santa Rita Corozal, Belize*. Pre-Columbian Art Research Institute Monograph 4, San Francisco, CA: Pre-Columbian Art Research Institute.

Chase, Diane Z., and Arlen F. Chase. 2004. "Archaeological Perspectives on Classic Maya Social Organization from Caracol, Belize." *Ancient Mesoamerica* 15 (01): 139–47. http://dx.doi.org/10.1017/S0956536104151080.

Chase, Diane Z., Arlen F. Chase, and William A. Haviland. 1990. "The Classic Maya City: Reconsidering the 'Mesoamerican Urban Tradition.'" *American Anthropologist* 92 (2): 499–506. http://dx.doi.org/10.1525/aa.1990.92.2.02a00210.

Childe, V. Gordon. 1936. *Man Makes Himself*. London: Watts.

Childe, V. Gordon. 1950. "The Urban Revolution." *Town Planning Review* 21: 3–17.

Childe, V. Gordon. 1956. *Piecing Together the Past: The Interpretation of Archaeological Data*. London: Routledge and Kegan Paul.

Chowning, Ann. 1956. "A Round Temple and Its Shrine at Mayapán." *Current Reports* 34: 443–62. Washington, DC: Carnegie Institution of Washington.

Chowning, Ann, and Donald E. Thompson. 1956. "A Dwelling and Shrine at Mayapán." *Current Reports* 33: 425–42. Washington, DC: Carnegie Institution of Washington.

Clark, John E. 2003. "Craftsmanship and Craft Specialization." In *Mesoamerican Lithic Technology: Experimentation and Interpretation*, edited by Kenneth G. Hirth, 220–33. Salt Lake City: University of Utah Press.

Clark, John E., and Stephen D. Houston. 1998. "Craft Specialization, Gender, and Personhood among the Post-conquest Maya of Yucatan, Mexico." In *Craft and Social Identity*, edited by Cathy Lynne Costin and Rita P. Wright, 31–46 Archaeological Papers of the American Anthropological Association 8. Washington, DC: American Anthropological Association. http://dx.doi.org/10.1525/ap3a.1998.8.1.31.

Cobos Palma, Rafael. 2004. "Chichén Itzá: Settlement and Hegemony During the Terminal Classic Period." In *The Terminal Classic in the Maya Lowlands: Collapse, Transition, and Transformation*, edited by Arthur A. Demarest, Prudence M. Rice, and Don S. Rice, 517–44. Boulder: University Press of Colorado.

Cobos Palma, Rafael, and Terance Winemiller. 2001. "The Late and Terminal Classic-Period Causeway Systems of Chichen Itza, Yucatan, Mexico." *Ancient Mesoamerica* 12 (2): 283–91. http://dx.doi.org/10.1017/S0956536101122066.

Coe, Michael D. 1965. "A Model of Ancient Maya Community Structure in the Maya Lowlands." *Southwestern Journal of Anthropology* 21: 87–119.

Connell, Samuel V. 2003. "Making Sense of Variability among Minor Centers: The Ancient Maya of Chaa Creek, Belize." In *Perspectives on Ancient Maya Rural Complexity*, edited by Gyles Iannone and Samuel V. Connell, 27–41. Los Angeles: Cotsen Institute of Archaeology, University of California, Los Angeles.

Connor, Judith G. 1983. *The Ceramics of Cozumel, Quintana Roo, Mexico*. PhD diss., University of Arizona. University Microfilms, Ann Arbor.

Costin, Cathy Lynne. 1991. "Craft Specialization: Issues in Defining, Documenting, and Explaining the Organization of Production." *Archaeological Method and Theory* 3: 1–56.

Cowgill, George L. 2007. "The Urban Organization of Teotihuacan, Mexico." In *Settlement and Society: Essays Dedicated to Robert McCormick Adams*, edited by Elizabeth C. Stone, 261–95. Los Angeles: Cotsen Institute of Archaeology, University of California, Los Angeles.

Cowgill, George L., Jeffery H. Altschul, and Rebecca S. Sload. 1984. "Spatial Analysis of Teotihuacan: A Mesoamerican Metropolis." In *Intrasite Spatial Analysis in Archaeology*, edited by Harold J. Hietala, 154–95. Cambridge: Cambridge University Press.

Coyston, Shannon, Christine D. White, and Henry P. Schwarcz. 1999. "Dietary Carbonate Analysis of Bone and Enamel for Two Sites in Belize." In *Reconstructing Ancient Maya Diet*, edited by Christine D. White, 221–43. Salt Lake City: University of Utah Press.

Craine, Eugene R., and Reginald C. Reindorp. 1979. *The Codex Pérez and the Book of Chilam Balam of Maní*. Norman: University of Oklahoma Press.

Crumley, Carole L. 1987. "A Dialectical Critique of Hierarchy." In *Power Relations and State Formation*, edited by Thomas C. Patterson and Christine W. Gailey, 155–69. Washington, DC: American Anthropological Association.

Crumley, Carole L. 1995. "Heterarchy and the Analysis of Complex Societies." In *Heterarchy and the Analysis of Complex Societies*, edited by Robert M. Ehrenreich, Carole L. Crumley, and Janet E. Levy, 1–5. American Anthropological Association Archaeological Papers no. 6. Arlington, VA: American Anthropological Association. http://dx.doi.org/10.1525/ap3a.1995.6.1.1.

Cruz Alvarado, Wilberth A. 2010. "Distribución y Cronología de sitios arqueológicos del centro-sur de Yucatán." Tésis profesional, Universidad Autónoma de Yucatán.

Cruz Alvarado, Wilberth A. 2012a. "Análisis preliminar de las modas cerámicas de Mayapán." In *Proyecto Los Fundamentos del Poder Económico de Mayapán, Temporadas 2008–2009: Informe final para el Consejo Nacional de Arqueología de México,* edited by Marilyn A. Masson, Carlos Peraza Lope, Timothy S. Hare, and Bradley W. Russell, 1163–90. Albany, NY: University at Albany–SUNY; Mérida, México: Centro INAH Yucatán.

Cruz Alvarado, Wilberth A. 2012b. "Las esculturas de roca caliza en Itzmal Ch'en." In *Proyecto Los Fundamentos del Poder Económico de Mayapán, Temporadas 2008–2009: Informe final para el Consejo Nacional de Arqueología de México,* edited by Marilyn A. Masson, Carlos Peraza Lope, Timothy S. Hare, and Bradley W. Russell, 1311–58. Albany, NY: University at Albany–SUNY; Mérida, Mexico: Centro INAH Yucatán.

Cruz Alvarado, Wilberth A., Luis Flores Cobá, Carlos Peraza Lope, and Marilyn A. Masson. 2009. "Análisis de cerámica, Temporada 2008." In *Proyecto Los Fundamentos del Poder Económico de Mayapán, Temporada 2008: Informe preliminario para el Consejo Nacional de Arqueología de México,* edited by Marilyn A. Masson, Carlos Peraza Lope, and Timothy S. Hare, 405–20. Albany, NY: University at Albany–SUNY; Mérida, México: Centro INAH Yucatán.

Cruz Alvarado, Wilberth A., Carlos Peraza Lope, Luis Flores Cobá, and Marilyn A. Masson. 2012. "Análisis de la cerámica – Temporadas 2008–2009." In *Proyecto Los Fundamentos del Poder Económico de Mayapán, Temporadas 2008–2009: Informe final para el Consejo Nacional de Arqueología de México,* edited by Marilyn A. Masson, Carlos Peraza Lope, Timothy S. Hare, and Bradley W. Russell, 1119–62. Albany, NY: University at Albany–SUNY; Mérida, México: Centro INAH Yucatán.

Culbert, T. Patrick. 2003. "The Ceramics of Tikal." In *Tikal: Dynasties, Foreigners, and Affairs of State; Advancing Maya Archaeology,* edited by Jeremy A. Sabloff, 47–82. Santa Fe, NM: School for Advanced Research Press.

Curtis, Jason H., David A. Hodell, and Mark Brenner. 1996. "Climate Variability on the Yucatan Peninsula (Mexico) during the Past 3500 Years and Implications for Maya Cultural Evolution." *Quaternary Research* 46 (1): 37–47. http://dx.doi.org/10.1006/qres.1996.0042.

Cyphers, Ann, and Kenneth G. Hirth. 2000. "Ceramics of Western Morelos: The Cañada through Gobernador Phases at Xochicalco." In *The Xochicalco Mapping Project: Archaeological Research at Xochicalco,* edited by Kenneth G. Hirth, 102–35. Salt Lake City: University of Utah Press.

D'Altroy, Terence N., and Christine A. Hastorf. 2001. *Empire and Domestic Economy.* New York: Springer.

Dahlin, Bruce H. 2009. "Ahead of its time: The remarkable Early Classic Maya economy of Chunchucmil." *Journal of Social Archaeology* 9 (3): 341–67. http://dx.doi.org/10.1177/1469605309338424.

Dahlin, Bruce H., and Traci Ardren. 2002. "Modes of Exchange and Regional Patterns: Chunchucmil, Yucatan, Mexico." In *Ancient Maya Political Economies*, edited by Marilyn A. Masson and David A. Freidel, 249–84. Walnut Creek, CA: AltaMira.

Dahlin, Bruce H., Daniel Bair, Tim Beach, Matthew Moriarty, and Richard Terry. 2010. "The Dirt on Food: Ancient Feasts and Markets Among the Lowland Maya." In *Pre-Columbian Foodways: Interdisciplinary Approaches to Food, Culture, and Markets in Mesoamerica*, edited by John Edward Staller and Michael Carrasco, 191–232. New York: Springer-Verlag. http://dx.doi.org/10.1007/978-1-4419-0471-3_8.

Dahlin, Bruce H., Timothy Beach, Sheryl Luzzadder-Beach, David Hixson, Scott Hutson, Aline Magnoni, Eugenia Mansell, and Daniel E. Mazeau. 2005. "Reconstructing Agricultural Sufficiency at Chunchucmil, Yucatan, Mexico." *Ancient Mesoamerica* 16 (2): 229–47. http://dx.doi.org/10.1017/S0956536105050212.

Dahlin, Bruce H., Christopher T. Jensen, Richard E. Terry, David R. Wright, and Timothy Beach. 2007. "In Search of an Ancient Maya Market." *Latin American Antiquity* 18 (4): 363–84. http://dx.doi.org/10.2307/25478193.

Davis, Mike. 2001. *Late Victorian Holocausts: El Niño Famines and the Making of the Third World*. London: Verso.

Deal, Michael. 1998. *Pottery Ethnoarchaeology in the Central Maya Highlands*. Salt Lake City: University of Utah Press.

Delgado Kú, Miguel Angél. 2009. *"La Pintura Mural de Mayapán, Yucatán: Una Interpretación Iconográfica."* Tésis profesional, Universidad Autónoma de Yucatán.

Delgado Kú, Miguel Angél. 2012a. "Casa Habitacional Q-39—al Oeste de la Zona Monumental." In *Proyecto Los Fundamentos del Poder Económico de Mayapán, Temporadas 2008–2009: Informe final para el Consejo Nacional de Arqueología de México*, edited by Marilyn A. Masson, Carlos Peraza Lope, Timothy S. Hare, and Bradley W. Russell, 771–56. Albany, NY: University at Albany–SUNY; Mérida, México: Centro INAH Yucatán.

Delgado Kú, Miguel Angél. 2012b. "Casa Habitacional Q-40a—al Oeste de la Zona Monumental." In *Proyecto Los Fundamentos del Poder Económico de Mayapán, Temporadas 2008–2009: Informe final para el Consejo Nacional de Arqueología de México*, edited by Marilyn A. Masson, Carlos Peraza Lope, Timothy S. Hare, and Bradley W. Russell, 757–88. Albany, NY: University at Albany–SUNY; Mérida, México: Centro INAH Yucatán.

Delgado Kú, Pedro C. 2004. "Estudio de la Arquitectura Pública del Núcleo Principal de Mayapán, Yucatán." Tésis profesional, Universidad Autónoma de Yucatán.

Delgado Kú, Pedro C., Bárbara del C. Escamilla Ojeda, and Carlos Peraza Lope. 2012a. "Itzmal Ch'en Sala Hipóstila H-15." In *Proyecto Los Fundamentos del Poder Económico de Mayapán, Temporadas 2008–2009: Informe final para el Consejo Nacional de Arqueología de México*, edited by Marilyn A. Masson, Carlos Peraza Lope, Timothy S. Hare, and Bradley W. Russell, 423–538. Albany, NY: University at Albany–SUNY; Mérida, México: Centro INAH Yucatán.

Delgado Kú, Pedro C., Bárbara del C. Escamilla Ojeda, and Carlos Peraza Lope. 2012b. "Templo Itzmal Ch'en H-17 y Altar H-17a." In *Proyecto Los Fundamentos del Poder Económico de Mayapán, Temporadas 2008–2009: Informe final para el Consejo Nacional de Arqueología de México*, edited by Marilyn A. Masson, Carlos Peraza Lope, Timothy S. Hare, and Bradley W. Russell, 257–422. Albany, NY: University at Albany–SUNY; Mérida, México: Centro INAH Yucatán.

Demarest, Arthur A. 2013. "Ideological Pathways to Economic Exchange: Religion, Economy, and Legitimation at the Classic Maya Royal Capital of Cancuén." *Latin American Antiquity* 24: 371–402.

Demarest, Arthur A., Prudence M. Rice, and Don S. Rice, eds. 2004. *The Terminal Classic in the Maya Lowlands: Collapse, Transition, and Transformation*. Boulder: University Press of Colorado.

Díaz, Gisele, Alan Rodgers, and Bruce E. Byland. 1993. *The Codex Borgia: A Full-Color Restoration of the Ancient Mexican Manuscript*. New York: Dover.

Dickson, D. Bruce. 2006. "Public Transcripts Expressed in Theatres of Cruelty: The Royal Graves at Ur in Mesopotamia." *Cambridge Archaeological Journal* 16 (2): 123–44. http://dx.doi.org/10.1017/S0959774306000084.

Diehl, Richard A., and Janet C. Berlo, eds. 1989. *Mesoamerica after the Decline of Teotihuacan, AD 700–900*. Washington, DC: Dumbarton Oaks.

Dietler, Michael, and Ingrid Herbich. 1998. "Habitus, Techniques and Style: An Integrated Approach to the Social Understanding of Material Culture and Boundaries." In *The Archaeology of Social Boundaries*, edited by Miriam T. Stark, 232–63. Washington, DC: Smithsonian Institution Press.

Drennan, Robert D. 1996. *Statistics for Archaeologists: A Commonsense Approach*. New York: Springer. http://dx.doi.org/10.1007/978-1-4899-0165-1.

Drennan, Robert D., Philip T. Fitzgibbons, and Heinz Dehn. 1990. "Imports and Exports in Classic Mesoamerican Political Economy: The Tehuacan Valley and the Teotihuacan Obsidian Industry." In *Research in Economic Anthropology*," vol. 12, edited by Barry L. Isaac, 177–99. Greenwich, CT: JAI Press.

Dunning, Nicholas, Timothy Beach, and Sheryl Luzadder-Beach. n.d. "Environmental Variability, Instability, and Ancient Maya Settlement." In *El Urbanismo en Mesoamerica/Urbanism in Mesoamerica*, vol. 3, edited by Robert H. Cobean, Eric Taladoire, Ángel García Cook, and Kenneth G. Hirth. México, DF: Instituto Nacional de Antropología e Historia; University Park: Pennsylvania State University.

Dunning, Nicholas, John G. Jones, Timothy Beach, and Sheryl Luzadder-Beach. 2003. "Physiography, Habitats, and Landscapes of the Three Rivers Region." In *Heterarchy, Political Economy, and the Ancient Maya: The Three Rivers Region of the East-Central Yucatán Peninsula*, edited by Vernon L. Scarborough, Fred Valdez, Jr., and Nicholas Dunning, 14–24. Tempe: University of Arizona Press.

Dyer, Christopher. 1989. *Standards of Living in the Later Middle Ages: Social Change in England c. 1200–1520*. Cambridge: Cambridge University Press. http://dx.doi.org/10.1017/CBO9781139167697.

Eaton, Jack D. 1974. "Shell Celts from Coastal Yucatan, Mexico." *Bulletin of the Texas Archaeological Society* 45: 197–207.

Edmonson, Munro S., annot. and trans. 1982. *The Ancient Future of the Itza: The Book of Chilam Balam of Tizimin*. Austin: University of Texas Press.

Einzig, Paul. 1949. *Primitive Money in Its Ethnological, Historical and Economic Aspects*. London: Eyre & Spottiswoode.

Eisenstadt, Shmuel. 1980. "Cultural Orientations, Institutional Entrepreneurs, and Social Change: Comparative Analysis of Traditional Civilizations." *American Journal of Sociology* 85 (4): 840–69. http://dx.doi.org/10.1086/227091.

Eisenstadt, Shmuel. 1981. "Cultural Traditions and Political Dynamics: The Origins and Modes of Ideological Politics." *British Journal of Sociology* 32 (2): 155–81. http://dx.doi.org/10.2307/589444.

Erickson, Clark L. 2006. "Intensification, Political Economy, and the Farming Community: In Defense of a Bottom-Up Perspective of the Past." In *Agricultural Strategies*, edited by Joyce Marcus and Charles Stanish, 334–63. Los Angeles: Cotsen Institute of Archaeology, University of California, Los Angeles.

Erickson, Clark L. 2009. "Precolumbian Causeways and Canals as Landesque Capital." In *Landscapes of Movement: Trails, Paths, and Roads in Anthropological Perspective*, edited by James E. Snead, Clark L. Erickson, and J. Andrew Darling, 232–52. Philadelphia: University of Pennsylvania Press.

Escamilla Ojeda, Bárbara. 2004. "Los artefactos de obsidiana de Mayapán." Tésis profesional, Universidad Autónoma de Yucatán.

Escamilla Ojeda, Bárbara. 2009. "Análisis de la obsidiana, temporada 2008." In *Proyecto Los Fundamentos del Poder Económico de Mayapán, Temporada 2008: Informe preliminario para el Consejo Nacional de Arqueología de México*, edited by Marilyn A.

Masson, Carlos Peraza Lope, and Timothy S. Hare, 385–94. Albany, NY: University at Albany–SUNY; Mérida, México: Centro INAH Yucatán.

Escamilla Ojeda, Bárbara. 2012. "Análisis de la obsidiana, temporadas 2008–2009." In *Proyecto Los Fundamentos del Poder Económico de Mayapán, Temporadas 2008–2009: Informe final para el Consejo Nacional de Arqueología de México*, edited by Marilyn A. Masson, Carlos Peraza Lope, Timothy S. Hare, and Bradley W. Russell, 953–1118. Albany, NY: University at Albany–SUNY; Mérida, México: Centro INAH Yucatán.

Fedick, Scott L. 1991. "Chert Production and Consumption among Classic Period Maya Households." In *Maya Stone Tools: Selected Papers from the Second Maya Lithic Conference*, edited by Thomas R. Hester and Harry J. Shafer, 103–18. Madison, WI: Prehistory Press.

Fedick, Scott L., ed. 1996. *The Managed Mosaic: Ancient Maya Agriculture and Resource Use*. Salt Lake City: University of Utah Press.

Feinman, Gary M., and Christopher P. Garraty. 2010. "Preindustrial Markets and Marketing: Archaeological Perspectives." *Annual Review of Anthropology* 39 (1): 167–91. http://dx.doi.org/10.1146/annurev.anthro.012809.105118.

Feinman, Gary M., and Linda M. Nicholas. 1993. "Shell-Ornament Production in Ejutla: Implications for Highland-Coastal Interaction in Ancient Oaxaca." *Ancient Mesoamerica* 4 (1): 103–19. http://dx.doi.org/10.1017/S095653610000081X.

Feinman, Gary M., and Linda M. Nicholas. 2000. "High-Intensity Household-Scale Production in Ancient Mesoamerica: A Perspective from Ejutla, Oaxaca." In *Cultural Evolution: Contemporary Viewpoints*, edited by Gary M. Feinman and Linda Manzanilla, 119–42. New York: Kluwer Academic/Plenum. http://dx.doi.org/10.1007/978-1-4615-4173-8_5.

Feinman, Gary M., and Linda M. Nicholas. 2004. "Unraveling the Prehispanic Highland Mesoamerican Economy: Production, Exchange, and Consumption in the Classic Period Valley of Oaxaca." In *Archaeological Perspectives on Political Economies*, edited by Gary M. Feinman and Linda M. Nicholas, 167–88. Salt Lake City: University of Utah Press.

Feinman, Gary M., and Linda M. Nicholas. 2007. "Household Production and the Regional Economy in Ancient Oaxaca: Classic Period Perspectives from Hilltop El Palmillo and Valley Floor Ejutla." In *Pottery Economics in Mesoamerica*, edited by Christopher A. Pool and George J. Bey, III, 184–211. Tucson: University of Arizona Press.

Feinman, Gary M., and Linda M. Nicholas. 2010. "A Multiscalar Perspective on Market Exchange in the Classic-Period Valley of Oaxaca." In *Archaeological Approaches to Market Exchange in Ancient Societies*, edited by Christopher P. Garraty and Barbara L. Stark, 85–98. Boulder: University Press of Colorado.

Feinman, Gary M., and Linda M. Nicholas. 2011. "Domestic Craft Production and the Classic Period Economy of Oaxaca." In *Producción artesanal y especializada en Mesoamérica: Áreas de actividad y procesos productivos*, edited by Linda R. Manzanilla and Kenneth G. Hirth, 29–58. México, D.F.: Instituto Nacional de Antropología e Historia, Universidad Nacional Autónoma de México, Instituto de Investigaciones Antropológicas.

Feldman, Lawrence H. 1978. "Moving Merchandise in Protohistoric Central Quauhtemallan." In *Mesoamerican Communication Routes and Cultural Contacts*, edited by Thomas A. Lee and Carlos Navarette, 7–17. Papers of the New World Archaeological Foundation no. 40. Provo, UT: New World Archaeological Foundation.

Feldman, Lawrence H. 1985. *A Tumpline Economy: Production and Distribution Systems in Sixteenth-Century Eastern Guatemala*. Culver City, CA: Labyrinthos.

Fernández de Oviedo y Valdés, Gonzalo. 1851. Vol. 1 of *Historia general y natural de las Indias, islas y tierra- firme del mar océano*, edited by Juan Amador de los Rios. Madrid: Real Academia de la Historia.

Fernández de Oviedo y Valdés, Gonzalo. 1853. Vol. 2 of *Historia general y natural de las Indias, islas y tierra-firme del mar océano*, edited by Juan Amador de los Rios. Madrid: Real Academia de la Historia.

Flannery, Kent V. 1983. "Major Monte Alban V Sites: Zaachila, Xoxocotlan, Cuilapan, Yagul, and Abasolo." In *The Cloud People: Divergent Evolution of the Zapotec and Mixtec Civilizations*, edited by Kent V. Flannery and Joyce Marcus, 290–94. New York: Academic Press.

Fletcher, Laraine A. 1983. "Coba and Mayapan: A Comparison of Solares, Household Variation, Sociopolitical Organization, and Land Tenure." In *Coba: A Classic Maya Metropolis*, edited by William J. Folan, Ellen R. Kintz, and Laraine A. Fletcher, 121–31. New York: Academic Press.

Fletcher, Laraine A., and Ellen R. Kintz. 1983. "Solares, Kitchen Gardens, and Social Status at Coba." In *Coba: A Classic Maya Metropolis*, edited by William J. Folan, Ellen R. Kintz, and Laraine A. Fletcher, 103–19. New York: Academic Press.

Fletcher, Roland. 2000–2001. "Seeing Angkor: New Views of an Old City." *Journal of the Oriental Society of Australia* 32–33: 1–27.

Fletcher, Roland. 2012. "Low-Density, Agrarian-Based Urbanism: Scale, Power, and Ecology." In *The Comparative Archaeology of Complex Societies*, edited by Michael E. Smith, 285–320. Cambridge: Cambridge University Press.

Foias, Antonia. 2002. "At the Crossroads: The Economic Basis of Political Power in the Petexbatún Region, Southwest Petén, Guatemala." In *Ancient Maya Political*

Economies, edited by Marilyn A. Masson and David A. Freidel, 223–48. Walnut Creek, CA: AltaMira.

Folan, William J. 1983. "Urban Organization and Social Structure of Coba." In *Coba: A Classic Maya Metropolis*, edited by William J. Folan, Ellen R. Kintz, and Laraine A. Fletcher, 49–63. New York: Academic Press.

Folan, William J. 1992. "Calakmul, Campeche: A Centralized Urban Administrative Center in the Northern Petén." *World Archaeology* 24 (1): 158–68. http://dx.doi.org /10.1080/00438243.1992.9980199.

Follett, Prescott H. F. 1932. "War and Weapons of the Maya." In *Middle American Papers*, 375–410. Middle American Research Series Publication 4. New Orleans, LA: Tulane University.

Forsyth, Donald W. 2004. "Reflexiones sobre la ocupación postclasica en Champotón a traves de la cerámica." *Los Investigadores de la Cultura Maya* 12 (1): 33–7.

Fotheringham, A. S., C. Brunsdon, and M. Charlton. 2000. *Quantitative Geography: Perspectives on Spatial Data Analysis*. Thousand Oaks, CA: Sage Publications.

Fox, John W. 1987. *Late Postclassic State Formation*. Cambridge: Cambridge University Press.

France, Elizabeth L. 2008. "Apéndice H." In *Proyecto Los Fundamentos del Poder Económico de Mayapán, Temporadas 2001–2004: Informe final para el Consejo Nacional de Arqueología de México*, edited by Marilyn A. Masson, Carlos Peraza Lope, and Timothy S. Hare, 908–24. Albany, NY: Department of Anthropology, University at Albany–SUNY; Mérida, México: Centro INAH Yucatán.

Freidel, David A. 1978. "Maritime Adaptation and the Rise of Maya Civilization: The View from Cerros, Belize." In *Prehistoric Coastal Adaptations: The Economy and Ecology of Maritime Middle America*, edited by Barbara L. Stark and Barbara Voorhies, 239–65. New York: Academic Press.

Freidel, David A. 1981. "The Political Economics of Residential Dispersion Among the Lowland Maya." In *Lowland Maya Settlement Patterns*, edited by Wendy Ashmore, 371–82. Albuquerque: University of New Mexico Press.

Freidel, David A. 1985. "New Light on a Dark Age: A Summary of Major Themes." In *The Lowland Maya Postclassic*, edited by Arlen F. Chase and Prudence M. Rice, 285–310. Austin: University of Texas Press.

Freidel, David A., Kathryn Reese-Taylor, and David Mora-Marin. 2002. "The Origins of Maya Civilization: The Old Shell Game, Commodity, Treasure, and Kingship." In *Ancient Maya Political Economies*, edited by Marilyn A. Masson and David A. Freidel, 41–86. Walnut Creek, CA: AltaMira.

Freidel, David, and F. Kent Reilly, III. 2010. "The Flesh of God: Cosmology, Food, and the Origins of Political Power in Ancient Southeastern Mesoamerica." In

Pre-Columbian Foodways: Interdisciplinary Approaches to Food, Culture, and Markets in Mesoamerica, edited by John E. Staller and Michael D. Carrasco, 635–80. New York: Springer-Verlag. http://dx.doi.org/10.1007/978-1-4419-0471-3_26.

Freidel, David A., and Jeremy A. Sabloff. 1984. *Cozumel: Late Maya Settlement Patterns*. New York: Academic Press.

Freidel, David A., and Linda Schele. 1988. "Kingship in the Late Preclassic Maya Lowlands: The Instruments and Places of Ritual Power." *American Anthropologist* 90 (3): 547–67. http://dx.doi.org/10.1525/aa.1988.90.3.02a00020.

Freidel, David , Linda Schele, and Joy Parker. 1993. *Maya Cosmos: Three Thousand Years on the Shaman's Path*. New York: William Morrow.

Freidel, David, and Justine Shaw. 2000. "The Lowland Maya Civilization: Historical Consciousness and Environment." In *The Way the Wind Blows: Climate, History, and Human Action*, edited by Roderick J. McIntosh, Joseph A. Tainter, and Susan Keech McIntosh, 271–300. New York: Columbia University Press.

Fry, Robert E. 2003. "The Peripheries of Tikal." In *Tikal: Dynasties, Foreigners, & Affairs of State*, edited by Jeremy A. Sabloff, 143–70. Santa Fe, NM: School for Advanced Research Press.

Gailey, Christine W., and Thomas C. Patterson. 1987. "Power Relations and State Formation." In *Power Relations and State Formation*, edited by Thomas C. Patterson and Christine W. Gailey, 1–27. Washington, DC: American Anthropological Association.

Galup, Sheila M. 2007. *Postclassic Maya Lithic Tool Maintenance, Recycling, and Consumption Patterns at Laguna de On Island*. Occasional Publication no. 13, Institute for Mesoamerican Studies. Albany, NY: Department of Anthropology, University of Albany–SUNY,.

Gann, Thomas W. 1900. *Mounds in Northern Honduras*. Nineteenth Annual Report of the Bureau of American Ethnology, 1897–1898, part 2: 655–92. Washington, DC: Smithsonian Institution.

Garber, James F. 1989. *Archaeology at Cerros, Belize, Central America*, vol. 2, *The Artifacts*. Dallas, TX: Southern Methodist University Press.

Garraty, Christopher P. 2010. "Investigating Market Exchange in Ancient Societies: A Theoretical Review." In *Archaeological Approaches to Market Exchange in Ancient Societies*, edited by Christopher P. Garraty and Barbara L. Stark, 3–32. Boulder: University Press of Colorado.

Gazdik, Karime F. 2009. "White-tailed Deer Management at the Ancient Maya City of Mayapán: An Osteometric Perspective." Paper presented at the University at Albany–SUNY Undergraduate Research Conference, Albany, NY, May 2009.

Gill, Richardson B. 2000. *The Great Maya Droughts: Water, Life, and Death.* Albuquerque: University of New Mexico Press.

Gill, Richardson B., and Jerome P. Keating. 2002. "Volcanism in Mesoamerican Archaeology." *Ancient Mesoamerica* 13 (1): 125–40. http://dx.doi.org/10.1017/S0956536102131051.

Gossen, Gary H., and Richard M. Leventhal. 1993. "The Topography of Ancient Maya Religious Pluralism." In *Lowland Maya Civilization in the Eighth Century A.D,* edited by Jeremy A. Sabloff and John S. Henderson, 185–218. Washington, DC: Dumbarton Oaks.

Graff, Donald H. 1997. "Dating a Section of the Madrid Codex: Astronomical and Iconographic Evidence." In *Papers on the Madrid Codex,* edited by Victoria R. Bricker and Gabrielle Vail, 147–67. Middle American Research Series Publication 64. New Orleans, LA: Tulane University.

Graham, Elizabeth. 1987. "Terminal Classic to Early Historic Period Vessel Forms from Belize." In *Maya Ceramics: Papers from the 1985 Maya Ceramic Conference,* edited by Prudence Rice and Robert Sharer, 73–98. BAR International Series 345. Oxford: BAR.

Graham, Elizabeth. 1991. "Archaeological Insights into Colonial Period Maya Life at Tipu, Belize." In *Columbian Consequences: The Spanish Borderlands in Pan-American Perspective,* vol. 3, edited by David Hurst Thomas, 319–36. Washington, DC: Smithsonian Institution Press.

Graham, Elizabeth. 2002. "Perspectives on Economy and Theory." In *Ancient Maya Political Economies,* edited by Marilyn A. Masson and David A. Freidel, 398–418. Walnut Creek, CA: AltaMira.

Graham, Elizabeth. 2011. *Maya Christians and Their Churches in Sixteenth-Century Belize.* Gainesville: University Press of Florida. http://dx.doi.org/10.5744/florida/9780813036663.001.0001.

Gunsenheimer, Antje. 2002. "Geschichtstradierung in den yukatekischen Chilam Balam-Büchern: Eine Analyse der Herkunft und Entwicklung ausgewählter historischer Berichte." PhD diss., Univeristät Bonn.

Hamblin, Nancy L. 1984. *Animal Use by the Cozumel Maya.* Tucson: University of Arizona Press.

Hansen, Mogens Herman. 2006. *The Shotgun Method: The Demography of the Ancient Greek City-State Culture.* Columbia: University of Missouri Press.

Hare, Timothy S. 2008a. "Reconocimiento y cartografiado en Mayapán." In *Proyecto Los Fundamentos del Poder Económico de Mayapán, Temporadas 2001–2004: Informe final para el Consejo Nacional de Arqueología de México,* edited by Marilyn A. Masson, Carlos Peraza Lope, and Timothy S. Hare, 7–128. Albany, NY: University at Albany–SUNY; Mérida, México: Centro INAH Yucatán.

Hare, Timothy S. 2008b. "Apéndice A. Albarradas en Cuadros de la Mapa de Mayapán: Archivos Electrónicos de la colección de William Bullard (del Museo Peabody de la Universidad Harvard)." In *Proyecto Los Fundamentos del Poder Económico de Mayapán, Temporadas 2001–2004: Informe final para el Consejo Nacional de Arqueología de México*, edited by Marilyn A. Masson, Carlos Peraza Lope, and Timothy S. Hare. Albany, NY: University at Albany–SUNY; Mérida, México: Centro INAH Yucatán.

Hare, Timothy S., and Marilyn A. Masson. 2010. "Pottery Assemblage Variation at Mayapán Residences." Paper presented at the 75th Annual Meeting of the Society for American Archaeology, St. Louis, MO, April 14–18.

Hare, Timothy S., and Marilyn A. Masson. 2012. "Intermediate-Scale Patterns in the Urban Environment of Postclassic Mayapán." In *The Neighborhood as a Social and Spatial Unit in Mesoamerican Cities*, edited by M. Charlotte Arnauld, Linda R. Manzanilla, and Michael E. Smith, 229–60. Tucson: University of Arizona Press.

Hare, Timothy S., Travis Ormsby, and Scott Speal. 2002. "Cartografiado con GPS de las estructuras al interior de la muralla." In *Proyecto Los Fundamentos del Poder Económico de Mayapán, Temporada 2002: Informe para el Consejo Nacional de Arqueología de México*, edited by Marilyn A. Masson, Carlos Peraza Lope, and Timothy S. Hare, 106–26. Albany, NY: University at Albany–SUNY; Mérida, México: Centro INAH Yucatán.

Hassig, Ross. 1981. "The Famine of One Rabbit: Ecological Causes and Social Consequences of a Pre-Columbian Calamity." *Journal of Anthropological Research* 37 (2): 172–82.

Hassig, Ross. 1988. *Aztec Warfare: Imperial Expansion and Political Control*. Norman: University of Oklahoma Press.

Haviland, William A. 1963. "Excavations of Small Structures in the Northeast Quadrant of Tikal, Guatemala." PhD diss., University of Pennsylvania.

Haviland, William A. 1970. "Tikal, Guatemala and Mesoamerican Urbanism." *World Archaeology* 2 (2): 186–98. http://dx.doi.org/10.1080/00438243.1970.9979473.

Haviland, William A. 1985. *Excavations in Small Residential Groups of Tikal, Groups 4F–1 and 4F–2*. Tikal Report no. 19. Philadelphia: University of Pennsylvania Museum of Archaeology and Anthropology.

Haviland, William A. 1992. "Status and Power in Classic Maya Society: The View from Tikal." *American Anthropologist* 94 (4): 937–40. http://dx.doi.org/10.1525/aa.1992.94.4.02a00140.

Haviland, William A., and Hattula Moholy-Nagy. 1992. "Distinguishing the High and Mighty from the Hoi Polloi at Tikal, Guatemala." In *Mesoamerican Elites: An Archaeological Assessment*, edited by Diane Z. Chase and Arlen F. Chase, 50–60. Norman: University of Oklahoma Press.

Headrick, Annabeth. 2007. *The Teotihuacan Trinity: The Sociopolitical Structure of an Ancient Mesoamerican City*. Austin: University of Texas Press.

Hendon, Julia A. 1991. "Status and Power in Classic Maya Society: An Archaeological Study." *American Anthropologist* 93 (4): 894–918. http://dx.doi.org/10.1525/aa.1991.93.4.02a00070.

Hendon, Julia A. 1992. "The Interpretation of Survey Data: Two Case Studies from the Maya Area." *Latin American Antiquity* 3 (1): 22–42. http://dx.doi.org/10.2307/971928.

Hendon, Julia A. 1996. "Archaeological Approaches to the Organization of Domestic Labor: Household Practice and Domestic Relations." *Annual Review of Anthropology* 25 (1): 45–61. http://dx.doi.org/10.1146/annurev.anthro.25.1.45.

Hester, Joseph A., Jr. 1952. "Agriculture, Economy, and Population Densities of the Maya." *Carnegie Institution of Washington Year Book* 51: 266–71.

Hester, Joseph A., Jr. 1953. "Agriculture, Economy, and Population Densities of the Maya." *Carnegie Institution of Washington Year Book* 52: 288–92.

Hester, Thomas R., G. Ligabue, Jack D. Eaton, Harry J. Shafer, and Richard E. W. Adams. 1982. "Archaeology at Colha, Belize: The 1981 Season." In *Archaeology at Colha, Belize: The 1981 Interim Report*, edited by Thomas R. Hester, Harry J. Shafer, and Jack D. Eaton, 1–10. San Antonio: Center for Archaeological Research, University of Texas at San Antonio.

Hester, Thomas R., and Harry J. Shafer. 1984. "Exploitation of Chert Resources by the Ancient Maya of Northern Belize, Central America." *World Archaeology* 16 (2): 157–73. http://dx.doi.org/10.1080/00438243.1984.9979925.

Hirth, Kenneth G. 1989. "Militarism and Social Organization at Xochicalco." In *Mesoamerica after the Decline of Teotihuacan, A.D. 700–900*, edited by Richard A. Diehl and Janet Catherine Berlo, 69–81. Washington, DC: Dumbarton Oaks.

Hirth, Kenneth G. 1993a. "The Household as an Analytical Unit: Problems in Method and Theory." In *Prehispanic Domestic Units in Western Mesoamerica: Studies of the Household, Compound, and Residence*, edited by Robert S. Santley and Kenneth G. Hirth, 21–36. Boca Raton, FL: CRC Press.

Hirth, Kenneth G. 1993b. "Identifying Rank and Socioeconomic Status in Domestic Units: An Example from Central Mexico." In *Prehispanic Domestic Units in Western Mesoamerica: Studies of the Household, Compound, and Residence*, edited by Robert S. Santley and Kenneth G. Hirth, 121–46. Boca Raton, FL: CRC Press.

Hirth, Kenneth G. 1998. "The Distributional Approach: A New Way to Identify Marketplace Exchange in the Archaeological Record." *Current Anthropology* 39 (4): 451–76. http://dx.doi.org/10.1086/204759.

Hirth, Kenneth G. 2003a. "The Altepetl and Urban Structure in Prehispanic Mesoamerica." In *El Urbanismo en Mesoamerica/Urbanism in Mesoamerica*, vol. 1, edited by William T. Sanders, Alba Guadelupe Mastache, and Robert H. Cobean, 57–84. México, D.F.: Instituto Nacional de Antropología e Historia; University Park: Pennsylvania State University.

Hirth, Kenneth G. 2003b. "Urban Structure at Xochicalco, Mexico." In *El Urbanismo en Mesoamerica/Urbanism in Mesoamerica*, vol. 1, edited by William T. Sanders, Alba Guadelupe Mastache, and Robert H. Cobean, 257–310. México, D.F.: Instituto Nacional de Antropología e Historia; University Park: Pennsylvania State University.

Houston, Stephen, Héctor Escobedo, Mark Child, Charles Golden, and René Muñoz. 2003. "The Moral Community: Maya Settlement Transformation at Piedras Negras, Guatemala." In *The Social Construction of Ancient Cities*, edited by Monica L. Smith, 212–53. Washington, DC: Smithsonian Institution.

Houston, Stephen D., and David Stuart. 2001. "Peopling the Classic Maya Court." In *Royal Courts of the Ancient Maya*, vol. 1, *Theory, Comparison, and Synthesis*, edited by Takeshi Inomata and Stephen D. Houston, 54–83. Boulder, CO: Westview Press.

Hutchinson, Robert H. H. 2010. "The Sociopolitical Structure of Mayapán: A Study of the City's Burial Patterns." Paper presented at the 75th Annual Meeting of the Society for American Archaeology, St. Louis, MO, April 14–18.

Hutchinson, Robert H. H., and Pedro Delgado Kú. 2012. "Casa Habitacional I-55a en el area de Itzmal Ch'en." In *Proyecto Los Fundamentos del Poder Económico de Mayapán, Temporadas 2008–2009: Informe final para el Consejo Nacional de Arqueología de México*, edited by Marilyn A. Masson, Carlos Peraza Lope, Timothy S. Hare, and Bradley W. Russell, 591–664. Albany, NY: University at Albany–SUNY; Mérida, Mexico: Centro INAH Yucatán.

Hutson, Scott R., Bruce H. Dahlin, and Daniel Mazeau. 2012. "Commerce and Cooperation among the Classic Maya: The Chunchucmil Case." In *Cooperation in Social and Economic Life*, edited by Robert Marshall, 81–103. Lanham, MD: AltaMira.

Hutson, Scott R., Travis W. Stanton, Aline Magnoni, Richard Terry, and Jason Craner. 2007. "Beyond the Buildings: Formation Processes of Ancient Maya Houselots and Methods for the Study of Non-architectural Space." *Journal of Anthropological Archaeology* 26 (3): 442–73. http://dx.doi.org/10.1016/j.jaa.2006.12.001.

Iannone, Giles. 2002. "Annales History and the Ancient Maya State: Some Observations on the 'Dynamic Model.'." *American Anthropologist* 104 (1): 68–78. http://dx.doi.org/10.1525/aa.2002.104.1.68.

Iannone, Giles, and Samuel V. Connell, eds. 2003. *Perspectives on Ancient Maya Rural Complexity*. Los Angeles: Cotsen Institute of Archaeology, University of California, Los Angeles.

Inomata, Takeshi. 2001. "King's People: Classic Maya Courtiers in a Comparative Perspective." In *Royal Courts of the Ancient Maya*, vol. 1, *Theory, Comparison, Synthesis*, edited by Takeshi Inomata and Stephen D. Houston, 27–53. Boulder, CO: Westview Press.

Inomata, Takeshi. 2003. "War, Destruction, and Abandonment: The Fall of the Classic Maya Center of Aguateca, Guatemala." In *The Archaeology of Settlement Abandonment in Middle America*, edited by Takeshi Inomata and Ronald W. Webb, 43–60. Salt Lake City: University of Utah Press.

Inomata, Takeshi, and Stephen D. Houston, eds. 2001. *Royal Courts of the Ancient Maya*, vol. 1, *Theory, Comparison, Synthesis*. Boulder, CO: Westview Press.

Inomata, Takeshi, and Laura Stiver. 1998. "Floor Assemblages from Burned Structures at Aguateca, Guatemala: A Study of Classic Maya Households." *Journal of Field Archaeology* 25 (4): 431–52.

Janusek, John Wayne 2002. "Out of Many, One: Style and Social Boundaries in Tiwanaku." *Latin American Antiquity* 13 (1): 35–61. http://dx.doi.org/10.2307/971740.

Janusek, John W. 2004. *Identity and Power in the Ancient Andes: Tiwanaku Cities through Time*. New York: Routledge. http://dx.doi.org/10.4324/9780203324615.

Janusek, John Wayne, and Deborah E. Blom. 2006. "Identifying Tiwanaku Urban Populations: Style, Identity, and Ceremony in Andean Cities." In *Urbanism in the Preindustrial World: Cross-Cultural Approaches*, edited by Glenn R. Storey, 233–51. Tuscaloosa: University of Alabama Press.

Jones, Grant D. 1989. *Maya Resistance to Spanish Rule: Time and History on a Colonial Frontier*. Albuquerque: University of New Mexico Press.

Jones, Grant D. 1998. *The Conquest of the Last Maya Kingdom*. Stanford, CA: Stanford University Press.

Jones, Morris R. 1952. "Map of the Ruins of Mayapán, Yucatán, Mexico." *Current Reports* 1: 2–5. Washington, DC: Carnegie Institution of Washington.

Jones, Morris R. 1962. "Map of the Ruins of Mayapán." In *Mayapán, Yucatán, Mexico*, by H. E. D. Pollock, Ralph L. Roys, Tatiana Proskouriakoff, and A. Ledyard Smith, rear inset. Carnegie Institution of Washington Publication 619, Washington, DC: Carnegie Institution.

Kaluzny, Stephen P., Silvia C. Vega, Tamre P. Cardoso, and Alice A. Shelly. 1998. *S+ SpatialStats: User's Manual for Windows and Unix*. New York: Springer.

Keegan, William, and Betsy Carlson. 2008/2009. "Blessed are the Beadmakers." *Times of the Islands: Sampling the Soul of the Turks and Caicos Islands*. Winter 2008/2009. http://www.timespub.tc/2009/01/blessed-are-the-beadmakers/

Kennett, Douglas J., Sebastian F. M. Breitenbach, Valorie V. Aquino, Yemane Asmerom, Jaime Awe, James U. L. Baldini, Patrick Bartlein, et al. 2012. "Development and Disintegration of Maya Political Systems in Response to Climate Change." *Science* 338 (6108): 788–91. http://dx.doi.org/10.1126/science.1226299.

Kent, Susan. 1990a. "A Cross Cultural Study of Segmentation, Architecture, and the Use of Space." In *Domestic Architecture and the Use of Space: An Interdisciplinary Cross-Cultural Study*, edited by Susan Kent, 127–52. Cambridge: Cambridge University Press.

Kent, Susan, ed. 1990b. *Domestic Architecture and the Use of Space: An Interdisciplinary Cross-Cultural Study*. Cambridge: Cambridge University Press.

Kepecs, Susan M. 1999. "The Political Economy of Chikinchel, Yucatán, Mexico: A Diachronic Analysis from the Prehispanic Era through the Age of Spanish Administration." PhD diss., University of Wisconsin–Madison.

Kepecs, Susan M. 2003. "Chikinchel." In *The Postclassic Mesoamerican World*, edited by Michael E. Smith and Frances F. Berdan, 259–68. Salt Lake City: University of Utah Press.

Kepecs, Susan M. 2007. "Chichén Itzá, Tula, and the Epiclassic/Early Postclassic Mesoamerican World System." In *Twin Tollans: Chichén Itzá, Tula and the Epiclassic to Early Postclassic Mesoamerican World*, edited by Jeff Karl Kowalski and Cynthia Kristan-Graham, 129–50. Dumbarton Oaks, Washington, DC.

Kepecs, Susan, and Sylviane Boucher. 1996. "The Pre-Hispanic Cultivation of Rejolladas and Stone-Lands: New Evidence from Northeast Yucatán." In *The Managed Mosaic: Ancient Maya Agriculture and Resource Use*, edited by Scott Fedick, 69–91. Salt Lake City: University of Utah Press.

Kepecs, Susan, Gary M. Feinman, and Sylviane Boucher. 1994. "Chichen Itza and Its Hinterland: A World-Systems Perspective." *Ancient Mesoamerica* 5 (2): 141–58. http://dx.doi.org/10.1017/S0956536100000115.

Kepecs, Susan M., and Phillip L. Kohl. 2003. "Conceptualizing Macroregional Interaction: World-Systems Theory and the Archaeological Record." In *The Postclassic Mesoamerican World*, edited by Michael E. Smith and Frances F. Berdan, 14–20. Salt Lake City: University of Utah Press.

Killion, Thomas W. 1992a. "Residential Ethnoarchaeology and Ancient Site Structure: Contemporary Farming and Prehistoric Settlement Agriculture at Matacapan, Veracruz, Mexico." In *Gardens of Prehistory: The Archaeology of Settlement Agriculture in Greater Mesoamerica*, edited by Thomas W. Killion, 119–49. Tuscaloosa: University of Alabama Press.

Killion, Thomas W. 1992b. "The Archaeology of Settlement Agriculture." In *Gardens of Prehistory: The Archaeology of Settlement Agriculture in Greater Mesoamerica*, edited by Thomas W. Killion, 1–13. Tuscaloosa: University of Alabama Press.

Killion, Thomas W., Jeremy A. Sabloff, Gair Tourtellot, and Nicholas Dunning. 1989.

"Intensive Surface Collection of Residential Clusters at the Terminal Classic Sayil, Yucatan, Mexico." *Journal of Field Archaeology* 16 (3): 273–94. http://dx.doi.org /10.2307/529834.

King, Eleanor. 1994. "Preliminary Report on the Colha Settlement Survey: The 1983 and 1984 Seasons." In *Continuing Archaeology at Colha, Belize*, edited by Thomas R. Hester, Harry J. Shafer, and Jack D. Eaton, 17–24. Studies in Archaeology 16. Austin: Texas Archeological Research Laboratory.

King, Eleanor M. 2000. "The Organization of Late Classic Lithic Production at the Prehistoric Maya Site of Colha, Belize: A Study in Complexity and Heterarchy." PhD diss., University of Pennsylvania, Philadelphia.

Kintz, Ellen. 1983. "Class Structure in a Classic Maya City." In *Coba: A Classic Maya Metropolis*, edited by William J. Folan, Ellen R. Kintz, and Laraine A. Fletcher, 161–77. New York: Academic Press.

Kohut, Betsy, Pedro C. Delgado Kú, Bárbara del C. Escamilla Ojeda, and Caroline Antonelli. 2012. "Taller I-57 en el área de Itzmal Ch'en." In *Proyecto Los Funda-mentos del Poder Económico de Mayapán, Temporadas 2008–2009: Informe final para el Consejo Nacional de Arqueología de México*, edited by Marilyn A. Masson, Carlos Peraza Lope, Timothy S. Hare, and Bradley W. Russell, 665–770. Albany, NY: University at Albany–SUNY; Mérida, México: Centro INAH Yucatán.

Koontz, Rex. 2002. "Terminal Classic Sacred Place and Factional Politics at El Tajin, Veracruz." In *Heart of Creation: The Mesoamerican World and the Legacy of Linda Schele*, edited by Andrea Stone, 101–17. Tuscaloosa: University of Alabama Press.

Kowalewski, Stephen A. 1990. "The Evolution of Complexity in the Valley of Oax-aca." *Annual Review of Anthropology* 19 (1): 39–58. http://dx.doi.org/10.1146/annurev .an.19.100190.000351.

Kowalski, Jeff Karl. 2003. "Evidence for the Functions and Meanings of Some Northern Maya Palaces." In *Maya Palaces and Elite Residences: An Interdisciplin-ary Approach*, edited by Jessica Joyce Christie, 204–52. Austin: University of Texas Press.

Kowalski, Jeff Karl. 2008. "What's 'Toltec' at Uxmal and Chichén Itzá? Merging Maya and Mesoamerican Worldviews and World Systems in Terminal Classic to Early Postclassic Yucatán." In *Twin Tollans: Chichén Itzá, Tula, and the Epiclassic to Early Postclassic Mesoamerican World*, edited by Jeff Karl Kowalski and Cynthia Kristan-Graham, 251–314. Washington, DC: Dumbarton Oaks.

Kristan-Graham, Cynthia. 2001. "A Sense of Place at Chichén Itzá." In *Landscape and Power in Ancient Mesoamerica*, edited by Rex Koontz, Kathryn Reese-Taylor, and Annabeth Headrick, 317–69. Boulder, CO: Westview Press.

Kurjack, Edward B. 1974. *Prehistoric Lowland Maya Community and Social Organization: A Case Study at Dzibilchaltún, Yucatán, Mexico.* Middle American Research Series Publication 38. New Orleans, LA: Tulane University.

Kvamme, Kenneth L. 1990. "Spatial Autocorrelation and the Classic Maya Collapse Revisited: Refined Techniques and New Conclusions." *Journal of Archaeological Science* 17 (2): 197–207. http://dx.doi.org/10.1016/0305-4403(90)90059-E.

Landa, Diego de. 1941. *Relación de las cosas de Yucatan.* Translated by Alfred Tozzer. Papers of the Peabody Museum of Archaeology and Ethnology 18. Cambridge, MA: Harvard University.

Lasalla, Gina. 2009. "Apéndice G, Lista de ornamentos y de estalactitas." In *Proyecto Los Fundamentos del Poder Económico de Mayapán, Temporada 2008: Informe preliminario para el Consejo Nacional de Arqueología de México*, edited by Marilyn A. Masson, Carlos Peraza Lope, and Timothy S. Hare. Department of Anthropology, Albany, NY: University at Albany–SUNY; Mérida, México: Centro INAH Yucatán.

Latimer, Jared R., and Pedro C. Delgado Kú. 2012. "Investigaciones en la Estructura H-11, una unidad habitacional en Itzmal Ch'en." In *Proyecto Los Fundamentos del Poder Económico de Mayapán, Temporadas 2008–2009: Informe final para el Consejo Nacional de Arqueología de México*, edited by Marilyn A. Masson, Carlos Peraza Lope, Timothy S. Hare, and Bradley W. Russell, 539–90. Albany, NY: University at Albany–SUNY; Mérida, México: Centro INAH Yucatán.

Le Plongeon, Augustus. 1882. *"Mayapan and Maya Inscriptions." Press of Chas Hamilton.* Worcester, MA.

Lee, Jay, and David W. S. Wong. 2001. *Statistical Analysis with ArcView GIS.* New York: John Wiley & Sons.

Lesure, Richard. 1999. "On the Genesis of Value in Early Hierarchical Societies." In *Material Symbols: Culture & Economy in Prehistory*, edited by John E. Robb, 23–55. Center for Archaeological Investigations Occasional Paper no. 26, Carbondale: Southern Illinois University.

Levi, Laura J. 2002. "An Institutional Perspective on Prehispanic Maya Residential Variation: Settlement and Community at San Estevan, Belize." *Journal of Anthropological Archaeology* 21 (2): 120–41. http://dx.doi.org/10.1006/jaar.2001.0394.

Leyden, Barbara W. 2002. "Pollen Evidence for Climatic Variability and Cultural Disturbance in the Maya Lowlands." *Ancient Mesoamerica* 13 (1): 85–101. http://dx.doi.org/10.1017/S0956536102131099.

Ligorred, Josep. 2009. "T'hó, una ciudad maya antigua bajo una ciudad maya moderna." *Revista del Instituto de Arqueología de la Facultad de Filosofía y Letras de la Universidad de Buenos Aires* 14: 137–72.

Liu, Li. 2006. "Urbanization in China: Erlitou and its Hinterland." In *Urbanism and the Preindustrial World: Cross-Cultural Approaches*, edited by Glenn R. Storey, 161–89. Tuscaloosa: University of Alabama Press.

Logan, Michael H., and William T. Sanders. 1976. "The Model." In *The Valley of Mexico: Studies in Pre-Hispanic Ecology and Society*, edited by Eric R. Wolf, 31–58. Albuquerque: University of New Mexico Press.

Lohse, John C., and Fred Valdez, Jr., eds. 2004. *Ancient Maya Commoners*. Austin: University of Texas Press.

Looper, Matthew G. 1991. "The Dances of Classic Maya Deities Chak and Hu Nal Ye." Master's thesis, University of Texas at Austin.

López Luján, Leonardo. 1998. "Recreating the Cosmos: Seventeen Aztec Dedication Caches." In *The Sowing and the Dawning: Termination, Dedication, and Transformation in the Archaeological and Ethnographic Record of Mesoamerica*, edited by Shirley Boteler Mock, 177–87. Albuquerque: University of New Mexico Press.

Love, Bruce. 1994. *The Paris Codex: Handbook for a Maya Priest*. Austin: University of Texas Press.

Luer, George M., David Allerton, Dan Hazeltine, Ron Hatfield, and Darden Hood. 1986. "Whelk Shell Tool Blanks from Big Mound Key (8Ch10), Charlotte County, Florida: With Notes on Certain Whelk Shell Tools." *Florida Anthropologist* 39:92–124.

Lynch, Kevin. 1960. *The Image of the City*. Cambridge, MA: MIT Press and Harvard University Press.

Mann, Charles. 2005. *1491: New Revelations of the Americas Before Columbus*. New York: Alfred A. Knopf.

Manzanilla, Linda. 1996. "Corporate Groups and Domestic Activities at Teotihuacan." *Latin American Antiquity* 7 (3): 228–46. http://dx.doi.org/10.2307/971576.

Manzanilla, Linda. 2003. "The Abandonment of Teotihuacan." In *The Archaeology of Settlement Abandonment in Middle America*, edited by Takeshi Inomata and Ronald W. Webb, 91–101. Salt Lake City: University of Utah Press.

Marcus, Joyce. 1983. "On the Nature of Mesoamerican City." In *Prehistoric Settlement Patterns: Essays in Honor Gordon R. Willey*, edited by Evon Z. Vogt and Richard M. Leventhal, 195–242. Albuquerque: University of New Mexico Press.

Marcus, Joyce. 1993. "Ancient Maya Political Organization." In *Lowland Maya Civilization in the Eighth Century A.D.*, edited by Jeremy A. Sabloff and John S. Henderson, 111–84. Washington, DC: Dumbarton Oaks.

Marcus, Joyce, and Jeremy A. Sabloff, eds. 2008. *The Ancient City: New Perspectives on Urbanism in the Old and New World*. Santa Fe, NM: School for Advanced Research Press.

Márquez Morfín, Lourdes, María Elena Peraza, José Gamboa, and Teresa Miranda. 1982. *Playa del Carmen: Una poblacíon de la costa oriental en el postclásico*. Coleccion Cientifica 119. Mexico, D.F.: Instituto Nacional de Antropologia e Historia.

Marquina, Ignacio. 1960. *El Templo Mayor de México*. México, D.F.: Instituto Nacional de Antropología e Historia.

Martin, Simon, and Nikolai Grube. 2008. *Chronicle of the Maya Kings and Queens: Deciphering the Dynasties of the Ancient Maya*. 2nd ed. New York: Thames & Hudson.

Martyr de Anglería, Peter. [1892] 1944. *Decadas del Nuevo Mundo*. Translated by Joaquin Torres Asensio. Reprint, Buenos Aires: Bajel.

Massey, Virginia, and D. Gentry Steele. 2006. "A Maya Skull Pit from the Terminal Classic Period, Colha, Belize." In *Bones of the Maya: Studies of Ancient Skeletons*, edited by Stephen L. Whittington and David M. Reed, 62–77. Tuscaloosa: University of Alabama Press.

Masson, Marilyn A. 1988. "Shell Celt Morphology and Reduction: An Analogy to Lithic Research." *Florida Anthropologist* 41 (3): 313–35.

Masson, Marilyn A. 1993. "Changes in Maya Community Organization from the Classic to Postclassic Periods: A View from Laguna de On, Belize." PhD diss., University of Texas at Austin.

Masson, Marilyn A. 1999a. "Animal Resource Manipulation in Ritual and Domestic Contexts at Postclassic Maya Communities." *World Archaeology* 31 (1): 93–120. http://dx.doi.org/10.1080/00438243.1999.9980434.

Masson, Marilyn A. 1999b. "Postclassic Maya Ritual at Laguna de On Island, Belize." *Ancient Mesoamerica* 10 (01): 51–68. http://dx.doi.org/10.1017/S0956536199101068.

Masson, Marilyn A. 2000. *In the Realm of Nachan Kan: Postclassic Maya Archaeology at Laguna de On, Belize*. Boulder: University Press of Colorado.

Masson, Marilyn A. 2001a. "Segmentary Political Cycles and Elite Migration Myths in the Postclassic Archaeology of Northern Belize." In *The Past and Present Maya: Essays in Honor of Robert M. Carmack*, edited by John M. Weeks, 89–106. Lancaster, CA: Labyrinthos.

Masson, Marilyn A. 2001b. "Changing Patterns of Ceramic Stylistic Diversity in the Pre-Hispanic Maya Lowlands." *Acta Archaeologica* 72 (2): 159–88. http://dx.doi.org/10.1034/j.1600-0390.2001.720207.x.

Masson, Marilyn A. 2001c. "The Economic Organization of Late and Terminal Classic Period Maya Stone Tool Craft Specialist Workshops at Colha, Belize." *Lithic Technology* 26: 29–49.

Masson, Marilyn A. 2002. "Introduction." In *Ancient Maya Political Economies*, edited by Marilyn A. Masson and David A. Freidel, 1–30. Walnut Creek, CA: AltaMira.

Masson, Marilyn A. 2003a. "The Late Postclassic Symbol Set in the Maya Area." In *The Postclassic Mesoamerican World*, edited by Michael E. Smith and Frances F. Berdan, 194–200. Salt Lake City: University of Utah Press.

Masson, Marilyn A. 2003b. "Laguna de On and Caye Coco: Postclassic Political and Economic Scales of Integration at Two Island Communities in Northern Belize." In *The Social Implications of Ancient Maya Rural Complexity*, edited by Gyles Iannone and Samuel V. Connell, 119–30. Cotsen Institute of Archaeology Monograph 49. Los Angeles: University of California, Los Angeles.

Masson, Marilyn A. 2004. "Fauna Exploitation from the Preclassic to the Postclassic Periods at Four Maya Settlements in Northern Belize." In *Maya Zooarchaeology: New Directions in Method and Theory*, edited by Kitty F. Emery, 97–124. Cotsen Institute of Archaeology Monograph 51. Los Angeles: University of California, Los Angeles.

Masson, Marilyn A. 2009. "Appendix: Inventory and Lot Descriptions from Carnegie Institution *Current Reports* on Mayapán." In *The Carnegie Maya II: Carnegie Institution of Washington* Current Reports, *1952–1957*, edited by John M. Weeks, 553–609. Boulder: University Press of Colorado.

Masson, Marilyn A. 2012. "Maya Collapse Cycles." *Proceedings of the National Academy of Sciences of the United States of America* 109 (45): 18237–8. http://dx.doi.org/10.1073/pnas.1213638109.

Masson, Marilyn A., and Henry Chaya. 2000. "Obsidian Trade Connections at the Postclassic Maya Site of Laguna de On, Belize." *Lithic Technology* 25: 135–44.

Masson, Marilyn A., Antonina M. Delu, and Carlos Peraza Lope. 2008. "Exploración de superficie en milpas y distribución de artefactos en Mayapán." In *Proyecto Los Fundamentos del Poder Económico de Mayapán, Temporadas 2001–2004: Informe final para el Consejo Nacional de Arqueología de México*, edited by Marilyn A. Masson, Carlos Peraza Lope, and Timothy S. Hare, 425–86. Albany, NY: University at Albany–SUNY, Mérida, México: Centro INAH Yucatán.

Masson, Marilyn A., Antonina M. Delu, Carlos Peraza Lope, and Clifford T. Brown. 2008. "Excavaciones de prueba en milpas de Mayapán." In *Proyecto Los Fundamentos del Poder Económico de Mayapán, Temporadas 2001–2004: Informe final para el Consejo Nacional de Arqueología de México*, edited by Marilyn A. Masson, Carlos Peraza Lope, and Timothy S. Hare, 273–424. Albany, NY: University at Albany–SUNY, Mérida, México: Centro INAH Yucatán.

Masson, Marilyn A., and David A. Freidel, eds. 2002. *Ancient Maya Political Economies*. Walnut Creek, CA: AltaMira.

Masson, Marilyn A., and David A. Freidel. 2012. "An Argument for Classic Era Maya Market Exchange." *Journal of Anthropological Archaeology* 31 (4): 455–84. http://dx.doi.org/10.1016/j.jaa.2012.03.007.

Masson, Marilyn A., and David A. Freidel. 2013. "Wide Open Spaces: A Long View of the Importance of Maya Market Exchange." In *Merchants, Trade and Exchange in the Pre-Columbian World*, edited by Kenneth G. Hirth and Joanne Pilsbury, 201–8. Washington, DC: Dumbarton Oaks.

Masson, Marilyn A., Timothy S. Hare, and Carlos Peraza Lope. 2006. "Postclassic Maya Society Regenerated at Mayapán." In *After Collapse: The Regeneration of Complex Societies*, edited by Glenn M. Schwartz and John J. Nichols, 188–207. Tucson: University of Arizona Press.

Masson, Marilyn A., and Shirley B. Mock. 2004. "Maya Cultural Adaptations from the Terminal Classic to Postclassic Period at Lagoon Sites in Northern Belize as Reflected in Changing Ceramic Industries." In *The Terminal Classic in the Maya Lowlands: Collapse, Transition, and Transformation*, edited by Arthur A. Demarest, Prudence M. Rice, and Don S. Rice, 367–401. Boulder: University Press of Colorado.

Masson, Marilyn A., and Carlos Peraza Lope. 2004. "A New Look at Household and Administrative Facilities at the Postclassic Maya City of Mayapán." Paper presented at the 69th Annual Meeting of the Society for American Archaeology Meetings, Montreal, Canada, March 31–April 4.

Masson, Marilyn A., and Carlos Peraza Lope. 2005. "Nuevas investigaciones en tres unidades residenciales fuera del area monumental de Mayapán." In *Investigadores de la Cultura Maya*, 2: 411–24. Campeche, México: Universidad Autónoma de Campeche.

Masson, Marilyn A., and Carlos Peraza Lope. 2007. "Kukulkan/Quetzalcoatl, Death God, and Creation Mythology of Burial Shaft Temples at Mayapán." *Mexicon* 29: 77–85.

Masson, Marilyn A., and Carlos Peraza Lope. 2008. "Animal Use at the Postclassic Maya Center of Mayapán." *Quaternary International* 191 (1): 170–83. http://dx.doi.org/10.1016/j.quaint.2008.02.002.

Masson, Marilyn A., and Carlos Peraza Lope. 2010. "Evidence for Maya-Mexican Interaction in the Archaeological Record of Mayapán." In *Astronomers, Scribes, and Priests: Intellectual Interchange between the Northern Maya Lowlands and Highland Mexico in the Late Postclassic Period*, edited by Gabrielle Vail and Christine Hernandez, 77–114. Washington, DC: Dumbarton Oaks.

Masson, Marilyn A., and Carlos Peraza Lope. 2012. "Figurillas y Diversidad Social en Mayapán." In *Localidad y Globalidad en el Mundo Maya Prehispánico e Indígena Contemporáneo: Estudios de Espacio y Genero*, edited by Judith Gallegos Gómora and Julia Ann Hendon, 119–38. Mexico, D.F.: Instituto Nacional de Antropología e Historia.

Masson, Marilyn A., and Carlos Peraza Lope. 2013. "The Distribution and Diversity of Faunal Exploitation at Mayapán: From Temple to Houselot." In *The Archaeology of Mesoamerican Animals*, edited by Christopher M. Götz and Kitty F. Emery, 233–80. Cambridge, MA: Cambridge Scholars Press.

Masson, Marilyn A., Carlos Peraza Lope, and Timothy S. Hare. 2008. *Proyecto Los Fundamentos del Poder Económico de Mayapán: Informe final de las Temporada 2001–2004 para el Consejo Nacional de Arquelogía.* D.F., México: Instituto Nacional de Antropología e Historia.

Masson, Marilyn A., Carlos Peraza Lope, Timothy S. Hare, and Bradley W. Russell. 2012. *Proyecto Los Fundamentos del Poder Económico de Mayapán: Informe final de las Temporada 2008–2009 para el Consejo Nacional de Arquelogía de México.* D.F., México: Instituto Nacional de Antropología e Historia.

Masson, Marilyn A., and Bárbara Escamilla Ojeda. 2012. "Análisis de Herramientas de Lítica, Temporadas 2008–2009." In *Proyecto Los Fundamentos del Poder Económico de Mayapán, Temporadas 2008–2009, Informe final para el Consejo Nacional de Arqueología de México*, edited by Marilyn A. Masson, Carlos Peraza Lope, Timothy S. Hare, and Bradley W. Russell, 1213–44. Albany, NY: University at Albany–SUNY; Mérida, Mexico: Centro INAH Yucatán.

Masson, Marilyn A., Bárbara Escamilla Ojeda, Miguel Delgado Kú, and Laura Tycz. 2008. "Análisis de la obsidiana." In *Proyecto Los Fundamentos del Poder Económico de Mayapán, Temporadas 2001–2004: Informe final para el Consejo Nacional de Arqueología de México*, edited by Marilyn A. Masson, Carlos Peraza Lope, and Timothy S. Hare, 647–60. Albany, NY: University at Albany–SUNY; Mérida, Mexico: Centro INAH Yucatán.

Masson, Marilyn A., Bárbara Escamilla Ojeda, and Carlos Peraza Lope. 2008. "Herramientas de pedernal, calcedonia y piedra verde." In *Proyecto Los Fundamentos del Poder Económico de Mayapán, Temporadas 2001–2004: Informe final para el Consejo Nacional de Arqueología de México*, edited by Marilyn A. Masson, Carlos Peraza Lope, and Timothy S. Hare, 661–89. Albany, NY: University at Albany–SUNY; Mérida, Mexico: Centro INAH Yucatán.

Masson, Marilyn A., and Robert M. Rosenswig. 2005. "Production Characteristics of Postclassic Maya Pottery from Caye Coco, Northern Belize." *Latin American Antiquity* 16 (4): 355–84. http://dx.doi.org/10.2307/30042505.

Mastache, Alba Guadalupe, Robert H. Cobean, and Dan M. Healan. 2002. *Ancient Tollan: Tula and the Toltec Heartland.* Boulder: University Press of Colorado.

McAnany, Patricia A. 1989. "Stone-Tool Production and Exchange in the Eastern Maya Lowlands: The Consumer Perspective from Pulltrouser Swamp, Belize." *American Antiquity* 54 (2): 332–46. http://dx.doi.org/10.2307/281710.

McAnany, Patricia A. 1994. "Operation 2033: Horizontal Exposure of a Terminal Classic Platform." In *Continuing Archaeology at Colha, Belize,* edited by Thomas R. Hester, Harry J. Shafer, and Jack D. Eaton, 79–89. Austin: Texas Archeological Research Laboratory, University of Texas.

McAnany, Patricia A. 1995. *Living with the Ancestors: Kinship and Kingship in Ancient Maya Society.* Austin: University of Texas Press.

McAnany, Patricia A. 2004. *K'axob: Ritual, Work, and Family in an Ancient Maya Village.* Los Angeles: Cotsen Institute of Archaeology, University of California, Los Angeles.

McAnany, Patricia A. 2010. *Ancestral Maya Economies in Archaeological Perspective.* Cambridge: Cambridge University Press.

McAnany, Patricia A., and E. Christian Wells. 2008. "Toward a Theory of Ritual Economy." In *Dimensions of Ritual Economy.* Research in Economic Anthropology, vol. 27, edited by E. Christian Wells and Patricia A. McAnany, 1–16. Bingley, UK: Emerald Group. http://dx.doi.org/10.1016/S0190-1281(08)00001-2.

McGuire, Randall H. 1983. "Breaking Down Cultural Complexity: Inequality and Heterogeneity." In *Advances in Archaeological Method and Theory,* vol. 6, edited by Michael Schiffer, 91–142. New York: Academic Press.

McKillop, Heather. 1996. "Ancient Maya Trading Ports and the Integration of Long-Distance and Regional Economies: Wild Cane Cay in South-Coastal Belize." *Ancient Mesoamerica* 7 (1): 49–62. http://dx.doi.org/10.1017/S0956536100001280.

Meggers, Betty J. 1954. "Environmental Limitation on the Development of Culture." *American Anthropologist* 56 (5): 801–24. http://dx.doi.org/10.1525/aa.1954.56.5.02a00060.

Meskell, Lynn. 1999. *Archaeologies of Social Life: Age, Sex, Class Etcetera in Ancient Egypt.* Oxford: Blackwell Press.

Michaels, George H. 1987. "A Description of Early Postclassic Lithic Technology at Colha, Belize." Master's thesis, Texas A&M University.

Milbrath, Susan, and Carolos Peraza Lope. 2009. "Survival and Revival of Terminal Classic Traditions at Postclassic Mayapán." *Latin American Antiquity* 20 (4): 581–606.

Milbrath, Susan, James Aimers, Carlos Peraza Lope, and Lynda Florey Folan. 2008. "Effigy Censers of the Chen Mul Modeled Ceramic System and Their Implications for Late Postclassic Maya Interregional Interaction." *Mexicon* 30 (5): 104–12.

Milbrath, Susan, and Carlos Peraza Lope. 2003a. "Revisiting Mayapan: Mexico's Last Maya Capital." *Ancient Mesoamerica* 14 (1): 1–46. http://dx.doi.org/10.1017/S0956536103132178.

Milbrath, Susan, and Carlos Peraza Lope. 2003b. "Mayapán's Scribe: A Link with Classic Maya Artists." *Mexicon* 25: 120–23.

Milbrath, Susan, and Carlos Peraza Lope. 2009. "Clash of Worldviews in Late May-apán." In *Maya Worldviews at Conquest*, edited by Leslie G. Cecil and Timothy W. Pugh, 183–204. Boulder: University Press of Colorado.

Milbrath, Susan, and Carlos Peraza Lope. 2013. "Mayapán's Chen Mul Modeled Effigy Censers: Iconography and Archaeological Context." In *Ancient Maya Pottery: Classification, Analysis, and Interpretation*, edited by James John Aimers, 203–28. Gainesville: University Press of Florida. http://dx.doi.org/10.5744 /florida/9780813042367.003.0012.

Milbrath, Susan, Carlos Peraza Lope, and Miguel Delgado Kú. 2010. "Religious Imagery in Mayapan's Murals." *PARI Journal* 10 (3): 1–10.

Miller, Arthur G. 1982. *On the Edge of the Sea: Mural Painting at Tancah-Tulum, Quintana Roo, Mexico*. Washington, DC: Dumbarton Oaks,.

Miller, Mary. 2000. "Understanding the Murals of Bonampak." In *Maya: Divine Kings of the Rainforest*, edited by Nikolai Grube, 235–43. Cologne, Germany: Konemann.

Miller, Mary, and Karl Taube. 1993. *An Illustrated Dictionary of the Gods and Symbols of Ancient Mexico and the Maya*. New York: Thames & Hudson.

Millon, René. 1976. "Social Relations in Ancient Teotihuacan." In *The Valley of Mexico: Studies in Pre-Hispanic Ecology and Society*, edited by Eric R. Wolf, 205–48. Albuquerque: University of New Mexico Press.

Millon, René. 1981. "Teotihuacan: City, State, and Civilization." In *Supplement to the Handbook of Middle American Indians*, vol. 1, *Archaeology*, edited by Jeremy A. Sabloff, 198–243. Austin: University of Texas Press.

Mock, Shirley B. 1994. *The Northern River Lagoon Site (NRL): Late to Terminal Classic Maya Settlement, Saltmaking, and Survival on the Northern Belize Coast*. PhD diss., University of Texas at Austin.

Mock, Shirley B., ed. 1998. *The Sowing and the Dawning: Termination and Dedication Processes in the Archaeological and Ethnographic Record of Mesoamerica*. Albuquerque: University of New Mexico Press.

Moholy-Nagy, Hattula. 1997. "Middens, Construction Fill, and Offerings: Evidence for the Organization of Classic Period Craft Production at Tikal, Guatemala." *Journal of Field Archaeology* 24 (3): 293–313.

Moholy-Nagy, Hattula. 2003. "Beyond the Catalog: The Chronology and Contexts of Tikal Artifacts." In *Tikal: Dynasties, Foreigners, & Affairs of State*, edited by Jeremy A. Sabloff, 83–110. Santa Fe, NM: School for Advanced Research Press.

Moholy-Nagy, Hattula. 2008. *The Artifacts of Tikal: Ornamental and Ceremonial Artifacts and Unworked Material*. Tikal Report 27A. Philadelphia: University of Pennsylvania Museum of Archaeology and Anthropology.

Moore, Jerry D. 2005. *Cultural Landscapes in the Ancient Andes: Archaeologies of Place*. Gainesville: University Press of Florida.

Nagao, Debra. 1989. "Public Proclamation in the Art of Cacaxtla and Xochicalco." In *Mesoamerica after the Decline of Teotihuacan, A.D. 700–900*, edited by Richard A. Diehl and Janet C. Berlo, 83–104. Washington, DC: Dumbarton Oaks.

Nichols, Deborah, and Thomas H. Charleton, eds. 1997. *The Archaeology of City-States: Cross-Cultural Approaches*. Washington, DC: Smithsonian Institution Press.

Novic, Juliana. 2008. "La clasificación de huesos modificados en Mayapán." In *Proyecto Los Fundamentos del Poder Económico de Mayapán, Temporadas 2001–2004: Informe final para el Consejo Nacional de Arqueología de México*, edited by Marilyn A. Masson, Carlos Peraza Lope, and Timothy S. Hare, 727–48. Albany, NY: University at Albany–SUNY; Mérida, México: Centro INAH Yucatán.

Nuttall, Zelia, ed. 1975. *The Codex Nuttall: A Picture Manuscript from Ancient Mexico*. New York: Dover.

Okoshi-Harada, Tsubasa. 2012. "Postclassic Maya 'Barrios' in Yucatán: An Historical Approach." In *The Neighborhood as a Social and Spatial Unit in Mesoamerican Cities*, edited by M. Charlotte Arnauld, Linda R. Manzanilla, and Michael E. Smith, 286–303. Tucson: University of Arizona Press.

Oland, Maxine. 2009. "Long-Term Indigenous History on a Colonial Frontier: Archaeology at a 15th–17th Century Maya Village, Progresso Lagoon, Belize." PhD diss., Northwestern University.

Olivier, Guilhem. 2003. *Mockeries and Metamorphoses of an Aztec God: Tezcatlipoca, "Lord of the Smoking Mirror"*. Translated by Michael Bisson. Boulder: University Press of Colorado.

Orr, Heather S. 2003. "Stone Balls and Masked Men: Ballgame as Combat Ritual, Dainzú, Oaxaca." *Ancient Mesoamerica* 5: 73–104.

Oudijk, Michael. 2002. "The Zapotec City-State." In *A Comparative Study of Six City-State Cultures*, edited by Mogens Herman Hansen, 73–90. Historisk-filosofiske Skrifter 27. Copenhagen: Royal Danish Academy of Sciences and Letters.

Paine, Richard R., and Glenn R. Storey. 2006. "Epidemics, Age at Death, and Mortality in Ancient Rome." In *Urbanism and the Preindustrial World: Cross-Cultural Approaches*, edited by Glenn R. Storey, 69–85. Tuscaloosa: University of Alabama Press.

Palka, Joel W. 2003. "Social Status and Differential Processes of Abandonment at the Classic Maya Center of Dos Pilas, Peten, Guatemala." In *The Archaeology of Settlement Abandonment in Middle America*, edited by Takeshi Inomata and Ronald W. Webb, 121–34. Salt Lake City: University of Utah Press.

Paris, Elizabeth H. 2008. "Metallurgy, Mayapan, and the Postclassic Mesoamerican World System." *Ancient Mesoamerica* 19 (1): 43–66. http://dx.doi.org/10.1017/S0956536108000291.

Paris, Elizabeth H. 2012. "Political Economy on the Postclassic Western Maya Frontier." PhD diss., University at Albany–SUNY.

Paris, Elizabeth H., and Wilberth A. Cruz Alvarado. 2012. "Análisis de Artefactos de Metal—Temporadas 2008–2009." In *Proyecto Los Fundamentos del Poder Económico de Mayapán, Temporadas 2008–2009: Informe final para el Consejo Nacional de Arqueología de México*, edited by Marilyn A. Masson, Carlos Peraza Lope, Timothy S. Hare, and Bradley W. Russell, 1265–96. Albany, NY: University at Albany–SUNY; Mérida, México: Centro INAH Yucatán.

Paris, Elizabeth H., and Bradley W. Russell. 2012. "Zona de Entierros Itzmal Ch'en." In *Proyecto Los Fundamentos del Poder Económico de Mayapán, Temporada 2008: Informe final para el Consejo Nacional de Arqueología de México*, edited by Marilyn A. Masson, Carlos Peraza Lope, Timothy S. Hare, and Bradley W. Russell, 71–236. Albany, NY: University at Albany–SUNY; Mérida, México: Centro INAH Yucatán.

Paso y Troncoso, Francisco del. 1939–1942. "Tasaciones de los pueblos (febrero de 1549)." In *Epistolario de Nueva España, 1505–1818*, vol. 5, 103–181 and vol. 6, 73–112. México, D.F.: Antigua Librería Robredo de José Porrúa e Hijos.

Paxton, Merideth. 2001. *The Cosmos of the Yucatec Maya: Cycles and Steps from the Madrid Codex*. Albuquerque: University of New Mexico Press.

Pendergast, David A. 1986. "Stability through Change: Lamanai, Belize, from the Ninth to the Seventeenth Century." In *Late Lowland Maya Civilization: Classic to Postclassic*, edited by Jeremy A. Sabloff and E. Wyllys Andrews V, 223–50. Albuquerque: University of New Mexico Press.

Pendergast, David A. 1993. "Worlds in Collision: The Maya/Spanish Encounter in Sixteenth and Seventeenth Century Belize." *Proceedings of the British Academy* 81:105–43.

Peraza Lope, Carlos Alberto. 1993. "*Estudio y secuencia del material cerámico de San Gervasio, Cozumel*." Tésis profesional, Universidad Autónoma de Yucatán.

Peraza Lope, Carlos. 1999. "Mayapán: Ciudad-Capital del Postclásico." *Arqueología Mexicana* 7 (37):48–53.

Peraza Lope, Carlos. 2005. "Ceramic Analyses and Sequence from San Gervasio, Cozumel." In *Quintana Roo Archaeology*, edited by Justine M. Shaw and Jennifer P. Mathews, 77–86. Tucson: University of Arizona Press.

Peraza Lope, Carlos, Pedro Delgado Kú, and Bárbara Escamilla Ojeda. 2002. "Trabajos de mantenimiento y conservacíon arquitectónica en Mayapán, Yucatán:

Informe de la tercera temporada 1998, tomo 1." In *Informe de actividades al Consejo de Arqueología del Instituto Nacional de Antropología e Historia*. Mérida, México: Centro INAH Yucatán.

Peraza Lope, Carlos, Pedro Delgado Kú, and Bárbara Escamilla Ojeda. 2003. "Trabajos de mantenimiento y conservación arquitectónica en Mayapán, Yucatán: Informe de la cuarta temporada 1999–2000." In *Informe de actividades al Consejo de Arqueología del Instituto Nacional de Antropología e Historia*. Mérida, México: Centro INAH Yucatán.

Peraza Lope, Carlos, Pedro Delgado Kú, Bárbara Escamilla Ojeda, and Mario Garrido Euán. 1999a. "Trabajos de mantenimiento y conservación arquitectónica en Mayapán, Yucatán: Informe de la temporada 1998." In *Informe de actividades al Consejo de Arqueología del Instituto Nacional de Antropología e Historia*. Mérida, México: Centro INAH Yucatán.

Peraza Lope, Carlos, Pedro Delgado Kú, Bárbara Escamilla Ojeda, and Mario Garrido Euán. 1999b. "Trabajos de mantenimiento y conservación arquitectónica en Mayapán, Yucatán: Informe de la segunda temporada 1997, tomo 1." In *Informe de actividades al Consejo de Arqueología del Instituto Nacional de Antropología e Historia*. Mérida, México: Centro INAH Yucatán.

Peraza Lope, Carlos, Pedro Delgado Kú, Bárbara Escamilla Ojeda, and Mario Garrido Euán. 1999c. "Trabajos de mantenimiento y conservación arquitectónica en Mayapán, Yucatán: Informe de la segunda temporada 1997, tomo 4." In *Informe de actividades al Consejo de Arqueología del Instituto Nacional de Antropología e Historia*. Mérida, México: Centro INAH Yucatán.

Peraza Lope, Carlos, Pedro Candelario Delgado Kú, Barbara Escamilla Ojeda, and Miguel Delgado Kú. 2003. "Trabajos de mantenimiento y conservación arquitectónica en Mayapán, Yucatán: Informe de la temporada 2001 y 2002, tomo 1." In *Informe de actividades al Consejo de Arqueología del Instituto Nacional de Antropología e Historia*. Mérida, México: Centro INAH Yucatán.

Peraza Lope, Carlos, Juvencia Escarela Rodríguez, and Pedro Delgado Kú. 2004. "Trabajos de mantenimiento y conservación arquitectónica en Mayapán, Yucatán: Informe de la temporada 2003, tomo 1." In *Informe de actividades al Consejo de Arqueología del Instituto Nacional de Antropología e Historia*. Mérida, México: Centro INAH Yucatán.

Peraza Lope, Carlos, Mario Garrido Euán, Pedro Delgado Kú, Bárbara Escamilla Ojeda, Mirza Lira Chim, and César García Ayala. 1997. "Trabajos de mantenimiento y conservación arquitectónica en Mayapán, Yucatán: Informe de la temporada 1996." In *Informe de actividades al Consejo de Arqueología del Instituto Nacional de Antropología e Historia*. Mérida, México: Centro INAH Yucatán.

Peraza Lope, Carlos, Marilyn A. Masson, Wilberth Cruz Alvarado, Luis Flores Cobá, and Timothy S. Hare. 2008. "Céramica." In *Proyecto Los Fundamentos del Poder Económico de Mayapán, Temporadas 2001–2004: Informe final para el Consejo Nacional de Arqueología de México*, edited by Marilyn A. Masson, Carlos Peraza Lope, and Timothy S. Hare, 749–864. Albany, NY: University at Albany–SUNY; Mérida, México: Centro INAH Yucatán.

Peraza Lope, Carlos, and Marilyn A. Masson, and Georgina Delgado Sánchez. 2008. "Investigación y restauración de la Estructura Y-45a." In *Proyecto Los Fundamentos del Poder Económico de Mayapán, Temporadas 2001–2004: Informe final para el Consejo Nacional de Arqueología de México*, edited by Marilyn A. Masson, Carlos Peraza Lope, and Timothy S. Hare, 487–572. Albany, NY: University at Albany–SUNY; Mérida, México: Centro INAH Yucatán.

Peraza Lope, Carlos, Marilyn A. Masson, Timothy S Hare, and Pedro Candelario Delgado Kú. 2006. "The Chronology of Mayapán: New Radiocarbon Evidence." *Ancient Mesoamerica* 17 (2): 153–75. http://dx.doi.org/10.1017/S0956536106060135.

Phillips, David A., Jr. 1979. *Material Culture and Trade of the Postclassic Maya*. PhD diss., University of Arizona. University Microfilms, Ann Arbor.

Piña Chan, Román. 1978. "Commerce in the Yucatec Peninsula: The Conquest and Colonial Period." In *Mesoamerican Communication Routes and Culture Contacts*, edited by Thomas A. Lee and Carlos Navarrete, 37–48. Papers of the New World Archaeological Foundation no. 40. Provo, UT: Brigham Young University.

Pirenne, Henri. [1925] 1969. *Medieval Cities: Their Origins and the Revival of Trade*. Princeton, NJ: Princeton University Press. Reprint, Princeton, NJ: Princeton University Press.

Pohl, John M. D. 1999. "The Lintel Paintings of Mitla and the Function of the Mitla Palaces." In *Mesoamerican Architecture as a Cultural Symbol*, edited by Jeff K. Kowalski, 177–97. New York: Oxford University Press.

Pohl, John M. D. 2003a. "Ritual Ideology and Commerce in the Southern Mexican Highlands." In *The Postclassic Mesoamerican World*, edited by Michael E. Smith and Frances F. Berdan, 172–77. Salt Lake City: University of Utah Press.

Pohl, John M. D. 2003b. "Creation Stories, Hero Cults, and Alliance Building: Confederacies of Central and Southern Mexico from A.D. 1150–1458." In *The Postclassic Mesoamerican World*, edited by Michael E. Smith and Frances F. Berdan, 61–66. Salt Lake City: University of Utah Press.

Pohl, John M. D., and Charles M. Robinson. 2005. *Aztecs and Conquistadores: The Spanish Invasion and the Collapse of the Aztec Empire*. Oxford: Osprey.

Pohl, Mary. 1981. "Ritual Continuity and Transformation in Mesoamerica: Reconstructing the Ancient Maya Cuch Ritual." *American Antiquity* 46 (3): 513–29. http://dx.doi.org/10.2307/280598.

Pohl, Mary. 1985a. "Osteological Evidence for Subsistence and Status." In *Prehistoric Lowland Maya Environment and Subsistence Economy*, vol. 77, edited by Mary D. Pohl, 109–13. Cambridge, MA: Peabody Museum of Archaeology and Ethnology.

Pohl, Mary. 1985b. "The Privileges of Maya Elites: Prehistoric Vertebrate Fauna from Seibal." In *Prehistoric Lowland Maya Environment and Subsistence Economy*, vol. 77, edited by Mary D. Pohl, 133–45. Cambridge, MA: Peabody Museum of Archaeology and Ethnology.

Pohl, Mary. 1990. "The Ethnozoology of the Maya: Faunal Remains from Five Sites in Peten, Guatemala." In *Excavations at Seibal, Department of Peten, Guatemala*, vol. 17, no. 3, edited by Gordon R. Willey, 142–74. Cambridge, MA: Harvard University Press.

Pollock, Harry E. D. 1936. *Round Structures of Aboriginal Middle America.* Carnegie Institution of Washington Publication 471. Washington, DC: Carnegie Institution.

Pollock, Harry E. D. 1951. *Carnegie Institution of Washington Year Book* 50: 221–29.

Pollock, Harry E.D. 1954. *Carnegie Institution of Washington Year Book* 53: 263–67.

Pollock, Harry E. D. 1956. "The Southern Terminus of the Principal Sacbe at Mayapán—Group Z-50." *Current Reports* 37: 529–50. Washington, DC: Carnegie Institution of Washington.

Pollock, Harry E. D. 1962. "Introduction." In *Mayapan, Yucatan, Mexico*, by Harry E. D. Pollock, Ralph L. Roys, Tatiana Proskouriakoff, and A. Ledyard Smith, 1–24. Washington, DC: Carnegie Institution of Washington Publication 619. Washington, DC: Carnegie Institution.

Pollock, Harry E. D., and Clayton E. Ray. 1957. "Notes on Vertebrate Animal Remains from Mayapán." *Current Reports* 41: 633–56. Washington, DC: Carnegie Institution of Washington.

Pollock, Harry E. D., Ralph L. Roys, Tatiana Proskouriakoff, and A. Ledyard Smith. 1962. *Mayapan, Yucatan, Mexico.* Carnegie Institution of Washington Publication 619. Washington, DC: Carnegie Institution.

Potter, Daniel R., and Eleanor M. King. 1995. "A Heterarchical Approach to Lowland Maya Socioeconomies." In *Heterarchy and the Analysis of Complex Societies*, edited by Robert M. Ehrenreich, Carole L. Crumley, and Janet E. Levy, 17–32. Washington, DC: Archeological Papers of the American Anthropological Association no. 6. http://dx.doi.org/10.1525/ap3a.1995.6.1.17.

Pounds, Norman J. G. 1973. *An Historical Geography of Europe: 450 B.C.–A.D. 1330.* Cambridge: Cambridge University Press. http://dx.doi.org/10.1017/CBO9781139163552.

Proskouriakoff, Tatiana. 1953. "Artifacts of Mayapan." *Carnegie Institution of Washington Year Book* 52: 281–83.

Proskouriakoff, Tatiana. 1955. "The Death of a Civilization." *Scientific American* 192 (5): 82–87. http://dx.doi.org/10.1038/scientificamerican0555-82.

Proskouriakoff, Tatiana. 1956. "Artifacts of Mayapan." *Carnegie Institution of Washington Year Book* 1955–1956: 339–41.

Proskouriakoff, Tatiana. 1962a. "Civic and Religious Structures of Mayapan." In *Mayapan, Yucatan, Mexico*, edited by Harry E. D. Pollock, Ralph L. Roys, Tatiana Proskouriakoff, and A. Ledyard Smith, 87–164. Carnegie Institution of Washington Publication 619. Washington, DC: Carnegie Institution.

Proskouriakoff, Tatiana. 1962b. "The Artifacts of Mayapan." In *Mayapan, Yucatan, Mexico*, edited by Harry E. D. Pollock, Ralph L. Roys, Tatiana Proskouriakoff, and A. Ledyard Smith, 321–515. Carnegie Institution of Washington Publication 619. Washington, DC: Carnegie Institution.

Proskouriakoff, Tatiana, and Charles R. Temple. 1955. "A Residential Quadrangle— Structures R-85 to R-90." *Current Reports* 29: 289–362. Washington, DC: Carnegie Institution of Washington.

Pugh, Timothy W. 2001. "Flood Reptiles, Serpent Temples, and the Quadripartite Universe: The *Imago Mundi* of Late Postclassic Mayapan." *Ancient Mesoamerica* 12 (2): 247–58. http://dx.doi.org/10.1017/S0956536101122042.

Pugh, Timothy W. 2002. "Remembering Mayapán: Kowoj Domestic Architecture as Social Metaphor and Power." In *The Dynamics of Power*, edited by Maria O'Donovan, 301–323. Center for Archaeological Investigations Occasional Paper no. 30, Carbondale: Southern Illinois University.

Pugh, Timothy W. 2003. "The Exemplary Center of the Late Postclassic Kowoj Maya." *Latin American Antiquity* 14 (4): 408–30. http://dx.doi.org/10.2307/3557576.

Pugh, Timothy W. 2009. "Residential and Domestic Contexts at Zacpeten." In *The Kowoj: Identity, Migration, and Geopolitics in Late Postclassic Petén, Guatemala*, edited by Prudence M. Rice and Don S. Rice, 173–91. Boulder: University Press of Colorado.

Pugh, Timothy W., and Prudence M. Rice. 1997. "Arquitectura estilo Mayapán y evidencias de organización dual en el sitio Postclásico de Zacpetén, Petén, Guatemala." In *X simposio de arqueología Guatemalteca*, edited by Juan Pedro Laporte and Hector Escobedo, 521–28. Guatemala City: Instituto de Antropología e Historia, Ministerio de Cultura y Deportes, y la Asociación Tikal.

Pugh, Timothy W., and Prudence M. Rice. 2009a. "Zacpeten and the Kowoj: Field Methods and Chronlogies." In *The Kowoj: Identity, Migration, and Geopolitics in Late Postclassic Petén, Guatemala*, edited by Prudence M. Rice and Don S. Rice, 85–122. Boulder: University Press of Colorado.

Pugh, Timothy W., and Prudence M. Rice. 2009b. "Kowoj Ritual Performance and Societal Representations at Zacpeten." In *The Kowoj: Identity, Migration, and Geopolitics in Late Postclassic Petén, Guatemala*, edited by Prudence M. Rice and Don S. Rice, 141–72. Boulder: University Press of Colorado.

Pugh, Timothy W., Prudence M. Rice, and Leslie G. Cecil. 2009. "Zacpeten Group 719, the Last Noble Residence." In *The Kowoj: Identity, Migration, and Geopolitics in Late Postclassic Petén, Guatemala*, edited by Prudence M. Rice and Don S. Rice, 192–216. Boulder: University Press of Colorado.

Puleston, Dennis E. 1982. "The Role of Ramon in Maya Subsistence." In *Maya Subsistence: Studies in Memory of Dennis E. Puleston*, edited by Kent V. Flannery, 353–66. New York: Academic Press.

Pyburn, K. Anne. 1997. "The Archaeological Signature of Complexity." In *The Archaeology of City-States: Cross-Cultural Approaches*, edited by Deborah L. Nichols and Thomas H. Charlton, 155–68. Washington, DC: Smithsonian Institution Press.

Pyburn, K. Anne. 2008. "Pomp and Circumstance before Belize: Ancient Maya Commerce and the New River Conurbation." In *The Ancient City: New Perspectives on Urbanism in the Old and New World*, edited by Joyce Marcus and Jeremy A. Sabloff, 247–72. Santa Fe, NM: School for Advanced Research Press.

Quezada, Sergio. 1993. *Pueblos y caciques yucatecos, 1550–1580*. México, D.F.: El Colegio de México.

Quiggin, Alison Hingston. [1949] 1970. *A Survey of Primitive Money: The Beginnings of Currency*. London: Methuen. Reprint, New York: Barnes and Noble.

Rapoport, Amos. 1988. "Levels of Meaning in the Built Environment." In *Cross-Cultural Perspectives in Nonverbal Communication*, edited by Fernando Poyatos, 317–36. Toronto: Hogrefe & Huber.

Rapoport, Amos. 1990. *The Meaning of the Built Environment: A Nonverbal Communication Approach*. Tucson: University of Arizona Press.

Rathje, William L. 1971. "Lowland Classic Maya Socio-political Organization: Degree and Form through Space and Time." PhD diss., Harvard University.

Rathje, William L. 1975. "The Last Tango in Mayapán: A Tentative Trajectory of Production-Distribution Systems." In *Ancient Civilization and Trade*, edited by Jeremy A. Sabloff and C. C. Lamberg-Karlovsky, 409–48. Albuquerque: University of New Mexico Press.

Rathje, William L. 1983. "To the Salt of the Earth: Some Comments on Household Archaeology among the Maya." In *Prehistoric Settlement Patterns: Essays in Honor of Gordon R. Willey*, edited by Evon Z. Vogt and Richard M. Levanthal, 23–34. Albuquerque: University of New Mexico Press, Albuquerque; Cambridge, MA: Peabody Museum of Archaeology and Ethnology.

Rathje, William L., David A. Gregory, and Frederick.M. Wiseman. 1978. "Trade Models and Archaeological Problems: Classic Maya Examples." In *Mesoamerican Communication Routes and Culture Contacts*, edited by Thomas A. Lee and Carlos Navarrete, 147–75. Papers of the New World Archaeological Foundation 40. Provo, UT: Brigham Young University.

Reents-Budet, Dorie. 1994. *Painting the Maya Universe: Royal Ceramics of the Classic Period*. Durham, NC: Duke University Museum of Art.

Reents-Budet, Dorie. 2006. "Power Material in Ancient Mesoamerica: The Roles of Cloth among the Classic Maya." In *Sacred Bundles: Ritual Acts of Wrapping and Binding in Mesoamerica*, edited by Julia Guernsey and F. Kent Reilly III, 105–26. Barnardsville, NC: Boundary End Archaeology Research Center.

Restall, Matthew. 1997. *The Maya World: Yucatec Culture and Society, 1550–1850*. Stanford, CA: Stanford University Press.

Restall, Matthew. 2001. "The People of the Patio: Ethnohistoric Evidence of Yucatec Maya Royal Courts." In *Royal Courts of the Maya*, vol. 2, *Data and Case Studies*, edited by Takeshi Inomata and Stephen D. Houston, 335–90. Boulder, CO: Westview Press.

Rice, Don S. 1986. "The Peten Postclassic: A Settlement Perspective." In *Late Lowland Maya Civilization: Classic to Postclassic*, edited by Jeremy A. Sabloff and E. Wyllys Andrews V, 301–46. Albuquerque: University of New Mexico Press.

Rice, Don S. 2006. "Late Classic Maya Population: Characteristics and Implications." In *Urbanism in the Preindustrial World: Cross-Cultural Approaches*, edited by Glenn R. Storey, 252–76. Tuscaloosa: University of Alabama Press.

Rice, Don S., and T. Patrick Culbert. 1990. "Historical Contexts for Population Reconstruction in the Maya Lowlands." In *Precolumbian Population History in the Maya Lowlands*, edited by T. Patrick Culbert and Don S. Rice, 1–36. Albuquerque: University of New Mexico Press.

Rice, Prudence M. 1983. "Serpents and Styles in Peten Postclassic Pottery." *American Anthropologist* 85 (4): 866–80.

Rice, Prudence M. 1986. "The Peten Postclassic: Perspectives from the Central Peten Lakes." In *Late Lowland Maya Civilization: Classic to Postclassic*, edited by Jeremy A. Sabloff and E. Wyllys Andrews V, 251–99. Albuquerque: University of New Mexico Press.

Rice, Prudence M. 1987. "Economic Change in the Lowland Maya Late Classic Period." In *Specialization, Exchange, and Complex Societies*, edited by Elizabeth M. Brumfiel and Timothy K. Earle, 76–85. Cambridge: Cambridge University Press.

Rice, Prudence M. 1999. "Rethinking Classic Lowland Maya Pottery Censers." *Ancient Mesoamerica* 10 (1): 25–50. http://dx.doi.org/10.1017/S0956536199101020.

Rice, Prudence M. 2004. *Maya Political Science: Time, Astronomy, and the Cosmos.* Austin: University of Texas Press.

Rice, Prudence M. 2009a. "Introduction to the Kowoj and Their Peten Neighbors." In *The Kowoj: Identity, Migration, and Geopolitics in Late Postclassic Petén, Guatemala*, edited by Prudence M. Rice and Don S. Rice, 3–16. Boulder: University Press of Colorado.

Rice, Prudence M. 2009b. "Who Were the Kowoj?" In *The Kowoj: Identity, Migration, and Geopolitics in Late Postclassic Petén, Guatemala*, edited by Prudence M. Rice and Don S. Rice, 17–20. Boulder: University Press of Colorado.

Rice, Prudence M. 2009c. "The Archaeology of the Kowoj: Settlement and Architecture at Zacpeten." In *The Kowoj: Identity, Migration, and Geopolitics in Late Postclassic Petén, Guatemala*, edited by Prudence M. Rice and Don S. Rice, 81–83. Boulder: University Press of Colorado.

Rice, Prudence M. 2009d. "The Kowoj in Geopolitical-Ritual Perspective." In *The Kowoj: Identity, Migration, and Geopolitics in Late Postclassic Petén, Guatemala*, edited by Prudence M. Rice and Don S. Rice, 21–54. Boulder: University Press of Colorado.

Rice, Prudence M. 2009e. "The Archaeology of the Kowoj: Pottery and Identity." In *The Kowoj: Identity, Migration, and Geopolitics in Late Postclassic Petén, Guatemala*, edited by Prudence M. Rice and Don S. Rice, 217–19. Boulder: University Press of Colorado.

Rice, Prudence M. 2009f. "Incense Burners and Other Ritual Ceramics." In *The Kowoj: Identity, Migration, and Geopolitics in Late Postclassic Petén, Guatemala*, edited by Prudence M. Rice and Don S. Rice, 276–315. Boulder: University Press of Colorado.

Rice, Prudence M. 2009g. "On Classic Maya Political Economies." *Journal of Anthropological Archaeology* 28 (1): 70–84. http://dx.doi.org/10.1016/j.jaa.2008.09.001.

Rice, Prudence M. 2009h. "Late Classic Maya Pottery Production: Review and Synthesis." *Journal of Archaeological Method and Theory* 16 (2): 117–56. http://dx.doi.org/10.1007/s10816-009-9063-2.

Rice, Prudence M., and Leslie G. Cecil. 2009. "The Iconography and Decorative Programs of Kowoj Pottery." In *The Kowoj: Identity, Migration, and Geopolitics in Late Postclassic Petén, Guatemala*, edited by Prudence M. Rice and Don S. Rice, 238–75. Boulder: University Press of Colorado.

Rice, Prudence M., and Don S. Rice. 1985. "Topoxte, Macanche, and the Central Peten Postclassic." In *The Lowland Maya Postclassic*, edited by Arlen F. Chase and Prudence M. Rice, 166–83. Austin: University of Texas Press.

Rice, Prudence M., and Don S. Rice, eds. 2004. "Late Classic to Postclassic Transformations in the Petén Lakes Region, Guatemala." In *The Terminal Classic in the Maya Lowlands: Collapse, Transition, and Transformation*, edited by Arthur A. Demarest, Prudence M. Rice, and Don S. Rice, 125–39. Boulder: University Press of Colorado.

Rice, Prudence M., and Don S. Rice. 2009. *The Kowoj: Identity, Migration, and Geopolitics in Late Postclassic Petén, Guatemala*. Boulder: University Press of Colorado.

Ringle, William M. 2004. "On the Political Organization of Chichen Itza." *Ancient Mesoamerica* 15 (2): 167–218. http://dx.doi.org/10.1017/S0956536104040131.

Ringle, William M., and George J. Bey III. 2001. "Post-Classic and Terminal Classic Courts of the Northern Maya Lowlands." In *Royal Courts of the Maya*, vol. 2, *Data and Case Studies*, edited by Takeshi Inomata and Stephen D. Houston, 266–307. Boulder, CO: Westview Press.

Ringle, William M., Tomás Gallareta Negrón, and George J. Bey III. 1998. "The Return of Quetzalcoatl." *Ancient Mesoamerica* 9 (2): 183–232. http://dx.doi.org/10.1017/S0956536100001954.

Robin, Cynthia. 2004. "Social Diversity and Everyday Life within Classic Maya Settlements." In *Mesoamerican Archaeology*, edited by Julia A. Hendon and Rosemary Joyce, 148–68. Oxford: Blackwell.

Robin, Cynthia. 2006. "Gender, Farming, and Long-Term Change: Maya Historical and Archaeological Perspectives." *Current Anthropology* 47 (3): 409–33. http://dx.doi.org/10.1086/503060.

Robles Castellanos, Fernando, ed. 1986a. "Informe anual del proyecto arqueológico Cozumel: Temporada 1980." *Cuaderno de Trabajo 2*. Mexico, D.F.: Instituto Nacional de Antropologia e Historia.

Robles Castellanos, Fernando, ed. 1986b. "Informe anual del proyecto arqueológico Cozumel: Temporada 1981." *3 Cuaderno de Trabajo 3*. Mexico, D.F.: Instituto Nacional de Antropologia e Historia.

Robles Castellanos, Fernando, and Anthony P. Andrews. 1986. "A Review and Synthesis of Recent Postclassic Archaeology in Northern Yucatan." In *Late Lowland Maya Civilization: Classic to Postclassic*, edited by Jeremy A. Sabloff and E. Wyllys Andrews V, 53–98. Albuquerque: University of New Mexico Press.

Rosado Escalante, José E., and Favila Ontiveros, eds. 1938. "Apéndice: Relación de Valladolid." In *Relación de las Cosas de Yucatán: Sacada de lo que escribió el padre Fray Diego de Landa de la Orden de San Francisco, M.D.LX.VI*, 213–47. Mérida, México: E. G. Triay e Hijos.

Rosenswig, Robert M., and Marilyn A. Masson. 2002. "Transformation of the Terminal Classic to Postclassic Architectural Landscape at Caye Coco, Belize." *Ancient Mesoamerica* 13 (2): 213–35.

Roys, Lawrence. 1941. "Masonry Traits Found at Mayapan." In *Los Mayas Antiguos: Monografías de arqueología, ethnografía y lingüísitica mayas, publicadas con motivo del centenario de la exploracion de Yucatán por John L. Stephens y Frederick Catherwood en los anos 1841–42*, edited by César Lizardi Ramos, 143–53. México, D.F.: El Colegio de Mexico.

Roys, Ralph L. 1933. *The Chilam Balam of Chumayel*. Norman: University of Oklahoma Press.

Roys, Ralph L. 1940. "Personal Names of the Maya of Yucatan." In *Contributions to American Anthropology and History* no. 31, 31–48. Carnegie Institution of Washington Publication 523. Washington, DC: Carnegie Institution.

Roys, Ralph L. 1957. *The Political Geography of the Yucatan Maya*. Carnegie Institution of Washington Publication 613. Washington, DC: Carnegie Institution.

Roys, Ralph L. 1962. "Literary Sources for the History of Mayapan." In *Mayapán, Yucatán, Mexico*. Carnegie Institution of Washington Publication 619, by Harry E. D. Pollock, Ralph L. Roys, Tatiana Proskouriakoff, and A. Ledyard Smith, 25–86. Washington, DC: Carnegie Institution.

Roys, Ralph L. [1933] 1967. *The Book of Chilam Balam of Chumayel*, 2nd ed. Norman: University of Oklahoma Press.

Roys, Ralph L. [1943] 1972. *The Indian Background of Colonial Yucatan*. Norman: University of Oklahoma Press.

Ruppert, Karl. 1931. "Temple of the Wall Panels, Chichén Itzá." In *Contributions to American Archaeology* 1 (3): 117–40. Washington, DC: Carnegie Institution.

Ruppert, Karl. 1943. "The Mercado, Chichen Itza, Yucatan." *Contributions to American Archaeology* 8 (43), 223–60. Washington, DC: Carnegie Institution.

Ruppert, Karl, and A. Ledyard Smith. 1952. "Excavation in House Mounds at Mayapan." *Current Reports* 4: 45–66. Washington, DC: Carnegie Institution of Washington.

Ruppert, Karl, and A. Ledyard Smith. 1954. "Excavations in House Mounds at Mayapan: III." *Current Reports* 17: 27–52. Washington, DC: Carnegie Institution of Washington.

Ruppert, Karl, and A. Ledyard Smith. 1957. "House Types in the Environs of Mayapan and at Uxmal, Kabah, Sayil, Chichen Itza, and Chacchob." *Current Reports* 39: 573–97. Washington, DC: Carnegie Institution of Washington.

Russell, Bradley W. 2000. "Postclassic Pottery Censers in the Maya Lowlands: A Study of Form, Function, and Symbolism." Master's thesis, University at Albany–SUNY.

Russell, Bradley W. 2007. "Colonnaded Hall Group Discovered Outside Mayapan City Walls." *Mexicon* 29 (4): 93–94.

Russell, Bradley W. 2008a. "Postclassic Maya Settlement on the Rural-Urban Fringe of Mayapán, Yucatán, Mexico." PhD diss., University at Albany–SUNY.

Russell, Bradley W. 2008b. "Investigaciones en las afueras de la ciudad amurallada de Mayapán: Muestreo, mapeo y pozos de prueba." In *Proyecto del Poder Económico de Mayapán, Temporadas 2001–2004: Informe final para el Consejo Nacional de Arqueología de México*, edited by Marilyn A. Masson, Carlos Peraza Lope, and Timothy S. Hare, 129–272. Albany, NY: University at Albany–SUNY; Mérida, Mexico: Centro INAH Yucatán.

Russell, Bradley W. 2013. "Fortress Mayapan: Key Defensive Features of a Postclassic Maya Fortification." *Ancient Mesoamerica* 24 (2): 275–94.

Russell, Bradley W., and Bruce H. Dahlin. 2007. "Traditional Burnt-Lime Production at Mayapán, Mexico." *Journal of Field Archaeology* 32 (4): 407–23. http://dx.doi.org /10.1179/009346907791071494.

Russell, Bradley W., Robert H.H. Hutchinson, and Pedro C. Delgado Kú. 2012. "Casa Habitacional Q-176 – al Oeste de la Zona Monumental." In *Proyecto Los Fundamentos del Poder Económico de Mayapán, Temporada 2008–2009: Informe final para el Consejo Nacional de Arqueología de México*, edited by Marilyn A. Masson, Carlos Peraza Lope, Timothy S. Hare, and Bradley W. Russell, 789–952. Albany, NY: University at Albany–SUNY; Mérida, Mexico: Centro INAH Yucatán.

Russell, Josiah Cox. 1972. *Medieval Regions and Their Cities*. Bloomington: Indiana University Press.

Sabloff, Jeremy A., ed. 2003. *Tikal: Dynasties, Foreigners, and Affairs of State*. Santa Fe, NM: School for Advanced Research Press.

Sabloff, Jeremy A. 2007. "It Depends on How We Look at Things: New Perspectives on the Postclassic Period in the Northern Maya Lowlands." *Proceedings of the American Philosophical Society* 151 (1): 11–26.

Sabloff, Jeremy A., and E. Wyllys Andrews V, eds. 1986. *Late Lowland Maya Civilization: Classic to Postclassic*. Albuquerque: University of New Mexico Press.

Sabloff, Jeremy A., and William L. Rathje. 1975. "The Rise of a Maya Merchant Class." *Scientific American* 233 (4): 72–82. http://dx.doi.org/10.1038/scientificamerican1075-72.

Sahlins, Marshall D. 1972. *Stone Age Economics*. Chicago, IL: Aldine-Atherton.

Sanders, William T. 1960. *Prehistoric Ceramics and Settlement Patterns in Quintana Roo, Mexico*. In *Contributions to American Anthropology and History* no. 60, 154–264. Carnegie Institution of Washington Publication 606. Washington, DC: Carnegie Institution.

Sanders, William T. 1962. "Cultural Ecology of the Maya Lowlands, Part 1." In *Estudios de Cultura Maya* 2: 79–121, Mexico, D.F.: Universidad Nacional Autónoma de México.

Sanders, William T. 1973. "The Cultural Ecology of the Lowland Maya: A Reevaluation." In *The Classic Maya Collapse*, edited by T. Patrick Culbert, 329–65. Albuquerque: University of New Mexico Press.

Sanders, William T., Alba Guadelupe Mastache, and Robert H. Cobean, eds. 2003. Vol. 1 of *El Urbanismo en Mesoamérica/Urbanism in Mesoamerica*. México, D.F.: Instituto Nacional de Antropología e Historia; University Park: Pennsylvania State University.

Sanders, William T., and Barbara J. Price. 1968. *Mesoamerica: The Evolution of a Civilization*. New York: Random House.

Sanders, William T., and Robert S. Santley. 1983. "A Tale of Three Cities: Energetics and Urbanization in Pre-Hispanic Central Mexico." In *Prehistoric Settlement Patterns: Essays in Honor of Gordon R. Willey*, edited by Evon Z. Vogt and Richard Leventhal, 243–91. Albuquerque: University of New Mexico Press.

Sanders, William T., and David Webster. 1988. "The Mesoamerican Urban Tradition." *American Anthropologist* 90 (3): 521–46. http://dx.doi.org/10.1525/aa.1988.90.3.02a00010.

Santley, Robert, Clare Yarborough, and Barbara Hall. 1987. "Enclaves, Ethnicity, and the Archaeological Record at Matacapan." In *Ethnicity and Culture*, edited by Réginald Auger, Margaret F. Glass, Scott MacEachern, and Peter H. McCartney, 85–100. Calgary, Canada: University of Calgary Archaeological Association, Calgary, Canada.

Santley, Robert S., and Ronald R. Kneebone. 1993. "Craft Specialization, Refuse Disposal, and the Creation of Spatial Archaeological Records in Prehispanic Mesoamerica." In *Prehispanic Domestic Units in Western Mesoamerica: Studies of the Household, Compound, and Residence*, edited by Robert S. Santley and Kenneth G. Hirth, 36–63. Boca Raton, FL: CRC Press.

Scarborough, Vernon L., and Fred Valdez, Jr. 2003. "The Engineered Environment and Political Economy of the Three Rivers Region." In *Heterarchy, Political Economy, and the Ancient Maya: The Three Rivers Region of the East-Central Yucatán Peninsula*, edited by Vernon L. Scarborough, Fred Valdez, Jr., and Nicholas Dunning, 3–13. Tucson: University of Arizona Press.

Scarborough, Vernon L., and Fred Valdez, Jr. 2009. "An Alternative Order: The Dualistic Economies of the Ancient Maya." *Latin American Antiquity* 20 (1): 207–27.

Scarborough, Vernon L., Fred Valdez, Jr., and Nicholas Dunning, eds. 2003. *Heterarchy, Political Economy, and the Ancient Maya: The Three Rivers Region of the East-Central Yucatán Peninsula*. Tucson: University of Arizona Press.

Schele, Linda, and David A. Freidel. 1990. *A Forest of Kings: The Untold Story of the Ancient Maya*. New York: William Morrow.

Schele, Linda, and Julia Kappelman. 2001. "What the Heck's Coatepec? The Formative Roots of an Enduring Mythology." In *Landscape and Power in Ancient Mesoamerica*, edited by Rex Koontz, Kathryn Reese-Taylor, and Annabeth Headrick, 29–53. Boulder, CO: Westview Press.

Schele, Linda, and Peter Mathews. 1998. *The Code of Kings: The Language of Seven Sacred Maya Temples and Tombs*. New York: Scribner.

Schellhas, Paul. 1904. *Representation of Deities of the Maya Manuscripts*. Papers of the Peabody Museum of Archaeology and Ethnology 4, no. 1. Cambridge, MA: Harvard University.

Scholes, France V. 1938. Vols. 14 and 15 of *Don Diego Quijada, Alcalde Mayor de Yucatán, 1561–1565*. México, D.F.: Biblioteca Histórica Mexicana de Obras Inéditas.

Scholes, France V., and Ralph L. Roys. 1938. "Fray Diego de Landa and the Problem of Idolatry in Yucatan." In *Cooperation in Research*, 585–620. Washington, D.C.: *Carnegie Institution*.

Serafin, Stanley. 2009. "Dental Caries at a Late Pre-Hispanic Regional Maya Capital." Paper presented at the 23rd Annual Conference of the Australasian Society for Human Biology, Rottnest Island, Western Australia, December 1–4.

Serafin, Stanley. 2010. "Bioarchaeological Investigation of Violence at Mayapan." PhD diss., Tulane University.

Serafin, Stanley, and Carlos Peraza Lope. 2007. "Human Sacrificial Rites Among the Maya of Mayapán: A Bioarchaeological Perspective." In *New Perspectives on Human Sacrifice and Ritual Body Treatments in Ancient Maya Society*, edited by Vera Tiesler and Andrea Cucina, 232–50. New York: Springer. http://dx.doi.org/10.1007/978-0-387-48871-4_10.

Serafin, Stanley, Bradley W. Russell, and Miguel Delgado Kú. 2012. "Análisis de Entierros." In *Proyecto Los Fundamentos del Poder Económico de Mayapán, Temporadas 2008–2009: Informe final para el Consejo Nacional de Arqueología de Mexico*, edited by Marilyn A. Masson, Carlos Peraza Lope, Timothy S. Hare, and Bradley W. Russell, 237–56. Albany, NY: University at Albany–SUNY; Mérida, Mexico: Centro INAH Yucatán.

Shafer, Harry J., and Thomas R. Hester. 1983. "Ancient Maya Chert Workshops in Northern Belize, Central America." *American Antiquity* 48 (3): 519–43. http://dx.doi.org/10.2307/280559.

Shafer, Harry J., and Thomas R. Hester. 1986. "Maya Stone-Tool Craft Specialization and Production at Colha, Belize: Reply to Mallory." *American Antiquity* 51 (1): 158–66. http://dx.doi.org/10.2307/280402.

Shafer, Harry J., and Thomas R. Hester. 1988. "Appendix III: Preliminary Analysis of Postclassic Lithics from Santa Rita Corozal, Belize." In *A Postclassic Perspective:*

Excavations at the Maya Site of Santa Rita Corozal, Belize, by Diane Z. Chase and Arlen F. Chase, 111–17. Pre-Columbian Art Research Institute Monograph 4, San Francisco: Pre-Columbian Art Research Institute.

Shafer, Harry J., and Thomas R. Hester. 1991. "Lithic Craft Specialization and Product Distribution at the Maya Site of Colha, Belize." *World Archaeology* 23 (1): 79–97. http://dx.doi.org/10.1080/00438243.1991.9980160.

Sharer, Robert J., and Charles W. Golden. 2004. "Kingship and Polity: Conceptualizing the Maya Body Politic." In *Continuities and Changes in Maya Archaeology: Perspectives at the Millennium*, edited by Charles W. Golden and Greg Borgstede, 23–50. New York: Routledge.

Shaw, Justine M. 2001. "Maya Sacbeob: Form and Function." *Ancient Mesoamerica* 12 (2): 261–72. http://dx.doi.org/10.1017/S0956536101121048.

Shaw, Leslie C. 1999. "Social and Ecological Aspects of Preclassic Maya Meat Consumption at Colha, Belize." In *Reconstructing Ancient Maya Diet*, edited by Christine D. White, 83–102. Salt Lake City: University of Utah Press.

Shaw, Leslie C. 2012. "The Elusive Maya Marketplace: An Archaeological Consideration of the Evidence." *Journal of Archaeological Research* 20 (2): 117–55. http://dx.doi.org/10.1007/s10814-011-9055-0.

Sheets, Payson. 2000. "Provisioning the Ceren Household: The Vertical Economy, Village Economy, and Household Economy in the Southeast Maya Periphery." *Ancient Mesoamerica* 11 (02): 217–30. http://dx.doi.org/10.1017/S0956536100112039.

Shennan, Stephen J. 1989. "Introduction: Archaeological Approaches to Cultural Identity." In *Archaeological Approaches to Cultural Identity*, edited by Stephen J. Shennan, 1–32. London: Unwin-Hyman.

Shiratori, Yuko. 2008. "Malacates." In *Proyecto Los Fundamentos del Poder Económico de Mayapán, Temporadas 2001–2004: Informe final para el Consejo Nacional de Arqueología de México*, edited by Marilyn A. Masson, Carlos Peraza Lope, and Timothy S. Hare, 865–70. Albany, NY: University at Albany–SUNY; Mérida, México: Centro INAH Yucatán.

Shook, Edwin W. 1952. "The Great Wall of Mayapán." *Current Reports* 2: 7–35. Washington, DC: Carnegie Institution of Washington.

Shook, Edwin W. 1953. "The X-Coton Temples at Mayapán." *Current Reports* 11: 207–21. Washington, DC: Carnegie Institution of Washington.

Shook, Edwin W. 1954a. "Three Temples and Their Associated Structures at Mayapán." *Current Reports* 14: 254–91. Washington, DC: Carnegie Institution of Washington.

Shook, Edwin W. 1954b. "The Temple of Kukulcan at Mayapán." *Current Reports* 20: 89–108. Washington, DC: Carnegie Institution of Washington.

Shook, Edwin W. 1954c. "A Round Temple at Mayapán." *Current Reports* 16: 15–26. Washington, DC: Carnegie Institution of Washington.

Shook, Edwin W. 1955. "Another Round Temple at Mayapán." *Current Reports* 27: 267–80. Washington, DC: Carnegie Institution of Washington.

Shook, Edwin M., and William N. Irving. 1955. "Colonnaded Buildings at Mayapán." *Current Reports* 22: 127–224. Washington, DC: Carnegie Institution of Washington.

Sidrys, Raymond V. 1983. *Archaeological Excavations in Northern Belize, Central America.* Monograph 17. Los Angeles: Institute of Archaeology, University of California, Los Angeles.

Simmons, Scott E. 1995. "Maya Resistance, Maya Resolve: The Tools of Autonomy from Tipu, Belize." *Ancient Mesoamerica* 6: 135–46. http://dx.doi.org/10.1017/S0956536100002145.

Smith, A. Ledyard. 1962. "Residential and Associated Structures at Mayapán." In *Mayapán, Yucatán, Mexico,* by Harry E. D. Pollock, Ralph L. Roys, Tatiana Proskouriakoff, and A. Ledyard Smith, 165–320. Carnegie Institution of Washington Publication 619. Washington, DC: Carnegie Institution.

Smith, A. Ledyard, and Karl Ruppert. 1953. "Excavations in House Mounds at Mayapán: II." *Current Reports* 10: 180–206. Washington, DC: Carnegie Institution of Washington.

Smith, A. Ledyard, and Karl Ruppert. 1956. "Excavations in House Mounds at Mayapán: IV." *Current Reports* 36: 471–528. Washington, DC: Carnegie Institution of Washington.

Smith, Carol A. 1976. "Introduction: The Regional Approach to Economic Systems." In *Regional Analysis,* vol. 1, *Economic Systems,* edited by Carol A. Smith, 1–61. New York: Academic Press.

Smith, Michael E. 1987. "Household Possessions and Wealth in Agrarian States: Implications for Archaeology." *Journal of Anthropological Archaeology* 6 (4): 297–335. http://dx.doi.org/10.1016/0278-4165(87)90004-3.

Smith, Michael E. 1992. "Braudel's Temporal Rhythms and Chronology Theory in Archaeology." In *Annales, Archaeology, and Ethnohistory,* edited by A. Bernard Knapp, 23–34. New York: Cambridge University Press. http://dx.doi.org/10.1017/CBO9780511759949.003.

Smith, Michael E. 1994. "Social Complexity in the Aztec Countryside." In *Archaeological Views from the Countryside: Village Communities in Early Complex Societies,* edited by Glenn M. Schwartz and Stephen E. Falconer, 143–59. Washington, DC: Smithsonian Institution Press.

Smith, Michael E. 1999. "On Hirth's 'Distributional Approach.'." *Current Anthropology* 40 (4): 528–30. http://dx.doi.org/10.1086/200049.

Smith, Michael E. 2002. "Domestic Ritual at Aztec Provincial Sites in Morelos." In *Domestic Ritual in Ancient Mesoamerica*, edited by Patricia Plunket, 93–114. Cotsen Institute of Archaeology Monograph no. 46. Los Angeles: University of California, Los Angeles.

Smith, Michael E. [1996] 2003a. *The Aztecs*. 2nd ed. Oxford: Blackwell.

Smith, Michael E. 2003b. "Small Polities in Postclassic Mesoamerica." In *The Postclassic Mesoamerican World*, edited by Michael E. Smith and Frances F. Berdan, 35–9. Salt Lake City: University of Utah Press.

Smith, Michael E. 2003c. "Key Commodities." In *The Postclassic Mesoamerican World*, edited by Michael E. Smith and Frances F. Berdan, 117–25. Salt Lake City: University of Utah Press.

Smith, Michael E. 2003d. "Economic Change in Morelos Households." In *The Postclassic Mesoamerican World*, edited by Michael E. Smith and Frances F. Berdan, 249–58. Salt Lake City: University of Utah Press.

Smith, Michael E. 2004. "The Archaeology of Ancient State Economies." *Annual Review of Anthropology* 33 (1): 73–102. http://dx.doi.org/10.1146/annurev.anthro.33.070203.144016.

Smith, Michael E. 2005. "City Size in Late Postclassic Mesoamerica." *Journal of Urban History* 31 (4): 403–34. http://dx.doi.org/10.1177/0096144204274396.

Smith, Michael E. 2007. "Form and Meaning in the Earliest Cities: A New Approach to Ancient Urban Planning." *Journal of Planning History* 6 (1): 3–47. http://dx.doi.org/10.1177/1538513206293713.

Smith, Michael E. 2008. *Aztec City-State Capitals*. Gainesville: University Press of Florida.

Smith, Michael E. 2010a. "The Archaeological Study of Neighborhoods and Districts in Ancient Cities." *Journal of Anthropological Archaeology* 29 (2): 137–54. http://dx.doi.org/10.1016/j.jaa.2010.01.001.

Smith, Michael E. 2010b. "Sprawl, Squatters and Sustainable Cities: Can Archaeological Data Shed Light on Modern Urban Issues?" *Cambridge Archaeological Journal* 20 (2): 229–53. http://dx.doi.org/10.1017/S0959774310000259.

Smith, Michael E. 2010c. "Aztec Taxation at the City-State and Imperial Levels." Paper presented at the Fiscal Regimes and the Political Economy of Early States Conference, Stanford University, Stanford, CA, May 27–29.

Smith, Michael E. 2011a. "Empirical Urban Theory for Archaeologists." *Journal of Archaeological Method and Theory* 18 (3): 167–92. http://dx.doi.org/10.1007/s10816-010-9097-5.

Smith, Michael E. 2011b. "Classic Maya Settlement Clusters as Urban Neighborhoods: A Comparative Perspective on Low-Density Urbanism." *Journal de la Société des Americanistes* 97 (1): 51–73.

Smith, Michael E., and Frances F. Berdan, eds. 2003a. *The Postclassic Mesoamerican World*. Salt Lake City: University of Utah Press.

Smith, Michael E., and Frances F. Berdan. 2003b. "Spatial Structure of the Mesoamerican World System." In *The Postclassic Mesoamerican World*, edited by Michael E. Smith and Frances F. Berdan, 21–34. Salt Lake City: University of Utah Press.

Smith, Michael E., and Cynthia Heath-Smith. 1994. "Rural Economy in Late Postclassic Morelos." In *Economies and Polities in the Aztec Realm*, edited by Mary G. Hodge and Michael E. Smith, 349–76. Albany, NY: Institute for Mesoamerican Studies.

Smith, Michael E., and Lisa Montiel. 2001. "The Archaeological Study of Empires and Imperialism in Pre-Hispanic Central Mexico." *Journal of Anthropological Archaeology* 20 (3): 245–84. http://dx.doi.org/10.1006/jaar.2000.0372.

Smith, Michael E., Jennifer B. Wharton, and Jan Marie Olson. 2003. "Aztec Feasts, Rituals, and Markets: Political Uses of Ceramic Vessels in a Commercial Economy." In *The Archaeology and Politics of Food and Feasting in Early States and Empires*, edited by Tamara Bray, 235–68. New York: Kluwer. http://dx.doi.org/10.1007/978-0-306-48246-5_9.

Smith, Philip E. 1955. "Excavations in Three Ceremonial Structures at Mayapán." *Current Reports* 21: 109–26 Washington, DC: Carnegie Institution of Washington.

Smith, Robert E. 1953. "Cenote X-Coton at Mayapán." *Current Reports* 5: 67–81. Washington, D.C.: Carnegie Institution of Washington.

Smith, Robert E. 1954. "Cenote Exploration at Mayapán and Telchaquillo." *Current Reports* 12: 222–33. Washington, DC: Carnegie Institution of Washington.

Smith, Robert E. 1971. *The Pottery of Mayapan*. Papers of the Peabody Museum of Archaeology and Ethnology 66. Cambridge, MA: Harvard University.

Snead, James E., Clark L. Erikson, and J. Andrew Darling. 2006. "Making Human Space: The Archaeology of Trails, Paths, and Roads." In *Landscapes of Movement: Trails, Paths, and Roads in Anthropological Perspective*, edited by James E. Snead, Clark L. Erikson, and J. Andrew Darling, 1–19. Philadelphia: University of Pennsylvania Museum of Archaeology and Anthropology.

Solís, Felipe. 2004. *The Aztec Empire*. New York: Guggenheim Museum.

Solomon, Char. 2002. *Tatiana Proskouriakoff: Interpreting the Ancient Maya*. Norman: University of Oklahoma Press.

Stanish, Charles. 1989. "Household Archaeology: Testing Models of Zonal Complementarity in the South Central Andes." *American Anthropologist* 91 (1): 7–24. http://dx.doi.org/10.1525/aa.1989.91.1.02a00010.

Stannard, David E. 1993. *American Holcaust: The Conquest of the New World*. Oxford University Press.

Stark, Barbara. 1997. "Gulf Lowland Settlement in Perspective." In *Olmec to Aztec: Settlement Patterns in the Ancient Gulf Lowlands*, edited by Barbara L. Stark and Phillip J. Arnold III, 278–309. Tucson: University of Arizona Press.

Stark, Barbara L., and Christopher P. Garraty. 2010. "Detecting Marketplace Exchange in Archaeology: A Methodological Review." In *Archaeological Approaches to Market Exchange in Ancient Societies*, edited by Christopher P. Garraty and Barbara L. Stark, 33–58. Boulder: University Press of Colorado.

Stephens, John L. 1843. Vols. 1 and 2 of *Incidents of Travel in Yucatan*. New York: Harper and Brothers.

Stephens, John L. [1843] 1963. *Incidents of Travel in Yucatan*. 2 vols. New York: Dover Publications. Reprint, New York: Harper and Brothers.

Stone, Elizabeth C., ed. 2007a. *Settlement and Society: Essays Dedicated to Robert McCormick Adams*. Los Angeles: Cotsen Institute for Archaeology, University of California.

Stone, Elizabeth C. 2007b. "The Mesopotamian Urban Experience." In *Settlement and Society: Essays Dedicated to Robert McCormick Adams*, edited by Elizabeth C. Stone, 213–34. Los Angeles: Cotsen Institute of Archaeology, University of California, Los Angeles.

Storey, Glenn R., ed. 2006. *Urbanism in the Preindustrial World: Cross-Cultural Approaches*. Tuscaloosa: University of Alabama Press.

Strömsvik, Gustav. 1953. "A Portal Vault and Temple at Mayapán." *Current Reports* 8: 136–43. Washington, DC: Carnegie Institution of Washington.

Strömsvik, Gustav. 1956. "Exploration of the Cave of Dzab-Na, Tecoh, Yucatan." *Current Reports* 35: 463–70. Washington, DC: Carnegie Institution of Washington.

Stuart, David. 1998. "'The Fire Enters His House': Architecture and Ritual in Classic Maya Texts." In *Function and Meaning in Classic Maya Architecture*, edited by Stephen D. Houston, 373–425. Washington, DC: Dumbarton Oaks.

Stuart, David. 2006. *Inscriptions from Temple XIX at Palenque*. San Francisco: Pre-Columbian Art Research Institute.

Sugiyama, Saburo. 2004. "Governance and Polity at Classic Teotihuacan." In *Mesoamerican Archaeology*, edited by Julia A. Hendon and Rosemary A. Joyce, 97–123. Malden, MA: Blackwell.

Suhler, Charles, Traci Ardren, David Freidel, and Dave Johnstone. 2004. "The Rise and Fall of Terminal Classic Yaxuna, Yucatán, Mexico." In *The Terminal Classic in the Maya Lowlands: Collapse, Transition, and Transformation*, edited by Arthur A. Demarest, Prudence M. Rice, and Don S. Rice, 551–87. Boulder: University Press of Colorado.

Taschek, Jennifer T. 1994. *The Artifacts of Dzibilchaltun, Yucatán, Mexico: Shell, Polished Stone, Bone, Wood, and Ceramics.* Middle American Research Series Publication 50. New Orleans, LA: Tulane University.

Taube, Karl A. 1992. *The Major Gods of Ancient Yucatan.* Studies in Pre-Columbian Art and Archaeology no. 32. Washington, DC: Dumbarton Oaks.

Taube, Karl. 1993. *Aztec and Maya Myths.* Austin: University of Texas Press.

Thompson, Donald E. 1955. "An Altar and Platform at Mayapán." *Current Reports* 28: 281–88. Washington, DC: Carnegie Institution of Washington.

Thompson, Donald E., and J. Eric S. Thompson. 1955. "A Noble's Residence and Its Dependencies at Mayapán." *Current Reports* 25: 225–52. Washington, DC: Carnegie Institution of Washington.

Thompson, Edward H. 1938. "The High Priest's Grave, Chichen Itza, Yucatán, Mexico." Prepared by J. Eric Thompson. Field Museum of Natural History Anthropological Series Publication 412, vol. 27, no. 1. Chicago, IL: Field Museum Press. http://dx.doi.org/10.5962/bhl.title.3502.

Thompson, J. Eric S. 1950. "Maya Hieroglyphic Writing." Carnegie Institution of Washington Publication 589. Washington, D.C.: Carnegie Institution.

Thompson, J. Eric S. 1954. "A Presumed Residence of the Nobility at Mayapán." *Current Reports* 19: 71–88. Washington, DC: Carnegie Institution of Washington.

Thompson, J. Eric S. 1957. "Deities Portrayed on Censers at Mayapán." *Current Reports* 40: 599–632. Washington: DC: Carnegie Institution of Washington.

Thompson, J. Eric S. 1970. *Maya History and Religion.* Norman: University of Oklahoma Press.

Tourtellot, Gair. 1988. *Excavations at Seibal, Department of Peten, Guatemala: Peripheral Survey and Excavation, Settlement and Community Patterns.* Memoirs of the Peabody Museum of Archaeology and Ethnology 16. Cambridge, MA: Harvard University Press.

Tourtellot, Gair, III. 1993. "A View of Ancient Maya Settlements in the Eighth Century." In *Lowland Maya Civilization in the Eighth Century A.D.*, edited by Jeremy A. Sabloff and John S. Henderson, 219–241. Washington, DC: Dumbarton Oaks.

Tourtellot, Gair, Francisco Estrada Belli, John J. Rose, and Norman Hammond. 2003a. "Late Classic Maya Heterarchy, Hierarchy, and Landscape at La Milpa, Belize." In *Heterarchy, Political Economy, and the Ancient Maya: The Three Rivers Region of the East-Central Yucatán Peninsula*, edited by Vernon L. Scarborough, Fred Valdez, Jr., and Nicholas Dunning, 37–51. Tucson: University of Arizona Press.

Tourtellot, Gair, Gloria Everson, and Norman Hammond. 2003b. "Suburban Organization: Minor Centers at La Milpa, Belize." In *Perspectives on Ancient Maya Rural*

Complexity, edited by Gyles Iannone and Samuel V. Connell, 95–107. Cotsen Institute of Archaeology Monograph 49. Los Angeles: University of California, Los Angeles.

Tourtellot, Gair, and Jason J. Gonzalez. 2004. "The Last Hurrah: Continuity and Transformation at Seibal." In *The Terminal Classic in the Maya Lowlands: Collapse, Transition, and Transformation*, edited by Arthur A. Demarest, Prudence M. Rice, and Don S. Rice, 60–82. Boulder: University Press of Colorado.

Tourtellot, Gair, and Jeremy A. Sabloff. 1994. "Community and Structure at Sayil: A Case Study of Puuc Settlement." In *Hidden Among Hills: Maya Archaeology of the Northwest Yucatan Peninsula*, edited by Hanns J. Prem, 71–92. Möckmuhl, Germany: Verlag von Flemming.

Tourtellot, Gair, and Jeremy A. Sabloff. 1999. "Community Structure at Sayil: A Case Study of Puuc Settlement." In *Hidden Among Hills: Maya Archaeology of the Northwest Yucatan Peninsula*. Acta Mesoamericana 7, edited by Hanns J. Prem, 71–92. Markt Schwaben, Germany: Verlag Anton Saurwein.

Townsend, Richard F. 1979. *State and Cosmos in the Art of Tenochtitlan*. Washington, DC: Dumbarton Oaks.

Tozzer, Alfred M. 1941. Notes to *Landa's Relación de las cosas de Yucatan*. Papers of the Peabody Museum of American Archaeology and Ethnology 18. Cambridge, MA: Harvard University.

Trigger, Bruce G. 1968. "The Determinants of Settlement Patterns." In *Settlement Archaeology*, edited by Kwang-chih Chang, 53–78. Palo Alto, CA: National Press Books.

Trigger, Bruce G. 1980. *Gordon Childe: Revolutions in Archaeology*. London: Thames & Hudson.

Tringham, Ruth. 1996. "But Gordon, Where are the People? Some Comments on the Topic of Craft Specialization and Social Evolution." *Craft Specialization and Social Evolution: In Memory of V. Gordon Childe*, edited by Bernard Wailes, 233–39. Philadelphia: MASCA Press, University of Pennsylvania.

Turner, Billie Lee, II, and Jeremy A. Sabloff. 2012. "Classic Period Collapse of the Central Maya Lowlands: Insights about Human-Environment Relationships for Sustainability." *Proceedings of the National Academy of Sciences of the United States of America* 109 (35): 13908–14. http://dx.doi.org/10.1073/pnas.1210106109.

Vail, Gabrielle. 2006. "Creation Mythology in Late Postclassic and Colonial Texts." Paper presented at the Annual Meeting of the Society for Ethnohistory, Williamsburg, VA, 1–5 November.

Vail, Gabrielle, and Andrea Stone. 2002. "Representations of Maya Women in Postclassic and Colonial Maya Literature and Art." In *Ancient Maya Women*, edited by Traci Ardren, 203–28. Walnut Creek, CA: AltaMira.

Vidal Guzmán, Cuauhtémoc. 2011. "Violence at Mayapán: The Taphonomy of Burned Remains from Itzmal Ch'en." Manuscript on file at the Department of Anthropology, University at Albany–SUNY.

Villacorta C., J. Antonio, and Carlos A. Villacorta. 1976. *Códices Mayas*. 2nd ed. Guatemala City: Tipografía Nacional.

Villela, Khristaan D., and Rex Koontz. 1993. "A Nose Piercing Ceremony in the North Temple of the Great Ballcourt at Chichén Itzá." Texas Notes on Pre-Columbian Art, Writing, and Culture no. 41. Austin: Center of the History and Art of Ancient American Culture, Department of Art, University of Texas, Austin.

Von Nagy, Christopher. 1997. "Some Comments on Madrid Deer-Hunting Almanacs." In *Papers on the Madrid Codex*, edited by Victoria R. Bricker and Gabrielle Vail, 27–71. New Orleans: Middle American Research Institute, Tulane University.

Voorhies, Barbara, and Janine Gasco. 2004. *Postclassic Soconusco Society: The Late Prehistory of the Coast of Chiapas, Mexico*. Albany, NY: Institute for Mesoamerican Studies, University at Albany–SUNY.

Wailes, Bernard. 1996. "V. Gordon Childe and the Relations of Production." *Craft Specialization and Social Evolution: In Memory of V. Gordon Childe*, edited by Bernard Wailes, 3–16. Philadelphia: MASCA Press, University of Pennsylvania.

Walker, Debra. 1990. "Cerros Revisited: Ceramic Indicators of Terminal Classic and Postclassic Settlement and Pilgrimage in Northern Belize." PhD diss., Southern Methodist University.

Wallace, Dwight T. 1977. "An Intra-site Locational Analysis of Utatlan: The Structure of an Urban Site." In *Archaeology and Ethnohistory of the Central Quiché*, edited by Dwight T. Wallace and Robert M. Carmack, 20–54. Institute for Mesoamerican Studies no. 1. Albany, NY: University at Albany–SUNY.

Webb, Malcolm C. 1964. *The Post-Classic Decline of the Peten Maya: An Interpretation in Light of a General Theory of State Society*. PhD diss., University of Michigan. University Microfilms, Ann Arbor.

Webb, Ronald W., and Kenneth G. Hirth. 2003. "Xochicalco: Abandonment of Households at an Epiclassic Urban Center." In *The Archaeology of Settlement Abandonment in Middle America*, edited by Takeshi Inomata and Ronald W. Webb, 29–42. Salt Lake City: University of Utah Press.

Webster, David. 2000. "The Not So Peaceful Civilization: A Review of Maya War." *Journal of World Prehistory* 14 (1): 65–119. http://dx.doi.org/10.1023/A:1007813518630.

Webster, David, and William T. Sanders. 2001. "The Ancient Mesoamerican City: Theory and Concept." In *Reconstruyendo la Ciudad Maya: El Urbanismo en Las Sociedades Antiguas*, vol. 6, edited by Andres Ciudad Ruiz, M. Josefa Iglesias Ponce de Leon, and María del Carmen Martinez, 34–64. Madrid: Sociedad Espanol de Estudias Mayas.

Weeks, John M., ed. 2009. *The Carnegie Maya II: Carnegie Institution of Washington Current Reports, 1952–1957*. Boulder: University Press of Colorado.

Weiner, Annette. 1992. *Inalienable Possessions: The Paradox of Keeping-While-Giving*. Berkeley: University of California Press. http://dx.doi.org/10.1525/california /9780520076037.001.0001.

Wells, E. Christian. 2006. "Recent Trends in Theorizing Prehispanic Mesoamerican Economies." *Journal of Archaeological Research* 14 (4): 265–312. http://dx.doi.org /10.1007/s10814-006-9006-3.

West, Georgia. 2002. "Ceramic Exchange in the Late Classic and Postclassic Maya Lowlands: A Diachronic Approach." In *Ancient Maya Political Economies*, edited by Marilyn A. Masson and David A. Freidel, 141–96. Walnut Creek, CA: AltaMira.

White, Jonathan, Marilyn A. Masson, Elizabeth H. Paris, and Gina Lasalla. 2012. "Análisis de artefactos especiales, Temporadas 2008–2009." In *Proyecto Los Fundamentos del Poder Económico de Mayapán, Temporada 2008–2009: Informe final para el Consejo Nacional de Arqueología de México*, edited by Marilyn A. Masson, Carlos Peraza Lope, Timothy S. Hare, and Bradley W. Russell, 1297–1310. Albany, NY: University at Albany–SUNY; Mérida, México: Centro INAH Yucatán.

Wilk, Richard R., and Robert McC. Netting. 1984. "Households: Changing Forms and Functions." In *Households: Comparative and Historical Studies of the Domestic Group*, edited by Robert McC. Netting, Richard R. Wilk, Eric J. Arnould, 1–28. Berkeley: University of California Press.

Wilk, Richard R., and Wendy Ashmore, eds. 1988. *Household and Community in the Mesoamerican Past*. Albuquerque: University of New Mexico Press.

Wilkerson, S. Jeffrey K. 1990. "El Tajín: Great Center of the Northeast." In *Mexico: Splendors of Thirty Centuries*, 155–85. New York: Metropolitan Museum of Art.

Winters, Howard D. 1955a. "A Vaulted Temple at Mayapán." *Current Reports* 30: 363–79. Washington, DC: Carnegie Institution of Washington.

Winters, Howard D. 1955b. "Excavation of a Colonnaded Hall at Mayapán." *Current Reports* 31: 381–96. Washington, DC: Carnegie Institution of Washington.

Winters, Howard D. 1955c. "Three Serpent Column Temples and Associated Platforms at Mayapán." *Current Reports* 32: 397–424. Washington, DC: Carnegie Institution of Washington.

Wolf, Eric R. 1982. *Europe and the People Without History*. Berkeley: University of California Press.

Wright, Lori E. 2007. "Ethnicity and Isotopes at Mayapán." Online research report to FAMSI. http://www.famsi.org/reports/05068/.

Wright, Rita. 1996. "Contexts of Specialization: V. Gordon Childe and Social Evolution." *Craft Specialization and Social Evolution: In Memory of V. Gordon Childe*, edited by Bernard Wailes, 124–32. Philadelphia: MASCA Press, University of Pennsylvania.

Ximenez, Francisco. [1929] 1999. *Historia de la provincia de San Vicente de Chiapa y Guatemala de la Orden de Predictadores*, edited by Carmelo Sáenz de Santa María. Guatemala City: Sociedad de Geografía e Historia de Guatemala.

Yaeger, Jason, and Cynthia Robin. 2004. "Heterogenous Hinterlands: The Social and Political Organization of Commoner Settlements near Xunantunich, Belize." In *Ancient Maya Commoners*, edited by Jon C. Lohse and Fred Valdez, Jr., 148–73. Austin: University of Texas Press.

Dr. Marilyn A. Masson is a professor of anthropology at the University at Albany–SUNY in Albany, New York.

Lic. Carlos Peraza Lope is an archaeologist and the project director with the Instituto Nacional de Antropología e Historia, Centro INAH Yucatán, Mexico.

Dr. Timothy Hare is an associate professor of anthropology at the Institute for Regional Analysis and Public Policy at Morehead State University, Morehead, Kentucky.

*Page numbers in boldface refer
to figures, maps, and tables.*

475–476; Temple H-17, 132. *See also* censers; colonnaded halls; felines; gods; Itzmal Ch'en group; religion; residences; sculptures; shrines; temples

Altepetl, 10, 153, 187

Amber, **272**, 278

Ancestors: apotheosized/patron gods, 35, 81–86, 102–103, 109, 426, 431, 433–**434**, 435–**437**, 422, 515; conjuring rites, 82, 469; effigy urn, 259–**260**; relics, 313; stone and ceramic sculpture frequency distributions, **481–510**, 511–515. *See also* elites; gods; priests; religion

Ancillary structures. *See* residences

Andrews, Anthony P., xxxii, 24; and chronology, 46, 60–61, 69; and Isla Cerritos, 408; and Postclassic settlement, 4, 42, 45, 408, 536

Andrews, E. Wyllys IV, 18

Andrews, E. Wyllys V, 24, 60–61, 69, 320

Animal pens. *See* pens

Animals: artistic renderings, 95, 130, 475–**477**; bone artifacts, 281–282, 302, **304–309**, 312–313; food (staples/consumption rituals), 122, 125–126, 249, 288, 290, 399–402, 428; headdresses and pelts (on censers), **432**, 435, 438, 456, 458–462; infectious disease, 198, 409–410; raising, 9, 243, 244, **252**, 295, 297, 399–402, 409–410, 544; sacrifice, 91–92; as tribute, 288–289. *See also* birds; bone objects; censers; coatimundi; deer; dogs; felines; females; figurines; gods; houselot enclosures; marine shell; monkeys; peccary; pens; reptiles; sacrifice, of animals; sculptures; turkeys; turtle

Architectural restoration, xxx, 20–21, 77; Itzmal Ch'en, 22, 128, **132**

Architecture. *See* altars; colonnaded halls; focal node architecture; oratories; residences; shrines; temples; urban planning

Astronomy, 53, 76, 78, 80–82, 84, 86, 88. *See also* priests, religion

Aveni, Anthony, 76, 82, 560

Axes, 59, 130, 273, 280–282, 285, 291, 329, **365**–366, **367–368**, 369–**371**, 372, **374**–377, **378–384**, 389–**391**, 392–**393**, **394–395**, 396–**397**, **398**, 410, 412, 423, 528. *See also* agriculture; chert/chalcedony; copper; greenstone

Aztec(s): central Mexican/Aztec art style, 77, 85, 88, 98; central Mexican gods (on censers), 284, 430, 445, 447, 459, 465–466; central Mexican imported goods (in Maya area), 278, 280; economy, 542–543; famine of

1 Rabbit, 527, 529; figurines, 34, 426; markets, 283; myths, 95–99, 103; variation among urban centers, 557. *See also* gods; ethnicity; Templo Mayor

Ballcourts: absence at Mayapán, 76, 553; at Chichén Itzá, 49, 57

Banners: name of Mayapán, 14; number banners (censer), 471; quincunx banners in art, 459; sculpture banners and banner holders, **432**, 476–477, **479**; war banners and marker stones, 478

Barrera Rubio, Alfredo, xxxii; and Mayapán art, 8, 31, 40, 76–77, 80–81, 88, 95, 553

Barrera Vásquez, Alfredo, 59–60

Basic ceremonial groups, 73, 127. *See also* colonnaded halls; focal node architecture, temples

Batab(ilob), 47, 49, 55, 101, 524

Beach, Timothy, xxxii, 6, 405, 407, 544

Beads, currencies, 247, 274, 280–281, 285–**286**, **287**, 299, 314, 318–**319**, 320, **324**, 326, 328, 335, 347–348, 420; distribution; 347–348, 366–**367**, 413–**414**, **416–417**; luxuries, 291; offerings, 114, 125–126, 144–145, 237, 348–349, 445; ornaments, **307–308**, 309–**311**, 312–313, 321, 323, **325–326**, 328, 423, 431, 439, 462, 474; preforms, 329–**330**, **331–332**; tribute, **271–272**, 278, 289, 347. *See also* bone objects; cache(s); currencies; greenstone; marine shell

Belize, xxx, 27, 42, 46, 62, 70, 76, **272**; cacao, 280, 289; Classic collapse, 409; lithic tools, 368, 370, 376–377; obsidian, 349, 363; Postclassic populations 536; Postclassic pottery, 69–70, 429–430, 461, 466, 548. *See also* Caracol; Caye Coco; censers; Chetumal; chronology; Laguna de On; Santa Rita

Benches, **210**, **227**, **233**

Berdan, Frances F.: and complex market and tribute systems, 270, 276, 284, 420, 542; and core cities, 546; and crafting and rites of passage, 297; and craft production heterogeneity (sites and regions), 6, 9, 294, 301; and Postclassic Mesoamerican world system, 5, 8, 24, 30, 50, 54, 270, 430, 549, 557; and post-Mayapán prosperity, 527–528, 550; and merchant suppression, 544

Bey, George: and censers, 430; and chronology, 69; and civic-ceremonial architecture, 107, 155, 185; and Feathered Serpent ideology/ elite interaction, 29, 47, 50, 82, 270, 430, 456, 548–549; and great houses, 56; and inves-

Campeche: 49, 50, 77, 100, **272**; Canpech, 41, 100, **279**

Cancuen, 96

Canul, 52, 53, 523; Ah Canul, 41, **271**, 278–**279**

Caracol (Belize), 28, 550, 557

Caracol (Chichén Itzá), 76

Caribbean sites: pottery, 14, 159, 265; trade, 26, **271–272**, **297**, 408, 422; spindle whorls, 299; use of *Chama* shells, 326. *See also* agriculture; Caye Coco; community specialization; economic interdependency; hinterlands; Laguna de On; market exchange; Santa Rita; settlement patterns; Tulum

Carmack, Robert, 76; and big houses (*nim ja*), 72, 109–110, 151; and interregional ties, 48, 481; and K'ich'e political organization, 33, 50, 55, 57, 110, 153; and K'ich'e religion, 47, 55–56, 100, 110, 515; and merchants, 48; and militarism, 48, 399; and quadripartite principles, 57, 110, 156; and Postclassic Maya society 24; and Utatlán project, 27

Carnegie Institution of Washington Project, xxix, xxx, 16, 21, 34, 51, 104, **516–519**, **533–536**; art, 34, 63–64, 72–73, 76, 87, 106, 126, **239–240**, **241**, 299, 347–348, 376, 412, 554; censers and sculptures, 113–**114**, **115**, 119, 425, 430–431, 453, 456, 459, 465, 467, 469, 472, 511, 513; elite and public architecture, 72–73, 76, 78, 87, 91, 99, 107, 126, 168, **237–238**, 428; settlement study, 18–**19**, 20–21, 32, 63–64, 154–155, 161, 182–184, 194, 196, 199; views of Postclassic Maya society, 2, 15, 20, 24, 30, 106, 119. *See also Current Reports*; Jones, Morris; Pollock, Harry E.D.; Proskouriakoff, Tatiana; Roys, Ralph; Shook, Edwin; Smith, A. Ledyard; Smith, Robert; Thompson, J. Eric

Caves. *See* cenotes

Caye Coco: architecture, 42, 548; censers, 119; deer bone mortuary offerings, 254; distribution of ritual paraphernalia, 428; figurine, 466; hinterland to Mayapán, 2, 549–550; lithic tools, 27; spindle whorls, 299; turtle sculpture, 58. *See also* community specialization; economic interdependency; hinterlands

Cehache, **272**

Cehac-Hunacti Composite, 116, **124**, 426–427; Cehpech, 47, **271**, 278–**279**

Cenote(s): 14–15, 21, 403; Acanbalam, 184; burials, 64, 255, 264; cacao cultivation, 280; catfish, 400; Chac Si Kin, 175; Ch'en

Chooch, 78; Ch'en Kulu, 181; Ch'en Max, 182; Ch'en Mul, **75**, 78–79, 90, 435–**437**, 438, **455**, **483**, **488**, **495**, **501**, **518**; Ch'en Pie, 181; Ch'en Uc, xxx; Colonial towns, **271**; Cosil, 175; daily life, 38, 123; deer bone taphonomy, 254; distribution, **166**, 175–176, 184–186, 190, 199, 202, 403; Dzab-Na (Tecoh), 366; entrances blocked, 199; excavators, 518, 519; as focal nodes, 21, 31, 36, 42, 78, 92, 102, 149, 151, 156–158, 161, 169, 177, 184–186, 189–191, 550, 552, 554; Hoal, 42; Itzmal Ch'en, 64, 123, 126, **128**, 158, 177, 186, 188; Polbox, 182; pre-Mayapán settlement, 64, 69, 202, 550; along roads, 181–182, 184, 209; Sac Uayum, 552; sacrifice, 29; of Sacrifice (Chichén Itzá), 289; at sites near Mayapán, **44–45**; stone and ceramic sculptures, **432**, 435–438, 455, 476–477, 483, 488, 495, 501; variable attributes, 161, 199; X-Coton, 64, 91, **94**, 177, 188, **432**, 476–**477**, **519**; Xot Zum Ch'en, 175, 181; X-te Toloc, 181–182; Xtoloc (Chichén Itzá), 92; Yax-nab, 181–182; Yo Dzonot, 181; Zuytun Cab, 175. *See also* agriculture; females; focal node architecture; Itzmal Ch'en group; residences; roads; temples

Censers, 7, 73, 102, 145–146, 189, 425–431, 436–437, 513–515; adornos, 139, 144, 453, 456, 513–**514**; animal vessels, 476; cacao pods, 513–**514**; chronology, 68, 70, 91, 427, 528; concentration at elite/public buildings, 106, 113–121, 197, 261–262; decentralized religious practice, 34, 119, 265, 428; excavators, **516–520**; gods, 318, 438–**440**, **441**–443, **444**–445, **446**–447, 448–**450**, **451**–453, **454**–455, 456–**457**, 458–**464**, 465–**466**, 467–**468**, 469–470, **471–472**, **474**–475; hinterland/ peripheral sites, 34, 427–430, 546, 548–549, 553; iconographic ties to architecture, 426; incomplete censer deposits, 429; manufacture, 117, 252, 254, **258**, 261–262, 265, 281, 291, **295–296**, **298**, 415, 419, 428, 430, 543, 546; Mayapán as nucleus of industry, 427, 429, 546, 548–549; mortuary contexts, 92–93, 113, 429, 469–**470**; non-effigy, 112–113, 115–117, 119, **121**, 144, 189, 426–427, 445, 448; restricted contexts, 36, **114**, **121**, **440**; revitalization movement, 70–71, 427, 527–528, 549; sacrificial and massacre contexts, 91–92, 98, 101, 117, **255**, 429, 524, 528–529, **530**, 532; spatial (frequency) distributions, 88, 106, 113, 117, 119–**120**, 145, 480–481, **482–510**, 511–515; termination rituals, 99, 130, 132, **134**, **135**, 139,

429, 532, **533**–**534**; and urns, 259–**260**; and Veracruz figurines, 430. *See also* ancestors; Aztec; birds; calendrical ceremonies; colonnaded halls; felines; gods; Itzmal Ch'en group; pottery; priests; religion; reptiles; sculptures; temples; termination rituals centralizing capacities, 37–38, 57–58, 71, 84, 110, 151, 153, 187, 191, 521, 524, 538, 541, 548–551, 554–555; council rule at other sites, 49, 56; dissolution, 522–**523**, 524–525, 529, 534, 537–538; paramount leaders, 47–51, 85, 102, 522, 555. *See also* collapse; divine kingship; elites; focal node architecture; governing elites; political organization; settlement patterns; urban planning

Ceramics. *See* Buff Polbox; censers; Chompoxte Red-on-cream; chronology; Mama Red; Matillas Fine Orange; Navula Unslipped; Pelé Polychrome; pottery; Tecoh Red-on-buff; Yacman Striated

Chac. *See* gods, censers

Chac masks, 20, 52, 64, **75**, 80, 113, 188, 448

Chacmool, **432**, 472, **473**

Chakan, **271**, 278–**279**, 290

Champotón, 41, 47, **272**, 278–**279**, 461, 513, 524

Chan Pixyah, **45**

Chanputun. *See* Champotón

Chase, Arlen, 5; and calendrical ceremonies, 146, 550; and censers, 146, 461, 550; and complexity of Maya cities, 2, 5–6, 8, 10, 28, 149–150, 189, 191, 550, 557; and craft production, 419; and figurines, 461; and interregional style, 77; and market exchange, 26, 272, 276, 543, 558; and Postclassic Maya society, 24, 538, 550, 557; and Postclassic site organization, 190, 265; and Santa Rita Corozal, 46, 425, 461

Chase, Diane, 5; and calendrical ceremonies, 58, 102, 146, 428, 514, 550; and censers, 146, 428, 461, 514, 550; and complexity of Maya cities, 2, 5–6, 8, 10, 28, 149–150, 189, 191, 550, 557; and craft production, 419; and figurines, 461; and interregional style, 77; and market exchange, 26, 272, 543, 558, 276; and Postclassic Maya society, 24, 538, 550, 557; and Postclassic site organization/administration, 107–108, 154–155, 157, 175, 185, 189–190, 265; and rotating political/religious duties, 56, 58, 111, 157, 176, 428, 514; and Santa Rita Corozal, 46, 111, 425, 428, 461

Chauaca, 45, 167, **271**, 278, 282

Chel, 51–52. *See also* Ah Kin Chel

Ch'en Mul Modeled. *See* censers

Ch'en Uc, **43, 44**

Chert/chalcedony, 125–126, **278**, 281, 294–**295**, 374, 376–377, **382**, **391**, **393**, 395, 418, 547; arrow shafts, 15; axes, 281, 285, 366, **368**–370, **371**–372, 374–377, **378**, 380, 382–**384**, 390–**391**, 392, **394**–**395**, 396, **397**–**398**; frequencies relative to obsidian, 27, **357**–358, **359**–**360**, 361, **362**–**364**; gravers and perforators, **369**–370, 372, **373**–**374**, 375, 377–**378**, 380–**381**, 384–**385**, 386, **387**–388, **391**–392, **393**–**395**; lithic production tools (cores, preforms, hammerstones), 281, 294, 320, 358, **368**, 370–**371**, **375**, **379**, **381**, 386, 388–**389**, 390, 392, **393**–**395**, 418, 420, **530**; pestles and polishers, 125; projectile points and knives (weaponry), 7, 125, 281, 284, **297**, 363, **368**, 370–**371**, **372**, **374**–**375**, 376–377, **378**–**379**, 381–**384**, 386, 389–390, **391**–392, **393**–**395**, 396, **397**–**398**, 399, 418, 525, 528–**530**; regional stylistic tool similarities, 42, 548–549; sources, 150, 281, 294; tools, **363**–**364**, **368**–**369**, 370, **371**–**375**, 411; unifaces, 358, **360**, 362, **368**–**369**, 370, **372**, **374**–**375**, **379**, **381**, **384**–**385**, 388, **391**–392, 528; workshop and non-workshop contexts, 215, 261, 291, **295**–296, **297**–**298**, 356–**357**, 377, **378**–**385**, 386, **387**–**389**, 390–**391**, 392, **393**–**395**, 396, 415–416, 418. *See also* agriculture; craft production; greenstone; obsidian; occupational specialization; residences; warfare; weapons

Chetumal, xxix, 14, 41, 46, **272**, 278–**279**

Chi, Gaspar Antonio, 60, 101, 289, 522

Ch'ibal(ob), 48, 56, 196

Chich'en Itzá: architectural features compared to Mayapán, 8, 10, 15, 27–29, 43, 49, 57–58, 76, 78, 89, 104, 546; Cenote Xtoloc, 92; Chacmool, 472; drought, 35, 525; during and after Mayapán's reign, 42, 271, 278, 280; dwellings, 202; Feathered Serpent priests and sun disks, 82; historical ties to Mayapán, 51, 52–53, 60–61, 63, 69, 75–76, 78, 522, 556; house society, 56; Kukulcan as founder, 87, 104; investiture and pilgrimage, 57, 82, 283; Isla Cerritos port, 408; jaguars in art, 135, 458–459; lords, lineages, and priests, 53–54, 56, 58, 271, 278, 435, 522; market exchange, 270, 283, 289; marketplace, 165; Osario burial shaft, 92–93, 96; Postclassic effigy censers, 93, 456, 460, 462; primate status, 270; regional road system, 280, 546;

role in Mayapán's founding, 29; serpent iconography, 89; site planning and focal nodes, 185; skull platform, 436, 513; Temple of the Jaguars, 82; Temple of the Warriors, 289; warrior orders, 458–459, 462

Chic Kaban festival. *See* Maní

Chicxulub crater, 15

Chikinchel, 6, 41–42, 46, **271**, 278–**279**, 537, 550

Chilam Balam books: 59, 96, 410, 526, 538; of Chumayel, 14, 68, 88, 405, 458, 521, 524; of Maní, 405

Childe, V. Gordon, 8, 542, 552, 555, 560

Chinamit, 56

Cholula, 29, 54, 57, 88, 435

Chompoxte Red-on-cream, 22, 111, 142, 143, 144

Chronology, 13–14, 24, 30–31, 35, 39, 41, 59, **63**, 69–70, 102, 194, 257, 427; archaeological, 61–71, 102; collapse and post-collapse, 37, 522–523, 524–525, 549; Hocabá and Tases phases, 69, 194; mythohistorical accounts, 59–61; Postclassic pottery distribution, 64–**65**, 68–69, **70**–**71**, 259; pre-Mayapán pottery spatial distributions, 62–64, **65**–**67**, 69, 102; problems with Early Postclassic, 69–70; radiocarbon, 61–**63**, 67, 71, 102, 143, 200, **523**–524, 532, **535**–**536**, 538; stelae dates, 79–80. *See also* censers; collapse; Hocaba ceramic phase; k'atun; pottery; radiocarbon dates; segmented century; settlement patterns; stela(e); Tases ceramic phase; termination rituals

Chunchucmil, xxxii, 10; atypical political organization, 49, 151, 547; craft production, 294, 419; houselot walls, 154, 180; marketplace and market exchange, 27, 165; population density, 28, 266

Cimatán, **272**, 278

Civic-Ceremonial architecture. *See* colonnaded halls; focal node architecture; governing elites; monumental center; oratories; shrines; temples; urban planning

Civlituk, 49

Clark, John E., 282, 288, 292, 295, 297, 419, 428

Classic Period, 8, 11, 15, 24, 28, 34, 53, 85, 92, 95–96, 99, 170, 176, 547; collapse of, 11, 37, 536–537, 556–557; earlier settlement near Mayapán, 30–31, **43**–**45**, 46, 60, 62–**63**, 64–**65**, **66**–**67**, 69, 102, 194, **255**–**256**, 299, 537, 546; importance of commercial exchange, 26–27, 270, 272–273, 277, 283, 294, 407, 419, 542, 544, 557; occupation of Mayapán area, 62–67; population density, 28; precursors

of Mayapán traditions, 2, 8, 10, 14, 23–24, 38, 48–49, 76, 103, 149–151, 188–189, 216, 254, 265–266, 301, 318, 376, 409, 430, 456, 475–476, 531, 539, 543, 555, 556–557. *See also* Chichén Itzá; chronology; market exchange; political organization; pottery; religion; settlement patterns

Climate change. *See* collapse; drought; environment

Cloth. *See* textiles

Coatimundi, 476–**477**

Cobá, 46, 51, 154, 185, 197, 245–246, **247**

Cochuah, 41, **271**–**272**, 278

Cocom: at Chichén Itzá, 51, 53, 61; association with Kukulcan, 53, 55, 555; as governing elites, 28, 39, 50, 51–53, 60, 101, **523**–524; mortuary patterns, 109; in Sotuta/Contact Period, 28, 42, 289; in Telchaquillo, 51; wars with the Xiu, 37, 52, 101, 522, **523**, 525–526, 538, 559. *See also* collapse; elites; governing elites; myths; political organization

Codex. *See* codices, central Mexico; codices, Maya

Codices, central Mexico: 456, 462, 467, 478; Borgia, 90, 95, 303, 370, 450; gender roles, 297; Kukulcan/Quetzalcoatl, 84, 88, 95, 462; quincunx banners, 459; Mendoza codex, 289, 297; Mixtec codices, 84, 95, 461–462; Nuttall codex 88, 95, 459, 461–462; weapons, 303, 370; Vindobonensis, 84, 462

Codices, Maya, 25, 110, 135; animals, 249, 399, 402; Dresden, 79, 95, 318, 370, 453, 456; gender roles, 295; Kukulcan/Quetzalcoatl, 95, 318, 456; Madrid , 95, 249, 284, 306, 370, 399, 402, 427; Paris, 59, 453; rotating offices, 59; gods, 79, 318, 425, 427, 439, 442, 445, 447, 449, 452–453, 460, 462–463, 465; warfare and sacrifice, 100, 399, 528; weapons, 306, 370, 386–387, 397

Colha: animal use, 399; chert source, **368**–**369**; craft specialization, 160, 216, 291, 293–294; mass grave, 96, 99–100; stone tool types, 370, 376

Collapse (Mayapán), 35, 52, 67–68, 515, 521–539, **523**–524, 541, 554–556; climate change, 405, 407, 521, **523**, 525–526, 537–538; destruction and abandonment events, 68, 428, 430, 521, **523**, 524–525, 531–532, **533**–**536**, 537; factional strife, 36–37, 54, 521–522, **523**, 538, 555, 559; post–Mayapán populations, 83, 527, 537, 539, 549, 556; prolongation of collapse, 521–522,

Copán, 28, 49, 478, 555

Copper: axes, 285; bells, **260**, 292; crafting, 252, **258**, 281, 291–**292**, **295–296**, **298**, 312, 348–349, 411–**413**, 416, 422, 543; currencies, 274, 285, 318, 348, 422; frequencies, **292**, 411–**413**; mortuary offerings, 93, 237, 252, **256**, **260**, 286; rings, **260**; sheets, **260**; trade goods, 36, 273, 282–283; tweezers, **260**. *See also* craft production; elites; luxury goods; residences; wealth

Cores. *See* chert/chalcedony; obsidian

Corn, 79, 283, 288, 376, 403, 405–**406**, 407, 409, 419, 421, 452–453; maize breads, 290, 421, 452, 544; trade, 36, 283, 288, 408, 421, 544; tribute, **271–272**, 278–**279**, 288. *See also* agriculture; censers; chert/chalcedony; gods; nonresidential enclosures; occupational specialization

Corvée labor, 36; agriculture, 288, 376; military service, 216, 294, 528; single dwellings, 216, 294, 421. *See also* occupational specialization

Cosmopolitan attributes, 1, 30, 40, 77, 102, 136, 194, 270, 469, 512, 546, 548. *See also* Aztec; ethnicity; urban planning

Cotecpan, 50. *See also* kings

Cotton. *See* agriculture; textiles

Council rule. *See* confederacy government

Cozumel: agglutinated structures, 215; allied to Mayapán, 41–42, 47; benches and altars, 232, 234; civic-ceremonial architecture, 49, 109, 111; dwellings, 194, 205, 211, 238, 548; hammocks, 202; merchants and commerce, 109, 196, 283; platforms, 213, 215; pottery, 159; products 6, 299, 399, 408; shrines and pilgrimage, 137, 277, 283, 511; spatial segregation of ritual buildings, 197; walled enclosures, 245, 247, 289. *See also* Freidel, David A.; hinterlands; Sabloff, Jeremy A.

Craft production: 9–10, 33, 151, 281, 292–294, 300–320, 415–416, 418–422, 542–544, 558; artisans drawn to urban centers, 299; crafts barrio, 6, 160, 187, 219, **355**, 416; crafting houselots, 127, **295**, **296**, **298**, 354, 358, 410, 412–**413**; frequencies of goods made and used, 261–262, **300**–301, 302–**303**, 304–**309**, 310–**315**, **316**–**317**, 318, **319**–321, **322**–**327**, 328, **329**–**335**, 336, **337**–**343**, 344, **345**–**346**, 347–349, **350**–**352**, 353–**357**, 358, **359**–**360**, **362**–**365**, 366, **367**–**369**, 370, **371**–**375**, 376, **378**–**385**, 386, **387**–**389**, 390, **391**–**395**, 396, **397**–**398**; and gender, 294–295; intensity and scale, 33, 269, 291–294, 354, 415, 419, 544, 558, 560; in

medieval towns, 12; mortuary offerings, **258**; multicrafting, 291–292, **295**, **298**; ordinary goods required for public events, 313–314; segregated stages of production, 9, 282, 301, 558; shared household tasks, 558; urban focus on final stages, 282, 299, 301, 419; and wealth, 259, 285, 294, 410–**413**, **414**–415, **416**–**417**, 419. *See also* bone objects; burials; censers; chert/chalcedony; Childe, V. Gordon; community specialization; copper; economic interdependency; figurines; honey; household economy; luxury goods; marine shell; market exchange; obsidian; occupational specialization; pottery; stucco; textiles; woodworking

Credit. *See* economic organization

Crocodile, 87; art, 95–**97**, 313, 476–**477**; bone objects, **307**, 309, 313. *See also* gods; myths

Cruz Alvarado, Wilberth, xxxi; censer production, 254, 261, 291, 543; metallurgy, 291, **298**, 348, 543; pottery analysis, 20–21, 63, 68–69, 112, 113, 115, 117, 119, 126, **140**, 143, 199, 257–259, 261, 263, 282, 427

Cuchcabalob, 47

Cuchcabob. *See* Ah Cuch Cab

Cuchteel, 55–56, 153, 197

Cupul, 6, 41, 52, **271**, 278–**279**; Naobon Cupul, **271**

Currencies, 36, 274, **279**, 280, 285, **286–287**, 299; cacao, 144, 274, 280, 285–**286**, 407; copper, 274, 280, **286**, 348–349; equivalencies, 285, **287**, 288; gradations of currency value, 285, 318, 320; jade, 274, **286**; mortuary contexts, **260**; shell, 274–275, 280, 285–**286**, 314, **316**, 318–**319**, 320, 326, 328, 334–336, 344, 347–348, 407; textiles, 274, **286**; use beyond Maya area, 287; wage labor, 288. *See also* cacao; copper; greenstone; marine shell; market exchange; textiles; value

Current Reports (Carnegie), 19, 21, 34, **114–115**, **297**, 347, 425, 430–431, 456, 472

Custodial houses, 72, **74–75**, 77, **93**, 108–109, 146, 171, 188, **346**–348, **360**, 421. *See also* copper; residence H-11; residences

Dahlin, Bruce H.: Chunchucmil, 5, 10, 15, 49, 151, 154, 165, 180, 189, 294, 419, 547; commons areas, 244; marketplaces and market economy, 26–27, 163, 165, 273–274, 283, 543, 560; PEMY project, xxix, xxxii, 22; plaster production, 281

Deane, Anne, xxxi, **80**, **81**, **97**
Death God. *See* censers; gods; myths; sculptures; stucco
Deer, xxx, 399–401, 428; bone mortuary offerings, 126, 254, **255–257**, 264; bone tools, 302, **303–304, 306–307**, 312; husbandry, 126, 249, 273, 281, 289, 399, 401–402, 409–410, 544. *See also* animals; bone objects; burials; females; market exchange
Deities. *See* gods
Defensive features. *See* wall; warfare
Degenerate model (Postclassic civilization), 2, 11, 20, 24; refutation, 24–25, 36, 102, 556–557. *See also* Freidel, David A.; political organization; Smith, A. Ledyard; Smith, Michael E.; urbanism
Delgado Kú, Miguel, xxxi; domestic architecture, 126–127, 237, 261, 281, monumental architecture, 20; murals, 21, 25, 31, 40, 46, 77, 80–82, **84**, 87–89, 95–96, 452, 553, 560
Delgado Kú, Pedro, xxxi; chronology, 63–64, 68–69; domestic architecture, 64, 126–127, 180, 261; monumental architecture, 16, 20–22, 52, 62, 64, 72–**74**, **75**–79, 85–87, 91, **93–94**, 95, 98, 100, 109, 122, 125, **128**, 130, 132, 145, 188, 190, 281, 436, 465, **516–518**, 532, 551
Divine kingship, 25, 48–49, 53, 560; divine lineages of Mayapán, 31, 49, 103. *See also* ancestors; elites; governing elites; myths; political organization
Diving god. *See* gods
Dogs, 101; in art, 130, **133**, 476–**477**; bone objects, **307**, 309, 312; faunal assemblage, 249, 281, 399, 400–402, 413, 428
Dresden codex. *See* codices, Maya
Drought(s), 35, 37, 405, 407, 410, 521, **523**, 525–526, 537–538, 545, 555
Dwellings. *See* residential groups *by name*
Dynasties: Classic era, 25, 38, 48, 85, 96, 99, 539, 555; at Mayapán, 25, 39–40, 50–53, 61, 83–85, 99, 102–103, 433, 461, 539; at other Postclassic sites, 85, 462–463. *See also* collapse; confederacy; governing elites; myths; political organization
Dzibilchaltun, 15, 154–155, 202, 216, 301

Earth lord. *See* gods
Ecab, 41, 45, **272**, 278–**279**, 282
Economic embeddedness. *See* market exchange
Economic Foundations of Mayapán Project. *See* PEMY

Economic interdependency, 5, 6, 8–10, 12–13, 26, 33, 150–151, 269–270, **271–272**, 273, 275, 277–288, **279**, 281–282, 289, 291, 415, 418–422, 542–547, 557–558; raw materials (local), 299, 273, 282; raw materials (non-local), 273, 282, 419–420; regional, 273, 290, **295**, 301, 545–547, 558; resource heterogeneity, 36, 277, 279, **295**, 419. *See also* community specialization; craft production; elites; market exchange; wealth
Economic organization, 415–416, 418–423; alliance networks and trade, 270, **271–272**, 277–278, 279, 281, 422–423; credit in pre-modern commerce, 274, 287–288; elite control of economic institutions, 275–276, 282–283, 416, 418; independence from elite control , 273, 416, 418, 560; overlapping exchange modes, 269, 275–276; redistribution, 275–276; wage labor, 288. *See also* community specialization; craft production; economic interdependency; elites; household economy; houselot enclosures; labor; market exchange; occupational specialization; political organization; wealth
Effigy censer(s). *See* censers
Ehecatl. See gods
Elites, 34, 196, 548; access to *Spondylus* shell, 346; assigning commodity value, **274**, 318, 320; balkanization, 35; coastal Caribbean elites, 548, 550; economic oversight, 36, 275–276, 282–283, 416, 418; elite sector growth and political stress, 54, 555; feasting and consumption, 7, 123, 125, 276, 290–291, 313–314, 409, 541–542; gifting, 269, 275, 290; hierarchy and heterarchy, 543–544; houselot size, 243–245; literati, 542, 559; luxury craft production, 254, 258, 261–262, 276, 291, 543; luxury goods exchange, 277, 558; occupations and official posts, 36, 54–57, 175–177, 185–187, 545, 547; political facilities, 38; portraits, 431, **432–434**, 435–**437**; regional interaction, 38; residences, 170, **171–174**, 176; rotating calendrical offices, 56–59, 102, 554–555; top-down processes, 3, 7, 11, 30, 106, 187, 191, 265, 268, 346, 541, 543–544, 551, 553; tribute exemptions, 288; ward leaders, 36. *See also* ancestors; censers; dynasties; emblematic style; focal node architecture; governing elites; hinterland; pottery; religion; residences; sculptures; urban planning; wealth
El Meco, 46
El Tajín, 93, 478

Laguna de On: censers, 428–429; lack of figurines, 466; lithic tools, 27, 299, 363, 376, 398;
Mayapán's hinterland, xxix, xxxii, 150, 428;
obsidian, 27, 363; spindle whorls, 299. *See also*
hinterlands
Land. *See* agriculture; houselot enclosures
Landa, Bishop Diego de: and animal use, 281,
289–290, 295, 400–401; and book burning, 25;
and cenotes, 175–176; censer rituals, 427–428,
514; and concentric model, 154, 175–176, 185,
252; and currencies, 280, 285, 347; and dwellings, 202; and epidemic, 527; and founding
of city, 14, 48, 51, 56, 60–61, 71–72, 151, 160, 187,
267, 281, 547, 552; and goods required for ceremonies, 7, 125, 290; and House of Commerce,
167, 282–283; and hurricane, 526; and k'atun
history, **523**, 524; and k'atun wheel, 58; and
Kukulcan Maní festival, 55, 83, 104, 290, 453;
and Mayapán's collapse, 14, 60, 521–**523**, 524,
526–527, 537; and mortuary patterns, 109, 252,
254, 529; and occupational specialization, 54,
252, 281, 295, 297, 428; and political organization, 48, 50–51, 56, 58, 151, 159–160, 176, 187,
267, 522, 537; and priests, 33, 53–54, 82–83, 176,
267, 290, 428; sacrifice, 99; and slaves, 280,
522; and Temple of Kukulcan, 78, 88; and
tooth modification, 461; and trade, 42, 270,
280–281, 284, 287, 289, 400–401, 407, 527; and
tribute, 281, 288; and young men's houses, 109
Landscape(s). *See* built environment
Lanes. *See* roads
Late Preclassic Period, 8, 11, 26–27, 48, 274, 326;
settlement around Mayapán, 30, 62, **67**, 102
Law of Environmental Limitation on Culture,
10
League of Mayapán. *See* confederacy
LiDAR survey, xxxi, 19, 181
Lithics. *See* chert/chalcedony; greenstone;
obsidian
Longue durée, 30, 539
Lords. *See* confederacy; elites; governing elites;
political organization
Love, Bruce, 55–56, 59, 515, 555
Luxury goods, 7, 13, 273–274, 276–277, 291, 366,
420, 548, 558–559; continuum of value, 274,
285, 290, 318, 320, 366, 420; determining
value, **274**, 318, 320; exchange, 273, 543, 546,
558–559; production, 36, 254, 258, 261–262,
291, 312. *See also* copper; elites; market
exchange; Residence Q-40a; wealth
Lynch, Kevin, 11, 31–32, 189, 190–191, 551–554

Maguey, 282, 301–302, 306
Maize. *See* corn
Maize God. *See* gods
Mama (settlement), 46
Mama Red pottery: burial offerings, 255;
Chichén Itzá Osario, 93; chronology, 68–69;
decorated, 115, **124**; Hall Q-88 assemblage,
112–113; high proportions across Mayapán,
117–118, 119, 259; House Y-45a assemblage,
124, 137, 139, **141–143**; pottery workshop
Q-176, 261; similarities to east coast, 42. *See
also* chronology; pottery
Mandibles, **80**; effigies, 78, **438**, 472, 474
Maní, 4, 41–42, **44**, 46–47, **271–272**, 278–**279**;
Chilam Balam book, 405; church, 537;
Kukulcan festival, 54–55, 83, 104
Manos: in art, 463; caches, 125; contexts and
uses 408–409; grave goods, 256, **258**, 409
Map (Carnegie map of Mayapán), **19**, 153–154.
See also Hare, Timothy S.; Jones, Morris
Marine shell, 274–275, 278–**279**, 280–281, 292,
295, **298**, 314, **315–317**, 318–**319**, 320–321,
322–323; in art, **432**, 453, 456, 471; beads in
altar caches, 114, 144–145, 348, 445; celts, 314,
321; chastity ornaments, 125, 254–**255**, 318;
conch shell trumpets, 92, 126, 396; currencies,
274–275, 280, 285–**286**, **287**, 299, 314, 318–**319**,
320, **324**, 326, 328, 334–336, 344, 346–349,
407, 413, 415, 420; deities emerging from
shells, 128, **131**, 442; finished objects, **325–326**,
328–329, 334, **335–336**, 339, **340–341**, **414**,
416–417; fossil shell artifacts, **327**–328, **333**;
gift exchange, 125; imported raw material, 151,
273, 281, 294, 314, 320, 420; INAH monumental center objects, **332**, 344, **345–346**; jewels
and ornaments, 237, 280, **286**, 291, 314, 318,
320, **325–326**, 328–**329**, **332**, 347–348, 413–**414**,
415–**416**, **417**, 420, 439; Kukulcan insignia, 92,
95, 318, 453, 456; manufacturing debris, **324**,
327–**328**, 329, 330–**335**, 326, 337–**338**; mortuary
contexts, 237, 254–**255**, **256**, **260**, 347–349;
palettes and cups, 291, 314, 321, **330**, 471; rings,
237, **329**, 348; trade commodity, 7, 36, 123, 410,
418, 422, 544; workshop and non-workshop
contexts and assemblages, 187, 261, 293–294,
296–297, **298**, 320–321, **324**, **327**–328, 336,
337–343, 344–**345**, **346**–347, 356, **373**, **387**, 392,
393–395, 413–**414**, 415, **416–417**, 418, 544. *See
also* craft production; community specialization; currencies; economic interdependency;
elites; market exchange; wealth

Market exchange, xxxii, 26–27, 33, 36, 146, 269–270, 274, 418, 420–422, 541–543, 545–547, 557–559; administration, 276, 282–283, 422; artifact densities, 200; Classic Period sites, 9–10, 26–27, 151, 163, 259, 270, 276, 283, 557; craft production, 10, 151, 269, 273, 276, 293, 418, 420, 559–560; currencies, 274, 280, 285; economic stability, 35, 557; embeddedness (in social institutions), 542; enmities and blockades, 278; equitable distribution of (access to) goods, 265; exchanged goods, 159, 259, 265, 277–**279**, 280–284, 289, 291, 366, 410–412, 415, 418, 420, 422–423, 557; food supply and trade, 35, 274, 405, 407–408, 421–422; maritime transport and ports, 270, 408; medieval towns, 12–13, 274; mundane, 7, 542; nested scales, 269–270, 272; organizational variation, 270, 275–276, 557–559; pilgrimage and market fairs 7, 197, 277, 282–283, 559; Postclassic amplification, 11, 26–27, 270, 272, 542–543; rules governing exchange, 7, 276, 282–283, 349, 543; slaves, 101; storage, 284; taxation, 558. *See also* community specialization; craft production; currencies; economic interdependency; economic organization; marketplace(s); ritual economy; roads; wealth

Marketplace(s): administrative features/institutions, 45, 165, 167, 215, 282–283, 558; archeological identification, 273, 283; associated shrines, 167, 197; associated with community wealth and prestige, 276–277, 299, 422, 559; association with major route within city, 158, 175, 177, 184–185, 187, 553; elite neighborhood by Square K marketplace, 6, **164**, 169, 171, **172–173**, 174–176, 185, 187, 190, 247, 418, 553; as focal nodes, 106, 158, 161, 177, 185, 189; ground level alignments (possible stall foundations), 165, 167, 283; market plazas at other sites, 45, 165, 167, 215, **271–272**, 282–283; market plaza spaces at Mayapán, 6, 32–33, 106, 149, 158, 163–167, **164**, **166**, 213, 215, 283, 554; neighborhood vendors, 543; nested hierarchies, 27, 418; open spaces suitable for markets, 163, 215; rules governing exchange, 7, 276, 349, 543. *See also* economic organization; focal node architecture; market exchange; neighborhoods

Masks. *See* Chac masks; pottery

Mass graves, 67, 99–101, 409, 528–529, 532; artifacts, 309, **360**, 376, 377, **382**, 386; desecration

of bones, 100, 529, **530**; Itzmal Ch'en, **63**, 100, 115, 117, **120**, 122–**123**, 127, 130, 252, **255**, 523–524, **530**, 532; pottery and censers, 101, 115, 117, **120**, 122–**123**, 429, 465; radiocarbon dates, **63**, 523–524, 538; Temple Q-80, 100, 465, **523**, 524. *See also* burial shaft temples; censers; chronology; collapse; Itzmal Ch'en group; sacrifice; Temple Q-58; Temple Q-80; Temple Q-95; warfare

Massive platform, 25, 205, 213–**214**, 215, **255**, 283. *See also* Cozumel

Mataya, **45**

Matillas Fine Orange: chronology 68; distribution across Mayapán, 115, 159, 259, 281–282, 284, 285; nonlocal trade good, 26, 159, 215, 272, 420, 423; poor ethnic indicator, 159, 215, 259, 281, 282, 284; shrine association, 157

May cycle, 14, 37–38, 56–59, 82, 158, 191, 290, 429

Medieval urban life, 12–13, 31, 266, 274, 547–548, 552, 555, 560

Mena, Fernando, xxx, 51

Mercantile model. *See* market exchange; merchants

Merchants, 12, 22, 26–27, 159, 163, 167, 197, 273–274, 276, 278, 280, 282, 284–285, 287, 422, 542–543, 546, 558–559; in art and religion, 79, 85, **87**, 116, 145, 197, 273, 430, 436, **439–440**, **449–450**, **451**, 452, 458, 465, 481, **482–487**, **494–499**, **506–507**, 508, 510–511, 513, 515, 544; hierarchies, 13, 24, 26–27, 163, 167, 176, 196, 270, 277, 422, 543; lodging, 109, 196; medieval town merchants, 12; military aspects, 101, 284; other towns, 48–49, 51, **272**, 278, 284; protection, 101, 274, 276, 284, 528, 558; storage, 195, 197, 215, 284; suppression by elites, 273, 544. *See also* community specialization; economic interdependency; gods; luxury goods; market exchange; marketplace; occupational specialization; wealth

Merchant God. *See* gods

Mérida: archaeological sites and routes, 15, 546; climate, 20, 408; Contact Period Maya center, 15, 46, 56, 539; museum objects, 460, 462. *See also* Tihó

Metates: abandonment, 531; in art, 79, 125, 463, 510; monumental buildings, 122; residences, 218, 408–409, 420–421

Migration: Kowoj, xxxii; 22, 52, 68; to Mayapán, 159, **523**, 547–548, 559; out of Mayapán, 68, 524. *See also* collapse; Kowoj; myths; urban planning

Milbrath, Susan: and archaeoastronomy, 76, 78, 81–82, 560; and censers, 119, 146, 426–430, 442–443, 445, 448, 452, 456, 461, 463, 465, 467, 471, 510–511, 513–514, 528, 546, 548–549; and creation mythology, 31, 77–79, 81, 84–85, 87–88, 95–96, 471; and ethnicity and politics, 22, 39, 50–52, 60, 64, 527; and interregional art themes, 8, 40, 48, 77, 91, 98, 135, 194, 445, 465, 467, 472, 475, 510, 513, 546, 553; and Kukulcan, 456, 467, 475; and monumental architecture and calendrical cycles, 25, 38–39, 59–61, 64, 68–71, 75, 78–79, 111, 525, 527–528, 532; and revitalization movements, 70–71; sacrifice, 100, 471

Military service. *See* warfare

Milpa mapping units (residential zones), xxx, 6, 22–**23**, 161–**162**, 163, 193, 196, 202, **203–204**, 205–**206**, **207**–208, **209–210**, 217, 219–**220**, 221–**222**, **223**, **224–227**, 228, **230–232**, 234–**235**, **236–237**, 240, **242**, 245–**247**, 249, 259, 347, 402–**404**; Milpa 1, 160, 187, 208, 213–**214**, 215, 219–**220**, 223, 236–237, 245, 261–262, **298**, 354–**355**, 356, 405–**406**, 415–416, 418, 543, 554; Milpa 2, **298**, 418; Milpa 4, 217–**218**, 219, 223, **298**, 356, 418; Milpa 5, 223, 236; Milpa 6, 219–**220**, 223, 236, 262; Milpa 7, **201**, 216, 219, 255; Milpa 8, 223, 229, 236, 262; Milpa 9, 219, 229, 236; Milpa 10, 216, 223, 234, 236, 262, **298**; Milpa 11, 223, 236, **298**, **304**, 356, 418; Milpa 12, 182–183, **209**–211, **212**, 216–217, 219, 223, 262–263; Milpa 13, 223, 229, 236; Milpa 14, 223; Milpa 15, **209**–211, 213, 219, 223, 229, 236, 263, **298**, 418; Milpa 16, 229, **298**, 356, 418; Milpa 17, 229, 262; Milpa 18, 223; Milpa 19, 183, 223; Milpa 20, 223, 229; Milpa 21, 211; Milpa 24, 183, 219; Milpa 26, 223, 262; Milpa 28, 157, 223, 229; Milpa 29, 177, 211, **213**, 244; Milpa 30, 223, 229; Milpa 32, 219, 223, 236, **298**, 356, 418; Milpa 33, 219, 223, 229, 236; Milpa 34, 223, 234; Milpa 35, 223, 229, 262. *See also* agriculture; houselot enclosures; Jones, Morris; neighborhoods; residences; roads; settlement patterns

Mitla, 84, 103

Mixtecs, 57, 84, 95, 461–462. *See also* codices; Kukulcan; Pohl, John M.D

Molds. *See* pottery

Money. *See* currencies

Monkeys: copper effigy bell, 237, 413; sculptures and façades, 128–129, **131**, 135, 136, 476–**477**; spider monkey bone, 400. *See also* monkey scribe

Monkey scribe, 98, 103, 437, **440**, 458, **468**, 471, **487**–**493**, **500**–**505**, **510**. *See also* gods

Monumental center (Mayapán), 15–**16**, **17**–**19**, 20–21, 24, 29, 39–40, 45–46, 59–64, 67–68, 71–**74**, **75**–79, **80**, 81–82, **83**–**84**, 85–**86**, **87**–89, **90**–92, **93**–**94**, 95–**97**, 98–104, 163, 528–529. *See also* altars; bone objects; burial shaft temples; censers; collapse; colonnaded halls; confederacy; elites; focal node architecture; gods; governing elites; INAH; marine shell; mass graves; murals; myths; sculptures; political organization; pottery; sculptures; shrines; temples; urban planning

Morley, Sylvanus G., 16, 59–60

Mortuary patterns. *See* burials; mass graves

Mosaic masks. *See* Chac masks

Multepal (council rule), 25, 31, 48–55, 85, 88, 102, 155, 176, 191, 196, 525, 555. *See also* confederacy; elites; governing elites; kings; political organization; urban planning

Murals, xxxiii, 21, 25, 40, 46, 77, 86, 88, 102–103, 107, 145, 194; Cacaxtla, 461; Chichén Itzá, 284, 289; Fisherman Temple (Q-95), 92, 95–**97**, 98–99, 111, 313, 456, 513; Santa Rita, 46, 450, 553; Sun Disk Hall (Q-161), 80–**83**, **84**–85; Temple of the Painted Niches (Q-80), 87–88, **90**, 448; Tulum, 46, 88, 425, 463, 465, 553. *See also* Delgado Kú, Miguel; Milbrath, Susan; myths; religion

Musical instruments: bone flutes and rasps, 302, **307**, 309–**311**, 313; ceramic drums, 113, 396; conch shell trumpet, 126, 396, 453; whistles, 252, 396

Myths: conjuring, 81–84; founding and creation mythology, 25, 29, 31, 38, 40, 52, 58–61, 70, 80–89, **90**, 92, 95–**97**, 98–99, 103, 156, 462–463, 471, 515, 559; international or foreign themes, 8, 40, 50. *See also* ancestors; censers; elites; gods; governing elites; Kukulcan; murals; religion; urban planning

Nachan Kan, xxix, **272**

Naco, 26

Nahuatl, 14, 50

Names of Mayapán, 14–15

Navula Unslipped pottery: Chichén Itzá Osario, 93; chronology, 68–69; Hall Q-88 assemblage, 112–113; high proportions across Mayapán, 117–**118**, 259, 262–263, **264**; non-effigy ritual ceramics, 145, 189; public

Paris, Elizabeth, xxxi, 24; and bone tools, 302; and copper production, 291, **298**, 312, 348–349, 411–412, 543; and effigy censers, 429–430; and Itzmal Ch'en mass grave, 67, 100, 117, 127

Paris Codex. *See* codices, Maya

Paths. *See* roads

Payil Red pottery, 159. *See also* pottery

Peabody Museum of Harvard, xxxi, **162**, **164**

Peccary: bone and tooth objects, **307**, 309, **311**; hunting, 249, 399; pens, 249; proportions of faunal assemblage, 400–401. *See also* animals, bone objects

Pelé Polychrome: chronology, 68; comparisons to Kowoj pottery, 22, 143–144, 159; distribution across Mayapán, 68, 115, 127, 259, 265, 515; fish designs, 111, **112**, 144, 515; Hall Q-88 assemblage, 111–112; House Y-45a assemblage, 111, **112–113**, **124**, 139, **140–143**; Palace R-86 assemblage, 515; turkey appliqué **113**; white pottery of Mayapán, 14; zoomorphic supports, 144. *See also* colonnaded halls; ethnicity; Kowoj; pottery; Residence Y-45a

PEMY (Proyecto Económico de Mayapán), xxix, xxx, 16, 21–**23**, 33–34, 51, 64, 516–519; bone objects, 302, **304**; burials, **255**, **257**, 259; craft production, **295**, **298**; fauna, 400; Itzmal Ch'en, **132**, **136**, **533**; lithics, **350**, **357**, **359–360**, 362, **366–367**, 369, 372, **374**, **378**, **382**, **387–389**, 393, 412–**413**; marine shell, 314–**315**, 321–**322**, 325, 328, **330**, **332–333**, 335, 336–**337**, **340**, **342**, 344, **414**, **416–417**; pottery results, 116–**118**, 119–**120**, **121**, 122–**123**, 513–**514**; settlement data, 153–154, 161–**162**, 182, 186, **203–204**, **237**, **242**, **247**, **249**, **251**, **253**, **296–297**, 402, **534**; spindle whorls, 299. *See also* agriculture; bone objects; chert/chalcedony; Colonnaded Hall H-15; craft production; focal node architecture; greenstone; house-lot enclosures; Itzmal Ch'en group; obsidian; marine shell; milpa mapping units; nonresidential fields; pottery; residences; spindle whorls; Temple H-17

Pens, 180, **201**, **212–214**, 218, 243, 248–250, **251–253**, 264, 401, 403. *See also* animals; houselot enclosures; nonresidential fields; residences

Perforators. *See* chert/chalcedony

Pestilence. *See* epidemic(s)

Petén, 41, 50, 76, 82, 96, 145, 266, **272**, 536, 549; censers, 429–430, 548–549; Classic collapse, 536; political organization, 54, 82; Kowoj, xxxii, 22, 40, 68, 82, 127, 144, 159, 191; pottery and ethnicity, 141, 144–145, 159; public buildings, 191. *See also* ethnicity; hinterlands; Itzá; Kowoj; Zacpetén

Peto Cream, 59. *See also* chronology; pottery

Pilgrimage, 37, 40, 55, 57, 79, 88, 167, 185, 188, 197, **272**, 289, 510–**511**; market fairs, 7, 197, 277, 283. *See also* market exchange

Piña Chan, Román, 6, 15, 26, 45, 51, 151, 153, 167, 178, 195–196, 270–**271**, **272**, 276–**279**, 280, 282–285, **287**, 290, 547, 558. *See also* community specialization; currencies; economic interdependency; economic organization; market exchange; marketplaces; tribute

Pixya, **44–45**

Planning. *See* urban planning

Playa del Carmen, 46

Pohl, John M. D.: elite interregional interaction, 29, 50, 57, 88, 151, 270, 277, 423, 548; dynastic heroic histories, 84, 103, 188, 459, 462; state-making and identity, 267

Polbox Buff pottery. *See* Buff Polbox

Pole (settlement), 46, 272

Political economy. *See* community specialization; craft production; economic interdependency; economic organization; political organization; market exchange; residences

Political organization, 8, 11–12, 14, 30–31, 39–43, 45–50, 60–61, 72, 99, 105, 149, 187, 415, 418, 529, 541, 551–552; alliance networks and trade, 2, **4**, 24, 27, 41–43, 50, 82, 150, 270, **271–272**, 277–278, 279, 281, 415, 422–423, 546, 549–550, 556; bureaucracy and administration, 6, 38, 40, 48–49, 55–57, 102–103, 106–108, 110–111, 122, 145, 152–153, 155, 160, 176, 187, 189, 196, 248, 262, 289, 422, 541, 559; capital cities, xxix, 1, 11, 14–15, 23, 27, 29, 35, 38–39, 43, 46–47, 60, 72, 102, 150–151, 158, 188, 265, 270, 415, 419, 521, 538–539, 546, 552, 557, 560; cycles of centralization and stability, 22–23, 36–38, 59, 61, 64, 101–102, 153, 407, 422, 427, 521–**523**, 524–525, 527, 531, 534, 537–**538**, 548–549, 554–557; factional strife, 61, 99, 153, 521–522, **523**, 538, 555, 559; historical groups and individuals, 49–53; investiture, 57; political and religious geography, **4**, 31, 36–38, 43, 46–48, 50, 54, 56–60, 64, 71, 158, 160, 176, 191, 270, 276, 290, 299, 548, 554–555; political economy, 3, 5, 7–9, 13, 35, 146, 272, 275, 289, 419–420, 542, 544, 558; power-sharing with priests, 33–35, 53–54,

Roads, 11, 15, **152**, 156–**157**, 158, **166**, 169–170, 185, 189–191, **198**, 229; bedrock pavement, 180, 182; from Gate AA (Minor), **166**, 182, **212**; from Gate B (Minor), **166**, 183; from Gate D, **157**, **164**, **166**, 177–179; from Gates EE (Major and Minor), **166**, 181–183; from Gate H, **157**, **165**–**166**, 169, 179–180; historical trails of possible antiquity, **162**, **166**, **168**, 178–179, 189, **212**; intersection at Cenotes Yax-nab and X-te Toloc, 181–182; intersection at northern sacbe terminus, 179; Mayapán's location amidst overland trade routes, 280, 299, 408; short residential zone lane segments, **183**–184; Tulum streets, 553. *See also* focal node architecture; houselot enclosures; neighborhoods

Robles Castellanos, Fernando, xxxii, 24, 46, 60–61, 69

Round temple(s). *See* Pollock, Harry E. D.; temples

Roys, Ralph L., **ii**, 4, **14**, 39, 88, 101, 108, 458, 522, 547; and chronology, 35, 59–61, 68, 101, 521–**523**, 524–529; and currencies, 278, 280, 282, 285, **287**; and exchange and labor, 288, 290; and Kukulcan rites, 54–55, 61, 555; and lords and officials, 50–53, 56–57, 555; and name of Mayapán, 14–15; and neighborhoods or wards, 152–153, 197; and overland trade routes, 26; and political and religious geography, **ii**, 30, 41, 43, 45, 47, 58, 67, 78, 127, 156; and property, 290; and sacrifice in the Colonial era, 99; and slaves, 196, 399; and tribute, 288–289; and war, 458, 461; and wooden masks, 365

Rubber, 461, 513

Ruppert, Karl: and Chichén Itzá, 165, 462; and Mayapán dwellings, 170, 177, 194, 263, 445, 469, **516**–**518**, **533**; and sites near Mayapán, 19, 42–**43**, **44**–**45**, 67, 537

Russell, Bradley W., **ii**, xxx, xxxi, 4, 11, 48, **74**, **87**, **128**, **136**, **140**–**142**, **152**, **157**, 405–**406**; and cenotes, 199, 202, 403; and censers and sculptures, 119, 427–430, **434**, **438**, **441**, **451**, **457**, **464**, **468**, 474; and city wall, 151, 264, 528, 552; and House Q-176 (pottery manufacture), 126, 254, 261; and Itzmal Ch'en mass grave, 67, 100, 117, 127, 429; and lime production, 281; and settlement beyond Mayapán's wall, 14, 18–19, 22, 28, 31, 49, 64, 67, 108, 127, 150, 154, 157, 168–169, 186, 194, 250, 266, 403, 421, 537, 545; and urban planning, 169, 186

Sabloff, Jeremy A., xxxii; and collapse, 536, 557; and Cozumel, 6, 32, 45–46, 57, 76, 107, 109, 111, 135, 137, 150, 167–168, 185, 194, 196–197, 202, 205, 211, 213, 215, 232, 234, 238, 247, 265, 277, 280, 283, 390, 511, 548; and importance of commercial exchange, 7, 11, 26, 197, 265, 270, 277, 283–284, 408, 542–553; and interregional ties, 8, 550; and Maya urbanism, 1, 10, 155, 165, 185, 186, 194, 196, 545; and medieval-Postclassic Maya comparisons, 13; and Postclassic Maya societal complexity, 24–26, 39, 48, 75, 77, 197, 557; and property, 289–290, 402; and sacrifice, 100; and Sayil 28, 155, 165, 186; and slaves, 399

Sacbe(ob), 49; at Mayapán, **157**–158, **166**, 168–171, **173**, 175, 179, 181, 184, 215–216, 237, 354, 418, 421, 480, 551–553

Sacrifice, 7, 40, 90–103, 125, 399, 471, 478, 513, 528–529, 551, 559; animals, 399–400; auto-sacrifice, 302, 306, 316; cenotes, 78; Contact Period, 99, 528; disembowelment, 438, **440**, 453; eye-gouging, 90, 303, 313; gods, 453; human bone trophy objects, 78, **80**, 96, 100, 102, **311**, 313, 528–529; and maize god, 453; monumental center as vast graveyard, 528–529; sacrificers, 55–56; sacrificial stones, 91, 100; victims, 196, 284, 287, 313, 410, 529. *See also* burial shaft temples, gladiatorial sacrifice; skulls; state terror; warfare

Salt, 6, 216, **271**–**272**, 277–278, 280–283, 288, 290, 397, 401, 420, 422, 538, 547

San Ángel, **43**, **44**, 158

Santa Cruz, **43**, 44

Santa Rita Corozal, 550; murals, 46, 425, 450, 553; rotating ritual burdens, 58, 111, 428–429; warrior effigies, 461

Sayil, 28, 165, 185–186, 266, 403

Schele, Linda, 11, 14, 39–40, 48–49, 58, 79, 82–83, 98–99, 430, 459, 461, 478, 548, 555–556

Schools (*calmecac*), 109, 168, 178

Sculptures (stone and stucco), xxxiii, 21, 34–35, 40, 51, 106–107, 125, 281, 291, 423, 425–431; abandonment and destruction, 532, **533**–**534**; anthropomorphic 25, 32, 73, 79, **81**, 83–86, 89–90, 103, 130, 133, 135, 431–**432**, **433**–**434**, 435–**437**, **439**, 452, 458, 463, **464**; banner stones, 478–**479**; bundles, 478–**479**; column balls, 478–**479**, 480; gods, 438–**439**, **440**, 463–**464**, 467–**468**, **471**, **473**–476, **477**–**478**, **479**–480; ring, **131**, 475; sacrifice, 100, 188; sculpted columns, 25, **86**; serpents, 89, 92,

ary graves, 109; tenoned heads, 98, 436–**437**, 512; trophies and relics, 73, 78, **80**, 96, 100, 102, 313, 528–529. *See also* ancestors; burials; gods; mass graves; oratories; shrines; skull platform; warfare

Slaves, 38, 40, 101, 196, 248, **271**, 278, 280, 285, 287–288, 396, 399, 405, 522, 527–529, 547

Smith, A. Ledyard, 5, 13, 19; and animal pens, 249; and "Cenote" Ch'en Chooch, 78; and cenotes, 175, 184, 199; and ceramic pectoral, 469; and colonnaded halls/men's houses, 108–109, 168, 171, 178; and decentralized religious practice, 197, 428; and degenerate civilization, 20; and effigy ceramics, **516–519**; and elite residences, 145, 170, **172–173, 175**, 177, 185; and farming, 376; and household archaeology, 18, 42, 194, 195, 197–198, 219, 263; and houselot enclosures, 154, 162, **165**, 179, 243, 402; and houselot ritual structures, 234, 236, **237**; and Mayapán house styles 202, 205, 208, 211, 215, 219, 221, 227–229, 232, 234, 236–237; and Mayapán king, 50; and offerings, 445, 532; and roads, 179–180, 182, 184; and mortuary patterns, 250, 252, 532, 551; and settlement around Mayapán, 42, **43–45**, 67, 537; and termination rituals, **533**; and urban settlement organization, 154–155, 168, 180; and X-Coton group structure T-70 burial, 92

Smith, Michael E., xxxii, 3; and archaeological political economy/household archaeology, 3, 5, 8–9, 193, 292, 358, 544, 558; and Aztec Quetzalcoatl myth, 96; and craft production, 9, 36, 287, 544; and degenerate Postclassic civilization, 557; and empires 48; and empirical urban theory, 3; and feasting, 111, 122, 446, 542; and figurines, 34, 426, 465; and market exchange, 146, 270, 276, 287, 410, 420, 542; and neighborhoods 6, 8, 56, 151, 155, 186–187, 267, 554; and Postclassic city sizes and layouts, 27–28, 43, 263, 266; and prestige goods, 558; and social diversity, 188; and tribute/taxation, 289; and Tzizimime shrines, 98; and urban functions/complexity, 2, 11, 150, 546, 560; and urban planning, 105, 150, 155–156, 187, 189–191, 265, 552–554; and world systems, 8, 24, 30, 50, 54, 270, 423, 430, 542, 546, 549

Smith, Robert E., 16, 19; and Cenote Ch'en Mul, 78, 259l and Postclassic pottery 14, 19, 68–69, 259, 299, 425, 426, 430–431, **468**, 472,

516; and settlement around Mayapán, 42, **43–44**, 60, 68–69

Social diversity, 30, 32, 50–53, 186–188, 194–196, 261–263, 265, 267; artifact and pottery stylistic homogeneity, 194, 548–549; mortuary patterns, 252, 254, 256, 263–264, 551; state and city identity, 36, 38, 51, 541, 545, 551. *See also* emblematic state style; ethnicity; residences; urban planning

Social memory, 11, 30, 560

Soconusco, 77

Soil, xxx, 20, 198, 403, 405, **406**; Mayapán anthropogenic soil, 198, 250, 405. *See also* agriculture

Solar disks. *See* astronomy; sun disks

Solare. *See* houselot enclosure

Solomon, Char, 20

Solstice, 76

Sotuta (ceramic complex), 69

Sotuta (province), 28, 41–42, 46–47, **279**, 281, 289, 526, 537

Spatial statistics, 200, 202, 245

Speleothems: climate record, 525–526; as framework for stucco statues, 291

Spindle whorls, 281–282, 296, 299–**300**, 301–302, 419; regional stylistic tool similarities, 548–549. *See also* craft production; females; textiles

Spondylus shell. *See* marine shell

Staple good, 7, 405, 407–408, 544; symbolic importance in public art and ritual, 125–126. *See also* agriculture; environment; market exchange

State terror, 31, 40, 99–101, 103, 267, 522, **523**, 551. *See also* sacrifice

Stela(e), 52, 71, 103; Itzmal Ch'en, 52, **128**, 136; Stela 1, 59, 79–80, **81**; Stela 5, 59, 80; Stela 6, 59, 80; Stela 7, 435; Stela 9, 79–80; Stela 14, 433; House Y-45, 138; Rancho San Ángel, 44

Stingray spine, **309**, 314

Storage, **139**, 195, 197, 213, 215, 284

Strömsvik, Gustav, 19, 49, 73, 91, 170, 178, 290, 366, **518**

Stuart, David, 96, 273–274, 478

Stucco: anthropomorphic and statues, 25, 34, 73, 103, 113, 129, **131**, 135, 188, 291, **432**, 436, **439**, 449–450, 462, 466, 475; art, 21, 25, 34, 40, 46, 102, 125, 423, 425, 480, **516**; columns, 25, 72, 84–**86, 87**, 107, 463–**464**, 467; covering and preserving murals under plaster, 80, 88; effigy mandible (trophy), 78; façades, 29, 40,

552; quadripartite principles, 57–58, 102, 146, 156–**157**, 186; residential zone planning, 154–155, 159; thirteen divisions, 58–59; top-down and bottom-up formation processes, 3, 7, 11, 30, 40, 105–107, 155, 159–160, 187–189, 191, 265–268, 281, 541, 543–544, 551, 553. *See also* colonnaded halls; focal node architecture; governing elites; temples; urbanism; urban life; urban models

Urn (effigy), 237, 259–**260**, 430

Utatlán: censers, 515; halls/lineage houses, 72, 109–110, 145, 151; quadripartite principles, 58; segmentary organization, 37, 153; similarities to Mayapán, 47–48, 50, 55, 100, 109, 145; size and importance, 27, 47, 153

Uxmal, 43, 185; council rule, 49; Feathered Serpent myth, 29; League of Mayapán, 60–61; Xiu, 51–52

Valladolid, 280, 408; Relación de Valladolid, 285, 288, 318

Value: continuum of, 269, 275, 285, 318, 320–321, 366, 420; currencies, 36, 285, 287, 415; determining value, 26, 36, **274**, 285, 287, 318, 320–321, 348–349, 366, 407, 415; increase in value with production steps, 294, 301. *See also* copper; currencies; greenstone; luxury goods; marine shell; market exchange; obsidian; wealth

Venus: astronomy, 81, 84, 88, 95; censers, 88, 437, 453, 458, 467–**468**, 487–505, 508, **510**, 515; serpent markings, 95

Wages. *See* currencies

Wall (Mayapán city wall), 14, 16, 18, 28–30, 49, 151, 153–154, 163, 552; as boundary, 9, 191, 402, 552, collapse, 522, 525, 528–529; hilltop enclosures, 247, **249**, 264; inner enclosure, 72, 154; intersecting features (parapets, gates, roads), 29, 49, 154, 156, **157**, 177, 179, 181–183, 191; murals, 553; other walled towns, 46, 56, 553; research beyond the wall, 18, 22, 28, 31, 42, **44–45**, 64, 67, 154, 157–158, 168, 250, 376, 421, 545; walled settlement attributes, 62, 64, 72, 102, 127, 161, 168, 176–177, 194, 196, **198**–200, **201**–202, 208–**210**, 211, **213**, 219, 221, **223–225**, 227–229, **232**, 245–247, 249, 263–264, **360**–361, 366, 402–**404**, 412, 421, 513. *See also* focal node architecture; gates; houselot enclosures; nonresidential fields; pens; roads; settlement patterns; warfare

Warfare, 29, 35, 48, 99–101, 376, **382**, 386, **397–398**, 399, 407, 409, 423, 554–555, 558; in art, 40, 78–79, **80**, 103; captives, 99–100, 196, 278, 399, 527, 529; collapse, 521, **523**–524, 527–528; defensible site locations, 546; defensive features, 29, 154, 247, **249**, 264, 525, 529; defining aspect of urban life, 29, 35, 101, 376, 529; importance to Mayapán state, 40, 396, 399, 409, 478, 528–529, 554; military service, 32, 101, 216, 288, 528, 546, 559; sacrifice, 78–80, 91–100, 521–**523**, 525–529, 538; slaves, 196, 278, 396, 399; weapons, 376, 397–398. *See also* collapse; burial shaft temples; chert/chalcedony; k'atun; mass graves; political organization; sacrifice; slaves; wall; warriors; weapons

Warriors, 389, 398–399; in art, 79, 98, 431, 435, 437, 453, 456, 458–461, 462, 476, **507**, 508; citizen militia, 376, 396, 529; guardhouse, 211; martially skilled merchants, 284; mercenaries, 458, 522–524, 547; military offices, 34; war captains, 458; warrior orders 54, 101, 458, 461. *See also* chert/chalcedony; obsidian; warfare; weapons

Wax, 6, **272**, 278, 284

Wealth, 5, 7, 9, 25–27, 33, 160, 193–194, 196, 240, 243, 265, 269, 410–411, 420, 555, 559; equitable distribution of valuables (via market exchange), 9–10, 33, 261, 265, 273, 281–282, **292**, 320, **346**–347, 348–**349**, 358, 362, 366, 410–412, **413–414**, 415, 419–420; houselot enclosure size, 243–244, 264, 402; mortuary offerings, **260**, 264–265, 349; status, 259, 261, 265; wealthy commoners, 225, 285, 259, 261, 410–411, 419, 547; wealthy elites, 25–27, 145, 187, 193, 237–238, 259, 270, 276–277, 415, 422, 547, 559. *See also* copper; elites; greenstone; luxury goods; marine shell; obsidian; pottery; religion; residences

Weapons, **382**; in art, 79–**80**, 461–462 axes, 370, 396–**397**, 398; bone, 303; points/knives, 15, **80**, **371–372**, 376, 386, 389, 394, 396–**397**, **397–398**, 525, 528, **530**; slings, **397**. *See also* chert/chalcedony; obsidian; warfare; warriors

Weaving. *See* bone objects; economic interdependency; females; spindle whorls

Weeks, John, 19, 34, 76

Whiskered God. *See* gods

Whistles. *See* figurines

Witschey, Walter, 21

Women. *See* females

Woodworking, 281, **365**, 370; cedar and mahogany, **272**, 278–**279**, 420; construction timbers, 62, 72, 100; fuelwood, 281, 544; platforms, 100; projectile shafts, 15; wooden objects, 125, 127, 280–282, 365–366, 427. *See also* agriculture; chert/chalcedony; community specialization; economic interdependency; greenstone

World system (Postclassic Mesoamerican), 1, 5, 24, 40, 54, 136, 270, 420, 549

Xcaret, 46
Xelha, 46
Xicalanco, 26, 50, 101, **272**, 278, 280
Xipe Totec. *See* gods
Xiu, 22, 39, 41, 50–52, 60, 101, 280, 448; collapse of Mayapán, 37, 52, 429, 522–**523**, 525, 532, 538; post-Mayapán, 52, 55, 60, **523**, 527
Xiuhcalli (Turquoise House), 54, 88
Xjujil, **45**

Xochicalco: economic organization, 9, 122, 190, 259, 314, 410, 418; Feathered Serpent, 29; military, 396; rapid abandonment, 531; urban organization, 10, 152–153, 185
Xochipilli, 85
Xtuki Ch'en, 45

Yacman Striated pottery, 117–**118**, 119, 261–262, **264**
Young face male effigies. *See* gods
Young men's houses, 108–109, 168–169, 211

Zaachila, 79
Zacal Actun, 14
Zacpetén: architecture, 110, 119, 145, 548; censers, 119, 130, 132, 144, 427, 429–430, 443, 447, 461, 470; decorated pottery, 22, 68–69, 111, 141, 423; figurines, 466–467; political organization, 191. *See also* Kowoj
Zaklaktun, 14